THE ATHENIAN AGORA

VOLUME XXVIII

THE LAWCOURTS AT ATHENS

SITES, BUILDINGS, EQUIPMENT, PROCEDURE, AND TESTIMONIA

THE ATHENIAN AGORA

RESULTS OF EXCAVATIONS
CONDUCTED BY
THE AMERICAN SCHOOL OF CLASSICAL STUDIES AT ATHENS

VOLUME XXVIII

THE LAWCOURTS AT ATHENS
SITES, BUILDINGS, EQUIPMENT, PROCEDURE, AND TESTIMONIA

BY

ALAN L. BOEGEHOLD

WITH CONTRIBUTIONS BY

JOHN MCK. CAMP II, MARGARET CROSBY, MABEL LANG, DAVID R. JORDAN, AND RHYS F. TOWNSEND

THE AMERICAN SCHOOL OF CLASSICAL STUDIES AT ATHENS

PRINCETON, NEW JERSEY

1995

Library of Congress Cataloging-in-Publication Data
Boegehold, Alan L. (Alan Lindley)
The lawcourts at Athens : sites, buildings, equipment, procedure, and testimonia / by Alan L. Boegehold with contributions by John McK. Camp II . . . [et al.].
p. cm. — (Athenian Agora ; v. 28)
Includes bibliographical references and index.
ISBN 0-87661-228-1 (hc. : alk. paper)
1. Courts—Greece—Athens—History. 2. Courthouses—Greece—Athens—History. 3. Procedure (Law)—Greece—Athens—History. 4. Athens (Greece)—Antiquities. 5. Athens (Greece)—Buildings, structures, etc. I. Title. II. Series
KL4115.A75B64 1995
347.495′1201—dc20
[344.9512071] 95-18926
CIP

TYPOGRAPHY BY THE AMERICAN SCHOOL OF CLASSICAL STUDIES PUBLICATIONS OFFICE
C/O INSTITUTE FOR ADVANCED STUDY, PRINCETON, NEW JERSEY
PLATES BY THE STINEHOUR PRESS, LUNENBURG, VERMONT
PRINTED IN THE UNITED STATES OF AMERICA
BY THE JOHN D. LUCAS PRINTING COMPANY, BALTIMORE, MARYLAND

For J. E. M. B.

PREFACE

THE PRESENT STUDY is intended to describe and identify objects, buildings, and sites that Athenians used in connection with their lawcourts, especially during the 5th and 4th centuries B.C.E. but also during the early 3rd century. The organization of the book is as follows. There are three parts.

In Part I, Chapter 1, names of courts are analyzed. There are twenty-five such names, excepting those of homicide courts, and a study of them all in context shows not surprisingly that Athenians had more than one name for some of their courts. If in fact all possible instances of polyonymy are authentic, there turn out to have been not twenty-five courts, that is, one for each preserved name, but perhaps as few as ten or twelve in all. These ten or twelve, moreover, were not all in use in the same period. Between, say, 422 and 322 B.C.E., no matter how one segments the whole span, there may have been functioning within any of the periods created thereby no more than four or five courts.

In Chapter 2, names of courts and structures plausibly identified as courts are reviewed and possibilities of identification explored. In Chapter 3, a prehistory of Athenian courts is hypothesized in a sketch in which the original meaning of "heliaia" is discussed. There follows in Chapter 4 a schematic presentation of three representative court days. The first is from an early time in the history of the courts, namely 460 (roughly) to 410/9 B.C.E. (pp. 23–30). A second is from a middle time, 410–340 B.C.E. (pp. 30–36). A third is from a late time, 340 to 322 B.C.E. (pp. 36–41). This last, however, is not the latest, and a note added as epilogue surveys various functions of popular courts at Athens from 322 until 106 B.C.E. I emphasize the word "schematic" because for practically any single procedural function, there are attested exceptions, variations, and alternatives. In Chapter 5 there is a brief resume of sites, equipment, and procedure in the Athenian homicide courts.

In Part II, an introduction is followed by seven chapters, each consisting of both an essay that defines and sets in context one kind of object associated with court procedures and a catalogue that lists all examples of that object found in excavations of the Agora. The order of presentation in Part II approximates the order in which the objects in question might appear or be used on a court day. The first item, a lead curse tablet, would, one supposes, have been consigned to its proper destination a day or so before the trial whose outcome it was to influence. Dikastic pinakia, of which there are twenty-four, are next, followed by a kleroterion (one) and balls (nine of bronze and one of terracotta), bronze tokens (fifty-eight), a klepsydra (one), an echinos (one), and bronze and lead ballots (fifty-four). Next, a catalogue of court sites includes brief descriptions of sites in and around Athens that have been identified with varying degrees of plausibility as places where courts met, both popular and homicide courts. In addition, all ways of referring to Athenian courts, whether formal or casual, are included in the same list, and various putative identifications of sites and building remains are assessed. Two essays follow, one presenting a description in detail of the Square Peribolos (which has more or less regularly been called Heliaia in the past), the other, descriptions in detail of various building remains under the Stoa of Attalos.

The volume concludes with a catalogue of 355 testimonia taken from literature and inscriptions and cited here by catalogue number in bold font. The major headings are general lists of courts, homicide courts, popular courts, architectural requirements, and equipment. This collection, the heart of the book, attests the use and identity of sites and objects used in the courts. Its scope and limits can be exemplified by two passages from 4th-century orators. Aischines 3.55–56 (**229**) is included because, in alluding to an audience that stands outside the court, he helps to situate material resources and equipment. [Demosthenes] 25.98, on the other hand, tells us principally that there were foreigners and metoikoi among the bystanders. This is welcome information, but because it does not help to define or limit an area or structure, it is not included as a testimonium.

In studying these texts I have undertaken various new interpretations and assessments. Some I have published elsewhere; others appear here as commentary to the testimonium in question. A few others are apparent as they are employed in discussion. I note the existence of new interpretations here because they are points at which students may want to concentrate their critical energies. The numbers are as follows: **1**, **5**, **14**, **21**, **64**, **65**, **70–75**, **81**, **82**, **84**, **93**, **104–111**, **148**, **176–185**, **255–277**, **283**, **288–305**, **317**, and **341–349**.

Detailed information concerning variety and density of laws, procedures, alternative procedures, modifications, and manoeuvres has continued to accumulate, thanks to major studies produced in this century. There is first the great compendium of Lipsius, whose good sense in evaluating literary sources continues in many cases to be paradigmatic. Other studies provide instruction concerning special topics, those by G. M. Calhoun, Gustav Colin, Hildebrecht Hommel, Robert Bonner and Gertrude Smith, Louis Gernet, H. T. Wade-Gery, Sterling Dow, Charles Hignett, A. R. W. Harrison, H. J. Wolff, Martin Ostwald, Eberhard Ruschenbusch, E. S. Staveley, D. M. MacDowell, John Triantaphyllopoulos, G. E. M. de Ste. Croix, Anthony Andrewes, John Kroll, Peter Rhodes, Michael Gagarin, Raphael Sealey, Mogens Hansen, Mortimer H. Chambers, Ronald Stroud, Sally Humphreys, and Robert Wallace.

The present essay differs from earlier studies in its systematic consideration of the material evidence and in the dates used as markers. Earlier studies had to be based almost exclusively on literary evidence because most of the relevant material evidence was lacking, and even until now most has been inaccessible to a wide public. Lipsius divided the history of Athenian lawcourt procedure roughly into that of the 5th and that of the 4th century. Hommel (1927, pp. 107–135) divided the history into three epochs (*Hauptepochen*), one beginning at a time he does not define and ending in 403/2, another lasting from 402 until 378/7, and a third, that of Aristotle, *Ath. Pol.* 63–69, beginning in 378/7 (following Keil 1902, p. 266) and ending in 322. Bonner and Smith (1928, pp. 372–374) reaffirm Hommel's scheme. Harrison himself (1971, pp. 239–241), without committing to the whole scheme, accepts dates like 403/2 and 378/7 as marking important changes, while objecting properly to Isokrates 7.54 as establishing any real boundary. Bonner and Smith in addition cite 346 B.C.E. as approximately the time when the organization described by Aristotle came into being at Athens. MacDowell (1978, pp. 297–254) distinguishes some 5th- and 4th-century procedures. All these dates have their uses in discussions of Athenian constitutions, and yet a case can be made for citing other dates and for using them as signs along a continuous way rather than as beginnings and ends of eras or epochs.

If an era can be said to have commenced, the time would have been when large panels of judges were instituted at Athens, whether it was Solon who was responsible, as Athenians of the 4th century B.C.E. and after believed, or someone later. The appointment of dikasts by lot, the use of the secret ballot, and payment for dikasts, all fundamentally important developments, came next, either all together or at least within a few years of each other. By mid-5th century B.C.E., that is, some time not long after Ephialtes' reforms in 462, these four features, *viz.*, large judging panels, allotment of dikasts, pay for dikasts, and the secret ballot, were the bases of the Athenian popular court system.

All other documented changes, whether they were new legislation or procedural modifications, are best regarded as ways to improve crowd control and to preserve the integrity of allotment procedures and the secret ballot.

The foregoing general observations form, when taken all together, a guiding assumption in the essay on representative court days. Admittedly, one can compose an account of court procedure wherein the changes and modifications that seem most telling are pegged to major constitutional changes. The method is old and known and approved. In fact the year 410/9, because so many major innovations can be associated with programs following the reestablishment of the democracy, marks the end of one period and the beginning of another in the essay under consideration. But overall a somewhat looser structure, one where most changes can be regarded as the result of one man's or a committee's perception of need, may produce a better account of what actually happened. It was not necessary for a whole constitution to be changed in order to modify operational procedures.

Professor Sterling Dow, supervisor of my doctoral dissertation at Harvard University, started me on a study of the courts in 1955 by turning over to me three looseleaf notebooks full of analyses, queries, abstracts, hypotheses, and citations he had collected in some twenty years of study. During my student years and after at the American School of Classical Studies at Athens, Eugene Vanderpool and Homer Thompson instructed me in the study of monuments and sites, and Homer Thompson entrusted me with the present publication of dikastic material from the Agora Excavations. Margaret Crosby at the time of her death in 1972 had already collected, translated, and put in order with explanatory essays 325 literary and epigraphical testimonia, an essential labor, which I have supplemented by revising most of her texts and translations, adding testimonia, and rewriting or reworking essays. At the same time, Mabel Lang had already completed catalogues and introductory essays for pinakia, ballots, bronze balls, and klepsydra with an essay introducing the dikastic small finds generally. She also directed my attention to the lid of the echinos. For permission to publish this lid, I thank T. Leslie Shear, Jr., the Director of the Agora Excavations until 1994. My own contribution, besides work with the testimonia, has been to assemble putative court sites and court names, suggest which courts were in use at given times, and create a context for sites and objects by composing three schematic court days. I have also catalogued and discussed the echinos and the dikastic bronze tokens and edited the whole. In this last capacity, I welcome David Jordan's publication of an Athenian dikastic curse tablet, Rhys Townsend's description of building remains under the Stoa of Attalos, and John Camp's description of the peribolos in the southwest corner of the Agora.

I gratefully acknowledge help in the preparation of this book from the following friends and colleagues, who have given me advice, learning, valuable observations, and criticism: Ernst Badian, Geoffrey Bakewell, Judith Binder, Nancy Bookidis, Dietrich von Bothmer, William M. Calder III, Abigail Camp, John Camp, Mortimer H. Chambers, Guy Cooper, Margaret Crosby, Carolyn Dewald, William Bell Dinsmoor, Jr., Sterling Dow, Thomas Drew-Bear, Colin Edmonson, Charles Fornara, Alison Frantz, Virginia Grace, Christian Habicht, Mogens Hansen, Evelyn B. Harrison, Joanne Heffelfinger, R. Ross Holloway, George L. Huxley, Henry Immerwahr, John Keaney, Peter Kalligas, Fred Kleiner, David Konstan, John Kroll, Hugh Lloyd-Jones, Douglas MacDowell, Craig Mauzy, Fordyce Mitchel, Harry Pleket, W. Kendrick Pritchett, Kurt Raaflaub, Peter Rhodes, Susan Rotroff, Adele Scafuro, Raphael Sealey, T. Leslie Shear, Jr., Marian Hartman Shotwell, James Sickinger, Ronald Stroud, Richard Swartz, Lucy Talcott, Leslie Threatte, Gerald Toomer, Rhys Townsend, Homer A. Thompson, Wesley Thompson, Stephen Tracy, Eugene Vanderpool, Robert Vincent, Alan Walker, Charles K. Williams, II, and William F. Wyatt, Jr. In addition I thank Elli Mylonas, Gwendolyn Jones, Thomas Pirrelli, Nancy Evans, Catherine Torigian, Frances Eisenhauer, Ruthann Whitten, and Walter Stevenson for help with preparation of the manuscript, and Paul Langmuir for his drawing of Figure 1. Marian McAllister, Nancy Moore, Elizabeth Bobrick, and Kathleen Krattenmaker have each made superior editorial contributions at different stages of the work.

I also record indebtedness to the George A. and Eliza Gardner Howard Foundation, the American Council of Learned Societies, the National Endowment for the Humanities, the American School of Classical Studies, and Brown University for grants of time and money that enabled me to work in Athens.

Mando Karamessini-Oikonomidou and Ioannis Touratsoglou of the Numismatic Museum of Greece, H.-D. Schultz of the Münzkabinett, Staatliche Museen zu Berlin, Dominique Guerin of the Cabinet des Médailles, Bibliothèque Nationale, Anne Kromann of the Mont-Og Medaillesamling, Nationalmuseet, Copenhagen, Martin Price of the Department of Coins and Medals, the British Museum, and Dr. Bernhard Overbeck of the Staatliche Münzsammlung, Munich, were friendly and generous in their responses to my requests for casts and for information concerning tokens.

A version of the chapter "Three Court Days" has had the benefit of informed discussion at a meeting of the Gesellschaft für griechische und hellenistische Rechtsgeschichte, held at Asilomar, California in September 1990. That version, which is without footnotes, appears as "Three Court Days" in *Symposion 1990. Vorträge zur griechischen und hellenistischen Rechtsgeschichte*, Cologne/Weimar/Vienna 1991, pp. 165–182.

ALAN L. BOEGEHOLD

Providence, RI
November 1994

TABLE OF CONTENTS

LIST OF ILLUSTRATIONS

ILLUSTRATIONS IN TEXT

FIGURES

PLATES

BIBLIOGRAPHY AND ABBREVIATIONS

SECONDARY SOURCES

ABV = J. D. Beazley, *Attic Black-figure Vase-painters*, Oxford 1956

Agora = *The Athenian Agora, Results of Excavations Conducted by the American School of Classical Studies at Athens*, Princeton

III = R. E. Wycherley, *Literary and Epigraphical Testimonia*, Princeton 1957

X = M. Crosby and M. Lang, *Weights, Measures and Tokens*, Princeton 1964

XII = B. A. Sparkes and L. Talcott, *Black and Plain Pottery of the 6th, 5th and 4th Centuries B.C.*, Princeton 1970

XIV = H. A. Thompson and R. E. Wycherley, *The Agora of Athens: The History, Shape and Uses of an Ancient City Center*, Princeton 1972

XV = B. D. Meritt and J. S. Traill, *Inscriptions: The Athenian Councillors*, Princeton 1974

XIX = G. V. Lalonde, M. K. Langdon, and M. B. Walbank, *Inscriptions: Horoi, Poletai Records, Leases of Public Lands*, Princeton 1991

XXVI = J. H. Kroll, *The Greek Coins*, Princeton 1993

XXVII = R. F. Townsend, *The East Side of the Agora: The Remains beneath the Stoa of Attalos*, Princeton 1995

*ARV*² = J. D. Beazley, *Attic Red-figure Vase-painters*, 2nd ed., Oxford 1963

Audollent, A. 1904. "Defixionum tabellae quotquot innotuerunt tam in Graecis Orientis quam in totius Occidentis partibus praeter Atticas in corpore Inscriptionum Atticarum editas" (diss. Université de Paris 1904)

Boegehold, A. L. 1960. "Aristotle's *Athenaion Politeia* 65,2: The 'Official Token'," *Hesperia* 29, pp. 393–401

———. 1963. "Toward a Study of Athenian Voting Procedure," *Hesperia* 32, pp. 366–374

———. 1967. "Philokleon's Court," *Hesperia* 36, pp. 111–120

———. 1972. "The Establishment of a Central Archive at Athens," *AJA* 76, pp. 23–30

———. 1974. "Ten Distinctive Ballots: The Law Court in Zea," *California Studies in Classical Antiquity* 9, pp. 7–19

———. 1982. "A Lid with Dipinto," in *Vanderpool Studies*, pp. 1–6

———. 1984. "Many Letters: Aristophanes *Plutus* 1166–1167," in *Dow Studies*, pp. 23–29

Bonner, R., and G. Smith. 1930. *The Administration of Justice from Homer to Aristotle* I, Chicago

———. 1938. *The Administration of Justice from Homer to Aristotle* II, Chicago

Beulé, C. E. 1858. *Monnaies d'Athènes*, Paris

Busolt, G., and H. Swoboda. 1920. *Griechische Staatskunde* I, Munich

———. 1926. *Griechische Staatskunde* II, Munich

Calhoun, G. M. 1919. "Oral and Written Pleading in Athenian Courts," *TAPA* 50, pp. 177–193

Camp, J. McK., II. 1986. *The Athenian Agora: Excavations in the Heart of Classical Athens*, London

Chambers, M. H. 1990. *Aristoteles. Staat der Athener*, Berlin

Chantraine, P. 1968. *Dictionnaire étymologique*, Paris

Colin, G. 1917. "Les sept derniers chapitres de l' Ἀθηναίων Πολιτεία (Organisation des tribunaux, à Athènes, dans la seconde moitié du IVᵉ siècle)," *REG* 30, pp. 20–87

Cohen, E. E. 1993. *Ancient Athenian Maritime Courts*, Princeton

Crosby, M. 1951. "The Poros Building," in Young 1951, pp. 168–187

Crux = *Crux: Essays Presented to G. E. M. de Ste. Croix on his Seventy-fifth Birthday*, P. A. Cartledge and F. D. Harvey, eds., Exeter 1985

Daremberg-Saglio = *Dictionnaire des antiquités*, Paris n.d.

Davies, J. K. 1971. *Athenian Propertied Families: 600–300 B.C.*, Oxford

Dontas, G. 1983. "The True Aglaurion," *Hesperia* 52, pp. 48–63

Dover, K. J. 1950. "The Chronology of Antiphon's Speeches," *CQ* 44, pp. 44–60

Dow, S. 1937. *Prytaneis: A Study of the Inscriptions Honoring the Athenian Councillors* (*Hesperia* Supplement 1), Athens

———. 1939. "Aristotle, the Kleroteria and the Courts," *HSCP* 50, pp. 1–34

———. 1963. "Dikasts' Bronze Pinakia," *BCH* 87, pp. 653–687

Dow Studies = *Studies Presented to Sterling Dow on His Eightieth Birthday* (*GRBM* 10), K. J. Rigsby, ed., Durham, North Carolina 1984
Ferguson, W. S. 1911. *Hellenistic Athens: An Historical Essay*, London
Frazer, J. G. 1898. *Pausanias's Description of Greece*, London/New York
Frisk, H. 1960–1972. *Etymologisches Wörterbuch*, Heidelberg
Gagarin, M. 1979. "The Prosecution of Homicide in Athens," *GRBS* 20, pp. 301–323
———. 1981. *Drakon and Early Athenian Homicide Law*, New Haven/London
———. 1986. *Early Greek Law*, Berkeley/Los Angeles
Garner, R. 1987. *Law and Society in Classical Athens*, New York
Gauthier, P. 1972. *Symbola. Les étrangers et la justice dans les cités grecques*, Nancy
Gernet, L. 1917. *Recherches sur le développement de la pensée juridique et morale en Grèce*, Paris
Grace, V. R. 1985. "The Middle Stoa Dated by Amphora Stamps," *Hesperia* 54, pp. 1–54
Habicht, C. 1979. *Untersuchungen zur politischen Geschichte Athens im 3. Jahrhundert v. Chr.* (*Vestigia* 30), Munich
Hansen, M. H. 1976. *Apagoge, Endeixis and Ephegesis against Kakourgoi, Atimoi and Pheugontes*, Odense
———. 1979. "Misthos for Magistrates in Classical Athens," *SymbOslo* 54, pp. 5–22
———. 1981. "The Prosecution of Homicide at Athens: A Reply," *GRBS* 22, pp. 11–30
———. 1981–1982. "The Athenian Heliaia from Solon to Aristotle," *ClMed* 33, pp. 9–47
———. 1987. *The Athenian Assembly in the Age of Demosthenes*, Oxford
———. 1989. *The Athenian Ecclesia II. A Collection of Articles 1983–1989*, Copenhagen
Harrison, A. R. W. 1971. *The Law of Athens*, II, *Procedure*, Oxford
Hignett, C. 1952. *A History of the Athenian Constitution*, Oxford
Hitzig, H., and H. Blümner. 1899. *Pausaniae Graeciae Descriptio* I, ii, Leipzig
Hommel, H. 1927. *Heliaia. Untersuchung zur Verfassung und Prozeßordnung des athenischen Volksgerichts, insbesondere zum Schlußteil der* Ἀθηναίων Πολιτεία *des Aristoteles* (*Philologus* Supplementband XIX, Heft II), Leipzig
Humphreys, S. 1983. "The Evolution of Legal Process in Ancient Attica," in *Tria Corda. Scritti in onore de Arnoldo Momigliano*, E. Gabba, ed., Como, pp. 229–256
Jacoby, F. 1949. *Atthis, the Local Chronicles of Ancient Athens*, Oxford
Jordan, D. 1985. "Survey of Greek Defixiones Not Included in the Special Corpora," *GRBS* 26, pp. 151–197
Judeich, W. 1931. *Topographie von Athen*, Munich
Kahrstedt, U. 1936. *Untersuchungen zur Magistratur in Athen*, Stuttgart
Keaney, J. J. 1970. "The Date of Aristotle's *Athenaion Politeia*," *Historia* 19, pp. 326–336
Keil, B. 1902. *Anonymus Argentinensis: Fragmente zur Geschichte des perikleischen Athens aus einem Strassburger Papyrus*, Strassburg
Kroll, J. H. 1972. *Athenian Bronze Allotment Plates*, Cambridge, Mass.
LSJ = H. G. Liddell, R. Scott, and H. S. Jones, *A Greek-English Lexicon*, 9th ed., Oxford 1940
Latte, K. 1920. *Heiliges Recht*, Tübingen (repr. Darmstadt 1964)
Lenschau, T., *RE* XVIII.3, 1949, cols. 168–171 (*s.v.* ἐπὶ Παλλαδίῳ)
Lipsius, J. R. 1905–1915. *Das attische Recht und Rechtsverfahren, mit Benutzung des attischen Processes von M. H. E. Meier und G. F. Schömann*, Leipzig
Lloyd-Jones, H. 1971. *The Justice of Zeus*, Berkeley
MacDowell, D. M. 1963. *Athenian Homicide Law in the Age of the Orators*, Manchester
———. 1971. See *Aristophanes. Wasps* under "Editions and Collections of Texts and Coins"
———. 1978. *The Law in Classical Athens*, London
———. 1985. "The Length of the Speeches on the Assessment of the Penalty in Athenian Courts," *CQ* n.s. 35, pp. 525–526
Meiggs, R., and D. Lewis. 1989. *A Selection of Greek Historical Inscriptions to the End of the Fifth Century B.C.*, 2nd ed., rev., Oxford/New York
Mikalson, J. D. 1975. *The Sacred and Civil Calendar of the Athenian Year*, Princeton
Miller, S. G. 1978. *The Prytaneion: Its Function and Architectural Form*, Berkeley/Los Angeles/London
Ostwald, M. 1986. *From Popular Sovereignty to the Sovereignty of Law: Law, Society, and Politics in Fifth-century Athens*, Berkeley/Los Angeles/London
Pritchett, W. K. 1979. *The Greek State at War*, III, *Religion*, Berkeley/Los Angeles/London
RAC = *Reallexikon für Antike und Christentum*, T. Klauser, ed., Stuttgart 1950–
RE = *Paulys Realencyclopädie der classischen Altertumswissenschaft, Neue Bearbeitung*, rev. G. Wissowa, Stuttgart 1894–1972

Rhodes, P. J. 1972. *The Athenian Boule*, Oxford

———. 1981. *Commentary on the Aristotelian* Athenaion Politeia, Oxford

Roscher, W. H. 1894–1897. *Ausführliches Lexikon der griechischen und römischen Mythologie*, Leipzig (repr. Hildesheim 1965)

Ruschenbusch, E. 1957. «Διкαστήριον πάντων кύριον», *Historia* 6, pp. 257–274

———. 1960. "Φόνος. Zum Recht Drakons und seiner Bedeutung für das Werden des athenischen Staates," *Historia* 9, pp. 129–154

———. 1965. "Ἡλιαία. Die Tradition über das solonische Volksgericht," *Historia* 14, pp. 381–384

Schwyzer 1923. See *Dialectorum Graecarum exempla epigraphica Potiora* under "Editions and Collections of Texts and Coins"

Sealey, R. 1987. *The Athenian Republic: Democracy or the Rule of Law?* University Park

Shear, T. L. 1933. "The Campaign of 1932," *Hesperia* 2, pp. 451–474

Shear, T. L., Jr. 1973. "The Athenian Agora: Excavations of 1971," *Hesperia* 42, pp. 121–179

———. 1978. *Kallias of Sphettos and the Revolt of Athens in 286 B.C.* (*Hesperia* Supplement 17), Princeton

———. 1984. "The Athenian Agora: Excavations of 1980–1981," *Hesperia* 53, pp. 1–57

Smith, S. B. 1925. "The Establishment of the Public Courts at Athens," *TAPA* 56, pp. 106–119

Staveley, E. S. 1972. *Greek and Roman Voting and Elections*, London/Southampton

Stroud, R. S. 1968. *Dracon's Law on Homicide* (*University of California Publications in Classical Studies* 3), Berkeley/Los Angeles

———. 1979. *The Axones and Kyrbeis of Drakon and Solon* (*University of California Publications in Classical Studies* 19), Berkeley/Los Angeles

Stumpf, G. 1987. "Zwei Gerichtsurteile aus Athen: *IG* II^2 1641 B und 1646 a," *Tyche* 2, pp. 211–215

Svoronos, I. N. 1898. «Περὶ τῶν εἰσιτηρίων τῶν ἀρχαίων», *JIAN* 1, pp. 37–120

———. 1923–1926. *Les monnaies d'Athènes*, Munich

Thompson, H. A. 1951. "Excavations in the Athenian Agora: 1950," *Hesperia* 20, pp. 45–60

———. 1954. "Excavations in the Athenian Agora: 1953," *Hesperia* 23, pp. 31–67

Thompson Studies = *Studies in Athenian Architecture, Sculpture and Topography Presented to Homer A. Thompson* (*Hesperia* Supplement 20), Princeton 1982

Threatte, L. 1980. *The Grammar of Attic Inscriptions*, I, *Phonology*, Berlin/New York

Thür, G. 1977. *Beweisführung vor den Schwurgerichtshöfen Athens. Die Proklesis zur Basanos* (Österreichischen Akademie der Wissenschaften, Philosophisch-historische Klasse, Sitzungberichte 317), Vienna

Travlos, J. 1971. *Pictorial Dictionary of Ancient Athens*, London

———. 1974. "The Lawcourt ἐπὶ Παλλαδίῳ," *Hesperia* 43, pp. 500–511

Travlos, J., and A. Frantz. 1965. "The Church of Dionysos the Areopagite and the Palace of the Archbishop of Athens in the 16th Century," *Hesperia* 34, pp. 157–202

Triantaphyllopoulos, J. 1985. *Das Rechtsdenken der Griechen* (*MünchBeitr* 78), Munich

Vanderpool, E. 1950. "The Apostle Paul in Athens," *Archaeology* 3, pp. 33–47

———. 1980. "The State Prison of Ancient Athens," in *From Athens to Gordion. The Papers of a Memorial Symposium for Rodney S. Young* (*University Museum Papers* 1), K. DeVries, ed., Philadelphia, pp. 17–31

Vanderpool Studies = *Studies in Attic Epigraphy, History and Topography Presented to Eugene Vanderpool* (*Hesperia* Supplement 19), Princeton 1982

Wachsmuth, C. 1874. *Die Stadt Athen im Alterthum* I, Leipzig

———. 1890. *Die Stadt Athen im Alterthum* II, Leipzig

Wade-Gery, H. T. 1958. *Essays in Greek History*, Oxford

Wallace, R. W. 1989. *The Areopagos Council, to 307 B.C.*, Baltimore/London

Wolff, H. J. 1946. "The Origin of Judicial Litigation among the Greeks," *Traditio* 4, pp. 31–87

———. 1966. *Die attische Paragraphe: Ein Beitrag zum Problem der Auflockerung archaischer Prozessformen* (*Graezistische Abhandlungen* 2), Weimar

Wünsch, R. 1897. *Defixionum Tabellae* [= *IG* III, iii], Berlin

Wycherley, R. E. 1955. "Two Notes on Athenian Topography," *JHS* 75, pp. 117–121

———. 1978. *The Stones of Athens*, Princeton

Wyse. 1904. See Isaios under "Editions and Collections of Texts and Coins"

Young, Rodney S. 1951. "An Industrial District in Athens," *Hesperia* 20, pp. 135–288

Young, Suzanne. 1939. "An Athenian Clepsydra," *Hesperia* 8, pp. 274–284

EDITIONS AND COLLECTIONS OF TEXTS AND COINS

(listed only where a particular edition or collection is necessary for identification or interpretation)

Aristophanes. Wasps, ed. D. M. MacDowell, Oxford 1971
Aristoteles. Ἀθηναίων Πολιτεία, ed. M. H. Chambers, Leipzig 1986
Bekker, *Anecdota Graeca.* See Λέξεις ῥητορικαί
BMC = *Catalogue of the Greek Coins in the British Museum*, London 1873–1927
CAF = *Comicorum Atticorum Fragmenta*, vols. I–III, ed. T. Kock, Leipzig 1880–1888
Deinarchos = *Dinarchus. Orationes cum Fragmentis*, ed. N. Conomis, Leipzig 1975
Demosthenes. Against Meidias, ed. D. M. MacDowell, Oxford 1990
Dialectorum Graecarum exempla epigraphica Potiora, ed. E. Schwyzer, Leipzig 1923 (repr. Hildesheim 1960)
Erotiani vocum Hippocraticum collectio, ed. E. Nachmanson, Göteborg 1918
Etymologicum Magnum, ed. T. Gaisford, Oxford 1848
Eubulus: The Fragments, ed. R. L. Hunter, Cambridge 1983
Eustathios, *Commentary on Homer, Iliad* = *Eustathii archiepiscopi Thessalonicensis commentarii ad Homeri Iliadem pertinentes ad fidem codicis Laurentiani editi*, vols. I–IV, ed. M. van der Valk, Leiden 1971–1987
———. *Commentary on Homer, Odyssey* = *Eustathii archiepiscopi Thessalonicensis commentarii ad Homeri Odysseam ad fidem exempli Romani editi*, ed. G. Stallbaum, Leipzig 1825–1826
FGrHist = F. Jacoby, *Die Fragmente der griechischen Historiker*, Berlin 1923–1930; Leiden 1940–1964
Gregory of Corinth = *Gregorii Corinthii et aliorum grammaticorum libri de dialectis linguae graecae*, ed. G. H. Schaefer, Leipzig 1811
Harpokration. Léxeis of the Ten Orators, ed. J. J. Keaney, Amsterdam 1991
Herodas. The Mimes and Fragments, with notes by W. Headlam, ed. A. D. Knox, Cambridge 1922
Hesychios = *Hesychii Alexandrini Lexicon* I–II, ed. K. Latte, Copenhagen 1953–1966; III–IV, ed. M. Schmidt, Jena 1861–1868
IG I^2 = *Inscriptiones Graecae*, I, editio minor, *Inscriptiones Atticae Euclidis anno anteriores*, ed. F. Hiller de Gaertringen, Berlin 1924
IG I^3 = *Inscriptiones Graecae*, I, i, editio tertia, *Inscriptiones Atticae Euclidis anno anteriores*, ed. D. M. Lewis, Berlin 1981
IG II^2 = *Inscriptiones Graecae*, II–III, i–iv, editio minor, *Inscriptiones Atticae Euclidis anno posteriores*, ed. J. Kirchner, Berlin 1913–1940
IG II, iv^2 = *Inscriptiones Graecae*, II, iv, *Inscriptiones Atticae aetatis quae est inter Euclidis annum et Augusti tempora*, indices, Berlin 1893
IG III, iii = *Inscriptiones Graecae*, III, appendix, *Inscriptiones Atticae aetatis romanae*, Berlin 1897
IG IX, i = *Inscriptiones Graecae*, IX, *Inscriptiones Graeciae septentrionalis voluminibus VII et VIII non comprehensae*, i, *Inscriptiones Phocidis Locridis Aetoliae Acarnaniae*, ed. G. Dittenberger, Berlin 1897
IG IX, ii = *Inscriptiones Graecae*, IX, *Inscriptiones Graeciae septentrionalis voluminibus VII et VIII non comprehensae*, ii, *Inscriptiones Thessaliae*, ed. O. Kern, Berlin 1908
IG XI, ii = *Inscriptiones Graecae*, XI, ii, *Inscriptiones Deli*, ed. F. Dürrbach, Berlin 1912
Isaios = *The Speeches of Isaeus*, ed. W. Wyse, Cambridge 1904
Lexicon Cantabrigiense, ed. E. O. Houtsma, Leiden 1870 (= *Lexica Vetera Minora*, ed. K. Latte, pp. 61–139)
Lexica Graeca Minora, eds. K. Latte and H. Erbse, Hildesheim 1965
Lexicon Patmense = M. Sakkélion, «Λέξεις μεθ' ἱστοριῶν ἐκ τῶν Δημοσθένους Λόγων», *BCH* 1, 1877, pp. 10–16, 137–154 (= *Lexica Vetera Minora*, ed. K. Latte, pp. 140–165)
Lexica Vetera Minora. See *Lexicon Patmense.*
Λέξεις ῥητορικαί, *Anecdota Graeca*, ed. I. Bekker, 3 vols., Berlin 1814–1821
Machon. The Fragments, ed. A. S. F. Gow, Cambridge 1965
McClean Collection = S. W. Grose. *Catalogue of the McClean Collection of Greek Coins, Fitzwilliam Museum*, Cambridge 1923–1929
Menander (Koe.) = *Menander quae supersunt*, ed. A. Koerte, Leipzig 1957
Menander = *Menandri Reliquiae Selectae*, ed. F. H. Sandbach, Oxford 1972
Menander, *Commentary* = A. W. Gomme and F. H. Sandbach, *Menander: A Commentary*, Oxford 1973
PA = *Prosopographia Attica*, ed. J. Kirchner, Berlin 1901–1903
Παυσανίου ᾿Ελλάδος Περιήγησις, I, Ἀττικά, ed. N. D. Papachatzis, Athens 1974

PCG = *Poetae Comici Graeci* II, Berlin 1991; IV, Berlin 1983; V, Berlin 1986; VII, Berlin 1989; ed. R. Kassel and C. Austin

PCG III.2 = *Poetae Comici Graeci. Aristophanes: Testimonia et fragmenta*, III.2, ed. R. Kassel and C. Austin, Berlin 1984

Photios, *Lexicon* = *Photii patriarchae lexicon*, ed. S. A. Naber, Amsterdam 1965

Photios, *Lexicon* I = *Photii patriarchae lexicon* I (α–δ), ed. C. Theodorides, Berlin/New York 1982

Photios, *Bibliotheca* = Photios, *Bibliotheca*, ed. R. Henry, 8 vols., Paris 1959–1977

Pollux = *Pollucis Lexicon*, ed. E. Bethe, Leipzig 1900–1937 (complete in W. Dindorf, Leipzig 1824 [repr. Teubner 1967])

POxy = *Oxyrhynchus Papyri*

Schol. Aeschines = *Scholia in Aeschinem*, ed. M. R. Dilts, Leipzig 1992

Schol. Aristophanes, *Acharnians* = *Scholia in Aristophanem. Scholia vetera et recentiora in Aristophanis Acharnes*, ed. N. G. Wilson, Groningen 1975

Schol. Aristophanes, *Birds* = *Scholia in Aristophanem. Scholia vetera et recentiora in Aristophanis Aves*, ed. W. J. W. Koster and D. Holwerda, Groningen 1978

Schol. Aristophanes, *Clouds* = *Scholia in Aristophanem. Prolegomena de comoedia. Scholia in Acharnenses Equites Nubes*, III, *Continens Scholia Vetera in Nubes*, ed. D. Holwerda, Groningen 1977

Schol. Aristophanes, *Ekklesiazousae* = *Scholia Graeca in Aristophanem*, ed. F. Dübner, Paris 1843

Schol. Aristophanes, *Knights* = *Scholia in Aristophanem. Scholia vetera et recentiora in Aristophanis Equites*, ed. D. Holwerda, Groningen 1991

Schol. Aristophanes, *Ploutos* = *Scholia Graeca in Aristophanem*, ed. F. Dübner, Paris 1843

Schol. Aristophanes, *Wasps* = *Scholia in Aristophanem. Scholia vetera et recentiora in Aristophanis Vespas*, ed. W. J. W. Koster, Groningen 1978

Schol. Demosthenes = *Scholia Demosthenica* I, Leipzig 1983; II, Leipzig 1986, ed. M. R. Dilts

SEG = *Supplementum Epigraphicum Graecum* I–XXV, ed. J. J. Hondius, Leiden 1923–1971; XXVI–XXXVIII, ed. R. Stroud and H. Pleket, Leiden 1976–1988

SNG = *Sylloge Nummorum Graecorum. The Royal Collections of Coins and Medals. Danish National Museum, Attica-Aegina*, Copenhagen 1944

Σόλωνος Νόμοι, *Die Fragmente des solonischen Gesetzeswerkes mit einer Text- und Überlieferungsgeschichte* (*Historia Einzelschriften* 9), E. Ruschenbusch, Wiesbaden 1966

Suda = *Suidae Lexicon*, ed. A. Adler, Lepizig 1928–1938

Theophrastos, *Characters* = *Theophrastus Characters, Herodas Mimes, Cercides and the Choliambic Poets*, ed. J. Rusten, I. C. Cunningham, and A. D. Knox, Cambridge, Mass./London 1993

Theophrastos, *Nomoi* = *The Nomoi of Theophrastus*, ed. A. Szegedy-Maszak, New York 1981

Thucydides, *Commentary* = A. W. Gomme, *A Historical Commentary on Thucydides*, vols. I–III; A. W. Gomme, A. Andrewes, and K. J. Dover, vols. IV and V, Oxford 1959–1981

TrGF = *Tragicorum Graecorum Fragmenta*, IV, *Sophocles*, ed. S. Radt, Göttingen 1977

PERIODICALS

Acme = *Annali della facoltà di filosofia e lettere dell'Università statale di Milano*

AdI = *Annali dell'Instituto di corrispondenza archeologica*

AJA = *American Journal of Archaeology*

AJAH = *American Journal of Ancient History*

AJP = *American Journal of Philology*

AM = *Mitteilungen des Deutschen Archäologischen Instituts, Athenische Abteilung*

AntK = *Antike Kunst*

ArchNews = *Archaeology News*

BCH = *Bulletin de correspondance hellénique*

BSA = *Annual of the British School at Athens*

ClMed = *Classica & Mediaevalia*

CP = *Classical Philology*

CQ = *Classical Quarterly*

CR = *Classical Review*

GRBM = *Greek, Roman and Byzantine Monographs*

GRBS = *Greek, Roman and Byzantine Studies*
HSCP = *Harvard Studies in Classical Philology*
JHS = *Journal of Hellenic Studies*
JIAN = *Journal international d'archéologie numismatique*
MünchBeitr = *Münchener Beiträge zur Papyrusforschung und antiken Rechtsgeschichte*
NC = *Numismatic Chronicle*
REG = *Revue des études grecques*
SymbOslo = *Symbolae Osloenses, auspiciis Societatis Graeco-Latinae*
TAPA = *Transactions of the American Philological Association*
ZN = *Zeitschrift für Numismatik*
ZöstG = *Zeitschrift für die österreichischen Gymnasien*
ZPE = *Zeitschrift für Papyrologie und Epigraphik*
ZRG = *Zeitschrift der Savigny-Stiftung für Rechtsgeschichte* (*Romanistische Abteilung*)

CATALOGUE ABBREVIATIONS

In the catalogues, the following abbreviations are used:

D. = diameter
est. = estimated
g. = gram
H. = height
L. = length
L.H. = letter height
obv. = obverse
p.D. = preserved diameter
p.L = preserved length
rev. = reverse
Th. = thickness
W. = width
Wt. = weight

All dimensions are given in meters, unless otherwise indicated.

GLOSSARY

Abacus (ἄβακος): Counting board of wood or stone on which sums could be reckoned with pebbles or in which bronze ballots could be inserted and counted.

Agora: Greek marketplace.

Agora of the Kerkopes (also Agora of Thieves): Putative market at Athens for the sale of stolen goods; mentioned by writers of later antiquity as having been near the Heliaia.

Amphictyony (Ἀμφικτυονεία): (1) Generally, a league of Greek cities in a particular area. (2) A league of Greek cities contracted for the protection and management of the oracle of Demeter near Thermopylai and, subsequently, the oracle of Apollo at Delphi.

Amphora: Two-handled vessel of terracotta used variously, mostly for transport and storage and regularly as receptacle for ballots in voting at Athens.

Anakrisis (ἀνάκρισις): Preliminary procedure in a case at law. Plaintiff and defendant present the documentation and basic argument of their respective cases to a magistrate for him to schedule a date for trial.

Ananke (ἀνάγκη, necessity): A reference, probably in comedy, to the klepsydra.

Anathyrosis: A mode of dressing masonry joints that sets one block with a smoothed margin against another block with a similarly smoothed margin

Antidikos (ἀντίδικος): An opposing litigant.

Antipatros (*ca.* 400–319 B.C.E.): Regent and general for Alexander of Macedon in European Greece. After defeating the marshaled troops of the Hellenic League in Thessaly and making terms with most of its members separately, he secured the unconditional surrender of Athens (summer, 322 B.C.E.). Antipatros introduced new property restrictions on the franchise at Athens and shut down the dikasteria.

Apollo Delphinios: Apollo in one aspect. A shrine dedicated to Apollo Delphinios at Athens was used as a homicide court: Delphinion. Compare Apollo Lykeios, tutelary at Argos, and Apollo Patroos, who protected ancestors and ancestral customs at Athens. Apollo Pythios, so called for his seat in Delphi, was called Apollo Patroos at Athens.

Arche (ἀρχή): (1) Any office or officer in the administration of a city. Archai at Athens under the democracy included the archonships, the boule of 500, and assorted other magistracies. (2) A period of rule, a reign.

Archon (ἄρχων): (1) One of the nine primary administrators of Athens, including the eponymous archon, the basileus, the polemarch, and the six thesmothetai. (2) The eponymous archon.

Ardettos: Hill south-southeast of the Periclean Odeion, outside the city wall of Classical Athens.

Areopagos (Ἄρειος Πάγος, the Hill of Ares): (1) Hill south of the Agora; (2) ἡ τοῦ Ἀρείου Πάγου βουλή, the Areopagos Council: Council consisting of the former archons of Athens, which met on the Areopagos. The Areopagos Council had wide-ranging authority before the reforms of Kleisthenes and Ephialtes and during periods of oligarchy. Its main function in the Athenian democracy was to judge cases of deliberate homicide, arson, and poisoning.

Artemis Delphinia: Honored jointly with Apollo Delphinios.

Astynomoi (ἀστυνόμοι): Board of ten magistrates, five in Athens proper, five in Peiraieus, responsible for the regulation of music-girls and the maintenance of streets and public land.

Atimia (ἀτιμία, dishonor): Penalty imposed at Athens for various reasons, e.g., on citizens with outstanding debts to the state and persons found guilty in the popular courts and the homicide courts. The *atimos* was denied some or all civil rights, including entrance to the Agora and state shrines.

Axon (ἄξων): (1) Rotating wooden tablet on which Drakon's and Solon's laws were written. (2) A section of a code of law, written on a single axon, and also as recorded anywhere else (e.g., on a stele).

Bakkhos ring: A circlet used to hold together the βάκχος, a leafy staff used in Eleusinian processions; also an emblem used on tokens.

Balanos (βάλανος, acorn): A ball. Balls of bronze (as well as terracotta) were used at Athens to allot dikasts to particular courts.

Batrachioun: Cited by Pausanias as a dikasterion at Athens: the Green Court.

Bema (βῆμα): A lectern in an Athenian court from which litigants addressed the dikasts.

Boukranion: A bull's head, stamped onto some bronze tokens.

Boule (βουλή, council): (1) A deliberative body common to most Greek cities, its number regulated by lot, by birth, or by some other criterion. (2) The council of 500 in the Athenian democracy.

Bouleusis (βούλευσις): The act of plotting the death of another person or of hiring a third party to kill someone.

Bouleuterion: (1) The meeting place of the council of a Greek city. (2) At Athens, the building on the west side of the Agora where the boule of 500 met, or the site on the Areopagos where the Areopagos council regularly met.

Chaironeia: A city of western Boiotia. Battle of Chaironeia, 338 B.C.E.: Battle fought between Philip II and the Greek alliance led by Athens and Thebes. The defeat of the Greek forces at Chaironeia marked the end of large-scale military efforts on behalf of the Greeks against Macedonian dominance during the lifetime of Philip.

Choirina (χοιρίνη, sea shell): A term for ballots used in 5th-century dikasteria at Athens.

Chous (χοῦς): A unit of liquid volume in ancient Greece, equivalent, in the case of the klepsydra found at Athens, to 3.276 liters.

Chytra (χύτρα): An unglazed, terracotta stew pot which could be closed and sealed to store documents for a case at law. *See* Echinos.

Clamp: Metal joint used to join blocks (horizontally) within the same course of a wall.

Coping course: Level of stone or masonry immediately above the cornice of a colonnade or wall and below the sima (gutter) of the roof overhead.

Cornice: The portion of the entablature of a colonnade or wall above the frieze and immediately below the roof or ceiling.

Delphinion: Shrine shared by Apollo Delphinios and Artemis Delphinia. It may have been located within a precinct of Pythian Apollo. Court at Delphinion: Court where ephetai judged claims of justified or lawful homicide.

Deme: One of 139 administrative and geographical units of the polis Athens; the base of an Athenian's franchise. After Kleisthenes, Athenian citizens included the name of their deme as the third element of their names. Hence NAME—FATHER'S NAME—DEME NAME.

Demetrios of Phaleron: Regent for Macedonians at Athens 317–307 B.C.E. Demetrios of Phaleron imposed a constitution on Athens similar to the one put in place by Antipatros.

Demetrios Poliorketes (Πολιορκητής, City-besieger): Macedonian king and liberator of Athens (307 B.C.E.). He entered Peiraieus with his fleet and compelled the garrison maintaining the regency of Demetrios of Phaleron in Mounychia to depart. He then negotiated an alliance for himself with the Athenians.

Demophon: In the legendary establishment of Palladion, he is the Athenian who is first tried there for unintentional homicide. The judges were Argive and Athenian ephetai.
Desmoterion (δεσμωτήριον): The jail or prison at Athens.
Diaitetes (διαιτητής): An arbitrator.
Diamartyria (διαμαρτυρία): A legal procedure used during trial at Athens wherein one of the litigants swears to the falsity of an assertion of fact by an opponent. If the litigant whose assertion is disputed concedes, the trial continues. Otherwise, a dikasterion must judge the particular assertion before the trial can continue.
Dikast (δικαστής, judge): A judge at Athens and elsewhere.
Dikasterion (δικαστήριον): (1) A panel of dikasts selected by lot, typically numbering 201, 401, or 501 men at Athens. (2) Any building or place where such a panel decided a case at law. (3) τὰ δικαστήρια: The buildings and procedures taken together as they were used in trials; (4) The whole system of popular courts.
Dike (δίκη): The abstract word for "justice" or "right"; also, at Athens, an action at law initiated on behalf of a private citizen.
Dokimasia (δοκιμασία): A review or scrutiny of a person, often in connection with eligibility to serve as a magistrate.
Dowel: Short bar used to join stones of different courses in walls and steps of Greek buildings.
Drakon: Eponymous archon (621/20 B.C.E.) and author of the first code of law (axones) at Athens. Drakon's law on homicide continued in use in the 4th century.
Dryphaktoi (δρύφακτοι): Temporary wooden fence surrounding the dikasteria, used to prevent unauthorized persons from participating in allotments and to keep bystanders at a distance.
Echinos (ἐχῖνος): In one sense, a receptacle in which to seal and store documents from an arbitration or an anakrisis.
Ekklesia (ἐκκλησία, assembly): In the Athenian democracy, the general assembly of citizens, which constituted the ultimate authority of the city.
Eleven, the (οἱ ἕνδεκα): Board of magistrates charged with maintenance of the desmoterion and the superintendance of state executions. The Eleven also presided over the trials of burglars, highwaymen, and kakourgoi. They are associated with the Parabyston.
Empektes (ἐμπήκτης, inserter): In the daily allotment of dikasts, he is the one of his phyle and section allotted by the draw of a pinakion to insert the pinakia of other members of his section into the kleroterion.
Enkentris (ἐγκεντρίς, sting): Cited by Pollux as a punning reference to the stylus as used in voting penalties.
Entablature: The portion of a colonnaded wall above the columns.
Epalxeis (ἔπαλξις, rampart): Reported as a homicide court only by mediaeval sources; possibly to be identified with the Prytaneion.
Ephesis (ἔφεσις, referral): The right to appeal or the act of appealing. Decisions of disputes public and private at Athens could be appealed to the dikastic (or heliastic) system (dikasteria).
Ephetai (ἐφέτης, consultant): At Athens, judges in trials of homicide cases. Panels of fifty-one ephetai sat in all the Athenian homicide courts except for the Areopagos and the Prytaneion.
Ephialtes: Athenian rhetor whose reforms in 462/1 B.C.E. resulted in more authority for the dikasteria and less for the Council on the Areopagos.
Epiklesis (ἐπίκλησις, extra title): An additional name given to a god or goddess, usually to designate one particular aspect of the divinity in question. *See* Apollo.

Episkepsis (ἐπίσκηψις): A formal challenge at law at Athens. If a litigant challenged another litigant's assertion of a fact and the litigant thus challenged did not concede, then by challenge the two litigants took the disputed assertion to a dikasterion for final settlement. After a dikasterion gave a decision in the episkepsis the original case could be retried.

Epistates (ἐπιστάτης, e.g., τῶν πρυτανέων, president of the prytaneis): Official allotted for one day and night from the prytaneis, responsible for the keys of state shrines, treasury, and archive. He allots the nine proedroi, who act as moderators and preside in meetings of the boule.

Eponymous Heroes: The ten heroes whose names were given to the ten tribes into which Kleisthenes divided Attika. Statues of the Eponymous Heroes stood to the east of the Metroon and Bouleuterion in the Agora.

Eukleides: First archon (403/2 B.C.E.) at Athens in the restored democracy after reconciliation with Sparta and the end of the regime of the Thirty.

Euthyna (εὔθυνα): An official examination of a magistrate's performance held during or after his term of office.

Forty, the (οἱ τεσσαράκοντα): Itinerant panel of judges allotted each year to hear and decide cases involving claims of less than ten drachmai. Judgments given by the Forty could be appealed to the arbitrators (diaitetai) for a new decision.

Geison: The uppermost member of the entablature of a colonnade or wall.

Gerra (γέρρα): Wattled screens or booths.

Glaukippos: Archon in 410/9.

Gorgoneion: A representation of a gorgon's head.

Grammateion (also grammateidion, little grammateion): (1) A whitened board on which an official document, declaration, or decree was written for public display and official recording. (2) A tablet for record keeping; a wax tablet.

Graphis (γραφίς): The stylus used to write on wax tablets.

Heliaia (ἡλιαία): (1) A panel of heliasts (dikasts) at Athens, consisting of at least 1,000 men. (2) The building where such a large panel met. Possible sites of the Heliaia include, in chronological order, the Rectangular Peribolos, Building A under the Stoa of Attalos, and the Square Peristyle. (3) The whole system of buildings, personnel, and procedures used in the trial of court cases before allotted dikasts at Athens.

Heliast: A term for dikast in the 5th century.

Herm: A head of Hermes on a square pillar, often placed at the entrance of a building or street.

Heroon: The shrine of a hero.

Hieropoioi (ἱεροποιοί): Boards of magistrates who tend to the sacrifices.

Hydria (ὑδριά): A water jar, which can also receive ballots in a voting.

Hymettos: Mountain east of Athens, source of accessible good marble.

Istor (ἵστωρ): A judge or referee who has some special competence(?).

Kainon: (1) τὸ Καινόν: Given as the name of a court by Aristophanes. (2) τὰ Καινά: *See* New Courts.

Kakourgos (κακοῦργος): Malefactor. At Athens, a petty thief, slaver, or highwayman.

Kalathos (κάλαθος): A reed basket, sometimes used in the storage of sacral objects. *See also* Bakkhos ring.

Kallion: A dikasterion at Athens, of uncertain identification.

Kalpis (κάλπις): Jar.

Kankelos (κάγκελος): The kinklis and dryphaktoi, transliteration of Latin *cancellus*.

Kanna (κάννα): A reed; hence a reed mat.

Kemos (κημός, wicker trap): In one sense, a long-necked wicker attachment that, when placed over tops of voting urns, hid the destination of ballots as they were deposited.
Ketharion (κηθάριον; also kethis, kethion): Box or jar used in the allotment of dikasts.
Kernos (κέρνος): A pot, designed for varied offerings to Demeter, used as an emblem on tokens.
Kibotos (κιβωτός): Chest used variously in allotment of dikasts.
Kinklis (κιγκλίς): Gate in the dryphaktoi.
Kleisthenes: Changed the structure of Athenian citizenship in 508/7 by establishing the ten tribes of Classical Athens.
Klepsydra (κλεψύδρα, water thief): Waterclock used *inter alia* to time speeches in the dikasteria at Athens.
Kleroterion (κληρωτήριον; also klerotris): Allotment machine used in sortition of dikasts at Athens.
Kolakretai (κωλακρέται): A board of financial magistrates in early Athens.
Kolonos Agoraios: Low hill just west of the Agora at Athens.
Krenophylakion (κρηνοφυλάκιον, guardianship of the spring): A magistracy at Athens.
Kyboi (κύβοι): Dice used in the kleroterion.
Kyrios (κύριος): At Athens, the appointed guardian of a widowed and fatherless woman or of an orphan. A kyrios represented his ward in any legal proceeding and had general charge of his ward's financial affairs.
Lithos (Stone of Outrage, Stone of Unforgiveness [λίθος ὕβρεως, ἀναιδείας]): The bemata of the defendant and plaintiff, respectively, at the Areopagos.
Logisterion (λογιστήριον): Regular meeting place of the logistai at Athens.
Logistai (λογισταί): Magistrates responsible for reviewing accounts of magistrates at Athens for the euthyna.
Lopas (λοπάς): A cooking pot; another name for the echinos, *q.v.*
Lykou Dekas (Λύκου δεκάς, Company of Lykos): A comic name for the general body of dikasts at Athens.
Lychneion (λυχνεῖον, lampstand): Stand from which dikasts took bronze ballots for voting.
Maltha (μάλθα): Mixture of pitch and wax, used to cover wax tablets.
Meizon (μείζων, Greater): Name for a court; used at Athens in 5th century B.C.E. Possibly the Heliaia.
Melite: An Attic city deme.
Meson: Middle Court. *See* New Courts.
Metoikos (μέτοικος, metic): A resident alien at Athens.
Meticheion (also Metichou Temenos): Large court building in use at Athens during the 5th century.
Metroon: Shrine of the Mother of the Gods. The central archive of Athens was housed in the old Bouleuterion in the last decade of the 5th century and came to be called the Metroon, which occupied a part of the site.
New Courts (Πρῶτον καὶ Μέσον τῶν Καινῶν, First and Middle of the New [Courts]): Possibly used to designate the 4th-century complex of court buildings located east of the Panathenaic Way.
Nomima, ta: In one sense, legal rights of an Athenian citizen.
Nomothetai (νομοθέται): Magistrates charged with drafting new laws.
Ochetos (ὀχετός): Water pipe or channel.
Odeion: Large theater built by Perikles for musical performances. Site of preliminary hearings held by the eponymous archon and perhaps of trials presided over by the archon.
Orthostate: Building block set on edge, with its longest edges vertical.
Oxybaphos (ὀξύβαφος): Small jar.

Palladion: (1) Temple of Athena at Athens. (2) Site of homicide court, possibly in Phaleron, that tried accidental homicide, bouleusis, and homicide of metics and slaves. (3) A wooden cult image of Athena.

Pallantidai: The sons of Pallas. In Athenian lore, rebels killed by Theseus.

Parabyston (Παράβυστον, squeezed in): Dikasterion at Athens, so-called for its shape or location; possibly to be identified with the Trigonon.

Paredros (πάρεδρος): Assistant to a magistrate. The archon, basileus, and polemarch each chose two paredroi; two paredroi were allotted to each of the ten euthynoi.

Peiraieus: The main port at Athens after the 6th century B.C.E.

Peisianakteios: An alternate name for the Stoa Poikile.

Peisistratos: Tyrant at Athens for nineteen years during the period beginning with his first attempt at rule (560 B.C.E.) and ending with his death (528/7 B.C.E.).

Periestekotes (περιεστηκότες, bystanders): The persons standing outside a dikasterion during a trial.

Perischoinisma (περισχοίνισμα): The roping off of an area outside a structure being used as a court.

Phoinikioun: Cited by Pausanias as a dikasterion at Athens: The Red Court.

Phratry (φρατρία): A unit of the tribal system at Athens.

Phreatto: Homicide court at Athens, said to be the venue for homicide trials when the accused was already in exile for homicide. Associated with the harbor, Zea.

Phyle (φυλή): (1) A tribe. (2) One of the ten tribes into which Kleisthenes divided the population of Attika.

Phylobasileis (φυλοβασιλεῖς): Tribe kings. In the democracy of the 4th century, the phylobasileis, along with the basileus, held inquiries in the Prytaneion in cases of death caused by an animal or an inanimate object.

Pinakion (πίναξ, πινάκιον): (1) A small plaque, of bronze or boxwood, used in kleroteria for the allotment of dikastai and bouleutai. (2) πινάκιον λελευκομένον: A whitened board on which an official document, declaration, or decree was written for public display and official recording.

Pinakion timetikon (τιμητικόν, assessing): Wax tablet used in votes on penalties in the 5th century.

Plinth (πλίνθος, brick): Block directly underneath a column in the colonnades of Greek buildings.

Pnyx: Meeting place of the Athenian ekklesia.

Polemarch: One of the chief archons at Athens. He presided at preliminary hearings in cases involving foreigners and metics.

Poletai (πωληταί, sellers): Board of ten magistrates at Athens, responsible for leasing silver mines at Laurion, selling rights to collect taxes, and disposing of the goods of atimoi.

Poros: Variety of limestone.

Prodikasia (προδικασία): One of the three preliminary hearings held in consecutive months by the basileus before a trial for homicide.

Proedroi (πρόεδροι): In one sense, nine men allotted each day to preside over the boule and ekklesia.

Proklesis (πρόκλησις): A summons to appear before an arbitrator or court.

Propylon (πρόπυλον): The building, or gatehouse, before a main entryway.

Prothesmia (προθεσμία): Date set as boundary for initiation of further proceedings in a case at law.

Prytaneis (πρυτάνεις): The fifty representatives of a tribe whose turn it was to be the Council's executive committee of Athens during a civic month.

Prytaneion: Building southeast of Agora used for state receptions; also site of hearings and possibly trials in cases of homicide where the killer was unknown and in cases of accidental death caused by animals or inanimate objects.

Psephos (ψῆφος, pebble, counter): (1) A ballot. (2) By synechdoche, a lawcourt or decision.

Psephisma (ψήφισμα): A decree.
Pseudomartyria (ψευδομαρτυρία): A charge lodged against one accused of making a false statement under oath in a case at law.
Psiathion (ψιάθιον): Mat used as cushion for sitting or sleeping.
Rebate block: Stone block with a recess cut in it.
Red and Green Courts: Two dikastic courts noted by Pausanias. *See also* Batrachioun; Phoinikioun.
Riser: The vertical face of a step.
Rubble packing: Filling of unworked stones used in walls and foundations.
Sanis (σανίς): Notice board. *See* Pinakion (2).
Socle: A band along the base of a wall.
Soffit: Lower surface of architrave and cornice, visible from the floor or steps of a building.
Solon: Lawgiver at Athens; archon in 594/3 B.C.E.
Stamnos (στάμνος): (1) A measure. (2) Jar or urn used as a standard of measure.
Sphekiskos (σφήκισκος, truss): (?) Lintel of a dikasterion.
Sphondylos (σφόνδυλος, vertebra): Bronze ballot.
Stoa of Attalos: Stoa east of Panathenaic Way built by King Attalos I of Pergamon beginning 158/7 B.C.E.
Stoa Basileios (Royal Stoa): Stoa in northwest section of Agora; occasionally used as meeting place of the Areopagos Council. As the Basileus' official seat, site of preliminary hearings in some murder cases.
Stoa Poikile (Painted): Stoa on northern side of Agora; used as seat of diaitetai and as a dikasterion.
Strategoi (στρατηγοί, generals): At Athens they were ten in number and elected.
Stylobate: The level of a Greek building on which columns are based.
Sycophant (συκοφάντης): An Athenian who prosecutes to extort money.
Symbolon (σύμβολον): A token, used in dikasteria (1) to allot dikasts to a section of seats within a court or (2) for the distribution of pay.
Synedrion (συνέδριον): The meeting place of a deliberative body.
Synegoros (συνήγορος): Witnesses and other speakers who testified on behalf of a litigant.
T-clamp: Metal clamp set into two building blocks to hold them together. *See also* Clamp.
Theseion: The shrine of Theseus, dubiously identified as a dikasterion.
Thesmothetai: Six of the nine archons, responsible *inter alia* for setting the calendar for the dikasteria.
Tholos: At Athens, a round building south of the Bouleuterion and Metroon where the prytaneis met and dined.
Timoleon: Syracusan king of mid-4th century B.C.E.; he prevented a Carthaginian conquest of Sicily in 343.
Tread: The horizontal surface of a step.
Trigonon (τρίγωνον, triangle): A court at Athens.
Triobol: (1) A coin worth three obols. (2) An emblem used on many bronze pinakia, perhaps to signify that the owner of a pinakion was eligible to serve as a dikast.
Tryblion (τρύβλιον): A small bowl.
Zea. *See* Phreatto.

PART I

HISTORY AND ANALYSIS

1

NOMENCLATURE OF COURTS AT ATHENS

IT IS VITAL TO ESTABLISH at the start what systems, structures, objects, and procedures the principal names and labels denote. For at Athens, a lively populace applied a refined appreciation of the complexities of judicial administration to an array of solutions. As a result, names of officers, buildings, procedures, and indeed the system as a whole acquired added or altered meanings as judicial life evolved. In this first chapter, names of courts are sorted and identified.

HOMICIDE COURTS

In nomenclature, as in other respects, homicide courts are differentiated from popular courts. For one thing, the nomenclature of homicide courts at Athens provides few instances of alternative names. Their judges are called ephetai or dikastai,[1] and a formal assembly of these judges is called dikasterion[2] or, in the case of the Areopagos, Council. A site or structure used by the Council of the Areopagos for assemblies was called synedrion or bouleuterion (**28**). Homicides, along with certain other associated crimes, fell into five classes, and each class was assigned to a particular homicide court. Athenians named the five courts after their locations. Hence one court sat somewhere on the Hill of Ares, another at the Palladion, a third at the Delphinion, a fourth at the Prytaneion, and a fifth (by tradition if not in practice) in the sanctuary of Phreatos.[3] Although the Council of the Areopagos sat on occasion not on the Hill of Ares but in the Stoa Basileios ([Demosthenes] 25.23; *Agora* III, no. 11), no alternate name for the council came into use as a result. One other name, ἐπάλξεις, found only in rhetorical lexica (**59**, **60**) as the name of a homicide court, may be an alternate designation for one of those just listed.[4] There are no references otherwise to a court of that name.

POPULAR COURTS

Athenian references to popular courts are various, and so an attempt to enumerate them requires careful analysis of nomenclature. To begin with basic terms, the old word ἡλιαία can mean a judging panel composed of an unknown number of heliastai (**97**) or (in the 4th century and after) an enhanced panel of 1,000 or more dikasts (**110**, **126**). "Heliaia" can furthermore denote the abstract concept "court system" or "lawcourt", which Athenians used in general rules or formulations having to do with the administration of justice (**114**, **123**, **130**–**138**). In time "heliaia" comes to mean one particular area or structure that is identified with the judging body (**110**, **116**–**122**, **124**, **125**,

[1] R. Sealey ("Athenian Courts for Homicide," *CP* 78, 1983, pp. 275–296) examines the place of ephetai in homicide courts. J. Burnet (*Plato's Euthyphro, Apology of Socrates and Crito*, Oxford 1924, p. 43) errs in assuming that the word δικασταί necessarily implies "an ordinary heliastic court."

[2] See, e.g., Hansen 1981, p. 16, note 10.

[3] See Boegehold 1974, pp. 14–16. It is also possible that "in Phreatto" (*vel sim.*) and "in Zea" were two different ways of referring to the same court.

[4] Miller (1978, pp. 18–19) suggests that this is another name for the Prytaneion.

127–129).[5] Presumably, it can also designate any area or structure whatsoever where the judging body called heliaia meets, particularly on the occasion when they meet there.

δικαστήριον and ἡλιαία are in most senses synonymous. "Dikasterion" means a judging panel of dikastai, that is, judges who cannot be differentiated from heliastai except in one respect, namely, that dikastai but not heliastai judge at homicide trials. "Dikasterion" also denotes the place, whatever the building or area may be, where empaneled dikasts sit. The word, often in its plural form, dikasteria, means "lawcourt" or "court system", that is, the whole system, as cited in laws, decrees, and general formulations.[6] In this last sense, the words dikasterion and heliaia are used to invoke a process. In the 4th century and later, *ta dikasteria* rather than *heliaia* was the way to denominate the system as a whole (including the heliaia *qua* enhanced dikastic panel) except for certain formal and ceremonial contexts where the old word, heliaia, was retained.[7] "Dikasterion" is sometimes personified, and so it can "stand up" at Demosthenes 21.221 or "thunder" in Aristophanes, *Wasps* (line 624 [**78**]), but "heliaia" is not.

At some time in the 4th century, one particular building at Athens came to be known as the Heliaia. (For a surmise that this was Building A, see pp. 11–12 below.) On occasions when one thousand or more dikasts convened to make up a single judging panel, they sat in that building. The building may have been used over a period of time as long as several generations for sittings of a combined panel called heliaia, but the name it acquired from these sessions is not attested until the middle of the 4th century. Previously and concurrently it could have had one or more other names.

The phrase τὰ δικαστήρια, after *ca.* 340 B.C.E., besides being used to invoke a process, seems to refer to a single complex of court buildings disposed in such a way that the complex as a whole could be closed off temporarily from its immediate surroundings. Aristotle's description of procedure (as clarified by modern scholarship; see Aristotle, *Ath. Pol.* 63–69 with Rhodes 1979) is the primary evidence from which we infer the existence of this complex, but in two other references as well, both from *ca.* 330 or after, speakers seem to assume such a unified cluster. They are Demosthenes 42.11, dated after 330 (**84**): "He came up to me in front of the courts"; and Deinarchos 2.13 (**80**), dated perhaps as late as 323. Certain other references to the courts as a whole might seem at a glance to have the same referent, but they are in fact equivocal. The topos "our forefathers built these courts" ([Demosthenes] 25.48, dated 338–324 B.C.E., and Demosthenes 18.123 [**81**], of 330 B.C.E.) can be understood as a widely inclusive reference. An accompanying gesture could show that courts both inside and outside the city wall were meant. The phrase πρὸ τῶν δικαστηρίων in Isokrates 7.54, of about 355 B.C.E. (**87**), and Demosthenes 21.4, of shortly after 350 (**82**), can be understood in the particular context of each oration to mean "now in front of this court and now in front of that." That is, the phrases were applicable at a time when, as we know, trials were being held in buildings like the Odeion and the Stoa Poikile, which were situated at considerable distances from each other (see Fig. 1).

[5] Hansen (1981–1982, pp. 9–47) has a helpful study with full collection of evidence and secondary literature. He shows that heliaia can be panel or institution (pp. 9–15), but of the four passages he cites to show heliaia as building, only two, namely, [Demosthenes] 47.12 (**118**) and Aristotle, *Ath. Pol.* 68.1 (**110**), are sure references to a building. Cf. Busolt and Swoboda 1920, pp. 1151–1152 with note 3. Of the other two references Hansen cites, I take ἐν ἡλιαίαι at Aristophanes, *Knights*, lines 894–898 (**104**) to mean "in court", and εἰς τὴν ἡλιαίαν τὴν τῶν θεσμοθετῶν of Antiphon 6.21 (**97**) refers to a dikastic panel that is to be convened and not to a building. Cf. *IG* I^3 40, lines 71–76 (**130**) and *Agora* III, p. 145. Further discussion is on pages 5–6 below.

[6] Note, e.g., the formula ὅταν πρῶτον πληρῶσι δικαστήριον; cf. Index, *IG* II^2, *s.v.* πρυτάνεις (fin.). As to the qualification δημόσια in τὰ δημόσια δικαστήρια of *IG* II^2 663, lines 29–30 (**93**), the word may serve to stipulate that these courts seat 500 dikasts. Cf. Hansen 1981–1982, pp. 33–35.

[7] See Agora I 7295, lines 101–104 (**132**). Cf. Hansen 1981–1982.

The basic terms δικαστήριον, δικαστήρια, and ἡλιαία therefore all need context to show exact sense. In addition to possible confusions caused by varying use, a given court might have more than one generally recognized name. A court could have names not only from its location (as was the case with homicide courts and possibly with the Parabyston) but also from a distinguishing feature, as, for instance, the Trigonon. Again, it could be named after a magistrate or architect or builder. The Stoa Poikile, where trials were held in mid-4th century, was known also as the Peisianakteios Stoa, after one Peisianax (*PA* 11775).[8]

An Athenian, in short, sometimes had options when he wanted to name a particular court. A survey of attested options, along with some that are inferential, will be helpful here.

Heliaia

No building called Heliaia is attested before mid-4th century, and so we cannot assign early sessions of a panel called heliaia to a building of that name. We do, however, have notice of a large court, one in which 1,000 dikasts sat, called Metiocheion or Μητίχου τέμενος (see **2**, **149–151**, with commentary on the spelling). Lexicographical tradition assigns the name to a Metiochos or Metichos as builder or underwriter. There was a Metiochos, contemporary of Perikles, about whom some comic lines survive.[9] Plutarch cites him as an example of the politician who wants to be responsible for everything and in doing so becomes ridiculous. If this Metiochos inspired the phrase "temenos of Metichos", the formulation may have a satiric or otherwise humorous basis.[10]

The Metiocheion can be the building in which the heliaia judged during the '40's, '30's, and '20's of the 5th century (**150**).[11] As for the interchangeable phrases ἡλιαία τῶν θεσμοθετῶν and δικαστήριον τῶν θεσμοθετῶν, they are best understood as particular elements of the whole system rather than as labels for a court building. In other words, dikasterion or heliaia of the thesmothetai is a panel of dikasts or heliasts that the thesmothetai convene. Witness a heliaia of the thesmothetai attested at *IG* I^3 40, lines 74–76 (**130**) and a dikasterion of the thesmothetai at Andokides 1.28 (**96**). That these are two ways of referring to the same sort of panel is shown by Antiphon 6.21–24 (**97**), where in one breath the speaker refers to a heliaia of the thesmothetai and in the next calls the same assembly a dikasterion. When in the early 3rd century the Athenians direct the thesmothetai to scrutinize a gift in the heliaia, the thesmothetai are being told to give the case in question to one of those days on the court calendar which they assign.[12]

There is a court called Μεῖζον, "greater", which Lysias and Deinarchos may have cited as though it were separate and independent (**2**). That adjective by itself, however, implies "heliaia", since no judging body or building other than the heliaia, except for the Metiocheion, is ever differentiated as being larger than the rest.

[8] See *Agora* III, nos. 13 and 22, with pp. 31, 45, note 1, on some corruptions of the name. Cf. Epilykeion (earlier called Polemarcheion), Boukoleion (which may have been called Basileion before; see Rhodes 1981, p. 103), Tholos (known also as Skias and conceivably also as Prytanikon [see *Agora* III, p. 184]), and the springs Klepsydra/Empedo and Kallirhoe/Enneakrounos. Cf. also the equivalence εἰς τὸ Μητρῷιον and εἰς τὸ δημόσιον.

[9] Plutarch, *Precepts of Statecraft* 811F.
Μητίοχος μὲν γὰρ στρατηγεῖ, Μητίοχος δὲ τὰς ὁδούς
Μητίοχος δ' ἄρτους ἐπωπᾶι, Μητίοχος δὲ τἄλφιτα,
Μητίοχος δὲ πάντ' ἀκεῖται, Μητίοχος δ' οἰμώχεται.

[10] Cf. *Agora* III, pp. 147–148 on Metiochos.

[11] Cf. *FGrHist* 324 F59, notes to commentary, p. 148.

[12] Shear (1978, p. 60) notes the equivalence of dikasterion and heliaia and assigns the difference to personal style in choice of words. For a suggestion that the word had a political resonance, see p. 41 below.

In sum, it is possible to conjecture that in the 5th century a large building named after Metiochos was one place where the heliaia (*qua* judging body) sat. That building, or a successor, came in time to be known as the Heliaia, that is, the building in which the heliaia customarily sat. Because of its size, or more probably because the heliaia *qua* enhanced panel was larger than other panels, the court or court building may have been called Meizon. There is, however, the Periclean Odeion, whose external dimensions (62.40 × 68.60 m.) establish it as the largest structure in which trials are attested as having taken place. In the absence of any apparent connection between the Odeion and the Heliaia, the term "greater" applies more easily to the size of the judging panel than to the building.

Odeion

The Odeion (Fig. 1), a famous monument of the Periclean building program, may well be the site that Aristophanes calls οὗπερ ἄρχων.[13] In the 4th century, suits for support (δίκαι σίτου) were heard in the Odeion (Pollux 8.33 [**170**], Demosthenes 59.52–54 [**169**]), and it was the archon who scheduled and introduced such suits (Lipsius 1905–1915, pp. 58–59). If in times as widely separated as 422 and *ca.* 340 archon and Odeion are associated, it is natural to assume that "archon's court" and "Odeion" were two separate and distinct ways of designating one court building. Formal arbitrations took place in the Odeion in the 4th century, but no dikastic trials other than those introduced by the archon are attested. If the heliaia did not meet here, the Odeion as court site could nevertheless have been called Meizon on the basis of its size.

Parabyston and Trigonon

Parabyston is a court building where a state committee of eleven men, styled simply the Eleven, supervised trials (**2**, **139**, **156**). This Parabyston may be Philokleon's Court of the Eleven and at the same time his "Court by the Walls".[14] A third equivalence needs to be discussed, the possibility that Trigonon was another name (possibly applied later) for the building called Parabyston.

While on the Hill of Ares, Pausanias (1.28.4–11) reflects on other courts at Athens, dikasteria first and then homicide courts (**1**). He makes it clear that he does not go in person to any of these courts, because his next topographical reference after talking about courts is at 1.29. There, upon leaving the Hill of Ares, he points to the Panathenaic ship. His list of courts, it has long been agreed, derives from a written account.[15] Or, if he heard of the courts from a local guide, he did not go and look at them. In either case, one item in his list of dikasteria, that is, the names Parabyston and Trigonon, has been problematic for editors, translators, and commentators. A clarification, however, is possible. First, consider the Greek text without 19th-century editorial changes.

> ἔστι δὲ ᾿Αθηναίοις καὶ ἄλλα δικαστήρια οὐκ ἐς τοσοῦτο δόξης ἥκοντα. τὸ μὲν οὖν καλούμενον παράβυστον καὶ τρίγωνον τὸ μὲν ἐν ἀφανεῖ τῆς πόλεως ὂν καὶ ἐπ᾽ ἐλαχίστοις συνιόντων εἰς αὐτό τὸ δὲ ἀπὸ τοῦ σχήματος ἔχει τὰ ὀνόματα. Βατραχιοῦν δὲ κὰι Φοινικιοῦν ἀπὸ χρωμάτων καὶ ἐς τόδε διαμεμένηκεν ὀνομάζεσθαι. τὸ δὲ μέγιστον. . .κτλ.

Curt Wachsmuth (1890, p. 366) adds a τὸ before τρίγωνον and prints τὰ ὀνόματα while adding in parentheses his preference for τὸ ὄνομα rather than τὰ ὀνόματα. Hitzig and Blümner (1896, p. 68) print Wachsmuth's added τὸ without brackets, change τὰ ὀνόματα to τὸ ὄνομα, and note

[13] See p. 173 below on the interpretation of Aristophanes, *Wasps*, lines 1108–1109 (**139**). Cf. *FGrHist* 324 F59, notes to commentary, p. 151, note 7.

[14] See *FGrHist, loc. cit.*, note 13 above.

[15] See, e.g., Hitzig and Blümner 1896, p. 314; *FGrHist* 324, F59, notes to commentary, p. 146. On views of Pausanias' reliability generally, see C. Habicht, *Pausanias' Guide to Ancient Greece*, Berkeley/Los Angeles/London 1985, pp. 165–175.

their changes in the apparatus criticus. Wachsmuth does not argue his alterations of the text. Hitzig and Blümner accept them without discussion. Wachsmuth may have given authority to lists such as are preserved in Pollux (**2**) or to Aristophanic scholia (**144**) and Photios (**167**), where Parabyston and Trigonon are cited as different courts. He consequently made two small but vital alterations in the text whose effect was to have Pausanias say that the two names designated two separate and distinct buildings. Hitzig and Blümner, subsequently in printing Wachsmuth's version, canonized Parabyston and Trigonon in Pausanias' account as separate. W. H. S. Jones in the Loeb edition (1918) and N. D. Papachatzis (1963) print τὸ ὄνομα (but with no warning that a plural form actually stands in the manuscript) without accepting Wachsmuth's proposed τὸ before τρίγωνον. James G. Frazer in *Pausanias's Description of Greece* accepts this interpretation when he translates: "The court called Parabyston (pushed aside) is so named because it is in an obscure part of the city and they resort to it only in the most trivial cases. The court called Trigonum (triangular) gets its name from its shape." Let his example stand for many.

The relevant sentences in their pre-Wachsmuth form (happily reinstated by Maria Helena Rocha-Pereira in the Teubner edition of 1973) can be construed as follows: "The Athenians have other lawcourts too, ones that are not so famous. The one called Parabyston and Trigonon has its names because it is situated in an obscure part of the city and men come together there on the least important occasions, and because of its shape. The green and red courts continue even now to be named from their colors. The most important court. . . . "

The structure of this short excursus is not very complex. The first μέν with οὖν is continuative. Then the particles μέν, δέ, δέ establish a sequence of three units. The first unit is a single court called by two names, *viz.* parabyston and trigonon, the second unit is two courts, each of which is labeled by its color, and the third unit is the Heliaia. The first of these three units is qualified by explanations of its double nomenclature. τὸ μὲν introduces an explanation of the name Parabyston, followed by an epexegetic καὶ, which introduces a circumstantial and therefore (it is intended) convincing detail. Next, a balancing τὸ δὲ introduces an explanation of the name Trigonon. It is Pausanias' manner of expression to use τὸ μὲν. . .τὸ δὲ . . . to qualify or explain a single entity. Compare 1.43.4, 2.3.2, 2.10.6, 2.19.3, 6.14.7, 8.7.3, 9.11.4, and 10.32.7.

Apart from Pausanias, a Parabyston and a Trigonon are attested elsewhere as separate and distinct courts: Parabyston in the late 5th and mid-4th century (**2**, **156**, **159**, **160**), Trigonon in the late 4th century (**2**, **166**). The clear difference in times prompts a conjecture that a court site or building or indeed merely the name, Trigonon, somehow succeeded Parabyston. But to return to Pausanias, if he does not say, as he does of the Red and Green Courts, that the Parabyston/Trigonon had its names in his day, the omission need not be relevant. The entire question of Pausanias' personal authority for the information he volunteers concerning the courts has not been answered satisfactorily. Two instances of awkwardness are apparent. First, he situates the Parabyston in an obscure part of the city. But if, as is credibly suggested, the Parabyston was situated in the Agora in the 5th and 4th centuries,[16] it was not in an obscure place at that time. Next, when he says that only the most trivial cases are tried there, he again contradicts what other evidence we have, for the Parabyston seems to have been a court in which important trials were held. The Eleven tried the malefactors who were called *kakourgoi* in that court, and a man convicted there could die. At least one trial held in the Parabyston may have been recorded on stone (**159**). This was an expensive form of publication, and it was not regular or usual to make a permanent public record of the outcome of a trial. Very few records of trials at Athens survive, and yet litigation under the

[16] See *Agora* III, p. 146.

democracy was unrelenting.[17] Moreover, if in the record of a trial possibly held at the Parabyston, 443 dikasts voted for acquittal (*IG* II^2 1646 [**159**]), a number as high as this shows that the judging panel was one of at least 501 dikasts, the number present, for example, at the trial of Sokrates. Again, a homicide could be tried at the Parabyston. Euxitheos at Antiphon 5.9–11 protests that he is being tried as a kakourgos rather than as a homicide, although the charge against him is really one of homicide.

To sum up, it is plain that the Parabyston in the 5th and 4th centuries B.C.E. was not in an obscure place where men convened on the least important occasions. As for Pausanias' time, the manner of his telling does not imply autopsy (see p. 6 above). It is likely that Pausanias heard or read a confused account, one whose author attempted some etymologizing.[18] If parabyston means "stuffed in a corner", an ancient commentator might extrapolate and state as fact that the court was obscure. This manner of reconstruction of early institutions can be seen in etymologies of "heliaia" and in the creation of ten-man companies of Lykos.[19]

Phoinikioun (Red) and Batrachioun (Green) Courts

Pausanias' Red and Green Courts, modern writers have generally agreed, get their names from courts in a complex of buildings which Aristotle calls τὰ δικαστήρια (**249**). In Aristotle's description of procedure, a dikast at one point receives a staff, which is the same color as some visible and painted architectural element of the court building in which he is to sit. At another point, officials are assigned to courts by an allotment in which dice and kleroteria are used. The dice, like the staves, are colored to match the identifying colors of the courts (see pp. 37, 199).

In an inscription that has been dated *ca.* 342/1, there is mention of a πρῶτον and a μέσον of the New Courts (Agora I 1749 [**147**]).[20] If the courts are new *ca.* 341, they may still have been sufficiently novel (or rather the system that was made complete with their construction was still sufficiently novel) for Aristotle to have given special care to their description even fifteen years later. The Red and Green Courts named by Pausanias and the courts that Aristotle describes as being identified by color could consequently have been the same buildings as the "First" and "Middle" courts. The Trigonon, since it is attested only for the time when the complex of courts existed, may likewise have been one of the three, situated, as conjectured above, on the site of the old Parabyston. The term "triangle" may alternatively in some unknown way refer to the disposition of all three (?) courts within the complex.

[17] U. E. Paoli ("Sull'esistenza di archivi giudiziari in Atene," in *Studi in onore di Emilio Betti* III, Milan 1962, pp. 4–13) postulates a special record-keeping office for the Athenian lawcourts, but the sort of business he instances could all have been handled by the relevant magistrates. It is the magistrates who set out the notices (Isokrates 15.237–238 [**342**]) at the beginning of an action. Where records of adjudications are preserved, they are found in the midst of an official's other published accounts. See **148**.

[18] Jacoby (*FGrHist* 324 F59, commentary, p. 154, notes to commentary, p. 146) postulates a common source for Pausanias and for Pollux *et al.* In the course of doing so, however, he must explain why Pausanias changed the order in which the names were given. He furthermore observes, without attempting an explanation, that Pausanias includes two names, *viz.* Batrachioun and Phoinikioun, which are not found in any other lists. In the face of these discrepancies, it seems as easy to suppose that Pausanias was using some different source of information.

[19] See Boegehold 1967, pp. 111–115.

[20] Wycherley (*Agora* III, p. 147) has the published date of this inscription fifty years too early. As a result, he erroneously places the dikasterion early in the 4th century (p. 148).

SUMMARY

In almost every case, an Athenian name for a lawcourt may be just one of two or three names for the same court. As a result, ten or more different names of courts or references to courts in the late 5th century may denominate five or fewer actual buildings or sites. They are the following: Metiocheion (which could also be called Heliaia and possibly Meizon), the Odeion (also called "where the archon sits" and possibly also Meizon because of its size), the Parabyston (also called the Court of the Eleven or the Court "by the Walls"), and perhaps the Kallion (**2**, **145**, **146**).[21] The existence of any particular court known to Athenians as the court "at Lykos" can be questioned (**176–185**). That is, the phrase may be an inference from Aristophanes' allusion to a court that was in normal parlance called by one or two other names. The same is true of his "Kainon" (**143**, **144**). Ardettos (**171–175**) and the Theseion (**186**, **187**) have been named as sites of trials, but their credentials as courts are dubious, and they will not be considered here as elements of the Athenian dikastic system. The stoas and dikasteria of Aristophanes, *Ekklesiazusae*, lines 681–686 (**64**), including the "stoa next to that" and the Alphitopolis, are not necessarily courts (see "Court Sites," p. 97 below, for the Stoa Basileios).

By mid-4th century, we might expect fewer courts. There were fewer citizens, and Athens no longer administered an empire. And we do in fact find just four, namely, a Heliaia (now unmistakably a building), the Odeion and the Parabyston (still), and a new addition, the Stoa Poikile.[22] If five or six courts sufficed in the 5th century, four were enough for the subsequently reduced volume of legal business.

The "First" and "Middle" courts can mark the beginning of a more coherent system. When Aristotle was writing his *Athenaion Politeia*, he could refer to the dikasteria as a single coherent complex of court sites: a first and a middle court, new in *ca.* 340, could have been courts in the complex, together perhaps with courts that already stood there. One of these courts accommodated the 1,000 or 1,500 dikasts Aristotle cites as constituting the heliaia (*qua* enhanced panel), and that building was called Heliaia. The Trigonon, of which authors speak around the time of the *Athenaion Politeia*, need not have been a separate, independent court site outside the complex. The name Trigonon could, for instance, have described or noted a distinctive feature in the physical disposition of a court within the complex.

[21] If the name Kallion (or Kalleion but not Kainon; see *FGrHist* 324 F59, notes to commentary, p. 152) reflects the influence or art of a Kallias, then it is possible that the court was called by other names as well.

[22] There was also at least one court in Peiraieus. See Boegehold 1974.

2
STRUCTURES THAT CAN BE INTERPRETED AS LAWCOURTS

IT HAS BEEN POSSIBLE to compose an account of Athenian dikastic procedures with enough circumstantial detail to discover changes and trends over a period that includes much of the 5th and 4th centuries (see "Three Court Days," pp. 21–42 below). The testimonies of poets, historians, orators, and philosophers who lived at about the same time as the procedures in question are crucial to attempts at reconstruction, as are the (usually) nameless authors of decrees, accounts, and notices preserved as inscriptions on stone. Later commentators, scholars, and lexicographers sometimes offer, it is true, mere speculation, based on little more primary evidence than is available today, but there are also occasions when their learning preserves unique sources of information. And such sources in turn provide bases for our understanding of objects and functions.[1]

In the account "Three Court Days" (pp. 27–38 below), it is noted that dikastic pinakia[2] changed from bronze to boxwood, and ballots, from pebbles to specially designed bronze voting implements. Another notable change was that of allotments, which became more numerous and more complex, necessitating in turn changes in the names and numbers of court sites and structural accommodations for trials. Since these changes in name and number are noted in contemporary literature and inscriptions and in works of later learning, these sources can be consulted for interpretation of certain architectural remains. Consideration of procedures will follow.

The remains in question are those of buildings whose ground plans and identities can be proposed with varying degrees of probability. Six of these structures were found under the Stoa of Attalos, and they are labeled Buildings A, B, C, D, E, and Square Peristyle (Figs. 2–4, 7–10). Another structure is that on the south side of the Agora, roughly square in plan and labeled over the past forty years or so sometimes "Heliaia" and sometimes "Heliaia(?)", and now in the present study, "Rectangular Peribolos" (Figs. 5, 6). There are in addition, on the west side of the Agora, four benches constructed of poros stone and set into the eastern slope of Kolonos Agoraios (Pl. 1) and, on the north side of the Agora, the Stoa Poikile. Finally there is the Periclean Odeion (Pl. 1), situated outside the Agora, just east of the Theater of Dionysos at the foot of the Akropolis. Our aim is to see whether these physical remains of structures can credibly be assigned places in the dikastic system as a whole.

It will be convenient here to consider two detailed descriptions, the first by John Camp, of the Rectangular Peribolos (pp. 99–103 below), and the second by Rhys Townsend, of the buildings under the Stoa of Attalos (pp. 104–113 below).

[1] See, e.g., **291**, **299**, **301**, **302**, with Boegehold 1982, pp. 3–4.

[2] Pinakion is a generic term, something like the English "plaque" or "tablet". The pinakia that are used in various dikastic procedures are of three sorts: (1) the πινάκιον τιμητικόν (**106**, **334**, **335**) on which dikasts would mark an assessment; (2) the tablets on which parties to an action would write down notes, memoranda, and challenges (**354**); (3) the tablets of bronze (later, boxwood) that served as dikasts' identification tags (see "Pinakia," pp. 59–64 below).

BUILDINGS A–E AND THE RECTANGULAR PERIBOLOS

The five buildings labeled A–E and the Square Peristyle are the structures that can be distinguished in a sometimes confusing complex of ancient wall foundations and footing trenches under the Stoa of Attalos. The earliest of them, Building A, seems to have been constructed around the end of the 5th century. It is also the single building of the six which can be associated by material evidence with judiciary procedures: within its walls and in what we shall with all due caution describe as a lined pit, the "Ballot Deposit" (Pl. 2) was found.[3] No single name for this building, where trials can have taken place, presents itself as immediate and obvious. Certainly, it housed none of the homicide courts, at least to the extent that one can speculate about their locations. The Council of the Areopagos met on the Areopagos and in the Stoa Basileios. The Delphinion was in the neighborhood of the Olympieion. The Palladion, whether near Ardettos or in Phaleron, was never located in the Agora.[4] Phreatos' (to use Theophrastos' spelling, or, as it may be, the court in Zea)[5] was near the sea. The Prytaneion was on the east slope of the Akropolis.[6]

Was Building A perhaps a heliastic court? Of these, there are four principal names, each with one or more alternate names, to be considered first. They are Heliaia, Parabyston, Odeion, and Stoa Poikile. "Heliaia", if not attested as a name of a structure in the 5th century,[7] can be associated by way of the lexicographers with a "precinct of Metiochos" and a "Meizon".[8] The name is accordingly convenient to use as that of one major structure. As argued above (pp. 6–8), Parabyston may be one in a succession of structures, not all necessarily in the same place. If the Parabyston received that particular name around the end of the 5th century, it could in an earlier form have been called "Court of the Eleven" or "Court at the Walls". The Odeion was also "where the archon sits". The Stoa Poikile (or Peisianakteios Stoa), explicitly attested as venue for trials in the 4th century, was built *ca.* 460 B.C.E. and can also be assumed to have been used as a court in the late 5th century. The names Kalleion, ἐπὶ Λύκωι, and Kainon, the first two cited in lexica, the third an allusion in Aristophanes, and all proposed in modern literature as 5th-century court sites,[9] do not have the same depth and variety of reference. Conceivably, they are yet other alternate designations for one or more of the four courts just listed.[10] Allusions to the Theseion and Ardettos as court sites are insubstantial (**171–175**, **186**, **187**). Some other names of courts or court sites, attested only in the 4th century, toward the middle of the century and later, are discussed below (pp. 14–15) in connection with later structures.

[3] See "Bronze Tokens," pp. 67–76 below, for a description of the "Ballot Deposit". "Lined pit", the interpretation of Rhys Townsend, can be compared with earlier attempts to reconstruct a box or table from the terracotta sections; see p. 105 below. Note token B 1169 (**T 11**), found just south of Building C, and token B 1170 (**T 12**), found in front of the north wall of Building D near its west end. Token B 1262 (**T 4**) was found at the southeast corner of the colonnade of the Square Peristyle. Ballot B 1000 (**B 11**) was found inside the southeastern corner of Building C.

[4] See pp. 47–48, 97–98 below for a discussion of the site of the Palladion.

[5] For the purpose of this particular discussion it does not matter whether the court in Zea is a homicide court or not; see "Sites," p. 98 below.

[6] See "Homicide Courts," pp. 50, 96 below.

[7] See "Nomenclature," pp. 5–6 above.

[8] Cf. *FGrHist* 324 F59, notes to commentary, p. 148.

[9] See *FGrHist* 324 F59, pp. 164–167. Cf. MacDowell 1971, commentary on line 1108.

[10] See "Nomenclature," p. 9 above.

Of the four principal names, two are fixed, for the Odeion and the Stoa Poikile have been located and partially excavated.[11] No structure is securely identified as the Heliaia or Parabyston, however, and so these two names can be tested as possibly applicable to otherwise unidentified architectural remains. To take the Heliaia first, the remains designated as Building A show a spacious floor plan of about 900 square meters.[12] If there was a structure in the Agora in the 5th century called the Heliaia, if that structure was the biggest of all the courts, and if it was hypaethral, then Building A might well be the Heliaia.

Another possibility for the identification of Building A presents itself. A square structure near the southwestern corner of the Agora, labeled on Agora plans for many years "Heliaia" or "Heliaia(?)", is named here (pp. 99–103 below) "Rectangular Peribolos", a useful, neutral term, which will be used generally hereinafter. The only substantial reason for calling the peribolos Heliaia was that it offered adequate space for 1,500 dikasts. Two considerations might have seemed to support this identification, but one is only valid when attended by certain almost arbitrary assumptions concerning the (really unknown) early functioning of the heliaia. The consideration is that the Rectangular Peribolos was first built shortly after the beginning of the 6th century B.C.E. The assumptions that give meaning to the date of construction are, first, that as early as the early 6th century, a body of 1,500 dikasts judged as heliaia and, second, that it was judging often enough to require a special, permanent enclosure. There is little in the literary and epigraphic sources, however, to support either assumption.[13] The second consideration is that the Rectangular Peribolos was unroofed: it could therefore be the object of word play with ἥλιος and ἡλιαία. But this consideration applies as well to any other large, unroofed building, for instance, to Building A. When, therefore, the full sum of indicators is displayed, exiguous as that sum may be, Building A more likely than the Rectangular Peribolos was the Heliaia.

Building A encloses an area roomy enough for 1,500 dikasts. In addition, an installation for dikastic equipment is associated with Building A. Furthermore, the ground plan of Building A is one that permits association with Aristophanes' humor. His jokes about sunning in the Heliaia, it is agreed, are etymologically unsound, and yet they may still be indexes to the absence of a roof over all or part of the actual building (**101**, **103**, **108**, **109**, **113**, **116**, **119**, **128**). Building A may at first have been completely open. After a period of use, roofed colonnades were added, which nevertheless left an open courtyard. The sun could still enter, and the same sort of reference was still possible.

Against this identification one might object that Building A was built sometime in the last two decades of the 5th century, whereas the heliaia was being regularly convened at least twenty or thirty years earlier. For those earlier panels one can point to a structure that was in use during the '40's, '30's, and '20's of the 5th century and was large enough for meetings of 1,500 dikasts. The structure in question at some point in its existence (a comic playwright could have invented the phrase) was dubbed "precinct of Metiochos". At the same time or as a result, a name "Metiocheion" was coined, which perhaps humorously evoked the notion of a heroon.[14] The court was also called μεῖζον because larger bodies of dikasts sat there. The Rectangular Peribolos might have been that structure. At the end of the 5th century, however, Building A, designed and built conceivably in the same spirit that occasioned kindred reforms in 410/9 B.C.E., became the place where dikastic panels,

[11] See Travlos 1971, pp. 378, 387–391 with fig. 91 on the Odeion, and Shear 1984, pp. 5–19 for a preliminary report on the Stoa Poikile.

[12] See "Square Peristyle and Its Predecessors," pp. 104–105 below.

[13] Cf. Smith 1925, pp. 106–119.

[14] Jacoby (*FGrHist* 324 F59, commentary, pp. 166–167) notes the possibility of comedy as origin for some of our notices.

whether single or multiple, convened henceforth. Building A subsequently came in the course of use to be called the Heliaia.[15]

Could Building A, however, have been not the Heliaia but the Parabyston? That is, the name may have been bestowed in some arbitrary way that had nothing to do with the situation of the building. Note that the east–west road that leads to the Dipylon Gate forms with the Panathenaic Way two sides of a triangle. If one assumes a third delimiter to the east, be it a north–south road or a structure intersecting these two ways, then a triangular area is formed. This triangular area could have been the basis for the name Trigonon[16] (see Fig. 3). Pausanias, in the reading I have recommended above ("Nomenclature," pp. 6–8), gives the Parabyston two names, *viz.* Parabyston and Trigonon. A Trigonon court is noted in lexicographers as having been mentioned by late 4th-century authors. The lexicographers' explanation that the name "Trigonon" came from the shape of the court may be mere inference from the name without any supporting factual information whatsoever. Another explanation seems equally plausible. Say that "Trigonon" came to be applied to the court because Athenians could see that it was situated on a triangle of land. An objection might seem to be that from *ca.* 340 B.C.E. on, there were other dikasteria in a complex of four court buildings. Why call one building in that area "Trigonon" but not others? An answer could be that the other buildings had not yet been built when the name was given. The building stood by itself in a triangular area, and the name "Trigonon" consequently reflects the situation of the building rather than its shape. In that particular respect, "Trigonon" could resemble "Parabyston" in that both names (for the same building, if we can believe Pausanias) signal site rather than shape. At the same time, Building A was clearly within the area of the Agora, and Antiphon 5.10–11 (**62**) shows that the Court of the Eleven was in the Agora, and the Court of the Eleven is associated somehow with (or may even be the same as) the Parabyston (**156**). Another reference in Antiphon (**156**) suggests a *terminus post quem* of *ca.* 412 B.C.E. for the Parabyston[17] and hence for Building A, if it was in fact the Parabyston.

Given uncertainties concerning the plan of one building, however, namely Building B, and the lack of data by which a secure chronology for Buildings A–E can be established, yet another possibility presents itself. Note that Building B is roughly contemporary with Building A, that is, it was built in the late 5th century. If Building A was not the Parabyston but was the Heliaia as conjectured above, could Building B have been the Parabyston? On the plan (Fig. 2), Building B looks as though it could have been regarded as "stuffed or squeezed in" to face the Panathenaic Way in front of Building A. A question of chronology, like that discussed above in connection with the Heliaia, also arises here. The Court of the Eleven, also known as the Court at the Walls, was in service in 422 B.C.E. (**139**). But if the Court of the Eleven is the same as the Parabyston, the physical remains of Building B are as much as twenty years too late to be identified with a court of the year 422. Is a sequence like the one postulated for the Heliaia imaginable, in which a Court of the Eleven becomes known as the Parabyston after it had been squeezed in between Building A and the Panathenaic Way?

The names Kalleion, Kainon, and "at Lykos" now come into the account. While hypothetically any one (or even two, or all) of these could have been the name(s) of Building A, there is no evidence

[15] Hansen's objection (1981–1982, p. 26) that Pausanias saw the Heliaia in the 2nd century C.E. is valid if Pausanias did actually see the Heliaia. But that may be a dubious assumption; see "Nomenclature," pp. 6–8 above.

[16] A suggestion made by T. L. Shear, Jr. to R. F. Townsend, personal communication.

[17] Not earlier than 419 B.C.E., according to Dover 1950, pp. 44–60, and not later than 411, when Antiphon was executed.

for such an equivalence.[18] Also, these names as well as Parabyston could have designated a court panel when it sat on the poros benches set into the east slope of Kolonos Agoraios. I have suggested that this court site (if it did serve as court) near a temenos of Apollo Patroos was identifiable by an oblique reference to Apollo in Aristophanes, *Wasps*, lines 389–394: Aristophanes, playing on similarities of sounds, has Philokleon appeal to a "Lykos" after having set up an expectation in the audience to hear "Lykeios", which is an epiklesis of Apollo (**176**). Eratosthenes and others subsequently extrapolated from that play on words a factitious court "at Lykos" (**177**, **178**, **181**–**185**). Whether or not these particular poros benches figured in Aristophanes' humor, they could nevertheless have offered seating space for 500 dikasts when they were first installed around the middle of the 5th century. Subsequently, the builders of the Stoa of Zeus Eleutherios may have truncated the northern extension of the benches and, in so doing, gave up an undeterminable amount of seating space. But even so, there remained room on the benches for a panel of 400 dikasts well into the 4th century.[19]

To sum up, it seems possible, without doing violence to documentary or archaeological evidence, to propose the following scheme: The Rectangular Peribolos became known in the mid-5th century as Metiocheion and Meizon; single and multiple panels of dikasts sat there. Toward the end of the 5th century, Building A was built, and it served the purposes of the heliaia (as court system) henceforth; it was probably the building called the Heliaia. Building B was squeezed in between Building A and the Panathenaic Way and became known as Parabyston. It continued to serve as the Court of the Eleven but was no longer the Court at the Walls, as it had been called in 422, when it was situated near or at some distinguishing but now unidentifiable walls.

In the mid-4th century, Athenians were still using Odeion, Parabyston, Heliaia (now indisputably a building [**118**]), and the Stoa Poikile for trials. If any two or three of these courts were in use on the same day, dikasts when allotted to one or the other had to make their way through a populous Agora and its environs. With so much space between buildings, there can be no question of an enclosed complex such as procedure of *ca.* 330 requires (see Fig. 1).

Not long after mid-century, perhaps as early as *ca.* 340, Athenians increased the numbers and kinds of allotment by which they assigned dikasts, magistrates, and venues. In a further implementation of measures designed to guard the integrity of the courts, they established a secure area within which allotted dikasts could proceed to allotted courts. For this system to work, there had to be three or four court buildings close enough to one another to be enclosed by a fence. This is the system that Aristotle describes in the last seven chapters of his *Athenaion Politeia*. With this system, all the court buildings in use on a given day were surrounded by a fence or barrier of some sort, at least until the allotments of the day were performed. The aim was to allot dikasts for service while they were still outside the circumscribed court area and to assign them to courts as they entered the circumscribed area. Since bystanders, or περιεστηκότες, are still mentioned as late as 323 (**193**), the fence must have been taken down or the gates opened after the allotments of dikasts to courts were performed.

In view of this major change in the use of space and structures for trials, it will be helpful now to consider Buildings C and D. Both were built in the third quarter of the 4th century, and Building D was oriented to form a southern boundary of the complex created by the four buildings, A, B, C, and D. As soon as four buildings were standing at the same time, the resulting configuration met the conditions required for the dikastic system of *ca.* 330, described by Aristotle. Building A, spacious enough to seat three dikastic panels of 500 each, could serve as the Heliaia in the system that Aristotle

[18] On a conjecture that Kainon could be another way of referring to the Metiocheion, see *FGrHist* 324 F59, commentary, p. 167.

[19] Boegehold 1967.

describes, whether or not it was called Heliaia earlier in the century. Note that Building A, as the largest of the four structures, is presumably the most important.

Buildings within this complex can account for two other names of courts. The Batrachioun and Phoinikioun courts are noted by Pausanias (**1**), and students now generally agree that the names derive from the colors that Aristotle said were used to distinguish the court buildings (**249**). If, then, Buildings A, B, C, and D made up the complex that Aristotle describes, any one of them could also have been called Green and any other, Red, no matter which was called First, Middle, Trigonon, or Parabyston.

A reader might ask how Pausanias in the 2nd century C.E. could have seen a Parabyston, Trigonon, or Heliaia, or any Red or Green Courts, if by 185 B.C.E. those courts and their successor, the Square Peristyle, were no more than vestiges, buried in the foundations of a great building, *viz.* the Stoa of Attalos. Certainly, Pausanias expresses himself in the manner of a traveler who is seeing monuments and buildings with his own eyes. His whole paragraph on the Athenian courts is written in the present tense, and in one instance he even cites names as enduring to his own day (ἐς τόδε). Note, however, that his animadversions on popular courts come in the middle of a digression that departs from where he is making seemingly firsthand observations on the Areopagos. What he says about popular courts at that point is not connected to any physical landscape. It becomes especially clear that Pausanias is getting his information at secondhand when immediately after his mention of the Heliaia, he goes on to list Athenian homicide courts. He continues to use the present tense, and one might believe that he is describing what he sees as he walks, except that some of the courts are at great distances from each other (Delphinion and Phreatto, for instance), and in one instance at least (Phreatto), the court is quite certainly long extinct.

To return to the cluster of four buildings that may have served as courts in Aristotle's description, two of the buildings, namely A and B, were built near the end of the 5th century, and two others, C and D, were built in the third quarter of the 4th century. Buildings C and D, therefore, can be seen as contemporaneous with two courts attested as new in an inscription of the year 342 B.C.E.[20] These are the First and Middle of the New Courts (**147, 148**). To explain the names First and Middle, we may want to refer to their siting in the complex. πρῶτον, to take the first, could be the court building that was first of the new courts built or the first in some arbitrarily designated spatial sequence; μέσον, a building that is in one way or another in the midst of the complex.[21] In that case, Building D could be the first of the New Courts, meaning either that it was the first to be built when the new complex was being formed or that it was the first of the new courts one saw when walking toward the complex from, say, the south. Building C by this hypothesis becomes the Middle Court, because in a plan of the four buildings, it can be construed as standing in the midst of the other buildings. A virtue of this hypothesis is that it eliminates the need to postulate an otherwise unattested "Third" court, which the term Middle might otherwise seem to prefigure (see "Sites," p. 94 below).

SQUARE PERISTYLE

Dikasteria as panels of 500 dikasts were working at Athens after 307/6 and well on into the 3rd century (see "After 322 B.C.E." pp. 41–42 below). If the dikasteria did not meet during the regime of

[20] Nothing suggests that Athenians at this time needed additional courts to cope with increased trial activity, and so it can be assumed that these new courts replace the Odeion and the Stoa Poikile. Because of their locations, these two particular accommodations cannot be reconciled with the new scheme of courts as Aristotle describes them, nor are they attested as courts after the mid-4th century.

[21] Jacoby (*FGrHist* 324 F59, commentary, p. 166) assumes that the courts called Meson and Parabyston had names that described their sites.

Demetrios of Phaleron, that is, the decade preceding 307/6, one might fairly suppose that when reestablished they took the same form they had when their functioning was interrupted. That is, the *patrios politeia* that Demetrios Poliorketes restored to Athens was in conception that of 322 B.C.E., or at least a constitution in which a system of popular courts was an integral element. A restored dikastic system accordingly might have used as a model one like that which Aristotle describes in *Ath. Pol.* 63–69. It is consequently of interest to find vestiges of a building, the Square Peristyle, a larger, later structure than the Rectangular Peribolos, built after Buildings A, B, C, and D[22] and suitable in size and design to house separately four dikasteria of 500 dikasts. One or two or three of these panels could have judged on a single day, all at the same time, or if there were need for a single enhanced body (which is not attested for the 3rd century), two or three panels could be combined in the spacious central area.

A schematic re-creation of how the Square Peristyle may have been used on a court day can be helpful here. A light fence was set up, which controlled the west entrance to the Peristyle. In the fence there were ten entrances (εἴσοδοι), one for each phyle (tribe),[23] and next to each entrance, there were two kleroteria, that is, two for each phyle, just as in Aristotle's description of procedure *ca.* 325 B.C.E. Dikasts approached their tribal entrances, dropped their pinakia into boxes, were allotted to judge that day, entered the area inside the fence, and were allotted at the same time to a court. The Square Peristyle offered under its colonnades space for four separate and distinct panels of 500 dikasts each. If one supposes there was ever a need after 300 B.C.E. for the enhanced judging body called heliaia, that is, if 1,000 or 1,500 dikasts were required for a particular case, the open area in the middle of the Square Peristyle was large enough for such numbers. There would also be room for bystanders, who were admitted after the outside fence was taken down.

It is not only the physical dimensions and arrangement of space in the Square Peristyle that lend plausibility to this reconstruction. In addition, the evidence of the letters that distinguish areas or bays in the colonnades indicate that the Square Peristyle was meant to accommodate such large numbers. The letters can be seen on krepidoma blocks taken from the Square Peristyle and reused in South Stoa II. Rho and omicron were cut into the faces of two stylobate blocks. The single letters eta, iota, zeta, kappa, and mu are preserved neatly and clearly cut into the top surfaces of separate step blocks, placed there, as Townsend observes (p. 111, note 23, with Pls. 3, 4), because the sloping floor of the court would have covered letters on the face of the blocks. The letters obviously were meant to be seen. On the two sides adjacent to each corner of the Square Peristyle, twenty-five letters can be restored on the step and stylobate blocks (using all the letters of the Attic alphabet plus the additional letter Ͳ, just as in the series of bronze tokens; see pp. 67–76 below). The letters label twenty-five seating areas, two for each intercolumnar area three meters wide and eight meters deep (the depth of the colonnade). It is a space in which 500 dikasts can be comfortably seated (pp. 110–111, with Ill. 5 and Fig. 10).

22 Building E (Fig. 7) was built after Buildings A and C were leveled. One can surmise that the conservative Athenians who were in power from 318 until 307 extirpated the physical evidence of an essential function of radical democracy on the grounds that there was no longer any need for such installations. But there is no literary or documentary evidence that gives a clue to the uses of Building E. Townsend discusses possiblilites of material evidence on p. 100 below, and more full in Townsend 1995.

23 There were, to be sure, twelve tribes by this time, and the system Aristotle describes accommodates ten. It may have been that two were disqualified each court day, by either allotment or rotation. Townsend envisions a slightly different allotment procedure: p. 110 below and Townsend 1995, pp. 92–93 with note 121.

3
HELIASTIC COURTS BEFORE 462 B.C.

IT IS IMPOSSIBLE to describe credibly an action at law in Athens before the production of Aristophanes' *Wasps* in 422 B.C.E., and it is venturesome to make such an attempt for the late 5th century. The basis for reconstruction is principally an assumption concerning what is and what is not taken for granted in a burlesque of the Athenian court system, enlightened from time to time by early commentators' attempts to explain obscure words or allusions. Nevertheless, whatever one thinks can be gleaned from such sources, the sources themselves appear rich and secure when compared with the available evidence concerning judges and courts for the preceding two hundred years. No contemporary author serves as a guide to that period. All accounts and quotations come from later authors, some of whom were heirs to traditional misinformation, while others had private reasons for invoking the past. Yet almost none of them had access to archival documentation.

If Drakon's axones, when republished in 408 B.C.E., preserved original substance and detail, valuable fragments of early legislation show a way to imagine how an early judicial action might have proceeded.[1] If Demosthenes preserves authentic tradition when he has Drakon be the founder of all the Athenian homicide courts (**6**), the basis exists for reconstruction of a site (the Areopagos) and some specified venues for specified trials (Palladion, Delphinion, Prytaneion, Phreatto). Given both conditions, a sketch like the following can be essayed: If one Athenian killed another in the years after publication of Drakon's code in 621/0 B.C.E., the decedent's kin (to a stipulated degree of relationship) or phyle must either prosecute the homicide or end by other means a quarrel that necessarily existed between families of the homicide and decedent. The decedent's kin could accept blood money and so agree to end the quarrel. If, however, the kin prosecuted, their way of phrasing the charge, together with the defendant's response, would determine in what homicide court the trial was to take place. A given death could, for instance, be represented or argued as having been voluntary, involuntary, or the result of an act of self-defense or of a legitimate attempt to protect the sanctity of one's home. How determination of venue finally was made can perhaps be inferred; possibly, the basileus was in the end bound to abide by the wishes of the prosecutor. Whatever the details of procedure, fifty-one ephetai acted as judges[2] and delivered a verdict (διαγνῶναι), and the basileus pronounced judgement (δικάζειν).[3]

[1] Stroud (1968, pp. 75–83) presents a case for responsible use by Aristotle of substantially authentic Draconian and Solonian texts. Cf., however, K. Walters, "The 'Ancestral Constitution' and Fourth Century Historiography in Athens," *AJAH* 1, 1976 [129–144], pp. 129–135.

[2] Homer and Hesiod, the earliest witnesses to juridical proceedings before the time of Drakon, do not attest Athenian practices: Wolff 1946, pp. 34–62. It is worth observing, however, that in the Homeric judging scene, *Iliad* 18, lines 497–508, a single, princely magistrate does not preside as judge; this function is served by a board or panel of elders attended by fellow citizens. In a later instance, Myron of Phlya and a court of 300 dikastai are chosen ἀριστίνδην: Plutarch, *Solon* 12. Jacoby (1949, p. 367, note 81) says the time is not after the expulsion of the Peisistratids. Note the account of 50 plus 50 judges (who become known as ephetai) at Palladion (**45**, **46**, **48**, **50**, **53**).

[3] See *IG* I^3 104 with Stroud 1968. Cf. Gagarin 1981, pp. 37–48. Humphreys (1983, pp. 231–251) lists assemblage of judges, arbitration, and self-help as the basic ways of resolving questions of justice in early days. At p. 235, note 11, she distinguishes between δικάζειν and διαγνῶναι in Drakon's homicide law: "... conceivably the ephetai decided between solutions proposed by the basileis." A different distinction can be suggested, however, namely, to utilize the force of δια- in διαγνῶναι as comparable to that in διακρίνειν, or διαφέρειν τὰς ψήφους, and the subsequent counting,

A truly extraordinary innovation at Athens was the large judging body composed of ordinary citizens, whatever the term citizen may be taken to mean in 590 B.C.E.[4] This was the heliaia,[5] which Aristotle describes as established for the first time by Solon (*Ath. Pol.* 7.3). Since the judges were numerous, it is a reasonable inference that they were not exclusively great landowners. This particular element of the Athenian judiciary system is one that endured (supposing that Solon did bring it into existence) for over four hundred years. It is extraordinary in concept, namely, that ordinary people have a right to judge, and in the very fact that it came to be without (so far as is known) generalized bloodshed. Judgments at Athens were those that allowed or disallowed life, death, freedom, exile, property ownership, trespass, family security; all, in short, that constituted existence both civic and personal. Where else in the history of human settlements has a king or ruling class, or anyone who has had power over others and has not been defeated in battle, relinquished peaceably a right to utter and execute such judgments? In the absence of any responsible account of the years that preceded these vital changes, unanswered questions remain.

An assembly of citizens (*ekklesia*) already established at Athens before Solon's time (exactly when is not known)[6] participated in some general decisions but perhaps did not, as later, decide all questions of state (whether to go to war or make peace, to send for ambassadors, or to ask for a new set of laws). One state function the ekklesia could not perform was that of judging questions of right and wrong where individuals were implicated. Another body, separate and distinct, was necessary for that: hence the heliaia.[7]

The word ἡλιαία as used in Athenian texts of the 5th, 4th, and 3rd centuries B.C.E. means quite different things in different contexts: a heliaia can be a panel of heliasts, which is to say dikasts. It can be two or three panels brought together to form an enhanced body of heliasts or dikasts (**110**). "Heliaia" as a site where trials are held provides a name for the site or building in which the trial takes place. It can also be the proper name of a known building (**118**). While these senses of the word have been generally recognized, one important use, persistently overlooked, has only recently been enucleated.[8] It is that "heliaia", as the entire system of popular courts, distinguishes that particular area of the state's functioning from that of the boule and the ekklesia (**114**, **123**). One could say "heliaia" to invoke "court" in its generic sense when, for example, defining court procedures for allies (**130**, **131**) or authorizing a scrutiny of qualifications for citizenship (**132**).

διαριθμεῖν. The sense is that a dikastic panel or a panel of 51 ephetai has only a yes or no decision to make. This highly restricted choice is the basis of Hippodamos' criticism of voting methods in the 5th century and a reason for his proposed reform (Aristotle, *Politics* 1267b22–1268b3). Whatever this yes or no decision may be, it is not official or applicable until pronounced by the basileus. When the basileus pronounces judgment, he states the right, i.e., δικάζει: see Wolff 1946, pp. 34–57 for this sense of the word. After the pronouncement of the basileus, the herald can then announce (ἀνακηρύττειν) the verdict to the judging panel and others assembled in court. A compound form of the verb, διαδικάζειν, which is used in inheritance cases and elsewhere (see, e.g., **96**) could mean that a presiding magistrate must distinguish between two or more claimants first and then state what the verdict is, i.e., δικάζειν. At Demosthenes 23.28 (**134**), I take this to be the distinction between prescribed duties of archons and heliaia. A prosecutor brings the homicide to whatever magistrate is competent to assign the case a place on a court calendar. After the magistrate has done that, he will on the proper day attend the trial. After a heliastic court has come to a decision, i.e., διαγιγνώσκειν, he pronounces judgment, i.e., δικάζει. In accordance with this sense of the verb, the clause ὧν ἕκαστοι δικασταί εἰσιν can be glossed, "charges concerning which each is authorized to pronounce judgement." Cf. Hansen 1981–1982, p. 27.

4 See, e.g., Hignett 1952, p. 79.

5 I use the familiar spelling. On "eliaia", see Ostwald 1986, p. 10, note 27.

6 See, e.g., Hignett 1952, p. 74, 84; Busolt and Swoboda 1920, p. 443; and Ostwald 1986, p. 77.

7 Hansen 1981–1982; Ostwald 1986; and Hansen 1989, "Addenda," pp. 258–262, present a productive exchange concerning the early heliaia. The following sketch draws on contributions made by both scholars.

8 Hansen 1981–1982, pp. 10–15.

In such uses, "heliaia" is interchangeable with τὰ δικαστήρια or even τὸ δικαστήριον.[9] Other components of the Athenian judicial system as a whole, such as public and private arbitration, trials at deme or phratry, δικασταὶ κατὰ δήμους, summary judgments by magistrates, and homicide courts are not included in the formulation "heliaia". Homicide courts, however, can be included under the term τὰ δικαστήρια (see "Nomenclature," p. 3 above). It is noteworthy that the earliest examples of "heliaia" in its generic sense are found in quotations from Solonian laws (**134**, **136**, **138**).[10]

The word *heliaia* is described by authorities today as cognate with an Ionian word ἁλής, "assembly".[11] "Heliaia" might be supposed therefore to denote from the start any sort of assembly. In recent studies it has been customary to appeal to cognates of "heliaia" and postulate, accordingly, a single, large judging assembly, sometimes even the full assembly of citizens that would be called ekklesia in another function.[12] But a cognate of words that denote "assembly" need not by itself imply only and exclusively the principal assembly of the city.[13] At Athens, an original assembly called heliaia would have been composed of heliasts, and a subdivision of that assembly (a panel of heliasts) would likewise have been called heliaia. That is, each court or panel (as Solon might have designed the system) was convened in accordance with the administrative responsibilities of a single magistracy or board. That Solon did design such a system is not a difficult supposition, since it does no more than retroject a practice of the 5th century.

Two post-Solonian citations of Solonian legislation can reflect Solon's actual language.[14] Although "heliaia" in these fragments has been construed as referring to the Athenian assembly acting in its judicial capacity, nothing in the laws as they are quoted need imply such an assembly. The heliaia is invoked in the 5th, 4th, and 3rd centuries when a certain kind of judicial action is to be judged within the system of popular courts. The word "heliaia" is not attested in the 5th century as necessarily presenting any information about size. As a denotation of the whole judiciary

[9] See Hansen 1981–1982, pp. 9–15. Cf. introduction to **133–138**. Cf. **98**, **130–132**. LSJ does not include this meaning, *s.v.* ἡλιαία. Note **136**, a law that directs the Eleven to take certain cases to the heliaia. The meaning of "heliaia" here may be "that department of the system as a whole to which the Eleven takes cases." The actual venue might have been the Parabyston. Cf. Hansen, *op. cit.*, p. 16: "We need not be surprised if a new source should turn up, telling us that an action was heard by the *heliaia* in the Parabyston."

[10] Jacoby (*FGrHist* 324 F59, commentary, p. 150) cites "an old suggestion of Th. Bergk in *Verh.* 9 *Philol. Vers.* 1847 which is *prima facie* attractive," that Kleisthenes can be assumed to have established four permanent courts, three of which were presided over by the three archons and the fourth by the thesmothetai. Bergk, it can be seen, took over the system as it seemed to him to have functioned (in its essentials) in the early 5th century, a system that could be referred to in its entirety as "heliaia", and assumed it to have been the one that existed in Kleisthenes' time. It seems a natural step to turn back a little further and postulate a similarly composed heliaia in Solon's day. That is, whether Solon or Kleisthenes established the heliaia, the term could have been used early in the 6th century B.C.E. as it was used in mid-5th century to denote four sorts of heliastic court. A body of heliasts, who were defined by the oath they swore, could have been divided by tribes, as soon as it became obvious that 5,000 or 6,000 heliasts when convened as a whole constituted an unwieldy mass. That assembly of sworn heliasts, however, could be *an* assembly without having to be *the* assembly; cf. Hansen 1981–1982, pp. 27–39.

[11] See Chantraine 1968 and Frisk 1960, *s.v.* ἁλής.

[12] The heliaia as the assembly acting in a judicial capacity is accepted by Staveley (1972, pp. 25–26), Bonner and Smith (1938, pp. 151–158), Hignett (1952, pp. 97–98), and Rhodes (1981, p. 160), to name only a few representative authorities. Cf. Hansen 1981–1982, p. 45, note 83.

[13] ἁλία can denote merely one sort of assembly, as in a 5th-century treaty between Knossos and Tylissos (Meiggs and Lewis 1989, no. 42, line 44). Hansen (1981–1982, pp. 28–30) makes this same point, citing other examples. Cf. Ostwald 1986, p. 10, note 29.

[14] Σόλωνος Νόμοι 1966, F16 (Lex ap. Dem. 23.28) τὴν δ' ἡλιαίαν διαγιγνώσκειν and F23c (Lysias 10.16) ἐὰν προστιμήσηι ἡ ἡλιαία (cf. F23d, Lex ap. Dem. 24.105).

system, it can refer to the meetings of separate courts all on the same day or one after another on different days. Note also that by the middle of the 5th century, Athenians could say "heliaia" for their system of popular courts as a whole and yet use the same word for a single panel within that system, one convened by the archon, basileus, or thesmothetai,[15] or (at some point) the Eleven, each meeting at a designated building. "Heliaia", therefore, possibly in Solonian laws and clearly in the 5th, 4th, and early 3rd centuries B.C.E., could denote at the same time the whole heliastic court system or a single heliastic panel, whether enhanced or not.

If "heliaia" is an abstract word for the whole system of popular courts, Aristotle, in saying that Solon founded the heliaia, could have meant that Solon founded the whole system of popular courts. Imagine accordingly a number of courts instituted by Solon, say, four, for the sake of example, each under the presidency of a magistrate.[16] Under Peisistratos, when these popular courts did not function, the Council of the Areopagos was chief (and conceivably the only) court. When Kleisthenes rearranged the administrative divisions of Athenian citizenry in 508/7 and made a democracy practicable, the Areopagos as established court continued to be preeminent. Until well after the Persian Wars and perhaps partly because of them, the Areopagos was the chief court at Athens. But in 462 Ephialtes in some way was responsible for limiting and transferring certain powers from the Areopagos to the popular courts (**86**). When this happened, that is, when there was again a system of popular courts, there was again a heliaia. Now its constituent parts were called dikasteria. To retreat briefly to Solon's time, it is within the realm of possibility that panels of the heliaia existed and were called dikasteria as early as 590 B.C.E., but there is no need to press the question: in Solon's Athens, density of population was not comparable to that of the 5th and 4th centuries. One therefore cannot very well postulate a press of legal business that would necessitate numerous panels of "judges".[17] The system as attested in the 5th and 4th centuries, when courts needed to meet many days of the year, surely came into being long after Solon. If, however, in Solon's time, the Court of the Archon met only one day a month, and the Court of the Basileus met once a month, and the Court of the Polemarch met two or three times a month (these are wholly arbitrary numbers), it would still be possible for Athenians to have called the system in which these various courts functioned "heliaia".

[15] ἡλιαία τῶν θεσμοθετῶν may be a particular panel of heliasts, but the phrase can also invoke the system: see "Nomenclature," pp. 3–4 above. Note that the phrase παρὰ τῶι πολεμάρχωι, cited by Wade-Gery in "The Judicial Treaty with Phaselis and the History of the Athenian Courts" (Wade-Gery 1958, pp. 185–186) as evidence for a summary court administered by a single magistrate, is like a phrase used by Aristophanes (*Ekklesiazusae*, line 655), *viz.* παρὰ τοῖς ἄρχουσι, at a time when the system of popular courts was fully established. A phrase consisting of the preposition παρά + magistracy in the dative case is not enough even in a judicial context to establish the existence of a summary tribunal. Cf. MacDowell 1978, p. 33.

[16] In Solonian laws, the formula ἂν ἡ ἡλιαία προστιμήσηι should not be taken to mean "if one huge assembly add a penalty" but rather "if one of the magistrates' courts add a penalty," i.e., if the trial goes from summary judgment to a trial. ἔφεσις in that case will be a transfer from summary judgment to trial before a heliaia, i.e., a panel of heliasts. Cf., however, E. Ruschenbusch, "Ἔφεσις, Ein Beitrag zur griechischen Rechtsterminologie," *ZRG* 78, 1961, pp. 386–390 and Hansen 1981–1982, p. 37.

[17] Smith 1925, pp. 106–119. Cf. Hommel 1927, p. 36, note 80a.

4
THREE COURT DAYS

AS A WAY OF SHOWING how court procedures changed over the course of a hundred and forty years or so, three schematic reconstructions are offered here of trials on three separate court days. The first is a day sometime between *ca.* 460 and 410 B.C.E.; the second represents a time between 410 and *ca.* 340 B.C.E.; the third, a time between *ca.* 340 and 322 B.C.E. The structures, disposition of personnel, and equipment are somewhat different in each.

The three segments of time that these dates bracket are not to be thought of as eras or as stages in the development of dikastic procedures at Athens. It happens that certain changes in procedure at or around these dates are known and that these changes are important enough to cite as markers, places to stop and take a focused look before continuing on in what is to be a comparatively long history.[1] But the points of demarcation offered here do not show when *all* the changes of the preceding years were effected. The change in voting procedure, for instance, from one pebble to two specially designed ballots, seems to have been made sometime after 405 B.C.E. but before the mid-4th century.[2] What might be called the old style of voting, therefore, obtained throughout the first of my (in some respects) arbitrary segments and during an undetermined part of the second.

Judicial procedures existed at Athens before 460, and the court system shows fluidity throughout the one hundred and fifty years (approximately) this account includes. And yet certain features, namely, large judging bodies, allotments, and secret balloting, remained constant, while Athenians modified ways by which they moved the judging bodies around, allotted courts and jurors, and guarded the integrity of voting. But any particular change can have been occasioned by more than one sort of person or event: perception of malpractice, or general constitutional upheaval or reform, or resentment at the outcome of a trial, or even just some particular Athenian's notion of how the system could be improved, any of these could have been a sufficient factor.

This account takes 460 (*ca.*) as a beginning, because in 462 Ephialtes occasioned an important if not satisfactorily documented shift of certain powers and responsibilities from the Council of the Areopagos to the dikasteria; not long after that, the earliest evidence for secret balloting appears.[3] Secret voting is such an important innovation in constitutional and judicial determinations that in the absence of reliable information about the conduct of earlier trials, Athenians' first use of a secret ballot helps to define a context for the first of the three court days.[4] Another distinctive Athenian

[1] Lipsius 1905–1915 does not present a systematic account of Athenian legal procedures as evolving process. Hommel (1927, pp. 109–135) distinguishes three principal eras, *viz.* 462–403/2, 402–388/7, 387–322. Cf. Bonner and Smith 1938.

[2] See *IG* II^2 1641, lines 25–33 (**163**); 1646, line 8 (**159**); and Aischines 1.79 (**252**).

[3] See Boegehold 1963. J. A. O. Larsen ("The Origin and Significance of the Counting of Votes," *CP* 44, 1949 [pp. 164–181], p. 172) reviews three early forms of assembly as credible venues for the beginnings of voting. But voting at first was open. Aristocrats rather than common folk made up these assemblies. They were proud men, who expected (and indeed took it as a prerogative of their nobility) to stand up and identify themselves with their votes. The Spartan Amompharetos (Herodotos 9.55) offers an example of the spirit if not the exact procedure one might have encountered at such meetings. Ordinary vulnerable people, once they could vote secretly, did not have to fear reprisals, but they needed the incentive of pay (see further, note 4 below).

[4] On variations and refinements of procedure, such as specially composed judging panels, ways of preferring charges, differing responsibilities of magistrates, the whole range of tactics and resources available to litigants, see, e.g.,

practice, that of paying dikasts, also began in these years and may be connected with the institution of the secret ballot.[5]

The year 410/9, when Athens had reestablished a democracy after the oligarchic coup of 411, is the time of another important change, namely, the procedure by which dikasts were assigned to courts and to seats in those courts. If it is not known exactly how these assignments were made, it is a likely inference that before 410 an Athenian citizen became a dikast or heliast by allotment and then was assigned (perhaps again by lot) to one particular court for a year or more at a time. Around or shortly after 410, however, dikasts began to be allotted to a different court each day and to seating places in the courts.[6] They may have been sworn into the eligible body once a year; they were in any case no longer assigned to particular courts: now daily allotments, whose outcome chance and the god (Apollo, presumably)[7] determined, reduced opportunities for corruption.

340 (again, roughly) is the time when Athenians organized their court buildings in accordance with the procedure Aristotle describes in *Ath. Pol.* 63–69. Before then, on a day when two or more courts functioned, all dikasts allotted to serve on that day were dispersed by panels to judge in separate buildings, which could be as far apart from each other as the Odeion (at the southeast foot of the Akropolis) and the Stoa Poikile (on the northern boundary of the Agora). But once Athens had a single, contained complex of structures, dikasts were in a protected area when they walked to their courts. As a consequence, litigants and anyone else who hoped to influence judgments beforehand could not easily make contact with dikasts and be sure they would be in the right place at the right time.

The year 322, when Antipater undid the dikasteria, is generally represented as the end of the Athenian democratic court procedures, at least in approximately the overall conformation they had during the preceding century.[8] Some features and equipment may have been the same as before, but the authority of the courts, widely recognized in the 5th and 4th centuries as paramount, appears from the time of Demetrios of Phaleron and after to be modified or diluted. The capacious Square

---

the relevant sections in Lipsius 1905–1915; Bonner and Smith 1938; Harrison 1971; MacDowell 1978; and Hansen 1976.

[5] Aristotle, *Ath. Pol.* 27.3–4 (cf. *Politics* 1274a8) has Perikles instituting pay for dikasts as a demagogic manoeuvre, and Plutarch, *Perikles* 9.4–5 cites him with approval. Modern scholars more or less follow Aristotle and Plutarch as to motivation, although Harrison (1971, p. 49) recognizes that pay was essential if poorer Athenians were to participate. As for chronology, scholars suppose that dikasts began to be paid shortly after the reforms of Ephialtes in 462. See Rhodes 1981, pp. 338–340; Hignett 1952, pp. 342–343; Thucydides, commentary, 1.112.1, p. 328. H. T. Wade-Gery ("Two Notes in Theopompos, *Philippika*, X," *AJP* 59, 1938 [129–134], pp. 131–134) accepts what he argues is Plutarch's date, namely, a time before Ephialtes' reforms, on the grounds that Plutarch's information comes from Theopompos. At first dikasts were paid two obols, and by 422 the sum was raised to three obols but no more thereafter. Hansen (1979, p. 11) points out that in a democracy like Athens, citizens received pay (*misthos*) as a supplement to income they had to earn elsewhere. The secret ballot was instituted some time close to the institution of pay for dikasts, between 462 and 458 (see Boegehold 1963). There may consequently be a causal connection between the two innovations. The secret ballot protected from bribery and reprisals judicial decisions of ordinary folk who were serving as dikasts. In the earliest kind of open balloting, one where a man voted by voice, by hand, or by means of a pebble or shell, his vote, if bartered or sold, was a commodity whose delivery could be verified. The secret ballot changed all this. If some were selling their votes, pay might have been a way of compensating these entrepreneurs for lost revenue.

[6] See Boegehold 1984, pp. 23–29.

[7] Apollo Pythios, *patroios* at Athens, played an important part in administrative decisions. Note, e.g., how Athenians went about naming the ten Kleisthenian tribes: Aristotle, *Ath. Pol.* 21.60. For the concept, cf. Plato, *Laws* 741B: ὁ νείμας κλῆρος ὢν θεός.... Cf. *id.* 759B.

[8] See note 61 below, p. 41.

Peristyle, which may represent the Athenians' most ambitious attempt to house all their courts in one area, seems never to have been totally functional.

In the present narrative, popular courts, as distinguished from homicide courts, provide the examples. Testimonia for homicide courts give information concerning sites, furnishings, and procedure at different times but not enough for a linear account in which changes or disruptions can be illustrated by circumstantial detail (see "Homicide Courts," pp. 43–50 below).

460 TO *CA.* 410 B.C.E.

By a law attributed to Solon, a citizen could indict anyone he perceived as doing wrong.[9] In cases where two parties disagreed about money, informal arbitration was possible, but there was no known formal, state-administered apparatus of arbitration.[10] To initiate an action as prosecutor, a citizen notified a defendant formally and with witnesses. He did this by sending a crier along with friends who would act as witnesses, or, since he knew the notification would be in a public place, he could hope to enroll casual bystanders as witnesses. This act of formal notification, once executed, required the defendant to appear before a magistrate. There he answered his prosecutor's charges. What magistrate to choose was the prosecutor's responsibility: it could be an archon, a general, or a committee such as the Eleven. After he identified a magistracy as appropriate for an initial hearing, that same magistrate would reserve him a place on the court calendar. A case that involved a foreigner or metoikos, for instance, would begin with a hearing before the polemarch,[11] who would then himself decide whether or not responsibility for that sort of case fell within his competence.

Let us say for the purposes of this reconstruction that the magistrate chosen by the prosecutor was an archon.[12] Once he acknowledged the case as one he was to administer, he fixed a day for the prosecutor (or prosecutors) and defendant to appear and swear charges and denials or counter-charges. If at this hearing (called *anakrisis* because there was questioning to determine when and where a trial should be held)[13] the archon determined his office did not superintend the sort of trial that the charge entailed, the prosecutor(s) could withdraw to find the right magistrate.

Or suppose the archon accepted responsibility. He had a scribe write charges and denials on a wax tablet.[14] He authorized a public notification of the impending trial. He had this notice printed in charcoal or black paint on a whitened wooden tablet (*sanis* [or *sanidon*]: notice board **[337]**), and its form was as follows: "So-and-so, son of Q, from deme R in a sworn indictment has charged Such-and-such, son of X, from deme Y with committing the following crime(s)." One or more

[9] Σόλωνος Νόμοι 1966, 40a–b. Ruschenbusch describes this particular fragment as "unzulässige Verallgemeinerung."

[10] A. Steinwenter, *Die Streitbeendigung durch Urteil Schiedspruch und Vergleich nach griechischem Recht* (Beiträge 8), Munich 1925, pp. 60–62. The evidence is admittedly weak, but as MacDowell (1978, p. 203) says, privately arranged arbitration "must have been common in Athens at all periods." Humphreys (1983, pp. 240–242) argues that state-organized arbitrations should be associated with Kleisthenes' reforms.

[11] See Lipsius 1905–1915, pp. 64–65.

[12] See Lipsius 1905–1915, pp. 53–120 on the relevant magistrates.

[13] On anakrisis, see MacDowell 1978, pp. 240–242; cf. Harrison 1971, pp. 94–105.

[14] He kept it as his own. At the end of a year in office, archons underwent a judicial review (*euthyna*) of transactions in which they had acted officially, and such notations on a wax tablet could have been helpful then as memoranda.

crimes were specified. After the crimes, a penalty, which may have been a money fine or death or exile, could be written. It was signaled by the single word "penalty".[15] The defendant's sworn denial may have been subjoined in some form such as follows: "I, Such-and-such, son of X, from deme Y, did not commit (whatever crime has been specified)." The tablet (or board, if it needed to be large enough to hold notices of other trials scheduled for the same day) would have been displayed before the statues of the Eponymous Heroes, which stood near the southwest corner of the Agora. A railed fence around the ten statues held the notices on display.[16]

Some litigants, giving vent to their feelings or hoping to improve their chances, used a curse. This bit of magic was directed against the principal antagonist and any of his friends or relations who might be thought to be coming to his aid. One form of curse was to scratch into a sheet of lead a formulaic prayer to Hermes or Demeter asking these gods to disarm So-and-so by freezing and stupefying his mind, his tongue, his arms, his legs, and (sometimes) his generative parts. If an average Athenian lacked savoir faire, he could go to the Agora and find an amanuensis who knew exactly what to do, namely, write out the proper words, commit them to the proper material, and explain how to post the message efficaciously. One way was to roll up the lead sheet on which the curse was scratched, drive a nail through it, and drop the package down a well or into a grave, preferably that of someone who had died prematurely (see "A Curse Tablet," pp. 55–57 and Ill. 4).

A magistracy, it appears, was consistently associated with a certain court, for instance, the Eleven with Parabyston (**156**) and the archon with the Odeion (**140**). The archon's court was accordingly a long way around from the Agora, where other, contemporary courts like the Parabyston and Stoa Poikile were situated. On occasions when a trial seemed to require a larger judging body, two or three panels met in combination to form a heliaia of 1,000 or 1,500 dikasts.[17] A total of 1,500 dikasts could have met in the Rectangular Peribolos at the southwest corner of the Agora (but this is not to say that the Rectangular Peribolos was the building known in the 4th century as Heliaia; see p. 12 above). The 1,500 could also have convened in the Odeion or the Theater of Dionysos, or (supposing an extraordinary heliaia of 6,000 heliasts was required) in the Pnyx.[18]

[15] Euripides, *Alkestis*, lines 30–31 (with A. M. Dale, *Euripides. Alcestis. Edited with Introduction and Commentary*, Oxford 1966, pp. 54–55) has Thanatos use the phraseology. Aristophanes uses the formula in his burlesque at *Wasps*, line 897. Note that the proposed penalty is added on to the charge without any connecting particle. The same asyndeton can be observed at Demosthenes 45.46 and at Diogenes Laertios 2.40. Whether the proposed penalty is one stipulated by law or one that the plaintiff puts forward is a question that is answered perhaps at the anakrisis. There existed various ways of describing, prosecuting, and punishing a given offense. See Antiphon 5.18–19. Cf. Hansen 1976, pp. 99–108; MacDowell 1978, pp. 214–219; and Wolff 1966, p. 120.

[16] A retrojection from Demosthenes 21.103. The *sanides*, or announcement boards, of Isokrates 15.237 (**342**) probably carried notices of impending trials, but possibly what they recorded were convictions. Cf. MacDowell 1990, p. 326 and Harrison 1971, p. 91, note 1.

[17] On one occasion at least, as many as 6,000 dikasts were thought to be the right number (Andokides 1.17). At other times the number might be 2,500, 2,000, 1,500, 1,000, 500, 400, or 200 (plus an odd man, after some point in the 4th century). See Harrison 1971, p. 47, with notes 2 and 3.

[18] Athenians did not restrict particular procedures exclusively to particular buildings. The Stoa Poikile, the Odeion, and the Theater of Dionysos were all used variously. Hansen (1981–1982, pp. 15–27) notes that judging panels larger than 1,500 dikasts could sit in the Odeion, but he does not discuss possibilities offered by areas that were not formally designated as courts. The thesmothetai presumably determined sizes of panels and days of meeting for panels, as later: Aristotle, *Ath. Pol.* 59.1.

To return to the archon, he had a list of days on which he could schedule trials in the Odeion.[19] Let us say the month was Maimakterion[20] and that the issue was alimony. The archon chose the tenth day of Maimakterion for the case in question. On that day, he, the prosecutor(s), and the defendant arrived at the Odeion early in the morning. About 500 dikasts also arrived singly or in groups. All of them had gotten up early. Most resided in the city, which means they spent much of each day in the Agora, whether judging or not. They, accordingly, had seen the notice posted before the statues of the Eponymous Heroes and so knew well in advance what the court days would be. Men from outlying areas, however, could also participate. For a man with a farm near Sounion or in Acharnai, going to Athens was a long trip, but farming in Attica allowed trips to the city. Grapes and olives required intensive work only at particular seasons; on many days a farm needed only someone to feed and water the livestock.

A dikast (or heliast, in the earlier terminology) had to be at least thirty years old and a citizen. These are what might be called generic qualifications for a dikast.[21] If he was listed as a state debtor, he was not allowed to judge, for a man in that category was not fully a citizen; he had lost certain rights of citizenship. To consider dikasts as a group, they may have been on average considerably older than thirty. Their means were modest enough, so that an obol or two or three for a day's judging was meaningful, but they also enjoyed their work. Every trial had its own drama, and it was exciting to be a participant in such dramas, many of which were literally life-and-death contests. It was not only the pay but also the excitement that brought countrymen from comparatively distant places like Sounion and Acharnai.

Dikasts who arrived late, after the archon had signaled that the gate was closed, would not judge that day. The gate in question (κιγκλίς) gave entrance through a wooden fence (δρύφακτοι) that ran around the whole court building. It was there to keep the world in general at a distance from the immediate area of the trial. Interested persons could nonetheless stand by this fence and still try to get the attention of approaching dikasts (Aristophanes, *Wasps*, lines 552–561 [**208**]).

Inasmuch as other magistracies were allotted at Athens starting well before the mid-5th century, it would be surprising if dikasts were not also allotted. At least as early as 422 B.C.E., dikasts depended on an allotment for work (and pay) in the courts: Aristophanes, *Wasps*, lines 673–674, describes them as rabble living off the κηθάριον (**264–266**),[22] that is to say, the wickerwork vessel that functioned in one or more allotments of dikasts to courts. Whatever the exact form of this allotment, it seems

[19] Not every day was open to him. Mikalson (1975, p. 201) concludes that at Athens, if all the festival days were known, the total "would probably be only slightly less than one half of all the days of the year." The ekklesia usually did not meet on monthly or annual festival days nor did the boule meet on annual festival days. The boule did, however, meet on monthly festival days. Working folk worked throughout festival days (*ibid.*, p. 203). We do not know if the dikasteria met on festival days, but it is surely an exaggeration when Aristophanes (*Wasps*, lines 660–663) says the courts met 300 days a year. M. H. Hansen ("How Often Did the Athenian Dicasteria Meet?" *GRBS* 20, 1979, pp. 243–246) calculates between 150 and 200 days per year. Cf. Pritchett 1979, p. 66 with note 83, pp. 220–229. See Cohen 1973, pp. 12–59 on trials to be held within a month, *dikai emmenai*, which met during the winter months.

[20] Philetairos, *Months* F12: A. τίς ἐστι Μαιμακτηρίων; B. μὴν δικάσιμος. Note also *IG* I³ 20, lines 32–33, where suits of a certain kind may be tried at Athens in the month(s) [Ἀνθεστε]ριõνι καὶ Ἐλαφεβολιõνι. Cf. *IG* I³, line 68: [Γαμε]λιõνι and *IG* I³ 41, line 90:]ν τõι αὐτõι μενὶ *h*οι ναυτοδ[...], and Aristophanes, *Birds*, line 1047, καλοῦμαι Πεισέταιρον ὕβρεως ἐς τὸν Μουνιχιῶνα μῆνα with Schol. to lines 1047 and 1478. Cf. Lipsius 1905–1915, p. 808.

[21] See R. Sealey, "How Citizenship and the City Began in Athens," *AJAH* 1983 [pp. 97–129], pp. 98–99. In certain cases, all members of the panel had to be especially qualified, e.g., cases where all dikasts had to be initiates of the Eleusinian mysteries (Andokides 1.17) or a defendant's fellow soldiers. See Harrison 1971, p. 32.

[22] Cf. the phrase κυαμόβολον δικαστήν from Sophokles' *Inachos* (**328**). Aristophanes' neologism κυαμότρωξ, "bean-weevil", applied to Demos (*Knights*, line 41) probably has a wider reference than dikastic service.

to have entitled a citizen to serve as dikast for one year rather than for just one day. It is clear, in any case, that in this period dikasts were not allotted to different courts on different days.[23] If all hopeful candidates assembled at Ardettos Hill once a year and some from this number were chosen by an allotment, "ketharion" could be a metaphorical way of referring to this allotment. On the other hand, citizens could have been assigned to panels by allotment the day they were to judge. There is no dependable contemporary account.

Dikasts, like citizens at a meeting of the ekklesia, were not accountable to any magistrate or any office for their judgments. They did not have to face euthynai at the end of their year.[24] They did swear an oath, possibly on the occasion when they were officially recognized as dikasts, possibly again on each court day, whereby they undertook to judge fairly.[25]

The number of dikasts was large enough to give substance to the legal fiction that a dikastic panel was the city of Athens sitting in judgment. (There could be, therefore, no higher tribunal to which one could appeal a verdict.) The number 500, however, to take one example, was not in itself absolute: it constituted one critical mass. That is, for a certain class of offense, that of Sokrates for instance, Athenians fixed the number of dikasts at 500 rather than 1,000 or 400 or 200 as aggregation proper for an authentic verdict. But the absence of one or two dikasts was not crucial: a panel that did not furnish its full complement of votes could nevertheless deliver a verdict.

To come into the Odeion, dikasts passed through a latticed gate, set in a wooden grillwork that defined a space beyond which unauthorized persons were not to go. Once inside, dikasts sat where they liked.[26]

The Odeion was big enough to seat easily 500 and more, even allowing for the numerous columns that held up its roof. Friends and cronies, people who had some interest in common, gathered in clusters. Many carried cushions or reed mats for comfort (**246**, **248**). They sat together and kept up a running commentary on all developments as the trial went on. When they chose to approve, they made themselves heard. They likewise made themselves heard when they did not approve.[27] On such occasions they might even order the speaker of the moment to step down from the *bema*, a raised area where a speaker stood while addressing the court (**227**–**244**).

When the archon decided that the panel was full, he signaled[28] that all was ready, and the opposing parties entered. There may have been one prosecutor or several, so long as each had an arguable complaint. Friends, relations, and witnesses may also have been in attendance. A defendant likewise brought as many supporters as he could find or manage. There was no apparent official control over number and identity of supporters. He would try to include some character witnesses. Litigants who wanted to record their own relevant memoranda might use wax tablets and a stylus, as in Demosthenes 46.11 (**354**), or papyrus, carried in ordinary stew pots (echinos, chytra, or lopas; see "Echinos," pp. 79–81 below). There may have been separate bemata, one for the prosecution and one for the defense. When these preliminaries were done, a herald or a

23 Aristophanes, *Wasps*, line 240 (with MacDowell 1971) shows that a dikast knew where he was going when he started out early in the morning for his court. Cf. Antiphon 6.21 (**97**): τοῖς αὐτοῖς δικασταῖς.

24 Artemidoros 2.27 (ed. Pack) preserves a simile that is doubtless proverbial: ἐοίκασι γὰρ οἱ ποταμοὶ δεσπόταις μὲν καὶ δικασταῖς διὰ τὸ πράττειν ὅσα ἂν βούλωνται ἀνυπευθύνως καὶ κατὰ γνώμην τὴν ἑαυτῶν. See Triantaphyllopoulos 1975, p. 176, note 177.

25 Σόλωνος Νόμοι 1976, 97a–d; Bonner and Smith 1938, pp. 152–155.

26 Epikrates F11 (*PCG* V = Pherekrates F11 [ed. Kock] F260 *PCG* VII [**247**]) commemorates as πρωτόβαθρος one who always made it his business to get a seat on the front bench. Cf. Aristophanes, *Wasps*, lines 89–90 (**106**).

27 Cf. V. Bers, "Dikastic *Thorubos*," in *Crux*, pp. 1–15.

28 Aristophanes, *Wasps*, line 690 with MacDowell 1979, *comm. ad loc.*

priest swore in the dikasts. They undertook by oath to judge without partiality, and they swore by Zeus, Demeter, and Apollo.[29]

Someone then manned the klepsydra, or "water thief" (**306–323** and pp. 77–78 below). This timekeeping device consisted of a terracotta pot with an overflow hole near its rim and a short bronze outlet pipe at its base. The pot was filled with water, which ran out into a similar pot while litigants were speaking (p. 31, Ill. 2). Different sorts of trials and speeches were assigned differing but stipulated amounts of time, the units of which were expressed as liquid measures. Two choes, for instance, were given to the second speech in a trial where 2,000 to 5,000 drachmai were at issue. In present terms, that would be six to eight minutes (see p. 77 below). If a klepsydra owned by a tribe was used in court, a member of that tribe might have supervised its functioning.

A secretary read the formal charge. The prosecutor spoke first. He tried to establish himself as a person whom the defendant's wrongdoing had affected directly and personally, for if he did not, 500 Athenian dikasts might well judge him a busybody or a sycophant and accordingly discount his accusation. It does not matter that Solon long before had established the right of "anyone who wants" to initiate a prosecution. The personal nature of the complaint therefore required a litigant to speak for himself in his own words, and as a consequence, it was impossible for him to appear with script in hand, not even one written by himself, to say nothing of having it written by another. Still, he would be only prudent if he availed himself of expert advice. Courtroom speeches (those of the orators that are extant, at least) had a recognizable form. In addition, they contained formulaic turns of speech. The same ones can be found in orations almost a century apart. To take a single instance, consider the speaker who asked for the dikasts' forbearance. He declared he was not a trained or practiced speaker, had never in fact been in a courtroom before: the dikasts therefore had to take him as he was, roughhewn but sincere.[30]

The defendant spoke second. In defending himself he invoked his whole life as testimony. Military service, liturgies, family friends, children, all could be presented to a dikastic panel as causes to find him not culpable. Since he, like the plaintiff or prosecutor, was timed by the outflow of water from a jar, he likewise wanted urgently to reach the end of his plea or defense before all his water ran out. A klepsydra could be, and was, called "necessity" (ἀνάγκη), and the allusion was clear (**250**). The defendant and prosecutor also worked under another limitation. If either of them angered the dikasts, the panelists could make enough hostile noise to force the speaker to step down from his bema before using all his time. Citizens as well as the general public could watch and listen to trials from outside (**97**, **188**, **190**, **191**). Speakers appealed to them regularly as περιεστηκότες (bystanders), and we can visualize them standing just outside whatever area or building has been delimited as the court for the day. This audience, too, may have shouted and influenced proceedings.

After the first (prosecutor) and second (defendant) speakers finished, the dikasts voted. No official stood up to give an objective summation of what had been said. The dikasts voted the

[29] See Bonner and Smith 1938, pp. 152–155.

[30] James Riddell (*The Apology of Plato*, Oxford 1877, p. xxi) cites a few instances of this sort of exordium. Euripides, *Hippolytus*, lines 986–987, which Riddell does not quote, gives notice that this sort of topos may have been in use as early as 428 B.C.E. Compare Aristophanes, *Wasps*, lines 959 (κιθαρίζειν γὰρ οὐκ ἐπίσταται), 989 (**271**) and MacDowell 1971, p. 256. Form and formulas, since they are regularly and manifestly elements of presentation, reveal what the dikasts expect. Another consideration that tells against purely extemporaneous speaking in court is the time recorded by the klepsydra. When a speaker's time is limited by it, he must, if he wants to protect his life and property, reach the middle and end of what he wants to say before his water runs out. And yet a man who had never had any instruction could hardly know what he needed to say or how long it would take him to enunciate it, nor could he assess degrees of irrelevance when time was measured and precious.

defendant innocent or guilty in an immediate response to speeches they had just heard. There were apparently two modes of voting, one of which was more general in its applications. In the more general mode, two urns were set up, touching each other but standing in such a way that one could be described as nearer and one as farther from the dikasts. The nearer of the two took votes to condemn; the other, farther away, votes to acquit. A dikast dropped his single pebble (or seashell) into one of the two urns, and when all the dikasts had done so, officials emptied one urn onto a flat stone for counting (**262**). They counted the ballots and awarded a verdict by simple majority. A tie favored the defendant.[31] A herald announced the result. The trial was over, and either the defendant exited free, or the proper functionaries, under the direction of the Eleven, immediately exacted the penalty.

The vote was secret: each dikast could vote without anyone else knowing for whom or against whom he had voted. References to an apparatus or fixture called κημός may provide hints as to how secrecy was made possible. A kemos (in some uses of the word) was a truncated cone of basketwork, open at both ends, and used as a trap for crabs and lobsters (**255**, **256**, **259**, **277**; see pp. 209–211 below and Ill. 1). A closely woven basketwork fixture of that shape could have kept voting secret in the following way. The large, open end rested on the shoulders of two urns that stood side by side. The kemos rose to a smaller opening, now at the top, which became in effect a single mouth for both urns. A heliast (to use Aristophanes' terminology) could approach the two urns (set up, it will be remembered, so that one was nearer, the other farther away), put his hand with its pebble inside the mouth of the kemos, and then drop his pebble into the urn he chose. His hand was hidden so that no one could see which urn he had chosen.[32] From time to time a pebble rattling against the inner wall of an urn could reveal what choice had been made (**317**), although straw could be used to deaden the sound. The method, whatever its shortcomings, was serviceable: it was in use until sometime after 405 B.C.E. (**279**).

When a charge carried a penalty already stipulated by law, the penalty (as noted above) was exacted without delay. In the case of some charges, however, like that for ἀσέβεια, for which Sokrates was tried, a second balloting was required, by which the same dikastic panel that had just voted to convict also had to judge what a culprit must pay or suffer. In such cases, the prosecutor again spoke first, and within a stipulated time proposed a penalty and argued exactly why that penalty was appropriate. Next, the defendant offered his own hope of a sufficient penalty, trying to find one severe enough to satisfy judges who had found him guilty less than an hour before but at the same time milder than that proposed by the prosecutor.

When a penalty was at issue a second mode of voting may have been used. Dikasts had wooden tablets covered with wax. A dikast, using a stylus (see pp. 240–241 below) or his fingernail, scratched a short line if he favored the defendant's proposed penalty, a long line for that proposed by the prosecutor. A dikast voted for one or the other. He had no other choice, except perhaps to abstain. Here, as in the first balloting, a simple majority ruled, with a tie going to the defendant. Aristophanes, in *Wasps,* lines 106–108 (**106**), 166–167 (**335**), with scholia (**334**, **336**), seems to allude to such a mode of voting in 422 B.C.E. Since penalties were acted upon immediately, no need (apparently) was felt for systematic record keeping. A trial was a definitive closure. The chief penalties were death, money fines, exile, and loss of citizenship (partial or full). Imprisonment seems not to have been a punishment in itself but rather a holding procedure, designed to last only until the verdict was

[31] See, e.g., M. Gagarin, "The Vote of Athena," *AJP* 96, 1975, pp. 121–127.

[32] See Illustration 1 for a conjectural representation of this procedure. The κημός, although not mentioned at Aischylos, *Agamemnon,* lines 814–818, can be imagined as in place over the two urns. I thank Sir Hugh Lloyd-Jones for recommending this particular application.

Ill. 1. How the χῆμος may have protected the secret ballot (drawing by Paul Langmuir)

executed. A magistrate might include a notation in his own accounts, against the coming judicial review of his year in office, but publication of the outcome of a trial was not a legal requirement.[33]

A single panel judged as many cases in a day as daylight allowed. The klepsydra put foreseeable limits on the amount of time any given trial would take. A dikast was paid for a day's work, two obols at first, then (thanks to Kleon in the 420's) three. If it was not a grand sum, it was enough to make a difference in the way a man lived and more than enough to sustain mere existence.[34]

[33] When details of an adjudication are published, they are found in a magistrate's general accounting. See **148**, *inter alia*, and the parallels noted there. Cf. Harrison 1971, p. 168, with note 5. Results of adjudications might also be published as lists. See, e.g., *IG* II^2 1928 with Lipsius 1905–1915, pp. 593–594, and D. M. Lewis, "Notes on Attic Inscriptions," *BSA* 49, 1954 [pp. 17–50], p. 37.

[34] Seven minae (4,200 obols) will keep 55 slaves for a year, i.e., an outlay of about one quarter of an obol per day (Demosthenes 27.36). Harrison (1971, pp. 48–49) surveys the brief history of pay for dikasts and accepts A. H. M. Jones's notion of the composition of an Athenian dikastic panel in the 4th century (*Athenian Democracy*, Oxford 1957, pp. 36–37). But Jones's reading (p. 31) of Demosthenes 21.83 and 21.95 is arbitrary: one could responsibly give the words quite a different sort of emphasis. Cf. F. W. Walbank, Rev. of C. Mossé, *La fin de la democratie athenienne*, in *CR* n.s. 13, 1963,

Furthermore, even in the 4th century, when other sorts of pay were raised, three obols remained the pay for dikasts.

To consider the magnitude of sums expended annually for dikasts by a 5th-century financial board called *kolakretai* (*FGrHist* Androtion F36), if courts sat, let us say for the sake of example, two hundred days a year, and on each of those days 2,000 dikasts judged, the total paid out per annum was around thirty-three talents (some of which was recovered from *prytaneia*, i.e., funds paid or deposited and forfeited by litigants).

410–340 B.C.E.

As far as one can tell, Athenians as citizens of a democracy continued to initiate lawsuits as they had in the past.[35] In the case of a homicide, a member of the decedent's family, as defined in Drakon's Code, but not just any member of the community, might initiate a prosecution.[36] In other kinds of wrongdoing, the injured person (or in the case of a woman, her male representative [*kyrios*]) issued the summons (*proklesis*). But when the best interests of the state were involved, anyone who wanted could be prosecutor. The prosecutor haled the defendant before a magistrate.[37] The magistrate asked enough questions to determine whether the proposed litigation fell within the area of his responsibilities, and if he decided that it did, he had a public notice posted on the railings that ran around the statues of the Eponymous Heroes.[38]

As in the time discussed above, notice of a trial started with a διωμοσία (*diomosia*), cast in some such form as the following, which is preserved in a Demosthenic oration: "Apollodoros, son of Pasion, from Acharnai [in a sworn indictment charges] Stephanos, son of Menekles, from Acharnai with giving false witness. Penalty: one talent. Stephanos testified falsely against me when he attested

p. 318; F. D. Harvey, "Literacy in the Athenian Democracy," *REG* 79, 1966 [585–635], p. 597, note 18; and M. M. Markle, "Jury Pay and Assembly Pay at Athens," in *Crux*, pp. 265–297. See now S. Todd, "Lady Chatterley's Lover and the Attic Orators," *JHS* 110, 1990, pp. 146–173 and W. T. Loomis, "Wages, Welfare Cost and Inflation in Classical Athens" (diss. Harvard University 1993), pp. 22–24, 31.

35 While the Thirty ruled (404/3), the dikasteria did not have their previous power and authority. Aristotle (*Ath. Pol.* 35.2) says of the Thirty: τὸ κῦρος ἐν δικασταῖς κατέλυσαν, i.e., they abrogated the authority that abided in the dikasts, but what that means precisely is not clear. On one occasion the Thirty, in a travesty of judicial procedure, required an open rather than a secret ballot and turned around the order of the dikasts' options. That is to say, a dikast was first given the option "acquit" and then "condemn", while earlier and later practice consistently shows the opposite order (**284**). Cf. MacDowell 1979, p. 259. The undesirable effect of an open ballot is easy to see, but that of reversing the order of a dikast's options is not so clear. It may be that the original order, condemn first, acquit second, was established because someone had discovered a tendency in judges to stop at the second option rather than return to the first. Whatever the original reason, by 404 B.C.E. a change to the reverse order was a patent distortion. Demosthenes 45.4 records a time between 371 and 362 when, because of the war, there were no private suits. The speaker at Demosthenes 39.17 tells of a time previous to that oration (before 348?) when there was no pay for dikasteria. If the dikasteria were accordingly closed, we are not told what if any juridical procedures took their place. We do know, however, that by that time the rules for official arbitration were well established, and so arbitration may have been the recourse when courts were closed. Ordinarily, the dikasteria seem to have met fewer than two hundred days a year (see note 19, p. 25 above).

36 See Stroud 1968. From 404/3 until 401, private suits, which category includes homicide, were not tried. See Wallace 1989, pp. 142–143 with note 32.

37 He should do so within five years of the offense. See Cohen 1973, pp. 10–12. Demosthenes 21.112 instances as a well-known inequity the capability of rich litigants to control the time of their trial.

38 These statues stood in their earlier place until after the middle of the century when their base was moved *ca.* 60 m. north to a site in front of the Metroön. See *Agora* XIV, pp. 38–41.

the written documents in the container." "I, Stephanos, son of Menekles, from the deme Acharnai, testified truly when I attested the written documents in the container" (Demosthenes 45.8; cf. 21.103).

The notice next told litigants when and where to be for their day in court. This was as it had been, as was the general response: the rest of town, always interested in something new, also wanted to know who was being tried, for what, and when. Spectators, although kept outside critical areas by dryphaktoi, could still stand close enough to see what was happening and to hear arguments and verdicts and to make themselves heard. They continued to participate, even if only marginally, in the conduct of trials (**197**).

What was different was the mode of assigning dikasts to courts. Earlier in the 5th century, citizens eligible for dikastic service were assigned somehow to their courts or panels; there is no testimony as to how this was done. Panels might at some time have followed affiliations by phyle. Note that the single klepsydra (see **306–323** and pp. 77–78 below) is labeled as the property "of Antiochis" (see Ill. 2, Pl. 6). But this one klepsydra may have been designated for use, for example,

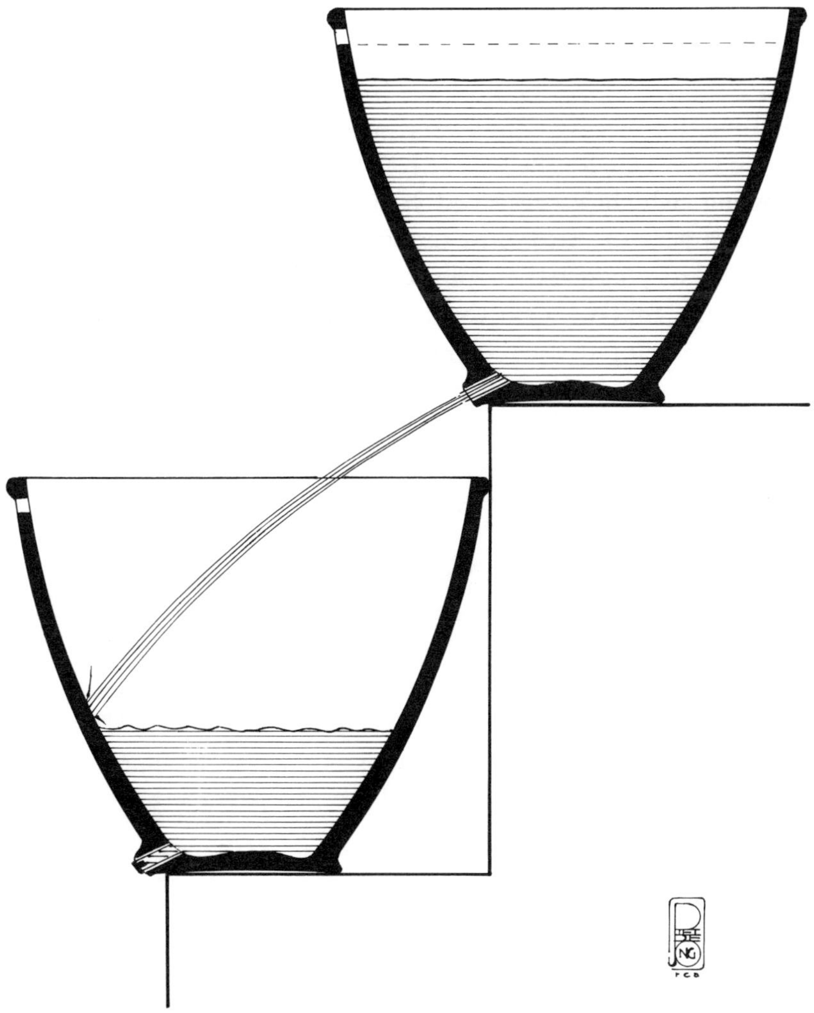

Ill. 2. Two klepsydrai, one above the other (drawing by Piet de Jong)

within the deme and have no function at all within the general system of popular courts. If, however, this klepsydra was dikastic, then other dikastic equipment such as staffs, tokens, and other allotment paraphernalia might have been maintained and disposed as property of the phyle. If the dikasts' panels had been assembled previously according to phyle, after a time (possibly as early as 410 B.C.E.) a new mode of identification and organization went into effect.[39] The eligible men of each phyle were allotted letters (A to K) that identified them as belonging to one of ten dikastic sections (**70–75**). These sections cut across phyle lines, and so each was made up of a roughly equal number of men from each of the ten phylai. An aim of this division was to prevent men from the same phyle from making combinations by which they could influence the outcome of a trial.

Assignment of section letters to dikasts could have been a simple procedure, such as drawing lettered balls from a container. It might have gone somewhat as follows:

The balls, lettered A to K, were shaken up in a wickerwork vessel called κηθίς or κήθιον or κηθάριον (see Aristophanes, *Wasps*, lines 673–674 [**264**], with scholia [**266**]). If there were two vessels to a tribe, there were perhaps 300 balls to a vessel. Each citizen who was eligible to be a dikast drew one letter. That letter was forthwith his section letter, and it was duly stamped into his pinakion.[40] These small bronze tags, into which some dikasts pierced holes for string to hang around their necks, were stamped, punched, or incised with the dikast's name, his father's name, his demotic, and a section letter.

Allotment machines, the kleroteria, could have been set up in the Agora, at locations specially designated for the receipt of the pinakia. These kleroteria were stelai of wood or stone, with columns of slots (Ill. 3, Pl. 6). Along one side a tube was affixed vertically (**326**).[41]

Suppose that there were two kleroteria for each phyle. Each kleroterion in that case would have five columns of slots, the first with A to E at the top, the second with I to K, making a total of ten columns. Would-be dikasts plugged their pinakia into appropriate columns.

A number of balls, some marked with the names of courts, some blank, were shaken up in a container and poured into the top of the tube at the side of the kleroterion.[42] The tube, stopped at the bottom, held the balls in the random order in which they entered. They were released from the bottom of the tube, one at a time, and each ball either assigned five dikasts to a court for the day or disqualified five, depending on whether or not the ball was marked with the name of a court. A dikast should now have received his staff (βακτηρία), a symbol of authority, for his passage to the court in which he would judge.

In the present illustration, that of a trial held sometime between 409 and *ca.* 340 B.C.E., trials continued to be held in buildings and localities widely separated from each other. On one and the same day, the Odeion and the Stoa Poikile could have been in use. The building in which the heliaia met could have been the same capacious structure in the southwest corner of the Agora, although by 400 or so Building A seems a better candidate (see pp. 11–15, 104–105). If a judging body of 2,000 or more dikasts were needed, that is to say, an assembly larger than could be accommodated in, let us say, Building A, archons theoretically could convene such a body in the Odeion or the

[39] Boegehold 1984, pp. 23–39 presents considerations in favor of this date, rather than 403/2, a year that is often proposed because of reforms associated with the archonship of Eukleides.

[40] See Kroll 1972. On the various meanings of pinakion, see p. 10 above, note 2.

[41] See pp. 58, 230–231 with Dow 1939.

[42] Aristotle (**325**) uses the word κύβοι, a word that means "cube" or "die", for the lots that are shaken up and dropped into the tube. But bronze balls (and two terracotta balls) found in the Agora excavations are of the right size to have been used the same way; see pp. 65–66 below.

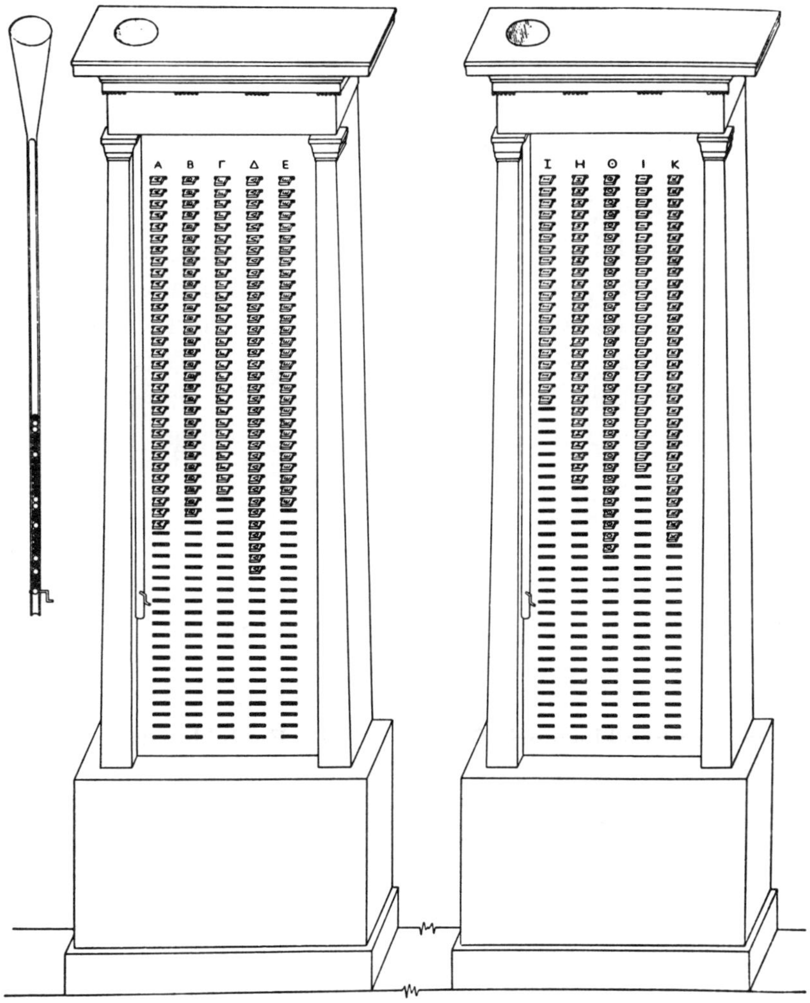

Ill. 3. Kleroterion, restored

Theater of Dionysos immediately west of the Odeion, or in the Pnyx, or in the Agora, where a fence would serve to mark the venue.

But to return to days on which two or more widely separated dikasteria were working: suppose the allotment of dikasts to courts took place in the Agora. How would the dikasts, after being allotted, not pass through open areas in the Agora in order to reach that court? Furthermore, if that court happened to be the Odeion, dikasts had to traverse parts of the town outside the Agora (Fig. 1). Aristotle, in his account of later procedure (*ca.* 325), describes courts as being within an enclosed area (**249**). Athenians, one can infer, had come to acknowledge the possibilities of corruption at this critical point. There may have been scandals. Think of Anytos, who Aristotle says became known in 409 as the first man ever to corrupt a whole dikasterion (*Ath. Pol.* 27.5). In the scheme under consideration here, when courts on any given day could be situated at good distances from each other, a staff was no protection. In fact, a staff in the hand of a dikast would make him a target for malefactors. Obviously, dikasts on their way to court were vulnerable to bribes or threats from litigants. This was surely a principal consideration when later Athenians planned an enclosed complex of courts (see p. 14 above).

Allotment of dikasts to ten sections of the whole body of dikastai was one innovation of the late 5th century. These sections, labeled by the letters A through K, each had a roughly equal number of dikasts from each phyle. Another innovation, that of allotment of dikasts to seating areas, likewise employed letters of the alphabet to designate sections. In this allotment, however, the letters used were all twenty-four plus an imported letter, ͳ. Also, the instruments of the allotment were tokens, that is, coin-shaped pieces of bronze (*symbola*), and the sections in question were seating areas. The reason for amplifying the alphabet was to provide twenty-five letters, this number a divisor of 200, 400, 500, and 1,000, numbers such as are found in dikastic panels.

Each dikast drew a lettered token as he entered his allotted court. He looked at the letter and went to a seating area labeled with the same letter. When a panel of 500 dikasts had been seated in this way, there would be twenty in each of twenty-five areas. This was apparently as much random dispersion as was thought enough to discourage the formation of blocs (see **70**, **249**, **276**, **341–349** and pp. 67–76 below).

In allotting dikasts to courts and assigning seating areas by chance, Athenians were guarding against two ways by which an evenhanded administration of justice could be spoiled. First, interested persons could not approach dikasts beforehand, since neither dikasts nor anyone else knew until the morning of their service where they would judge. (As discussed above, however, dikasts could still be approached en route to their courts.) Secondly, unlike during the previous period (p. 26 above), dikasts could not sit where they liked and so form blocs of friends or relations with kindred interests.

The trial itself seems to have followed the established, earlier plan. A magistrate (say that this time he is the basileus) ascertained that the dikastic panel was full. Early in the 4th century, 500 dikasts would have made up a full panel, but by the '80's an odd man had been added. A panel now needed 501 dikasts to be full, ostensibly to make tie votes impossible (Schol. Demosthenes 24.9). There was no need for such a measure, however, since Athenians had long before established a principle that tie votes were in favor of the defendant. The addition of an odd man may consequently attest some formal consideration or look to tradition. The 51 ephetai, for instance, may have provided a model of a judging body made up of an odd number of judges.[43]

In any case, the basileus gave a signal to the herald, who in turn brought in the prosecutor (with supporters) and the defendant (likewise with supporters). Say, for example, that the court in question was meeting in the Stoa Poikile. A railing or grill (the dryphaktoi) fixed between columns defined an area within which the trial would take place. Prosecutor and defendant entered through a gate (the kinklis) in those railings. The herald announced charges and denials. A man was posted at the klepsydra, and the prosecutor began his address to the judging panel. He was standing on the bema, and the herald stood next to him as he spoke (Aischines 1.79 [**252**]). The man in charge stopped the flow whenever a prosecutor was having laws, ordinances, or testimonies read aloud (**315**). Anyone speaking in behalf of the prosecutor did so within the time allotted to the prosecution. There was apparently some constraint on all litigants to keep to the point while speaking, but it is not known what the sanctions were if they did not; nor can it be clear from preserved orations, which were surely edited and sometimes augmented after having been used in court, that the injunction was consistently effective.

[43] The number 401 in Aristotle, *Ath. Pol.* 4 has been judged one of several anachronisms in the same chapter. It may be so for Athens. Outside Athens, however, there were other early administrative or judicial bodies that specified an odd man in their composition: 61 dikasts in a decree from Erythrae (Schwyzer 1923, no. 701, lines 22–25); 101 in one decree from Lokris (Meiggs and Lewis 1989, no. 13, lines 7–8); judging bodies of 9 and 15 in *IG* IX i 334, line 15.

The defendant followed, speaking under the same rules and with the same time limits. He tried to show how unlikely the accusation against him was. Neither he nor the prosecutor cited precedents to provide necessary legal force. A precedent cited in court served only as a reminder or for some other such rhetorical end.

One new control was now available for the plaintiff and the defendant. If the disputants had come to this trial by way of an arbitration that failed, neither party to the action was allowed to use any law, testimony, witness, oath, or the like that had not been brought forward at arbitration or anakrisis. This prohibition was meant to stop litigants from adding new and different documents and arguments and possibly thereby changing the actual question to be judged. In a larger context, this new procedure tells of a time when men had come to desiderate the fixity and precision of a written text, as compared with the fluidity of speech. They recognized, therefore, that there was such a thing as a true text, a text, that is, that could be agreed upon to form the basis of arguments on both sides. For if laws and oaths used in the trial must be the same as those cited at arbitration or anakrisis, two kinds of sameness were necessary. First, the documents had to be of the same sort. That is to say, one testimony of X and one oath of Y could not be discarded and replaced by an oath sworn by a hitherto unknown Z or augmented by citation of a law. Second, the wording of those documents also had to be the same. As a control, both parties had access to sealed copies of all the documents, for at the close of a failed arbitration, each contestant deposited copies of all documents in echinoi (see **288–305** and pp. 79–81 below). These plain, unglazed terracotta (or bronze) cooking vessels had lids that could be tied on with string and sealed with wax. The echinoi were then entrusted to the public arbitrators (διαιτηταί) of the litigant's own tribe and kept against the trial that was to follow.[44]

If, at the trial, one party heard cited some law, testimony, or oath that had not figured in the arbitration, he could challenge his opponent. A response to that challenge might be for a litigant to demonstrate to the dikasterion that the seal on his echinos was unbroken (**293**). Once he had done that, he had the echinos opened. The texts would be taken out, identified, and read aloud, and the dikasts in their deliberations would weigh what they had heard. Such confrontations could establish a basis for a challenge at the end of a trial, an important capability in view of the paramount authority of the dikasterion. There was no appeal from its judgment, although a successful challenge could lead to a trial in which false witness was charged, and that trial in turn could lead to a reversal. The whitened tablet (*pinakion*) on which a witness might write his deposition (at home, if he liked) and the wax tablet, which a witness might use to make (and erase) notes in responding to challenges ([Demosthenes] 46.11 [**354**]), attest literacy and a concern for written documentation.

When the defendant (and supporters) had said as much as his stipulated time allowed, the panel of dikasts received ballots and formulaic voting instructions, which did no more than define the two different kinds of ballot. There was no charge given to the panel and no time for conferring or deliberation.[45]

The manner of voting was different from that described in the preceding period, when the kemos and pebbles were used (pp. 27–28 above). Sometime after 405 B.C.E., but not later than

[44] Aristophanes has an ἐχῖνος in his *Danaids* (F274, *PCG* III.2 [**299**]), and an ancient commentator explains the word as being exactly this container. Cf. Aristophanes, *Wasps*, lines 1435–1437 (**288**) and a similar explanation in the scholion (**289**). The explanation may be inferential and an anachronism, but the word could in fact have been used *qua* repository of documents in both plays. If that is so, the date for the introduction of written evidence in Athenian lawcourts, generally cited in modern studies with all due caution as having become required in 388/7 B.C.E., can be dated somewhat earlier than that. See MacDowell 1978, pp. 242–243. Some ancient commentators have been encouragingly dependable when transmitting information concerning the echinos; see Boegehold 1982.

[45] Aristotle, *Politics* 1268b.3–11 has most lawgivers making specific provisions against such opportunities.

345, Athenian dikasts began to cast votes using two official ballots (**252**), one of which signified "vote for the defendant", the other, "vote against the defendant". Both ballots were bronze disks pierced at the center, one by a short, hollow tube, the other by a short, solid peg (see pp. 82–90 below). Tube and peg constituted the essential difference between ballots, which in Greek are called, accordingly, τετρυπημένη ("pierced") and πλήρης ("full"). A pierced ballot represented a vote for the party who spoke first, that is, prosecutor or plaintiff. A full ballot was a vote for the defendant. A dikast received one of each sort and held them in either hand, thumb over one end of the axle, a finger over the other. When he held his ballots this way, no one could see which ballot was which.[46]

The herald's instructions amounted to no more than a reminder of the unchanging convention that "pierced" was a vote for the prosecutor, "full" a vote for the defendant. Carrying both ballots, the dikasts walked to one of two amphoras, which stood near the bema at the front of the court (Demosthenes 19.311 [**240**]). They dropped one ballot into that amphora, and this was the ballot that counted. The ballot that was not meant to count went into the other amphora, which took discards. When all the dikasts had voted, ballots from the validating amphora were emptied out and counted. A simple majority ruled, and ties favored the defendant.

In the case of a second vote, as in Plato's representation of Sokrates' trial (*Apology* 36–38b), when alternate penalties were proposed and determined, the voting was again by ballot, a change from the special assessing tablets of twenty years or so earlier (**106**, **250**, **334–336**). Penalties were exacted immediately after the vote, unless, as in the case of Sokrates, special circumstances caused a delay.[47] The Eleven had responsibility for execution of verdicts, unless the verdict was of a sort that authorized a plaintiff to employ self-help.[48]

The same dikastic panel might hear a second or even third trial on the same day, so long as there was daylight. In some instances, one whole day was given to a single trial,[49] and a regular formula for the division of such days is fragmentarily preserved at Aristotle, *Ath. Pol.* 67 (**315**).

CA. 340–322 B.C.E.

Sometime around 340, Athenians consolidated their court buildings.[50] We may have references to these structures in Agora inscriptions I 1749, lines 12–13, 116–117 (**147**), and I 5656, lines 12–21 (**148**), where a First and a Middle "New Court" are named.

What would be the architectural requirements for such a complex?[51] As noted above (pp. 14–15), at least three buildings stood close enough together to be enclosed by a fence of some sort

[46] A scholiast on Aristophanes, *Wasps*, line 95 explains that the thumb, index, and middle fingers are the three that Philokleon used to hold his ballot. That grip is right for the 420's. Cf. voters on the earlier Dijon Cup, Pl. 5.

[47] Whether or not Sokrates could have addressed the dikasterion after he had been sentenced, as reported in Plato, *Apology* 38c–42 and Xenophon, *Apology* 24, cannot be demonstrated.

[48] See MacDowell 1978, pp. 153–154.

[49] See Rhodes 1981, pp. 719–728; MacDowell 1985; and I. Worthington, "The Duration of an Athenian Political Trial," *JHS* 109, 1989, pp. 204–207.

[50] See Aristotle, *Ath. Pol.* 63–69 (**110**, **249**, **276**, **315**, **325**) for the basis of the following: there seems to have been no major disruption in the functioning of the courts during these years. *IG* II^2 1629, lines 204–217 preserves a direction that certain trials be funded by the Treasurers of Athena, but it is not clear whether this was a regular practice or an extraordinary subvention.

[51] It is tempting to associate the buildings under the Square Peristyle (pp. 104–113 below) with this putative complex. The concentration of psephoi and symbola from the 4th century B.C.E. found in the area has no like elsewhere in the

that defined an area where unauthorized persons were not supposed to be. Just outside each of the ten entrances, one for each phyle, stood the two kleroteria. Near them were the ten boxes, each labeled with one of the letters from A to K (**249, 251, 325**). At or inside each entrance stood a hydria, and somewhere nearby (just inside, it would seem) a different set of boxes. The number of this second set of boxes varied with the number of courts in session on any given day. Two or three would be the usual number.

Would-be dikasts assembled by phylai, each phyle before the two kleroteria outside their one gate. Each dikast introduced and validated himself as a candidate by producing his pinakion. At the time of Aristotle's account, these identification tags were made of boxwood. The information they carried was nonetheless the same as that on the earlier ones of bronze, *viz.* section letter, name, father's name, and demotic.[52] A prospective dikast, on approaching his phyle's entrance, threw his pinakion into one of ten boxes that was labeled with his section letter. This action initiated the allotment that determined whether he would serve at all that day. Next, at the archon's signal, a slave picked up the boxes, each containing dozens of pinakia, and shook them well.

The archon then picked up a single pinakion at random out of each box and summoned its owner to step forward and act as an *empektes*, a dikast who inserted all dikastic pinakia bearing the same section letter as his own into appropriate slots in the kleroterion (**249, 325**) . Ten empektai consequently were chosen in this simple form of allotment, and with this assignment each of the ten was assured of a place on a dikastic panel for that day.

When all pinakia had been plugged in, the next phase of this allotment began: The archon shook up black and white dice (κύβοι) in a cup (*oxybaphos*) or wickerwork vessel (*ketharion*) and poured them into a tube, which was, as before, affixed vertically to one side of the kleroterion. Since the end of the tube had been stopped, the dice were now stacked one on top of the other. The archon released dice one by one and matched each die as it came out with a horizontal row of five pinakia. If a white die came out, five dikasts (one from each one of the five section letters on that kleroterion) were allotted as dikasts for the day. A black die meant that five would-be dikasts would not work that day. No one touched the invalidated pinakia: they were left in their slots until the whole allotment was over.

The archon took the validated pinakia one by one and, by calling out the names written on them, summoned the dikasts one at a time to the next step in their progress toward a court for the day, a new allotment. This procedure allotted dikasts to specific dikastic panels, using a new piece of equipment, which Aristotle calls an "acorn" (βάλανος [**249**]). The allotment was simple: Each dikast reached into a hydria and withdrew an acorn. Whatever this piece might actually have been or looked like, it bore one letter of the alphabet, lambda, mu, nu, or xi (this series begins with lambda to make it distinct from that of the dikastic sections, where the series runs A–K).[53]

An allotted dikast showed the letter on his balanos to the archon, and the archon threw the dikast's pinakion (marked, it will be remembered, with his section letter) into a box marked with the same letter (lambda, mu, nu, or xi) as that on the balanos; this was one of the two or three letters that labeled one of the day's courts. The dikast then showed his balanos again to a functionary, entered the enclosure through the gate, and received a colored staff whose color matched that of some visible part of the entrance to the court to which he had been assigned. The staff was a badge, easy to recognize, that would admit him to his allotted court and deny him entrance to any other court.

Agora. But no means of identification with the new, consolidated dikasteria are sure. See Plates 3, 7 and pp. 110–113 below for plans and speculations concerning procedure.

[52] On the earlier bronze examples and their times of use, see pp. 59–64 below.

[53] Aristotle says "from lambda on," but one may doubt that on any given day there was a need for letters beyond xi, for no more than three or four courts were normally in use on any one day (see "Nomenclature," pp. 3–9 above).

At the beginning of day each court received by allotment as a label for the day one of the letters, lambda to nu. But while letters changed every day, the court colors remained constant. According to Aristotle, the σφήκισκος of a court carried the court's distinctive color.[54] A thesmothetes, himself chosen by allotment for this task, had already allotted letters to courts for that day. The procedure was simple; Aristotle does not mention kleroteria or any other apparatus such as jars or boxes in connection with this allotment. It was probably traditional and well known to any Greek reader and not worth discussing. In any case, by the time an allotted dikast received his staff, his court building had been suitably identified by an allotment that prevented any sort of foreknowledge of that aspect of the day's proceedings.

Once he had arrived in his court for the day, the dikast gave up to another functionary his balanos and staff, receiving in turn a token that told him by means of a letter of the alphabet where to sit (see pp. 67–76). The dikast in question proceeded, let us say, to area A.

An allotment of magistrates to courts was meanwhile being performed by means of two kleroteria that were set up in the first of the courts.[55] Two new sets of dice, bronze ones now, came into play, one with names of offices painted on or incised, the other with colors of courts.[56] Two thesmothetai, allotted to the task, shook up the dice, poured them into the tubes, released them one by one, and matched the name of the office on one ball as it came out with the color on the other, which came out at the same time. As the magistrates in question were matched with colors, a herald announced the results, and they went off to their courts.

At about this time, the fence that surrounded the court complex was disassembled, or the gates in it were opened so that Athenians who wanted to watch and listen could approach the courts. Aischines (3.55–56 and 207 [**229**, **231**]) refers to this audience. Most were citizens, but there were foreigners in it as well (Demosthenes 25.98).

Once at their courts, the magistrates allotted dikasts to tend to ballots, klepsydra, and pay-tokens. To do this they used the pinakia that were dropped into boxes just inside the enclosure. Ten of them, one from each tribal entrance, were brought to each court. One held all the pinakia marked alpha, another all the betas, and so on to the kappas. The archon had the ten boxes shaken and took at random one pinakion out of each. He dropped the ten pinakia collected this way into a single empty box, which was shaken in its turn. From this box the archon drew five pinakia. The owner of the first pinakion would tend the klepsydra, and the next four would oversee the distribution, counting, and collection of ballots. The five remaining pinakia identified the dikasts who would supervise the payment of dikasts at the end of the trial.

The four dikasts allotted to ballots would be responsible for 1,002 bronze ballots, 501 pierced and 501 full. Their job was to set them out, using what Aristotle calls a lampstand (λυχνεῖον),[57] and at the end they collected them. The man at the klepsydra was responsible for stopping and starting the water when it was time. At the end of the trial, the five men allotted to pay out tokens

[54] See T. L. Shear, Jr., "The Demolished Temple at Eleusis," in *Thompson Studies* [pp. 128–140], pp. 129–130. Cf. Chambers 1990, *comm. ad* 65.2. Modern readers have more or less agreed to translate σφήκισκος as "lintel", but the usage is singular. Usually the word means "beam".

[55] Earlier in the 4th century, the *epistates* of a court could have been the magistrate who first heard the case. In Aristotle's time, there seems to have been no clear and necessary connection between the kind of magistracy and the kind of trial (**94**, **95**, **249**).

[56] The colors were surely red and green (see Batrachioun and Phoinikioun at **1**) and one or two others of the remaining few that could easily be distinguished, e.g., black, white, yellow, blue, and purple.

[57] Such bronze lampstands as survive from the 4th century do not make clear how this was done.

would give them to the dikasts who had voted. Those who had not voted did not receive a token, which meant they received no pay.

The trial was now ready to begin. It would be consistent with the seriousness of the undertaking for dikasts to swear their oath at the beginning of the trial, and for there to be an altar and a sacrifice, but no such sacramental or ceremonial functions are attested. The trial itself was like those of earlier times, except for the ballots.

The herald announced the names of the litigants and repeated from the notice posted by the Eponymous Heroes the sworn charges and denials. The prosecutor, or plaintiff, stood and gave the details of his accusation. His friends and relations, if he felt he needed them, also spoke, but they would occupy time in which he could speak. His time was measured by the klepsydra or by a division of the daylight hours of the month Posideion (**308**, **315**),[58] and so he had to decide where other speakers could help him most. When he was through, the defendant had in his turn to decide how much of the time given him he could use for his own speech and how much to apportion to persuasive friends and relations.

When the defendant (and supporters) had finished speaking, the herald announced that any challenge of testimony had to be presented before voting began. Such challenges offered to a litigant the possibility of a review of the judgment, for there was otherwise no appeal from the judgment of a dikasterion. If a panel of dikasts could be thought of as the city, and if there could be no higher tribunal than the city, then it followed that no appeal to a higher authority was possible. If, on the other hand, testimony could be shown to be perjured or wrong, then a man who had been judged as culpable had access to a whole new set of legal manoeuvres.[59] After the announcement concerning challenges, the herald enunciated a convention, venerable by now, that a pierced ballot represented a vote for the prosecutor, or plaintiff, a full ballot, a vote for the defendant. There was no summation by a presiding officer, nor was there any officially designated time for dikasts to confer among themselves. They stood up from their benches and walked to the lampstand to receive their two ballots, one of each sort, and then proceeded to the voting urns. Note, however, that in the time it took 500 dikasts to do all the foregoing, they had opportunity to talk informally with their neighbors and much to talk about.

In the course of receiving ballots, they gave up the bronze token that designated their seating area. They dropped a single ballot into an urn that held valid ballots and the remaining ballot into an urn that took discards. One urn was of bronze, could be disassembled, and had a fitting on the top that allowed only one ballot to go through at a time. The other urn was of wood. As each dikast voted, he received a bronze token marked with a gamma or some other sign for three obols. This was his pay-token. When all the dikasts had voted, a functionary emptied out the bronze urn, and all the ballots were displayed for counting. An abacus, a counting board with at least 500 holes in it, received the ballots, whose axles fit in those holes. When they were plugged in, the full and pierced axles were easy to distinguish. A magistrate counted them through, and a simple majority determined the outcome. A tie favored the defendant.[60]

If the defendant was found innocent, he went free. If he was found guilty, and the charge was of a sort where the dikasterion had to decide upon a penalty, then each dikast received his staff back

58 Posideion contained the shortest days of the year, and so any division that used those days as standard would serve for any other month.

59 What exactly they were in different circumstances is not perfectly clear. See MacDowell 1978, pp. 244–245.

60 A tie vote continued to be a possible contingency, since even after an odd man was added to dikastic panels, it would happen now and again that not all 501 were present or that not everybody voted (**163**). On one occasion, the opposed parties agreed to mix up the ballots, so that there would be no official count: Isaios 5.18.

again (presumably because the act of voting took him out of the court area and he needed a badge to return) and went back into the court to hear arguments about a penalty. The prosecutor (first) and the defendant (second) proposed their notions of a suitable punishment and justified their proposals as far as they could in the time it took a half-chous of water to run out of the klepsydra. After hearing these arguments, the dikasts voted again, using the same ballots and amphoras as before. The pay-token, when a second balloting was in view, would not be handed out until there had been a vote on the penalty.

Again, upon voting they received a pay-token, and this time they would be able to turn the token in for their pay of three obols. Those five dikasts, who at the beginning of the day had been allotted to the task of paying, now went to work. Ten boxes of pinakia had been brought to the court, one from each tribal entrance, and each of the five dikasts assumed control of two boxes. The dikast in charge of a given box picked out a pinakion at random. He read out the owner's name, and the owner collected both pinakion and pay. The chance selection of each pinakion constituted yet another allotment, the last one of the day, the one that determined the order in which the dikasts were paid.

To summarize, the three foregoing sketches of court days show consistency in the principal elements that establish the identity of Classical Athenian popular court procedure. For as far back as our evidence goes, the judging panels were composed of many citizens. Dikasts who sat in judgment could therefore be thought of, by virtue of their number, as constituting an assembly that was in some sense the city itself. Also, in having been chosen by allotment, they had been chosen by chance (or they may have thought of Pythian Apollo as the agent). Litigants were supposed to speak their own minds in their own words, but they had to know how to do so within a certain span of time measured out by the timekeeping device. A degree of expertise was therefore almost a necessity, whether one acquired it oneself by training or used texts prepared by more proficient friends or political allies. The citizens, acting as judge and jury alike, registered by means of a secret ballot judicial decisions, which each was considered to have reached essentially by himself.

What changes in procedure can be observed over time were technical refinements, better ways to protect the integrity of the characterizing principles. The early ways by which secrecy in voting was effected needed improvement. A kemos hid a voter's hands from view at the crucial moment he deposited his ballot, but pebbles made a sound as they went into the voting urns (**317**), and despite the fact that sounds are hard to locate, some Athenians thought they were hearing which urn the pebble entered. As a result, someone designed two distinct bronze psephoi and a validating urn with a special cover. The waxed tablets on which a dikast scratched a line to signal his vote for one penalty or another seem not to have been in service for long (see pp. 234–235 below). One reason for this may have been that such records could easily be altered after they had left a dikast's hands; another, that one man's long line could seem short to another.

Allotment procedures showed need to be refined again and again, and Athenians may have found the study of such problems congenial. In any case, a basic rearrangement of the topography of the courts was at last found practicable. At first, so far as one can tell, there was only an allotment by which a citizen gained the right to serve as heliast. In that capacity, he was assigned to one particular court and would judge there possibly half the days of the year. But since his appearance at that court was predictable, litigants could identify him and try to influence him before their trial. Another thing that made this sort of manipulation easy was the known association between magistrates, the kinds of litigation they supervised, and certain courts. Furthermore, if dikasts were assigned originally to courts by phyle, members of the same phyle could arrange themselves to form like-minded seating blocs. This sort of abuse at least can be inferred from a reform that by *ca.* 409 B.C.E. divided the whole body of Athenian dikasts into ten sections. Dikasts thereafter were allotted to courts by section, and the sections were allotted to courts by the day on the very day they were to judge.

But these precautionary measures turned out not to be fully effective. The Athenians next (*ca.* 340 B.C.E.) enclosed their courts within a fenced area and multiplied the number of allotments it took to get magistrate, dikastic panel, and litigants to formal resolutions of legal differences. If we do not hear of any further important changes after the time Aristotle describes, it might be because the city had undergone a transformation. Some of the old forms, to be sure, survived, but Athenians did not use the courts for the same variety of business and with the same unrelenting passion.

AFTER 322 B.C.E.

Antipater is said to have closed down the lawcourts in 322, but surely during the brief and ill-founded restoration of democratic institutions in 318, the courts were again in service.[61] Subsequently, after the collapse of this government, and under Demetrios of Phaleron, citizenship was restricted, and the Council of the Areopagos did much of the work that had been done by the courts. We hear nothing of dikasteria during the time of Demetrios of Phaleron.[62] He may have raised the number of dikasts necessary to judge in the special form of indictment called an *eisangelia* from 1,000 to 1,500, but such tribunals were not the same as popular courts.[63] In 307/6 Demetrios Poliorketes restored to Athens an "ancestral constitution" (Plutarch, *Demetrios* 7). The phrase πάτριος πολιτεία is admittedly susceptible of a wide range of applications, some of them serviceable for oligarchs, but in the context of government at Athens in 307/6 it seems natural to suppose that a democratic ancestral constitution was being invoked, one close in form to that just preceding the changes of 322. (Note the use of the fine old word ἡλιαία, possibly as buttress for the concept of an ancestral constitution [**132**].) The popular courts therefore would have been included in such a constitution as an integral function of democracy. Whether they had anything like their earlier powers is doubtful: certainly, as those troubled times continued, their sphere of influence and activity lessened.

The people of Athens possibly did not have the same conception of themselves as formerly. They were willing, to an extent, to submerge their civic identities in the numinous presence of some magnified personage, as they seem to have done in the case of Demetrios Poliorketes. Yet to decree him king seems politic and innovative, not the cringing response of an enslaved populace.[64]

[61] Hommel 1927, p. 134 cites Suda, *s.v.* Δημάδης to signal the end in 322/1 of the earlier Athenian court system. The Suda has Δημάδης. . .τελευτᾶι δὲ κατ' 'Ολυμπιάδα ριε ἐπὶ Ἀντιπάτρου ὃς κατέλυσε τὰ δικαστήρια καὶ τοὺς ῥητορικοὺς ἀγῶνας. But the word κατέλυσε says no more than "terminate (for a while)." Cf., e.g., Aristotle (*Ath. Pol.* 35.2), who uses the same word in recounting what happened to the courts in the time of the Thirty. After the Thirty, the dikasteria, immediately reestablished, had a long and vigorous life, another eighty years or so. From other evidence, moreover, it is patent, as Hommel himself notes *loc. cit.*, that the courts, although their influence on public life had diminished, did not disappear forever after 322. When Theophrastos says in his *Laws* that dikasts no longer swore an official oath on Ardettos (**173**), it is not clear whether he meant to say that there were no more dikasts, that there were dikasts and they had stopped taking an oath, or that they were taking the oath but not on Ardettos Hill.

[62] A comic threat to take a dispute to law, *viz.* δικάσομαι in Menander, *Kolax*, line 132 (produced *ca.* 315, according to Gomme and Sandbach [*Menander, Commentary*, p. 422]), a generic allusion to δικαστήρια in Menander, *Dyskolos* (316/5 B.C.E.), lines 743–744, and a phrase without context, *viz.* δικάσιμοι ἡμέραι in Menander, F840 (ed. Koerte), are reminders that some sort of court system had to be functioning.

[63] Demetrios of Phaleron may have written a description of such a procedure in his own time. See F141a (ed. Wehrli) and H.-J. Gehrke, "Politik und Philosophie bei Demetrios von Phaleron," *Chiron* 8, 1978 [pp. 149–193], p. 154, with note 24.

[64] Cf. Shear 1978, p. 16.

During the twenty years or so when Demetrios Poliorketes had a proprietary interest in Athens, democratic institutions such as the boule and ekklesia continued to exist, if sometimes only nominally. The working of the courts, not perfectly continuous even under the fully developed democracy of the 4th century, can be imagined to have been sporadic. As control of the city's administration shifted, so various powers of adjudication might go to the dikasteria or to the Areopagos. But the system of popular courts, τὰ δικαστήρια, was still working as panels in 288/7 B.C.E., when a Phyleus was praised for supervising the allotment of the courts (**94**),[65] and in 286/5, when thesmothetai were expected to introduce a scrutiny (*dokimasia*) the next time they manned the courts (**93**).

There is also adequate material evidence from excavations in the Agora to show that dikastic panels continued to sit in the 3rd century and that they continued to use the same sort of equipment. There are psephoi from mid-3rd-century contexts,[66] as well as lead tokens (see p. 68 below). Of numerous lopades unearthed in the course of excavation in the Agora, only one example (**E 1**), a fragmentary lid of *ca.* 300 B.C.E., is inscribed and identifiable as that of an echinos, that is, a sealed receptacle for documents that could be used as control during a trial before a dikasterion (**305**; see pp. 79–81 below). The most important single monument may be the Square Peristyle, an ambitious attempt to bring together the whole dikastic system within the confines of a single structure (see pp. 110–113 below).

Athenian judicial practices were widely known, and traces of their influence are visible outside Athens in the 4th century and after. From Thasos and Rhodes there are dikastic pinakia.[67] Herodas in his second mime has a pimp charge one Thales with beating one of his girls. The scene of the action may be a lawcourt in Kos in the 3rd century B.C.E., but details throughout evoke an Athenian trial as we know its form to have been in the 4th century (**318**).[68] Machon Comicus, who sets his scene in 3rd-century Alexandria, presents not a courtroom but a refined dinner table (**349**). He expects his readers to appreciate play on the words *psephoi*, *symbola*, and *lopas*, characteristic pieces of Athenian dikastic equipment.

[65] He had been called a ἱερεύς, but he is a thesmothetes when he performs that particular service. See the commentary in *IG* II^2 1163. *IG* II^2 847, lines 27–30 (*ca.* 215/4) preserves a formula τούς τε λόγους ἀπενέχθησαν πρὸς τοὺς λογιστὰς καὶ εἰς τὸ μητρῷιον καὶ τὰς εὐθύνας δεδώκασιν ἐν τῶι δικαστηρίωι κατὰ τοὺς νόμους where the singular δικαστηρίωι denotes a generic court. When a reference to the court is left out of a similar formula at *IG* II^2 958, lines 17–18, an ellipse in presentation is to be presumed rather than an absence of courts. Note comparable formulae in *IG* II^2, iv (Index), *s.v.* πρυτάνεις (p. 61), where, throughout the 3rd century, singular and plural forms of δικαστήριον are used without distinction.

[66] If the psephoi stamped with the single letters lambda and mu attest the added two tribes, Antigonis and Demetrias, as Mabel Lang suggests (pp. 84–86 below), we have additional evidence for traditional forms of lawcourt activity after 307/6, the year when those tribes were created in honor of Demetrios Poliorketes; see **B 35**, **B 36**, **B 52** and lead tokens in *Agora* X, nos. L 144–L 166.

[67] See Dow 1963, pp. 676–685 on the identification and use of a pinakion from Sinope and of three from Thasos; and P. M. Fraser, "Notes on Two Rhodian Institutions," *BSA* 67, 1972 [113–124], pp. 119–124, on five Rhodian pinakia. See also *SEG* XXX 1037.

[68] See *Herodas*, pp. 70–107. Cf. I. C. Cunningham, *Herodas. Mimiamboi*, Oxford 1971, pp. 80–81.

5

PROCEDURE, EQUIPMENT, AND SITES OF HOMICIDE COURTS

THE FOLLOWING OUTLINE provides a convenient reference for points of comparison between heliastic and homicide courts. When Athenians spoke of a "homicide court", they had in mind one of five separate and distinct courts, namely, the Court or Council of the Areopagos,[1] the court at Palladion, the court at Delphinion, the court in Phreatto, and the court at Prytaneion. These five dikasteria (for so they are called; never, however, heliaia or heliastic) were in theory the principal components of a system of judicial procedure that functioned apart from that of the heliastic or popular courts. The term "homicide courts" is a convenient but not comprehensively accurate way to refer to this system, since dikasts in these courts heard not only trials that came about as a result of a death but certain others as well, wounding, for instance, or poisoning.[2] The nomenclature "homicide" in any case recommended itself to Athenians of the time and continues to be used in modern studies. The system as a whole differs enough from that of the popular courts to require a separate description of procedure, topography, and court furnishings. It is apparent, especially in the case of the Areopagos, that spheres of jurisdiction might be enlarged, diminished, or displaced in accordance with a change in the city's government. Overall, however, given a characteristic Athenian conservatism in matters of religion, and in the absence of circumstantial narrative accounts, reconstructions of the system of homicide courts necessarily lack diachronic scope.[3]

It will be helpful to consider first how these homicide courts are named. They are courts "on" or "at" the Areopagos, "at" Palladion, "at" Delphinion and Prytaneion, or "in" Phreatto. In other words, a homicide court does not have a name other than that of the site or structure in whose area the dikastai sit and judge. The manner of naming reflects a basic need of the homicide courts: it is that of being "in a holy place and in the open air."[4] The prepositional phrases also reveal a characteristic of both the homicide and heliastic systems, namely, that all the homicide courts and most of the heliastic courts deliberated at sites that were not in the first place designed to accommodate trials: sites and structures alike were originally shrines, temples, stoas, or places for other sorts of gathering (cf. pp. 91–98 below).

Tradition as preserved in Pausanias and various lexicographers has trial proceedings first taking place on the Areopagos, and at Palladion, Delphinion, and Prytaneion in the times of Orestes, Erechtheus, Aigeus, Theseus, and Demophon, which is to say, those mythical times just before and after the Trojan War. The sites, so far as one can speculate, were at varying and considerable distances from each other: The Areopagos and Prytaneion were situated within the city walls (as those walls defined Athens in the 5th century), Delphinion was outside the walls and to the

[1] The Council of the Areopagos becomes the Court of the Areopagos when it is sitting in judgment.

[2] See Gagarin 1979, pp. 301–323; Hansen 1981, pp. 11–30.

[3] For the Court of Areopagos as a possible exception, see Wallace 1989. Cf. MacDowell 1963, pp. 6–7. A change from ephetai to (heliastic) dikasts in the court at Palladion has been surmised as having taken place as a result of reforms connected with the archonship of Eukleides in 403/2, but the evidence proposed is not adequate. See, e.g., Lenschau 1949, and cf. MacDowell 1963, pp. 52–56.

[4] Aristotle, *Ath. Pol.* 57.4 (**3**): ἐν ἱερῶι καὶ ὑπαίθριοι. The accused was not to be under the same roof as the accuser (Antiphon 5.11 [**62**]).

east, Palladion was possibly in the same general neighborhood but more likely near Phaleron, and Phreatto was by the sea. No obvious pattern of disposition emerges nor any easy way to account for the differing physical situation of each court. If before Drakon's time Attica was unified (at least that part of Attica including Athens and the territory to the south and east), Athenians could have established various separate areas as venues for certain kinds of homicide trial. Drakon was the lawgiver responsible *ca.* 620 B.C.E. for a long-lived code at Athens that fixed categories of homicide. It may be, however, that he did not invent those categories. The sites may have been of immemorial antiquity by the 5th century B.C.E., and the sorts of trial associated with them, whether invented by Drakon or not, could likewise seem to have come into existence in legendary times.[5]

Athenians recognized different kinds of homicide: they made distinctions between voluntary homicide, involuntary (accidental) homicide, and self-defense. They also included among related juridical determinations two special procedures for deaths happening in two sets of tightly defined circumstances. The first was when an inanimate object was the immediate cause of death and no responsible person could be identified; the second, when a convicted homicide, while in exile for homicide, killed an Athenian. But Athenians also used the homicide courts to try charges of arson, wounding, and plotting, even where it was not clear that a death resulted. I present now a more or less summary account of sites, furnishings, and procedure in the five homicide courts, noting but not analyzing or judging (for the most part) some relevant interpretations and discussions of Athenian homicide law.

AREOPAGOS

To Athenians looking back from the 4th century, the court of the Areopagos seemed to have been an important agency of moral and administrative supervision in early Athens. Whatever its powers and jurisdiction before 462 B.C.E., the year in which Ephialtes reduced the dimensions of its authority, the Council seems thereafter, until 307, at least, to have been principally a court whose jurisdiction included crimes committed, attempted, or projected against the lives and persons of Athenians.[6]

Like all the other homicide courts, the Court of the Areopagos takes its name from the place where it met. The dikasts sat in judgment somewhere on the Hill of Ares, a low hill just northwest of the Akropolis and joined to it by a saddle. Where exactly on the hill they judged is not obvious. Pausanias speaks of monuments in the neighborhood, such as the tomb of Oedipus, an altar of Warlike Athena, and a sanctuary of the Semnai Theai, but no remains of these have ever been identified. Two house-sized boulders, which sit today on a shoulder of the hill where they fell, may hide the eponymous meeting place.[7]

The Council of the Areopagos used the Stoa Basileios as an alternate meeting place on certain occasions. This comparatively small stoa was situated near the northwestern corner of the Athenian Agora, and from its excavated remains a ground plan and certain dimensions have been recovered. When the Council of the Areopagos met there, a rope barrier would on occasion have kept the public at a distance. Whatever the business of those meetings, it would not have been the trial

[5] Stroud (1968, pp. 65–83) discusses the date and circumstances of Drakon's reforms.

[6] Demosthenes 23.22 (**20**) and Aristotle, *Ath. Pol.* 57.3 (**3**) list deliberate homicide, deliberate wounding, homicide by poisoning, and arson as crimes judged by the Court of the Areopagos. Destruction of sacred olive trees, however, was another charge within its competence. See Wallace 1989, pp. 109–111.

[7] With Vanderpool 1950, pp. 34–47, cf. Travlos and Frantz 1965, pp. 159–163.

of a homicide, which required that a defendant not be under the same roof as blood relations of the person who was killed.[8]

If the number of councillors was maintained solely through the accession of ex-archons, no more than 9 new members could be added in a year. There would have been even fewer in a year when 1 or more archons had been disqualified for misconduct in office. Tenure, once an Areopagite was appointed, was lifelong. Suppose, then, that in the first thirty years of the council's existence, 9 archons were added annually: 270 ex-archons at most would have made up the Council, although naturally there were fewer, since some would have died in a span of thirty years. Whatever the actual number first was, say, 200 to 250, it ought to have remained more or less constant thereafter. The number of councillors can accordingly be put at over 200.[9] This number is smaller than the judging complements of most heliastic courts, but so too are the numbers for the other homicide courts, where 51 ephetai judged or, in the case of the Prytaneion, where the basileus and tribal kings judged.

The initiation of a prosecution for homicide was not open to all. To prosecute a homicide, one had to be an Athenian citizen, related to the decedent to a degree stipulated as cousin, or associated by membership in the same phratry. All those outside the defined relationships had no part in such actions.[10] If, as seems to have been the case, all members of the decedent's family participated in preliminary oath-takings (Antiphon 6.16), one mature male member of the family should have been designated to appear in court and perhaps to perform some of the other legal, sacral, and ceremonial functions designed to preserve family honor, avenge the decedent, deter homicides generally, and protect the city from disruptions of a continuing vendetta and from a possibly infectious miasma. Since there was no set time by which he had to accomplish this, he (and presumably in the event of his death or incapacity, a successor) had the lifetime of the perpetrator in which to meet his responsibility.[11]

The prosecutor first made a proclamation at the decedent's tomb and then a formal proclamation in the Agora, banning the perpetrator from functions, places, and ceremonies defined by custom and law.[12] He made out a formal charge and presented it to the basileus, who in turn proclaimed the accused killer banned from τὰ νόμιμα.

The basileus coordinated the calendars of the homicide courts. In the case of a charge of, for example, premeditated killing, he first scheduled three preliminary hearings (προδικασίαι), each to take place in the Prytaneion a month apart.[13] The function of these hearings was to test the validity of the charge and determine the proper venue of the trial. If in the course of these hearings

[8] See *Agora* III, pp. 21–25.

[9] Humphreys (1983, p. 236, note 15) estimates 150 to 200 members of the Council in Classical Athens and a smaller number for the time before Peisistratos. Jacoby (1949, p. 367, note 81) thinks of 300 (in connection with Myron of Phlyeus and others at Plutarch, *Solon* 12) as being "the aristocratic normal number."

[10] D. M. MacDowell, "The *Oikos* in Athenian Law," *CQ* n.s. 39, 1989 [pp. 10–21], pp. 18–19 discusses degrees of relationship. For further discussion concerning who could prosecute, see Gagarin and Hansen, *locc. citt.*, note 2 above, p. 43.

[11] See MacDowell 1963, p. 10 on προθέσμια.

[12] This is an expanded translation of the expression εἴργεσθαι τῶν νομίμων found in Antiphon 6.35–36, Aristotle, *Ath. Pol.* 57.2 (**3**). Cf. Rhodes 1981, pp. 640–641. Theophrastos, *Nomoi* F10 attests a proclamation at the border: ἐφορία. ἡ ἐπὶ τῶν ὅρων γινομένη προαγόρευσις ὡς Δημοσθένης διδάσκει ἐν τῶι κατ' Ἀριστοκράτους καὶ Θεόφραστος ἐν ⟨ι⟩γ τῶν νόμων. Szegedy-Maszak *ad loc.* notes that προαγόρευσις had two functions. Before a homicide trial it was a public declaration of the impending trial. It was made by the family of the victim. Afterwards it was the official ban, pronounced by the basileus, who ordered the murderer to stay away from temples, the agora, and other public places.

[13] MacDowell 1963, p. 43.

it became clear that the question at issue was one of intent, and what had to be determined was whether or not the death was accidental or justifiable, then the trial would be held in the court at Palladion or in the court at Delphinion. The accuser, one supposes, had to stipulate the nature of the homicide in question. If an accused should urge that the death was accidental and if an accuser insisted it was not, the trial would necessarily take place on the Areopagos. The Court of the Areopagos heard legal cases only on the last three days of the month. Appropriate times had to be scheduled for trials at the other courts; the basileus had the right to decline on technical grounds.[14]

On a day given to a trial by the Court of Areopagos, prosecutor and defendant walked up the hill to the court site. The prosecutor, in the case of a homicide, was a relative of the decedent, but in the case of wounding or arson, the prosecutor would be the injured person himself, if he was able, or a relation, when the injured party was not qualified. If the charge was one of destroying sacred olive trees, the prosecutor could be any citizen who wanted to act in the public interest. Homicide trials were heard in open air to avoid pollution from any possible miasma that might attach to the person who has killed.

Within the court area, to which there were two entrances, seating for approximately 250 dikasts can be imagined. The meeting place was called *synedrion* or *bouleuterion*, neither word necessarily entailing the existence of any sort of roofed structure (**28**). In the area where the trial took place, two "unworked stones" (ἀργοὺς λίθους, as Pausanias calls them: 1.28.4 [**1**]) could be low eminences formed by the natural limestone of the hill. They served as bemata. One, called the Rock of Outrage (Ὕβρεως), was where the defendant stood, and the other, the Rock of Unforgiveness (Ἀναιδείας), where the prosecutor stood (**1**). Both parties swore an oath, first the accuser, "invoking destruction on himself and his family and his house, and no ordinary oath either, but one which no one swears on any other subject, standing over the cut pieces of a boar, a ram, and a bull, which have been slaughtered by the right persons and on the proper days, so that every religious requirement has been fulfilled both as regards the time and as regards the executants" (Demosthenes 23.67–68, trans. MacDowell [1963, p. 91]).

Whatever the order and length of speeches given at a trial before the Court of the Areopagos, both parties undertook to speak to the point. They were not allowed to present a formal introduction (προοίμιον) or to lament. Witnesses before giving testimony took an oath.[15] Whether women, slaves, and children could give testimony in such a trial is not clear.[16] The accuser spoke first, explaining how the accused was identified and detailing whatever circumstances and probabilities seemed useful to the prosecution of his case. The accused answered, citing another and different train of circumstances and probabilities. After finishing this speech, he could leave the court and voluntarily go into exile, if it seemed prudent to do so. If he did not, his accuser had a second opportunity to refute his arguments and strengthen his own attack. The accused then answered this rebuttal, and the dikasts voted immediately thereafter, without consulting each other. They did on occasion, or perhaps regularly, take their ballots from an altar.[17] Aischines 1.92 (**12**) implies that members of the

[14] If, for instance, a basileus is due to retire from office within three or four months of a time when a charge is first lodged, he will not have time himself to officiate at each of three prodikasiai on succeeding months and at a trial in the fourth month. See Antiphon 6.41–43. Cf. Gagarin 1978, p. 306, note 18.

[15] MacDowell 1963, pp. 98–100.

[16] MacDowell 1963, pp. 101–109.

[17] Demosthenes 18.134 has Areopagites take ballots from an altar, but it is not clear whether the practice is particular to that trial or general in homicide trials. It seems clearly to be a way of sanctifying a vote. Cf. Latte 1920, p. 45: "Ein feierliches Glanz soll das Urteil umkleiden und es über die Sphäre eines rein menschlichen Meinungsäusserung

Council of the Areopagos did some of their own investigating. He does not make it clear, however, just how they did this. Wolff (1946, pp. 37–38) has suggested that the *istores* of the trial described by Homer on the shield of Achilles had that name because they had special information concerning the dispute they attended. Aischines may refer to some phase or tradition of such circumstances.

The basileus did not cast a vote: he simply pronounced justice (δικάζει),[18] that is, he pronounced the defendant acquitted or condemned in accordance with the judgment of the court, and he stated what the defendant, if guilty, had to pay or suffer. The herald received this information from the basileus and made the announcement. The man who prevailed then swore that he had done so fairly, invoking destruction on himself, his family, and his house if he had not.[19]

PALLADION

The use of the name "Palladion" to mean a locality for a homicide court is generally understood to be a way of referring to one particular sanctuary or temple of Athena Pallas and Zeus. This was the temenos situated outside the city wall, possibly east of the the Akropolis, in the neighborhood of Ardettos Hill (**52**). Note, however, the prominence of Phaleron as a topographical detail in Pausanias (**1**), Pollux (**2**), and Phanodemos (**53**). According to the scholiast to Aischines 2.87 (**41**), Phaleron is where tradition places a battle at night, in which the Argives met the Athenians and in ignorance killed them; the scholiast has the Palladion set up in the sanctuary of Athena at Phaleron and a dikasterion established there as well.[20] A natural interpretation of ἐν τούτωι τῶι τόπωι in the commentary on Demosthenes 23.71 (**51**) is that it means "Phaleron". The same is true of αὐτόθι δ' ἱδρύθη in Pollux (**2**). Possibly, there were two quite separate sanctuaries called Palladion. One Palladion, the one just east of the walls, a sanctuary or temple of Athena Pallas and of Zeus, was named Palladion from Athena's epiklesis Pallas. The other Palladion, however, the one near

hinausheben." We hear of it once on the Akropolis; see Plutarch, *Perikles* 32. (Jacoby, in saying that this motion of Drakontides is unique, presumably refers to the site and not the procedure: *FGrHist* 324 F59, notes to commentary, p. 152.) Otherwise, in questions of citizenship, even at deme level, ballots were taken from the altar ([Demosthenes] 43.14, 82; *IG* II^2 1237). Herodotos 8.123 has the Greek generals cast their ballots on or at an altar of Poseidon at the Isthmos to determine who was best at Salamis. Plutarch (*Themistokles* 17.1), describing the same event, has them taking their ballots from the altar. Paintings on Attic red-figured cups show Achaian heroes voting Achilles' armor to Odysseus. Those heroes are depositing on an altar the pebbles that represent their votes. See commentary to **21** and Plate 23.

[18] At Aristotle, *Ath. Pol.* 52.3 the basileus states the right. Wolff (1946, pp. 67–78) explains how the verb δικάζειν must be understood in this and like contexts, and his explanation makes unnecessary an assumption that the basileus voted and was consequently the odd man of fifty-one ephetai. For this assumption, see, e.g., Lenschau 1949. Cf. Rhodes 1981, pp. 586–587, 648. The usage is clear in the wording of Andokides 1.78 (**14**) and Plutarch, *Solon* 19.3 (**27**), where the basileus has pronounced the verdict but the courts are named as judging bodies. Cf. M. Talamanco, "Δικάζειν e Κρίνειν nelle testimonianze greche piu antiche," in *Symposion 1974. Vorträge zur griechischen und hellenistischen Rechtsgeschichte*, A. Biscardi, ed., Cologne/Vienna 1979, pp. 103–105.

[19] Photios (*Lexicon* I, *s.v.* διωμοσία) assigns this oath to homicide trials generally: ὤμνυον καὶ οἱ φόνου ἀγῶνα διώκοντες καὶ οἱ φεύγοντες καὶ μετὰ τὸ εἰπεῖν κτλ. MacDowell (1963, pp. 92–93) had arrived at more or less the same conclusion. Note that Photios' version does not present the textual problems of Bekker, *Lex Rhet.* 239.29–30, discussed in MacDowell 1963, pp. 97–98.

[20] Cf. Kleitodemos (**53**). Jacoby (*FGrHist* 323 F20, notes to commentary, p. 75) says that Pausanias (the lexicographer, not the Periegete) is responsible for the assertion about the dikasterion.

Phaleron, received its name from having housed the legendary Palladion,[21] and it was there that homicide trials were held.

When a homicide was on trial, proceedings would take place under the open sky. A single prosecutor, we can assume, was recognized, although all family members were in some way involved. There would be a declaration at the grave and then proclamations banning the killer from τὰ νόμιμα. The basileus performed the same administrative functions as he did when a trial was to be heard on the Areopagos: he scheduled the *prodikasiai* (pretrial hearing) and heard what prosecutor and defendant had to say about the circumstances surrounding the death. And when the prosecutor determined a proper charge, the basileus assigned an appropriate venue and scheduled a day on his calendar. To take one sort of example, the court at Palladion was appropriate when a prosecutor agreed to test by trial a defendant's claim that the death in question was accidental. Trials there also took place when the decedent was a foreigner, metic, or slave, or again when someone's counsel or plan (βούλευσις) had resulted in a death. The prosecutor spoke first, the defendant second. After their presentations, each gave a second, shorter talk. Then fifty-one dikastai, known also as ἐφέται, judged. The basileus, as in trials on the Areopagos, did not vote: he pronounced justice. When that pronouncement had been made, the man who prevailed took an oath that he did so honestly, calling down destruction on himself and his family if he was swearing falsely (**40**). This brought the trial to an end. A defendant found guilty of ἀκούσιος φόνος went immediately into exile by a prescribed route (τακτὴν ὁδόν), which had to be covered within a stipulated period of time (ἔν τισιν εἰρημένοις χρόνοις: Demosthenes 23.72). This particular detail of procedure may reflect a wish to minimize exposure to possible infection from miasma. If so, it prompts a speculation: If the Palladion were situated in Phaleron, then the prescribed route would start at Phaleron rather than at Athens. A convicted homicide would in that case reach the sea, which is to say, pass beyond Athens' border, sooner than he would if he had started from the city. He would accordingly represent a possible threat to the health of the community for a shorter time.

Only a modest area need be defined for judicial hearings where the judging panel is composed of fifty-one men.[22] In the court at Palladion, there was also room for bystanders. Their presence is attested in Antiphon 6.14 (**190**).[23] A stoa enhanced (possibly) with a propylon[24] is not what was wanted for such trials, whose proper venue was an open-air site associated with some consecrated area: a temenos, a shrine, or a temple.

DELPHINION

The court at Delphinion, according to Demosthenes 23.74 (**6**), was the holiest and most awesome of the homicide courts. The ephetai judged there (**7**, **8**). A man defended himself at Delphinion when he claimed that he had killed justly or lawfully.[25] He had first to establish that claim, however,

[21] L. Ziehen (*RE* XVIII.3, 1949 [cols. 171–201], cols. 172–178, *s.v.* Palladion) cites more than one Palladion *qua* cult image at Athens. Note that "Agbatana" in Herodotos 3.64 and "Shrine of Zeus in Nemea" at Thucydides 3.96.1 each denote more than one place (lending themselves nicely to stories about the inscrutability of oracles).

[22] It is not necessary to find explanations for a panel of 500 dikasts (brought into existence by editorial emendation of a text) at the Palladion. See MacDowell 1963. Cf. note 3 above, p. 43.

[23] Cf. MacDowell 1963, p. 97.

[24] The identification proposed by Travlos (1971, pp. 412–413). Cf. pp. 94, 97–98 below.

[25] MacDowell (1963, pp. 80–81) distinguishes "justly" and "lawfully", but cf. M. Gagarin, "The Prohibition of Just and Unjust Homicide in Antiphon's *Tetralogies*," *GRBS* 19, 1978 [pp. 291–306], pp. 292–293.

in the course of the three prodikasiai. If his accuser would not accept that claim, the trial was held on the Areopagos. Certain homicides, when committed under stipulated circumstances, were defined as within the law: An Athenian could with impunity kill a man whom he found having sexual intercourse with his wife, mother, sister, daughter, or any concubine with whom he begat free children. He was likewise exempted from punishment if he caused death by accident in an athletic contest or by ignorance in war, mistaking an ally for an enemy. A doctor in whose care a patient died was not liable to punishment. Killing in defense of one's person or property was within the law, given specified conditions: a thief who steals by night, or a robber using force, could be killed with impunity. Quite apart from person and property, one also could kill certain offenders against the state, such as a man who, although sentenced to exile for homicide, is found within Athenian boundaries. There were also times when persons attempting to subvert the democracy at Athens could be killed with impunity.[26]

As in the case of the Palladion, a modest area was sufficient to serve as a court in which fifty-one ephetai acted as judges. The court at Delphinion likewise had to be in the open air.

PHREATTO

The court variously called Phreattys, Phreattos, Phreatos, among others, presents an enigmatic face, not only because of uncertainties regarding name and site.[27] The sort of trial that is reported to have been held there has no recorded examples. It is accordingly not surprising to find in two amnesty decrees, one from *ca.* 590 B.C.E. (**27**), the other from 405 (**14**), that among exiled homicides who are excepted from the general amnesty, no provision is made for men in exile after a trial in Phreatto. The specific set of circumstances, moreover, for which that model of procedure was devised are so tightly defined that Aristotle's observation, "There are not many such trials even in big cities" (**4**), has the look of understatement. Consider what a particular confluence of events must have preceded a trial in Phreatto. An Athenian kills someone whose family has the means and power to prosecute or settle.[28] He is judged to have killed unintentionally (ἄκων), and he has not been able to reach a reconciliation with the family of the decedent. He must, therefore, live outside the borders of Attica. While he is in exile, he kills another Athenian, this time in circumstances that point to an intentional killing. But he wants someday to return to Athens, and so he agrees to travel by sea to a point off the coast somewhere near Peiraieus, and there he presents his defense from a boat moored offshore. If he is found guilty, he is put to death. If he is acquitted, he goes back into exile, hoping one day to be reconciled with the relations of the first man he has killed.

The specifications are exact, and not one of them can be removed without changing the whole character of the situation (seen as a matter for trial, that is). One asks whether need for such a trial might not have arisen just once. Could one single Athenian have been tried that way, possibly generations before Drakon's codification of homicide law in 620 B.C.E.? A named place, a temenos,

[26] See MacDowell 1963, pp. 77–81.

[27] On the name, see commentary preceding **54** and **55** and MacDowell 1963, pp. 82–83. Papachatzis 1963, fig. 25 (pp. 100–101) shows a Phreattys on the west side of the entrance to the harbor of Zea. I do not know the basis for this siting. Judeich (1931, p. 436) had connected Phreattys with some cuttings in the rocks along the coast, but they are shown on Papachatzis' figure as on the other side of the entrance to the harbor.

[28] Harpokration, *s.v.* ὑποφόνια (= Deinarchos [ed. Conomis], F10.5 and F19.12; Theophrastos, *Nomoi*, F19). MacDowell (1963, p. 9) calls such settlements "bribes", hence illegal, but the matter is not perfectly clear. Cf. Bonner and Smith 1938, pp. 196–198.

or conceivably a mere landing in the neighborhood of Phaleron was chosen. (Peiraieus seems not to have been a usual landing place in the 7th and 6th centuries.) It could have been named and consecrated long before its use as trial site, or indeed at some time after the first trial there. In any case, by the 5th and 4th centuries the dikasterion in Phreatto had a legendary look.

An actual court, to distinguish it from that putative site, existed near the small harbor called Pashalimani in recent years but Zea in antiquity. Trials were held there in the 4th century B.C.E. Ten distinctively marked bronze ballots, showing signs of use, were found in a well near the harbor, and there is no reason to assume that they were far from home. The court to which they point may later have become identified in the lexicographical tradition with the traditional homicide court in Phreatto.[29]

PRYTANEION

The Prytaneion, on the other hand, had a vital, central function in the life of the city; its governmental and ceremonial uses are well documented.[30] The prodikasiai were held there (**58**), and the reason for this surely is that it was a neutral place, one that did not predispose an issue. If the prodikasiai were held on the Areopagos, at Delphinion, or at Palladion, the association of a court with a specified kind of homicide trial could be thought to establish a frame of reference that might be prejudicial. As for the types of homicides actually tried in the Prytaneion, there is no need for modern students to consign judgments uttered at the Prytaneion to legend or mere ceremonial function. When an Athenian died by an instrumentality and not by an identifiable hand, the community wanted a formal judgment that would close the case. Without such a judgment, an unresolved homicide presented opportunities over an undefined passage of time for prosecutions founded on malice alone. The basileus consequently declared the sentence, forbidding the perpetrator the holy places of Attica. In doing this, he put an end to the question.

The site of the Prytaneion, thanks to discovery of an inscribed stele, can now be located on the eastern side of the Akropolis.[31] The stele, which is reported as having been found in its original place on the eastern slope of the Akropolis, records a decree of the council and demos in 247/6 or 246/5 regarding matters in the sanctuary of Aglauros. A direction at lines 33–36, that the stele be erected in the Aglaurion, should identify the site of the Aglaurion. When this information is combined with Pausanias 1.18.2–3, where he says that the Prytaneion is next to the temenos of Aglauros, the site of the Prytaneion can be placed conjecturally somewhere on the eastern side of the Akropolis.

[29] See Boegehold 1974, pp. 7–19. Only the "Ballot Deposit" in the Agora is in any way comparable (see p. 68 below).
[30] See Miller 1978, pp. 4–23.
[31] Dontas 1983, pp. 48–63.

PART II

EQUIPMENT, FURNISHINGS, AND BUILDINGS

A.

SMALL FINDS ASSOCIATED WITH TRIALS

ARISTOTLE'S ACCOUNT of the Athenian lawcourts *(Ath. Pol.* 63–69) both made possible and provoked much detailed study of Athens' judicial machinery.[1] Furthermore, the examination of material remains in the light both of Aristotle's description and of its various interpretations has proved unusually fruitful,[2] since the understanding of a complicated process either from a verbal description or from the relevant paraphernalia alone is like reading the text of an archaeological work without reference to the plates or ignoring the text and looking only at the illustrations.

Literary and epigraphical sources provide evidence both for the location of lawcourts in the Agora and for the use of various stoas there for particular sessions of courts (see pp. 7–20 above). It was therefore to be expected that the Agora would be rich in dikastic remains. The material uncovered there includes pinakia, kleroteria, bronze and lead ballots, an echinos lid, and a klepsydra. Also present, but perhaps not exclusively dikastic, were bronze balls, possibly used in the kleroteria, and stamped bronze tokens. The klepsydra, the echinos lid, and pinakia have already been published[3] but will be included here for the sake of completeness; much of the other material has not been previously published.

The distribution of findspots of the dikastic equipment (pinakia **P 1–P 24**; ballots **B 1–B 54**; bronze balls **BB 1–BB 9**; klepsydra **M 1**; echinos **E 1**) in the Agora may be seen in Figure 4.[4] Since the pinakia were personal possessions, the places at which they were found[5] may not have the same significance for their use as those of court furniture. One-third of the ballots and balls were found within a 40-meter radius of the Tholos, suggesting that they were either used in the Bouleuterion by members of the boule acting in their legislative or judicial capacities or stored in the Tholos or Bouleuterion.

A second concentration is that of objects in or near the "Ballot Deposit" (Pl. 2) under the north end of the Stoa of Attalos. Two terracotta water-channel sections standing upright a short distance apart, their interiors facing one another, thus delineating a rectangular area, have been variously interpreted. At first it was thought that they served as supports for a tabletop on which a voting jar was placed or for an abacus on which ballots were counted. There is also the suggestion that they represent remains of a lined pit (see p. 105 below). The pit will have been sunk into the floor for storage, and dikastic paraphernalia of different kinds could have been stored there. No matter that there is an open space between the two terracotta segments: the ballots, tokens, balls, and the like would in any case have been held in cloth or leather sacks. Associated with the channels

[1] Much of the earlier work culminates in, and is reviewed by, Hommel 1927.

[2] Good examples are Dow 1939 and Kroll 1972.

[3] Young 1939, pp. 274–284; Kroll 1972, nos. 15, 32, 40, 45, 47, 48, 96, 97, 101, 112, 113, 130, 131, 133, 137, 141, 160, 162, 169, 175, 180, 181; Boegehold 1982, pp. 1–6.

[4] Because of the small scale of the plan, the objects have been located only by grid square and are not accurately spotted within each square. They are indicated by Agora inventory number, not by the catalogue numbers used here.

[5] Most of the complete pinakia actually come from graves, presumably of their last owners. The irrelevant contexts in which fragments are found suggest that they may have been discarded in antiquity after breaking.

were several kinds of dikastic implements found in mixed contexts: bronze ballots, balls (bronze and terracotta), part of a dikastic pinakion, tokens (bronze and terracotta), and a stylus.[6]

Since pinakia and styli, at least, seem to have been personal rather than city or phyletic property, an area where they are found mixed with dikastic equipment could be interpreted as one of general dikastic activity, rather than as a storage place. At the same time, even if the channels did form a storage pit rather than a structure for some courtroom device, Athenians stored their equipment where it was going to be used. These channels were found embedded in the clay floor of a room that appears to date from the close of the 5th century B.C.E. and that was partly destroyed to make way for the Square Peristyle at the end of the 4th century B.C.E.[7] The concentration of six ballots, one bronze token, and one bronze ball in the storage pit and other pieces of dikastic equipment from the neighborhood, making a total of twenty-five dikastic implements (see p. 68 below), seems to point to the presence of a lawcourt here beginning late in the 5th century and continuing on into the 4th century B.C.

[6] This last is admittedly not exclusively associated with dikastic procedures, but styli did have a place in courtroom activity (**250**, **352–355** and Pl. 22), and so when one is found near indubitable dikastic implements, its presence is notable.

[7] Thompson 1954, pp. 58–61, *Agora* XIV, pp. 52–56.

6

A CURSE TABLET AGAINST OPPONENTS AT LAW

IF FREQUENT RECOURSE to the courts was a feature of life in ancient Athens, apparently so too was the feeling that the machinery of the law would not necessarily produce the desired result without one's own intervention into its working. Evidence is the use of the lead curse tablet against opponents at law.[1] Some twenty-five Attic curse tablets, dating in the late 5th and the 4th centuries B.C.E., are recognizable as being intended to influence the outcome of trials, for there are *antidikoi* ("opponents"), *synêgoroi* ("assisting speakers"), and the like among their intended victims.[2] One such tablet (Ill. 4), which curses *synêgoroi*, was among several lead curse tablets (the others unfortunately too damaged to yield texts) found in 1972 among objects of the 4th and 3rd centuries B.C.E. in a dump fill in a well beside the Panathenaic Way at the crossroads in front of the Royal Stoa.[3] The text consists of a list of names of six intended victims in the nominative case, all but one (who is qualified as a *synêgoros*) with his father's name in the genitive; there follows a generalizing phrase in the accusative case but no verb; 4th- and possibly 5th-century parallels exist for this arrangement of nominatives plus accusatives in curse texts.[4] The text is written retrograde, no doubt to throw the intended victims' plans into reverse; the inscriber's discomfort with this type of writing is evident. Retrograde curse texts are rare in Attica, the practice of merely reversing spelling (e.g. ΣΑΙΛΛΑΚ for ΚΑΛΛΙΑΣ) being much commoner.[5] Most curse texts with reversed spelling seem to be of

[1] For an introduction to the study of lead curse tablets, see K. Preisendanz, "Fluchtafel (Defixion)," *RAC* VIII, cols. 1–24, Stuttgart 1972. There are two corpora of curse tablets, Wünsch 1897 and Audollent 1904. Greek tablets that have appeared more recently are listed in Jordan 1985, pp. 151–197.

[2] See Wünsch 1987, index IV, and Audollent 1904, index IIB3, *s.vv.* δικαστής, μάρτυς, ῥήτωρ, σύνδικος, συνήγορος. Further Attic examples include Jordan 1985, 6, 9, 19, 42, and 48. C. A. Faraone ("Aeschylus' ὕμνος δέσμιος [*Eum.* 306] and Attic Judicial Tablets," *JHS* 105, 1985, pp. 150–154) argues that Aischylos' account of the Furies' use of a hymn to bind Orestes' wits before his trial on the Areopagos is an early attestation (458 B.C.E.) of magical coercion to ensure the outcome of litigation.

[3] For the excavation of the well (J 5:1), see Shear 1973, pp. 360–369. Some of the fill in the well consisted of objects discarded from a nearby rectangular shrine whose cult was female.

H. A. Thompson adds *per litt.*: "It should be pointed out that the well belongs with the shrine (which I continue to believe was in all probability the Leokorion). This is shown by the relationship of peribolos and well on the plan as well as by the great number of offerings from the shrine that were found in the well. But in addition to serving the shrine, the well served also as a place for discarding material relevant to other aspects of religious or civic life, notably the tablets and tokens from the Hipparcheion and the great number of loom-weights which, I venture to suggest, are to be related somehow to the wearing of Athena's peplos done under the authority of the Basileus."

[4] Wünsch 1897, nos. 38 and 39 (5th or 4th century); Jordan 1985, no. 19 (Attica, early 4th century?); Audollent 1904, nos. 60 and 61 (Attica, 4th century); Jordan 1985, no. 171 (Olbia, no published date, but letter forms suggest 4th century).

[5] I know of only two other Attic examples of curse tablets inscribed retrograde, Wünsch 1897, nos. 26 (six lines, retrograde throughout, 5th or 4th century) and 33 (five lines, parts of two retrograde, 4th century). For examples of reversed spelling, see Wünsch 1897, index VE, *s.vv.* "Litterarum ordo a dextra incipit." It happens that the Agora excavations have yielded a black-glazed lamp of the 4th century (see M. Lang, *Graffiti and Dipinti* [*The Athenian Agora* XXI], Princeton 1976, no. C 32) with six men's names, spelled backwards, inscribed on its nozzle. Its purpose, as Lang speculates, was no doubt magical; cf. D. Jordan, Rev. of M. Lang, *Graffiti and Dipinti* in *ArchNews* 7, 1978 [pp. 92–94], p. 94.

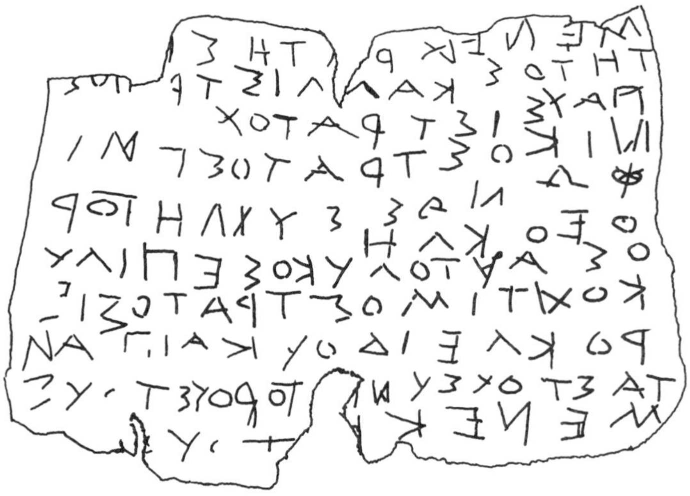

Ill. 4. Curse tablet

the 4th century. Taken together, the aim, the context, the syntax, and the reversed spelling of the tablet suggest a 4th-century date.

CATALOGUE

C 1 (IL 1695) Lead curse tablet Ill. 4
Dump fill in well in front of Royal Stoa.
4th century.
H. 0.0615; W. 0.0905.
Written retrograde:

Μενεκράτης Κ[ρά-]
τητος, Καλλίστρατος
Παυσιστράτου,
Νικόστρατος Γνί-
φωνος,
Θεοκλῆ⟨ς⟩ συνήγορ-
ος, Αὐτόλυκος Ἐπιλύ-
χου, Τιμόστρατος Ἱε-
ροκλείδου, καὶ πάν-
τας τοὺς συνηγόρους τοὺς
Μενεκράτους.

Menekrates son of K[ra]tes, Kallistratos son of Pausistratos, Nikostratos son of Gniphon, Theokles *synêgoros,* Autolykos son of Epilykos, Timostratos son of Hierokleides, and all the *synêgoroi* of Menekrates.

Presumably, Menekrates was the principal in the lawsuit, and all the other men served as his *synêgoroi*. None of the men is identifiable with any Athenian on record, although Timostratos son of Hierokleides (*PA* 7463) may be the father or the son of a Hierokleides son of Timostratos who proposed two honorific decrees, *IG* II^2 206 and 209, in 349/8 B.C.E.

7
KLEROTERION

FRAGMENTS OF KLEROTERIA found in excavations in The Athenian Agora were the subject of an unfinished study by Sterling Dow. An introduction to the form and function of the kleroterion precedes testimonia **324–333** in this book.

CATALOGUE

A fragment of a kleroterion came to light in 1986 in excavations conducted by the Greek Archaeological Service. The piece, which was subsequently kept in the storeroom within the Library of Hadrian, had at the time of finding been used in the building of the "post-Herulian" wall near the so-called Diogeneion. I thank Alkestis Choremi, Archaeologist, for informing me of this find, for sending me a photograph, and for giving me valuable assistance in my study of the stone at first hand. I thank the Α′ Ἐφορεία Προϊστορικῶν καὶ Κλασικῶν Ἀρχαιοτήτων of the Akropolis for permission to describe it here.

K 1 (ΠΛ 367) Kleroterion fragment Pl. 6

Fragment as whole: H. 0.193; W. 0.18; max. p. Th. 0.11.

Preserved face: H. 0.123; W. 0.145.

Vertical distance between slots, as measured on center: 0.215.

Distance between columns of slots: 0.035.

Slots: H. (at face) 0.009; L. 0.035; Depth 0.02.

Pentelic marble, broken all around except for an area of the face which preserves in three columns three complete slots for pinakia and traces of eleven others. The three complete slots are in the middle column of the three.

Dimensions, spacing, and workmanship of the slots, when compared with those of nine kleroteria in Athens (namely, Dow 1937, nos. II–VI, VIII–XI), show that the fragment under discussion was never a part of any of those nine. The measurements do not coincide, and the workmanship is less careful than that in all others examined, except perhaps for Dow's no. II. The slots were fashioned by drilling two shallow holes *ca.* 0.035 m. apart and then chipping out the marble between. Then a second pair of holes was drilled in the shallow slot, a little closer together, and then a third pair, a little closer again, with the result that in one measurable case the length of the slot at bottom is less than half what it is at the face.

Of the kleroteria published by Dow, all could have been designed for use in dikasteria. Not enough of the present kleroterion is preserved to recommend a particular application.

8
PINAKIA

IN THE PRESENT ESSAY "pinakion" designates a small inscribed plaque of bronze or boxwood that Athenians (and others)[1] used in various allotments during the 4th century B.C.E. A characteristic pinakion was inscribed with the owner's name, his father's name, and his demotic. The letters were either incised or punched. Separate and distinct from these letters, a single letter, one of the first ten of the Attic-Ionic alphabet (Α, Β, Γ, Δ, Ε, Ζ, Η, Θ, Ι, Κ), served to designate dikastic section. One or more seals might, in addition, be stamped into the metal. These seals might show an owl, an Athena head, or a gorgoneion. Pinakia tend to measure *ca.* 0.11 m. in length, 0.02 m. in width, and from 0.0015 to 0.0025 m. in thickness, depending partly on the number of times one owner's name had been erased and a new owner's name inscribed in its place. Between *ca.* 348 B.C.E. and 330–326 B.C.E., that is, between the time of Demosthenes 39.10–12 and Aristotle's *Athenaion Politeia*, Athenians changed from bronze to boxwood for their dikastic pinakia. No example, needless to say, of a boxwood pinakion has survived. The datum, however, is helpful because it establishes a *terminus ante quem* for bronze pinakia, whose use in the first half of the 4th century B.C.E. is also indicated by the shapes of their inscribed letters.

By size and shape, the pinakia (both bronze and boxwood) were fit for insertion into slots of an allotment machine, or kleroterion. Aristotle (*Ath. Pol.* 63–65 [**249**]) describes in detail the procedure by which dikasts were allotted to service on a court day.[2] In a simple allotment, however, a number of pinakia could be shaken up in a receptacle from which one or more were taken at random. See, for instance, the allotments described by Aristotle (*Ath. Pol.* 65 and 69).

Since not all such pinakia carry a dikastic section letter, it may be that not all were used in dikastic allotments. Only those that have such section letters conform with Aristotle's description of allotment procedures at the dikasteria. The pinakia that do not carry a section letter could have been used in any of the numerous other allotments that the Athenian system of administration made necessary. The use of pinakia for allotment in the boule can be envisioned from Aristotle's description at *Ath. Pol.* 44.2: "And whenever the prytaneis bring together the boule or the demos this man (epistates of the prytaneis) allots the nine proedroi, one from each tribe except that holding the prytany, and again from these nine, one epistates, and he hands over the agenda to them." There is explicit testimony, for instance, that bronze pinakia were used in allotments to the boule and to archonships (Demosthenes 39.10–12).

The complete and exhaustive study of all known Athenian pinakia by John H. Kroll (1972) makes it unnecessary here to go into detailed examination of these pieces and the significance of their various characteristics for our understanding of their use. They are included here to give a complete picture of dikastic operations in the Agora.

[1] See "After 322 B.C.E.," pp. 41–42 above.

[2] See Dow 1937, pp. 198–215; *idem* 1939, pp. 1–34; *idem*, *RE* Supplement VII, 1940, cols. 322–328, *s.v.* Kleroterion; and J. D. Bishop, "Cleroterium," *JHS* 90, 1970, pp. 1–14. A description of this allotment is given in "Three Court Days," pp. 32–34, 37 above.

Twenty-three of the twenty-four pinakia and fragments catalogued below[3] were found in the Agora, more scattered over the whole area than were other sorts of dikastic equipment. Pinakia, since they were personal possessions, moved about with their owners, and so pinakia have also been found outside the Agora, especially in graves, far more frequently than other dikastic material.[4]

Pinakia with section letters were obviously designed for use in the kleroteria, where the columns of slots were marked by section letters and a whole row could be allotted or excluded by a single ball. The kleroteria thus simplified and speeded up the process of allotting a group or groups of men to achieve equal representation from a number of different sections of the population. This "mechanization" was ideal for allotting courts ranging in size from 200 up, from ten roughly equal sections of potential dikasts, but would only have been cumbersome where the desired result was proportional representation from groups of different sizes.[5] Or, since pinakia seem to have been designed for use in a kleroterion, allotments that did not require the use of that specialized equipment might well have been carried out more simply with black and white beans in a jar from which individuals themselves drew.

Many pinakia have other kinds of stamping in addition to the section letter. According to an older view,[6] the different stamps represented various offices, so that as a result, a man's pinakion served as a kind of pocket *curriculum vitae.* But there are too few varieties of stamps to represent the multiplicity of offices open to Athenian citizens, and there seems to be no criterion by which some offices should be so denoted and others not. Furthermore, the fact that some of the stamps were impressed before the name was inscribed and others were certainly added later has now been established by Kroll, who was able to distinguish between primary and secondary seals on the basis of relative location, symmetry, orientation, and form.[7] His conclusions about their respective functions are perhaps more open to question, namely, that the (primary) triobol seal, representing as it does the dikast's daily stipend, appropriately authenticates dikastic pinakia, while the (primary) gorgoneion seal merely certifies citizenship; and that the secondary seals were validating stamps applied to the pinakia of all dikasts registered at a particular time. It seems certain that the primary seals give original certification and the secondary seals represent some kind of renewal, but the differentiation between dikastic and nondikastic pinakia depends in large part on the hypothesis that there was an annual allotment of 6,000 dikasts, as a result of which those citizens who were not reallotted had

[3] The twenty-fourth (**P 24**) was catalogued with Agora material when it was brought in from a cremation burial near Daphni.

[4] See Kroll 1972, pp. 9–11.

[5] For example, in the allotment of a tribal contingent to the boule, where the demes were represented according to their population, the allotment had to be more discriminating. Thus Kroll's description (1972, pp. 92–94) of the use of dikastic section letters and kleroteria in the allotment of offices seems not to take into account the need for deme distribution to which Aristotle (*Ath. Pol.* 62.1) testifies for a whole group of offices or boards for some not very distant earlier period and for the bouleutai and phrouroi continuing into his own time. Kroll's interpretation of his Class III and Class IV pinakia as nondikastic requires him to suggest a nondikastic use for the sections. There remains some doubt, however, both as to the necessity of their being nondikastic and as to the likelihood of annual reallotment to achieve a standing body of 6,000 dikasts and of an annual reissue of tickets, with newly allotted dikasts turning in nondikastic pinakia and former dikasts excluded by the lot exchanging dikastic pinakia for nondikastic. If so much care was to be taken to insure a properly limited and authenticated pool of dikasts, there would have to have been strict requirements about the turning in of "last year's" pinakia. And if those controls were so lax as to allow so many Athenians to take their pinakia into the next world, there was nothing to prevent a live Athenian keeping his dikastic *pinakion* and using it year after year without benefit of reallotment.

[6] T. Teusch, *De sortitione iudicum apud Athenienses*, Göttingen 1894, pp. 54–58, cited by Lipsius 1905–1915, p. 150, note 50 and Hommel 1927, p. 42.

[7] Kroll 1972, pp. 41–59.

to exchange dikastic pinakia for nondikastic, and *vice versa*. It may be that differences in the primary seals resulted from nothing more significant than different issuing authorities (like mint marks) or from changes of symbols over a period of years. Since Kroll has clearly determined that his latest class of pinakia exhibits no seals at all, their function was not essential to the dikastic allotment as described by Aristotle.[8]

Turning to what is, at least in origin, the specifically dikastic part of the pinakia, one should note that on some of these the section letter is stamped and on others it is incised. Kroll argues[9] that the difference was chronological, with the stamped letters having been applied to the earlier pinakia before the names were inscribed and the incised section letters added to later pinakia along with the owners' names and "regularly changed with each change of name." Mode of application, however, is not a sound basis for chronological distinctions. Compare the bronze ballots: some have a stamped letter while others have a large letter in relief (see pp. 87–88 below), and both kinds were contemporary (see pp. 82–83 below).

CATALOGUE

The pinakia are arranged as follows: (1) alphabetically by names (of last use) where the first part is preserved; (2) ends of names; (3) middles of names. Findspots are generally indicated by the square or squares of the Agora grid (e.g., I 16 for **P 1**), with a context date where available; for dated deposits that are also groups, the grid designation is followed by the number of the deposit (e.g., B 19:14 for **P 13**) within the square. All letters are incised, except where otherwise indicated. All dates are B.C.E.

See Kroll 1972 for a full treatment of earlier uses and possible readings.

P 1 (B 56) Fragment of pinakion Pl. 7
Kroll, no. 45, Class III.
I 16.
P.L. 0.032; W. 0.023; Th. 0.0013; L.H. 0.006–0.008.
Only left end preserved, with upper left corner broken away.
Earlier use(s): almost completely erased gorgoneion stamp (0.01 m. in diameter) at lower left; partially erased section letter, Δ, was incised at upper left; traces only of other erased letters.
Last use: Ἀβρ̣[– – –]
Κι[ϰ̣ιννεύς]
The absence of a section letter at the left end (in the last use) suggests either that this pinakion was like *IG* II² 1869 (Kroll, no. 38) in having its section letter at the right end or that it should be compared to *IG* II² 1899 (Kroll, no. 182), which may have had no section letter at all.

P 2 (B 822) Fragment of pinakion Pl. 7
Kroll, no. 130, Class VI.
B 19. Mid-4th century.
P.L. 0.102; W. 0.021; Th. 0.001; L.H. 0.007.
Broken at right.
Young 1951, p. 216, pl. 71:b.
Earlier use(s): erasure evidenced by thinness and uneven edges (from hammering).
Last use: Δημοφάνης : Φιλι[– – –]
Κηφισιεύς
Perhaps an ancestor of Demophanes of Kephisia, who appears in a prytany list of *ca.* 210 (*IG* II² 913, line 17). For the absence of the section letter, see **P 1**.

P 3 (B 242) Fragment of pinakion Pl. 7
Kroll, no. 32, Class III.
D 9.
P.L. 0.063; W. 0.024; Th. 0.002; L.H. 0.006–0.008.
Broken at right.
Earlier use: traces of letters in second line: . . EIO, partially erased gorgoneion stamp at lower left.

[8] 1972, pp. 63–68, 104. If it is objected that Aristotle writes of boxwood pinakia, of which no material remains exist, one may answer that it is hard to imagine indelible stamps on wooden pinakia.

[9] 1972, pp. 36–40.

Last use: Εὐθύμα[χος]
'Ερυξιμ[άχου]

Perhaps *PA* 5634, Euthymachos, son of E----- (*IG* II² 1622d, line 444, 347/6). For the absence of the section letter, see **P 1**.

P 4 (B 62) Fragment of pinakion Pl. 7

Kroll, no. 133, Class VI.
F 16. Last quarter 4th century.
P.L. 0.059; W. 0.021; Th. 0.0015; L.H. 0.004–0.009.
Broken at right.

Section letters of all three uses are incised in center of left end.

First use: N[---]
Γ̣
Φα̣λη̣ρ̣[εύς]

Second use: Ἀντιχ[άρης]
Θ
Ἀχαρν[εύς]

Third use: 'Ιππο[.?.]
Ι
Φαλη[ρεύς]

For the last name, see *IG* II² 2423, line 17, where 'Ιππο *vac.* is listed with other men from Phaleron. For Antichares, see *IG* II² 1926, line 101, where an Antichares Acharneus appears as diaitetes in 325/4. But a bronze pinakion could not have been reused at that date, since pinakia were then of boxwood. We must either imagine that this Antichares gave up his pinakion at an earlier date to be reused by Hippo-- or that the pinakion belonged to his eponymous uncle in the second quarter of the century.

P 5 (B 974) Pinakion Pl. 7

Kroll, no. 131, Class VI.
J 11. 4th century.
L. 0.057; W. 0.022; Th. 0.002; L.H. 0.006.
Several joining fragments; both ends preserved.

Only certain use: Κρατι̣άδης
Κ̣
Θοραι[ε]ύς

The section letter (?) is quite uncertain.

P 6 (B 1212) Fragment of pinakion

Kroll, no. 162, unclassified.
Found on the Pnyx.
P.L. 0.028; W. 0.023.
Broken at both ends.
Lost before photographing.

Only certain use: [Λ]υσισ[---]
[Ἀ]πολλ̣[---]

P 7 (B 1047) Fragment of pinakion Pl. 7

Kroll, no. 137, Class VI.
I 12. Late 4th–early 3rd centuries.
P.L. 0.034; W. 0.022; Th. 0.001; L.H. 0.01.
Only upper left corner preserved.

Only one use: Στ̣ [---]
Ι
[---]

The sigma is malformed.

P 8 (B 60) Fragments of pinakion Pl. 7

Kroll, no. 47, Class IV.
F 16. 4th–early 3rd centuries.
L. (est.) 0.08; W. 0.022; Th. 0.002; L.H. 0.004–0.006.

Two pieces preserve most of the pinakion; that they belong together is almost certain, since they were found in the same place on the same day.

Earlier use: remains of erased gorgoneion stamp at right center.

Later use: Φ[ι]λοχ̣[ύ]δης
Κ[ρ]ω(πίδης)

Upper left corner is damaged, but even so there can have been no section letter; see **P 1**. Kroll reads Ἀλω(πεκῆθεν), arguing from the break along the diagonal of the lambda, but the kappa is clear and the lambda line may belong to the earlier use.

P 9 (B 1352) Pinakion Pl. 7

Kroll, no. 96, Class V.
I 5.
L. 0.139; W. 0.021–0.025; Th. 0.0025.

Earlier uses: remains of punched-letter name and demotic; traces of three incised section letters (successively gamma, kappa, and beta); three stamps (triobol at lower left, gorgoneion at right, double owl at lower right).

Next to last use: Κιχων[ίδ]ης
Η
Γαργήτ( )

Last use: Φιλόμνηστος
Κ
'Ικαριεύς

Section letters in the last two uses stamped.

P 10 (B 111) Fragment of pinakion Pl. 7

Kroll, no. 160, unclassified.
K 7. Second half 4th century.
P.L. 0.034; W. 0.022; Th. 0.0015; L.H. 0.005–0.008.
Broken at both ends.

Only certain use: Φ̣ρυνι[---]
Εἰρε[σίδης]

The break at the left end follows the line of the phi's vertical stroke above; below, the break is straight for part of its course, as if following the line of an earlier letter.

P 11 (B 12) Fragment of pinakion Pl. 7

Kroll, no. 97, Class V.

H 5. 5th–2nd centuries.

P.L. 0.056; W. 0.023; Th. 0.002; L.H. 0.004–0.006.

Broken at left.

T. L. Shear, "The American Excavations in the Athenian Agora: The Campaign of 1932," *Hesperia* 2, 1933 [pp. 451–474], p. 474.

First use: only punched holes at ends of letter strokes remain, probably to be read as

[– – –]αχος
[– – –]ι

Partly erased stamp of gorgoneion (0.008 m. in diameter) at right end; on reverse, traces of rectangular stamp (0.01 m. in width) with double-bodied owl.

Second use: [– – –]ν

Third use: [– – –]ς

Last use:]Νικίο(υ)

For later uses, no letters are visible in the second line. It is likely that the last use records the father's name and that only the right end of the pinakion is preserved, since the demotic would appear in the second line at the beginning of the pinakion. Abbreviation of the father's name is common practice.

P 12 (B 700, B 110) Fragments of pinakion Pl. 7

Kroll, no. 48, Class IV.

K 8. Second half 4th century.

P.L. 0.022 (left) plus 0.053 (right); W. 0.021; Th. 0.0015–0.0018; L.H. 0.004–0.01.

One piece preserves the left end, the other the right end.

Earlier use: an erased gorgoneion stamp at right end;

[– – –]ς
[– – –]εύς

Later use: Γ (deeply incised section letter at left end);
(at right end) [– – –]μίδης
[– – –]

The end of the demotic has been assigned to the earlier use because it is less deeply incised.

P 13 (B 847) Fragment of pinakion Pl. 8

Kroll, no. 101, Class V.

B 19:14. 4th century.

P.L. 0.026; W. 0.022; Th. 0.0015; L.H. 0.006.

Broken at both ends.

Young 1951, p. 201, pl. 67:c.

First use: (punched holes at ends of strokes give pattern of letters)

[– – –]ος
[– – –]υ

Partly erased at right is half a rectangular stamp 0.008 m. in height with a double-bodied owl and Α[Α].

Second use: [– – –]
[– – –] ε̣ύ̣ς [– – –]

Last use: [– – –]λείδ[ης]
[– – –]ρρι(ος)

The demotic may be read as Φρεάρριος or Κυθήρριος. In the former case the owner of the pinakion may have been Diokleides, father of a trierarch of 325/4 (*PA* 3979); in the latter, Timokleides, father of a Timotheus of the end of the 4th century (*PA* 13722).

P 14 (B 1104) Fragment of pinakion Pl. 8

Kroll, no. 15, Class II.

H 15. Hellenistic–Early Roman.

P.L. 0.06; W. 0.023; Th. 0.002; L.H. 0.008.

Broken at left.

First use: erased round stamp with traces of owl below end of a patronymic, which belongs to last use.

Second use:]ης Η̣[
ε]ύς [

Last use:]ς ⁝ Διονυσίο(υ)
ε]ύς

Pierced with a hole below the nu.

P 15 (B 1003) Fragment of pinakion Pl. 8

Kroll, no. 169, unclassified.

R 10. 2nd century.

P.L. 0.093; W. 0.021; Th. 0.002; L.H. 0.008.

Broken at both ends.

Thompson 1954, p. 59, note 42.

Earlier use: only trace is seen in upright crossing epsilon.

Later use: [– – –]λος Εὐ[– – –]
[– – ε]ύς [– – –]

P 16 (B 898) Fragment of pinakion Pl. 8

Kroll, no. 140, Class VI.

D 16. 4th century.

P.L. 0.057; W. 0.022; Th. 0.001; L.H. 0.008–0.01.

Left end broken away.

Earlier use: possible traces of erased round stamp at right.

Later use: (letters incised with punch marks at ends of strokes)

[– – –]λης
[– – –]σιος

P 17 (B 987) Fragment of pinakion Pl. 8

Kroll, no. 112, Class V.

J 11.

P.L. 0.039; W. 0.02; Th. 0.0015; L.H. 0.009.

Broken at both ends.

Earlier use: (many slanting strokes of uncertain letters)
Later use: [– – –]κος
[– – –]ος
(Letters incised with punch marks at ends of strokes)

P 18 (B 1083) Fragment of pinakion Pl. 8
Kroll, no. 141, Class VI.
N 16. Hellenistic.
P.L. 0.059; W. 0.022; Th. 0.0006; L.H. 0.006.
Bent; left end probably broken away.
Only certain use: [– – –]όδημος

P 19 (B 1397) Fragment of pinakion Pl. 8
T 13.
P.L. 0.049; W. 0.022; Th. 0.01; L.H. 0.006.
Broken at both ends.
Only certain use: [– – –]στοκλη[ς]
[– – –]αθ( ) [– – –]

P 20 (B 76) Fragment of pinakion Pl. 8
Kroll, no. 175, unclassified.
I 13. Hellenistic.
P.L. 0.034; W. 0.021; Th. 0.001; L.H. 0.006–0.007.
Broken at both ends.
Earlier use(s): traces of erasure.
Last use: [– – –]ης [– – –]
[– – –] [– – –]

P 21 (B 863) Fragment of pinakion (?) Pl. 8
Kroll, no. 181, unclassified.
A–B 19–20.
P.L. 0.057; W. 0.026; Th. 0.001; L.H. 0.007.
Five pieces; very fragmentary.
Only certain use: [– – –]διο[– – –]
[– – –]ịπο[– – –]

Possible trace of section letter (?) in break at left. Unusual width, apparent lack of demotic, and the square omicron combine to make it doubtful that this is a dikastic pinakion.

P 22 (B 1028) Fragment of pinakion (?) Pl. 8
Kroll, no. 180, unclassified.
I 13.
P.L. 0.018; W. 0.105; Th. 0.002; L.H. 0.009.
Small fragment preserving only one edge.
Only certain use: [– – –]ụφι[– – –]

Note the square phi.

P 23 (B 1485) Fragment of pinakion Pl. 8
I 5.
P.L. 0.027; W. 0.023; Th. 0.002; L.H. 0.007.
Broken at both ends; nicks in edges.
Earlier use(s): traces of erasure.
Last use: [– – –]ουφ[– – –]
[– – –]ει[– – –]

P 24 (B 1276) Pinakion Pl. 8
Kroll, no. 113, Class V.
Cremation burial at Daphni. 4th century.
L. 0.095; W. 0.02–0.028; Th. 0.0015.

Damaged and fragmented by fire; punch marks for letters are visible, but the text is illegible.

9
BALLS

OF THE NINE BRONZE BALLS found in the Agora, six were found in the immediate area of the Tholos and one in the "Ballot Deposit" under the north end of the Stoa of Attalos (p. 105 below). These locations point to use in both lawcourts and the Bouleuterion. Only three of the nine balls preserve incised letters; whether the others were never inscribed at all or were labeled with paint or some other fugitive substance, the present state of the surface does not permit us to ascertain. The terracotta ball (**CB 1**) is included here because of its size. It has neither letters nor context. Of the three balls with inscribed letters, one has a single letter (**BB 3**: N) and two have two (**BB 1**: N N; **BB 6**: X X). If the double letters are merely a device whereby the letter can be read in whatever way the ball is held, all three may be analogous to the dikastic bronze tokens. That is, the letters could be labels in a series of twenty-five (assuming an added letter as in the case of the tokens), and the balls would be instruments of allotment for some group of men, perhaps dikasts, divisible by twenty-five. If the two letters are to be read together and so make up an additional series of twenty-five, so that there are fifty in all, a similar allotment can be imagined.

The balls could also have been used for allotment of seats in the Bouleuterion. We know from Philochoros (*FGrHist* 328 F140 [**73**]) that the boule was seated for the first time by letter in 410/9 B.C. and that bouleutai continued to swear that they would sit in the section to which each was allotted by letter. If we ask how the allotment of seats in the Bouleuterion might have been made with bronze balls lettered from single alpha through at least double chi (which is what our three inscribed balls might allow), one solution would be to have the pinakia of all 500 bouleutai inserted by tribes in the ten columns (50 slots each) of a kleroterion. Fifty bronze balls lettered from single alpha through double sampi (on the analogy of the tokens; see pp. 69–70 below) would be thrown in the funnel. As each ball was let out, it would assign one row of ten men (one from each tribe) to one row of a defined seating area. Such an answer presumes, however, that the seating was arranged in sections and rows and that each group of ten seats was lettered consecutively. It further presumes that mixing up the tribal contingents was one of the aims of the seating allotment. Other solutions might be devised to satisfy other presumptions, but however it was done, the only way of enforcing it would have been to make a seating chart from which a check could be made. (There is no evidence that such a chart was made. It is also less likely that every ten seats had a separate section number [so 50 different sections] than that the 500 seats were divided into ten sections, corresponding to the ten section numbers in the pinakia of the bouletai: in that case all the checking needed would be to match a man's pinakia with his section.)

The scantiness of our evidence and the general usefulness of small bronze balls in a variety of capacities make it impossible to come to any one conclusion about their function. It is wholly possible that they were used in more than one way. But the fact that they are balls instead of cubes makes it difficult to identify them with the bronze *kuboi* which Aristotle *Ath. Pol.* 64.3 (**325**) describes as being used in the tribal kleroteria for the lawcourts.

CATALOGUE

Findspots are indicated by the square of the Agora grid; for dated deposits that are groups, the grid designation is followed by the number of the deposit within the square.

BB 1 (B 105) Inscribed bronze ball Pl. 9
J 12.
D. 0.017.
Letters incised: N N.

BB 2 (B 500) Bronze ball Pl. 9
H 12:11.
D. 0.016.

BB 3 (B 539) Inscribed bronze ball Pl. 9
H 12:11.
D. 0.015.
Letter incised: N. The ball is pierced and has an incised scale pattern, and so it may have been reused as a bead.

BB 4 (B 540) Bronze ball Pl. 9
H 12:11.
D. 0.016.

BB 5 (B 541) Bronze ball Pl. 9
H 12:11.
D. 0.017.

BB 6 (B 593) Inscribed bronze ball Pl. 9
H 12:11.
D. 0.016.
Letters incised: X X.

BB 7 (B 594) Bronze ball Pl. 9
H 12:11.
D. 0.017.

BB 8 (B 1060) Bronze ball Pl. 9
Q 8:3. "Ballot Deposit". *Ca.* 300.
D. 0.016.

BB 9 (B 1379) Bronze ball Pl. 9
P 6.
D. 0.016.

CB 1 (MC 856) Terracotta ball Pl. 9
H 12:11.
D. 0.017.

10
BRONZE TOKENS

A TOKEN[1] is a small object of little or no intrinsic worth that can serve as a means of exchange for goods and services. Shape, material, and insignias of ancient Greek tokens are seemingly arbitrary and usually do not by themselves tell anything about their function. If the widely varying insignias on Greek and Roman bronze, terracotta, and lead tokens ever do suggest a particular function, there rarely exists any independent literary, epigraphical, or lexicographical evidence to explain what that function might be.[2] As a result, even when an insignia is very distinctive, we seldom know what it meant to those who used it.

In the present study, there are included fifty-eight coin-shaped bronze tokens recovered in the course of archaeological excavations in the Athenian Agora. Of this number, forty-four are formally catalogued; fourteen are noted as comparanda. Of the total fifty-eight, forty can be associated with the uses of Athenian dikasteria during the 4th century B.C.E. by means of literary evidence in connection with one or more clues provided by context or special characters.[3] All these forty have a single letter on one or both sides, and the letters are predominantly those of a 4th-century Attic-Ionic alphabet. Of the remaining eighteen tokens, most carry similar letters and are accordingly included in this catalogue of dikastic tokens, although they admittedly lack significant context or special stamped characters. Even if there is no other clue to their use (three, for instance, do not even have letters), they are nevertheless included as additional examples of the same sort of object.

In the 18th and 19th centuries, scholars and collectors catalogued bronze tokens as coins, because they interpreted single letters that appeared on one or both sides of the tokens as initial letters of Greek cities. Charles E. Beulé, however, saw that the "coins" were actually tokens[4] and furthermore that they were Athenian. He thought they would have been used at meetings of the ekklesia, the dikasteria, and in the theaters.[5] Not long after, Achilleus Postolacca published 1,121 coinlike lead tokens,[6] some three hundred of which he thought Athenians used in governmental procedures. In succeeding years, Friederich Imhoof-Blumer, Otto Brendel, Julius Friedländer, Max Fränkel, and Alexandros Meletopoulos[7] acknowledged the tokens as tickets to lawcourts, boule, ekklesia, or theaters or as vouchers by which various necessities of communal life could be obtained.

[1] σύμβολον in Greek, *tessera* in Latin: Gauthier (1972, pp. 62–75) discusses the word σύμβολον *inter alia* and its applications.

[2] A token labeled, e.g., ΘΕΣΜΟΘΕΤΩΝ does not thereby tell how it is to be used.

[3] **T1–T30** plus 10 uncatalogued tokens in these series. (The uncatalogued tokens are noted where appropriate as duplicates.)

[4] 1858, pp. 78–79.

[5] Beulé (1858, p. 79) ends his discussion by saying, "Si les tessères d'hospitalité et les tessères de théâtre ont été l'objet de travaux particuliers, on remarquera que les tessères politiques ou judiciaires sont un sujet beaucoup plus neuf et digne de sérieuses recherches."

[6] In *AdI* 38, 1866, pp. 339–356, with drawings on pl. XXXII in *Monumenti Inediti* VIII; *idem* 40, 1868, pp. 268–316, with drawings on tav. di agg. K and pl. LII in *Monumenti Inediti* VIII.

[7] F. Imhoof-Blumer, "Beiträge zur Münzenkunde und Geographie von Alt-Griechenland und Kleinasien," *ZN* 1, 1874 [pp. 93–162], pp. 123–124; O. Benndorf, *ZÖstG* 26, 1875, pp. 579–618; J. Friedländer, "Alphabete und Syllabarien auf römischen Münzen," *Hermes* 9, 1875 [pp. 251–253], p. 253; M. Fränkel, "Eine Marke der Thesmotheten," *ZN* 3, 1876 [pp. 383–393], p. 383; and A. Meletopoulos, Κατάλογος τῶν ἀρχαίων νομισμάτων συμβόλων καὶ κερμάτων τῆς συλλογῆς, Athens 1884, p. 100 (as a correction).

Jean N. Svoronos, however, in 1898 catalogued 134 Athenian bronze tokens and argued that they served as entrance tickets to the Theater of Dionysos. He enshrined them as such in his comprehensive *Les monnaies d'Athènes* (pls. 100–102), and studies of the Athenian theater thereupon included as illustrations of theater tickets these bronze tokens.[8] Oscar Broneer, however, removed the basis of Svoronos' argument when he observed that the letters cut into the inner curb of the gutter of the Theater of Dionysos do not distinguish seating areas, as Svoronos thought, but places where covering slabs for a drain were to be set.[9]

In 1954, Homer A. Thompson described a level excavated in the northeastern corner of the Athenian Agora. It was a hard-packed floor, partly enclosed by a wall. In the floor, two terracotta sections of a water channel stood on end facing each other with a little distance between, to define, if not enclose absolutely, a small space (Pl. 2). Between and around the channel sections there lay five bronze ballots close together with a sixth nearby (**B 12**–**B 17**), a bronze token (**T 1**), and a bronze ball (**BB 8**).[10] Elsewhere within traces of the same building complex at comparable levels, three more ballots (**B 6**, **B 10**, and **B 17**) were found, and thirteen more bronze tokens (**T 3**, **T 4**, **T 8**, **T 9**, **T 11**, **T 12**, **T 14**, **T 19**, **T 20**, **T 26**–**T 29**), as well as a single terracotta token (*Agora* X, no. C 18, p. 129). In the Agora, this is a singular concentration of such objects, each of which as a type can be associated by literary, epigraphical, or archaeological evidence with dikastic uses. This deposit will be cited as the "Ballot Deposit" throughout this book.

In 1960, tokens from Series A, D, and E of the present study were interpreted as instruments of an allotment that Athenians used to seat their dikasts in court randomly (Boegehold 1960, pp. 393–401). In 1964, Margaret Crosby (*Agora* X, pp. 83–84) reviewed various attested and hypothetical uses of Athenian tokens in civic, festal, and private life. She suggested that numbers L 1 through L 19 in her catalogue of 335 lead tokens (from a total of over 900) might be Hellenistic successors to the bronze dikastic tokens of the 4th century. The lead tokens present single letters in differing formats. They do not preserve any instances of two or more letters on tokens of the same design, as the bronze tokens do, and yet single letters of the alphabet ought to be in themselves a patent index to the existence of series. However one explains the lack (given the high number of examples, "accidents of preservation" can hardly be invoked), numbers L 144–L 146, as Crosby says, would be appropriate as dikastikon or ekklesiastikon (pay-token).

Crosby's suggestion that symbola were in use in Athenian lawcourts during the 3rd century is strengthened by evidence that had not had widespread scrutiny when she composed her study. Machon Comicus (*Chreia* 5 [ed. Gow], vv. 25–45), writing in Alexandria in the 3rd century B.C.E., assumes that Athenians are as litigious as ever. He ends his anecdote with a play on the words λοπάς, ψῆφος, and ἀσύμβολον. They can be dikastic and nondikastic references at the same time (**349**).

[8] See, e.g., M. Bieber, *Die Denkmäler zum Theaterwesen im Altertum*, Berlin/Leipzig 1920, p. 84; M. Bieber, *The History of the Greek and Roman Theater*, Princeton 1939, p. 127; A. Pickard-Cambridge, *The Dramatic Festivals of Athens*, Oxford 1953, pp. 273–274 (not, however, the second revised edition of J. Gould and D. M. Lewis [1968, pp. 270–271]). For discussions of tokens in more general contexts, see W. Müri, *Symbolon. Wort- und Sachgeschichtliche Studien*, Bern 1931, pp. 5–6, 35–36; K. Regling, *RE* IV A.1, 1931 [cols. 1091–1093], col. 1092, *s.v.* Symbolon; G. Lafaye, "Tesserae," Daremberg-Saglio 130–132; E. Caillemer, "Dikastai," Daremberg-Saglio 189–201; Gauthier 1972; J. H. Kroll and F. W. Mitchel, "Clay Tokens Stamped with the Names of Athenian Military Commanders," *Hesperia* 49, 1980, pp. 86–96.

[9] O. Broneer, "The 'Ὀχετός in the Greek Theater," in *Classical Studies Presented to Edward Capps on His Seventieth Birthday*, Princeton 1936, pp. 29–41.

[10] Thompson 1954, pp. 58–59. Cf. *Agora* XIV, p. 56; "Small Finds Associated with Trials," pp. 53–54 above. The pottery was late 4th century B.C.E., with a 2nd-century B.C.E. intrusion. The ballots, token, and bronze ball belong to series that can be dated by alphabetic and literary references to the 4th century B.C.E. For this reason, it is convenient to treat the deposit as practically homogeneous in discussions where purity is not a meaningful issue.

SERIES A–E

Turn now to the forty tokens of Series A through E, those for which use in dikasteria can be postulated on various grounds, and consider first Series A. **T 1** was found with the ballots and bronze ball noted above (note 10, p. 68) in the "Ballot Deposit". **T 3** was in an associated context. **T 2** carries a distinctive monogram form of eta (H). It is composed of the two letters that begin HTA as it is spelled in Greek, with the crossbar of eta supplying a horizontal hasta for tau as well.[11] The resulting monogram differentiates eta (H) from zeta (I), which otherwise, as when set in the circular frame of a token or ballot, would not be distinguishable from eta. The same monogram is in fact used for eta on dikastic ballots,[12] where the letter likewise stands in a circle. Dikastic pinakia, however, present a frame where names establish a line for top and bottom. With these directions for orientation, there is no need for any distinctive form of eta. And yet, when the section letter eta is stamped into a pinakion, a monogram form, H, is used (**P 9**). Why this should be so is not obvious. It may be relevant that section letters were stamped into pinakia separately. If a stamper was not always to be trusted to orient a single letter properly, the monogram could be useful.[13]

At the same time, there are other ways to orient letters. In the case of sigma and mu, where confusion in a circular frame is inevitable, mu is spelled out by the addition of an upsilon under the mu (**T 3**: M). The bakkhos ring of Series B, to take another instance, is parallel to a ground line no matter whether it is high or low in relation to the letter it accompanies. An upright owl orients the letters of Series F. It may be that the ligature eta and tau (H) first appeared as a practical design on tokens and psephoi and then, because of its association with dikastic paraphernalia, seemed appropriate as a sign on dikastic pinakia.

Obviously, no single clue leads by itself to sure identification. Context, to return to the first clue cited at the beginning of this section, does not suffice. Terracotta sherds, if found in closed contexts with dikastic equipment, cannot for that reason alone be identified as belonging to pots that Athenians used in courts, and the same holds true for bronze objects. Again, the monogram form of eta is not exclusively dikastic. By combining the initial letters of *hεκατόν* (H in the old Attic alphabet) and τάλαντα, it signifies one hundred talents (ἑκατὸν τάλαντα) in financial texts of the 5th century B.C.E. (cited in note 11).

The character (Ͳ) on **T 5**, however, is also suggestive. Called sampi in another form (ϡ) in later Greek, it is found a few times as a letter in early Ionian inscriptions and later in papyri as the number 900. It was not used in Attic writing, but in the 5th and 4th centuries artisans at Athens sometimes used it as a letter label to denote one item in a series.[14] In the case of these tokens, Series A and others include a sampi, and the addition of this exotic figure to the twenty-four letters

[11] W. F. Wyatt, Jr. and C. N. Edmonson ("The Ceiling of the Hephaisteion," *AJA* 88, 1984 [pp. 135–167], p. 165), in objecting that "evidence from the fifth century for ligatures or monograms of the sort envisioned by Boegehold [such as H] is not compelling," do not note the occurrence of that monogram in 5th-century documents, where it combines the initial letters of *hεκατόν* and τάλαντα. See, e.g., *IG* I^3 363, 365, 366, 369, 370, 371 and Threatte 1980, p. 111. For some other appearances of the ligature, see A. Postolacca, "Piombi Inediti del Nazionale Museo Numismatico di Atene," *AdI* 40, 1868 [pp. 268–316], p. 272, pl. K 51. I. N. Svoronos, «Περὶ τῶν εἰσιτηρίων τῶν ἀρχαίων. Μέρος Δ΄. τὰ μολύβδινα σύμβολα», *JIAN* 3, 1900 [pp. 319–343], p. 324, pl. IZ′:30, may list another.

[12] See Boegehold 1974, p. 9 with pl. 3:2.

[13] See Kroll 1972, pp. 36–37 on the stamping.

[14] See Threatte 1980, index, *s.v.* Sampi. Cf. A.-M. Bon and A. Bon, *Les timbres amphoriques de Thasos* (*Études Thasiennes* IV), Paris 1975, p. 345, no. 378, where, however, the figure is not correctly identified; also L. Talcott and B. Philippaki, "Figured Pottery," in L. Talcott, B. Philippaki, G. R. Edwards, and V. R. Grace, *Small Objects from the Pnyx: II* (*Hesperia* Supplement 10), Princeton 1956 [pp. 1–77], no. 131, p. 34.

of the Attic-Ionic alphabet creates a series of twenty-five. To go a little further, the series that have a sampi do not have koppa (Ϙ) or digamma (ϝ), two other letters that were still current (and therefore easily accessible) in the neighboring Greek alphabets. Since the Athenians did not import these letters for their tokens, we may suppose that they did not want more than a total of twenty-five letter labels in these particular series. If twenty-five is the desired number, then it may be relevant that 25 is a divisor of numbers like 200, 400, 500, and so on, which are the numbers of dikasts in certain dikasteria.

To sum up, tokens in Series A were found with dikastic paraphernalia. One token (**T 2**) has the monogram Ͱ that is used distinctively on other, independently identified dikastic equipment. Two (**T 5** and **T 6**) are stamped with a character (Ͳ) that extends the total number of labels to twenty-five, a divisor of the total number of dikasts in a dikasterion. These clues, combined with references in 4th-century Athenian authors to the use of tokens in dikasteria, permit a working hypothesis concerning the identity of these particular bronze tokens: they are dikastic. Given this hypothesis, tokens of other series, principally Series B through E, can also be regarded as dikastic, even if single examples in those series lack one or more of the clues we find in tokens of Series A.

Tokens of Series B are called dikastic because of their generic likeness to those of Series A and because of contexts in which they were found. **T 8**, **T 11**, and **T 12** were found at levels and in areas that associate them with the Ballot Deposit, hence with Series A.

From Series C, **T 17**, stamped with the distinctive sampi, was found in a context associated with the Ballot Deposit.

From Series D, **T 19**, **T 20**, and **T 26** were found in contexts associated with the Ballot Deposit. **T 28** has the sampi.

From Series E, **T 29** was found in a context associated with the Ballot Deposit. In addition, a token from this series in Berlin (Svoronos 1923–1926, pl. 100.33) has the distinctive monogram form of eta. (For a discussion of the lion's head stamp and its possible connection with dikasteria, see p. 75 below.)

SERIES F–J

It is possible to argue that Series F, G, H, I, and J do not constitute separate series. Note that Series D includes some letters in incuse squares and some not. Svoronos (1898) makes of these incuse squares a criterion that establishes a separate series. But Svoronos (1898, no. 22, πιν. Γ:19) shows an alpha in an incuse square on one side and a plain alpha on the other. If, consequently, one holds up one side, the token belongs to one Svoronos series, but if one holds up the other side, the token belongs to another Svoronos series. There was therefore no intention on the part of the designer to differentiate one series from another by means of the framing of a letter. In the face of such ambivalence where easy differentiation is the aim, it seems best to include in a single series all tokens with the same letter on each side. In addition, one might ask whether letters accompanied by pellets or owls were used to differentiate series for different courts. Possibly not, for if tokens with a letter on each side were to be used on a stipulated day, letters in various dispositions and frames could have served. The variations, accordingly, may attest protracted use and a lack of regard for meticulous consistency rather than series to be used on different days or in different courts.

It may well be that Athenians used no more than five or perhaps six series at a time, namely, (1) Athena head left/letter; (2) Athena head right/letter; (3) lion's head right/letter; (4) letter/letter; (5) ΘΕΣΜΟΘΕΤΑΙ and four owls in chi formation/letter; and (6) (?) blank/letter. All other variations in design or size reflect changes by die makers and not new ways of differentiating series. Small variations, such as a bakkhos ring, plemochoe, or owl, to orient a letter could have been introduced and discontinued in the lifetime of a series. The changes signal no more and no less than do the different forms of lion's head in Series E.

CHRONOLOGY

The tokens of Series A through E were made and used during the 4th century, as various indicators show. The number and variety of these indicators are such that it will be helpful to consider them one at a time.

Some tokens of Series A are struck over a Syracusan bronze litra: **T 5** is one such. The Syracusan coins had long been dated to the time of Timoleon (*fl. ca.* 340 B.C.E.), but examples found in earlier contexts are now being announced. One found in the destruction fill at Motya, for instance, implies a date of issue early in the 4th century or even late in the 5th.[15] No context in which tokens of Series A were found, however, is earlier than the 4th century. This series therefore can have been initiated as early as the first decade of the 4th century and continued in use for two or three generations.

Dikastic tokens may have been used for the first time somewhat earlier than our earliest explicit testimony. Philochoros (*FGrHist* 328 F140 [**73**]) records that in 410/9 Athenian bouleutai began to be allotted to seating places that were labeled by letters and that the practice continued to his own day (4th/3rd century B.C.E.). He can be saying, however, depending on how one construes the Greek, not just that bouleutai were being allotted lettered seats in 410/9 but that they *also* were being allotted ἐπὶ Γλαυκίππου, καὶ ἡ βουλὴ κατὰ γράμμα τότε πρῶτον ἐκαθέζετο. And if we ask what "also" implies, that is, in addition to what or whom, the answer "dikasts" presents itself as self-evident. The cause for such an innovation can be deduced from contemporary references to an abuse that might have prompted corrective innovation. Like-minded Athenians, if they sat together in clusters at assemblies, could cheer in unison or drown out speakers' voices with shouts and so wreck pretensions to objective deliberation (Thucydides 6.13.1; Aristophanes, *Ekklesiazusae*, lines 292a–299; Plutarch, *Perikles* 11.2). If, owing to the accidents that preserve or destroy testimonies from the past, one has notice only that Athenians recognized the problem in their ekklesia but had no sure solution,[16] one can rationally suppose that Athenians proposed corrective procedures to be applied to what must have been some such abuse in the boule. The combination of problems (in the ekklesia) and solution (in the boule) points to tokens as evidence for the same problem and the same solution in the dikasteria.

References in literature to tokens *qua* dikastic paraphernalia begin in 388 with Aristophanes, *Ploutos*, lines 277–278 (**70**), where Chremylos tells the chorus leader to go to the grave, for that is where the latter's section has been allotted to judge. Aristophanes adds as corollary detail that Charon is handing out tokens; it is corollary because Aristophanes does not add Charon's function

[15] See C. Boehringer, "Zu Finanzpolitik und Münzprägung des Dionysius von Syrakus," in *Greek Numismatics and Archaeology, Essays in Honor of Margaret Thompson,* O. Mørkholm and N. M. Waggoner, eds., Wetteren 1979 [pp. 9–32], pp. 21–22 and R. R. Holloway, "Le Origini della Monetazione di Bronzo in Sicilia e in Magna Grecia," in *Atti del VI Convegno del Centro Internazionale di Studi Numismatica,* Rome 1979 [pp. 123–144], p. 133.

[16] Tokens were distributed in meetings of the ekklesia in mid-4th century, and their function was so obvious to those who used them that their purpose did not have to be written down (*IG* II^2 1749, line 76). Such tokens may have been pay vouchers, or they could have assigned ekklesiasts to benches within the meeting place.

in order to summarize or explain the allotment he has announced with the word ἔλαχες. Rather, he has added a second detail of procedure to strengthen his allusion to a court day. The first allusion is to allotment of one dikastic section; the second, to a dikast's allotment of a seating place in the court.

Demosthenes in 330 B.C.E. speaks of the staff and token as a dikast's authenticating badges (Demosthenes 18.210 [**346**]). Aristotle, *ca.* 325 B.C.E., refers to two quite different sorts of bronze token. One a dikast receives as he enters his court (*Ath. Pol.* 65.2 [**249**]), the other, after he has voted (*Ath. Pol.* 68.2 and 69.2 [**276**]). The first of these tokens, it is suggested here, carried a letter of the alphabet, which designated a bench or seating area where the dikast was to sit. The other, carrying a gamma or III, was a pay voucher, to be turned in when it became time to collect the day's pay.

Machon's punning reference to tokens shows that they were still in use in the early years of the 3rd century (**349**). The archaeological context and appearance of many lead tokens support this interpretation (*Agora* X, pp. 83–84).

Archaeological criteria are in accord with the literary references. The letters on the tokens are those of a post-Eucleidean Attic-Ionic alphabet and are formed in ways one sees elsewhere in the 4th century at Athens. Omega in particular, with its high, well-defined bow (Ω), belongs to the earlier years rather than the later years of the century. (The rho of Svoronos 1923–1926, pl. 102.45, however, looks later because of the serifs.) Where tokens were found in closed contexts, the pottery was consistently that of the 4th century; note **T 5**, **T 6**, **T 11**, **T 15**, **T 17**, **T 25**, and **T 29**.

CATALOGUE

All references in the following catalogue to Svoronos are to the plates of *Les monnaies d'Athènes* (1923–1926) unless otherwise indicated. Findspots are generally indicated by the square or squares of the Agora grid (e.g., D 15 for **T 2**), with a context date where available; for dated deposits that are also groups, the grid designation is followed by the number of the deposit (e.g., Q 8:3 for **T 1**) within the square. All dates are B.C.E.[17]

Series A

Head of Athena left, in crested helmet/Letter.[18]

T 1 (B 1176) Epsilon (chip missing from Athena's helmet) Pl. 9
Q 8:3. Ballot Deposit.
D. 0.018. Wt. 4.9 g. (partial)
Noted in Boegehold 1960, p. 398 (wrongly as B 3172); *Agora* XIV, pp. 54, 56, pl. 40:b.
Same as Svoronos 101.6.

T 2 (B 1132) Eta (with tau in monogram) Pl. 9
D 15. 4th century.
D. 0.020. Wt. 5.3 g.
Same as Svoronos 101.7.

T 3 (B 1172) Mu (with upsilon beneath) Pl. 9
Q 7.
D. 0.0185. Wt. 4.8 g.
Noted in Boegehold 1960, p. 398 (wrongly as B 3168).
Same as Svoronos 101.12; B 1264.

[17] In the Catalogue, the heading letters A through M serve to distinguish series of tokens but do not signal any chronological or qualitative distinctions. References to Svoronos 1923–1926, pls. 100–102 offer convenient access to photographs of many series of tokens. Note, however, that the tightly dated nine periods of manufacture that Svoronos prints at the bottom of his plates should be disregarded. "Same as", when establishing an equivalence to a token that appears in Svoronos, means that the obverse and reverse have the same letter or head but are not necessarily identical.

[18] Weights are noted in descriptions of tokens in this series because some pieces have been visibly struck over coins. Cristof Boehringer informs me (*per litt.*, 8 April 1990) that Syracusan hippocamps can be identified as belonging to earlier and later emissions, the earlier weighing 4–5 grams, the later 7–8.

T 4 (B 1262) Rho (chip missing at tail) Pl. 9
P 8.
D. 0.019. Wt. 4.1 g. (partial).
Same as Svoronos 101.16.

T 5 (B 1564) Sampi Pl. 9
T 13. Early 4th century.
D. 0.0195. Wt. 4.9 g.
Obverse struck off-center to lower left. Token overstruck. Under sampi on the reverse there is visible a vestige of Syracusan bronze (*BMC*, nos. 289–296, p. 187, *McClean Collection* I, nos. 15–17, p. 98: head of Athena in Corinthian helmet, ΣΥΡΑ; hippocamp modeled on Pegasos). Lower strands of Athena's hair visible. Same as Svoronos 101.24 and B 1133, both similarly overstruck. On the overstrikes, see Svoronos 1898, nos. 48–71, pp. 50–52 (although he does not note this particular overstrike at 71α).

T 6 (B 1133) Sampi Pl. 9
D 15. 4th century.
D. 0.0185. Wt. 5.3 g.
Overstruck in same way as **T 5**. Below and across bottom of sampi, front of Athena's Corinthian helmet can be seen.

T 10 (B 1135) Lambda with ring to left Pl. 10
I 9.
D. 0.0175.
Same as Svoronos 102.26. On obv. die, see **T 8**. More distance between letter and ring than lambda on *SNG* 412.

T 11 (B 1169) Mu with ring beneath Pl. 10
Q 8. 325–300.
D. 0.018.
Noted in Boegehold 1960, p. 398 (wrongly as B 3165); *Agora* XV, p. 54, pl. 39:c, d.
Same as Svoronos 102.27. On obv. die, see **T 8**.

T 12 (B 1170) Mu with ring beneath Pl. 10
Q 9.
D. 0.0175.
Noted in Boegehold 1960, p. 398 (wrongly as B 3166).
Same as Svoronos 102.27 and **T 11** but in poor condition. On obv. die, see **T 7**.

T 13 (B 1163) Nu backward with ring beneath Pl. 10
C 10. Hellenistic fill.
D. 0.019.
Same as Svoronos 102.28 and B 1565. On obv. die, see **T 8**.

Series B

Head of Athena right, in close-fitting crested helmet/ Letter with bakkhos ring[19]

T 7 (B 1179) Beta with ring at upper right Pl. 9
D. 0.018.
Obv. illegible. Chip missing.
Cf. Svoronos 102.23–29.

T 8 (B 1263) Theta with ring Pl. 10
Q 10.
D. 0.0165.
Same as Svoronos 102.24. Same obv. die as **T 9**–**T 13**; Svoronos 102.24–29, 102.35.

T 9 (B 1165) Iota with ring at side Pl. 10
P 7.
D. 0.0185.
Same as Svoronos 102.25. On obv. die, see **T 8**.

Series C

Head of Athena left, in crested helmet/Letter in incuse square

T 14 (B 1177) Pi Pl. 10
Q 18. Hellenistic and 4th/3rd-century coins.
D. 0.0255.
Same as Svoronos 100.9 and B 1142. Same obv. die as **T 17**.

T 15 (B 1158) Phi Pl. 10
B 19. 5th/4th century.
D. 0.0255.
Same as Svoronos 100.13 and B 1143, B 1145, B 1157, B 1178.

T 16 (B 1125) Psi Pl. 10
G 11.
D. 0.026.
Same as Svoronos 100.14 and B 1168.

[19] J. D. Beazley ("Bakchos Rings," *NC*, ser. 6, 1, 1941, pp. 1–7) considers the object usually called kalathos by earlier scholars a bakkhos ring, such as those represented in vase paintings and elsewhere binding the bundle of leafy branches held by Eleusinian initiates; John Kroll (*Agora* XXVI, p. 28) prefers "Eleusis Ring". A bronze ballot (Athens National Museum 7496) inscribed ΨΗΦΟΣ ΔΗΜΟΣΙΑ has stamped into it a delta with a bakkhos ring in an incuse square. See Boegehold 1974, no. 4, p. 9.

T 17 (B 1174) Sampi — Pl. 10
Q 7. 325–300.
D. 0.0245.
Poor condition.
Noted in Boegehold 1960, p. 398 (wrongly as B 3170).
Same as Svoronos 100.16. Same obv. die as **T 14**.

Series D[20]

Letter/Letter

T 18 (B 1137) Alpha (chip missing) — Pl. 10
H 11.
D. 0.018.

T 19 (B 1175) Beta — Pl. 10
Q 7.
D. 0.015.
Noted in Boegehold 1960, p. 398 (wrongly as B 3171).
Same as **T 20** and Svoronos 101.26.

T 20 (B 1164) Beta — Pl. 11
Q 7.
D. 0.0175.
Same as **T 19**.

T 21 (B 1154) Zeta — Pl. 11
G 3. 3rd century.
D. 0.0165.
Surface flaked on both sides. The letter is identified as zeta rather than eta on the assumption that eta (of which we do not have an example) would have had the special monogram form ⊢H.
See Svoronos 100.26, 33; 101.7; cf. 101.25–39; 100.20.

T 22 (B 1124) Theta — Pl. 11
G 6.
D. 0.0175.
Belongs in Svoronos 101.25–39.

T 23 (B 1260) Lambda — Pl. 11
D 17.
D. 0.016.
Obv. worn quite smooth.
Same as Svoronos 101.30.

T 24 (B 1140) Omicron — Pl. 11
I 13.
D. 0.0155.
Same as Svoronos 101.33.

T 25 (B 1159) Tau — Pl. 11
A 20. 4th-century context at southwest corner of section.
D. 0.0175.
A vertical line that descends from one crossbar of tau seems accidental.
Svoronos 101.35.

T 26 (B 1171) Phi (chips missing) — Pl. 11
Q 7.
D. 0.0195.
Noted in Boegehold 1960, p. 398 (wrongly as B 3167).
Same as Svoronos 100.25 and 101.37, and like B 1139. Obv. and rev. seem to be from same die as Svoronos 101.37.

[20] Svoronos 1898 presents four different series of bronze tokens with a single letter stamped on each side. They are 22–30, ἓν γράμμα τοῦ ἀλφαβήτου *Rev.* τὸ αὐτὸ γράμμα ἀλλ' ἐν τετραγώνωι ἐγκοίλωι. 72–88, ἓν γράμμα τοῦ ἀλφαβήτου *Rev.* τὸ αὐτὸ γράμμα ἐν πεδίωι ἐγκοίλωι κατὰ τὸ μᾶλλον ἢ ἧττον. 100–101, ἓν γράμμα τοῦ ἀλφαβήτου *Rev.* τὸ αὐτὸ γράμμα ἐν πεδίωι ἐγκοίλωι μικρᾶς διαμέτρου καὶ λίαν εἰσέχοντι. 128–129, ἓν γράμμα τοῦ ἀλφαβήτου *Rev.* τὸ αὐτὸ γράμμα. Easy differentiation seems to be the aim of designing tokens in different ways. One series is in use at one court, another at another. To take the other four series described previously, namely Series A, B, C, and E, Athena heads and a lion's head are easy to recognize. But in the case of Series D, can one say the same of letters that stand in a roughly square shallow concavity, a roughly circular shallow concavity, or a slightly smaller circular concavity? I prefer to believe that these changes come from protracted use. When one die wears out, another is put in its place; the second die is not exactly like the first. Unfortunately, there are not enough examples here to make a proper study of die sequences. I note, however, that even in terms of the distinction Svoronos (1923–1926) makes, the obverse of pl. 100.17–25 is hard to distinguish from obverse and reverse of pl. 101.25–39. Also, in Series E, at least three different lions' heads can be distinguished: Svoronos, *op. cit.*, pl. 100.29 shows one; pl. 100.30 another; and pl. 100.31 yet another. This last token is also interesting in that the lion and the letter epsilon have been stamped over another sort of lion and a different letter (omega?). If a lion's head can vary and still emblematize one series, a single letter can do the same.

T 27 (B 1167) Psi Pl. 11
O 11.
D. 0.0165.
Same as Svoronos 101.39.

T 28 (B 1166) Sampi Pl. 11
O 8.
D. 0.0165.
Cf. Svoronos 101.25–39.

Series E

Lion's head right/Letter of alphabet[21]

T 29 (B 1173) Gamma Pl. 11
Q 7. 325–300.
D. 0.017.
Noted in Boegehold 1960, p. 398 (wrongly as B 3169).
Same as Svoronos 100.29.

T 30 (B 1626) Rho Pl. 11
D. 0.017.
Cf. Svoronos 100.29–41.

Series F[22]

Blank/Letter with owl

T 31 (B 1156) Delta Pl. 11
A–B 22.
D. 0.026.
Same as Svoronos 102.20 and B 1141.

T 32 (IL 1161) Kappa Pl. 12
H 13.
D. 0.027.

T 33 (B 1129) Lambda Pl. 12
F 14. Hellenistic.
D. 0.024.

[21] Svoronos (1898, p. 48) observes that one lion's head (πιν. Δ:1) of the series I have designated E looks earlier than others in the series and is clearly a protome. Furthermore, the tongue hangs out as is necessary if a lion's head is a fountain spout. Since tokens of Series E can be associated with dikastic procedures on other grounds, this particular insignia merits a further surmise. Pollux 8.113 (**322**) names a magistracy called fountain guardianship (χρηνοφυλάκιον). The name prompts him to note a certain bronze lion that Athenians called fountain guard (χρηνοφύλαξ). Through this lion, water was conveyed in trials where flow of water regulated time given to speakers. Pollux then passes, by a natural transition, to discussion of the klepsydra. A man was allotted to maintain the equitable working of the water. He was called "the man at the water", and the phrase πρὸς ὕδωρ in a context where trials are mentioned is a clear reference to the timing of speeches by klepsydra. Cf. LSJ, *s.v.* πρός, C III, 4; Aristotle, *Ath. Pol.* 67.2 (**315**): ὕδωρ πρὸς ὃ δεῖ λέγειν τὰς δίκας; Aischines 2.126 (**307**): πρὸς ἕνδεκα γὰρ ἀμφόρας ... κρίνομαι. Most of the data Pollux records here can be corroborated. At Athens (and elsewhere in Greece) there was a highly honored, elective office whose incumbent was styled ἐπιμελητὴς κρηνῶν (Aristotle, *Ath. Pol.* 43.1; cf. Rhodes 1981, pp. 516–519; C. Habicht, "Pytheas von Alopeke, Aufseher über die Brunnen Attikas," *ZPE* 77, 1989, pp. 83–87). Spouts at Athens were more often than not in the form of a lion's head: see B. Dunkley, "Greek Fountain Buildings before 300 B.C.," *BSA* 36, 1935/1936 [1939] [pp. 142–204], pp. 192–193. During trials at Athens, a dikast was allotted to work the klepsydra. Aristotle calls him the man ἐπὶ τὸ ὕδωρ (*Ath. Pol.* 66.2–67.2), while Pollux fails to make a clear differentiation between magistrate and dikast. For the rest, what cannot be corroborated is at least credible. A lion's head spout at a fountain might well be called fountain guard: F. Muthmann, "Weihrelief an Acheloos und Naturgottheiten," *AntK* 11, 1968 [pp. 24–44], p. 31; F. Hölscher, *Die Bedeutung archaischer Tierkampfbilder*, Würzburg 1972, p. 80. But how does Pollux come to associate a lion's head spout with a certain kind of trial? (Pollux says "lion" and not "lion's head", a usual way of speaking.) There may have been a fountain with a lion's head spout from which officials drew water for klepsydrai (*inter alia*) when courts were in session, but from what is known of the water supplies and the topography of the ancient city, it is unlikely that there was a fountain given exclusively to dikastic uses. It may be, however, that one fountain with a lion's head spout was close enough to an area where suits were usually heard to be associated by propinquity. An orator's casual reference to the fountain and an explanatory note by a later commentator provided Pollux with his information. One die maker may have taken that lion's head spout as model for the insignia he designed, knowing of the association. Other die makers for whatever reason were content to represent a lion, thinking of it (if they thought of it at all) as a protective talisman generally and not as having a specific reference.

[22] Cf. Hermippos, F13 (*PCG* V): οἴμοι τί δράσω σύμβολον κεχαρμένος, and Pollux's explanation (9.71): "He seems to have been half-shorn, and so we must think of this little coin as having been struck on one side only, or to be divided. . . . "

Same as B 1155. B 1162 may be stamped with a tau in this series.

T 34 (B 1130) Chi Pl. 12
F 14. Hellenistic.
D. 0.0245.
Cf. *Agora* X, no. L 9.
Owl is to right of chi. There may be one more secondary mark right of the owl. Like B 1128 and B 1131.

Series G

Athena head left/Letter

T 35 (B 1168) Psi Pl. 12
O 7.
D. 0.021.
Like Svoronos 100.14.

Series H

Athena head right/Letter with plemochoe

T 36 (B 1160) Kappa Pl. 12
M 11.
D. 0.017.
Kernos to right of kappa.
Same as Svoronos 102.18.

Series I

Athena head right/Letter with plemochoe

T 37 (B 1161) Chi Pl. 12
D. 0.026.
Cf. Svoronos 102.18.

Series J

Athena head right/Letter with owl

T 38 (B 1146) Lambda Pl. 12
D. 0.0195.
Owl is between legs of lambda.
Same as Svoronos 102.21. Cf. the owl stamp on an official ballot (Boegehold 1974, nos. 1–10, pp. 8–13).

Series K

Illegible/Letter in small, low-relief square

T 39 (B 1138) Phi Pl. 12
H 13. Hellenistic.
D. 0.018.
Differs from Svoronos in that letter is not incuse but inside a square indicated in low relief.

Series L

Head right/Letter

T 40 (B 1261) Delta Pl. 12
H 12.
D. 0.022.

Series M

Janiform mask/Letter

T 41 (B 1126) Nu Pl. 12
F 13. Hellenistic.
D. 0.0225.
The head looking left is an older, bearded man; the head looking right is of a younger man with a full chin. He may be a Ptolemy. Cf. G. M. A. Richter, *The Portraits of the Greeks*, New York 1984, nos. 197–199 on pp. 230–231. Both heads appear to be portraits.
See Crosby in *Agora* X, no. L 44, p. 90, for a discussion of Janiform heads on tokens.

Tokens without letters

T 42 (B 1127) Illegible: Boukranion(?) Pl. 12
G 13. Hellenistic.
D. 0.0234.
Cf. Crosby in *Agora* X, nos. 164, 165, p. 102 for Hellenistic boukrania on lead tokens; see also a terracotta token from a 4th-century context, *ibid.*, no. C 18, p. 128 (found on the top of the wall by the terracotta water channels of the Ballot Deposit). Cf. *SNG Denmark* under Cephallenia 45839 (with caveat that it may be an Athenian tessera) in both *McClean Collection* II, pl. 190:20 and *BMC, Peloponnesos*, pl. xvii:4, 5.

T 43 (B 1644) Bearded male head in wolf-skin headdress right: Blank Pl. 12
N 16.
D. 0.019.
There is a small A to the left behind his head. Lykos? Dolon?

T 44 (B 1136) Illegible: Large bakkhos ring Pl. 12
H 10.
D. 0.018.
Same as Svoronos 102.30.

11

KLEPSYDRA

THE IDENTITY of the klepsydra (**306–323**; Ill. 2, Pl. 13) was established by Suzanne Young.[1] It is enough here to quote from Aristotle's account (*Ath. Pol.* 67.2 [**315**]):

> There are klepsydras with small tubes for outflow into which they pour the water against [whose flow] the litigants must speak at their trials. Ten choes are given for cases involving over 5,000 drachmai and three choes for the second speech, seven choes for those up to 5,000 drachmai and two choes for the second speech, five choes for those under 1,000 and two choes for the second speech, and six choes for suits involving rival claims for which there is no second speech. He who has been chosen by lot to measure the water stops up the tube when the secretary is about to read a statute or law or testimony or agreement.

The klepsydra is well adapted for this kind of measurement since it holds two choes, as the painted inscription indicates (XX). Two such vessels appropriately placed (see Pl. 13) could be used for all the private cases specified by Aristotle that involve two choes or a multiple of two. When the upper klepsydra had discharged its contents into the lower, their positions could be reversed in a moment, a plug inserted in the empty one so that it could be refilled and another removed from the full one to make it operative. Most convenient for all cases would be a combination of three klepsydras, two of two-chous capacity and one holding three choes.

The chous on which the klepsydra is based is very close to that generally accepted, that is, it held 3.276 liters (3.462 quarts). But the length of time represented by the contents of a chous flowing out of this particular bronze pipe is less by at least one-quarter than that calculated on the basis of the "measured day". The text of Aristotle's *Athenaion Politeia* is badly damaged at this point (67.4), but it seems clear[2] that in describing how public cases are timed by the part of a day rather than by choes, he says that the days of Posideon (December/January) were used as a standard and that the day was taken as eleven amphoras, divided into three parts, of which one was for the dikasts to collect and vote, and the other two for the plaintiff and the defendant. If, it is argued, the measured day of eleven amphoras was equal to the approximate length of daylight in Athens at that time of year ($9\frac{1}{2}$ hours or 570 minutes),[3] it is necessary to assume that one amphora is equal to almost 52 minutes, so that one chous (one-twelfth amphora) is equal to more than 4 minutes.[4]

Six minutes is the mean time for the two-chous klepsydra to discharge its water. An eleven-amphora day at the rate of 3 minutes to the chous is only 6 hours 36 minutes. Three possible solutions to this discrepancy between a chous of 3 minutes and a chous of something over 4 minutes may be mentioned: (1) the measured day may not have been from dawn to dusk, even though it is hard otherwise to see why the shortest days of the year are used as a standard; (2) the bronze tube in this klepsydra may have lost a millimeter or so from its internal diameter by corrosion and so now provides a faster flow than originally; (3) it may be, apart from reading laws or testimony, for

[1] 1939, pp. 274–284.

[2] On the basis of Xenophon, *Hellenika* 1.7.23 and Aischines 2.126.

[3] See literature quoted in Rhodes 1981, pp. 723–728.

[4] If the day was really measured by twelve amphoras, and it always took one amphora for the dikasts to assemble, the court's actual business would be measured by eleven amphoras. In that case the chous would be almost exactly 4 minutes. Cf. Rhodes 1981.

which the water was not stopped in cases held on measured days, that there were other periods of time when the water was not running.

The second inscription, Ἀντιοχ[ίδος], indicates tribal ownership. The findspot, a well deposit of about 400 B.C.E., just two meters to the southeast of the Tholos precinct wall, suggests nearby use or storage. The former would probably be in the Bouleuterion; the latter in some unidentified building used for the storage of dikastic equipment and perhaps also for the semiofficial dry measures made of terracotta.[5]

CATALOGUE

M 1 (P 2084) Klepsydra Pl. 13

H 12:11. Beginning of 4th century.

H. 0.232; D. of base 0.117; D. of rim as restored 0.28; L. of bronze tube *ca.* 0.026; inside D. of tube 0.006–0.008; D. of overflow hole 0.01. Capacity: 6.400 liters. Time of discharge: 6 minutes (in several tests the vessel was filled several times with water, and the time of discharge ranged from somewhat under 6 minutes to somewhat over, giving a mean time of 6 minutes).

Profile preserved complete with outlet tube and overflow hole; restored in plaster. Pail-shaped vessel with heavy flat base, steep flaring walls, and plain thickened rim. Horizontal handles may be assumed from the remains of one attachment. Just beneath the rim is a small hole, which prevented the vessel from being filled above this point. At one side of the base a clay spout houses a small bronze tube, which could be plugged to hold in the water. Painted in glaze on outside, (1) around upper wall: Ἀντιοχ[ίδος]; (2) on lower wall: X X, i.e., two choes. Fine, reddish buff clay; glaze wash inside and on rim; thinner wash carelessly daubed on outside.

[5] Lang, in *Agora* X, p. 41.

12
ECHINOS

THE WORD "ECHINOS" denominates *inter alia* a container with a lid, which Athenians used in the 4th century B.C.E. and perhaps as early as the late 5th century to safeguard documents. The container, when it did not hold legal documents, was called *chytra* or *lopas* (**299**, **300**, **303**), a round, large-mouthed, unglazed pot that had no base, since it was to sit in the embers as a stewpot. "Lopas" could in context suggest "echinos" (see p. 80 below). As container for documents, at least three sorts of use can be distinguished.

First and best known is the use of an echinos to safeguard documents after an attempt at arbitration has failed and a dispute is going to be taken to a trial before a dikasterion. Aristotle described in detail the procedure by which diaitetai and the Forty heard disputes and, when they failed to compose them, sealed copies of documents in echinoi against the day when a dikasterion would hear the same arguments, witnesses, and evidence in court (**290**). When Demosthenes refers to an echinos (**292**–**297**), the context seems to entail arbitrations such as Aristotle describes.

An inscribed lid from the Agora excavations shows another area for use of the echinos.[1] Litigants at Athens appeared at a pretrial hearing, the questioning (*anakrisis*). At this hearing, a magistrate determined whether or not he was the competent official to give the disputants a time and place for trial. In opening, parties to the dispute made sworn statements, and then they produced as much evidence and as many witnesses as the magistrate needed to make his decision. At this point, a litigant could stop the proceedings by swearing that something essential in his opponent's presentation was not true. When, for instance, A must be the son of B for resolution of a given question to be possible, one litigant might swear that A is not the son of B. Such a protest under oath was called a *diamartyria,* and once it was introduced, the hearing stopped. The question had to be settled so that all parties agreed that A was or was not the son of B. If all agreed that A was not the son of B, there was no longer an adjudicable question. If, however, all did not agree, a challenge (ἐπίσκηψις) was made, and the question went before a dikasterion. The man who made the protest was charged with perjury (δίκη ψευδομαρτυρίων). If he was found to have testified falsely, he was duly sentenced, and then the original dispute could be resumed, the relationship of A and B now a *res judicata.*

In the case of an echinos lid of the late 4th century B.C.E. (**E 1**: **305**), it may be that a challenge has been made and that all documents relating to the diamartyria, or copies of them, have been sealed in an echinos. The contents of the echinos are listed on the lid along with (it can be conjectured) names of officiating magistrates and litigants. At a trial for perjury, these documents served as controls over the wording in charges, testimonies, supporting documents, and oaths, none of which ought to have changed between hearing and trial.

A third area of use may be that of undertakings not immediately relevant to court trials or arbitrations. A private contract, for instance, could be sealed in an echinos. Two signatories would then agree to have a disinterested third party keep the echinos in his possession so that neither could change language or figures in his own copy of the contract and claim that it was the true text. When Theophrastos has his Reckless Man (**304**) characteristically appear at court trials with an echinos, the point may be that he regularly let himself act as a person with whom others would deposit sealed

[1] See **291**, **299**, **301**, and **302**. On the identification, see Boegehold 1982, pp. 1–6.

documents, especially wills,[2] and that he took on the sort of custodial responsibility that led almost inevitably to days in court.

The earliest attested association of echinos (and, in a special context, lopas) with legal procedures may be an allusion in Aristophanes, *Wasps*, produced in 422. Early in the play, Aristophanes characterizes his central figure, Philokleon, in terms of his love for various sorts of dikastic paraphernalia (**106**), and in a later scene (lines 820–862), an interplay between ordinary household objects and dikastic equipment is the point of the fun. Again, earlier in the play (line 511), Philokleon has an appetite for a nice jugged little trial (δικίδιον . . . ἐν λοπάδι πεπνιγμένον). The word πεπνιγμένον (stifled) implies a lid that, if not sealed, was at least set fast in place, as the lid on an echinos should have been. When Philokleon later produces his nonsense tale of an echinos hailing a witness (**288**), it may be another instance of the same sort of joke. That is to say, "echinos" is in 422 a known piece of equipment in the dikasteria. In Aristophanes' fragmentary *Danaides* an echinos was mentioned, but the play has no date.

Two considerations reinforce a surmise that Athenians used an echinos in judicial procedures well before the time of Demosthenes. First, there is the tradition, a long one by the 5th century, that honored oath-taking as an art. That is, when some critical decision was to be determined by oath, one could disarm or frustrate antagonists by the use of careful phrasing: Autolykos, Odysseus' maternal grandfather, surpassed humankind in theft and oath (ἀνθρώπους ἐκέκαστο κλεπτοσύνῃ θ' ὅρκῳ τε).[3] His superiority in oath consisted in his being able to swear an oath that in no literal way was untrue but whose tight and precise qualifications neutralized it in whatever particular case it was sworn. If Greeks could admire such virtuosity, they could also develop counter-measures. A good memory for what one heard would not always have been enough. The essential importance of every word in an oath was therefore widely recognized. Second, there is the diamartyria, generally agreed to be an old-fashioned legal tactic by the end of the 5th century.[4] In circumstances where it could be foreseen that an oath would be tested in court days or weeks after it had been sworn, provision for the continuing integrity of the text would seem only prudent. And so, in view of these considerations, together with the pervasiveness of reference to dikastic equipment in *Wasps*, it seems likely that the echinos was in use at Athens in lawcourts as early as the 420's.

CATALOGUE

E 1 (P 28470) Fragment of echinos lid Pl. 14
H. 0.054; p.W. 0.113; est. D. 0.19.

About one-quarter of a shallow-domed, unglazed lid, mended from ten pieces; orange, slightly micaceous clay; knob handle at top center; rounded edge.

Context: 350–300; fill used to level a floor.[5]

Dipinto (**305**).

The lid is like that in *Agora* XII, pl. 95, nos. 1963 and 1981, from 4th-century contexts.

[2] Cf. Aristophanes, *Wasps*, line 585. Possibly, a lid was plastered onto the pot with wax or clay, and then the whole was bound with string or straps whose knots would be waxed, stamped, and enclosed in a protective shell (κόγχη). See W. J. M. Starkie, *The Wasps of Aristophanes*, London 1897, p. 236; MacDowell 1979, p. 212.

[3] Homer, *Odyssey* 19, line 396. Cf. *Hymn to Hermes*, lines 368–384; Herodotos 4.201; Thucydides 3.34.3; and especially Lasos of Hermione *ap.* Athenaeus 8.338c.

[4] See, e.g., MacDowell 1978, p. 213.

[5] See Shear 1973, pp. 138–144 on the building.

Inscription
fin. saec. IV

[– – –]δ̣ε̣: τετταρ̣[. . .]ν̣: ἐκ[– – –]
[– – – δ]ιαμαρτυρία: ἐξ ἀνακρίσεως
[– – –]ν κακώσε̣ω̣[– – –]
[– – –]ιδ̣ι̣[– – –]ρ: ἐπέθ̣[ηκε]
[– – –]Θ[– – –]
[– – –]Υ̣[– – –]

Epigraphical Commentary

Letters (except omega) are 0.004 to 0.005 m. high, painted neatly in black with a brush. In some places, pigment is gone but prints of letters can still be seen; see, for example, ΝΚΑΚΩΣ in line 3. Elsewhere, as in the space before rho in line 4, where letters ought to have been, no trace remains. A left margin cannot be fixed. ἀνακρίσεως and ἐπέθηκε may end lines 2 and 4. A photograph and a drawing (Pl. 14) of all the shapes and lines I have been able to see supplement the epigraphical commentary. There is no trace of writing above line 1. The dotted nu in line 1 could be an eta; the dotted iota in line 4 is uncertain because of an ancient smudging of the paint.

Restored Text

On the assumption that Lid P 28470 once closed an echinos, I present the following restored text, *exempli gratia:*

[ἔνεστι: τά]δε: τέτταρα [τῶ]ν: ἐκ[γεγρα]-
[μμένων: δ]ιαμαρτυρία: ἐξ ἀνακρίσεως[:]
[νόμος: ἐπικλήρω]ν κακώσεω[ς: ἐπίσκηψις:]
[ὅρκοι: ἀντ]ιδί[κων: Ἀντήνω]ρ: ἐπέθ[ηκεν:]
NOMINA
NOMINA

Translation of Restored Text

"Of the written copies,[6] the following four are inside: diamartyria from the anakrisis, law on abuse of heiresses, challenge of testimony, oaths of litigants. Antenor put the lid on." (Names of litigants and possibly other relevant persons follow.)

[6] Gabriele Soritz-Handler ("Ein Echinos aus einer Anakrisis," in *Festschrift für Arnold Kränzlein: Beiträge zur antiken Rechtsgeschichte*, G. Wesener, ed., Graz 1986, p. 103), in offering an alternative set of restorations (see also *SEG* XXXVI 296), objects: "In einem Echinos sind doch in erster Linie Originale zu erwarten." But in fact copies were sometimes sealed in echinoi; see [Demosthenes] 48.48 (**296**).

13
BALLOTS

THE FIFTY-FOUR BALLOTS found in the Agora cannot be treated as a homogeneous group since they differ from one another in a variety of ways: (1) Although most are bronze, a few are lead (**B 50–B 54**). (2) The shapes fall readily into four fairly distinct classes on the basis of diameter of wheel and length of axle. (3) Some are inscribed "official ballot" (ψῆφος δημοσία: **B 7–B 12, B 14–B 16, B 18**), but most are not. (4) Only a few are additionally distinguished with a "single letter", sometimes in an incuse stamp (**B 8–B 12, B 14–B 16, B 18**), sometimes large and in relief (**B 13, B 17, B 21, B 22**). (5) They come from contexts ranging from the mid-4th century B.C.E. down. (6) Most are from one of two fairly small areas, one around the Tholos and Bouleuterion, the other in or near the "Ballot Deposit" (Pl. 2), while the rest are somewhat more scattered (Fig. 4).[1] It seems clear from this distribution that the ballots were used both in the courts and in the Bouleuterion.

Most of these criteria divide the group along different lines, but some correspondences should be noted: (1) None of the lead ballots are marked either as an official ballot or with a letter. (2) Only **B 54** approximates the measurements of any class of bronze ballots (IV); **B 50–B 53** have the same diameter but long axles. (3) Although all inscribed examples belong to Class I, not all ballots of that class are inscribed. (4) All examples that are inscribed as official ballots also have an incuse letter,[2] but those with a relief letter have no "ballot" inscription. (5) Several of the inscribed ballots of Class I have a context date in the second half of the 4th century B.C.E.; one of Class II (**B 32**) came from a 4th-century B.C.E. context; two of Class III (**B 35, B 36**) have a context of the 3rd century B.C.E.; and no example of Class IV can be dated by context. (6) All the ballots but one (**B 6**) from the "Ballot Deposit" area (**B 6, B 10–B 17**) are inscribed either with a letter or as an official ballot, or both, while none from the Tholos-Bouleuterion area is inscribed.

From these coincidences and differences it is possible to formulate a few hypotheses. That the ballots of Class I with their large diameters (0.055–0.065 m.) and long axles (0.024–0.038 m.) are the earliest (4th century B.C.E.) seems clear not only from context dates but also from letter shapes on the inscribed examples. But since Class I itself includes three different types (uninscribed; inscribed as official ballots and marked with incuse letter; and marked only with letter in relief), we must ask if these differences also are chronological. Between the latter two it seems reasonable to suppose a slight chronological difference, with the large letter in relief replacing the small incuse letter to improve legibility. The relief letter would at the same time obviate the necessity for the official inscription, since as part of the very fabric of the ballot it serves as an adequate guarantee. But the chronological difference cannot be important since ballots of both kinds were used together and found together in the "Ballot Deposit". To determine whether the uninscribed ballots of Class I must be thought of as chronologically different from the inscribed pieces, it is necessary to consider briefly other known ballots with respect to the nature and function of the letter that distinguishes both types of inscribed ballots from the uninscribed.

[1] Tholos and Bouleuterion: **B 1–B 5, B 23–B 26, B 33, B 34, B 38, B 40, B 41, B 47–B 50, B 53**. "Ballot Deposit": **B 6, B 10–B 17**. Somewhat more scattered: **B 7–B 9, B 18–B 22, B 27–B 32, B 39, B 42–B 46, B 51, B 52, B 54**. Grid locations are indicated on the plan, Figure 4.

[2] **B 7** is almost certain to have had such a letter, but two-thirds of the wheel is lost.

Twenty-five ballots in the Athens National Museum are now published in Boegehold 1974. Of this number, nineteen carry letter stamps, many of them more than one. Often only one stamp remains readable, while another one or two have been deliberately effaced by gouging. Sometimes it is possible to identify these earlier letters. The total number of preserved letters is as follows: alpha (1), beta (1), gamma (4), delta (2), zeta (1), eta (2), theta (2), iota (1), kappa (1), lambda (2), mu (4), omicron (1, although it is possibly a theta). Alfred Koerte,[3] who at the time of his study had only sixteen inscribed ballots to examine, read fewer letters but did see one lambda and four mus. Since he had expected to find letters from A to K only, the letters representing the ten dikastic sections, he explained the additional letters as coming from a time when there were twelve tribes at Athens and consequently (he reasoned) a corresponding twelve dikastic sections. In support of his hypothesis, he pointed out that one ballot shows mu superimposed on delta and another has a mu stamped on the inscribed side and traces of an obliterated stamp on the side where a stamp is usually found. It is very difficult to check this hypothesis, since the only other appearance of section letters is on the bronze dikasts' pinakia, which were replaced by boxwood before the introduction of the twelve tribes. But the difficulties inherent in such an increase in the number of sections are serious. For although the two new tribes were filled by transferring demes from the old tribes, a corresponding increase to twelve sections, if each of the twelve tribes was to be equally represented in each of the twelve sections, would have required that the entire potential dikastic population be individually reallotted. Furthermore, numbers to be allotted for courts of 200, 400, or 500 from twelve tribes by twelve sections would have required computers, rather than kleroteria, for each tribe. That is, when the first white cube came out of each of 24 kleroteria of 6 columns each, 144 men would have been allotted.

The convenience of the ten sections for achieving courts of varying round numbers thus militates against the introduction of twelve sections. At the same time, the presumption that the demesmen transferred to the new tribes would take with them their pinakia with section letters obviates any need for new sections. It is obvious that the dikastic sections were by Aristotle's time a device to facilitate allotment within the tribe. They no longer functioned as a unit, as in the 5th century, when a section sat together for a year in a single court, or in the early 4th century, when a section was allotted as a whole to a court. In the later procedure, the section was no longer a corporate whole that sat in a court and might therefore have had equipment of its own; it had become a means whereby the members of one tribe were divided into ten groups, and so allotment could proceed by tens (or fives, since two kleroteria were used for each tribe) rather than by ones. If the section had not been inherited, the same end could have been achieved by requiring each potential dikast to deposit his pinakion in the next box after his predecessor as he came up to the tribal entrance, and when all had come all ten boxes would have an almost equal number.[4] Members of a section from one tribe had no connection in this later procedure with members of the same section from

[3] A. Koerte, "Attische ψῆφος," *AM* 21, 1896, pp. 450–453. Cf. *IG* II[2] 1923a; J. N. Svoronos, «Ἠπειρώτων ψῆφοι δικαστικαὶ ἐκ Δωδώνης», *JIAN* 13, 1911, pp. 121–130. A similar ballot, marked as sacred (IEPA) was found in Olbia (*Kratkie Soobshcheniia Instituta Arkheologii* 130 (Academy of Science, U.S.S.R.), 1972; cf. *AR* 1971–1972, p. 50.

[4] Such a system, though perhaps harder to police, would have obviated the inequalities that Dow notes (1939, pp. 30–34), namely, that sections within a tribe must always have been unequally represented, so that those whose pinakia were put in slots below the last full row were automatically excluded from the allotment by cubes. That is, the sections are vestigial and make for small inefficiencies and inequities that a brand new device would have avoided. But it may be that one useful development of the earlier system was brought over into the procedure of Aristotle's time: the registration of one man in more than one section. If this was the case, the sections on the kleroterion could be easily equalized. See **73** and **74** and Boegehold 1984, pp. 23–29 for an interpretation of that sort of registration; also pp. 32–33 above.

another tribe. There were no officials in charge of sections, and so it is very difficult to imagine such amorphous groups owning anything.

The paraphernalia mentioned initially by Aristotle in his account of the procedure (*Ath. Pol.* 63.1–2 [**249**]) seems all to belong either to the tribes or to the courts. Each tribe had two kleroteria, ten boxes for section letters, other boxes for the dikasts allotted to the court, and two hydriai. For each court there were colored staves and lettered balanoi that were given to the dikasts as they were allotted at their tribal entrances. Is it likely that these latter were the property of the individual courts? The courts had no continuing existence as far as personnel was concerned; they were permanent places, but both their dikasts and presiding officers changed from day to day. So just as the dikastic sections had permanent personnel but no corporate function, the courts had a corporate function but no permanent personnel. Owning and caring for large amounts of equipment does not seem appropriate to either sections or courts, partly because maintenance and replacement require a treasury which neither could have had.

There were, of course, public slaves who might store and maintain equipment, but these ordinarily seem to have worked under the direction of elected or allotted officials.[5] The bodies that had permanent personnel who were both section members and dikasts in the courts, and that had responsible officials who were also the presiding officers of the courts, were the logical owners of all the equipment used not only in the allotting of dikasts to courts but in the courts themselves. The archon or thesmothetes of each tribe had public slaves to handle the equipment and physical aspects of the allotment (*Ath. Pol.* 63–65). When either was allotted to a court (*Ath. Pol.* 66.1), it is natural to assume that his slaves accompanied him to handle the equipment and physical aspects of the session there. They would therefore be the logical people to provide the ballots and klepsydrai for the dikasts allotted to take charge of these (*Ath. Pol.* 66.2).

Ownership of dikastic equipment by the tribes seems eminently reasonable and desirable. It may be that kleroteria, section-letter boxes, and hydriai, in addition to klepsydrai and ballots, were owned by individual tribes, but it is likely that the boxes that were taken to the courts, and also staves and balanoi, all marked with either the colors or the letters of specific courts, were held in common by all the tribes, since these ended up in the courts and could more easily be taken from there to a common store than sorted into ten tribal stores. The common store would be especially convenient, since the same number of courts (hence of balanoi, staves, and boxes) would not be used every day. One imagines that the archons and thesmothetai met very early in the morning and not only determined the number and size of the courts (and so also the number of dikasts each was to allot from his own tribe) but also collected with their public slaves the appropriate number of boxes (for the courts) and staves and balanoi (for the dikasts). It must have been at this time also that one thesmothetes allotted the letters to the courts for that day (**249**). As far as ballots and klepsydrai are concerned, public slaves serving the presiding officer, whose position was basically tribal, would be responsible not only for providing the proper number but also for collecting them afterwards. Furthermore, the ballots are stamped with letters, which should indicate ownership, and the fact that both letters and tribes were twelve in number makes the invention of twelve dikastic sections gratuitous.

The use of letters to indicate tribes cannot at present be proved, but there is evidence that is at least suggestive. The boundary stones that read simply ὅρος α´ (*IG* II^2 2515) and ὅρος κ´ (*IG* I^2 876) must belong to a group (perhaps of ten) that had a recognized order, easily expressed by letters. If these were the tribes, the stones would have marked the position or headquarters of

[5] W. L. Westermann, *The Slave Systems of Greek and Roman Antiquity*, Philadelphia 1955, p. 10.

each in some place where all the tribes met for some official or military purpose. Since more formal documents avoid the use of abbreviated forms like those letters, little more certain evidence can be expected. The danger of confusion with section letters seems minimal because of the decisive nature of the context in any imaginable use.

Tribal ownership of dikastic equipment seems to be confirmed by the inscription on the klepsydra (**M 1**), which identifies it as the property of the tribe Antiochis. In the original publication,[6] Suzanne Young suggested that tribes may have owned klepsydrai for use when they were acting as prytaneis in trials held either in the boule or in the ekklesia or for use by the Thirty Judges, who were organized by tribes. It seems easier to assume that the tribes were responsible for providing klepsydrai to the courts through and for their thesmothetai. That the klepsydra from the Agora dates from a time (*ca.* 400) when the dikastic sections were still functioning as corporate units does not seem to be an objection, since they were even then headless bodies, without funds or officials necessary for effective stewardship.

If use in the Bouleuterion is not required for a tribally owned klepsydra, it is reasonable to assume that the building was furnished with only one set of equipment for whatever kind of business it was conducting. So where the voting was secret, there would have been one lot of ballots,[7] which might be used by all tribes acting as prytaneis. There was no need to mark these ballots as official, since they stayed in the Bouleuterion, and this was sufficient guarantee of their official nature. It is possible then that the uninscribed ballots of Class I, all of which came from the Tholos-Bouleuterion area, belong to the boule rather than to the tribes, in which case the absence of inscription need not imply a difference in date.[8] There would be no danger of anyone removing such unidentified ballots, since the count after a vote was a sufficient check on numbers.

Ballots used in the lawcourts were more exposed to meddling on the part of a larger number and more mixed lot of people who might try to introduce "reasonable facsimiles" in order to stuff the ballot box or to make away with official ballots for later illegal use. It therefore seems reasonable to suppose that the inscribed ballots of Class I were designed for use in the lawcourts. In this case, we should expect their findspots to tie in with other evidence on the location of the courts. Since six of them come from the "Ballot Deposit" (**B 12**–**B 17**) and three from nearby (**B 6**, **B 10**, **B 11**), they are themselves evidence that a lawcourt or storage area for courts was located there. Two others (**B 8**, **B 9**) were found close by the large Poros Building immediately to the southwest of the Agora once tentatively identified as a lawcourt,[9] more recently as an official place of confinement called the desmoterion.[10] The other inscribed ballot of Class I (**B 7**) came from the immediate vicinity of the large early structure for many years labeled Heliaia.[11]

Of the twenty-five ballots in the Athens National Museum, twenty-one are like those of the Class I defined in this essay. Ten of them, all inscribed and all bearing owl stamps of one sort or another, were found in the neighborhood of Mounychia and may have been used in a lawcourt in Peiraieus. The rest are not catalogued as having useful proveniences. The fact that no Class I

[6] Young 1939, pp. 282–284. See "Klepsydra," pp. 77–78 above.

[7] Five hundred, if both "for" and "against" jars were used; 1,000, half of which were pierced, half solid, if "valid" and "invalid" jars were used.

[8] **B 6**, **B 19**, and **B 20** do not come from that area, but their poor condition may well account for their apparent lack of inscription.

[9] Crosby 1951, pp. 184–187.

[10] Vanderpool 1980, pp. 17–31. Cf. pp. 95–96 below.

[11] Thompson 1954, p. 38; *Agora* XIV, pp. 62–65.

ballots that are definitely without inscription have been reported from elsewhere suggests that they are peculiarly at home in the Tholos-Bouleuterion area.

That Class I ballots belong to the 4th century is likely from the fact that several come from 4th-century contexts and that they are generally uniform. Those that are stamped with the letter lambda (**B 9**, **B 16**) may come from the end of the century, after the introduction of the two new tribes.

Two ballots (**B 21**, **B 22**), which can belong neither to Class I because of their smaller diameter (0.049–0.056 m.) and thicker wheel nor to Class II because of their medium-long axles (0.021–0.03 m.) and their "section" letters in relief, are inserted here as Class I variants, which may be regarded as transitional to Class II.

Ballots of Class II are slightly smaller in diameter (0.051–0.056 m.) than those of Class I, but the real distinguishing feature is the short axle (0.015–0.02 m.). None is inscribed as official, and none is marked with a letter. Six of the twelve examples were found in the Tholos-Bouleuterion area (**B 23**–**B 26**, **B 33**, **B 34**), but the other six were widely scattered. The very poor condition of **B 32** makes its classification doubtful, as does its 4th-century context date.

Ballots of Class III are somewhat smaller still in diameter (0.046–0.05 m.) and have axles of medium length (0.022–0.031 m.), that is, for the most part longer than those of Class II but generally shorter than those of Class I. None is inscribed as official, and none is marked with a letter. Only two (**B 40**, **B 41**) of the ten came from the immediate area of the Tholos and Bouleuterion.

Ballots of Class IV are the smallest in diameter (*ca.* 0.04 m.) and have short axles (*ca.* 0.018 m.), except for **B 49**, whose axle is 0.027 m. None is inscribed as official, and none is marked with a letter. All four examples were found in the Tholos-Bouleuterion area.

The only ballots in Classes II–IV that have context dates are **B 32** (II) in the 4th century and **B 35** and **B 36** (III) in the 3rd century. On the present evidence it seems reasonable to assume that the decrease in size is related to the chronology of the ballots and that the first decrease in size was accompanied by what can have been another measure of economy, the dropping of both kinds of inscriptions. That this change may well have been related to the increase in the number of tribes is suggested not only by the 4th-century context of **B 32** but also by ballots in the Athens National Museum on which the mu has been substituted for another letter and by **B 16**, where two stamped letters (iota and lambda) appear side by side. That is, tribes at first continued to mark their dikastic ballots, even making new ones like **B 9**, with a lambda stamped in incuse square. It is possible that when the old order changed, with the two new tribes Antigonis and Demetrias ranking first and second, there was a new distribution of old ballots to fit the new tribal order, with only Aiantis and Antiochis (now XI and XII, or Lambda and Mu) having to convert old ballots by adding the new letter. It seems likely that the complications were such that it seemed easier to drop the identifying symbol and the official inscription completely. Certainly the distribution of Classes II–IV shows that more than half of them were probably used in the courts rather than in the Bouleuterion.

That the decrease in the size of the ballots was an economy measure is suggested by the lead ballots (**B 50**–**B 54**), which are most like the smallest of the bronze ballots and must have been still cheaper. Absolute dates for Classes II–IV and for the lead ballots cannot even be conjectured, but two of Class III (**B 35**, **B 36**) have 3rd-century context dates, and it is possible that the latest pieces belong to the 2nd century.

CATALOGUE

The bronze ballots are arranged by classes; the lead ballots are grouped at the end. Findspots are generally indicated by the square or squares of the Agora grid, with a context date where available; for dated deposits that are also groups, the grid designation is followed by the number of the deposit within the square.

Presumably because of the inaccuracy of the molds or the mismatching of the two halves, all the ballots show axles whose two ends have slightly (but in varying degrees) different centers. Thickness refers to the total thickness, which is therefore the same as length of axle.

All dates are B.C.E., unless otherwise indicated.

Class I: all ballots in this class have thin wheels

B 1 (B 146) Pierced axle Pl. 15
G 10.
D. 0.06; Th. 0.037.
Good condition.

B 2 (B 182) Solid axle Pl. 15
G 13. Hellenistic.
D. 0.055; Th. 0.03.
Fair condition; piece of rim missing.

B 3 (B 429) Pierced axle Pl. 15
H 12.
D. 0.061; Th. 0.036.
Poor condition; most of edge missing.

B 4 (B 431) Pierced axle Pl. 15
H 12.
D. 0.059; Th. 0.034.
Fair condition.

B 5 (B 493) Pierced axle Pl. 15
G 11:2. Roman fill.
P.D. 0.036; Th. 0.039.
Poor condition; most of edge broken away.

B 6 (B 947) Pierced axle Pl. 15
P 7. 4th century.
D. 0.061; Th. 0.023.
Poor condition; edge broken away.
Thompson 1954, p. 59, note 42.

B 7 (B 43) Solid axle: inscribed Pl. 15
G 14:2. 4th, 3rd, 2nd centuries.
P.D. 0.061; Th. 0.038.
Poor condition; nearly two-thirds of wheel broken away.
Incised letters: [ψῆφ]ος · δημο[σία]. Stamped letter presumably lost.

B 8 (B 728) Pierced axle: inscribed Pl. 16
B 20. Hellenistic.
D. 0.062; Th. 0.032.
Fair condition.
Incised letters, unusually far in from edge: ψῆφος ⁝ δημοσία. On other side, just before beginning of inscription, zeta stamped in incuse square, with top toward axle.

B 9 (B 783) Pierced axle: inscribed Pl. 16
B 19. Hellenistic.
D. 0.061; Th. 0.031.
Fair condition.
H. A. Thompson, "The Excavation of the Athenian Agora, Twelfth Season: 1947," *Hesperia* 17, 1948 [pp. 149–196], pl. 46:4.
Incised letters around edge on one side: ψῆφος · δημοσία. On other side, just before beginning of inscription, lambda stamped in incuse square, with top toward axle.

B 10 (B 992) Pierced axle: inscribed Pl. 16
Q 8. Hellenistic.
D. 0.063; p.Th. 0.02.
Good condition except for axle broken off on one side.
Thompson 1954, p. 59.
Incised letters around edge on one side: ψῆφος : δημοσία. On other side, just before beginning of inscription, theta stamped in incuse square.

B 11 (B 1000) Solid axle: inscribed Pl. 16
R 9. Late 4th century.
D. 0.06; Th. 0.025.
Good condition.
Thompson 1954, p. 59.
Incised letters around edge on one side: ψῆφος : δημοσία. On other side, just before beginning of inscription, theta stamped in incuse square.

B 12 (B 1055) Solid axle: inscribed Pl. 16
Q 8:3. *Ca.* 300.
D. 0.063; Th. 0.033.

Good condition.
Thompson 1954, p. 59.
Incised letters around edge on one side: ψῆφος · δημοσία. On other side, just before beginning of inscription, theta stamped in incuse square.

B 13 (B 1056) Solid axle: inscribed Pl. 17
Q 8:3. *Ca.* 300.
D. 0.063; Th. 0.031.
Good condition.
Thompson 1954, p. 59.
Large epsilon in relief on one side.

B 14 (B 1057) Solid axle: inscribed Pl. 17
Q 8:3. *Ca.* 300.
D. 0.062; Th. 0.037.
Good condition.
Thompson 1954, p. 59, pl. 17.
Incised letters around edge on one side: ψῆφος ⁝ δημοσία. On other side, just before beginning of inscription, small epsilon stamped in incuse square, with upright toward axle.

B 15 (B 1058) Solid axle: inscribed Pl. 18
Q 8:3. *Ca.* 300.
D. 0.064; Th. 0.032.
Good condition.
Thompson 1954, p. 59, pl. 17.
Incised letters around edge on one side: ψῆφος δημοσία. On other side, halfway between end and beginning of inscription, small epsilon stamped in incuse square, with upright toward axle.

B 16 (B 1059) Solid axle: inscribed Pl. 18
Q 8:3. *Ca.* 300.
D. 0.061; Th. 0.036.
Part of wheel missing.
Thompson 1954, p. 59, pl. 17.
Incised letters around edge on one side: ψῆφ[ος δημοσί]α. On other side, halfway between end and beginning of inscription, two small rectangular stamps: one is certainly iota in incuse; the other is most probably lambda in incuse.

B 17 (B 1061) Solid axle: inscribed Pl. 17
Q 8:3. *Ca.* 300.
D. 0.063; Th. 0.028.
Pieces of edge missing.
Thompson 1954, p. 59, pl. 17.
Large gamma in relief on one side.

B 18 (B 1374) Pierced axle: inscribed Pl. 18
J 5:1. Second half 4th century.
P.D. 0.062; Th. 0.032.
Edges disintegrated; poor condition.
Incised letters around preserved edge on one side: ψ[ῆ]φος δημοσία. On other side a square incuse stamp with uncertain letter, possibly iota.

B 19 (B 1375) Pierced axle Pl. 18
J 5:1. Second half 4th century.
P.D. 0.04; Th. 0.025.
Poor condition, much disintegrated.

B 20 (B 1380) Solid axle Pl. 19
J 5:1. Second half 4th century.
P.D. 0.046; Th. 0.022.
Poor condition, much disintegrated.

Class I Variants

B 21 (B 1235) Solid axle: inscribed Pl. 19
Q 17:7. Roman fill.
D. 0.056; Th. 0.03.
Good condition. Thick wheel.
Medium-sized gamma in relief on one side.

B 22 (B 1357) Pierced axle: inscribed Pl. 19
Q 21.
D. 0.049; Th. 0.021.
Good condition. Thick wheel.
Large beta in relief on one side.

Class II: all ballots in this class have short axles

B 23 (B 100) Solid axle Pl. 19
H 12.
D. 0.053; Th. 0.019.
Good condition. Thick wheel.
H. A. Thompson, "The Athenian Agora: Excavation and Reconstruction," *Archaeology* 6, 1953 [142–146], p. 143.

B 24 (B 157) Pierced axle Pl. 19
H 11.
D. 0.056; Th. 0.018.
Good condition. Thick wheel.

B 25 (B 165) Pierced axle Pl. 19
F 11.
D. 0.052; Th. 0.017.
Good condition. Thick wheel.
Thompson, *loc. cit.* (**B 23** above).

B 26 (B 166) Pierced axle Pl. 19
F 11.
D. 0.056; Th. 0.017.
Good condition.
Thick wheel.

B 27 (B 255) Pierced axle Pl. 19
M 10.

D. 0.052; Th. 0.017.
Fair condition. Thick wheel.

B 28 (B 582) Solid axle Pl. 20
O 18.
D. 0.051; Th. 0.016.
Good condition. Thin wheel.

B 29 (B 697) Solid axle Pl. 20
B 20.
D. 0.055; Th. 0.02.
Good condition. Thin wheel.
Thompson, *loc. cit.* (**B 23** above).

B 30 (B 698) Pierced axle Pl. 20
N 17.
D. 0.053; Th. 0.015.
Fair condition. Thick wheel.

B 31 (B 699) Pierced axle Pl. 20
N 17.
D. 0.055; Th. 0.018.
Fair condition. Thin wheel.

B 32 (B 988) Solid axle Pl. 20
J 11. 4th century.
P.D. 0.031; p.Th. 0.009.
Very poor condition; axle missing on one side; much of wheel gone.

B 33 (B 1078) Solid axle Pl. 20
H 12–13.
D. 0.051; Th. 0.017.
Good condition. Thick wheel.

B 34 (B 1086) Solid axle Pl. 20
H 13.
D. 0.051; Th. 0.016.
Good condition. Thick wheel.

Class III: all ballots in this class have medium axles

B 35 (B 233) Solid axle Pl. 20
E 14:1. 3rd century.
D. 0.047; Th. 0.026.
Good condition. Thin wheel.

B 36 (B 234) Solid axle Pl. 20
E 14:1. 3rd century.
D. 0.049; Th. 0.028.
Good condition. Thin wheel.

B 37 (B 295) Solid axle Pl. 21
D 7.
D. 0.05; Th. 0.022.
Good condition. What may have been a pierced hole near edge is now broken open. Thin wheel.

B 38 (B 355) Solid axle Pl. 21
J 10.
D. 0.046; Th. 0.028.
Good condition. Thick wheel.

B 39 (B 449) Solid axle Pl. 21
J 18:2. Roman fill.
D. 0.048; Th. 0.031.
Fair condition. Thin wheel and very thin axle.

B 40 (B 790) Solid axle Pl. 21
I 12.
D. 0.05; Th. 0.028.
Fair condition. Thin wheel.

B 41 (B 791) Solid axle Pl. 21
I 12.
D. 0.047; Th. 0.03.
Poor condition. Thin wheel.

B 42 (B 871) Pierced axle Pl. 21
D 17.
D. 0.05; Th. 0.022.
Good condition. Thin wheel.

B 43 (B 969) Solid axle Pl. 21
P 13.
D. 0.05; Th. 0.029.
Good condition. Thin wheel.

B 44 (B 1013) Solid axle Pl. 21
I 14.
D. 0.047; Th. 0.029.
Fair condition. Thick wheel.

B 45 (B 1230) Solid axle Pl. 21
Q 16.
D. 0.046; Th. 0.016.
Good condition. Thick wheel.

Class IV: all ballots in this class have small diameters

B 46 (B 54) Solid axle Pl. 22
I 9.
D. 0.04; Th. 0.017.
Good condition. Thin wheel.
Shear 1933, p. 474.

B 47 (B 72) Solid axle Pl. 22
G 13.
D. 0.039; Th. 0.0175.
Fair condition. Thick wheel.

B 48 (B 99) Pierced axle Pl. 22
H 12.
D. 0.039; Th. 0.0185.
Poor condition; edge partially corroded. Thin wheel.

B 49 (B 430) Solid axle Pl. 22
H 12.
D. 0.039; Th. 0.027.
Fair condition. Thick wheel.

Lead Ballots

B 50 (IL 578) Pierced axle Pl. 22
H 11.
D. 0.043; Th. 0.04.
Fair condition with axle longer on one side and bent. A groove runs around the edge of the wheel.

B 51 (IL 579) Pierced axle Pl. 22
H 14.
D. 0.04; Th. 0.038.
Poor condition; edge partially corroded. Axle longer on one side; not pierced through.

B 52 (IL 971) Solid axle Pl. 22
C 16. Late Hellenistic.
D. 0.04; Th. 0.025.
Fair condition. On one side of wheel, a small circular stamp (D. 0.014 m.) with thunderbolt; cf. L 74 in Crosby, *Agora* X.

B 53 (IL 1075) Solid axle Pl. 22
G–H 11–12.
D. 0.041; Th. 0.038.
Fair condition; wheel somewhat bent.

B 54 (IL 1266) Pierced axle Pl. 22
K 9–10:1. 1st century C.E.
D. 0.045; Th. 0.018.
Good condition. This is very much more like the bronze ballots (Class IV) than are **B 50**–**B 53**.

B.
COURT SITES

IN VIEW of the variety of ways Athenians referred to their courts, it will be helpful here to list all the names and phrases together with all the monuments, sites, or remains of buildings that have suggested themselves for one reason or another as lawcourts. As explained above (pp. 3–9), a given court could have two or three different names, sometimes used contemporaneously, sometimes one succeeding another. The following catalogue, arranged alphabetically, includes names, sites, building remains, and monuments, all interspersed. Cross references to discussions within this chapter are indicated by the italicized heading of the appropriate section and a page number; cross references to another chapter in this volume are indicated by the chapter name (usually shortened) in quotation marks and a page number. In all, they document an ancient diversity and multiplicity of labels as well as the conjectures of scholarship, both modern and that of late antiquity. The sum of these cross references will show that there are fewer courts than there are names. Although no single identification of archaeological remains with court name, or names, can be said to be beyond dispute, some are more likely than others. An attempt to evaluate proposed identifications is accordingly entered under each appropriate rubric.

Alpha, Beta, Gamma, Delta, Epsilon . . . Kappa (**71**). As names for courts, these letters represent an erroneous attempt by a scholar in late antiquity to explain certain Aristophanic allusions.

Archaic building south of the Olympieion. Remains of a structure described as having been built *ca.* 500 B.C.E. just west of foundations of a Doric temple built in the mid-5th century B.C.E. John Travlos (1971, p. 83), while conceding that "no conclusive evidence as to the identification" can be cited, proposed the temple as that of Apollo Delphinios. Four potsherds that preserve the first letters of Apollo's name, and a mention by Pausanias (1.19.1) of a shrine of Apollo Delphinios in the neighborhood of the Olympieion, form the basis of Travlos' proposal. The Archaic building (older than the mid-5th-century temple) is close enough to that structure to appear to be within a putative temenos. The building was capacious, its exterior dimensions 21.50 × 11.20 m., and in plan shows a large central hall flanked by two smaller halls (Travlos 1971, figs. 113, 114). Although the function this plan was designed to serve is not clear, Travlos argued from the site and from the good quality of workmanship and materials that the Archaic building was the homicide court called "at the Delphinion". Wycherley (1978, pp. 166–167) pronounces the identification "convincing", but the physical remains are not consistent with such modest needs for space as the functions of the court presume. The judging body was comparatively small, and a roofed structure would in any case be inappropriate for a homicide trial; see "Homicide Courts," pages 43–49 above.

Archon's Court (**139**–**142**). Possibly an alternate designation of the Odeion, *q.v.*; cf. "Nomenclature," p. 6 above.

Ardettos Hill (**171**–**175**). A low hill southeast of the Olympieion and just across the Ilissos River. Dikasts swore their annual oath here, and Pollux names Ardettos a lawcourt (**171**), but there is no evidence that trials were held on or near the hill; see Judeich 1931, p. 42.

Areopagos (**1**–**6**, **8**–**28**). This low eminence joined by a saddle to the slightly higher Akropolis to the southeast is, in fact, a spur of the Akropolis. It was conventionally called the Hill of Ares, although a connection with ἀρά is sometimes invoked. See, e.g., Frisk 1960–1972, *s.v.* Ἄρης. Paul Chantraine also proposes a connection with ἀρείων (1968, *s.v.*; cf. Wallace 1989, pp. 213–214). The council met on this hill, surely when it was first called the Council of the Areopagos, and presumably thereafter even when other meeting places, such as the Stoa Basileios, were possible. No sure trace remains to show where a meeting place on the hill could have been. For a suggestion that the council originally met on the plateau or terrace northeast and somewhat lower than the highest part of the hill, where in later years a Church of St. Dionysios stood, see Vanderpool 1950, pp. 34–37; cf., however, Travlos and Frantz 1965, pp. 159–163.

By the middle of the 5th century B.C.E. and as late as 337/6 (**28**), the council met in a bouleuterion. The word in itself means no more than "place where a council convenes". It does not, therefore, refer to the Bouleuterion where the Council of 500 met, nor does it necessarily even imply a single building given uniquely to the uses of the Council of the Areopagos. Any building, the Stoa Basileios, for instance, when the Council of the Areopagos was convened there, became for that time a bouleuterion or synedrion. Any structure within which the council met for the purpose of judging homicide cases, however, must have been hypaethral, since a man accused of homicide presented danger of pollution to any member of the victim's family under the same roof; cf. Wycherley 1955, pp. 118–121.

Basilica at the northeast corner of the Agora. This basilica, like others at Rome and elsewhere, may have served sometimes as a meeting place for court trials; see *Agora* XIV, pp. 71–72.

Batrachioun (**1**). A name given to an Athenian lawcourt, preserved only in Pausanias 1.29; see "Nomenclature," p. 8 above.

Bouleuterion (**28**). Usually in Athenian contexts, this word denominates the building in which the Council of 500 met, and Aristotle (*Ath. Pol.* 45.1) assigns certain judicial functions to that body; cf., however, Rhodes 1981 and Chambers 1990, p. 356. Note also a travesty of judicial proceedings enacted by the Thirty in 404/3 (**284**). On the Bouleuterion as site of judgments made by the Council of the Areopagos, see *Areopagos*, pp. 91–92 above.

Buildings under the Square Peristyle. Remains of buildings under the peristyle can be interpreted as those of five structures; see *Agora* XIV, pp. 56–61. Initially labeled A–E, the largest of them, Building A, could have been the 4th-century Heliaia, and B, the Parabyston/Trigonon. See pp. 12–15 above. The four buildings A–D were at one point in their joint history close enough together to construe as a complex and, accordingly, as having had at least one common use. Rhys F. Townsend describes the remains on pages 104–113 below. If the work that made these structures a complex was done around the middle of the 4th century B.C.E., two of them could have been the First and the Middle of the New Courts in 342/1; see "Nomenclature" and "Structures," pp. 8–16 above. Two of them could also have come to be known as Batrachioun (Green) and Phoinikioun (Red). See also next entry.

Courts, The: τὰ δικαστήρια (**61–95**). The phrase sometimes designates Athenian judicial administration as a whole and sometimes the actual buildings used as courts singly and together; or it can designate one coherent, generally recognized architectural complex of courts as in Aristotle, *Ath. Pol.* 63–69. In these last two senses, the phrase has a place in this catalogue.

Buildings within this last-defined complex can have been called, for example, Batrachioun and Phoinikioun in accordance with the colors that Aristotle says distinguished one court from another. The same buildings could also have had names like First (Πρῶτον) and Middle (Μέσον); see "Nomenclature," p. 8 above.

Delphinion, at (**1, 2, 3, 14, 29–39**). See *Archaic building south of the Olympieion* (p. 91 above) for a proposed identification of Delphinion and court at Delphinion.

Dikasterion of the Thesmothetai (**97**). A panel of dikasts rather than a specific building, synonymous with Heliaia of the Thesmothetai; see "Nomenclature," pp. 5–6 above.

East Building. This structure, designed *ca.* 150 B.C.E., measures 13.80 × 39.80 m. and joins Middle Stoa and South Stoa II at their eastern extremities. A spacious terrace along the east front of the building once accommodated large numbers of people. Thompson and Wycherley (*Agora* XIV, pp. 69–70) interpret this building as the formal entrance to the South Square (*q.v.*), where courts sat in the 2nd century B.C.E.

Eleven, Court of the (**139, 156**). An alternate designation of the Parabyston; see "Nomenclature," pp. 6–7. When in the law quoted by Demosthenes 24.105 (**136**) the Eleven are directed to introduce a certain kind of case εἰς τὴν ἡλιαίαν, they are being authorized to take the case to court but not to a particular building called Heliaia; see Hansen 1981–1982, p. 14. Aristophanes' reference to a court at the walls (*Wasps*, line 1109 [**139**]) can be read as an alternate designation of the court where the Eleven judge; see "Nomenclature," pp. 6–7 above.

Epalxeis. See *Prytaneion*, p. 96 below.

Ephetai or *The Fifty-One.* A court that sat in judgment on certain kinds of homicide case could be cited in formal contexts by naming its judges, the ἐφέται or Fifty-One; see Stroud 1968, pp. 47–49.

First and Middle of the New Courts (**148**). πρῶτον καὶ μέσον τῶν καινῶν δικαστηρίων are mentioned circumstantially in an inscription of 342/1 (**147**). Dow (1939, p. 23) postulates a Third Court; cf. *Buildings under the Square Peristyle*, p. 92 above.

Heliaia (**1, 2, 96–138**). Foundations of a capacious, unroofed structure, square in plan, situated in the southwest corner of the Agora, have been labeled "Heliaia" with or without a question mark since being excavated; see *Agora* XIV, pp. 62–65. For a complete description of the physical remains, see "Rectangular Peribolos," pp. 99–103 below.

The building called Heliaia, whether it was this one or another that housed such assemblies, had no roof in its early phases, a circumstance that led to comic punning such as we find at Aristophanes, *Wasps*, lines 771–772 (**108, 109**), where ἡλιάζεσθαι and ἥλιος are associated. The word ἡλιαία is, in fact, cognate with Ionic ἁλής, or "assembly of people", and has nothing to do with ἥλιος, sun, but such nice etymological distinctions are beside the point for a comic poet. Scholiasts, however, accepted a connection between ἡλιαία and ἥλιος as fact and took it to demonstrate that the Heliaia was unroofed. To use the scholiasts' etymologizing as a support for the identification of this particular unroofed building as *the* Heliaia is not credible. The identification of the building remains could be correct, and scholiasts may even have known or heard that the building was unroofed, but the false etymology is not relevant to the question. Rhys Townsend (pp. 104–105 below) describes the remains of Building A under the Stoa of Attalos. Building A is also a possible Heliaia; see "Structures," pp. 10–15 above.

Heliaia of the Thesmothetai (**97, 130**). A phase of court administration rather than the name of a specific court. It is synonymous with the dikasterion of the thesmothetai; see "Nomenclature," pp. 5–6 above.

Kainon (**143, 144**). This single court, named just once in Aristophanes' *Wasps*, line 120, has not been located. It is not to be confused with the First and Middle of the New Courts, which are attested in the mid-4th century. Note, however, Wycherley's caution (1978, p. 60) that the title "New" can last for many years.

Kallion (**2**, **145**, **146**). See "Nomenclature," p. 9 above.

Klepsydra (**323**). A note in the *Suda, s.v.,* construes what may have been a synecdoche as actual name of a court.

Lower Court (**83**, **85**, **86**). A speculative entity, product of ancient attempts by commentators on Demosthenes to explain κάτωθεν νόμος.

Lykos (**176–185**). See *Poros Benches*, p. 95 below.

Meizon (**2**). Possibly another way of referring to the Heliaia or the Odeion; see "Nomenclature," pp. 5–6 above.

Meson (**2**, **144**, **147**, **148**, **167**). The name of this court can represent the time when it was built (given a sequence of three courts) or its location in a complex of courts; cf. *First and Middle of the New Courts*, p. 93 above, and "Structures," p. 15 above.

Metiocheion or *Temenos of Metiochos* (**2**, **149–151**). Possibly alternate designations of the Heliaia; see "Nomenclature," pp. 5–6 above.

Middle Stoa. Designed perhaps as early as 183 B.C.E. and built ten or twenty years after, this great stoa (146.63 m. long × 16.96 m. deep) does not, as it might seem, sequester the southern quarter of the Agora, since it opens south and north. Virginia R. Grace (1985, pp. 26–30) sees the building as a municipal granary, with the whole complex of buildings that make up the South Square serving attendant functions. Homer Thompson (*Agora* XIV, pp. 65–71), on the other hand, interprets the Square as a complex of courts; see *South Square*, p. 96 below, on the date; see also S. Rotroff, "The Long-Petal Bowl from the Pithos Settling Basin," *Hesperia* 57, 1988, pp. 87–93.

Odeion (**139–141**, **168–170**). The Periclean Odeion has been identified as a considerable building that stood at the foot of the southeastern slope of the Akropolis, just east of the Theater of Dionysos. Only partially uncovered by excavators, its exterior dimensions have been calculated to be *ca.* 62.40 × 68.60 m. (Travlos 1971, p. 387). The roof was supported by a great number of columns. Although the building's original intended function was to serve as a hall for musical entertainments, it is generally agreed that the Odeion cited in Aristophanes' *Wasps*, lines 1008–1009 as a lawcourt by Philokleon's fellow heliasts (**139**) is this Periclean Odeion. It is likely, moreover, that the Archon's Court, mentioned in the same lines of Aristophanes and elsewhere, was also situated in the Periclean Odeion. In the 4th century, diaitetai used the building for formal hearings, and dikastic panels convened by the archon heard trials for support there; see "Nomenclature," p. 6 above.

Palladion (**1**, **2**, **40–53**). See *Stoa on Makri Street*, pp. 97–98 below, for a proposed identification of the Palladion and the lawcourt at Palladion.

Parabyston (**62**, **139**, **144**, **152–161**). See *Eleven, Court of the* and *Buildings under the Square Peristyle*, pp. 92–93 above, and "Nomenclature," pp. 6–8 above.

Peiraieus, Court in. There are references to τὸ δικαστήριον in a few inscriptions from Peiraieus, but it is not clear whether the references are generic or specific; see *IG* II^2 244, line 36, and *IG* II^2 1669, lines 18, 21, and 38. The notion of a court in Peiraieus offered in an ancient lexicon (**85**) need have no substantive basis. While no remains of building can be identified as a dikasterion, there is nevertheless cause to assume the existence of dikastic activity in Peiraieus. A deposit of ten bronze ballots, recovered in the 19th century from a well near Zea, points to a court in use nearby. Since, moreover, there was need for a court in a busy port town like Peiraieus, we can suppose that at least one lawcourt was working there in the 4th century. Note also that Aristotle (*Ath. Pol.* 39.6) may be assuming the existence of such a court when he describes measures for rehabilitating oligarchs in 402. The relevant phrase can be translated: "to a court comprising men who can show their taxable property is in Peiraieus" (cf. Rhodes 1981, pp. 470–471 *ad loc.*). Such a dikastic panel could have convened in a building called "the lawcourt in Zea", but in the lexicographical tradition the phrase "in Zea" appears as an alternate way of referring to the court in Phreatto; see Boegehold 1974, pp. 7–19.

Peisianakteios Stoa. Another way of referring to the Stoa Poikile (p. 98 below).

Phoinikioun (**1**). See *Buildings under the Square Peristyle*, p. 92 above.

Phreatos' or *Phreatto, Court in* (**1–8**, **54**, **55**). This homicide court may also have been called "the Court in Zea", but there is reason to argue that the Court in Zea was not a homicide court but in fact a regularly functioning popular lawcourt in Peiraieus; see *Peiraieus*, p. 94 above, and *Zea*, p. 98 below.

Pnyx, Court in. In a scholion to Aristophanes (*Acharnians*, line 683 [**234**]), the notion of a court in the Pnyx is perhaps a mistaken inference.

Poros benches. Sometime after the middle of the 5th century, four benches, made of cut poros blocks and deep enough for comfortable seating, were set into the east slope of Kolonos Agoraios (Pl. 1). They extended north–south for at least the 37 meters that are preserved today, and so each of them could seat 100 adults in a line. While there is no evidence for a fifth bench that would assure seating for a total of 500, there was room for such a bench between the lowest preserved blocks and the 5th-century ground level to the east in front. On this level ground, there was ample room for all speakers who might appear in the course of a dikastic trial. The existence of a nearby shrine of Apollo and some hints in Aristophanes, *Wasps*, lines 387–394, have led to a suggestion that this area could have been the site of the court that scholars of the 3rd century B.C.E. and after dubbed ἐπὶ Λύκωι (**176–185**); see Boegehold 1967, pp. 111–120. Thompson and Wycherley (*Agora* XIV, p. 71) object that no arrangements to insure privacy are evident. What needs for privacy there were, however, could have been supplied by temporary fences or γέρρα (cf. *Agora* III, p. 191, Wycherley 1978, p. 58). MacDowell (1979, pp. 184–185) objects that Athenians would not have confused "Lykos" and "Lykeios" in Philokleon's prayer (cf. J. Rusten, "Γείτων Ἥρως: Pindar's Prayer to Herakles [N.7.86–101] and Greek Popular Religion," *HSCP* 94, 1983 [pp. 287–297], pp. 295–296). Note, however, that the reference πατρῴοισι θεοῖσι immediately preceding Philokleon's prayer creates an expectation in the audience that they are going to hear Λύκειε, an epiklesis of Apollo, rather than Λύκε, which comes παρὰ προσδοκίαν; cf. Sophokles, *Elektra*, lines 1374–1379 for the sort of sequence an appeal to paternal gods at Athens might initiate. Note also a proverbial saying at Athens, namely, ἐπὶ Πυθίωι κρεῖττον ἦν ἀποπατῆσαι (it would have been better to defecate in the Pythion), based on the nuisance Philokleon promises at line 394 not to commit. Explanations of the proverbial saying have Athenians urinating and defecating at the Athenian sanctuary of Pythian Apollo; see J. P. Lynch, "Hipparchos' Wall in the Academy at Athens," in *Dow Studies*, pp. 173–179.

Poros Building. A complex structure built south of the southwest corner of the Agora in the mid-5th century has its name from poros blocks found in its scanty foundations. Margaret Crosby (1951, pp. 179–180) notes that the building was used by marble workers in the 4th century B.C.E. She also speculates briefly on the possibility that this complex of rooms, associated with a courtyard and an annex, might accommodate a number of dikasteria such as Aristotle describes in *Ath. Pol.* 63–69. Eugene Vanderpool subsequently argued that the ground plan of the sizable complex (37.56 m. long on its north–south axis and 16.50 m. wide at the south) is compatible with the sorts of activity Andokides (*On the Mysteries*) and Plato (*Phaedo*) note circumstantially as going on in Athens' place of confinement; see Vanderpool 1980, pp. 17–21 and Camp 1986, pp. 113–116, 182. Cf., however, S. N. Koumanoudes, "Perhaps>Usually>Certainly," *Horos* 2, 1984, pp. 71–81.

Proton (**148**). See *First and Middle of the New Courts*, p. 93 above.

Prytaneion (**1–3**, **5–7**, **14**, **27**, **57–60**). No remains are currently recognized as belonging to the Prytaneion. It may be helpful, however, to note here, in view of sporadic yet persistent confusions in modern literature, that at Athens the Prytaneion and the Tholos are separate and distinct structures; see, e.g., Miller 1978, pp. 38–66. The Tholos is located toward the southern extremity of the west side of the Agora, whereas the Prytaneion, which Pausanias described as near the sanctuary of the Dioskouroi, may have been at the eastern foot of the Akropolis; see Dontas 1983, pp. 48–63. Epalxeis (**59–60**), mentioned as a homicide court in connection with the Prytaneion, may be an alternate name for the Prytaneion *qua* lawcourt, or it may be, as Miller (1978, pp. 18–19) suggests, an annex.

Rectangular Peribolos. See the essay by John McK. Camp, pp. 99–103 below.

South Square. Four structures define the "South Square". They are the Middle Stoa, East Building, South Stoa II, and Rectangular Peribolos. From some time after 183 until 86 B.C.E., they formed an architectural complex in the southernmost quarter of the Agora, which Homer Thompson interprets as serving the needs of courts; see *Agora* XIV, pp. 65–71.

Two lines of reasoning make this an attractive interpretation. First, Athens continued in the 3rd century to need space for panels of 500 dikasts. Once provision had been made (as presumably it had been with the erection of the Square Peristyle) to seat such panels in a complex of buildings, Athenians continued to provide similar appointments after the Square Peristyle had been razed. South Square is the only complex in the Agora that appears able to serve such needs at this period.

The second line of reasoning is that the South Square was created roughly at the same time as the Stoa of Attalos was being built. Since the Stoa of Attalos occupied the site where the Square Peristyle previously stood, the earlier structure had to have been disassembled, and the functions it served had to be accommodated elsewhere. Athenians took various sorts of worked stone architectural elements out of the Square Peristyle when it was demolished and used them in building South Stoa II. This continuity of use in matters of material may be a clue to continuity of function; see "The Square Peristyle and Its Predecessors," pp. 104–113 below.

There are, however, other considerations to weigh. First, the complex provides more space than Athens apparently needed, even in the 5th and 4th centuries, when more courts met apparently more often. Second, the stone fragments of kleroteria found along the northwest end of the Middle Stoa were not necessarily from allotment machines such as can be shown to have served lawcourts. They could have served the uses of the Boule or of other administrative committees. In any case, the South Square should be thought of as having more than one function, since its great size admitted a variety of social, administrative, and mercantile uses. At the same time, there would also have been room for one or more dikastic panels to meet somewhere within its arcades. Twelve marble bedding blocks in the East Building could have offered places for dikastic equipment, as Thompson suggests

(*Agora* XIV, p. 70), but they could also have supported tables that were used in accounting or banking transactions; cf. Grace 1985, p. 29.

South Stoa (II). A one-aisled Doric colonnade 93 meters long, it was built some time after the East Building, that is, some time after 150 B.C.E. Homer Thompson (*Agora* XIV, p. 68) observes that material for the steps, columns, entablature, and facing of the rear wall was salvaged from the Square Peristyle. (Note, especially, the single letters of the alphabet cut into stylobate blocks; see "Structures," p. 16 above, and "The Square Peristyle," pp. 108–109 below.) South Stoa II succeeds South Stoa, which was demolished to make room for it. Its orientation, unlike that of South Stoa, is aligned with that of the Rectangular Peribolos (*Agora* XIV, p. 68).

Square Peristyle. Partly over Buildings A–E in the northeast corner of the Agora and partly under the succeeding Stoa of Attalos, there are foundations of an enormous square peristyle (or pi-shaped peristyle, since its south side was never finished). The structure was built around the beginning of the 3rd century B.C.E. and was dismantled to make way for the Stoa of Attalos shortly after the beginning of the 2nd century B.C.E. Although it was never finished, it nevertheless reached a stage of building, like many another major structure in antiquity, where it could serve its intended function. Given the singular concentration of dikastic paraphernalia associated with one of the Square Peristyle's predecessors in this corner of the Agora, namely, Building A, it is tempting also to see Buildings B, C, and D as courts. Further, it is a natural inclination to identify a structure that succeeded them in roughly the same area as one intended to serve the same ends. Note that each of the Square Peristyle's four colonnades was deep enough and long enough to seat a dikastic panel of 500 men; see "The Square Peristyle," pp. 108–113 below.

Stoa Basileios. A small (*ca.* 7.57 × 17.72 m.) but important stoa at the northwest corner of the Agora; see *Agora* XIV, pp. 83–90. Its identification is assured by the text of Pausanias 1.3.1, as well as by a group of herms in front of the building, five of them dedicated by men who had served as basileus. This was the official residence of the basileus, and here at a pre-trial hearing, the anakrisis, he would hear charges and counter-charges from citizens whose need for an official response seemed to them to fall within his range of competence. The building was too small to hold a dikastic panel of 500, but the Council of the Areopagos met there on occasion, and when that happened, the Stoa became in effect a bouleuterion. Again, if the council on that occasion was acting as a judging body, which happened sometimes in cases where the Eleusinian Mysteries were involved, the Stoa would become for the time of that trial a dikasterion. On such occasions, a rope barrier kept the uninitiated at a distance (Demosthenes 25.23; *Agora* III, no. 11). Homer Thompson suggests (*per litt.*, Feb. 12, 1990): "Arrangements for a klepsydra are perhaps to be recognized on the ground (*Hesperia* 40 [1971], pp. 245, 246). Just behind the stylobate and just to the north of the axis of the stoa is a light rectangular foundation suitable for the support of a table. From in front of this base a terracotta drain ran off toward the Great Drain. The only obvious source of water is something resting on this table."

Stoa on Makri Street. John Travlos supervised excavation of this stoa in 1962 and proposed to identify it as the lawcourt at the Palladion (**1**, **2**, **40–53**; Travlos 1971, pp. 412–413; *idem* 1974, pp. 500–511). The stoa, whose exterior dimensions Travlos calculates as 21.61 × 5.80 m., faced south. Along its interior and exterior colonnades there were rectangular cuttings, which he interpreted as sockets for stanchions that would support light barriers, the dryphaktoi. From the use of such barriers he inferred that the stoa served as a lawcourt. The stoa, however, cannot have served as a lawcourt for trials that were to be held "in a holy place and in the open air," as Aristotle stipulates (**3**). A separate but contemporary structure, whose total plan and dimensions could not be recovered, extends west from the stoa. Travlos, using hints from old legends and aetiological stories, locates the Palladion west of the Ilissos River on the level land at the foot of the Mouseion Hill, hence in the area where this structure and its associated stoa stood. It is possible (although Travlos does not say so) that the prepositional phrase ἐπί with the dative encouraged him to find support for his conjecture in the circumstance that here (as in the case of the Archaic Building southwest of the Olympieion) the remains show two adjacent or attendant structures. The prepositional phrase, however, need not point to an annex or other building. An open-air court could be so styled while located by or near the Palladion, or even in the Palladion if that name designated an unroofed area. Travlos' proposed identification therefore is best regarded as conjecture; see pp. 47–48 above.

Stoa of Peisianax. An alternate designation of the Stoa Poikile; see next entry. On the name, see, especially, *Agora* III, pp. 31 and 95 with note 1, also p. 5 above.

Stoa Poikile. This stoa, also called the Stoa of Peisianax, is well attested as having various uses at Athens, among them that of a lawcourt; see *Agora* III, pp. 31–45 for a complete collection of testimonia, and **162–164** (pp. 183–184 below) for testimonia relating to use of the stoa as a court. The partly excavated stoa northeast of the Stoa Basileios has been identified as the Stoa Poikile; see Shear 1984, pp. 5–19 for a preliminary report. So far, the west end of the stoa has been exposed to reveal a structure that by its placement and orientation (it faces south) defined a segment of the northern boundary of the Agora. Comparable in size to the Stoa of Zeus, it measures 11.51 m. from front to back at the stylobate and may turn out to be about 46 m. long.

Street of Marble Workers. Plutarch (*de genio Socratis* 10.580d–f [**90**]) notes a path or road that passes by sculptors and lawcourts. This literary reference is not to be connected with a road southwest of the Agora whose metal when excavated yielded abundant marble chips and other industrial detritus (see Young 1951, pp. 139, 151 and A. Boegehold, Rev. of R. E. Wycherley, *The Stones of Athens,* in *AJP* 101, 1980, p. 126).

Theseion (**186, 187**). Of four sanctuaries of Theseus in and around Athens, one is noted in lexica as having been a place where suits were pleaded. For discussion concerning sites for these sanctuaries, see *FGrHist* 328 Philochoros F18, text and *comm. ad loc.*; *Agora,* XIV, p. 66, note 179; and K. A. Christensen, "The Theseion: A Slave Refuge," *AJAH* 9, 1984, pp. 23–32.

Triangle or *Trigonon* (**1, 2, 117, 144, 165–167**). See *Buildings under the Square Peristyle,* p. 92 above, and "Nomenclature," pp. 6–8 above.

Upper Court (**83, 85, 86**). See *Lower Court,* p. 94 above.

Walls, Court at (**139**). Cited at Aristophanes, *Wasps,* line 1109, this court is perhaps the same as the Court of the Eleven or Parabyston, *q.v.*

Zea. In *Anecdota Graeca* 311.17–22 (**5**), articles explaining the phrases "in Phreatto" and "in Zea" seem to be referring to the same homicide court. It is possible, therefore, that Athenians did refer to this court, as they did to others, in more than one way. Judeich (1931, p. 436) speculated that certain cuttings in the rock entrance to the harbor at Zea might be a clue to the location of the court "in Phreatto". I have suggested that a "court in Peiraieus" as a regularly functioning court could have been called "the court in Zea", and that the court then became identified mistakenly with the court in Phreatto later in the lexicographical tradition; see Boegehold 1974, pp. 7–19.

14
RECTANGULAR PERIBOLOS

REMAINS OF A BUILDING often labeled "Heliaia" on Agora plans lie on sloping ground at the southwest corner of the Agora (Figs. 2, 3). Earlier discussions of the identity of the building can be found in *Agora* XIV, pages 62–65. The following account is an abstract of the full publication of the building, which will appear in a separate volume of the Agora series entitled *The South Side of the Agora: The Earlier Buildings.*

The building is almost square in plan, measuring *ca.* 26.50 m. north–south by *ca.* 31.00 m. east–west (Fig. 5). As is the case with all the buildings along the south side, it has suffered considerable damage, and little remains *in situ* above foundation level.

The north side is the best-preserved element of the building. It takes the form of a stairway leading up from the lower levels at the north. Three steps remain *in situ*, risers and treads both measuring *ca.* 0.36 m., and the bedding for a fourth step may be seen on the top of the third step. The width of the foundations suggests the restoration of a fifth step as well. The steps are of hard, cream-colored limestone, the individual blocks set in a polygonal style with oblique joints at both the vertical and horizontal faces. The blocks were set without clamps or dowels, although there are shallow pry holes. The joint surfaces were treated with anathyrosis, and the faces of the risers were lightly picked; where they can be made out, the tool marks suggest the use only of the drove and point. The construction of the stairway is of some interest. The lowest step rests on a packing of large irregular limestone blocks set on a horizontal shelf of dressed bedrock. Behind, to the south, the bedrock has been dressed to a 45-degree slope. Each step course is *ca.* 0.80 m. deep, the front part made up of dressed blocks *ca.* 0.50 m. deep with a rubble packing *ca.* 0.30 m. wide behind.

This unusual arrangement of steps set on sloping bedrock perhaps suggests that no great weight was to be supported and that if anything rested on the topmost step it would have been of light construction. Heavy foot wear all along the preserved sections of the steps also indicates general access along the length of the stairway to the higher area to the south. This southern area was presumably leveled by dressing down the bedrock. The limits of the other three sides of the area are represented by the lowest course of rubble foundations, preserved only for short stretches at the east and west but for most of their length along the south side. These foundations take the form of a packing of irregularly shaped chunks of limestone set in a cutting in bedrock *ca.* 0.80–0.90 m. wide and 0.15–0.20 m. deep. The individual pieces are rough picked with a point on their upper surfaces, which are remarkably level, varying no more than 0.02 m. over the length of the foundations. This packing is made up of pieces of various sizes, but an effort was made to place a particularly large piece at regular intervals of *ca.* 1.25 m. The four large pieces at the east end of the south foundations have pry holes cut into their upper surfaces.

These arrangements suggest that the foundations were intended to carry large squared blocks. One such block survives, apparently in its original position, at the east end of the south wall. It measures *ca.* 1.20 m. long by 0.59 m. wide by 0.49 m. high. The joint surfaces are treated with anathyrosis, the south face was left rough picked, and the other faces are finished smooth with a drove. The discovery of this one block *in situ* has permitted a fair degree of certainty in assigning other blocks found in the area to the building. Like the block *in situ*, they are all of hard, gray limestone, finished with a drove and treated with deeply cut anathyrosis on the joint surfaces. Many show signs of having been plastered on one face with a thin layer of fine marble-dust stucco.

These blocks allow a reconstruction of the enclosure wall. The lowest course was 0.58–0.60 m. wide and *ca.* 0.50 m. high. On top of that rested a course *ca.* 0.51 m. wide and 0.725 m. high, with a low rebate along the bottom of one face and stucco on the opposite face. Above lay blocks 0.48 m. wide by 0.48 m. high. There is no way of determining how high the wall may have risen.

The wall was topped by a coping course that projected some 0.15 m. beyond each face. It took the form of a double cornice, rising to a peak in the middle. On one face the transition from soffit to vertical wall surface was decorated with a carved hawksbeak molding painted with a Doric leaf pattern in red and either blue or green. Several fragments of this course were found reused in a predecessor of the Square Peristyle, Building C under the north end of the Stoa of Attalos (see "The Square Peristyle," pp. 104–113 below). The fragments are associated with the wall blocks of the Rectangular Peribolos on the basis of material, workmanship, and scale. Several smaller fragments of the coping were found within the enclosure itself.

Thus the original plan of the structure seems to have consisted of a stairway of five steps along the north side leading into an enclosure defined on east, south, and west by a freestanding wall of large squared blocks crowned by a coping. There is no clear evidence of how the north side was closed off at the top of the steps. For this original phase, we have no evidence of internal divisions of any sort, nor of any roof. At that time the south wall was not parallel to the front steps, and the enclosure measured 25.20 m. north–south at the east and *ca.* 26.90 m. at the west (measured from the inner faces of the foundations). Although poorly preserved, the east and west walls seem to have been almost parallel, set *ca.* 30.30 m. apart.

CHRONOLOGY

The date of Phase I is not easy to determine, in large part because much of the floor lies at virtually the level of dressed bedrock. The best stratigraphic evidence comes from the north side of the building. There, two Archaic rubble walls, presumably of modest private houses, were found running south of and roughly parallel to the northern steps of the building (Fig. 5). At the east end of the more northern of these two walls, a cutting in bedrock runs farther east for 1.10 m. and then turns north for 1.15 m., beyond which point it was apparently cut by the foundations for the stairway. Pottery found above the floors associated with these walls and from the trench in bedrock dates to the first half of the 6th century B.C.E. (Lots K 181, K 184, and K 315; P 23316). This would seem to provide a *terminus post quem* for the building in the second quarter of the 6th century B.C.E. Whether construction of the whole square enclosure immediately followed abandonment of the private house remains an open question, but two wells within the limits of the building (I 14:1 and J 14:3; see *Agora* XII, pp. 393–394) also went out of use in the second quarter of the 6th century, further indicating that this area saw a shift from private to public use at this time. There are other indications of a 6th-century date as well, though perhaps after the middle of the century. The hawksbeak molding on the soffit of the coping blocks finds its closest parallel in a raking geison dated to the time of the so-called Peisistratid temple on the Akropolis,[1] sometime late in the second half of the 6th century. Similarly, the polygonal setting of the steps, the gray limestone, and the use of a drove rather than claw chisel would all seem to favor a date in the 6th century for the original phase of the peribolos.

[1] L. Shoe, *The Profiles of Greek Mouldings*, Cambridge, Mass. 1936, pl. LII, no. 2.

MODIFICATIONS

South Wall

The enclosure underwent several changes in its long history. One change occurred at the southeast corner, which shows signs of extensive rebuilding (Fig. 5). The main effect of this work seems to have been to bring the south wall into alignment with the front steps. To achieve this, an additional packing of limestone blocks was added along the south foundations at their east and for a distance of 8.20 m. These supplementary foundations differ from the originals in the finer smoothing of their top surfaces. In this second phase a block originally carved as a wall block was cut in half along its long axis and placed along the south face of the easternmost block of the original south wall. It measures 0.25 m. wide at the west and 0.30 m. wide at the east, its south face thus giving the line of the later reorientation of the south wall. Several other blocks used in the rebuilding have double-T clamps, unlike any blocks from the original phase. There is no sure way of dating this rebuilding, but because it so extensive, it seems probable that it was occasioned by severe damage to the building, presumably in the Persian destruction of 480/79.

Propylon

Also to be dated later than the initial phase is the addition of a propylon or staircase along the central part of the north side. Foundations measuring 12.10 m. east–west and 1.40 m. north–south were set up against the old steps, which were recut to join them properly. The upper surfaces of the steps were cut down *ca.* 0.08 m. and reworked with a claw chisel, the faces of the steps were cut back and treated with anathyrosis, and the new superstructure was attached to the old steps by means of double-T clamps. Thus the old building was given a more monumental entrance, although we have no way of knowing if the new foundations supported a columnar porch or simply steps leading up to a series of doorways. The new entrance is set almost exactly on the axis of the building.

West Wall

The west wall, too, seems to have been extensively rebuilt. The northwest corner is made up of two courses of blocks of a softer poros rather than the hard limestone of the original construction. In addition, they are squared blocks rather than the polygonal ones used elsewhere on the north. At euthynteria level the steps were extended 0.60 m. farther west. The westernmost first-step block is also a replacement. This westward shift is discernible farther south, where two east–west crosswalls (see below) run over the cutting in bedrock for the original west wall. This rearrangement of the west wall would seem to be associated with the construction of the adjacent Southwest Fountainhouse. The state of preservation is not sufficient for certainty, but the west wall of the square enclosure and the east wall of the fountainhouse may well have been a party wall. The Southwest Fountainhouse, and therefore the resetting of the west wall of the enclosure, can be dated on the basis of associated pottery to the third quarter of the 4th century.

Western Rooms

Other changes to the peribolos included a series of rooms added along the west side. A long north–south wall was built running the full length of the building *ca.* 5 to 6 meters east of the west wall. It was of rubble construction, *ca.* 0.65–0.70 m. wide. In the southern half of this western area are two east–west crosswalls of similar construction and width. They form two rooms in the southwest corner, a southern one measuring *ca.* 4.20 m. north–south and a northern one measuring 3.25 m. north–south. No further crosswalls have been noted farther north. At their western ends both crosswalls run over the line of the original west peribolos wall and should therefore date to the period of the rebuilding in the 4th century, or later. Resting in a north–south line *ca.* 1.80 m. to the east was a series of four isolated square bases, perhaps for a simple colonnade. The bases consist of individual blocks of limestone on a rubble packing, *ca.* 0.70–0.80 m. on a side. The southernmost base *in situ* is a single block that shows traces of weathering, indicating the position of a column *ca.* 0.50 m. in diameter. The bases are set somewhat irregularly *ca.* 2.50–3.50 m. apart.

As noted, these additions to the west side can be dated to the second half of the 4th century B.C.E. In addition to the association of the west wall with the Southwest Fountainhouse, deposits of pottery found in the floor levels of the building itself indicate a substantial rebuilding in the 4th century (Deposit I 15:2, P 26867 [black-glazed plate], P 26828 [rim of a plate], L 5409, L 5410 [globular lamps]).

With the resetting of the west wall and the construction of rooms along the west side, it seems probable that the original coping blocks on that side, at least, became available for reuse in Building C, a predecessor of the Square Peristyle underneath the north end of the Stoa of Attalos.

Peristyle Court

A final addition to the building was the construction of an interior peristyle within the peribolos. It consisted of six freestanding piers or columns on each of four sides. The foundations of the piers are preserved as cuttings in bedrock, packed with rubble and often including large square blocks of poros or conglomerate. The footing trenches were filled with working chips of Hymettian marble and plaster. The cuttings for the piers are *ca.* 1.80 m. square, and the actual foundations within them are *ca.* 1.40–1.50 m. on a side. The four corner pieces are L-shaped, measuring 2.10–2.40 m. on a side. The centers of the piers are about 2.50 m., measured from center to center. This results in an open square courtyard *ca.* 13.00 m. on a side, with covered aisles *ca.* 4.60–5.40 m. wide around it. No trace of the superstructure has been recognized, and it is not clear how it is to be restored. The large corner piers, set farther away from the other piers, would seem to preclude a normal colonnade. A cutting in bedrock along the south and west side of the courtyard indicated to the excavator the position of a gutter to carry off rainwater, suggesting that the court was open to the sky. The larger corner piers, however, suggest to Homer Thompson (*Agora* XIV, pp. 62–65) the presence of a clerestory arrangement, with the entire area fully roofed.

The date of construction of the peristyle should be after that of the western rooms with their light colonnade, although how much later is not entirely clear. Originally dated also to the late 4th century, the peristyle has been most recently assigned to the mid-2nd century B.C.E., when the entire South Square was being constructed.

Later History

The building was apparently badly damaged in the Sullan siege of 86 B.C.E., and the western rooms were extensively rebuilt, with thicker walls incorporating large conglomerate blocks. The area was used for industrial activity from the 1st century B.C.E. into the 2nd century C.E.. Pits with emery powder suggest marble working in the area, and a kiln and another pit full of yellow clay suggest the manufacture of pottery. A large lime-slaking pit was also cut into the southeast area of the building. A general leveling of the area brought this industrial activity to a halt in the 2nd century C.E., although there is no clear evidence for the use of the area until after the Herulian sack of 267 C.E., when there is evidence of bronzeworking. The final abandonment of the old building occurred in the 5th century C.E., perhaps as a result of Alaric's incursion in 395 C.E., following which the great south wall was robbed out.

IDENTIFICATION AND FUNCTION

The identification of the building, and therefore its function, remain to be considered. No literary or epigraphical evidence sheds clear light on the matter, nor was anything found within the structure to give a clue to its use. We are left with the remains themselves, the location, and the date. In scale, the square enclosure exceeds most other major public buildings of its time. Its construction, of well-cut squared blocks, carefully finished and decorated with stucco and paint, is equal to that of any Athenian secular building of the period. Dominating the southwest corner of the great Agora square, alongside a main thoroughfare that led to populous demes such as Melite and the assembly area (Pnyx), the building is noteworthy for its prominent location. On the basis of generally invoked criteria it can be supposed that the square enclosure was one of the major public buildings of Archaic and Classical Athens.

Can one go further? The ground plan leaves little to go on and few, if any, parallels. Most enclosure walls of this sort surround sacred areas, but in this case no internal structures, no altars, and no appropriate small finds were recovered to encourage such a religious identification, although the peribolos has recently been proposed as a candidate for the Aiakeion, a large sanctuary of Archaic date that stood in the Agora.[2] The basic ground plan, a large, open, square building with ample room and access for numerous people, suggests a building intended to accommodate meetings or assemblies of some sort. With the Bouleuterion and meeting place of the ekklesia already identified, the remaining basic need in the civic administration of the city for a building of this sort is a lawcourt. In trying to establish the form of an early lawcourt, it is instructive to consider Building A, located under the Stoa of Attalos. Dating to the early 4th century B.C.E., it is identified as a lawcourt on the basis of the "Ballot Deposit" and other dikastic items (pp. 10–15, 110–113). Its principal points of comparison with our building are noteworthy: it is a large rectangular enclosure (22 × 41 m.; 902 sq. m. as opposed to *ca.* 800 sq. m.), has only the slightest interior appointments, and was also unroofed in its original phase. If Building A may be identified as a lawcourt and preserves the basic characteristics of an early Athenian court building, then the identification of the Rectangular Peribolos as a court building becomes more probable.

[2] R. Stroud, "The Sanctuary of Aiakos in the Athenian Agora" (lecture, New Orleans 1992), abstract in *AJA* 97, 1993, pp. 308–309.

15
THE SQUARE PERISTYLE AND ITS PREDECESSORS

THE FOLLOWING ACCOUNT provides a summary description of the buildings at the northeast corner of the Agora that may have served as lawcourts.[1] The full archaeological history of this area is presented in Volume XXVII of the *Agora* series, *The East Side of the Agora: The Remains beneath the Stoa of Attalos*.

The northeast quadrant of the Agora is formed by the intersection of the major thoroughfare that crossed the square at its northern end and the Panathenaic Way, which bisected it on a northwest–southeast diagonal (Fig. 1). Until the end of the 5th century, this area, essentially comprising that later occupied by the Stoa of Attalos, remained outside the public sector of the ancient city center. After the formation of the Agora proper around 600 B.C.E. and throughout the next one hundred years,[2] the area came to house residences and workshops, similar, it would seem, to the region southwest of the Agora.[3] Heavy damage by the Persians in 479 led to the abandonment of these properties, but no extensive effort was made at that time to use the space for communal purposes. In fact, other than a small roadside shrine, which was erected in the area below the north end of the terrace of the Stoa of Attalos,[4] there is very little evidence for renewed occupation of the land following the war. At the end of the third quarter of the 5th century, a number of small, haphazard structures sprang up. Built hurriedly and without regard to existing structures (the little shrine was destroyed), these may have been refugee shelters, built to accommodate Athenians coming into the city soon after the Peloponnesian War began in 431.[5]

After the conclusion of that conflict, at the turn of the 5th to 4th century, the ramshackle buildings were swept away to make room for the first of four loosely grouped structures. Despite their ruinous state, these are clearly recognizable by their size and plan as public buildings, and a patchwork of evidence indicates more specifically that they served as lawcourts.

BUILDING A

The plan, Figure 7, shows the basic form and position of the four buildings, A–D. In addition, a fifth, temporary structure, Building E, is indicated. Building A, the first to be erected, was also the largest. A simple rectangle in form, its internal dimensions of *ca.* 41 × 22 m. enclose an area of approximately 900 square meters. The building was set close to the triangular area formed by the intersection of the east–west road at the north and the Panathenaic Way to the west, its north wall

[1] For an earlier description of this area, with references to preliminary excavation reports in *Hesperia*, see *Agora* XIV, pp. 56–61.

[2] For the early formation of the Agora, see *Agora* XIV, pp. 19–20; *Agora Guide*, 4th ed., pp. 17–43; and Camp 1986, pp. 37–38. For the east side of the Agora, see *Agora* XXVII, pp. 9–14.

[3] Young 1951, pp. 135–288.

[4] *Agora* XXVII, pp. 14–18; earlier reports in Thompson 1951, p. 49; *idem*, "Excavations in the Athenian Agora: 1951," *Hesperia* 21, 1952 [pp. 83–113], pp. 103–104; and *Agora* XIV, p. 123.

[5] *Agora* XIV, p. 57; *Agora* XXVII, pp. 18–23. For a similar situation at the southwest corner of the Agora, see G. V. Lalonde, "A Fifth Century Hieron Southwest of the Athenian Agora," *Hesperia* 37, 1968, pp. 123–133. For the refugees flooding into the city, see Thucydides 2.16–17.

closely aligned with the edge of the road on that side. So placed, it occupied an advantageous position at the junction of two major thoroughfares and left open, almost certainly by design, a large area in front of it. Of the structure itself little was found *in situ*, and no remains can be securely associated with its superstructure. The line of its walls, however, can be traced through stretches of foundation trenches preserved on its east, south, and west sides, in areas not disturbed by later construction; actual blocks remain only in two isolated patches, approximately in the middle of the west side and at the southeast corner. The only possible trace of an entrance was found along the south wall, about 10.5 m. west of the southwest corner of the building. Here, two bases, aligned with the south wall, may conceivably have served as the support for a small porch. There may have been other entrances as well, but nothing of them survives.

Evidence for the interior arrangement of Building A is equally scanty. Originally, it may have been an open enclosure, with the exception, perhaps, of a room in the southeast corner. Later, perhaps in the third quarter of the 4th century, a peristyle was added. Two rows of columns, spaced *ca.* 2.90–3.00 m. on centers, surrounded a central courtyard approximately 27 m. long and 11.5 m. wide. The most enigmatic feature of Building A is found within the eastern colonnade. Here, two terracotta water channels were set on end with their hollow sides facing, separated from each other by a few centimeters.[6]

Within and just outside the two channels was found a concentration of 4th-century dikastic equipment, which undoubtedly is to be associated with them. How long the channels may have functioned in conjunction with the room and how long the room may have remained in use during the lifetime of Building A are both uncertain. The channels appear to have been connected with the room at one time because they are anchored in its floor and are set parallel to one of its walls. It has been suggested that they served as a base for a table,[7] and it could be that the room was used as a storage facility when Building A was still an open enclosure. Such an arrangement would have been awkward, however, since the floor of Building A, set some centimeters higher than that of the room, would have covered the socle of its walls, which showed no signs of being remodeled to accommodate the new floor level. The room could certainly no longer have continued in use once the colonnade of Building A was constructed, first, because the walls would have interfered with the positions of the columns, and second, because the colonnade demanded that the higher floor level of Building A be maintained throughout the interior of the structure. The upright channels, however, functioned until Building A was dismantled. They were sunk into its floor, all except the top few centimeters, which were exposed above ground, placed precisely level with the tops of the pier supports for the columns. It is not likely that such agreement in level of floor, water channels, and column supports is coincidental. It seems that the channels now, if not earlier, formed a lined pit, sunk into the floor of the building near one of the columns. A similar lined pit was found in connection with Building C. If indeed the complex of structures A–D were used for the courts, such lined pits could have served as suitable receptacles for wooden containers holding the many and varied items of equipment used in dikastic proceedings. For instance, a container with the internal dimensions of the tile-lined pit in Building A (*ca.* 0.60 × 0.22 × 0.55 m.) would hold approximately 1,000 bronze ballots, enough for a dikasterion of 500.[8]

[6] This has been called a "ballot box", but an alternative interpretation is proposed below. For full discussion, see *Agora* XXVII, pp. 27–28, with pl. 4. For an illustration, see Plate 2; *Agora* XIV, pl. 40:b; and Camp 1986, fig. 81.

[7] *Agora* XIV, p. 57.

[8] A calculation made by Homer A. Thompson and recorded in notes on file in the Records Room of the Stoa of Attalos.

BUILDING B

Of Building B only a bare stretch of stripped foundation trench remains, some 8.5 m. long, just to the west of the west wall of Building A. Earth packing within the trench contained sherds of the late 5th century B.C.E. Building B thus would seem to be contemporary with Building A, but it is very difficult to determine the original form of the structure. It has been reconstructed as a triangular enclosure,[9] with the extant wall abutting the southwest corner of Building A, its second wall shared with the west wall of Building A, and its third formed by an extension of the north wall of Building A. This reconstruction relies on the alignment of the one actual trace of wall with the southwest corner of Building A. Although previous plans have shown the remains of this stretch of wall extending to the corner of Building A,[10] in fact they do not. Both this corner and as much as 4 meters of bedrock to the west were dug away in the 4th century to lay foundations for a monument base; as a result, the southern termination of the wall of Building B is not known. The possibility of another plan suggests itself when it is observed that the surviving wall trench of Building B lies nearly parallel to the line of the Panathenaic Way, an alignment that would create a rectangular enclosure, its west wall bordering the Panathenaic Way, its east snugged close to Building A in order to maximize space. The resulting building would be approximately 16 × 11.5 m. internally, insufficient, probably, for a dikastic panel of 500 but large enough for one of 400. There is no evidence regarding its superstructure; it is not even possible to determine whether or not it was roofed.

BUILDING C

Some time in the third quarter of the 4th century, Building C was added along the east side of Building A. Although it abutted the southern part of the east wall of Building A, the long axis of this stoalike structure was shifted slightly from that of its neighbor so as to face in towards the open area to the south of the earlier building. Little of Building C remains but enough to be reasonably certain of its form. Its area can be estimated at 210 square meters. Best preserved is the southern wall. This consisted of a socle of coarse stone masonry, made to a large extent of reused material, below a mud-brick superstructure. In at least two places the excavators found the socle preserved above the level of the floor within the building; elsewhere the mud brick was discovered collapsed at the base of the wall, in places as much as three quarters of a meter thick. At intervals of *ca.* 2.70–2.80 m. the socle was interrupted by bases for columns. The wall thus can be reconstructed as a closed colonnade, its intercolumniations filled by a screen wall, reaching partway up the height of the columns. There is no way to determine how high this wall reached, although presumably it did not extend to the entablature, since such an arrangement would effectively preclude the need for columns. A screen of this sort would assure some degree of privacy for the activities inside the building, without sacrificing welcome light and ventilation.

The building was entered from both the south and north. On the south the entrance originally lay at the east end of the building. Here, where the ground outside lay at a higher level, bedrock was cut back, and low flights of stairs were built into the newly formed scarp at both the east and south. These led down to the entrance positioned in the second intercolumniation from the east. A light fence continued the line formed by the stairs and scarp on the south, running to the end of the

[9] *Agora* XIV, p. 57.
[10] Cf. *Agora* XIV, fig. 17, p. 58.

building at the west. The four extant post holes, which attest its existence, show that it was a modest but practicable affair. They are small, obviously intended for wooden uprights; the easternmost one had to be repaired or replaced at some point, to judge from the two closely spaced holes for it. The fence seems to have been maintained throughout the life of the building, but the original entrance apparently was abandoned. Earth from the higher ground to the east and south gradually gathered over the stairs, and eventually the doorway was intentionally blocked up. In its place, a second entrance was made in the eighth intercolumniation from the east.

The east and north walls of the building were less well preserved. That at the east is indicated by a shallow cutting in bedrock. Of the north wall only the east end remains, in the area directly behind the Stoa of Attalos. Here, a light porch afforded another entrance to the building at the very northeast corner. Immediately to the west stood a small room, whose size and narrow proportions suggest that it may have served as a storage closet (or possibly a guard room?). The rest of the north wall was lost when the foundations of the Stoa of Attalos were laid, although slight indications exist that there may have been at least one other entrance on this side. The area to the north of Building C, between it and the road on this side, served the building in some fashion, to judge from the clay floor that ran without a break from the building to the road and was maintained throughout the life of Building C.[11]

It was in this floor, just north of the small room, that another tile-lined pit was discovered.[12] Corinthian pan tiles were placed on edge to form a small rectangular container set into the floor, the top edges of the tiles protruding slightly above ground level. The pit contained only destruction debris and general refuse, roof tiles from the building and a few goats' horns. Its similarity in form and position to the pit in Building A nevertheless suggests that this one too may have held a storage container for use in the courts. Building C was large enough to accommodate a dikasterion of 400.

BUILDING D

To the south of Buildings A and C, across an open, graveled area, lay Building D. Of this structure, the only substantial remains belong to the north wall, in the area where it lay below the colonnade of the Stoa of Attalos. Here were found a few blocks from the lowest course of the wall together with remnants of a water channel that ran directly in front; of this installation, one catch basin and bits of its waterproof stuccoing survived. Farther west, only the cuttings in bedrock for the wall and channel remained at the time of excavation. Additional traces of cuttings gave slight indications of the western and southern extents of the building. Nothing of the east wall survived; it is lost under the foundations of the shops for the Stoa of Attalos. These scanty remains suggest the form of a stoa or more probably a hall-like structure approximately 42 meters long and 17 meters deep. The building will have been entered through the north side, either by means of a colonnade or by a series of doors pierced through a continuous wall. Within, as many as 1,500 dikasts could have gathered.

With the construction of Building D, probably around 325 B.C.E., the group of four buildings at the northeast corner of the Agora takes its final form (Fig. 8). Although a relatively loose assemblage constructed over the course of some seventy-five years, the buildings nevertheless give the impression of a related complex. They all face the same open, graveled area and are clustered so as to give positive form to this space. Buildings A, B, and C define the northern limit, while Building D is

[11] The so-called northern part of Building C, referred to in *Agora* XIV, pp. 57 and 59, seems instead to have formed part of an earlier structure put out of use at the time Building A was constructed, or perhaps even earlier.

[12] For a full description, see *Agora* XXVII, p. 33.

oriented so as to close the area at the south. The main approach to the buildings will have been from the Panathenaic Way at the west, with secondary access from the east.

BUILDING E

Although Buildings A–D can have functioned as a cluster, they have no architectural monumentality. They were replaced before long by a much more imposing structure, the Square Peristyle. In the early stages of this effort, while Buildings A–D were being dismantled, an intermediary structure, Building E, was erected in the center of what was to be the court of the Square Peristyle. Pieces of three walls, east, north, and west, survive. No evidence of a fourth wall exists, and it is likely that the structure remained open on this side. Its area can be estimated at 206.5 m., that is, very near the area of Building C. Within, slight traces of a colonnade allow Building E to be reconstructed in the form of a Π-shaped stoa. The building overlapped the south wall of Building C and the southeast corner of Building A, clear indication that these two structures were no longer in service when Building E was built. The construction was very similar to that of Building C. Each of the surviving walls consisted of a screened colonnade (with an interaxial equivalent to that of Building C), the space between columns closed by a wall made up of a rubble socle supporting mud brick. The presence of reused material, similarity of form and construction, and the duplication of dimensions all suggest that Building E was built from material salvaged from Building C and that it was intended to continue the functions of that structure. In time, however, Building E was itself taken down and the base of its walls buried under the deep construction fill of the Square Peristyle.

SQUARE PERISTYLE

The new building, the Square Peristyle, was designed to include virtually the same elements as its predecessors but to present them with a formal unity and quality of endurance wholly lacking in the earlier buildings. The plan (Fig. 9) called for four Doric colonnades around a central square courtyard, with a main entrance in the middle of the west side and a secondary opening in the middle of the east wall. The building provided as much open, unobstructed space as possible. Each colonnade measured 40 m. long on axis and 8 m. deep (from the inside edge of the stylobate to the face of the back wall), without any internal division or support. The axial spacings between columns were a generous 3 m., increased to 3.5 m. at the corners. With outer dimensions of 58.56 m. on a side, the building encompassed a total area of 3,429 square meters, over three-quarters of an acre.

Very little of this great edifice remains *in situ*. Foundations for the outer wall and stylobate at the north were preserved under the construction fill of the Stoa of Attalos, but elsewhere only the very lowest courses or just the empty foundation trench remained at the time of excavation. And for some 17 meters in the middle of the outer wall on the west side, where the main entrance was intended, not even the foundation trench had been dug. Of the superstructure, two isolated step blocks were found in place, one at the northeast corner, in the first columnar space on the east side, the other, more fragmentary block under the position for the fourth column from the east on the north side. Additional fragments of the order were found scattered around the Agora and beyond; most, however, were concentrated in late contexts near South Stoa II. Many elements of that building, including its steps, back wall, and (probably) roof structure, were originally used in the

Square Peristyle. It is now clear that the Square Peristyle, never finished in its original form, was eventually dismantled and reerected to form South Stoa II, the last of the group of buildings forming the South Square of the Agora, a complex that was built over the course of the first half of the 2nd century B.C.E.[13]

How much of the Square Peristyle was completed in its original location? It seems that most of three sides (the north, west, and east) probably were erected to roof level, but the south colonnade was never constructed,[14] nor was the entrance on the west side. If this was intended to be approached by a formal propylon, a separate building contract may have been drawn, one that was never fulfilled. The east entrance also remained as a simple break in the outer wall; still, it was used, to judge from the traffic wear visible where the original ground level was preserved. Haste in construction is evident throughout the building. The outer walls, of mud brick, rested directly on top of the foundations without the benefit of orthostates. Two large drains were built under the north colonnade to carry off rainwater from the great clay floor of the court, which sloped gently downward in their direction. But no water channel was constructed around the edge of the court to catch water flooding from the shed roofs of the colonnades. Although one fragment of molding found in the destruction debris of the building indicates that at least some parts of the order had received the final touches of decorative paint, it is also clear that other elements of the superstructure remained unfinished. Step blocks still retained their protective surfaces, and column drums were never fluted. Nevertheless, care was taken to inscribe letters on the top surfaces of at least some intercolumnar step blocks and on the front faces of stylobate blocks positioned under the columns, presumably to indicate bays.

Evidence for these letters is preserved on several intercolumnar step blocks and two stylobate blocks from the Square Peristyle that remain in place today where they were reused in South Stoa II (Pls. 3, 4).[15] On some of these blocks, single carved letters are preserved; on the step blocks they appear in the center of the tread, on the stylobate blocks in the middle of the front face. In both cases, they can be interpreted to indicate seating sections in the colonnade of the Square Peristyle.[16]

Recent analysis of the ceramic and numismatic evidence from the construction fill of the Square Peristyle indicates that the building was begun at the turn of the 4th to 3rd century B.C.E., and not around 325 as previously suggested.[17] It was used in its abbreviated form until the beginning of the 2nd century. At that time the building was dismantled, its blocks carried off and eventually rebuilt early in the third quarter of the 2nd century to form South Stoa II. The site of the Square Peristyle, dug up and disordered from the process of its demolition, was covered over with a layer of fill. The small Brick Building went up at its southeast corner. Otherwise, the area seems to have remained largely untouched until the construction of the Stoa of Attalos, *ca.* 157 B.C.E.[18]

13 *Agora* XIV, pp. 65–71.

14 Post holes were found at the southeast corner of the court of the Square Peristyle. Mentioned in *Agora* XIV, p. 61 as part of a rope barrier to control access to the colonnades, instead they may have held scaffolding intended for use in the construction of the colonnade; or they may have been for fence posts, designed to prevent unauthorized access to the building from the open area to the south. For full discussion of the Square Peristyle as originally designed and as actually built, see *Agora* XXVII, pp. 68–80.

15 Two of the stylobate blocks seen in Plate 3 are replacement blocks made at the time of construction of South Stoa II.

16 See pp. 110–111 below.

17 325: *Agora* XIV, p. 61. 4th to 3rd century: *Agora* XXVII, pp. 90, 143–153.

18 For the date, see Grace 1985, pp. 14–15. For the Brick Building, see *Agora* XXVII, pp. 107–112.

FUNCTION

The archaeological evidence for the use of Buildings A–D and the Square Peristyle as lawcourts is twofold. First, there is the concentration of dikastic equipment found in conjunction with the pit defined by upright water channels within Building A, including six bronze ballots, a bronze token, and a bronze ball. This represents the single greatest concentration of such paraphernalia in the Agora and the only case where it was found *in situ*. In addition, three more ballots and sixteen more tokens were found in the area of the Square Peristyle and its predecessors (Fig. 4), a total of some twenty percent of such dikastic equipment found in the Agora.[19] Second, the combination of a large central space and surrounding enclosures, which is basic to both the group of Buildings A–D (Fig. 8) and the Square Peristyle (Fig. 10), is appropriate for use by the courts, as they are understood to have operated in the late 5th through 4th centuries.[20]

The Square Peristyle in particular appears to have been designed specifically to accommodate an arrangement of the courts similar to that described by Aristotle. The building was planned using a design module of $3\frac{1}{8}$ Doric feet, with each foot equivalent to 0.32 m.[21] Simple multiples both of the module and of the foot unit itself appear in the building in a way that suggests their conscious application to meet the complex needs of the court system. First, the main entrance of the Square Peristyle in the middle of the west side, although unfinished, apparently was to have been five intercolumniations wide. If each of these column spacings were divided in two, there would result ten entrances, each precisely one module in width. The number ten corresponds to the number of entrances described by Aristotle, through which dikasts would proceed to their allotted courts.[22]

In the case of the Square Peristyle, the dikasts, once they were through the entrance, would make their way to the court to which they had been assigned on the basis of its color, painted (it can be conjectured) on the roof beams of the colonnades that surrounded the central court. Most court procedures required dikastic panels of 500, apparently divided into twenty-five seating sections, each section identified by a letter. On entering the court building, a dikast was given a token inscribed with a letter which he matched with that of a section. In the Square Peristyle, the columns and intercolumniations on each side of the peristyle adjacent to the four corners comprised the seating sections, up to a total of twenty-five for each court. (There would be eleven sections on one side of the corner, twelve on the other; two benches shared the corner column.) As has been noted, the intercolumniations in the building were marked by letters on the top surface of the step blocks, and the columns were identified by letters inscribed on the faces of individual stylobate

[19] See "Bronze Tokens," p. 68 above. See *Agora* XXVII, Table I, p. 42, for precise stratigraphic contexts.

[20] For full discussion, see *Agora* XXVII, pp. 40–49, 90–103.

[21] The determination of the module is based on the frequent occurrence of this measurement in various dimensions of the building. The length of a Doric foot, which could vary considerably from one structure to another, is likewise established by the repeated use of a given unit (in this case, 0.32 m.), throughout various elements of the building. Complete evidence for both the module and the foot unit in the Square Peristyle, and for their application in the use of the building as a lawcourt, is explained in Agora XXVII, pp. 68–72, 93–96.

[22] The selection of dikasts by allotment would have taken place outside the entrances, where there was room for kleroteria and other necessary paraphernalia. There was a sufficient open area in front of the Square Peristyle for all the tribes. Only after having been selected would the dikasts have been ushered through the ten entrances of the propylon itself, each entering by way of the gateway designated for his tribe. At this time, so Aristotle tells us (*Ath. Pol.* 65.1; **249**), the dikasts would have shown the acorn or token given them in the allotment process and assigning them to a particular court; in return they received a colored stave. Through the checking of "credentials" in this manner, no unauthorized person could enter the court.

blocks beneath the columns (Illustration 5 shows the arrangement of letters).[23] Behind each column and at the center of each intercolumniation, wooden benches would have extended to the back wall of the colonnade. For a dikastic panel of 500, each bench would need to seat twenty men. With colonnades 8.00 m. deep (equivalent to eight modules), a dikast would thus have a seat 0.40 m. wide, an adequate allowance,[24] corresponding to $1\frac{1}{4}$ feet (Fig. 10).

Each corner of the peristyle would have been given over to the litigants and magistrates attending the trial. Here, too, would be arrayed the varied items of equipment necessary for the proceedings: bemata, klepsydra, box with ballots, and something Aristotle calls a lampstand (λυχνεῖον; **276**). This design arranged the courts very neatly and symmetrically within the peristyle. The benches all faced the corners, so that the dikasts had their backs to the other courts in order to reduce any interference from the sounds of other trials. In addition, each court was separated from that next to it by a break in the line of benches: a gap of one axial spacing in the middle of the north and south sides and a gap of two axial spacings in the middle of the west and east sides, where the entrances to the building were located. Variations of this "standard" design could be accommodated if larger or smaller dikastic panels were required. The peristyle arrangement was flexible enough to manage a variety of needs, and it represented a natural choice when a complex of courts was desired, since individual courts had long been accustomed to meeting in stoas. In fact, the module used in the Square Peristyle is the same as that employed in the Stoa Poikile,[25] a structure known to have accommodated dikastic panels of 500.[26] It is possible, then, that the architect of the Square Peristyle had studied the earlier building when working on his own design and found it convenient to make use of the same building unit.

In addition to the evidence presented by the dikastic equipment and design of the buildings, support for association of the buildings at the northeast corner of the Agora with the courts has also been sought through reference to names of attested dikasteria. The archaeological evidence for such connections is speculative. In the destruction debris of Building C, and deriving from it or from one of its neighbors, were found two roof tiles (**161**). The first, a fragment of a Laconian pan tile, preserves parts of two letters painted on its upper surface, PA; the second, a Laconian cover tile, has traces of three, perhaps TOΠ. It has been suggested that these letters are part of the name of the building to which they belonged, *viz.*, the Parabyston: [πα]ρά[βυστον] and τὸ π[αράβυστον]. This dikasterion at Athens may be attested as early as *ca.* 424–415 B.C.E. by Antiphon.[27] With the reconstruction of Building B as a triangular enclosure, its association with the court known as the

[23] The Square Peristyle did not have a continuous stylobate; blocks were set only beneath the columns, in the manner of plinths. The letters were marked on the top surface, or tread, of the step blocks, rather than on the front face, or riser, because the sloping floor of the court of the Square Peristyle covered the face of these blocks toward the southern end of the building where the court floor was higher than at the north.

[24] Compare the widths of seats in the Theater of Dionysos, marked by incised lines *ca.* 0.41 m. apart: see W. Dörpfeld and E. Reische, *Das Griechische Theater,* Athens 1896, pp. 49–50; A. W. Pickard-Cambridge, *The Theater of Dionysos in Athens,* Oxford 1946, pp. 140–141; W. Wurster, "Die neuen Untersuchungen am Dionysostheater in Athen," *Architectura. Zeitschrift für Geschichte der Baukunst* 9, 1979 [pp. 58–76], p. 70 and fig. 5, pp. 64–65. (A second set of markings in the theater, 0.327 m. wide and equal to the Pheidian Doric foot, is too narrow for practical use and may have been used in some manner to define a seating area for groups; cf. Wurster, *op. cit.*, p. 70.)

[25] Stoa Poikile, 0.999 m.; Square Peristyle, 1.00 m. For the module employed in the Stoa Poikile, see Shear 1984, p. 9.

[26] For references to the Stoa Poikile holding trials with 500 dikasts, see **163** and **164** (*IG* II^2 1641, lines 25–33 and *IG* II^2 1670, lines 34–35).

[27] Antiphon 5.10–11 (**62**); cf. **156**. For discussion of this reference in relation to the courts and to these tiles in particular, see Thompson 1954, pp. 60–61; *Agora* III, p. 146; *Agora* XIV, p. 59; *Agora* XXVII, pp. 47–48.

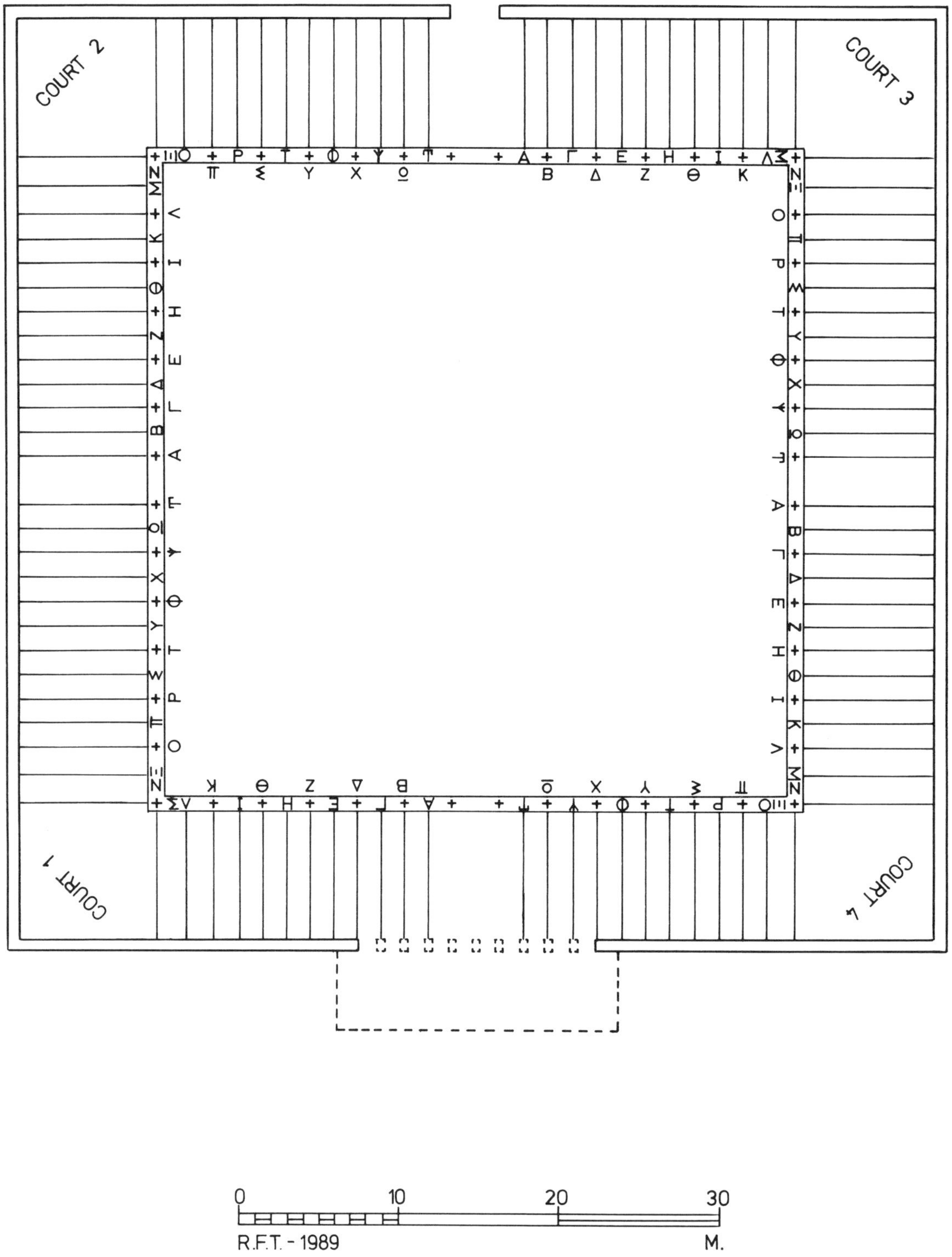

Ill. 5. Square Peristyle: seating plan

Trigonon was inevitable.[28] The archaeological evidence for such a design is tentative, however, and as has been seen, there is at least as much support for a more canonical rectangular form. If, however, the reference to the Trigonon could refer to the area where the court met rather than to the shape of the enclosure per se, an association with Buildings A–D would still be possible. Finally, the size of Building A, and later the Square Peristyle, has suggested their identification with the largest of the Athenian courts, the Heliaia. The various possibilities for connecting these and other known names of courts with the Square Peristyle and its predecessors are explored by Boegehold, pages 14–20 above.

[28] *Agora* XIV, pp. 59–60.

PART III

TESTIMONIA

III
TESTIMONIA

THESE TESTIMONIA are intended to include all references in ancient sources to Athenian lawcourt buildings and other buildings in which courts met, to their probable location, their names, the architectural requirements of the buildings, and the court equipment. Since *dikasterion* can mean site, building, judging panel, or system as a whole, not all references to dikasterion as judging panel have been included in this compilation. The material is arranged as follows:

- General lists (**1**, **2**)
- The Homicide Courts (**3**–**60**)
  - General (**3**–**9**)
  - The Court of the Areopagos (**10**–**28**)
  - The Court at Delphinion (**29**–**39**)
  - The Court at Palladion (**40**–**53**)
  - The Court in Phreatto (**54**, **55**)
  - The Court at the Prytaneion (**56**–**60**)
  - The Court in Zea (**5**)
- The Heliaia and the Other Dikastic Courts (**61**–**187**)
  - General References to Dikasteria (**61**–**95**)
  - The Heliaia (**96**–**138**)
  - Other Buildings Used by Dikastic Panels (**139**–**170**)
  - Dikasteria(?) (**171**–**187**)
- Architectural Requirements (**188**–**249**)
- Court Equipment: Minor Movable Objects (**250**–**355**)

The quotations under each heading are arranged alphabetically by author, following the system used by Wycherley in *Agora* III, with the epigraphical references following the literary. Testimonia are assigned a boldface catalogue number in the section where they seem most relevant. Here the Greek text and full translation will be found. When relevant to more than one category, a testimonium is repeated (with its catalogue number italicized and in parentheses), sometimes with only a reference to the original, sometimes with part of or all the translation. See, for example, the references under **18**. The translations can all be regarded as either mine or Margaret Crosby's.

The following conventions are used in the Greek: Words left out by me as editor are indicated with ellipses: . . . . Words dropped from the text itself, which may have resulted, for example, from a hole in a papyrus, are indicated with square brackets and ellipses: [. . .]. The number of letters missing, if this can be determined, is indicated above the ellipses: [. .$^{5-6}$. .]. Conjectures by the editor to fill such a gap, for example, with τοῦτο, are placed within the brackets: τ[οῦτο]. A letter or word added by the editor to make sense of a passage, even if there is no physical gap in the text, is indicated with angle brackets: ⟨τοῦτο⟩. Braces are used to indicate a word presumed not to belong.

Margaret Crosby expressed in her manuscript a wish to thank Professor Homer A. Thompson and R. E. Wycherley, "who have generously given time to read through the manuscript, and have made suggestions and corrections. Very special thanks are due Miss Aziza Kokoni for her care and interest in typing an accurate copy of a difficult manuscript."

GENERAL

1. Pausanias 1.28.4–11 *ca.* 150 C.E.

καταβᾶσι δὲ οὐκ ἐς τὴν κάτω πόλιν ἀλλ' ὅσον ὑπὸ τὰ προπύλαια πηγή τε ὕδατός ἐστι καὶ πλησίον Ἀπόλλωνος ἱερὸν ἐν σπηλαίωι. . . . ἔστι δὲ Ἄρειος πάγος καλούμενος, ὅτι πρῶτος Ἄρης ἐνταῦθα ἐκρίθη καί μοι καὶ ταῦτα δεδήλωκεν ὁ λόγος ὡς Ἁλιρρόθιον ἀνέλοι καὶ ἐφ' ὅτωι κτείνειε. κριθῆναι δὲ καὶ ὕστερον Ὀρέστην λέγουσιν ἐπὶ τῶι φόνωι τῆς μητρός· καὶ βωμός ἐστιν Ἀθηνᾶς Ἀρείας, ὃν ἀνέθηκεν ἀποφυγὼν τὴν δίκην. τοὺς δὲ ἀργοὺς λίθους, ἐφ' ὧν ἑστᾶσιν ὅσοι δίκας ὑπέχουσι καὶ οἱ διώκοντες, τὸν μὲν Ὕβρεως τὸν δὲ Ἀναιδείας αὐτῶν ὀνομάζουσι.

Πλησίον δὲ ἱερὸν θεῶν ἐστιν ἃς καλοῦσιν Ἀθηναῖοι Σεμνάς, Ἡσίοδος δὲ Ἐρινῦς ἐν Θεογονίαι. πρῶτος δέ σφισιν Αἰσχύλος δράκοντας ἐποίησεν ὁμοῦ ταῖς ἐν τῆι κεφαλῆι θριξὶν εἶναι· τοῖς δὲ ἀγάλμασιν οὔτε τούτοις ἔπεστιν οὐδὲν φοβερὸν οὔτε ὅσα ἄλλα κεῖται θεῶν τῶν ὑπογαίων. κεῖται δὲ καὶ Πλούτων καὶ Ἑρμῆς καὶ Γῆς ἄγαλμα· ἐνταῦθα θύουσι μὲν ὅσοις ἐν Ἀρείωι πάγωι τὴν αἰτίαν ἐξεγένετο ἀπολύσασθαι, θύουσι δὲ καὶ ἄλλως ξένοι τε ὁμοίως καὶ ἀστοί. ἔστι δὲ καὶ ἐντὸς τοῦ περιβόλου μνῆμα Οἰδίποδος, πολυπραγμονῶν δὲ εὕρισκον τὰ ὀστᾶ ἐκ Θηβῶν κομισθέντα· τὰ γὰρ ἐς τὸν θάνατον Σοφοκλεῖ πεποιημένα τὸν Οἰδίποδος Ὅμηρος οὐκ εἶα μοι δόξαι πιστά, ὃς ἔφη Μηκιστέα τελευτήσαντος Οἰδίποδος ἐπιτάφιον ἐλθόντα ἐς Θήβας ἀγωνίσασθαι.

Ἔστι δὲ Ἀθηναίοις καὶ ἄλλα δικαστήρια οὐκ ἐς τοσοῦτο δόξης ἥκοντα. τὸ μὲν οὖν καλούμενον Παράβυστον καὶ Τρίγωνον, τὸ μὲν ἐν ἀφανεῖ τῆς πόλεως ὂν καὶ ἐπ' ἐλαχίστοις συνιόντων ἐς αὐτό, τὸ δὲ ἀπὸ τοῦ σχήματος ἔχει τὰ ὀνόματα. Βατραχιοῦν δὲ καὶ Φοινικιοῦν ἀπὸ χρωμάτων καὶ ἐς τόδε διαμεμένηκεν ὀνομάζεσθαι. τὸ δὲ μέγιστον καὶ ἐς ὃ πλεῖστοι συνίασιν, ἡλιαίαν καλοῦσιν.

ὁπόσα δὲ ἐπὶ τοῖς φονεῦσιν, ἔστιν ἄλλα· καὶ ἐπὶ Παλλαδίωι καλοῦσι καὶ τοῖς ἀποκτείνασιν ἀκουσίως κρίσις καθέστηκε. καὶ ὅτι μὲν Δημοφῶν πρῶτος ἐνταῦθα ὑπέσχε δίκας, ἀμφισβητοῦσιν οὐδένες· ἐφ' ὅτωι δέ, διάφορα ἐς τοῦτο εἴρηται. Διομήδην φασὶν ἁλούσης Ἰλίου ταῖς ναυσὶν ὀπίσω κομίζεσθαι, καὶ ἤδη τε νύκτα ἐπέχειν ὡς κατὰ Φάληρον πλέοντες γίνονται καὶ τοὺς Ἀργείους ὡς ἐς πολεμίαν ἀποβῆναι τὴν γῆν, ἄλλην που δόξαντας ἐν τῆι νυκτὶ καὶ οὐ τὴν Ἀττικὴν εἶναι. ἐνταῦθα Δημοφῶντα λέγουσιν ἐκβοηθήσαντα, οὐκ ἐπιστάμενον οὐδὲ τοῦτον τοὺς ἀπὸ τῶν νεῶν ὡς εἰσὶν Ἀργεῖοι, καὶ ἄνδρας αὐτῶν ἀποκτεῖναι καὶ τὸ Παλλάδιον ἁρπάσαντα οἴχεσθαι, Ἀθηναῖόν τε ἄνδρα οὐ προϊδόμενον ὑπὸ τοῦ ἵππου τοῦ Δημοφῶντος ἀνατραπῆναι καὶ συμπατηθέντα ἀποθανεῖν· ἐπὶ τούτωι Δημοφῶντα ὑποσχεῖν δίκας οἱ μὲν τοῦ συμπατηθέντος τοῖς προσήκουσιν, οἱ δὲ Ἀργείων φασὶ τῶι κοινῶι.

ἐπὶ Δελφινίωι δὲ κρίσις καθέστηκεν ἐργάσασθαι φόνον σὺν τῶι δικαίωι φαμένοις, ὁποῖόν τι καὶ Θησεὺς παρεχόμενος ἀπέφυγεν, ὅτε Πάλλαντα ἐπαναστάντα καὶ τοὺς παῖδας ἔκτεινε· πρότερον δὲ πρὶν ἢ Θησεὺς ἀφείθη, καθειστήκει πᾶσι φεύγειν κτείναντα ἢ κατὰ ταὐτὰ θνήσκειν μένοντα.

τὸ δὲ ἐν Πρυτανείωι καλούμενον, ἔνθα τῶι σιδήρωι καὶ πᾶσιν ὁμοίως τοῖς ἀψύχοις δικάζουσιν, ἐπὶ τῶιδε ἄρξασθαι νομίζω. Ἀθηναίων βασιλεύοντος Ἐρεχθέως, τότε πρῶτον βοῦν ἔκτεινεν ὁ βουφόνος ἐπὶ τοῦ βωμοῦ τοῦ Πολιέως Διός· καὶ ὁ μὲν ἀπολιπὼν ταύτηι τὸν πέλεκυν ἀπῆλθεν ἐκ τῆς χώρας φεύγων, ὁ δὲ πέλεκυς παραυτίκα ἀφείθη κριθεὶς καὶ ἐς τόδε ἀνὰ πᾶν ἔτος κρίνεται. λέγεται μὲν δὴ καὶ ἄλλα τῶν ἀψύχων αὐτόματα ἐπιθεῖναι σὺν τῶι δικαίωι τιμωρίαν ἀνθρώποις· ἔργον δὲ κάλλιστον καὶ δόξηι φανερώτατον ὁ Καμβύσου παρέσχετο ἀκινάκης.

ἔστι δὲ τοῦ Πειραιῶς πρὸς θαλάσσηι Φρεαττύς· ἐνταῦθα οἱ πεφευγότες, ἢν ἀπελθόντας ἕτερον ἐπιλάβηι σφᾶς ἔγκλημα, πρὸς ἀκροωμένους ἐκ τῆς γῆς ἀπὸ νεὼς ἀπολογοῦνται· Τεῦκρον πρῶτον λόγος ἔχει Τελαμῶνι οὕτως ἀπολογήσασθαι μηδὲν ἐς τὸν Αἴαντος θάνατον εἰργάσθαι.

τάδε μὲν οὖν εἰρήσθω μοι τῶνδε ἕνεκα, ὁπόσοις μέτεστι σπουδῆς γνῶναι τὰ ἐς τὰ δικαστήρια.

On descending [from the Akropolis] not to the lower city but to just below the Propylaia, there is a spring of water and nearby a sanctuary of Apollo in a cave (here follows the story of Apollo meeting Kreusa here and of Philippides and Pan).... There is the hill called that of Ares, because Ares was the first to be tried there. I have already told how he killed Halirrothios, and why he did so. They say that Orestes was afterwards tried for the murder of his mother, and there is an altar of Warlike Athena which he dedicated after his acquittal. The unwrought stones on which the accused and the accusers stand are named respectively the Stone of Injury and the Stone of Ruthlessness.

Nearby is a sanctuary of the goddesses whom the Athenians call Semnai, but whom Hesiod in the *Theogony* calls the Erinyes. Aischylos was the first to represent them with snakes in their hair. But there is nothing terrible in their images nor in the other images of the gods of the underworld. There are images also of Pluto and Hermes and Earth. Persons who have been acquitted on the Hill of Ares sacrifice here, and sacrifices are offered on other occasions both by strangers and citizens. Within the enclosure is the tomb of Oedipus. After much inquiry I found that his bones were brought from Thebes; for Sophokles' version of the death of Oedipus is, in my opinion, rendered incredible by Homer's statement that when Oedipus died, Mekisteus went to Thebes and took part in the funeral games.

The Athenians have other, though less famous, courts of justice. The one called Parabyston and Trigonon has its names from the fact that it is in an obscure part of the city—on the most trivial occasions do dikasts convene there—and from its shape. The Batrachioun [Green] and the Phoinikioun [Red] are named after their colors and retain their names to the present day. The largest court and the one in which the greatest number assemble is called Heliaia.

The courts that deal with homicide are different. There is the one called "at Palladion" where cases of involuntary homicide are tried. Nobody denies that Demophon was the first person tried here, but there is a difference of opinion as to the crime for which he was tried. They say that after the capture of Ilion, Diomedes was sailing homeward, and night fell when they arrived off Phaleron; the Argives disembarked as in an enemy's country, taking it in the dark for some land other than Attica. Here Demophon, they say, unaware that the men from the ships were Argives, came out against them and killed some of them and carried off the Palladion. But an Athenian who did not see him coming was knocked down by Demophon's horse and trampled to death. For this Demophon was brought to trial, some say by the kinsmen of the man who had been trampled underfoot, others say by the Argive community.

At Delphinion there are held the trials of persons who plead that the homicide which they committed was justifiable. On such a plea Theseus was acquitted when he had slain the rebel Pallas and his sons. But in former days, before the acquittal of Theseus, the custom for all was for a homicide to go into exile or to stay and be killed the same way as he killed.

The court called "in the Prytaneion", where iron and all lifeless things are brought to trial, originated, I believe, on the following occasion: When Erechtheus was king of the Athenians, the Ox-slayer slew an ox for the first time on the altar of Zeus Polieus; and having done so he left his axe there and fled from the country; but the axe was tried and acquitted, and every year it is tried down to the present time. Other lifeless things are said to have inflicted of their own accord a righteous punishment on men. The best and most famous instance is that of the sword of Kambyses.

In Peiraieus beside the sea there is Phreattys. Here exiles, against whom in their absence another charge has been brought, make their defense from a ship, the judges listening on the shore. The legend runs that Teukros was the first to plead thus in his defense before Telamon, asserting that he had nothing to do with the death of Ajax.

Let this account suffice for those who are interested to learn about the lawcourts.

2. Pollux 8.117–121 (includes Lysias F116, Androtion F59) 2nd century C.E.

Δικαστήρια τὰ Ἀθήνησιν. Ἄρειος πάγος· ἐδίκαζε δὲ φόνου καὶ τραύματος ἐκ προνοίας, καὶ πυρκαϊᾶς, καὶ φαρμάκων, ἐάν τις ἀποκτείνηι δούς. ἐγίνετο δὲ διωμοσία, καὶ μετὰ τὴν διωμοσίαν κρίσις· προοιμιάζεσθαι δὲ οὐκ ἐξῆν, οὐδ' οἰκτίζεσθαι. μετὰ δὲ τὸν πρότερον λόγον ἐξῆν φυγεῖν, πλὴν εἴ τις γονέας εἴη ἀπεκτονώς. καθ' ἕκαστον δὲ μῆνα τριῶν ἡμερῶν ἐδίκαζον ἐφεξῆς, τετάρτηι φθίνοντος, τρίτηι, δευτέραι. οἱ δ' ἐννέα ἄρχοντες οἱ καθ' ἕκαστον ἐνιαυτὸν μετὰ τὸ δοῦναι τὰς εὐθύνας ἀεὶ τοῖς Ἀρεοπαγίταις προσετίθεντο. ὑπαίθριοι δ' ἐδίκαζον. φόνου δὲ ἐξῆν ἐπεξιέναι μέχρις ἀνεψιῶν, καὶ ἐν τῶι ὅρκωι ἐπερωτᾶν τίς προσήκων ἐστι τῶι τεθνεῶτι· κἂν οἰκέτης ἦι, ἐπισκήπτειν συγκεχώρηται.

τὸ ἐπὶ Παλλαδίωι. ἐν τούτωι λαγχάνεται περὶ τῶν ἀκουσίων φόνων· μετὰ γὰρ Τροίας ἅλωσιν Ἀργείων τινὰς τὸ Παλλάδιον ἔχοντας Φαληρῶι προσβαλεῖν, ἀγνοίαι δὲ ὑπὸ τῶν ἐγχωρίων ἀναιρεθέντας ἀπορριφῆναι. καὶ τῶν μὲν οὐδὲν προσήπτετο ζῶιον, Ἀκάμας δὲ ἐμήνυσεν ὅτι εἶεν Ἀργεῖοι τὸ Παλλάδιον ἔχοντες. καὶ οἱ μὲν ταφέντες ἀγνῶτες προσηγορεύθησαν τοῦ θεοῦ χρήσαντος, αὐτόθι δ' ἱδρύθη τὸ Παλλάδιον, καὶ περὶ τῶν ἀκουσίων ἐν αὐτῶι δικάζουσιν. τὸ ἐπὶ Δελφινίωι ἱδρῦσθαι μὲν ὑπὸ Αἰγέως λέγεται Ἀπόλλωνι Δελφινίωι καὶ Ἀρτέμιδι Δελφινίαι, ἐκρίθη δὲ ἐν αὐτῶι, πρῶτος Θησεὺς ἀφοσιούμενος τὸ ἄγος τῶν ὑπ' αὐτοῦ ἀνῃρημένων ληιστῶν καὶ τῶν Παλλαντιδῶν, οὓς ὡμολόγει μὲν ἀποκτεῖναι, δικαίως δ' ἔφη τοῦτο δεδρακέναι. τὸ ἐπὶ Πρυτανείωι δικάζει περὶ τῶν ἀποκτεινάντων, κἂν ὦσιν ἀφανεῖς, δικάζει δὲ καὶ περὶ τῶν ἀψύχων τῶν ἐμπεσόντων καὶ ἀποκτεινάντων. προειστήκεσαν δὲ τούτου τοῦ δικαστηρίου οἱ φυλοβασιλεῖς, οὓς ἔδει τὸ ἐμπεσὸν ἄψυχον ὑπερορίσαι. τὸ ἐμ Φρεαττοῖ. ἐν τούτωι ἐκρίνετο εἴ τις τῶν φευγόντων ἐπ' ἀκουσίου φόνου αἰτίαι δευτέραν αἰτίαν ἑκουσίου προσλάβοι. ἦν δ' ἐπὶ θαλάττηι τὸ δικαστήριον, καὶ τὸν ἐν αἰτίαι προσπλεύσαντα τῆς γῆς οὐ προσαπτόμενον ἀπὸ τῆς νεὼς ἐχρῆν ἀπολογεῖσθαι, μητ' ἀποβάθραν μητ' ἄγκυραν εἰς τὴν γῆν βαλλόμενον.

γνώριμα δικαστήρια ἡ Ἡλιαία, τὸ Τρίγονον οὗ μέμνηται Δείναρχος, Μέσον, Παράβυστον, Μεῖζον· Παραβύστου καὶ Μείζονος δὲ μέμνηται Λυσίας· ἐν μέντοι τῶι Παραβύστωι οἱ ἕνδεκα ἐδίκαζον. Τὸ Μητίχου, Κάλλιον οὗ μνημονεύει Ἀνδροτίων, τὸ ἐπὶ Λύκωι ἀφ' οὗ καὶ ἡ Λύκου δεκάς, καὶ ἥρως δὲ ἵδρυτο αὐτόθι ἔχων τοῦ θηρίου μορφήν· πάλαι δ' ἐκεῖ συνήιεσαν οἱ συνδεκάζοντες τὰ δικαστήρια. τὸ δὲ Μητίχου δικαστήριον μέγα, οὕτω κληθὲν ἀπὸ ἀρχιτέκτονος Μητίχου.

> The text and punctuation of the last paragraph are those given by Lipsius 1905–1915, p. 170, note 19, following George F. Schömann and followed by Otto Schulthess (*RE* XV.1, 1931, col. 362, *s.v.* μεῖζον). Jacoby (*FGrHist* 324 Androtion F59) shifts the position of the first Παράβυστον, but his reading does not change the sense or the number of courts named. For an emendation Μητιχεῖον, see **151**.

The lawcourts at Athens: the Areopagos used to try cases of homicide and wounding with intent, arson, and poison, if the one who gave the poison succeeded in killing. An oath was taken by both parties, and the trial was held after the oath. Neither an introductory speech nor lamenting was permitted. After the first speech the accused could go into exile, but not if he had killed his parents. They would judge every month on three successive days, namely, the fourth, third, and second days from the end of the month. The nine annual archons, after giving their accounts, were on each occasion always added to the Areopagites. They held the trials under the open sky. Cousins [and closer relatives only] could prosecute for homicide, and in the oath they could ask who was related to the man who had been killed. And if he be a house servant, one is allowed to denounce him.

The [court] at Palladion: in this court, cases of involuntary homicide are tried. After the sack of Troy, some Argives who had the Palladion landed at Phaleron and were killed and their bodies cast away by some natives who did not know who they were. And no living creature would touch them. But Akamas gave information that they were Argives and that they had the Palladion. After they were buried they were called the Unknown at the command of an oracle; on that spot the Palladion was set up, and cases of involuntary homicide are tried there.

The [court] at Delphinion is said to have been founded by Aigeus for Apollo Delphinios and Artemis Delphinia. The first to be tried there was Theseus, who was averting the curse of the robbers and the Pallantidai he killed. He admitted that he had killed them but said that he had done it justly.

The [court] at Prytaneion judges cases of homicides whose identity is unknown and of inanimate objects that have fallen and killed someone. The *phylobasileis* [tribal kings] presided at this court, and it was their duty to cast beyond the border the inanimate object which had fallen.

The [court] in Phreatto: here was tried a person in exile by reason of an involuntary homicide who received in addition a second charge of voluntary homicide. The court was on the seacoast, and the accused had to make his defense from a ship, sailing close to land but not touching it. Neither a gangway nor an anchor could be thrown to the land.

Well-known lawcourts are the Heliaia; the Trigonon, which Deinarchos mentions; the Middle; the Parabyston; the Greater. Lysias mentions the Parabyston and the Greater. The Eleven pronounced judgment in the Parabyston. [Others are] that of Metichos; the Kallion, which Androtion mentions; and that at Lykos from which comes the phrase "the company of Lykos". A statue of a hero in the form of the animal was set up there, and formerly those who bribed dikastic panels assembled there. The court of Metichos is large and is named from the architect Metichos.

THE HOMICIDE COURTS

General

3. Aristotle, *Ath. Pol.* 57.2–4 *ca.* 329–322 B.C.E.

λαγχάνονται δὲ καὶ αἱ τοῦ φόνου δίκαι πᾶσαι πρὸς τοῦτον, καὶ ὁ προαγορεύων εἴργεσθαι τῶν νομίμων οὗτός ἐστιν. εἰσὶ δὲ φόν[ο]υ δίκαι καὶ τραύματος, ἂν μὲν ἐκ προνοίας ἀποκτείνηι ἢ τρώσηι, ἐν Ἀρείωι πάγωι, καὶ φαρμάκων, ἐὰν ἀποκτείνηι δούς, καὶ πυρκαϊᾶς· [τ]αῦτα γὰρ ἡ βουλὴ μόνα δικάζει. τῶν δ' ἀκουσίων καὶ βουλεύσεως, κἂν οἰκέτην ἀποκτείνηι τις ἢ μέτοικον ἢ ξένον, οἱ ἐπὶ Πα[λ]λαδίωι. ἐὰν δ' ἀποκτεῖναι μέν τις ὁμολογῆι, φῆι δὲ κατὰ τοὺς νόμους, [οἷ]ον μοιχὸν λαβών, ἢ ἐν πολέμωι, ἀγνοήσας, ἢ ἐν ἄθλωι, ἀγωνιζόμενος, τούτωι̣ ἐ̣π̣ὶ̣ Δελφινίωι δικάζουσιν· ἐὰν δὲ φεύγων φυγὴν ὧν αἴδεσίς ἐστιν, αἰτίαν ἔχ[ηι] ἀποκτεῖναι ἢ τρῶσαί τινα, τούτωι δ' ἐν Φρεάτου δικάζουσιν. ὁ δ' [ἀπ]ολογεῖται προσορμισάμενος ἐν πλοίωι. δικάζουσι δ' οἱ λαχόντες ταῦ[τ']α.[.].[.]ς πλὴν τῶν ἐν Ἀρείωι πάγωι γιγνομένων, εἰσάγει δ' ὁ βασιλεύς, καὶ δικάζουσιν . . . καὶ ὑπαίθριοι, καὶ ὁ βασιλεὺς ὅταν δικάζηι περιαιρεῖται τὸν στέφανον. ὁ δὲ τὴν α̣ἰ̣τ̣ί̣α̣ν̣ ἔχων τὸν μὲν ἄλλον χρόνον εἴργεται τῶν ἱερῶν, καὶ οὐδ' εἰς τὴν ἀγορὰν νόμο̣ς̣ ἐμβαλεῖν αὐτῶι. τότε δ' εἰς τὸ ἱερὸν εἰσελθὼν ἀπολογεῖται. ὅταν δὲ μὴ εἰδῆι τὸν ποιήσαντα, τῶι δράσαντι λαγχάνει, δικάζει δ' ὁ βασιλεὺς καὶ οἱ φυλοβασιλεῖς καὶ τὰς τῶν ἀψύχων καὶ τῶν ἄλλων ζώιων.

All cases of homicide are assigned to him [the basileus], and it is he who makes the proclamation that the [defendant] is to keep away from the customary things prescribed by law. Trials for homicide and wounding, if the killing or wounding is intentional, are held on the Hill of Ares; and so are those for poison, if one causes death by giving it, and arson. These are the only cases which the council tries.

Cases of unintentional homicide and of a counsel or plan that results in a death, and anyone who kills a slave or a metic or a foreigner, the [judges] at Palladion judge. If a man admits killing, but says that he did it in accordance with the laws—for example catching an adulterer [with his wife], or unknowingly in war, or competing in a contest—they judge him at Delphinion. If a man living in banishment on a charge for which reconciliation is possible is accused of killing or wounding someone, he is tried in [the court] of Phreatos and makes his defense from a boat, anchored near the shore. These cases, except those held in the Areopagos, are judged by [?fifty-one] men who are appointed by lot. The basileus brings in the case and the trials are held in a [sanctuary] and in the open air, and the basileus when he judges removes his crown. The defendant must keep away from the sanctuaries for the rest of the time, and the law is for him not ever to enter the Agora. Entering the sanctuary at the time of the trial he makes his defense. When one does not know who did it, one brings a case against "the perpetrator", and the basileus and phylobasileis try the case, and also the cases of inanimate objects and of animals as well.

The last sentence refers to cases tried at the Prytaneion. See Demosthenes 23.76 *et al.* and Rhodes 1981, pp. 648–650. The second sentence repeats almost verbatim a law quoted by Demosthenes 23.22 (**20**).

4. Aristotle, *Politics* 1300b24–30 *ca.* 336–322 B.C.E.

Aristotle, in listing the various kinds of courts according to the types of cases they tried, includes the following note on homicide courts:

φονικοῦ μὲν οὖν εἴδη, ἄν τ' ἐν τοῖς αὐτοῖς δικασταῖς ἄν τ' ἐν ἄλλοις, περί τε τῶν ἐκ προνοίας καὶ περὶ τῶν ἀκουσίων καὶ ὅσα ὁμολογεῖται μὲν ἀμφισβητεῖται δὲ περὶ τοῦ δικαίου, τέταρτον δὲ ὅσα τοῖς φεύγουσι φόνου ἐπὶ καθόδωι ἐπιφέρεται, οἷον Ἀθήνησι λέγεται καὶ τὸ ἐν Φρεαττοῖ δικαστήριον, συμβαίνει δὲ τὰ τοιαῦτα ἐν τῶι παντὶ χρόνωι ὀλίγα καὶ ἐν ταῖς μεγάλαις πόλεσιν.

The homicide courts are of these kinds, whether the dikasts are the same or different, namely, for cases of deliberate homicide, of involuntary homicide, of homicide admitted but where there is a question of legality, and fourth, to deal with charges of homicide brought against men [already] in exile from their country for homicide with a view to their return, such as the dikasterion in Phreatto at Athens is said to be, although in all time such cases are few, even in the great cities.

MacDowell (1963, p. 84) translates ἐπὶ καθόδωι as "with a view to their return".

These subdivisions of the homicide courts are based on the Athenian system. The first is that on the Areopagos, the second the one at the Palladion, and the third the court at the Delphinion. An explicit reference to the court in the sanctuary in Phreatto confirms the Athenian identity of the other three kinds of courts.

5. Bekker, *Anecdota Graeca* 1.311.3–22

ἐπὶ Παλλαδίωι. Οἱ ἀκούσιοι φόνοι ἐν τούτωι ἐκρίνοντο. φάσι γὰρ Δημοφῶντα, ἁρπάσαντα Διομήδους τὸ Παλλάδιον, φεύγειν ἐφ' ἅρματος, πολλοὺς δὲ ἐν τῆι φυγῆι ἀνελεῖν, συμπατήσαντα τοῖς ἵπποις. ὅθεν πρῶτον γενέσθαι ταύτην δίκην ἀκουσίων φόνων ἐπὶ Παλλαδίωι. δικάζουσι δὲ ἐν τούτωι οἱ ἐφέται.

περὶ Ἀρείου πάγου. αὕτη κρίνει τὰς φονικὰς δίκας καὶ φαρμάκων καὶ πυρκαϊᾶς. εἰς ταύτην ἀναβαίνουσιν οἱ καλῶς ἄρξαντες θεσμοθέται, ἀνυπεύθυνοι γενόμενοι.

ἐπὶ Δελφινίωι. ὁμολογούμενος φόνος ἔννομος δικάζεται.

ἐπὶ Πρυτανείωι. ἐὰν λίθος ἢ σίδηρος ἢ ξύλον φανῆι, τὸν δὲ δράσαντα ἀγνοῆι.

ἐν Ζέαι. τόπος ἐστὶ παράλιος. ἐνταῦθα κρίνεται ὁ ἐπ' ἀκουσίωι μὲν φόνωι φεύγων, αἰτίαν δὲ ἔχων ἐπὶ ἑκουσίωι φόνωι.

ἐν Φρεαττοῖ. οἱ ἐπ' ἀκουσίωι φόνωι φεύγοντες, ἐπ' ἄλλωι δέ τινι κρινόμενοι· οἱ ἐπὶ πλοίωι ἑστῶτες ἀπολογοῦνται.

At Palladion: involuntary homicides were tried in this court. They say that Demophon robbed Diomedes of the Palladion and fled in a chariot, killing many in his flight by trampling them down with his horses. Hence for the first time there came into existence this trial for involuntary homicide at Palladion. The ephetai serve as judges in it.

About the Areopagos: this [council] judges homicide cases and those of poison and arson. Thesmothetai who have completed their magistracies well go up to this council after having become no longer liable to an official accounting [of their archonship].

At Delphinion: a homicide confessed as lawful is judged here.

At Prytaneion: if a stone or piece of iron or wood [that caused a death] is in sight but it is not known who did the deed, [the case is tried here].

In Zea: it is a place on the seashore. Here one who is in exile for unintentional homicide is tried when he is charged with intentional homicide.

In Phreatto: those who are in exile for unintentional homicide and are being tried for some other [homicide are tried here]. They make their defense standing in a boat.

The Palladion as a court in which the ephetai serve is named in another entry in Bekker, *Anecdota Graeca* 1.257.23, *s.v.* ἐφέται, not quoted here. On the court "in Zea" and "in Phreatto", see "Sites," pp. 95, 98 above.

6. Demosthenes 23 (*Aristokrates*) 63, 65–67, 70–71, 73–78 352 B.C.E.

63 Ἀλλ' ἐν κεφαλαίωι λέγω· ὁπόσοι νόμοι περὶ τῶν φονικῶν δικαστηρίων εἰσίν, καλεῖσθαι λέγοντες ἢ μαρτυρεῖν ἢ διόμνυσθαι τοὺς ἀγωνιζομένους ἢ ἄλλ' ὁτιοῦν προστάττοντες, πάντας ὑπερβέβηκε τούτους καὶ πᾶσιν ἐναντίον εἴρηκεν τὸ ψήφισμα τουτί ... καίτοι ταῦτα πάντ' ἐπὶ πέντε δικαστηρίοις γίγνεται προστεταγμένα τοῖς νόμοις....

65 Ἡμεῖς, ὦ ἄνδρες Ἀθηναῖοι, Χαρίδημον ἐποιησάμεθα πολίτην, καὶ διὰ τῆς δωρειᾶς ταύτης μετεδώκαμεν αὐτῶι καὶ ἱερῶν καὶ ὁσίων καὶ νομίμων καὶ πάντων ὅσων περ αὐτοῖς μέτεστιν ἡμῖν. πολλὰ μὲν δὴ παρ' ἡμῖν ἐστι τοιαῦθ' οἷ' οὐχ ἑτέρωθι, ἓν δ' οὖν ἰδιώτατον πάντων καὶ σεμνότατον, τὸ ἐν Ἀρείωι πάγωι δικαστήριον, ὑπὲρ οὗ τοσαῦτ' ἔστιν εἰπεῖν καλὰ παραδεδομένα καὶ μυθώδη καὶ ὧν αὐτοὶ μάρτυρές ἐσμεν ὅσα περὶ οὐδενὸς ἄλλου δικαστηρίου· ὧν ὡσπερεὶ δείγματος εἵνεχ' ἄξιόν ἐστιν ἓν ἢ δύ' ἀκοῦσαι.

66 τοῦτο μὲν τοίνυν τὰ παλαιά, ὡς ἡμῖν ἀκούειν παραδέδοται, ἐν μόνωι τούτωι τῶι δικαστηρίωι δίκας φόνου θεοὶ καὶ δοῦναι καὶ λαβεῖν ἠξίωσαν καὶ δικασταὶ γενέσθαι διενεχθεῖσιν ἀλλήλοις, ὡς λόγος, λαβεῖν μὲν Ποσειδῶν ὑπὲρ Ἁλιρροθίου τοῦ υἱοῦ παρ' Ἄρεως, δικάσαι δ' Εὐμενίσι καὶ Ὀρέστηι οἱ δώδεκα θεοί. καὶ τὰ μὲν δὴ παλαιὰ ταῦτα, τὰ δ' ὕστερον, τοῦτο μόνον τὸ δικαστήριον οὐχὶ τύραννος, οὐχ ὀλιγαρχία, οὐ δημοκρατία τὰς φονικὰς δίκας ἀφελέσθαι τετόλμηκεν, ἀλλὰ πάντες ἀσθενέστερον ἂν τὸ δίκαιον εὑρεῖν ἡγοῦνται περὶ τούτων αὐτοὶ τοῦ παρὰ τούτοις εὑρημένου δικαίου. πρὸς δὲ τούτοις τοιούτοις οὖσιν, ἐνταυθοῖ μόνον οὐδεὶς πώποτε οὔτε φεύγων ἁλοὺς οὔτε διώκων ἡττηθεὶς ἐξήλεγξεν ὡς ἀδίκως ἐδικάσθη τὰ κριθέντα.

67 ταύτην τοίνυν τὴν φυλακὴν καὶ τὰς ἐν ταύτηι νομίμους τιμωρίας παραβὰς ὁ γράφων τὸ ψήφισμα τοδί, ζῶντι μὲν ἐξουσίαν γέγραφε τῶι Χαριδήμωι ποιεῖν ὅ τι ἂν βούληται, παθόντος δέ τι τοῖς οἰκείοις συκοφαντίαν δέδωκεν. σκέψασθε γὰρ οὑτωσί. ἴστε δήπου τοῦθ' ἅπαντες, ὅτι ἐν Ἀρείωι πάγωι, οὗ δίδωσιν ὁ νόμος καὶ κελεύει τοῦ φόνου δικάζεσθαι, πρῶτον μὲν διομεῖται κατ' ἐξωλείας αὑτοῦ καὶ γένους καὶ οἰκίας ὅ τιν' αἰτιώμενος εἰργάσθαι τι τοιοῦτον....

70 καὶ πρῶτον μὲν παρ' ἑνὸς τούτου δικαστηρίου καὶ [παρὰ] τοὺς γεγραμμένους νόμους καὶ τἄγραφα νόμιμα τὸ ψήφισμ' εἴρηται.

71 Δεύτερον δ' ἕτερον δικαστήριον τὸ τῶν ἀκουσίων φόνων φανήσεται συγχέων, τοὐπὶ Παλλαδίωι, καὶ τοὺς παρὰ τούτωι νόμους παραβαίνων. Καὶ γὰρ ἐνταῦθ' ὑπόκειται πρῶτον μὲν διωμοσία, δεύτερον δὲ λόγος, τρίτον δὲ γνῶσις τοῦ δικαστηρίου, ὧν οὐδέν ἐστιν ἐν τῶι τούτου ψηφίσματι....
73 ταῦτα μὲν δὴ δύο τηλικαῦτα καὶ τοιαῦτα δικαστήρια καὶ νόμιμ' ἐκ παντὸς τοῦ χρόνου παραδεδομένα οὕτως ἀναιδῶς ὑπερπεπήδηκεν.
74 Τρίτον δ' ἕτερον πρὸς τούτοις δικαστήριον, ὃ πάντων ἁγιώτατα τούτων ἔχει καὶ φρικωδέστατα, ἄν τις ὁμολογῆι μὲν κτεῖναι, ἐννόμως δὲ φῆι δεδρακέναι. τοῦτο δ' ἐστὶ τοὐπὶ Δελφινίωι....
75 τρίτον τουτὶ δικαστήριον καὶ τὰ τούτου νόμιμα παραβεβηκὼς φαίνει.
76 τέταρτον τοίνυν ἄλλο πρὸς τούτοις τοὐπὶ Πρυτανείωι. τοῦτο δ' ἐστὶ τί; ἐὰν λίθος ἢ ξύλον ἢ σίδηρος ἤ τι τοιοῦτον ἐμπεσὸν πατάξηι, καὶ τὸν μὲν βαλόντ' ἀγνοῆι τις, αὐτὸ δ' εἰδῆι καὶ ἔχηι τὸ τὸν φόνον εἰργασμένον, τούτοις ἐνταῦθα λαγχάνεται....
77 ἔτι τοίνυν πέμπτον δικαστήριον ἄλλο θεάσασθ' οἷον ὑπερβέβηκε, τὸ ἐν Φρεαττοῖ. ἐνταῦθα γάρ, ὦ ἄνδρες Ἀθηναῖοι, κελεύει δίκας ὑπέχειν ὁ νόμος ἐάν τις ἐπ' ἀκουσίωι φόνωι πεφευγώς, μήπω τῶν ἐκβαλόντων αὐτὸν ἠιδεσμένων, αἰτίαν ἔχηι ἑτέρου φόνου ἑκουσίου....
78 τί οὖν ἐποίησεν; ἤγαγε τοὺς δικάσοντας οἷ προσελθεῖν οἷον τ' ἐκείνωι, τῆς χώρας ἀποδείξας τόπον τιν' ἐν Φρεαττοῖ καλούμενον ἐπὶ θαλάττηι. εἶθ' ὁ μὲν ἐν πλοίωι προσπλεύσας λέγει τῆς γῆς οὐχ ἁπτόμενος, οἱ δ' ἀκροῶνται καὶ δικάζουσιν ἐν τῆι γῆι· κἂν μὲν ἁλῶι, τὴν ἐπὶ τοῖς ἑκουσίοις φόνοις δίκην ἔδωκε δικαίως, ἂν δ' ἀποφύγηι, ταύτης μὲν ἀθῶιος ἀφίεται, τὴν δ' ἐπὶ τῶι πρότερον φόνωι φυγὴν ὑπέχει.

Aristokrates had passed a decree by which the person of Charidemos should be inviolable, that is, anyone who killed him could be summarily arrested. Demosthenes argues here that Aristokrates thus ignores and bypasses the five homicide courts and their provisions for fair trials. Demosthenes lists the five courts and their special functions.

To summarize: however many laws there are about the homicide courts regulating the summonses, the testimony, and the oaths of the contestants, and whatever else they prescribe, all these this present decree steps over and contradicts.... And yet all these matters are assigned by the laws to five courts....

We, Athenians, have made Charidemos a citizen, and through this gift we have given him a share in all that is sacred and proper and lawful and in whatever we ourselves have a share. The like of many of these are not found elsewhere. One especially is most peculiarly our own and is the most venerable, namely, the court on the Hill of Ares. Of no other court is it possible to tell so many fine traditions and stories, to which we ourselves are witnesses. By way of illustration, it is worth your while to listen to one or two of these.

First, then, in ancient times, as we are told by tradition, the gods saw this court alone as fit for them both to submit to trial and to exact punishment for homicide, and to sit in judgment when they had quarreled with each other, Poseidon, according to the legend, expecting to get justice from Ares on behalf of his son Halirrothios, and the twelve gods finding it appropriate to adjudicate between the Eumenides and Orestes. These are ancient stories; let us pass to a later date. This is the only tribunal which no despot, no oligarchy, no democracy has ever dared to deprive of its jurisdiction in cases of homicide, all men agreeing that in such cases no jurisprudence of their own devising could be more effective than that which has been devised in this court. In addition to these great merits, here alone no convicted defendant and no defeated prosecutor has ever made good any complaint that the court reached its finding unjustly.

And so in circumvention of this safeguard, and of the lawful penalties that it awards, the author of this decree has offered to Charidemos a free license to do what he likes so long as he lives, and to his kinsmen the right of extraordinary prosecution when he is dead. Look at it this way. You are all aware, of course, that on the Hill of Ares, where the law both permits and orders the trial of homicide, first, the man who accuses someone of such a crime must make an oath invoking destruction upon himself, his family, and his house. . . .

This then is my first point: here is one court whose written laws and unwritten usages have been violated by the decree.

There is a second court, that for the trial of unintentional homicide, that at Palladion, which he [Aristokrates] will manifestly confound and whose laws he will transgress. Here also there is the oath, secondly the debate, and third the judgment of the court, and there is no sign of any of these in his decree. . . . These two great and ancient courts and the customs handed down from time immemorial he has thus shamelessly bypassed.

There is a third court, in addition to these, which is the most sacred and awe inspiring of all, for cases in which a man admits the act of slaying, but claims that it was done lawfully. This is the court at Delphinion. . . . This then is a third court with its lawful usages that he has manifestly bypassed.

There is a fourth court in addition to these, that at the Prytaneion. What is this? If a stone or stick or piece of iron or something else of the same sort falls on a person and hits him, and one does not know who threw it, but knows and has the object that worked the death, one brings a case there against the object. . . .

And now consider the character of another court, a fifth one, which he has walked over, that in Phreatto. There, Athenians, the law orders cases brought in which a man, in exile for unintentional homicide and not yet reconciled with those who caused his banishment, is accused of committing another homicide intentionally. . . .

(The author of the laws, *scil.* Drakon, arranged a trial in spite of all the difficulties.) How did he [the lawmaker] manage it? He brought the judges who were to serve to a place to which the accused was able to go, appointing a place within the country but on the seacoast called "in Phreatto". The defendant approaches the shore in a boat and makes his defense without touching land, while the judges listen and pass judgment on shore. If found guilty, the man suffers the penalty of intentional homicide as he deserves; if acquitted, he is released innocent of this charge, but still in banishment for the earlier homicide.

7. Harpokration, *s.v.* ἐφέται — 2nd century C.E.

ἐφέται: Δημοσθένης ἐν τῶι κατ' Ἀριστοκράτους. οἱ δικάζοντες τὰς ἐφ' αἵματι κρίσεις ἐπὶ Παλλαδίωι καὶ ἐπὶ Πρυτανείωι καὶ ἐπὶ Δελφινίωι καὶ ἐν Φρεαττοῖ ἐφέται ἐκαλοῦντο.

Ephetai: Demosthenes in the speech against Aristokrates (23). Those serving as judges in trials of bloodshed at Palladion and at Prytaneion and at Delphinion and in Phreatto were called ephetai.

The reference is to a law quoted by Demosthenes 23.37, which states that "anyone who kills a slayer or is responsible for his being killed, as long as he keeps away from the frontier and games and Amphictyonic rites, is to be liable to the same treatment as one who kills an Athenian, and the ephetai are to decide." This law is part of the law of Drakon of 409/8 B.C.E. (*IG* I^3 104).

8. Photios, *Bibliotheca* 535a22–34 9th century C.E.

ὅτι ἐν ταῖς Ἀθήναις καὶ οὗτος τέσσαρα δικαστήρια φονικὰ εἶναι λέγει, α′ τὸ ἐν Ἀρείωι πάγωι, ὃ δικάζει τοὺς ἐκ προνοίας τὸν φόνον δεδρακότας, β′ τὸ ἐπὶ Παλλαδίωι, ὅπερ ἐτάζει τοὺς ἀκουσίως, γ′ τὸ δὲ ἐπὶ Δελφινίωι ὃ συνίσταται ἐπὶ τῶν λεγόντων δικαίως τὴν ἀναίρεσιν πεποιηκέναι, καὶ τέταρτον τὸ ἐν Φρεατοῖ, ὃ δικάζει τὸν χρόνον μέν τινα φεύγοντα ῥητόν, αἰτίαν δὲ πρότερον ἔχοντα φόνου· ὃς καὶ κρινόμενος ἐπὶ νηὸς ἔξωθεν τοῦ Πειραιῶς ἀπολογούμενος ἄγκυραν καθίει, διότι ὁ νόμος αὐτὸν οὐκ ἐδίδου τῆς γῆς ἐπιβῆναι. Ἀρεοπαγῖται μὲν οὖν ἐκαλοῦντο οἱ τὸν ἑκούσιον φόνον κρίνοντες, οἱ δὲ ἐν τοῖς ἄλλοις δικαστηρίοις κοινῶς ἐφέται.

[Helladios] says that in Athens there are four homicide courts, the first the one on the Hill of Ares that judges those who have killed intentionally, the second the one at Palladion that tries those who have killed unintentionally, the third the one at Delphinion that is constituted for cases involving those who say that they have done the killing justly, and the fourth the one in Phreatto that hears the case of one who, having been guilty earlier of homicide, is in banishment for a stated period of time. Tried on a boat outside Peiraieus, he lets down his anchor and makes his defense, for the law does not permit him to set foot on the land. Those who serve as judges for intentional homicide were called Areopagites, while those who serve in the other courts were all called ephetai.

Helladios, from whom Photios is quoting in this section of the *Bibliotheca*, was a grammarian of the 4th century C.E. whose home was in Egypt. Excerpts survive, such as this from his *Chrestomatheia*, a miscellaneous collection of information probably originally in verse. See A. Gudeman, *RE* VIII.1, 1912, cols. 98–103, *s.v.* Helladios (2).

9. Pollux 8.125 2nd century C.E.

ἐφέται τὸν μὲν ἀριθμὸν εἷς καὶ πεντήκοντα, Δράκων δ' αὐτοὺς κατέστησεν ἀριστίνδην αἱρεθέντας· ἐδίκαζον δὲ τοῖς ἐφ' αἵματι διωκομένοις ἐν τοῖς πέντε δικαστηρίοις. Σόλων δ' αὐτοῖς προσκατέστησε τὴν ἐξ Ἀρείου πάγου βουλήν. κατὰ μικρὰ δὲ κατεγελάσθη τὸ τῶν ἐφετῶν δικαστήριον.

The ephetai were fifty-one in number. They were established by Drakon and appointed according to birth (or merit?). They tried men being prosecuted for homicide in the five courts. Solon established in addition to them the Council of the Areopagos. The dikasterion of the ephetai gradually became an object of ridicule. . . .

Pollux adds another sentence, not quoted here, in which he gives the same explanation of the origin of the word ephetai as does Harpokration, *s.v.* ἐπὶ Παλλαδίωι (**48**). Pollux errs in stating that ephetai served in all five of the homicide courts. They acted only in three: the ones at Palladion, at Delphinion, and in Phreatto; see Aristotle, *Ath. Pol.* 57.4 (**3**). He may also be in error in stating that Solon established the Areopagos; see *Ath. Pol.* 3.6 (**17**) and Plutarch, *Solon* 19.1–4 (**27**), with commentary.

The Court of the Areopagos

The Areopagos, the oldest and most revered council in Athens (possibly successor to a council of elders, the nobles who advised kings), was guardian of the laws and supervisor of morals and at times had great judicial and political powers. Ephialtes, however, in 461 was an agent in the transfer of many of these powers to the system of popular courts. The council as homicide court was left with certain powers, principally those of judging charges of specified homicide and wounding and cases involving those who destroyed the olive trees belonging to Athena. (On a pre-Solonian Council of the Areopagos, see Plutarch, *Solon* 19.1–4 [**27**].) Even after this, in times of crisis or oligarchical reaction the Areopagos could take independent action, as in 338 B.C.E. after the battle of Chaironeia, when it tried and condemned to death some of those who had fled the city (Aischines 3.252 [**13**]; Lykourgos, *Leokrates* 52).

This is not the place to try to trace these various changes nor to discuss or quote the numerous and often confused testimonia used by both ancient and modern authorities in their efforts to construct a history of the Areopagos. Here there are assembled some testimonia that bear directly on its functions and fame as a homicide court. Even when meeting as a court, its official title seems to have been the boule of the Areopagos (Demosthenes 23.22 [**20**], a direct quotation from law), although occasionally it was referred to as a dikasterion (*ibid.*, 65 [**6**]) and as a synedrion (Aischines 1.92 [**12**], Agora I 6524 [**28**]; for discussion of the various uses of the word *synedrion*, see *Agora* III, pp. 126–128). Speakers at trials there addressed the court as boule (Lysias 3.7).

The Council of the Areopagos sitting as a homicide court tried cases of deliberate homicide, of wounding with intent, of poison, and of arson (Demosthenes, Aristotle, Pollux). It was named, by one derivation, from the Hill of Ares just below the Akropolis. This was its normal meeting place, and according to Athenian tradition the first trial for bloodshed was held here, whether that of Ares (Demosthenes, Pausanias, *et al.*) or that of Orestes (Aischylos). Meeting as a homicide court, the council had to sit in an unroofed area (Antiphon 5.10–11 [**62**]). Possibly, there was also a covered meeting place within the precinct on the hill; see comment on Agora I 6524 (**28**).

10. Aischylos, *Eumenides*, lines 570–571 — 458 B.C.E.

Ἀθηναία: πληρουμένου γὰρ τοῦδε βουλευτηρίου
σιγᾶν ἀρήγει καὶ μαθεῖν θεσμοὺς ἐμούς.

Athena: For while this bouleuterion is filling it is well to be silent
and come to know my decrees.

Athena is organizing the trial of Orestes on the Areopagos, continued below with the next quotation (**11**).

These two lines are cited as an example of the use of the word *bouleuterion* with reference to the Areopagos: compare comment on Agora I 6524 (**28**).

11. Aischylos, *Eumenides*, lines 681–693 — 458 B.C.E.

Ἀθηναία: κλύοιτ' ἂν ἤδη θεσμόν, Ἀττικὸς λεώς,
πρώτας δίκας κρίνοντες αἵματος χυτοῦ.
ἔσται δὲ καὶ τὸ λοιπὸν Αἰγέως στρατῶι
αἰεὶ δικαστῶν τοῦτο βουλευτήριον.
πάγον δ' Ἄρειον τόνδ', Ἀμαζόνων ἕδραν
σκηνάς θ', ὅτ' ἦλθον Θησέως κατὰ φθόνον
στρατηλατοῦσαι, καὶ πόλει νεόπτολιν
τήνδ' ὑψίπυργον ἀντεπύργωσαν τότε,
Ἄρει δ' ἔθυον, ἔνθεν ἔστ' ἐπώνυμος
πέτρα πάγος τ' Ἄρειος· ἐν δὲ τῶι σέβας
ἀστῶν φόβος τε ξυγγενὴς τὸ μὴ ἀδικεῖν
σχήσει τό τ' ἦμαρ καὶ κατ' εὐφρόνην ὁμῶς,
αὐτῶν πολιτῶν μὴ 'πικαινούντων νόμους·

δικαστῶν in line 684 is Canter's emendation of δ'ἑκάστων (W. Canter. *Aeschyli Tragoediae* VII. Antwerp 1580 [ante decennium paratus est liber]). μὴ 'πικαινούντων (line 693) is Stephanos' emendation of 'πικαινόντων.

Athena: People of Athens, hear now my decree as you judge the first trial for bloodshed. This place of counsel for judges will exist for all future time for the host of Aigeus. This hill of Ares was the seat and tent site of the Amazons when they invaded in envy of Theseus. They raised here then a newly fortified city with high towers over against the Akropolis, and they sacrificed to Ares, whence this rock gets its name, the Hill of Ares. Citizens' reverence for this court and related fear will keep them from evil night and day, if the citizens themselves do not make new and additional laws.

12. Aischines 1 (*Timarchos*) 92 345 B.C.E.

χρήσασθε δὴ παραδείγματι τῆι βουλῆι τῆι ἐξ Ἀρείου πάγου, τῶι ἀκριβεστάτωι συνεδρίωι τῶν ἐν τῆι πόλει. πολλοὺς γὰρ ἤδη ἔγωγε τεθεώρηκα ἐν τῶι βουλευτηρίωι τούτωι εὖ πάνυ εἰπόντας καὶ μάρτυρας πορισαμένους ἁλόντας· ἤδη δέ τινας κακῶς πάνυ διαλεχθέντας καὶ πρᾶγμα ἀμάρτυρον ἔχοντας οἶδα νικήσαντας. οὐ γὰρ ἐκ τοῦ λόγου μόνον οὐδ' ἐκ τῶν μαρτυριῶν, ἀλλ' ἐξ ὧν αὐτοὶ συνίσασι καὶ ἐξητάκασι, τὴν ψῆφον φέρουσι, τοιγάρτοι διατελεῖ τοῦτο τὸ συνέδριον εὐδοκιμοῦν ἐν τῆι πόλει.

Take the example of the boule of the Areopagos, the most scrupulous synedrion in the city. By now I have seen many men convicted in this bouleuterion, though they spoke most eloquently and presented witnesses; and I know by now that certain men have won their cases, although they spoke most feebly and had no witnesses to testify. For it is not on the strength of pleading alone, nor of the testimony alone, but from what they comprehend and have investigated that they [the members of the Areopagos] give their verdict. And this is the reason why this synedrion maintains its high repute in the city.

13. Aischines 3 (*Ktesiphon*) 252 330 B.C.E.

ἐνταῦθ' ἀνὴρ ἰδιώτης ἐκπλεῖν μόνον εἰς Σάμον ἐπιχειρήσας ὡς προδότης τῆς πατρίδος αὐθημερὸν ὑπὸ τῆς ἐξ Ἀρείου πάγου βουλῆς θανάτωι ἐζημιώθη.

At that time a certain private citizen who only undertook to sail to Samos was on the same day punished with death by the Council of the Areopagos as a traitor to his country.

Compare Lykourgos, *Leokrates* 52, which reports the same action of the Areopagos. This was just after the battle of Chaironeia, in 338 B.C.E. This passage is cited to show that the Areopagos did occasionally take action not concerned with homicide even after the reforms of Ephialtes. Note also that although it was acting as a court it is called the boule rather than a dikasterion.

14. Andokides 1 (*On the Mysteries*) 78 399 B.C.E.

Πατροκλείδης εἶπεν ... ψηφίσασθαι τὸν δῆμον ... πλὴν ὁπόσα ἐν στήλαις γέγραπται τῶν μὴ ἐνθάδε μεινάντων ἢ ἐξ Ἀρείου Πάγου ἢ τῶν ἐφετῶν ἢ ἐκ Πρυτανείου ἢ Δελφινίου ἐδικάσθη ὑπὸ τῶν βασιλέων, ἢ ἐπὶ φόνωι τίς ἐστι φυγὴ ἢ θάνατος κατεγνώσθη ἢ σφαγεῦσιν ἢ τυράννοις τὰ δὲ ἄλλα πάντα ἐξαλεῖψαι. . . .

Patrokleides proposed that the people decree ... except all the names on stelai of persons who did not stay here, whether judgment was pronounced on them by the basileis after trial by [the Courts of] Areopagos, Ephetai, Prytaneion, or Delphinion; or if someone is an exile because of a homicide, or because of a death sentence pronounced on mass-murderers or tyrants—erase all the other names. . . .

Andokides quotes from an amnesty decree proposed in 405 B.C.E. by Patrokleides, who by having names removed from stelai, enfranchised persons who had suffered full or partial loss of citizens' rights. Patrokleides introduced his measure as the same as one the Athenians passed during the Persian Wars, but it cannot have been literally the same, for the exceptions reflect Athenian judicial procedures of the late 5th century. His choice of words shows affinities with Plutarch, *Solon* 19.4 (**27**). On text and translation, see A. Boegehold, "Andokides and the Decree of Patrokleides," *Historia* 39, 1990, pp. 149–162.

15. Androtion (*FGrHist* 324 F3 = *FGrHist* 328 Philochoros F4, F20) 4th century B.C.E.

ἐδίκαζον οὖν Ἀρεοπαγῖται περὶ πάντων σχεδὸν τῶν σφαλμάτων καὶ παρανομιῶν, ὡς ἅπαντά φησιν Ἀνδροτίων ἐν πρώτηι καὶ Φιλόχορος ἐν δευτέραι καὶ τρίτηι τῶν Ἀτθίδων.

Now the Areopagites acted as judges on almost all faults and illegal acts, as Androtion says absolutely in the first book of his *Atthis*, and Philochoros in the second and third of his [*Atthis*].

16. Androtion (*FGrHist* 324 F4a = *FGrHist* 328 Philochoros F20) 4th century B.C.E.

ἐκ γὰρ τῶν ἐννέα καθισταμένων ἀρχόντων Ἀθήνησι τοὺς Ἀρεοπαγίτας ἔδει συνεστάναι δικαστάς, ὥς φησιν Ἀνδροτίων ἐν δευτέραι τῶν Ἀτθίδων· ὕστερον δὲ πλειόνων γέγονεν ἡ ἐξ Ἀρείου πάγου βουλή, τουτέστιν ἡ ἐξ ἀνδρῶν περιφανεστέρων πεντήκοντα καὶ ἑνός, πλὴν ἐξ εὐπατριδῶν, ὡς ἔφημεν, καὶ πλούτωι καὶ βίωι σώφρονι διαφερόντων, ὡς ἱστορεῖ Φιλόχορος διὰ τῆς τρίτης τῶν αὐτοῦ Ἀτθίδων.

Maximus Confessor, in *Prooemio ad S. Dionysii Areopagitae Opera* II, Antwerp 1634, p. xxxiv, has τῶν αὐτῶν Ἀτθίδων.

At Athens the Areopagite judges had to be drawn from the nine men who were appointed archons, as Androtion says in the second book of his *Atthis*. Later the Council of the Areopagos was formed from a larger number, that is, the council of fifty-one, composed of eminent men, but only of Eupatrids, as we said, and men distinguished for wealth and sober life, as Philochoros records in the third book of his *Atthis*.

The number fifty-one for the Council may be a confusion with the fifty-one ephetai. This passage has been used by some modern scholars as proof that the ephetai were drawn from the Areopagos; see, for example, Bonner and Smith 1930, p. 100, and compare MacDowell 1963, pp. 51–52. It is quoted here merely as one of the relatively few texts in which Areopagites are called dikasts. Compare *FGrHist* 324 Androtion F3–F4, note 32.

17. Aristotle, *Ath. Pol.* 3.6 *ca.* 329–322 B.C.E.

ἡ δὲ τῶν Ἀρεοπαγιτῶν βουλὴ τὴν μὲν τάξιν εἶχε τοῦ διατηρεῖν τοὺς νόμους, διώικει δὲ τὰ πλεῖστα καὶ τὰ μέγιστα τῶν ἐν τῆι πόλει, καὶ κολάζουσα καὶ ζημιοῦσα πάντας τοὺς ἀκοσμοῦντας κυρίως. ἡ γὰρ αἵρεσις τῶν ἀρχόντων ἀριστίνδην καὶ πλουτίνδην ἦν, ἐξ ὧν οἱ Ἀρεοπαγῖται καθίσταντο· διὸ καὶ μόνη τῶν ἀρχῶν αὕτη μεμένηκε διὰ βίου καὶ νῦν.

The Council of the Areopagites had the position of guarding the laws. It administered most of the most important functions in the city, and with full authority it punished and fined all those who disrupted public order. The archons, from whom the Areopagites were appointed, were chosen according to merit and wealth. For this reason [the Areopagite] is the only office that continues to be for life to the present day.

On 4th-century Athenian views of the Council, see *FGrHist* 324 Androtion F4–F5, commentary and notes.

18. Aristotle, *Ath. Pol.* 16.8 *ca.* 329–322 B.C.E.

καί ποτε προσκληθεὶς φόνου δίκην εἰς Ἄρειον πάγον αὐτὸς μὲν ἀπήντησεν ὡς ἀπολογησόμενος, ὁ δὲ προσκαλεσάμενος φοβηθεὶς ἔλιπεν.

And once when [Peisistratos] was summoned on a charge of homicide to the Areopagos and presented himself to make his defense, the man who had brought the accusation became frightened and abandoned the case.

Compare Aristotle (*Politics* 1315b21) and Plutarch (*Solon* 31.2) for this same story of Peisistratos.

(3) Aristotle, *Ath. Pol.* 57.2–4

(4) Aristotle, *Politics* 1300b25–26
See **4** above, where the function of the court is described but the court is not named.

(237) Bekker, *Anecdota Graeca* 1.219.28–31
For a full text of this passage, see **237**; compare **242**.

(85) Bekker, *Anecdota Graeca* 1.253.26

(5) Bekker, *Anecdota Graeca* 1.311.5

19. Bekker, *Anecdota Graeca* 1.444.1–12 (= *FGrHist* 323a Hellanikos F1)

Ἄρειος πάγος· δικαστήριον Ἀθήνησιν. ἦσαν οὖν Ἀθήνησι βουλαὶ δύο, ἡ μὲν τῶν πεντακοσίων . . . ἡ δὲ εἰς βίον τῶν Ἀρεοπαγιτῶν. ἐδίκαζε δὲ τὰ φονικά, καὶ τὰ ἄλλα πολιτικὰ διώικει σεμνῶς. ἐκλήθη δὲ Ἄρειος πάγος ἤτοι ὅτι ἐν πάγωι ἐστὶ καὶ ἐν ὕψει τὸ δικαστήριον, Ἄρειος δὲ ἐπεὶ τὰ φονικὰ δικάζει, ὁ δὲ Ἄρης ἐπὶ τὸν φόνον· ἢ ὅτι ἔπηξε τὸ δόρυ ἐκεῖ ὁ Ἄρης ἐν τῆι πρὸς Ποσειδῶνα ὑπὲρ Ἁλιρροθίου δίκηι ὅτε ἀπέκτεινεν αὐτὸν βιασάμενον Ἀλκίππην, τὴν αὐτοῦ καὶ Ἀγραύλου τῆς Κέκροπος θυγατρός, ὥς φησιν Ἑλλάνικος ἐν πρώτωι.

Areopagos: a lawcourt in Athens. There were two councils in Athens, one of the Five Hundred . . . the other of the Areopagites, who served for life. [The Council of the Areopagos] tried cases of homicide and administered the rest of the functions of state in a high-minded way. It was called the *Hill* of Ares because it is on a rocky hill and the lawcourt is high up, *Areios* because it judges homicide cases, and Ares is concerned with homicide; or because Ares stuck his spear there in the trial with Poseidon over Halirrothios, when he [Ares] had killed Halirrothios, who had raped Alkippe the daughter of Ares and Agraulos the daughter of Kekrops, as Hellanikos says in his first book.

See *Suda, s.v.* Ἄρειος Πάγος, and *Etymologicum Magnum* for similar notices, not quoted here.

20. Demosthenes 23 (*Aristokrates*) 22 352 B.C.E.

λαβὲ δὴ τοὺς νόμους αὐτοὺς καὶ λέγε, ἵν' ἐξ αὐτῶν ἐπιδεικνύω τούτων τὸ παράνομον.

ΝΟΜΟΣ ΕΚ ΤΩΝ ΦΟΝΙΚΩΝ ΝΟΜΩΝ ΤΩΝ ΕΞ ΑΡΕΙΟΥ ΠΑΓΟΥ

Δικάζειν δὲ τὴν βουλὴν τὴν ἐν Ἀρείωι πάγωι φόνου καὶ τραύματος ἐκ προνοίας καὶ πυρκαϊᾶς καὶ φαρμάκων, ἐάν τις ἀποκτείνηι δούς.

Take the laws themselves and read them aloud so that I can demonstrate from them the illegality of these men's proposal.

A LAW FROM THE HOMICIDE LAWS FROM THE HILL OF ARES

The council on the Areopagos is to try cases of homicide and wounding committed deliberately, and of arson and of poisoning, if anyone causes death by giving poison.

Compare **3** above, Aristotle, *Ath. Pol.* 57.3. Note above that in the law dealing with homicide, the Areopagos is called a boule, not a dikasterion.

(6) Demosthenes 23 (*Aristokrates*) 65–67

21. Euripides, *Iphigeneia in Tauris*, lines 961–969 *ca.* 414–412 B.C.E.

'Ορέστης: ὡς δ' εἰς Ἄρειον ὄχθον ἧκον, ἐς δίκην
ἔστην, ἐγὼ μὲν θάτερον λαβὼν βάθρον,
τὸ δ' ἄλλο πρέσβειρ' ἥπερ ἦν 'Ερινύων.
εἰπὼν δ' ἀκούσας θ' αἵματος μητρὸς πέρι,
Φοῖβός μ' ἔσωσε μαρτυρῶν, ἴσας δέ μοι
ψήφους διηρίθμησε Παλλὰς ὠλένηι·
νικῶν δ' ἀπῆρα φόνια πειρατήρια.
ὅσαι μὲν οὖν ἕζοντο πεισθεῖσαι δίκηι
ψῆφον παρ' αὐτὴν ἱερὸν ὡρίσαντ' ἔχειν.

Orestes: When I came to Ares' Hill, I stood trial,
I took one of the places to stand,
she who was oldest of the Erinyes took the other.
About my mother's blood, Phoibos spoke and listened
and testified and saved me. Pallas
Athena with [a gesture of] her arm certified as sum
equal votes on either side.
I left the murder trial a winner.
Now all the Erinyes who accepted the verdict
were assigned a shrine by the very court . . .

The two βάθρα are the unworked stones of Pausanias 1.28.5 (**1**). Note the translation "certified as sum" for διηρίθμησε. The idea is that Athena has counted through the ballots, has found them equal in number on either side, and so now makes a gesture with her hand that tells all present that Orestes has won. An amplified translation could be presented as follows: "Pallas sorted out the ballots as equal . . . to my advantage . . . [and signaled that she had done so by a gesture made] with her arm."

Three Attic, Late Archaic red-figured vases with paintings of the *krisis hoplon* show Athena supervising an open vote wherein Achilles' weapons and armor are being awarded to Odysseus rather than Aias (Douris, Vienna 3695, *ARV*² 429.26, the Painter of Louvre G265, Leiden PC 75, *ARV*² 416.7 [bis]). In these paintings, Athena, standing behind an altar, seems to identify Odysseus as winner by means of her outstretched right arm, despite clear indications that the voting is still in progress (Pl. 23). Visible accumulations of psephoi at each end of the altar show a majority of ballots for Odysseus. In another painting of the same judgment, Athena turns left and makes a forbidding gesture to Aias, telling him he has lost (Brygos, London E 69, *ARV*² 369.2).

The portmanteau effect of the paintings, that is, their compression of a sequence of actions into a single frame, may be analogous to Euripides' expression here: he has combined the idea of "counting all the way through" (διηρίθμησε) and the signal of the outcome of the counting (ὠλένηι). Athena's gesture in the paintings may be one that painters saw in actual life, a herald, for instance, announcing the result of a vote in assembly, lawcourt, or at dramatic competitions. For more details, see A. Boegehold, "A Signifying Gesture: Euripides *IT* 965–966," *AJA* 93, 1989, pp. 81–83. Note ψῆφος as synecdoche for tribunal.

22. Euripides, *Electra*, lines 1268–1272 *ca.* 413 B.C.E.

Διόσκουροι: καὶ τοῖσι λοιποῖς ὅδε νόμος τεθήσεται
νικᾶν ἴσαις ψήφοισι τὸν φεύγοντ' ἀεί.
δειναὶ μὲν οὖν θεαὶ τῶιδ' ἄχει πεπληγμέναι
πάγον παρ' αὐτὸν χάσμα δύσονται χθονός,
σεμνὸν βροτοῖσιν εὐσεβὲς χρηστήριον.

Dioskouroi: And for time to come this law shall be
that a defendant win if the votes are equal.
Now then the fearsome goddesses, stricken by this pain,
will go down into earth's chasm, by the very [same] hill,
a holy oracle, object of veneration for mortals.

Compare Euripides, *Iphigeneia in Tauris*, line 969 (**21**).

(47) Harpokration, *s.v.* βουλεύσεως

Of bouleusis: . . . Isaios . . . [says] that these trials were at the Palladion, but Deinarchos . . . that they were on the Areopagos. Aristotle in the *Constitution of Athens* agrees with Isaios.

For the full text of this passage, see **47**.

23. Lykourgos, *Leokrates* 12–13 330 B.C.E.

τούτων δ' αἴτιοι ὑμεῖς ἐστε, ὦ ἄνδρες· τὴν γὰρ ἐξουσίαν ταύτην δεδώκατε τοῖς ἐνθάδ' εἰσιοῦσι, καὶ ταῦτα κάλλιστον ἔχοντες τῶν Ἑλλήνων παράδειγμα τὸ ἐν Ἀρείωι πάγωι συνέδριον, ὃ τοσοῦτον διαφέρει τῶν ἄλλων δικαστηρίων, ὥστε καὶ παρ' αὐτοῖς ὁμολογεῖσθαι τοῖς ἁλισκομένοις δικαίαν ποιεῖσθαι τὴν κρίσιν. πρὸς ὃ δεῖ καὶ ὑμᾶς ἀποβλέποντας μὴ ἐπιτρέπειν τοῖς ἔξω τοῦ πράγματος λέγουσιν.

You yourselves are to blame, gentlemen. You have given the means to the speakers who come in here, you who possess as noblest example among the Greeks the synedrion on the Areopagos, which is so much better than other lawcourts that even those whom it convicts admit that its judgments are fair. You should look to it and not permit the speakers to speak beside the point.

For just decisions on the part of the Areopagos, see Demosthenes 23.66 (**6**). That speakers before the Areopagos must keep to the point is also noted in Lysias 3.46 and Lucian, *Anacharsis* 19.

Note that the Areopagos here is called a synedrion. For discussion of the word, see *Agora* III, pp. 126–127.

24. Lysias 1 (*On the Murder of Eratosthenes*) 30 *ca.* 400–380 B.C.E.

ἀνάγνωθι δέ μοι καὶ τοῦτον τὸν νόμον ἐκ τῆς στήλης τῆς ἐξ Ἀρείου πάγου. ΝΟΜΟΣ. ἀκούετε, ὦ ἄνδρες, ὅτι αὐτῶι τῶι δικαστηρίωι τῶι ἐξ Ἀρείου πάγου, ὧι καὶ πάτριόν ἐστι καὶ ἐφ' ἡμῶν ἀποδέδοται τοῦ φόνου τὰς δίκας δικάζειν, διαρρήδην εἴρηται τοῦτον μὴ καταγιγνώσκειν φόνου, ὃς ἂν ἐπὶ δάμαρτι τῆι ἑαυτοῦ μοιχὸν λαβὼν ταύτην τὴν τιμωρίαν ποιήσηται.

Read this law also from the stele on the Areopagos. (The law is read.) You hear, gentlemen, that for the very court of the Areopagos, to which it has been given by ancestral custom and in our own time to try cases of homicide, it is expressly forbidden to find guilty of homicide a man who catches an adulterer with his wife and punishes him in this way.

Note that the Areopagos is here referred to as a dikasterion. This speech can have been delivered at Delphinion, since the defendant claims that his action was justified. If, however, Eratosthenes' family did not agree to that line of defense, the trial would take place on the Areopagos.

25. [Lysias] 6 (*Andokides*) 14 soon after 399 B.C.E.

καίτοι καὶ ἐν Ἀρείωι πάγωι, ἐν τῶι σεμνοτάτωι καὶ δικαιοτάτωι δικαστηρίωι, ὁμολογῶν μὲν ἀδικεῖν ἀποθνήισκει, ἐὰν δὲ ἀμφισβητῆι, ἐλέγχεται, καὶ πολλοὶ οὐδὲν ἔδοξαν ἀδικεῖν.

And yet on the Areopagos, in that most august and just dikasterion, a man who admits his guilt is put to death, while if he contests the charge he is put to the proof, and many have been judged to have done no wrong at all.

26. Lysias 26 (*Evandros*) 11–12 382 B.C.E.

ταύτης δὲ τῆς ἀρχῆς ἀξιούμενος αὐτὸς καθ' αὑτὸν ἄρξει, καὶ μετὰ τῆς ἐν Ἀρείωι πάγωι βουλῆς τὸν ἅπαντα χρόνον τῶν μεγίστων κύριος γενήσεται ... καὶ φόνου δίκας δικάζοντα, ὃν ἔδει αὐτὸν ὑπὸ τῆς ἐν Ἀρείωι πάγωι βουλῆς κρίνεσθαι;

But if he is approved for this office, he will hold it by himself, and as a member of the council on the Areopagos he will control the most important matters for unlimited time ... [what will the citizens think when they find] ... a judge in homicide trials who should have been tried himself by the council on the Areopagos?

(1) Pausanias 1.28.4–7

(8) Photios, *Bibliotheca* 535a22–34

27. Plutarch, *Solon* 19.1–4 *ca.* 40–*ca.* 120 C.E.

Συστησάμενος δὲ τὴν ἐν Ἀρείωι πάγωι βουλὴν ἐκ τῶν κατ' ἐνιαυτὸν ἀρχόντων ... ἔτι δ' ὁρῶν τὸν δῆμον οἰδοῦντα καὶ θρασυνόμενον τῆι τῶν χρεῶν ἀφέσει, δευτέραν προσκατένειμε βουλήν, ἀπὸ φυλῆς ἑκάστης, τεττάρων οὐσῶν, ἑκατὸν ἄνδρας ἐπιλεξάμενος, οὓς προβουλεύειν ἔταξε τοῦ δήμου καὶ μηδὲν ἐᾶν ἀπροβούλευτον εἰς ἐκκλησίαν εἰσφέρεσθαι. τὴν δ' ἄνω βουλὴν ἐπίσκοπον πάντων καὶ φύλακα τῶν νόμων ἐκάθισεν.... οἱ μὲν οὖν πλεῖστοι τὴν ἐξ Ἀρείου πάγου βουλήν, ὥσπερ εἴρηται, Σόλωνα συστήσασθαί φασι· καὶ μαρτυρεῖν αὐτοῖς δοκεῖ μάλιστα τὸ μηδαμοῦ τὸν Δράκοντα λέγειν μηδ' ὀνομάζειν Ἀρεοπαγίτας, ἀλλὰ τοῖς ἐφέταις ἀεὶ διαλέγεσθαι περὶ τῶν φονικῶν. ὁ δὲ τρισκαιδέκατος ἄξων τοῦ Σόλωνος τὸν ὄγδοον ἔχει τῶν νόμων οὕτως αὐτοῖς ὀνόμασι γεγραμμένον. ἀτίμων ὅσοι ἄτιμοι ἦσαν πρὶν ἢ Σόλωνα ἄρξαι, ἐπιτίμους εἶναι πλὴν ὅσοι ἐξ Ἀρείου πάγου ἢ ὅσοι ἐκ τῶν ἐφετῶν ἢ ἐκ Πρυτανείου καταδικασθέντες ὑπὸ τῶν βασιλέων ἐπὶ φόνωι, ἢ σφαγαῖσιν ἢ ἐπὶ τυραννίδι ἔφευγον ὅτε ὁ θεσμὸς ἐφάνη ὅδε. ταῦτα δὴ πάλιν ὡς πρὸ τῆς Σόλωνος ἀρχῆς καὶ νομοθεσίας τὴν ἐξ Ἀρείου πάγου βουλὴν οὖσαν ἐνδείκνυται. τίνες γὰρ ἦσαν οἱ πρὸ Σόλωνος ἐν Ἀρείωι πάγωι καταδικασθέντες, εἰ πρῶτος Σόλων ἔδωκε τῆι ἐξ Ἀρείου πάγου βουλῆι τὸ κρίνειν;

After [Solon] had established the Council on the Areopagos, consisting of those who had been archons each year ... seeing that the demos was uneasy and bold because of their release from debt, he established another council by choosing 100 men from each of the four tribes. To these he assigned the duty of deliberating on public matters before the people did, and they were not to allow any matter to come before the ekklesia without such previous deliberation. Then he made the upper council an overseer of everything and guardian of the laws....

Now most say that Solon established the Council on the Areopagos as has been stated. And their view seems to be supported by the fact that Drakon nowhere speaks of or names the Areopagites, but always addresses the ephetai in cases of homicide. But the thirteenth tablet of Solon contains the eighth of his laws written in these very words: "Of the disfranchised, all who were disfranchised before Solon became archon shall be restored to the franchise except those who having been found guilty on the Areopagos or by the ephetai or in the Prytaneion of murder or bloodshed or attempted tyranny were in exile by action of the basileis when this law was made known." This surely proves that the Council of the Areopagos was in existence before the archonship and legislation of Solon. For how could men have been condemned on the Areopagos before the time of Solon, if Solon was the first to give the council of the Areopagos its jurisdiction?

Pollux 8.125 (**9**), in stating that the Areopagos was established by Solon, may have been using as a source one of the majority (πλεῖστοι) cited by Plutarch. But Aristotle's descriptions in the *Athenaion Politeia* of a pre-Solonian council of the Areopagos and Plutarch's reasoning, if his quotation from the amnesty law preserves the original wording, seem persuasive. Most modern authorities believe in a very early date for the Areopagos (Bonner and Smith 1930, pp. 88–89; MacDowell 1963, p. 39; Wade-Gery 1958, "Eupatridai, Archons and Areopagos," pp. 86–115). See above, Andokides 1.78 (**14**), for similar language and exceptions to an amnesty law included in the decree of Patrokleides (405 B.C.E.).

(2) Pollux 8.117

The lawcourts [dikasteria] at Athens: the Areopagos used to try cases of homicide and wounding with intent, arson, and poison, if the one who gave the poison succeeded in killing. An oath was taken by both parties and the trial was held after the oath. Neither an introductory speech nor lamenting was permitted. After the first speech, the accused could go into exile, but not if he had killed his parents. They would judge every month on three successive days, namely, the fourth, third, and second days from the end of the month. The nine annual archons, after giving their accounts, were on each occasion always added to the Areopagites. They held the trials under the open sky. Cousins [and closer relatives only] could prosecute for homicide, and in the oath they could ask who was related to the man who had been killed. And if he be a house servant, one is allowed to denounce him.

(9) Pollux 8.125

28. Agora I 6524, lines 11–16 and 22–26 — 337/6 B.C.E.

... μὴ ἐξεῖναι δὲ τῶν βουλευτῶν τῶν τῆς βουλῆς τῆς ἐξ Ἀρείου πάγου καταλελυ[μ]ένου τοῦ δήμου ἢ τῆς δημοκρατίας τῆς Ἀθήνησιν ἀνιέναι εἰς Ἄρειον πάγον μηδὲ συνκαθίζειν ἐν τῶι συνεδρίωι μηδὲ βουλεύειν μηδὲ περὶ ἑνός....

ἀναγράψαι δὲ τόνδε τὸν νόμον ἐν στήλαις λιθίναις δυοῖν τὸν γραμματέα τῆς βουλῆς καὶ στῆσαι τὴμ μὲν ἐπὶ τῆς εἰσόδου τῆς εἰς Ἄρειον πάγον τῆς εἰς τὸ βουλευτήριον εἰσιόντι τὴν δὲ ἐν τῆι ἐκκλησίαι....

... If the demos and the democracy at Athens are overthrown, the members of the Council of the Areopagos are not to be allowed to go up to the Areopagos nor to sit together in the synedrion nor to deliberate about anything....

The secretary of the boule is to inscribe this law on two stone stelai and set one up at the entrance to the Areopagos, the entrance for a person going to the bouleuterion, and the other in the ekklesia....

A decree containing provision for action to be taken or not taken in case the government is overthrown, inscribed on a marble stele. Found under the north end of the Stoa of Attalos, it is the antityranny decree of 336 B.C.E.; see B. D. Meritt, "Greek Inscriptions," *Hesperia* 23, 1952 [pp. 340–380], pp. 355–359; *SEG* XII 87.

This decree, which has no direct bearing on the homicide court, is cited because of the topographical points it raises. The bouleuterion (lines 25–26) beyond the entrance to the Areopagos is probably a meeting place of the Council of the Areopagos on the hill and is the same as the synedrion of line 15; see Wycherley 1955, pp. 118–121 and *Agora* III, pp. 126–128. If this bouleuterion/synedrion was a covered building, there had to be another meeting place within the precinct that was open to the sky, as was required for homicide trials (Antiphon 5.10–11 [**62**]). But neither word, *bouleuterion* or *synedrion*, necessarily implies "roofed structure".

THE COURT AT DELPHINION

The Delphinion was a sanctuary shared by Apollo Delphinios and Artemis Delphinia and is said to have been founded by Aigeus. The court that met at Delphinion tried persons who admitted that they had killed but claimed that they had done it justly.

Pausanias, after mentioning the statue of Pythian Apollo near the Olympieion, continues, "There is also another sanctuary of Apollo with the epithet Delphinios," but he uses no connecting place word. According to Plutarch, the house of Aigeus stood "where now is the periphrakton in the Delphinion" and "the Hermes to the east of the sanctuary is called that at Aigeus' gate." There was a temple in the sanctuary, according to Pausanias, which was being built when Theseus came to Athens.

John Travlos, in excavations conducted in 1962, uncovered the foundations of a large temple and a public building just south of the Olympieion. He sees in this complex the Temple of Apollo Delphinios and the lawcourt at Delphinion (1971, p. 83). This location is in accord with Pausanias in that it is near the Olympieion and (inferentially) the sanctuary of Pythian Apollo, close to the city wall (and so a gate), and in the region of other early sanctuaries between the Olympieion and the Ilissos. Wolf Aly ("Delphinios. Beiträge zur Stadtgeschichte von Milet und Athen," *Klio* 11, 1911 [pp. 1–25], p. 8, note 2) suggested that the Pythion and Delphinion were one and the same. This suggestion, based on a passage in Hesychios which states that Peisistratos built the temple in the Pythion, is rejected by Judeich (1931, p. 386, note 5), who believes that there was no temple at the Pythion.

Orators do not indicate any case specifically as being or having been tried at the Delphinion. This is perhaps not surprising, because the name of the specific court in which a case was being tried rarely appears in any of the speeches. Lysias' first oration (*On the Killing of Eratosthenes*) provides an example of a trial for justifiable homicide, which, according to Aristotle and Demosthenes, should be tried at the Delphinion. It is generally agreed by modern scholars that the trial was held there, although the court is not specifically named (MacDowell 1963, pp. 71–72; Bonner and Smith 1930, p. 271).

The Delphinion is named in two speeches, however, as the place at which an oath was taken before a *diaitetes*, or arbitrator. In both cases a mother is testifying as to the paternity of her sons, that is, in a question of family relationship or citizenship ([Demosthenes] 40.11 [**30**] and Isaios 12.9 [**33**]). Neither has any connection whatsoever with homicide. Lipsius (1905–1919, p. 228, note 33) points out that in these two texts the Delphinion is named only as the place in which an oath was taken before an arbitrator and that it does not necessarily follow that a panel of diaitetai held regular meetings at the Delphinion. The panels of diaitetai acting for the tribes Oineis and Erechtheis met in the Heliaia ([Demosthenes] 47.12 [**118**], *ca.* 353 B.C.E.), and a meeting of diaitetai is recorded at the Stoa Poikile (Demosthenes 45.17 [**162**], *ca.* 351 B.C.E.). Assuming, however, that the diaitetai did witness oaths at their regular meeting place, one might suggest that the panels for the tribes

Akamantis (all the Thorikians of [Demosthenes] 40) and Aigeis (Erchians of Isaios, hypothesis to 12) met regularly at the Delphinion. The arbitration at the Stoa Poikile possibly was being held by the panel acting for the tribe Aiantis (if Amphias, who deposited the document in question, was in fact from Aphidna). See Lipsius, *op. cit.*, p. 227 for the ten panels of diaitetai, one from each tribe.

As further testimonia for the cult and sanctuary of Apollo Delphinios and Artemis Delphinia, two inscriptions are often cited, both fragmentary and uninformative.

(1) *IG* II–III^2 3725 (= III 939), known only "ex schedis Fourmonti", has been much restored and emended to read as a dedication by a priestess to Apollo Delphinios and Artemis Delphinia.

(2) *IG* II–III^2 4743 (= III 138), formerly built into the Akropolis wall, seems to be a dedication of the 1st and 2nd century C.E. by a herald who has recovered from an illness. The dedication may be to Δελφ[ινίωι θεῶι . . .].

(14) Andokides 1 (*On the Mysteries*) 78

(3) Aristotle, *Ath. Pol.* 57.3

(4) Aristotle, *Politics* 1300b27–28

See **4** above, where functions of the court at Delphinion are described, but the court is not named.

29. Bekker, *Anecdota Graeca* 1.255.19–21

ἐπὶ Δελφινίωι· δικαστήριον ἓν τῶν φονικῶν, ὅ φασιν Αἰγέα ἱδρύσασθαι αὐτὸ ἀπὸ Δελφῶν ἥκοντα Ἀπόλλωνι Δελφινίωι καὶ Ἀρτέμιδι Δελφινίαι.

At Delphinion: one of the homicide courts, which they say Aigeus founded when he arrived from Delphi and dedicated to Apollo Delphinios and Artemis Delphinia.

Compare Pollux 8.119 (**2**).

(5) Bekker, *Anecdota Graeca* 1.311.13

(6) Demosthenes 23.74

30. [Demosthenes] 40 (*Boiotos* II) 11 — 347/6 B.C.E.?

ὡς γὰρ πρὸς τὸν διαιτητὴν ἀπήντησε, παραβᾶσα πάντα τὰ ὡμολογημένα ἡ Πλαγγὼν δέχεταί τε τὴν πρόκλησιν καὶ ὄμνυσιν ἐν τῶι Δελφινίωι ἄλλον ὅρκον ἐναντίον τῶι προτέρωι.

As he met her before the arbitrator, Plangon, contravening everything that she had agreed to, accepted the challenge and swore another oath in the Delphinion opposite to the former one.

With this oath in the Delphinion, Plangon declared that the father of Boiotos and Pamphilos, her sons, was Mantias.

31. *Etymologicum Magnum*, *s.v.* ἐπὶ Δελφινίωι — 12th century C.E.

ἐπὶ Δελφινίωι· Δικαστήριον Ἀθήνησιν, ἐπὶ τῶν ὁμολογούντων φόνους δεδρακέναι. οἱ δὲ φασίν, ὅτι Κρητῶν χειμαζομένων, εἰκασθεὶς δελφῖνι ὁ Ἀπόλλων ἔσωσεν αὐτοὺς εἰς τὴν Ἀττικὴν κομίσας· ἀνθ' ὧν Ἀπόλλωνι Δελφινίωι ἱδρύσασθαι ἱερόν. δικαστήριον γενέσθαι τῶν φονικῶν ἐν ὧι καὶ Θησέα κεχρίσθαι ὑπὲρ τῶν φόνων τῶν περὶ Σκείρωνα καὶ Σίνιν.

At Delphinion: a dikasterion at Athens for those who admit that they have committed a homicide. The story goes that when some Cretans were struck by a storm, Apollo in the form of a dolphin saved them by bringing them to Attica. In return for this, they founded a sanctuary of Apollo Delphinios. It became a lawcourt for homicide trials, and in this court even Theseus was tried for killing Skiron and Sinis.

The scholion on Demosthenes 23.74 (**34**) includes a story of Apollo appearing as a dolphin as the explanation of the epithet Delphinios but does not associate that transformation with Attica, as is done here.

32. Harpokration, *s.v.* ἐπὶ Δελφινίωι 2nd century C.E.

ἐπὶ Δελφινίωι· δικαστήριόν ἐστιν οὕτω καλούμενον Ἀθήνησι. δικάζονται δὲ ἐνταῦθα οἱ ὁμολογοῦντες μὲν ἀπεκτονέναι, δικαίως δὲ πεποιηκέναι τοῦτο λέγοντες, ὡς Δημοσθένης ἐν τῶι κατ' Ἀριστοκράτους δηλοῖ καὶ Ἀριστοτέλης ἐν τῆι Ἀθηναίων πολιτείαι.

At Delphinion: there is a court called this in Athens. There those who admit that they have killed but say that they have done it justly are tried, as Demosthenes makes clear in the speech against Aristokrates and as Aristotle says in the *Constitution of Athens*.

(7) Harpokration, *s.v.* ἐφέται

33. Isaios 12 (*Euphiletos*) 9 344/3 B.C.E.?

ἡ τοῦ Εὐφιλήτου μήτηρ, ἣν οὗτοι ὁμολογοῦσιν ἀστὴν εἶναι, ὅρκον ὀμόσαι ἐπὶ τοῦ διαιτητοῦ ἐβούλετο ἐπὶ Δελφινίωι ἦ μὴν τουτονὶ Εὐφίλητον εἶναι ἐξ αὑτῆς καὶ τοῦ ἡμετέρου πατρός.

The mother of Euphiletos, who they admit is a citizen, was willing to swear an oath in the presence of the arbitrator at Delphinion that Euphiletos, then present, was the issue of herself and our father.

Euphiletos had been crossed off the list of deme members of Erchia and was suing his fellow demesmen to recover his citizenship.

See Bonner and Smith 1938, p. 113 for the suggestion that this speech may be some ten years earlier than 344/3, a date that is usually given.

34. *Lexicon Patmense*, *s.v.* ἐπὶ Δελφινίωι
Commentary on Demosthenes 23.74.

ἐπὶ Δελφινίωι· τοῦτο τὸ δικαστήριον ἐγένετο μετὰ τὸ Ἀρεοπαγιτικὸν ἐπὶ Αἰγέως ὃς καὶ ἱδρύσατο ἱερὸν Ἀρτέμιδος καὶ Ἀπόλλωνος Δελφινίου. οὕτω δὲ ὁ θεὸς ἐκλήθη, ὅτι ὤφθη τοῖς ἀπὸ Κρήτης Κνιδίοις ἐπὶ μαντείαν πλέουσιν εἰς Δελφοὺς μεταβαλὼν τὴν μορφὴν εἰς δελφῖνα. ἐκρίθη δὲ Θησεὺς ἐνταῦθα ὑπὲρ ὧν ἀπέκτεινεν ἐκ Τροιζῆνος εἰς Ἀθήνας πορευόμενος, καὶ ἐπὶ τοῖς Παλλαντίδαις· ἀπελογεῖτο δὲ ὁμολογῶν μὲν τὸν φόνον, δικαίως δὲ φάσκων δεδρακέναι. ὅθεν καὶ οἱ ἐνταῦθα κρινόμενοι ἐπὶ φόνοις ὁμολογουμένοις μέν, δικαίως δὲ γεγονόσι δικάζονται.

At Delphinion: this court was established after that of the Areopagos at the time of Aigeus who also founded the sanctuary of Artemis and Apollo Delphinios. The god was called thus because he was seen in the form of a dolphin by the Knidians as they sailed from Crete to Delphi to seek an oracle. Theseus was tried here for those whom he had killed on his way from Troizen to Athens, and for the Pallantidai. His defense was to admit that he had done the murder, but to claim that he had done it justly. Wherefore those tried here are judged for homicides they admit but that were done justly.

35. Pausanias 1.19.1 *ca.* 150 C.E.

μετὰ δὲ τὸν ναὸν τοῦ Διὸς τοῦ 'Ολυμπίου πλησίον ἄγαλμά ἐστιν Ἀπόλλωνος Πυθίου· ἔστι δὲ καὶ ἄλλο ἱερὸν Ἀπόλλωνος ἐπίκλησιν Δελφινίου. λέγουσι δὲ ὡς ἐξειργασμένου τοῦ ναοῦ πλὴν τῆς ὀροφῆς ἀγνὼς ἔτι τοῖς πᾶσιν ἀφίκοιτο Θησεὺς ἐς τὴν πόλιν· οἷα δὲ χιτῶνα ἔχοντος αὐτοῦ ποδήρη καὶ πεπλεγμένης ἐς εὐπρεπές οἱ τῆς κόμης, ὡς ἐγίνετο κατὰ τὸν τοῦ Δελφινίου ναόν, οἱ τὴν στέγην οἰκοδομοῦντες ἤροντο σὺν χλευασίαι, ὅτι δὴ παρθένος ἐν ὥραι γάμου πλανᾶται μόνη· Θησεὺς δὲ ἄλλο μὲν αὐτοῖς ἐδήλωσεν οὐδέν, ἀπολύσας δὲ ὡς λέγεται τῆς ἁμάξης τοὺς βοῦς, ἥ σφισι παρῆν, ἀνέρριψεν ἐς ὑψηλότερον ἢ τῶι ναῶι τὴν στέγην ἐποιοῦντο.

After the temple of Olympian Zeus there is nearby a statue of Pythian Apollo. There is also another sanctuary of Apollo with the epithet Delphinios. The story has it that when the temple was finished except for the roof, Theseus arrived in the city and was not yet recognized by anyone. Wearing a tunic that reached to his feet and with his hair neatly plaited, he came to the temple of the Delphinian; those who were building the roof mockingly asked what a maiden of marriageable age was doing wandering about alone. The only answer Theseus made was to loose, it is said, the oxen from their cart and to throw them (or the cart?) higher than the roof of the temple the men were building.

(1) Pausanias 1.28.10

At Delphinion there are held the trials of persons who plead that the homicide which they committed was justifiable. On such a plea Theseus was acquitted when he had slain the rebel Pallas and his sons. But in former days, before the acquittal of Theseus, the custom for all was for a homicide to go into exile or to stay and be killed the same way as he killed.

(8) Photios, *Bibliotheca* 535a25–26

36. Plutarch, *Theseus* 12.6 1st–2nd century C.E.

λέγεται δὲ τῆς κύλικος πεσούσης ἐκχυθῆναι τὸ φάρμακον ὅπου νῦν ἐν Δελφινίωι τὸ περίφρακτόν ἐστιν, ἐνταῦθα γὰρ ὁ Αἰγεὺς ὤικει, καὶ τὸν 'Ερμῆν τὸν πρὸς ἕω τοῦ ἱεροῦ καλοῦσιν ἐπ' Αἰγέως πύλαις.

And it is said that as the cup fell, the poison was spilled where now is the enclosure in Delphinion, for that is where the house of Aigeus stood, and the Hermes to the east of the sanctuary they call the Hermes at Aigeus' gate.

At Medea's suggestion Aigeus had been persuaded to entertain Theseus as a stranger guest and to poison him. Aigeus, however, recognized Theseus by his sword and knocked the cup of poison to the ground.

37. Plutarch, *Theseus* 14.1 1st–2nd century C.E.

καὶ χειρωσάμενος ἐπεδείξατο ζῶντα διὰ τοῦ ἄστεος ἐλάσας, εἶτα τῶι Ἀπόλλωνι τῶι Δελφινίωι κατέθυσεν.

After [Theseus] had mastered [the Marathonian bull], he made a display, driving it alive through the city, and then sacrificed it to the Delphinian Apollo.

38. Plutarch, *Theseus* 18.1 1st–2nd century C.E.

γενομένου δὲ τοῦ κλήρου παραλαβὼν τοὺς λαχόντας ὁ Θησεὺς ἐκ τοῦ Πρυτανείου, καὶ παρελθὼν εἰς Δελφίνιον, ἔθηκεν ὑπὲρ αὐτῶν τῶι Ἀπόλλωνι τὴν ἱκετηρίαν. . . . εὐξάμενος δὲ κατέβαινεν ἕκτηι μηνὸς ἐπὶ θάλασσαν ἱσταμένου Μουνυχιῶνος, ἧι καὶ νῦν ἔτι τὰς κόρας πέμπουσιν ἱλασομένας εἰς Δελφίνιον.

When the lot was cast [for the youths to be sent to Crete], Theseus took those upon whom it fell from the Prytaneion and went to the Delphinion, where he dedicated his suppliant's branch to Apollo in their behalf. . . . After he had finished his prayers, he went down to the sea on the sixth day of Mounychion, on which day even now [the Athenians] still send their maidens to the Delphinion to propitiate the god.

(2) Pollux 8.119

The [court] at Delphinion is said to have been founded by Aigeus for Apollo Delphinios and Artemis Delphinia. The first to be tried there was Theseus, who was averting the curse of the robbers and the Pallantidai he killed. He admitted that he had killed them but said that he had done it justly.

39. *Suda, s.v.* ἐπὶ Δελφινίωι 10th century C.E.

ἐπὶ Δελφινίωι· δικαστήριον Ἀθήνησιν ἐπὶ τῶν ὁμολογούντων μὲν δεδρακέναι φόνους, κατὰ νόμους δέ.

At Delphinion: a dikasterion in Athens for those who admit that they have committed a homicide but claim that it is lawful.

The Court at Palladion

According to legend, the first trial at Palladion was that of Demophon, or whichever Athenians had stolen the Palladion from Argives returning from Troy and in so doing had killed some of the Argives. The trial was held at the place where the Palladion was in due course established, presumably within a sanctuary of Athena. In later times, at least, this sanctuary was shared by Zeus.

A location of this first trial (and so of the original sanctuary of the Palladion) at or near Phaleron is implied, and sometimes stated, in the story of the origin of the court, told in slightly varying forms by Pausanias, Pollux, Phanodemos, Kleitodemos, and in a scholion to Aischines. Plutarch, however, in a description of the battle between the Athenians and the Amazons, quotes "Kleidemos" (= Kleitodemos), the Atthidographer of the 4th century B.C.E., as saying that the Athenians, attacking from the Palladion and Ardettos and the Lykeion, drove back the wing of the Amazons based on the Pnyx. This combination of localities suggests a location for the Palladion somewhere along the southeast edge of the city and to the west of Ardettos, that is, in the general region of the early sanctuaries near the Olympieion. John Travlos in 1962 and 1966 discovered foundations of a stoa and part of a peristyle about one hundred meters west of the southwest corner of the terrace wall of the Olympieion. He believes these remains belong to the Palladion: 1971, pp. 412–413 and 1974, pp. 500–511; compare, however, "Sites," pp. 97–98 above. For a suggestion that there were two sanctuaries called Palladion, see pp. 47–48 above.

Cases of involuntary homicide, of plotting to kill (bouleusis), and of murders of a slave, metic, or foreigner were tried in the court at the Palladion, according to Aristotle, *Athenaion Politeia* and a scholion to Aischines. Harpokration mentions only cases of involuntary homicide and bouleusis. Demosthenes, in his listing of the homicide courts, mentions only cases of involuntary homicide, as do Pausanias, Pollux, and later writers.

The court at the Palladion still served as a homicide court in the late 5th and 4th centuries, as shown by several contemporary references (Aristophanes as quoted by Eustathios [**46**], Aischines 2.87 [**40**], Demosthenes 47.70 [**42**] and 59.9 [**43**], and Isokrates 18.52 [**49**]).

Originally, fifty-one ephetai served as judges in this court. Some modern authorities believe that by the 4th century the ephetai had been replaced by ordinary heliastic juries of larger size (G. Smith, "Dicasts in the Ephetic Courts," *CP* 19, 1924, pp. 353–358; Bonner and Smith 1930, pp. 270–274; Lipsius 1905–1915, p. 413). Part of the evidence for the replacement is mention of a dikasterion of 700 in Isokrates 18.54 (**49**), usually interpreted as referring to the case at the Palladion just described, and a passage in [Demosthenes] 59.9 (**43**) about another case at the Palladion. In Demosthenes, the manuscript reading is that Stephanos got few votes out of 500 drachmai, and many editors delete the "drachmai" and present the passage as "few votes out of 500." MacDowell (1963, pp. 52–57), however, argues that since ephetai are mentioned in other 4th-century texts, they did continue to serve as dikasts. He suggests that Isokrates' reference to a panel of 700 applies to a different trial, perhaps one for perjury, and not to the murder case tried at the Palladion, and that there is no real justification for deleting the word "drachmai" from the Demosthenes manuscript. For detailed arguments and full references on this question, see MacDowell, *op. cit.*, pp. 54–55. (Note that the number 700 is unparalleled as the sum of dikasts in a single panel. Φ [500] for Ψ [700] would be an easy emendation.)

In the 2nd century B.C.E., Kleitomachos, a pupil of Karneades, had his own school of philosophy at the Palladion for eleven years starting in the archonship of Hagnotheos, 140/39 B.C.E. (*FGrHist* 244 Apollodoros of Athens F55–F56 and Ferguson 1911, pp. 337–338). Plutarch, *On Exile* 14, includes the Palladion among the schools of the wise men along with the Academy, the Stoa, and the Odeion. This may be a reference only to the school of Kleitomachos, or it may mean, as seems more probable, that the Palladion did continue to be a resort of philosophers for a longer period of time.

Information relating to the cult and so to the sanctuary proper is found in four inscriptions:

(1) *IG* I³ 369, *logistai* accounts of money borrowed from the other gods; Athena at the Palladion is named in lines 73 and 90, in 423/2 B.C.E.

(2) *IG* II–III² 1096, a letter of the time of Augustus from an Attic genos to Delphi, is dated by the priest of Zeus at the Palladion (partly restored).

(3) *IG* II–III² 3177, of the Augustan period; the priest of Zeus at the Palladion, on orders of an oracle of Pythian Apollo, set up and dedicated another statue of Pallas.

(4) *IG* II–III² 5055; the priest of Zeus in the Palladion is named on one of the theater seats.

From these later citations, particularly that mentioning a dedication of a statue of Pallas, it seems clear that Zeus and Athena were closely associated at the Palladion, although whether in a single or in separate shrines is uncertain. Thus the Palladion, at least as a sanctuary, had a very long existence from the earliest days of Athenian civic life well down into Roman times.

40. Aischines 2 (*The False Embassy*) 87 — 343 B.C.E.

. . . οἱ πατέρες ἡμῶν ἐν ταῖς φονικαῖς δίκαις ταῖς ἐπὶ Παλλαδίωι . . . κατέδειξαν τέμνοντα τὰ τόμια τὸν νικῶντα τῆι ψήφωι ἐξορκίζεσθαι, καὶ τοῦτο ὑμῖν πάτριόν ἐστι ἔτι καὶ νῦν. . . .

Our fathers, in the trials for bloodshed at Palladion, prescribed that he who wins his case must cut in pieces the sacrificial flesh and take a solemn oath, and the custom of your fathers is in force to this day. . . .

Compare Photios, *Lexicon* I, *s.v.* διωμοσία (p. 47, note 19 above).

41. Schol. Aischines 2 (*The False Embassy*) 87

ἐπὶ Παλλαδίωι· ἐπὶ τούτωι ἐκρίνοντο οἱ ἀκούσιοι φόνοι. οἱ δὲ ἐν τούτωι τῶι δικαστηρίωι δικάζοντες ἐκαλοῦντο ἐφέται, ἐδίκαζον δὲ ἀκουσίου φόνου καὶ βουλεύσεως καὶ οἰκέτην ἢ μέτοικον ἢ ξένον ἀποκτείναντι. ὠνομάσθη δὲ ἐντεῦθεν. Ἀργεῖοι τὸ Παλλάδιον ἔχοντες τὸ ἀπὸ Ἰλίου καὶ ἐκ Τροίας ἀνακομιζόμενοι ὡρμίσαντο Φαληροῖ, καὶ αὐτοὺς τῶν ἐγχωρίων τινὲς ἀκουσίως ἀναιροῦσιν. μενόντων δὲ ἐπὶ πολὺν χρόνον τῶν νεκρῶν ἀδιαφθόρων καὶ ἀψαύστων ὑπὸ θηρίων, πολυπραγμονήσαντες οἱ ἐγχώριοι ἔγνωσαν παρ' Ἀκάμαντος ὅτι Ἀργεῖοι ἦσαν καὶ τὸ Παλλάδιον εὑρόντες ἱδρύσαντό τε παρὰ τῆι Ἀθηνᾶι τῆι Φαληροῖ, καὶ τοὺς νεκροὺς θάψαντες δικαστήριον ἐποίησαν ἐκεῖ τοῖς ἐπὶ ἀκουσίωι φόνωι φεύγουσιν.

At Palladion: here, cases of involuntary homicide were tried. Those who judge in this court were called ephetai, and they tried cases of involuntary homicide and conspiracy and cases in which someone killed a slave or metic or foreigner. It was so named for the following reason. Some Argives with the Palladion from Ilion on their way back from Troy put in at Phaleron, and some of the natives through ignorance killed them. When the bodies remained without decay for a long time and untouched by wild animals, the natives made inquiries and learned from Akamas that they were Argives. They found the Palladion and set it up at the sanctuary of Athena at Phaleron, and after they had buried the bodies, they established a lawcourt there for those charged with involuntary homicide.

See Pollux (**2**) and the *Suda* (**53**) for a similar story of the origin of the court, taken from Phanodemos, according to the *Suda*. The statement that the Palladion was set up in a sanctuary of Athena at Phaleron is found only in this scholion.

(3) Aristotle, *Ath. Pol.* 57.3

(4) Aristotle, *Politics* 1300b27
See **4** above. The function of the court is described, but the court is not named.

(5) Bekker, *Anecdota Graeca* 1.311.3–22

(6) Demosthenes 23.71

42. [Demosthenes] 47 (*Euergos and Mnesiboulos*) 70 — *ca.* 353 B.C.E.
(The speaker is quoting a reply given him by the exegetai.)

εἶτα πρὸς τὸν βασιλέα μὴ λαγχάνειν· οὐδὲ γὰρ ἐν τῶι νόμωι ἔστι σοι· οὐ γάρ ἐστιν ἐν γένει σοι ἡ ἄνθρωπος, οὐδὲ θεράπαινα, ἐξ ὧν σὺ λέγεις, οἱ δὲ νόμοι τούτων κελεύουσιν τὴν δίωξιν εἶναι· ὥστ' εἰ διομεῖ ἐπὶ Παλλαδίωι αὐτὸς καὶ ἡ γυνὴ καὶ τὰ παιδία . . . χείρων τε δόξεις πολλοῖς εἶναι. . . .

Further, do not bring a case before the basileus; it is not legally your concern, since from what you say, the woman is not a relative or slave of yours, and it is by a master or a relative that the laws order prosecution to be undertaken; so that if you yourself and your wife and children take the oath at the Palladion . . . many will think you ignoble. . . .

43. [Demosthenes] 59 (*Neaira*) 9 — *ca.* 340 B.C.E.

παρασκευασάμενος ἀνθρώπους δούλους καὶ κατασκευάσας ὡς Κυρηναῖοι εἴησαν, προεῖπεν αὐτῶι ἐπὶ Παλλαδίωι φόνου.

[Stephanos] suborned slaves and represented them as Kyreneans, and charged [Apollodoros] at the Palladion with homicide.

These two passages and one from Isokrates (**49**) show the court at the Palladion in use at the end of the 5th and during the 4th century.

44. [Demosthenes] 59 (*Neaira*) 10 — *ca.* 340 B.C.E.

ὀλίγας ψήφους μεταλαβὼν ἐκ πεντακοσίων δραχμῶν, ἀπῆλθεν ἐπιωρκηκὼς καὶ δόξας πονηρὸς εἶναι.

He received as his share a few votes from his outlay of 500 drachmai and left as a perjured man with a bad name.

See the introduction to "Palladion," p. 140 above, concerning the text here. "Five-hundred" has been taken to mean "500 votes cast by 500 dikasts."

45. *Etymologicum Magnum, s.v.* ἐπὶ Παλλαδίωι (= *FGrHist* 323 Kleidemos F20) 4th century B.C.E.

ἐπὶ Παλλαδίωι· Δικαστήριον Ἀθήνησιν, ἐν ὧι περὶ ἀκουσίου φόνου ἐδίκαζον. Κλειτόδημός φησιν ὅτι Ἀγαμέμνονος σὺν τῶι Παλλαδίωι προσενεχθέντος Ἀθήναζε, Δημοφῶντα ἁρπάσαι τὸ Παλλάδιον· τοῦ δὲ Ἀγαμέμνονος δυσχεραίνοντος, κρίσιν ὑποσχεῖν ἐπὶ πεντήκοντα Ἀθηναίων καὶ ν′ Ἀργείων· οὓς ἐφέτας κληθῆναι, διὰ τὸ παρ' ἀμφοτέρων ἐφεθῆναι αὐτοῖς περὶ τῆς κρίσεως.

At the Palladion: a lawcourt at Athens in which they tried cases of involuntary homicide. Kleitodemos says that when Agamemnon landed at Athens with the Palladion, Demophon stole the Palladion. Since Agamemnon was angry, Demophon underwent a trial with fifty Athenians and fifty Argives as judges; these were called ephetai from the fact that the matters of the case were referred to them from both sides.

Compare Harpokration (**48**) and *Suda* (**53**).

46. Eustathios, *Commentary on Homer, Odyssey* 1.321 (1419, 52–59) 12th century C.E.
(contains Aristophanes F602 [*PCG* III.2] + *FGrHist* 323 Kleidemos F20)

(οἱ παλαιοὶ) δικαστήριον ἱστοροῦσιν Ἀθήνησιν ἐπώνυμον τῆς Παλλάδος. Ἀριστοφάνης·
ἄκων κτενῶ σε, τέκνον. ὁ δ' ὑπεκρίνετο,
ἐπὶ Παλλαδίωι τἄρ', ὦ πάτερ, δώσεις δίκην.
ἐδίκαζον δὲ κατὰ Παυσανίαν ἐκεῖ ἀκουσίους φόνους οἱ ἐφέται. Ἀργεῖοι γὰρ (φησίν) ἀπὸ Ἰλίου πλέοντες, ἡνίκα προσέσχον Φαλήροις, ὑπὸ Ἀθηναίων ἀγνοούμενοι ἀνηιρέθησαν. ὕστερον δὲ Ἀκάμαντος γνωρίσαντος καὶ τοῦ ἱστορουμένου Παλλαδίου εὑρεθέντος κατὰ χρησμόν, αὐτόθι τὸ δικαστήριον ἀπέδειξαν. Κλειτόδημος δέ φησιν, Ἀγαμέμνονος σὺν τῶι Παλλαδίωι προσενεχθέντος ταῖς Ἀθήναις Δημοφῶντα τὸ Παλλάδιον ἁρπάσαι, καὶ πολλοὺς τῶν διωκόντων ἀνελεῖν. τοῦ δὲ Ἀγαμέμνονος δυσχεραίνοντος, κρίσιν αὐτοὺς ὑποσχεῖν ἐπὶ πεντήκοντα Ἀθηναίων καὶ τοσούτων Ἀργείων, οὓς ἐφέτας κληθῆναι διὰ τὸ παρ' ἀμφοτέρων ἐφεθῆναι αὐτοῖς περὶ κρίσεως. καὶ τὸ δικαστήριον ἐπώνυμον τῆι Παλλάδι γενέσθαι.

(The ancients) tell of a lawcourt at Athens named after Pallas, [as in these lines] from Aristophanes (F602 [*PCG* III.2]):
"Unwillingly I shall kill you my lad." The boy replied, "In that case, father, you'll be punished for it at the Palladion."
According to Pausanias, ephetai tried cases there of involuntary homicide. Argives, he says, sailing back from Ilion, were not recognized by the Athenians when they put ashore at Phaleron and were killed. Later, when Akamas recognized [them], and the famed Palladion was found, following the instructions of an oracle, they established the dikasterion at that spot. But Kleitodemos says that when Agamemnon put in at Athens with the Palladion, Demophon stole the Palladion and killed many of those pursuing him. Since Agamemnon was angry [about this], they underwent a trial with fifty Athenians and the same number of Argives as magistrates, whom they called ephetai because the matters of the trial were referred to them from both sides (*FGrHist* 323 Kleidemos F20). And the dikasterion was named after Pallas.

Except for the quotation from Aristophanes and the last sentence, the *Suda* presents virtually the same text. The latter, however, assigns the first version of the founding of the court to Phanodemos.

47. Harpokration, *s.v.* βουλεύσεως 2nd century C.E.

βουλεύσεως· ἐγκλήματος ὄνομα ἐπὶ δυοῖν ταττόμενον πραγμάτοιν· τὸ μὲν γάρ ἐστιν ὅταν ἐξ ἐπιβουλῆς τίς τινι κατασκευάσηι θάνατον, ἐάν τε ἀποθάνηι ὁ ἐπιβουλευθεὶς ἐάν τε μή, τὸ δ' ἕτερον ὅταν ἐγγεγραμμένος ὡς ὀφείλων τῶι δημοσίωι αὐτὸς δικάζηταί τινι ὡς οὐ δικαίως αὐτὸν ἐγγεγραφότι. τοῦ μὲν οὖν προτέρου μάρτυς 'Ισαῖος ἐν τῶι πρὸς Εὐκλείδην, ἐπὶ Παλλαδίωι λέγων εἶναι τὰς δίκας, Δείναρχος δὲ ἐν τῶι κατὰ Πιστίου ἐν Ἀρείωι πάγωι. Ἀριστοτέλης δ' ἐν τῆι Ἀθηναίων πολιτείαι τῶι 'Ισαίωι συμφωνεῖ....

"Of bouleusis": the name of an indictment drawn up on one of two matters. The first is when a man arranges death for another by a plot, whether the one plotted against dies or not. The second is when a person listed as being in debt to the state brings a charge against someone else on the grounds that this second person has wrongly listed him as debtor. Of the first type of indictment, Isaios in the speech in reply to Eukleides (F62) is a witness, saying that these trials were at the Palladion, but Deinarchos in the speech against Pistios (15 F2) says that they were on the Areopagos. Aristotle in the *Constitution of Athens* agrees with Isaios....

Neither of the two speeches referred to has survived. For a discussion of the meaning of bouleusis (planning, contriving), see MacDowell 1963, pp. 60–62, where it is suggested that Harpokration possibly misunderstood Deinarchos, for there is no other evidence to suggest that such cases were tried at the Areopagos.

48. Harpokration, *s.v.* ἐπὶ Παλλαδίωι 2nd century C.E.

ἐπὶ Παλλαδίωι· Δημοσθένης ἐν τῶι κατ' Ἀριστοκράτους, δικαστήριόν ἐστιν οὕτω καλούμενον, ὡς καὶ Ἀριστοτέλης ἐν Ἀθηναίων πολιτείαι, ἐν ὧι δικάζουσιν ἀκουσίου φόνου καὶ βουλεύσεως οἱ ἐφέται. ἔσχε δὲ καὶ τὸ δικαστήριον τὴν τοῦ Παλλαδίου ἐπωνυμίαν καὶ οἱ δικασταὶ τὴν τῶν ἐφετῶν ἐντεῦθεν. Ἀγαμέμνονος μετὰ τῶν Ἀργείων σὺν τῶι Παλλαδίωι προσενεχθέντος Ἀθήναις ἐξ 'Ιλίου Δημοφῶν ἁρπάζει τὸ Παλλάδιον καὶ πολλοὺς τῶν διωκόντων ἀναιρεῖ. Ἀγαμέμνων δὲ δυσχεράνας δίκην τὸν ἁρπάσαντα ἀπαιτεῖ, καὶ συνίσταται τὸ δικαστήριον ἐπὶ πεντήκοντα μὲν Ἀθηναίων, πεντήκοντα δὲ Ἀργείων, οὓς ἐφέτας ἐκάλεσαν διὰ τὸ παρ' ἀμφοτέρων ἐφεθῆναι αὐτοῖς τὰ τῆς κρίσεως.

At the Palladion: used by Demosthenes in the speech against Aristokrates (23). It is the name of a dikasterion, also mentioned in Aristotle's *Constitution of the Athenians*, in which the ephetai try cases of involuntary homicide and of bouleusis. The court had the name Palladion and the dikasts the name of ephetai for the following reasons. When Agamemnon and the Argives with the Palladion put in at Athens on the way back from Ilion, Demophon stole the Palladion and killed many of those pursuing him. An angry Agamemnon demanded a trial of the thief and established a court of fifty Athenians and fifty Argives, whom they called ephetai from the fact that the matters of the case were referred to them from both sides.

See *Suda* (**53**), which ascribes this story of the establishment of the court to Kleitodemos (*scil.* Kleidemos), the Atthidographer of *ca.* 350 B.C.E. It is repeated by Eustathios (**46**) and in the *Etymologicum Magnum* (**45**). The commentary on Demosthenes (**50**) mentions the court of an equal number of Argives and Athenians and suggests the same derivation for the word *ephetai* but names Diomedes instead of Agamemnon as leader of the Argives.

(7) Harpokration, *s.v.* ἐφέται

49. Isokrates 18 (*Kallimachos*) 52, 54 402 B.C.E.

ὑποκρυψάμενοι θεράπαιναν ᾐτιῶντο τὸν Κρατῖνον συντρῖψαι τῆς κεφαλῆς αὐτῆς, ἐκ δὲ τοῦ τραύματος φάσκοντες ἀποθανεῖν τὴν ἄνθρωπον λαγχάνουσιν αὐτῶι φόνου δίκην ἐπὶ Παλλαδίωι. . . . ἐλθόντες εἰς τὴν οἰκίαν ἵν' ἦν κεκρυμμένη, βίαι λαβόντες αὐτὴν καὶ ἀγαγόντες ἐπὶ τὸ δικαστήριον ζῶσαν ἅπασι τοῖς παροῦσιν ἐπέδειξαν. ὥσθ' ἑπτακοσίων μὲν δικαζόντων, τεττάρων δὲ καὶ δέκα μαρτυρησάντων ἅπερ οὗτος, οὐδεμίαν ψῆφον μετέλαβε.

Having hidden away a female slave, they accused Kratinos of having crushed her head. They claimed that she died as a result of the wound and brought suit against him at Palladion on the charge of homicide. . . . [Kratinos and his friends] went to the house where she had been hidden, seized her by force and, bringing her into court, presented her alive to all present. The result was that in a tribunal of seven hundred judges, after fourteen witnesses had given the same testimony as that of Kallimachos, he failed to receive a single vote.

On arguments that there were 700 dikastai at Palladion, see MacDowell 1963, pp. 52–54.

50. *Lexicon Patmense*, *s.v.* ἐφέται
Commentary on Demosthenes 23.37.

ἐφέται ἦσαν ἄνδρες τὸν ἀριθμὸν ν' ἐξειλεγμένοι, ἐδίκαζον δὲ τοὺς ἀκουσίους φόνους, ἐὰν ξένος ἢ δοῦλος ἦν ὁ ἀναιρεθείς. ἐκλήθησαν δὲ οὕτως ἀπὸ τοιαύτης αἰτίας. εἰς Φάληρον τῆς Ἀττικῆς κατέπλευσαν ἀπὸ Τροίας πλέοντες οἱ μετὰ Διομήδους Ἀργεῖοι· ἀγνοήσαντες δὲ αὐτοὺς τῶν ἐπιχωρίων τινὲς καὶ ἐπιθέμενοι ὡς λησταῖς, νυκτὸς οὔσης, τοὺς πλείστους ἀπέκτειναν. ἡμέρας δὲ γενομένης ἐνεκάλουν οἱ μετὰ Διομήδους ὡς δεινὰ πεπονθότες. Ἀθηναῖοι δὲ συνθήκας ἐποιήσαντο καθίσαι δικαστήριον ἔκ τε Ἀργείων καὶ Ἀθηναίων ἴσων· καὶ τῆς δίκης γενομένης ἀφείθησαν οἱ τὸ ἔργον δεδρακότες ὡς κατὰ ἄγνοιαν ποιήσαντες. ἐπεὶ οὖν ἑκάτεροί τισιν ἐφῆκαν δικασταῖς περὶ τοῦ πράγματος, ἐφέται ἐκ τούτου ἐκλήθησαν οἱ τῶι ἀκουσίωι δικάζοντες.

Ephetai were fifty chosen men who judged cases of involuntary homicide, if the killed person was a foreigner or a slave. They were called ephetai for the following reason. Diomedes and his Argives sailing back from Troy landed at Phaleron in Attica. Some of the natives, not knowing who they were, attacked them as pirates, since it was night, and killed most of them. When day came, those with Diomedes complained that they had been treated terribly. Then the Athenians made a treaty to establish a court of an equal number of Argives and of Athenians. And when the trial was held those who had done the deed were acquitted as having acted through ignorance. Since both sides referred (ἐφῆκαν) the matter to dikasts, those who served as dikasts for involuntary homicide were called ephetai.

Harpokration and *Suda* give the same explanation of the word *ephetai*, and *Suda* cites Kleitodemos as the source, but in that account Agamemnon rather than Diomedes is named as leader of the Argives. Diomedes, however, is named by Pausanias and also in Bekker, *s.v.* ἐπὶ Παλλαδίωι (**5**).

51. *Lexicon Patmense*, *s.v.* ἐπὶ Παλλαδίωι
Commentary on Demosthenes 23.71.

ἐπὶ Παλλαδίωι· τοῦτο τὸ δικαστήριον ἱδρύσατο Δημοφῶν ὁ Θησέως κατὰ μαντείαν τοῦ ἐν Δελφοῖς Ἀπόλλωνος. μαθὼν γὰρ παρὰ Ἀλκμαίωνος Ἀργείου περὶ τῶν ἐν Φαλήρωι ἀνῃρημένων ἔθαψεν αὐτούς, καὶ ἱδρύσατο τὸ δικαστήριον τοῦτο. ἐκλήθη δὲ ἐπὶ Παλλαδίωι ὅτι τὸ Παλλάδιον τὸ ἐκ Τροίας κεκομισμένον ὑπὸ τῶν Ἀργείων τῶν περὶ Διομήδην λαβὼν ὁ Δημοφῶν καὶ καταγαγὼν ἐπὶ θάλατταν καὶ ἁγνίσας διὰ τοὺς φόνους ἱδρύσατο ἐν τούτωι τῶι τόπωι. ὥρισται δὲ ἐπὶ τῶι δικαστηρίωι τούτωι φυγὴ καὶ αἴδεσις.

At Palladion: Demophon son of Theseus founded this court at the order of an oracle of Apollo at Delphi, for having learned from Alkmaion the Argive about those killed at Phaleron, he buried them and established this court. It was called "at Palladion" because Demophon took the Palladion which had been brought from Troy by the Argives with Diomedes, brought it down to the sea and purified it because of the homicides, and established the court in this place. Exile and reconciliation are determined at this court.

(1) Pausanias 1.28.8–9

There is the one called "at Palladion" where cases of involuntary homicide are tried. Nobody denies that Demophon was the first person tried here, but there is a difference of opinion as to the crime for which he was tried. They say that after the capture of Ilion, Diomedes was sailing homeward, and night fell when they arrived off Phaleron; the Argives disembarked as in an enemy's country, taking it in the dark for some land other than Attica. Here Demophon, they say, unaware that the men from the ships were Argives, came out against them and killed some of them and carried off the Palladion. But an Athenian who did not see him coming was knocked down by Demophon's horse and trampled to death. For this Demophon was brought to trial, some say by the kinsmen of the man who had been trampled underfoot, others say by the Argive community.

Much the same version of the story of the origin of the court, with Diomedes as leader of the Argives, is given in the commentaries to Demosthenes (**50**, **51**) and is also found in Bekker (**5**).

(8) Photios, *Bibliotheca* 553a24–25

52. Plutarch, *Theseus* 27.3–5 (includes *FGrHist* 323 Kleidemos F18) 1st–2nd century C.E.

ἱστορεῖ δὲ Κλείδημος, ἐξακριβοῦν τὰ καθ' ἕκαστα βουλόμενος, τὸ μὲν εὐώνυμον τῶν Ἀμαζόνων κέρας ἐπιστρέφειν πρὸς τὸ νῦν καλούμενον Ἀμαζόνειον, τῶι δὲ δεξιῶι πρὸς τὴν Πνύκα κατὰ τὴν Χρύσαν ἥκειν. μάχεσθαι δὲ πρὸς τοῦτο τοὺς Ἀθηναίους ἀπὸ τοῦ Μουσείου ταῖς Ἀμαζόσι συμπεσόντας, καὶ τάφους τῶν πεσόντων περὶ τὴν πλατεῖαν εἶναι τὴν φέρουσαν ἐπὶ τὰς πύλας παρὰ τὸ Χαλκώδοντος ἡρῶιον, ἃς νῦν Πειραϊκὰς ὀνομάζουσι. καὶ ταύτηι μὲν ἐκβιασθῆναι μέχρι τῶν Εὐμενίδων καὶ ὑποχωρῆσαι ταῖς γυναιξίν, ἀπὸ δὲ Παλλαδίου καὶ Ἀρδηττοῦ καὶ Λυκείου προσβαλόντας ὤσασθαι τὸ δεξιὸν αὐτῶν ἄχρι τοῦ στρατοπέδου καὶ πολλὰς καταβαλεῖν.

Kleidemos, who wishes to be precise, writes that the left wing of the Amazons extended to what is now called the Amazoneion, and that with their right wing they touched the Pnyx at Chrysa; that with this right wing the Athenians fought, having attacked the Amazons from the Mouseion, and that the graves of those who fell are along Broad [Street], which leads to the gate by the heroon of Chalkodon, now called the Peiraieus gate. Here he says the Athenians were routed and driven back by the women as far as the shrine of the Eumenides, but those who attacked from the Palladion and Ardettos and the Lykeion drove back their Amazons' right (or left?) wing as far as their camp and slew many of them.

Jacoby accepts Reiske's emendation (*FGrHist* 323 F18, notes to commentary, p. 74, note 8) of "left" for the text's "right" wing of the Amazons in the last line.

The positions of the battle lines of Amazons and Athenians, as Kleidemos imagined them, are far from exact; see *FGrHist* IIIb, Suppl. I, pp. 76–83. The association of Palladion with Ardettos and the Lykeion does not square with a Palladion in Phaleron; see p. 139 above.

(2) Pollux 8.118

> The [court] at Palladion: in this court, cases of involuntary homicide are tried. After the sack of Troy, some Argives who had the Palladion landed at Phaleron and were killed and their bodies cast away by some natives who did not know who they were. And no living creature would touch them. But Akamas gave information that they were Argives and that they had the Palladion. After they were buried they were called the Unknown at the command of an oracle; on that spot the Palladion was set up, and cases of involuntary homicide are tried there.

According to the *Suda*, this version of the story of the origin of the court, with Akamas identifying the unknown bodies, was told by Phanodemos (late 4th century B.C.E.). This version is also given in a scholion on Aischines and is repeated by Eustathios.

53. *Suda, s.v.* ἐπὶ Παλλαδίωι (= *FGrHist* 323 Kleidemos F20) 10th century C.E.

> ἐπὶ Παλλαδίωι· δικαστήριον Ἀθήνησιν, ἐν ὧι οἱ Ἐφέται ἀκουσίου φόνου ἐδίκαζον. Ἀργεῖοι γὰρ ἀπὸ Ἰλίου πλέοντες, ἡνίκα προσέσχον Φαλήροις, ὑπὸ Ἀθηναίων ἀγνοούμενοι ἀνηιρέθησαν. ὕστερον δὲ Ἀκάμαντος γνωρίσαντος καὶ τοῦ Παλλαδίου εὑρεθέντος, κατὰ χρησμὸν αὐτόθι τὸ δικαστήριον ἀπέδειξαν, ὡς Φανόδημος. Κλειτόδημος δέ φησιν, Ἀγαμέμνονος σὺν τῶι Παλλαδίωι προσενεχθέντος Ἀθήναις, Δημοφῶντα ἁρπάσαι τὸ Παλλάδιον καὶ πολλοὺς τῶν διωκόντων ἀνελεῖν· τοῦ δὲ Ἀγαμέμνονος δυσχεραίνοντος, κρίσιν ὑποσχεῖν ἐπὶ ν' Ἀθηναίων καὶ ν' Ἀργείων, οὓς Ἐφέτας κληθῆναι, διὰ τὸ παρ' ἀμφοτέρων ἐφεθῆναι αὐτοῖς περὶ τῆς κρίσεως.
>
> At Palladion: a dikasterion at Athens in which the ephetai try cases of involuntary homicide. The Argives sailing back from Ilion, when they put ashore at Phaleron, were not recognized by the Athenians and were killed. Later, when Akamas recognized them and the Palladion was found, following the instructions of an oracle they established the dikasterion at that spot, according to Phanodemos (*FGrHist* 325 F16). But Kleitodemos (*scil.* Kleidemos [*FGrHist* 323 F20]) says that when Agamemnon with the Palladion put in at Athens, Demophon stole the Palladion and killed many of those pursuing him. Because Agamemnon was angry, Demophon submitted to judgment with fifty Athenians and fifty Argives [as judges] whom they called Ephetai because of the fact that the trial was referred to them from both sides.

Both these versions of the story of the origin of the court are found in earlier lexicographers but not credited to Phanodemos (late 4th century B.C.E.) and Kleitodemos (mid-4th century B.C.E.). For Phanodemos' version, see Pollux and the scholion on Aischines. For that of Kleidemos, see Harpokration (**48**) and the commentary on Demosthenes in the *Lexicon Patmense* (**50**). Eustathios (**46**) repeats this entry giving both stories almost verbatim. The *Etymologicum Magnum* repeats the version of Kleidemos.

The Court in Phreatto

If a man in exile for unintentional homicide was charged with an intentional homicide, he was tried at the court in Phreatto. Because he was in exile he could not set foot on Attic ground and therefore had to make his defense from a boat anchored near the shore where the court was meeting. Aristotle's comment in *Politics* 1300b (**4**) that cases such as those assigned to this court "are very few in the whole course of history even in the great cities" is undoubtedly true.

The name as preserved in the manuscripts is found in various forms, ἐν Φρεαττοῖ, ἐν Φρεάτου, and in a nominative form, Φρεαττύς. Theophrastos, as quoted by Harpokration, states that the court was named from a hero Phreatos, which if true would support ἐν Φρεάτου (or Φρεάττου) as the correct form. An association with the word φρέαρ (well) seems likely. On the evidence, it is hard to be sure that a single, original, correct form existed; see MacDowell 1963, pp. 82–83; John E. Sandys, *Aristotle's Constitution of Athens*, London 1912, p. 228; Judeich 1931, p. 436.

The physical requirements of procedure demand a location on the seacoast. Pausanias places the court at Peiraieus, as does Helladios, quoted by Photios. In the list of homicide courts found in Bekker, the rubric "court at Zea" is followed by "court in Phreatto", and both are said to try cases of those in exile for unintentional homicide. The two different names with one specialized function may reflect different conceptions of the word "dikasterion": the dikasterion in Phreatto could have been the judging panel, while the dikasterion in Zea was a physical structure, a building in which trials were held. That court would have been in Zea, in the eastern part of Peiraieus; see Boegehold 1976, pp. 8–19.

Near the southern tip of the east side of Zea harbor there are some oval, tub-shaped cuttings possibly used in antiquity for collecting salt or drying fish. It has been suggested that these cuttings were called *phreata* and that the court in Phreatto met here. Judeich (1931, p. 436, note 3) further points out that there seems to be an opening in the sea wall at this point that could be explained by the fact that the court met here. On the likelihood of any permanent installation to serve such rare combinations of circumstances, see pp. 49–50 above.

(3) Aristotle, *Ath. Pol.* 57.3–4

(4) Aristotle, *Politics* 1300b24–30

(5) Bekker, *Anecdota Graeca* 1.311.17–22

(6) Demosthenes 23.77–78

54. Harpokration, *s.v.* ἐν Φρεαττοῖ 2nd century C.E.

ἐν Φρεαττοῖ· Δημοσθένης ἐν τῶι κατ' Ἀριστοκράτους περὶ τοῦ ἐν Φρεαττοῖ δικαστηρίου ἀκριβῶς διεξελήλυθε, λέγων οὕτως. ἔτι τοίνυν πέμπτον δικαστήριον .... καὶ μετ' ὀλίγον φησὶν ... ἐπὶ ἑτέρωι φόνωι φυγὴν ὑπέχει. ὠνομάσθαι δ' ἔοικε τὸ δικαστήριον ἀπό τινος Φρεάττου ἥρωος, καθά φησι Θεόφραστος ἐν ις' τῶν Νόμων.

In Phreatto: Demosthenes in his speech against Aristokrates (23.77–78) described the court in Phreatto accurately, saying, "and now consider the character of a fifth court. . . . " And a little further on he says, " . . . but is still in banishment for the earlier homicide." It seems likely that the court is named for some hero Phreattos, as Theophrastos says in the 16th book of the *Laws*.

See **6** above for the quotation from Demosthenes.

(7) Harpokration, *s.v.* ἐφέται

(1) Pausanias 1.28.11

In Peiraieus beside the sea there is Phreattys. Here exiles, against whom in their absence another charge has been brought, make their defense from a ship, the judges listening on the shore. The legend runs that Teukros was the first to plead thus in his defense before Telamon, asserting that he had nothing to do with the death of Ajax.

(8) Photios, *Bibliotheca* 535a28–32

(2) Pollux 8.120

The [court] in Phreatto: here was tried a person in exile by reason of an involuntary homicide who received in addition a second charge of voluntary homicide. The court was on the seacoast, and the accused had to make his defense from a ship, sailing close to land but not touching it. Neither a gangway nor an anchor could be thrown to the land.

55. *Suda s.v.* ἐμφρεάτοι 10th century C.E.

ἐμφρεάτοι· δικαστήριον τῶν ἀκουσίων φόνων ἐν Ἀθήναις. Δημοσθένης ἐν τῶι κατὰ Ἀριστογείτονος ἀκριβῶς διέρχεται περὶ αὐτά. ὠνομάσθαι δὲ τὸ δικαστήριον ἔοικεν ἀπό τινος Φρεάτου ἥρωος, ὡς Θεόφραστος ἐν ις′ νόμωι μαρτυρεῖ.

In Phreatto: a dikasterion for involuntary homicide at Athens. Demosthenes in the speech against Aristogeiton describes it accurately. It seems likely that the court is named from some hero [named] Phreatos, as Theophrastos testifies in the 16th book of the *Laws*.

A shortened and garbled account apparently derived from Harpokration (**54**). It was not the court for involuntary homicide, and the speech is that against Aristokrates, not Aristogeiton. This entry is repeated almost verbatim in the *Etymologicum Magnum*, *s.v.* ἐν Φρεατοῖ.

(75) Schol. Aristophanes, *Ploutos*, line 1166

THE COURT AT THE PRYTANEION

Full testimonia on the Prytaneion in Athens are given in *Agora* III, nos. 541–571, pp. 166–174. Compare Miller 1978, pp. 132–218, for full testimonia on the Prytaneion in antiquity. Located (it now appears) on the east slope of the Akropolis (see Dontas 1983, pp. 60–61), it served as the central hearth of the city; it was a major community dining hall, as well as being the site of a homicide court. Only those texts that refer to the court are included here.

The court at the Prytaneion took action on homicide cases in which a person had been killed by an inanimate object, an animal, or an unknown person (as in Aristotle [**3**], Demosthenes [**6**], Harpokration [**56**], *Lexicon Patmense* [**57**], Pausanias [**1**], and Pollux [**2**]. Aristotle is the only one to include animals; Demosthenes and Pausanias mention only inanimate objects).

The function of the court was to take cognizance of homicides when there was no individual to be tried. The suggestion that it corresponds in some ways to the modern coroner's court (MacDowell 1963, p. 89) makes the picturesque details of the condemnation of inanimate objects and animals seem less absurd.

Although Harpokration (*s.v.* ἐφέται [**7**]) specifically includes the Prytaneion among the courts in which ephetai served as judges, and Pollux states that ephetai served in the five homicide courts, which would include the Prytaneion, probably cases were decided here by the basileus and phylobasileis, as stated by Aristotle, and without a panel of judges. The Prytaneion is also separated from the ephetai in the amnesty law in Plutarch, *Solon* 19 (**27**) and Andokides 1.78 (**14**). See Bonner and Smith 1930, p. 91; MacDowell 1963, p. 88. Since there was no known defendant present at cases brought before the court at the Prytaneion, there would seem to be no need for a panel of ephetai.

A homicide court called Ἐπάλξεις or Ἔπαλξις is mentioned only in Bekker and in the *Etymologicum Magnum*. The Bekker entry states that it was built beside (against?) the Prytaneion. Possibly, the court at the Prytaneion, situated on the steep east slope of the Akropolis, was called "court of" or "at the battlement". It does not seem in any case to have been a separate court, and so the relevant testimonia are cited as a sort of appendix to those on the court of the Prytaneion.

(14) Andokides 1.78

(3) Aristotle, *Ath. Pol.* 57.4

(5) Bekker, *Anecdota Graeca* 1.311.15

(6) Demosthenes 23.76

56. Harpokration, *s.v.* ἐπὶ Πρυτανείωι 2nd century C.E.

ἐπὶ Πρυτανείωι· δικαστήριόν ἐστι καὶ τοῦτο φονικόν, δικάζει δὲ ἄν τι τῶν ἀψύχων ἐμπεσὸν ἀποκτείνηι τινά, τοῦτο δέ ἐστιν, ἐὰν λίθος ἢ ξύλον ἢ σίδηρος ἤ τι τοιοῦτον, καὶ τὸν μὲν βαλόντα ἀγνοῆι, αὐτὸ δὲ εἰδῆι καὶ ἔχηι τὸ τὸν φόνον εἰργασμένον.

At the Prytaneion: this also is a court for homicide. It pronounces judgment if an inanimate object falls on someone and kills him, that is, a stone or stick or piece of iron or something else of the same sort, and one does not know who threw it, but knows and has the object that worked the death.

Compare Demosthenes 23.76 (**6**), which this repeats almost verbatim, and the *Suda, s.v.* ἐπὶ Πρυτανείωι for the same information.

(7) Harpokration, *s.v.* ἐφέται

57. *Lexicon Patmense, s.v.* ἐπὶ Πρυτανείωι
Commentary on Demosthenes 23.76.

ἐπὶ Πρυτανείωι· ἐν τούτωι τῶι δικαστηρίωι δικάζονται φόνου, ὅταν ὁ μὲν ἀνηιρημένος δῆλος ἦι, ζητεῖται δὲ ὁ τὸν φόνον δράσας. καὶ ἀποφέρει τὴν γραφὴν πρὸς τὸν βασιλέα, καὶ ὁ βασιλεὺς διὰ τοῦ κήρυκος κηρύττει καὶ ἀπαγορεύει τόνδε τὸν ἀνελόντα τὸν δεῖνα μὴ ἐπιβαίνειν ἱερῶν καὶ χώρας Ἀττικῆς. ἐν τῶι αὐτῶι δὲ τούτωι δικαστηρίωι κἄν τι ἐμπεσὸν πατάξηι τινὰ καὶ ἀνέληι τῶν ἀψύχων, δικάζεται τούτωι καὶ ὑπερορίζεται.

At the Prytaneion: in this court they are tried for homicide whenever it is clear who the person killed is, but the killer is being sought. One delivers the accusation to the basileus, and the basileus makes the announcement through the herald and forbids the man who killed So-and-so to set foot in the sanctuaries and land of Attica. Also, if an inanimate object falls on someone and hits him and kills him, a trial is held for it in this same court, and it is cast beyond the frontier.

(1) Pausanias 1.28.10

The court called "court in the Prytaneion", where iron and all lifeless things are brought to trial, originated, I believe, on the following occasion: When Erechtheus was king of the Athenians, the Ox-slayer slew an ox for the first time on the altar of Zeus Polieus; and having done so he left his axe there and fled from the country; but the axe was tried and acquitted, and every year it is tried down to the present time. Other lifeless things are said to have inflicted of their own accord a righteous punishment on men. The best and most famous instance is that of the sword of Kambyses.

58. Photios, *Lexicon, s.v.* προδικασία 9th century C.E.

προδικασία· οἱ τὰς ἐπὶ φόνωι δίκας ἐγκαλούμενοι ἐν Πρυτανείωι πρὸ τῆς δίκης διατελοῦσιν ἐπὶ τρεῖς μῆνας, ἐν οἷς ἐξ ἑκατέρου μέρους λόγοι προάγονται· τοῦτό φασι προδικασίαν.

Preliminary hearing: men who are being charged with homicide continue to be charged in the Prytaneion for three months before the trial, during which time speeches are brought in for both sides. This is called a preliminary hearing.

This entry is repeated verbatim in the *Suda, s.v.* προδικασία. On the translation, compare Miller 1978, p. 182. MacDowell (1963, p. 36) translates the passage as "persons accused on charges of homicide live at the prytaneion for three months before the trial . . ." and adds that there is no other evidence to confirm or refute the statement.

In homicide trials three preliminary hearings were to be called by the basileus in each of three successive months, and then the case was to be brought to trial in the fourth (Antiphon 6.42). This association of the preliminary hearings with the Prytaneion, found in Photios and in the *Suda, s.v.* προδικασία, is questioned by Lipsius (1905–1915, p. 840, note 39). The misstatement, if it is one, may have arisen from the fact that the basileus and phylobasileis presided over the court at the Prytaneion, and a lexicographer, knowing that the basileus held the preliminary hearings on all homicide cases, inferred that the basileus held these in the Prytaneion. On the other hand, the Prytaneion constituted a venue that would not prejudice the outcome of the deliberations. It seems therefore to be the right place.

(27) Plutarch, *Solon* 19.3

(2) Pollux 8.120

> The [court] at Prytaneion judges cases of homicides whose identity is unknown and of inanimate objects that have fallen and killed someone. The phylobasileis presided at this court, and it was their duty to cast beyond the border the inanimate object which had fallen.

Two testimonia on a homicide court called "the battlements", ἐπάλξεις, follow. They may refer to the court at the Prytaneion (see p. 96 above).

59. Bekker, *Anecdota Graeca* 1.243.16–18

> ἐπάλξεις· ἐξοχαὶ τειχῶν, προμαχῶνες, ἀψίς. ἔστι δὲ καὶ δικαστήριον τῶν φονικῶν, ᾠκοδόμηται δὲ πρὸς τῶι Πρυτανείωι.
>
> Battlements: projecting heights of walls, breastworks, vault. It is also a homicide court, and it is built beside the Prytaneion.

60. *Etymologicum Magnum, s.v.* ἔπαλξις 12th century C.E.

> ἔπαλξις· ὁ προμαχῶν τοῦ τείχους. . . . ἔστι δὲ ἐξοχὴ τειχῶν, ἀψίς. ἔστι δὲ καὶ δικαστήριον τῶν φονικῶν.
>
> Battlement: the breastwork of the wall. . . . It is the projecting height of the walls, vault. And it is also a homicide court.

THE COURT IN ZEA

(5) Bekker, *Anecdota Graeca* 1.311.3–22

THE HELIAIA AND THE OTHER DIKASTIC COURTS

This section includes references to dikasterion and dikasteria where the name of a specific court or building is not given. Dikasterion in these passages usually means a heliastic court.

The Heliaia as court, court building, meeting place, or judging body was the largest and most important court in Athens, as all sources agree (Harpokration, Pollux, Scholion to Demosthenes, *et al.*). (For specification of the various meanings of "Heliaia", see pp. 3–6 above.) It was almost certainly located in or near the Agora, but the only specific information is that the Thieves' Market was near the Heliaia (Hesychios, Eustathios). That it was unroofed, or at least that the main assembly room was unroofed, in the 5th and 4th centuries may follow from Aristophanes' play on words, ἡλιάσει πρὸς ἥλιον (*Wasps*, line 772), and from the fact that it was large enough to hold at least 1,500 dikasts (Aristotle, *Ath. Pol.* 68.1 [**110**]). Much smaller meetings were also held there on occasion. Thus the diaiteitai for the tribes of Oineis and Erechtheis met in the Heliaia ([Demosthenes] 47.12 [**118**]). The panels of diaitetai for each tribe, composed as they were of men in their sixtieth year, cannot have been large. The only complete list of diaitetai, *IG* II^2 1926, of the year 325/4 B.C.E., records 103 names, and panels acting for a single tribe were accordingly around one-tenth of this number. (For the diaitetai, see Busolt and Swoboda 1920, pp. 1111–1112 and Lipsius 1905–1915, p. 227.) They may have met on one or two of the benches in the Heliaia, as suggested by Kahrstedt (1936, p. 299), but a smaller adjoining area, a colonnade or attached room of some sort, is another possibility. Since, however, diaiteitai also met in the Stoa Poikile (Demosthenes 45.17 [**162, 293**]), in which a panel of 499 dikasts could convene (**163**), there is no real need to postulate a smaller meeting room. Arbitrators may also have held meetings in the Delphinion (**33**).

These seem to be the only specific facts about the Heliaia to be found in ancient written sources. Later commentators and lexicographers concentrate on the derivation of the word and on the number of dikasts who met there. For the derivation, two alternate suggestions are made: Heliaia comes from ἥλιος because "it is open to the sky and the sun shines on it," or it comes from ἁλίης, an Ionic word for assembly. The latter recommends itself as the more probable. (See Wade-Gery 1958, p. 173, and note 4.) An argument can be made to use the spelling Eliaia in discussions of the court (see, e.g., MacDowell 1971, pp. 273–275), but there is a convenience to the traditional spelling. Both derivations are suggested in the scholion to Demosthenes (**116**; also Bekker, *Anecdota Graeca* 1.310 [**113**] and *Etymologicum Magnum* [**119**]). Stephanos of Byzantion (**127**) gives a derivation only from ἁλία. The derivation from ἥλιος is akin to and may stem from the play on words in the *Wasps*. It is found in various scholia to Aristophanes and in the *Suda* almost verbatim. Note that the long scholion on *Wasps*, line 772 (**109**), which quotes Didymos on the play on words, does not attribute the suggested derivation from ἥλιος to Didymos.

The Heliaia was used for trials in which 1,000 dikasts (two panels of 500 each) or 1,500 (three panels) came together (Aristotle, *Ath. Pol.* 68.1 [**110**] and Harpokration [**121**]). The lacunae in the text of *Athenaion Politeia* at this point make it uncertain whether Aristotle actually connects the single dikasterion of 500 with the Heliaia or not; the number 500 is mentioned in line 1. Harpokration does not state that dikastic panels of 500, the standard unit at least for the 5th century, did in fact also meet there. Pollux (**126**) states that the Heliaia was of 500 (see also Schol. Aristophanes, *Wasps*, line 88 [**107**]), and one can safely assume that the building was used for many cases with a panel of 500. The later sources, reflecting perhaps Harpokration's and possibly Aristotle's omission, name only the higher numbers (Stephanos of Byzantion [**127**], Photios [**125**], the *Suda* [**128**], *Etymologicum Magnum* [**119**], Bekker [**111**]).

These references suggest that the Heliaia and most of the other buildings used by the dikastic courts were in or near the Agora. Lysias (**88**) states that the dikasterion was in the Agora, and Plato (**89**) and Athenaeus (**79**), quoting Euboulos, imply the same, as does a long passage from Aristophanes, *Ecclesiazusae* (**84**). Antiphon (**62**) states that a case was being tried in a roofed building in the Agora (probably the Parabyston; see pp. 178–179). According to a scholion to *Ploutos* (**71**), the dikasts were allotted in the Agora; according to Isokrates (**87**) they were allotted in front of the dikasteria (which need not be perceived as forming a complex, as they did later in the 4th century). Allotments were performed at ten entrances to a complex of dikasteria, according to Aristotle.

A conspicuous public place for the allotment is also implied in the *Ecclesiazusae.* The dikasteria, according to Plutarch (**90**), were in the district of the herm carvers.

The speculations on upper and lower courts started by Demosthenes' phrase ὁ κάτωθεν νόμος are included in this section (Demosthenes [**83**], Harpokration [**86**] and Bekker [**85**]), as are the long scholia to *Ploutos* on the use of letters on the separate courts.

Finally, several items indicating the important role played by the dikastic courts in Athens will be found here, such as the passage from Alkiphron (**61**), lines 206–208 of Aristophanes, *Clouds* (**63**), and several quotations from the *Wasps* (**76–78**) and the *Knights* (**68**, **69**).

General References to Dikasteria

61. Alkiphron, *Epistles* 2.3.11 (4.18.11) 2nd century C.E.

ποῦ γὰρ ἐν Αἰγύπτωι ὄψομαι ἐκκλησίαν καὶ ψῆφον ἀναδιδομένην; ποῦ δὲ δημοκρατικὸν ὄχλον οὕτως ἐλευθεριάζοντα; ποῦ δὲ θεσμοθέτας ἐν τοῖς ἱεροῖς κώμοις κεκισσωμένους; ποῖον περισχοίνισμα; ποίαν αἵρεσιν; ποίους Χύτρους; Κεραμεικόν, ἀγοράν, δικαστήρια, τὴν καλὴν ἀκρόπολιν. . . .

Where in Egypt shall I see the assembly and the ballot being distributed? Where shall I see a democratic mob acting free in this way? Or the thesmothetai garlanded with ivy at the sacred revels? What roped enclosure shall I see? What election of officers? What feast of pots? Where shall I see the Kerameikos, the agora, the lawcourts, the noble Akropolis. . . ?

Alkiphron composed the *Epistles* as though they were written in the 4th century B.C.E.

62. Antiphon 5 (*Herodes*) 10–11 *ca.* 424–415 B.C.E.

ἐμοὶ δὲ πρῶτον μέν, οὗ τοῖς ἄλλοις εἴργεσθαι προαγορεύουσι τοῖς τοῦ φόνου φεύγουσι τὰς δίκας, ἐνταυθοῖ πεποιήκασι τὴν κρίσιν, ἐν τῆι ἀγορᾶι. . . . Ἔπειτα δὲ . . . ἅπαντα τὰ δικαστήρια ἐν ὑπαίθρωι δικάζει τὰς δίκας τοῦ φόνου, οὐδενὸς ἄλλου ἕνεκα ἢ ἵνα τοῦτο μὲν οἱ δικασταὶ μὴ ἴωσιν εἰς τὸ αὐτὸ τοῖς μὴ καθαροῖς τὰς χεῖρας, τοῦτο δὲ ὁ διώκων τὴν δίκην τοῦ φόνου ἵνα μὴ ὁμωρόφιος γίγνηται τῶι αὐθέντηι. σὺ δὲ τοῦτο μὲν παρελθὼν τοῦτον τὸν νόμον τοὐναντίον τοῖς ἄλλοις πεποίηκας.

In my case the prosecution has first of all caused the trial to be held in the one place from which those charged with murder are always debarred by proclamation, the Agora. . . . Furthermore . . . all courts try cases of homicide under the open sky for no other purpose than that first the dikasts not enter the same place as those with unclean hands, and secondly that he who prosecutes the case for homicide not be under the same roof with the killer. But you contravening this law have made an opposite to the others.

These two passages from Antiphon's fifth oration show that the case in question was being tried in a covered building in the Agora (probably the Parabyston; see page 179).

63. Aristophanes, *Clouds*, lines 206–208 423 B.C.E.

Μαθητής: αὕτη δέ σοι γῆς περίοδος πάσης. ὁρᾶις;
αἵδε μὲν Ἀθῆναι.
Στρεψιάδης: τί σὺ λέγεις; οὐ πείθομαι,
ἐπεὶ δικαστὰς οὐχ ὁρῶ καθημένους.

Student: This is a chart of the whole world. See? This is Athens.
Strepsiades: What do you mean? I don't believe it, since I see no dikasts sitting.

64. Aristophanes, *Ecclesiazusae*, lines 675–690 393 B.C.E.

(Praxagora is explaining to her husband Blepyros how all Athenians will eat when her socialist state is established.)

Βλέπυρος: τὸ δὲ δεῖπνον ποῦ παραθήσεις;
Πραξαγόρα: τὰ δικαστήρια καὶ τὰς στοιὰς ἀνδρῶνας πάντα ποιήσω.
Βλέπυρος: τὸ δὲ βῆμα τί σοι χρήσιμον ἔσται;
Πραξαγόρα: τοὺς κρατῆρας καταθήσω
καὶ τὰς ὑδρίας, καὶ ῥαψωιδεῖν ἔσται τοῖς παιδαρίοισιν
τοὺς ἀνδρείους ἐν τῶι πολέμωι, κεἴ τις δειλὸς γεγένηται,
ἵνα μὴ δειπνῶσ' αἰσχυνόμενοι.
Βλέπυρος: νὴ τὸν Ἀπόλλω χαριέν γε.
τὰ δὲ κληρωτήρια ποῖ τρέψεις;
Πραξαγόρα: εἰς τὴν ἀγορὰν καταθήσω.
κἆιτα στήσασα παρ' Ἁρμοδίωι κληρώσω πάντας, ἕως ἂν
εἰδὼς ὁ λαχὼν ἀπίηι χαίρων ἐν ὁποίωι γράμματι δειπνεῖ·
καὶ κηρύξει τοὺς ἐκ τοῦ βῆτ' ἐπὶ τὴν στοιὰν ἀκολουθεῖν
τὴν βασίλειον δειπνήσοντας· τὸ δὲ θῆτ' ἐς τὴν παρὰ ταύτην,
τοὺς δ' ἐκ τοῦ κάππ' ἐς τὴν στοιὰν χωρεῖν τὴν ἀλφιτόπωλιν.
Βλέπυρος: ἵνα κάπτωσιν;
Πραξαγόρα: μὰ Δί', ἀλλ' ἵν' ἐκεῖ δειπνῶσιν.
Βλέπυρος: ὅτωι δὲ τὸ γράμμα
μὴ ἐξελκυσθῆι καθ' ὃ δειπνήσει, τούτους ἀπελῶσιν ἅπαντες;
Πραξαγόρα: ἀλλ' οὐκ ἔσται τοῦτο παρ' ἡμῖν.
πᾶσι γὰρ ἄφθονα πάντα παρέξομεν·

Blepyros: Where will you serve dinner?
Praxagora: I shall make all the lawcourts and stoas dining halls.
Blepyros: How will you use the bema?
Praxagora: I shall place the mixing bowls and pitchers on it, and little boys can recite poems about men who have been brave in war and whoever has been a coward so that these will be ashamed and not dine.
Blepyros: Charming, by Apollo! Where will you put the kleroteria?
Praxagora: I shall put them in the Agora, set them up beside Harmodios, and allot everybody until each man gets his lot, and goes off happy knowing in what letter he is dining. And the herald will proclaim that those of section beta go along to the Stoa Basileios to dine, those of theta to the stoa beside it, and those of section kappa shall go to the stoa alphitopolis.
Blepyros: To gobble?
Praxagora: No, by Zeus, to dine.
Blepyros: Those for whom a letter in which to dine has not been drawn, will everyone drive them away?
Praxagora: It will not be so with us. We shall offer everything in abundance.

See Boegehold 1984, pp. 23–29 for a discussion of these lines.

65. Schol. Aristophanes, *Ecclesiazusae*, line 683 (ed. Dübner)

γράμματι δειπνεῖ: Δέον εἰπεῖν δικάζειν, εἶπε δειπνεῖν.

In what letter he is dining: where one should say "to judge" he said "to dine".

66. Schol. Aristophanes, *Ecclesiazusae*, line 685 (ed. Dübner)

βασίλειον· ἐπεὶ τὸ βασίλειον ἀπὸ τοῦ β ἄρχεται. ἐς τὴν παρὰ ταυτήν· τοὺς θῆτας, τοὺς μισθωτοὺς εἰς τὸ Θησεῖον· ἐπεὶ πάλιν ἀπὸ τοῦ θῆτα ἄρχεται.

Basileion [royal]: because basileion begins with a beta. To the one beside it: the thetes, the hired men, to the Theseion, since this begins with a theta.

The scholiast wants to find a correlation between section letters and names of stoas at Athens. In the case of beta and basileion, he has a point. The Theseion may be an attempt to continue the pattern, but it seems mistaken, despite the following kappa and κάπτωσιν; compare *Agora* III, no. 8.

67. Schol. Aristophanes, *Ecclesiazusae*, line 687 (ed. Dübner)

τὸ κάπτωσιν ἀπὸ τοῦ κάππα, διὸ ἐπὶ τῶν ἐκ τοῦ κ ἔφη.

κάπτωσιν [gobble], from the letter kappa, since he said those from section kappa.

See the section on court furnishings and equipment for scholia to *Ecclesiazusae*, line 677 on the bema (**235**), and to line 681 on the kleroteria (**324**).

68. Aristophanes, *Knights*, lines 1316–1318 424 B.C.E.
(The Sausage Seller is speaking.)

εὐφημεῖν χρὴ καὶ στόμα κλείειν, καὶ μαρτυριῶν ἀπέχεσθαι,
καὶ τὰ δικαστήρια συγκλείειν, οἷς ἡ πόλις ἥδε γέγηθεν,
ἐπὶ καιναῖσιν δ' εὐτυχίαισιν παιωνίζειν τὸ θέατρον.

One ought to be quiet, close his mouth, hold off from witness, and close up the courts this city loves, and the theater should sing a paean in consequence of the new good luck.

69. Schol. Aristophanes, *Knights*, line 1317

οἷς ἡ πόλις· Ὅτι φιλόδικοι ἦσαν 'Αθηναῖοι.

In which the city: because Athenians loved trials.

70. Aristophanes, *Ploutos*, lines 277–278 388 B.C.E.

ἐν τῆι σορῶι νυνὶ λαχὸν τὸ γράμμα σου δικάζειν,
σὺ δ' οὐ βαδίζεις; ὁ δὲ Χάρων τὸ ξύμβολον δίδωσιν.

Now that you have been allotted your letter to act as judge in the grave, go. Charon is handing out the token.

Allusions to two separate and distinct allotments are included here. The letter designates the court site; the token, a seating area within the court. For interpretation of these lines, see Boegehold 1984, pp. 23–29.

71. Schol. Aristophanes, *Ploutos*, line 277

Most of the long, somewhat repetitious scholia on this passage derive indirectly from Aristotle's account of the allotment of the dikasts in *Athenaion Politeia*. Since the scholiasts were trying to explain procedures of 388 B.C.E. in terms of a later, changed procedure, there is considerable confusion in the following extracts; see also **341**.

(The text is that of L. M. Positano, *Scholia in Aristophanem*, IV, *Jo. Tzetzae Commentarii in Aristophanem*, eds. L. M. Positano, D. Holwerda, W. J. W. Koster, Groningen 1969, p. 79)

ἐν ταῖς Ἀθήναις πολλὰ ἦν δικαστήρια. καὶ ἔν τισι μὲν ἐδίκαζον περὶ φονικῶν πραγμάτων, ἔν τισι δὲ περὶ δημοτικῶν· καὶ ἕκαστον δὲ τούτων εἶχεν ἕν τι τῶν στοιχείων ἰδικὸν ὄνομα. οἷον ἦν τι τῶν δικαστηρίων λεγόμενον ἄλφα, ὁμοίως ἄλλο βῆτα, ἄλλο γάμμα, καὶ ἑξῆς τὸ δ καὶ τὸ ε καὶ τἄλλα. δέκα γὰρ ἦν τὰ δικαστήρια ἐν Ἀθήναις, τὰ πάντα καὶ πρὸ θυρῶν δὲ ἑκάστου δικαστηρίου ἐγέγραπτο πυρρῶι βάμματι τὸ στοιχεῖον, ὧιτινι τὸ δικαστήριον ὠνομάζετο.

In Athens there were many dikasteria. In some they tried homicide cases, in others, public cases. And each of these had one of the letters as its own name. Thus one of the dikasteria was called alpha, likewise one beta, another gamma, and then in order delta and epsilon, and the rest. For there were ten dikasteria in all in Athens, and before the doors of each dikasterion, the letter with which the dikasterion was named was written in red dye.

ὅτε οὖν συνέβαινε καιρὸς τοῦ δικάζειν, ἀπήρχοντο πάντες οἱ δικασταὶ εἰς τὴν ἀγοράν, κἀκεῖ κλήρους ἔβαλλον· καὶ ὅστις ἂν ἐκληροῦτο κλῆρον τὸν ἔχοντα τὸ α, ἀπήρχετο εἰς τὸ α δικαστήριον, καὶ ὁμοίως εἰς τὸ β καὶ τὰ ἐφεξῆς.

When it was time to judge, all the dikasts came to the Agora, and there they cast the lots; and whoever received a lot marked alpha went to the alpha dikasterion, likewise to the beta, and so on.

Dübner 1843, p. 340, lines 20–36, prints a garbled version (not in Positano) of Aristotle's account of the allotment procedure equating the ten dikastic panels with the ten tribes and speaking of five dikasteria with letters alpha to epsilon. Lines 31–32 are quoted because the Heliaia is mentioned, since the scholiast has assumed that the trial the old man will judge would be in the Heliaia.

(Dübner 1843, p. 340, lines 31–32)

ἀνθυπήλλαξε γὰρ εἰπὼν ἐν τῆι σορῶι, δέον ἐν τῆι Ἡλιαίαι.

He changed the word, saying "in the grave" when it should have been "in the Heliaia".

72. Aristophanes, *Ploutos*, line 972 — 388 B.C.E.

ἀλλ' οὐ λαχοῦσ' ἔπινες ἐν τῶι γράμματι;

But were you drinking without having been allotted in the letter?

See Boegehold 1984, p. 28.

73. Schol. Aristophanes, *Ploutos*, line 972 (contains *FGrHist* 328 Philochoros F140)

Παρ' ὑπόνοιαν ἀντὶ τοῦ ἐδίκαζες. ὅτι δὲ κατὰ γράμματα ἐκληροῦντο, προείρηται· οὐ μὴν ἀλλὰ καὶ ἐβούλευον οὗτοι τῶι πρὸ τούτου ἔτει ἀρξάμενοι. φησὶ γὰρ Φιλόχορος, ἐπὶ Γλαυκίππου, καὶ ἡ βουλὴ κατὰ γράμμα τότε πρῶτον ἐκαθέζετο· καὶ ἔτι νῦν ὄμνυσιν ἀπ' ἐκείνου καθεδεῖσθαι ἐν τῶι γράμματι ὧι ἂν λάχωσι. Ἄλλως. τοῦτο ἀφ' ἑτέρου ἐστὶν ἑρμηνεῦσαι· Ἀθηναῖοι γὰρ ἀπὸ τῶν φυλῶν ἐποίουν τοὺς δικαστὰς κατὰ γράμμα, οἷον ἡ πρώτη τὸ α ἔσχε σημεῖον, καὶ ἡ δευτέρα τὸ β, καὶ αἱ ἄλλαι ὁμοίως ἕως τοῦ κ. δέκα γὰρ φυλῶν οὐσῶν δέκα ἐγίνοντο δικασταί· ὁ οὖν λαχὼν τὸ α πρῶτος ἐδίκαζε, καὶ οἱ ἄλλοι ὁμοίως.

The scholiast explains an unexpected turn (παρὰ προσδοκίαν) in Aristophanes' line.

[Were you drinking] by imputation instead of did you act as judge. That they were allotted by letters has already been said; these [Athenians] in fact would also sit [allotted by letter] as bouleutai having started this system the year before [the production of *Ploutos*] (see below). For Philochoros says that in the archonship of Glaukippos the boule also first sat by letter, and they still take an oath from his time to sit in the letter to which they are allotted. Or this can be explained in another way: The Athenians made up the dikasts from the tribes according to letter: for example, the first tribe got the symbol alpha, the second beta, and the others similarly up to kappa. For since there were ten tribes there were ten dikasts. The one allotted alpha was the first to judge, and the others similarly. (The scholiast continues with further discussion of letters and allotment, the possible implication that the women are wine lovers, and so on.)

Glaukippos was archon in 410/9 B.C.E. The scholiast refers to Aristophanes' first *Ploutos*, produced in 408 B.C.E., and not the second *Ploutos*, the text of which survives.

74. Aristophanes, *Ploutos*, lines 1166–1167 388 B.C.E.

οὐκ ἐτὸς ἅπαντες οἱ δικάζοντες θαμὰ
σπεύδουσιν ἐν πολλοῖς γεγράφθαι γράμμασιν.

No wonder all the men who judge a lot are eager to be enrolled in many letters.

A reduced pool of candidates and a corresponding reduced volume of legal business may have encouraged informal solutions to the question of filling dikastic panels; see Boegehold 1984, pp. 26–28.

75. Schol. Aristophanes, *Ploutos*, line 1166

(After a verbose explanation of the fact that the dikasts try to get enrolled in several dikasteria so that their chances of being chosen to serve will be better, the scholia continue [Dübner 1843, p. 384, lines 44–50]):

περὶ δὲ τῶν γραμμάτων καὶ δικαστηρίων Ἀθηναίων ἔφημεν ὄπισθεν, πῶς ἐν ἑκάστωι ἦν γεγραμμένον στοιχεῖον· ἐν μὲν τῶι τοῦ Ἀρεοπάγου δικαστηρίωι πρὸ τῶν θυρῶν ἐπιγέγραπτο α ἐν δὲ τῆι Ἡλιαίαι η· ἐν δὲ τῶι ἐν Φρεαττοῖ δ, καὶ ἐν τοῖς λοιποῖς ὡσαύτως· διὰ τοῦτο ἔφη, σπεύδουσιν ἐν πολλοῖς γεγράφθαι γράμμασιν.

We have said above about the letters and the Athenian dikasteria that there was a letter written in each. In the court of the Areopagos before the doors there is written alpha, in the Heliaia eta, in that at Phreatto a delta, and similarly at the others. For this reason [Aristophanes] said, "They are eager to be enrolled in many letters."

The delta was perhaps written in error for phi. In any case, the scholiast's notes appear to be idiosyncratic amplifications of references in Aristophanes and Aristotle.

76. Aristophanes, *Wasps*, lines 581–582 422 B.C.E.

(This and the two following entries are from Philokleon's descriptions of the glories of serving as a dikast.)

κἂν αὐλητής γε δίκην νικᾶι, ταύτης ἡμῖν ἐπίχειρα
ἐν φορβειᾶι τοῖσι δικασταῖς ἔξοδον ηὔλησ' ἀπιοῦσιν.

And if a flute-player wins his case, he in harness pays us dikasts by playing us an exit tune as we go out.

77. Aristophanes, *Wasps*, lines 594–595 422 B.C.E.

χἂν τῶι δήμωι γνώμην οὐδεὶς πώποτ' ἐνίκησεν, ἐὰν μὴ
εἴπηι τὰ δικαστήρι' ἀφεῖναι πρώτιστα μίαν δικάσαντας.

And no one ever could carry a proposal in the assembly unless he moved to dismiss the dikasteria as soon as they judged a single case.

78. Aristophanes, *Wasps*, lines 622–625 422 B.C.E.

ἢν γοῦν ἡμεῖς θορυβήσωμεν,
πᾶς τίς φησιν τῶν παριόντων,
οἷον βροντᾶι τὸ δικαστήριον,
ὦ Ζεῦ βασιλεῦ.

If we shout, every passerby says, "How the court thunders, O King Zeus."

(249) Aristotle, *Ath. Pol.* 63.1–2, 5; 65.2

A few passages from Aristotle's description of court procedure and allotment are cited here as examples of the use of the plural form τὰ δικαστήρια for the single court complex required by that system. The Greek text and fuller quotations and comments will be found at **249**.

The nine archons by tribes fill the dikasteria, and the secretary of the thesmothetai represents the tenth tribe. There are ten entrances to the dikasteria, one for each tribe, and twenty kleroteria. (63.1–2)

After the thesmothetes has chosen by lot the letters which are to be attached to the dikasteria, the attendant takes the allotted letter and places it on the proper dikasterion. (63.5)

For at each of the dikasteria, a color is painted on the lintel of the entrance. (65.2)

79. Athenaeus 14.640b–c (contains Euboulos F74 [*PCG* V]) 2nd–3rd century C.E.

ὁ Εὔβουλος δ' ἐν 'Ολβίαι ἔφη
ἐν τῶι γὰρ αὐτῶι πάνθ' ὁμοῦ πωλήσεται
ἐν ταῖς Ἀθήναις, σῦκα, (B.) κλητῆρες, (A.) βότρυς
γογγυλίδες, ἄπιοι, μῆλα, (B.) μάρτυρες, (A.) ῥόδα,
μέσπιλα, χόρια, σχαδόνες, ἐρέβινθοι, (B.) δίκαι,
(A.) πυός, πυριάτη, μύρτα, (B.) κληρωτήρια,
(A.) ὑάκινθος, ἄρνες, (B.) κλεψύδραι, νόμοι, γραφαί.

As Euboulos says in *Olbia*: "You will find everything sold together in the same place at Athens: figs, (B.) summoners, (A.) bunches of grapes, turnips, pears, apples, (B.) witnesses, (A.) roses, medlars, haggis, honeycombs, chickpeas, (B.) lawsuits, (A.) beestings, beestings pudding, myrtle, (B.) allotment devices, (A.) *hyakinthos*, lambs, (B.) waterclocks, laws, indictments."

See *Agora* III, no. 610, for comment on the text. The letters A and B are arbitrary designations of two different speakers. Euboulos is a comic poet of the mid-4th century B.C.E. The place in Athens where everything was sold together is surely the Agora. Buildings such as lawcourts are not named explicitly, but mention of lawsuits, kleroteria, klepsydrai, and indictments implies the presence of lawcourts there.

80. Deinarchos 2 (*Aristogeiton*) 13 338–323 B.C.E.?

. . . περιπατῶν ἔμπροσθεν τῶν δικαστηρίων⟨. . .⟩

. . . walking around in front of the lawcourts.

81. Demosthenes 18 (*On the Crown*) 123 330 B.C.E.

οἰκοδομῆσαι δὲ τοὺς προγόνους ταυτὶ τὰ δικαστήρι' ὑπείληφα, οὐχ ἵνα συλλέξαντες ὑμᾶς εἰς ταῦτα ἀπὸ τῶν ἰδίων κακῶς τἀπόρρητα λέγωμεν ἀλλήλους,

Our ancestors, I think, did not build these courts for us to gather you into them and abuse each other with secrets from our private lives.

For the topos, compare [Demosthenes] 25.48: οὐδὲ γὰρ τοὺς προγόνους ὑπολαμβάνω τὰ δικαστήρια ταῦθ' ὑμῖν οἰκοδομῆσαι, ἵνα τοὺς τοιούτους ἐν αὐτοῖς μοσχεύητε (because I do not suppose that your ancestors built these courts for you to plant such creatures in them).

82. Demosthenes 21 (*Meidias*) 4 347 B.C.E.

ἃ δ' ἐν ὑμῖν μετὰ ταῦτ' ἔσθ' ὑπόλοιπα, ὅσωι πλείοσιν οὗτος ἠνώχληκε καὶ παρήγγελκεν (ἑώρων γὰρ αὐτὸν ἄρτι πρὸ τῶν δικαστηρίων οἶ' ἐποίει), τοσούτωι μᾶλλον ἐλπίζω τὸ δίκαιον ἕξειν.

As to what yet remains in your hands, my hope is that the more people this [defendant] has troubled with his recruiting (I saw just now what sorts of things he was doing in front of the dikasteria), the more likely I am to obtain justice.

Demosthenes is addressing the dikasts. This speech, which some students think was merely written and never delivered in court, has been accepted by H. Erbse ("Über die Midiana des Demosthenes," *Hermes* 84, 1956 [pp. 135–151], p. 150) as having been spoken at a trial that took place in 347/6 B.C.E.; compare M. H. Hansen, "Seven Hundred *Archai* in Classical Athens," *GRBS* 21, 1980 [pp. 151–173], p. 159, note 20, and MacDowell 1990, pp. 23–28.

83. Demosthenes 23 (*Aristokrates*) 28 352 B.C.E.

(Euthykles is speculating on the ramifications of a proposal to make the person of Charidemos inviolable. The putative transgressor would be denied the customary safeguards of law.)

καίτοι πάντα ταῦτ' ἀπείρηκεν ἄντικρυς καὶ σαφῶς ὁ κάτωθεν νόμος μηδὲ τοὺς ἑαλωκότας καὶ δεδογμένους ἀνδροφόνους ἐξεῖναι ποιεῖν. λέγε δ' αὐτοῖς αὐτὸν τὸν νόμον τὸν μετὰ ταῦτα.

[When they have got him they are to be allowed to torture him or maltreat him or extort money from him.] Yet the law below definitely and clearly forbids such treatment even of men caught and found guilty of murder. Now read to them the actual law that follows.

The κάτωθεν νόμος refers to the law next lower on the list (or on the axon) as stated in an entry in Bekker, *Anecdota Graeca* 1.269.14: κάτωθεν νόμος ἐστὶν ὁ ἑξῆς καὶ μετὰ τοῦτον κάτωθεν ἄξονος γεγραμμένος ("The law below is the one next in series and written after it lower on the axon").

Demosthenes is cited here because of later speculations (see **85** and **86**) on the meaning of the phrase "the law below" or "lower law" in relation to the location of various courts. See **134** for the text of the law.

84. Demosthenes 42 (*On the Estate of Phainippos*) 11 after 330 B.C.E.

ἐδεῖτό μου προσελθὼν πρόσθε τῶν δικαστηρίων μετὰ Πολυεύκτου τοῦ Κριωέως καὶ ἑτέρων τινῶν, πρῶτον μὲν περὶ διαλύσεως συνελθεῖν αὐτῶι.

He came up to me in front of the courts, and in the company of Polyeuktos, son of Krioeus, and some other people first asked me to get together with him concerning a settlement.

85. Bekker, *Anecdota Graeca* 1.253.26–254.2

ἐπάνω δικαστήριον καὶ ὑποκάτω· ἐπάνω μὲν δικαστήριον τὸ ἐν Ἀρείωι πάγωι· ἔστι γὰρ ἐν ὑψηλῶι λόφωι· κάτω δὲ τὸ ἐν κοίλωι τινὶ τόπωι. ἢ ἄνω μὲν ἐν ἀκροπόλει, κάτω δὲ ἐν πόλει. ἢ ἄνω μὲν ἐν ἄστει, κάτω δὲ τὸ ἐν Πειραιεῖ. ἢ ἄνω μὲν τὸ ἄνω βλέπον εἰς τὴν ἀκρόπολιν, κάτω δὲ τὸ κάτω βλέπον εἰς ἄστυ ἢ τὸν Πειραιᾶ. ἢ ἰδίως οὕτω καλεῖσθαι ἄνω καὶ κάτω δικαστήριον. ἢ ἄνω μὲν τὸ ἐν ὑπερῴοις, κάτω δὲ τὸ ἐν ὑπαίθρωι.

The upper dikasterion and the lower: the upper dikasterion is that on the Areopagos. It is on a high hill; the lower is in a hollow place. Or the upper is on the Akropolis, the lower in the city. Or the upper is in the city and the lower in Peiraieus. Or the upper is the one looking up towards the Akropolis, the lower looking down towards the city or the Peiraieus. Or it is called by special usage the upper and the lower dikasterion. Or the upper is in an upper story and the lower is under the open sky.

86. Harpokration, *s.v.* ὁ κάτωθεν νόμος — 2nd century C.E.

ὁ κάτωθεν νόμος· Δημοσθένης ἐν τῶι κατ' Ἀριστοκράτους. Δίδυμος ἤτοι, φησί, τὴν ἡλιαίαν λέγει ὁ ῥήτωρ διὰ τὸ τῶν δικαστηρίων τὰ μὲν ἄνω τὰ δὲ κάτω ὀνομάζεσθαι, ἢ διὰ τὸ σχῆμα τῆς ἐν τοῖς ἄξοσι γραφῆς βουστροφηδὸν γεγραμμένης ἧι τὸν ἀπὸ τῶν εὐωνύμων ἀρχόμενον νόμον κάτωθεν ὀνομάζει ὁ Δημοσθένης· ὅτι γάρ, φησί, βουστροφηδὸν ἦσαν οἱ ἄξονες καὶ οἱ κύρβεις γεγραμμένοι, δεδήλωκεν Εὐφορίων ἐν τῶι Ἀπολλοδώρωι. ἢ ἐπεί, φησί, τοὺς ἄξονας καὶ τοὺς κύρβεις ἄνωθεν ἐκ τῆς ἀκροπόλεως εἰς τὸ βουλευτήριον καὶ τὴν ἀγορὰν μετέστησεν Ἐφιάλτης, ὥς φησιν Ἀναξιμένης ἐν Φιλιππικοῖς.

The law below (or lower law), Demosthenes in the speech against Aristokrates: Didymos says, "Either the orator is referring to the Heliaia because some of the dikasteria are called upper, others lower, or Demosthenes calls the law beginning at the left the lower one because of the pattern of the writing on the axones which is boustrophedon. That the axones and kyrbeis were written boustrophedon," Didymos says, "Euphorion has made clear in his Apollodoros. Or [the reason may be]," he says, "that the axones and kyrbeis were moved by Ephialtes from above on the Akropolis to the bouleuterion and the agora, as Anaximenes says in his *Philippics*."

Pollux 8.128 (= *Agora* III, no. 561) also states that the kyrbeis and axones were moved, but he says from the Akropolis to the Prytaneion and the Agora, and διὰ τοῦτο ἔλεγον τὸν κάτωθεν νόμον ἀντιτιθέντες πρὸς τὴν ἀκρόπολιν ("Therefore they would say 'the lower law' when making a contrast to the Akropolis"). On axones and kyrbeis generally, see Stroud 1979, with references to this passage on pp. 12, 32, and 37.

87. Isokrates 7 (*Areopagiticus*) 54 — 355 B.C.E.?

ὅταν ἴδηι πολλοὺς τῶν πολιτῶν αὐτοὺς μὲν περὶ τῶν ἀναγκαίων, εἴθ' ἕξουσιν εἴτε μή, πρὸ τῶν δικαστηρίων κληρουμένους.

[A rhetorical question, in which he asks who does not suffer] when he sees many of the citizens being allotted in front of the dikasteria to see whether they will have the necessities or not.

88. Lysias 19 (*Aristophanes*) 55 — 387 or 386 B.C.E.

ἐγγύς τε οἰκῶν τῆς ἀγορᾶς οὔτε πρὸς δικαστηρίωι οὔτε πρὸς βουλευτηρίωι ὤφθην οὐδεπώποτε.

Although I live near the Agora, never at any time was I seen at the dikasterion or bouleuterion.

A similar boast is found in Isokrates 15.38 (*Antidosis*, 354/3 B.C.E.), where the speaker claims that no one has seen him in the synedria nor around the examinations nor near the lawcourts (ἐπὶ τοῖς δικαστηρίοις) nor before the diaiteitai. The Agora is not mentioned.

89. Plato, *Theaetetus* 173c–d 4th century B.C.E.

οὗτοι δέ που ἐκ νέων πρῶτον μὲν εἰς ἀγορὰν οὐκ ἴσασι τὴν ὁδόν, οὐδὲ ὅπου δικαστήριον ἢ βουλευτήριον ἤ τι κοινὸν ἄλλο τῆς πόλεως συνέδριον.

In the first place, suppose that from childhood they do not know which is the road to the Agora, nor where dikasterion or bouleuterion is or any other public meeting place of the city.

Although the text does not necessarily state that a dikasterion was in the Agora, it can be construed in such a way as to suggest that ignorance of the way to dikasterion, bouleuterion, and any other public meeting place is a specification, an illustration of his ignorance of the Agora. In that case, a translation could be: ". . . they do not know which is the road to the Agora, not where dikasterion or bouleuterion or any other public building is."

90. Plutarch, *de genio Socratis* 10.580d–f 1st–2nd century C.E.

ἔτυχε μέν, ὦ Σιμμία, μέμνησαι γάρ, ἄνω πρὸς τὸ Σύμβολον Σωκράτης καὶ τὴν οἰκίαν τὴν Ἀνδοκίδου βαδίζων, ἅμα τι διερωτῶν καὶ διασείων τὸν Εὐθύφρονα μετὰ παιδιᾶς· ἄφνω δὲ ἐπιστὰς καὶ σιωπήσας προσέσχεν αὑτῶι συχνὸν χρόνον, εἶτ' ἀναστρέψας ἐπορεύετο τὴν διὰ τῶν κιβωτοποιῶν. . . . οἱ μὲν οὖν πολλοὶ συνανέστρεφον . . . νεανίσκοι δέ τινες τὴν εὐθεῖαν βαδίζοντες. . . . πορευομένοις δ' αὐτοῖς διὰ τῶν ἑρμογλύφων παρὰ τὰ δικαστήρια, σύες ἀπαντῶσιν ἀθρόοι βορβόρου περίπλεοι, καὶ κατ' ἀλλήλων ὠθούμεναι διὰ πλῆθος· ἐκτροπῆς δὲ μὴ παρούσης, τοὺς μὲν ἀνέτρεψαν ἐμβαλοῦσαι, τοὺς δ' ἀνεμόλυναν.

It happened, as you remember, Simmias, that Sokrates was walking up towards the Symbolon and the house of Andokides, putting some questions to Euthyphron and making fun of him. Suddenly he stopped and fell silent, lost in thought for some time. Then turning back, he went by way of the box makers. . . . Most turned back with him . . . but some of the young men went straight ahead. . . . As they were walking along through the herm carvers, past the lawcourts, a herd of pigs covered with filth and jostling one another met them and, since there was no place to turn aside, knocked some of them down, and covered others with dirt.

The imaginary setting of the *de genio* is in Athens shortly after the liberation of Thebes in 379 B.C.E. The Symbolon, of which no further mention is known, and the house of Andokides are generally assumed to have been near the Agora (Judeich 1931, pp. 178 and 353).

The mention of the herm carvers, or their shops, may be borrowed from Plato's *Symposium* 215a, where Alkibiades compares Sokrates to the silenes ἐν τοῖς ἑρμογλυφείοις (215a). Note that ἑρμογλυφιων in the manuscript has been emended to ἑρμογλύφων. LSJ lists ἑρμογλυφεῖον, ἑρμογλύφος, and ἑρμογλυφεύς as uncommon words, rarely found in classical authors.

One would like to know whether τὰ δικαστήρια in the district of the herm carvers represents the scene as it was in Plutarch's day, added by Plutarch from personal observation, or whether it is a topographical detail from some earlier source. Excavations in the Agora have shown that in the 5th and 4th centuries B.C.E. many marble workshops were located in the industrial area southwest of the Square (Young 1951, pp. 139, 151, and 160); compare Wycherley 1978, pp. 97–98, with a caution expressed by A. Boegehold (Rev. of R. E. Wycherley, *The Stones of Athens*, in *AJP* 101, 1980, p. 126). For a later period, however, between the destruction wrought by Sulla in 86 B.C.E. and the building done by Hadrian, there is evidence of marble workers along the south side of the Square, as well as a sculptors' workshop at the southeast corner.

91. Pollux 8.6 2nd century C.E.

Δικαστικὰ ὀνόματα εἴη ἄν, ὡς ἐγῷμαι, τάδε. δίκη μὲν ... ὁ δὲ δικάζων δικαστής, τὸ δὲ χωρίον δικαστήριον.

The dikastic words would be, it seems to me, these. Trial (there follow some synonyms, and then) ... he who serves as dikast, a dikast, the place a dikasterion.

92. Pollux 8.15 2nd century C.E.

κοινὰ δ' ἐπὶ δικαστῶν ... ἔστι δ' εἰπεῖν ἐκάθισε δικαστήριον καὶ ἀπεκληρώθη δικαστήριον.

The common words related to the dikasts (there follow some words and phrases having to do with verdicts and voting, and then) it is possible to say that the dikasterion sat, and that the dikasterion was chosen by lot.

93. *IG* II^2 663 286/5 B.C.E.
(A grant of Athenian citizenship, lines 24–30 = *SEG* XXVIII 56)

[... τοὺ]ς δὲ πρυτάνεις [τ]οὺς [πρυτανεύοντα]ς τοῦ Μουνιχιῶνος μην- [ὸς δοῦναι περ]ὶ αὐτοῦ τὴν ψῆφον εἰς τή- [ν πρώτην ἐκκλ]ησίαν κα[ὶ τοὺ]ς θεσμοθέ- [τας εἰσαγαγ]εῖν αὐτῶι [τὴν δοκιμασ]ία- [ν ὅταν πληρῶ]σιν τὰ δημόσι[α δικαστή]ρ- [ια

[The] prytaneis for the month Mounichion [are to] present a balloting concerning him at the first meeting of the ekklesia, and the thesmothetai to introduce his dokimasia when they man the people's courts.

On τὰ δημόσια δικαστήρια, compare Aristotle *Ath. Pol.* 59.5. The formulae listed in *IG* II^2 4, line 1, p. 61 have εἰς τὸ δικαστήριον or ὅταν πληρῶσι δικαστήρια for τὰ δικαστήρια; see **94** and **95**. Ferguson (1911, p. 130, note 4) sees here oligarchic judicial control of citizenship. Possibly, the phrase τὰ δημόσια δικαστήρια can be taken to mean "courts convened in panels of 501 dikasts," the normal number for trial of charges classed as δημόσια; compare Aristotle, *Ath. Pol.* 68.1 (**110**).

94. *IG* II^2 1163, lines 2–14 *ca.* 288/7 B.C.E.

Πρόξενος Πυλαγόρου Ἀχερδούσι- ος εἶπεν· ἐπειδὴ Φυλεὺς λαχὼν ἱε- ρεὺς τοῦ Ἀσκληπιοῦ ἐπὶ Ἰσαίο[υ ἄ]- ρχοντος τάς τε θυσίας ὅσας πρ[οσ] [ῆ]κεν αὐτὸν θῦσαι πάσας καλῶς κα- [ὶ] φιλοτίμως τέθυκεν ὑπὲρ τοῦ δή- μου τοῦ Ἀθηναίων, ἐπιμελεῖται δ- ὲ καὶ τῆς κληρώσεως τῶν δικαστ[η]- [ρ]ίων καὶ τῶν ἄλλων ὧν αὐτῶι οἵ τ[ε] νόμοι καὶ τὰ ψηφίσματα προστάτ- τουσιν δικαίως καὶ κατὰ το[ὺ]ς νό- μους καὶ διὰ ταῦτα ἥ τε βουλὴ καὶ ὁ δῆμος ἐπεινέκασιν αὐτόν·

Proxenos, son of Pylagoros, from the deme Acherdous moved: inasmuch as Phyleus as allotted priest of Asklepios in the archonship of Isaios has performed well and honorably all the sacrifices it was his duty to perform for the Athenian people, and inasmuch as he is superintending honestly and in accordance with the laws the allotments of the lawcourts and other things that the laws and ordinances enjoin, for these reasons, both boule and people commend him.

95. Agora I 3625 (B. D. Meritt, "Greek Inscriptions," *Hesperia* 7, 1938 [pp. 77–160], p. 95, no. 15) 327/6 B.C.E.

Δημοκράτης Δημοκλέ-
ους Ἀφιδναῖος εἶπε·
ἐπειδὴ ὁ θεσμοθέτη-
ς ὁ τῆς Αἰαντίδος ἐπ-
ιμεμέληται τῆς τε κ-
ληρώσεως τῶν ἀρχῶν
καὶ τῶν δικαστηρίω-
ν τῆς πληρώσεως καὶ
τῶν ἄλλων ἁπάντων τ-
ῶν περὶ τὴν Αἰαντίδ-
α φυλήν, ἐπαινέσαι Τ-
ηλέσκοπον Ἀριστοκ-
ρίτου Ῥαμνούσιον.

Demokrates, son of Demokles, from the deme Aphidna, moved: since the thesmothetes of the phyle Aiantis has been responsible for the allotment of offices and the manning of the dikasteria and everything else concerning the tribe Aias, praise be given to Teleskopos, son of Aristokratos, from the deme Rhamnous.

THE HELIAIA

96. Andokides 1 (*On the Mysteries*) 28 399 B.C.E.

ἔδοξεν οὖν τῶι δήμωι ἐν τῶι τῶν θεσμοθετῶν δικαστηρίωι τοὺς μεμυημένους ἀκούσαντας τὰς μηνύσεις ἃς ἕκαστος ἐμήνυσε διαδικάσαι.

The demos then decreed that initiates hear in the court of the thesmothetai the information that each informer had given and adjudicate between them.

The question to be decided was the amount of the rewards to be given to the various informers on the violation of the Mysteries. The form of the inquiry is that of a διαδικασία, a judicial procedure in which more than two opposed parties are involved and rankings or eliminations are at issue. The court of the thesmothetai may appear to be a topical reference but again may be a panel convened by the thesmothetai; compare **97**.

97. Antiphon 6 (*Choreutes*) 21–24 419/18 B.C.E.

Ἔλεξε μὲν γὰρ Φιλοκράτης οὑτοσί, ἀναβὰς εἰς τὴν ἡλιαίαν τὴν τῶν θεσμοθετῶν, τῆι ἡμέραι ἧι ὁ παῖς ἐξεφέρετο, ὅτι ἀδελφὸν αὐτοῦ ἀποκτείναιμι ἐγὼ ἐν τῶι χορῶι, φάρμακον ἀναγκάσας πιεῖν. Ἐπειδὴ δὲ οὗτος ταῦτα ἔλεγεν, ἀναβὰς ἐγὼ εἰς τὸ δικαστήριον τοῖς αὐτοῖς δικασταῖς ἔλεξα ὅτι. . . . Καὶ εἶπόν τε ταῦτα ἐν τῶι δικαστηρίωι, καὶ προὐκαλούμην αὐτὸν εὐθὺς τότε, καὶ αὖθις τῆι ὑστεραίαι ἐν τοῖς αὐτοῖς δικασταῖς. . . . Καὶ ταῦτα ἐμοῦ προκαλουμένου καὶ λέγοντος ἐν τῶι δικαστηρίωι, οὗ καὶ αὐτοὶ οἱ δικασταὶ καὶ ἕτεροι ἰδιῶται πολλοὶ μάρτυρες παρῆσαν.

ἡλιαίαν is recorded as the correction of John Taylor for ἡλιακην codd. See F. Blass, *Antiphontis Orationes et Fragmenta*, Leipzig 1892, p. 103.

For Philokrates here appeared before the heliaia of the thesmothetai the day of the boy's funeral and said that I had killed his brother in the chorus by making him drink poison. Since he was saying this, I went before the dikasterion and told the same dikasts that [Philokrates was making his false accusations to compromise the other suits] and I both said this in the dikasterion and challenged him immediately at that time and again the following day before the same dikasts . . . and I made this challenge in the dikasterion, where the dikasts themselves and many other private persons were present as witnesses.

Note that "heliaia of the thesmothetai" and "dikasterion" are synonymous; also that the same dikasts are judging on two successive days; also that many private persons besides dikasts are present. These are presumably the *periestekotes* of, for example, Plato, *Apology* 24e, Aischines 3.56 (**229**), Demosthenes 30.32 (**195**), 54.41.

98. Aristophanes, *Birds*, lines 109–111 414 B.C.E.

Τηρεύς: μῶν ἡλιαστά;
Πεισέταιρος: Μάλλὰ θατέρου τρόπου
ἀπηλιαστά.
Τηρεύς: σπείρεται γὰρ τοῦτ' ἐκεῖ τὸ σπέρμ';
Πεισέταιρος: ὀλίγον ζητῶν ἂν ἐξ ἀγροῦ λαβοῖς.

Tereus: You are not heliasts, are you?
Peisetairos: No, the other sort, we're anteliasts.
Tereus: Is this seed sown there?
Peisetairos: If you look, you might get a little out of the country.

A scholiast clarifies: ὡς ὀλίγον ὄντων τῶν μισοδίκων, καὶ τούτων ἀγροίκων ("As though those who hate the courts are few, and they are country folk").

99. Schol. Aristophanes, *Birds*, line 109

ἡλιαστά· δικασταί, ἀπὸ τοῦ μεγάλου δικαστηρίου τῆς ἡλιαίας· οὕτω δὲ ἐκλήθη διὰ τὸ ἐν ὑπαίθρωι εἶναι τόπωι καὶ ὑπὸ ἡλίου βάλλεσθαι.

Heliasts: dikasts, from the great lawcourt the Heliaia; it is so called because it is in a place open to the sky and is hit by the sun.

Compare scholia on *Clouds*, *Knights*, *Wasps*, and the *Suda*.

100. Aristophanes, *Clouds*, line 863 423 B.C.E.
(Strepsiades is speaking.)

ὃν πρῶτον ὀβολὸν ἔλαβον ἡλιαστικόν.

. . . with the first obol I got as heliastic pay.

101. Schol. Aristophanes, *Clouds*, line 863

ἡλιαστικὸν δέ, ἀντὶ τοῦ ἐκκλησιαστικόν· ἡλιαία δὲ τὸ δικαστήριον, διὰ τὸ ὑπαίθριον εἶναι καὶ τῶι ἡλίωι βάλλεσθαι. οὐχ ἵστατο δὲ τῶν δικαστῶν ὁ μισθός.

Heliastikon instead of ekklesiastikon: the lawcourt is heliaia because it is open to the sky and is hit by the sun. There was not a "pay of the dikasts".

The clause διὰ . . . βάλλεσθαι is assigned by Koster to a recension by Thomas Magister and Demetrius Triclinius in *Scholia Recentiora in Nubes.* Compare scholia on the *Birds*, *Wasps*, *Knights*, and the *Suda.*

102. Aristophanes, *Knights*, lines 255–256 424 B.C.E.

Παφλαγών: ὦ γέροντες ἡλιασταί, φράτερες τριωβόλου,
οὓς ἐγὼ βόσκω κεκραγὼς καὶ δίκαια κἄδικα.

Paphlagonian: You old heliasts, members of the brotherhood of the triobolon,
Whom I feed whether what I shout is right or wrong.

103. Schol. Aristophanes, *Knights*, line 255

Ἡλιαία γὰρ μέγιστον δικαστήριον Ἀθήνησιν . . .

(The scholiast then says that the dikasts are supported by the demagogues who give them the triobol dikasts' pay and digresses from "triobol" to discuss the meanings of φράτορες [a later form of φράτηρ] and συγγενεῖς. Then he adds a final sentence.)

Ἡλιαία δὲ καλεῖται, διὰ τὸ ὑπαίθριον αὐτὸ εἶναι καὶ ὑπὸ τῶι ἡλίωι καθέζεσθαι τοὺς συνελθόντας δικαστάς.

Heliaia is the great lawcourt at Athens. . . . It is called Heliaia because it is open to the sky and the dikasts meeting there sit in the sun.

Compare scholia on *Clouds*, line 863; *Wasps*, lines 88 and 772; *Birds*, line 109; also *Suda*, *s.v.* ἡλιαστής; Schol. on Demosthenes 24.21; Bekker, *Anecdota Graeca* 1.310.32; and *Etymologicum Magnum*, *s.v.* ἡλιαία.

104. Aristophanes, *Knights*, lines 897–898 424 B.C.E.

Ἀλλαντοπώλης: κἄπειτ' ἐν ἡλιαίαι
βδέοντες ἀλλήλους ἀποκτείνειαν οἱ δικασταί.

Sausage-seller: and then in court
the dikasts would fart each other to death.

105. Schol. Aristophanes, *Knights*, line 898

οἱ δικασταί· οἱ ἡλιασταί. τὸ μέγα δὲ δικαστήριον ἐν τῆι Ἀττικῆι Ἡλιαία, καὶ οἱ δικασταὶ ἡλιασταί.

The dikasts: the heliasts. The great lawcourt in Attica was the Heliaia, and the dikasts were heliasts.

This is repeated almost verbatim in the *Suda.*

(71) Schol. Aristophanes, *Ploutos*, line 277

He changed the word, saying "in the grave" when it should have been "in the Heliaia".

(75) Schol. Aristophanes, *Ploutos*, line 1166

We have said above about the letters and the Athenian dikasteria that there was a letter written in each . . . in the Heliaia, eta.

106. Aristophanes, *Wasps*, lines 88–110 422 B.C.E.
(Xanthias is describing Philokleon.)

φιληλιαστής ἐστιν ὡς οὐδεὶς ἀνήρ,
ἐρᾶι τε τούτου τοῦ δικάζειν, καὶ στένει,
ἢν μὴ ’πὶ τοῦ πρώτου καθίζηται ξύλου.
ὕπνου δ’ ὁρᾶι τῆς νυκτὸς οὐδὲ πασπάλην.
ἢν δ’ οὖν καταμύσηι κἂν ἄχνην, ὅμως ἐκεῖ
ὁ νοῦς πέτεται τὴν νύκτα περὶ τὴν κλεψύδραν.
ὑπὸ τοῦ δὲ τὴν ψῆφόν γ’ ἔχειν εἰωθέναι
τοὺς τρεῖς ξυνέχων τῶν δακτύλων ἀνίσταται,
ὥσπερ λιβανωτὸν ἐπιτιθεὶς νουμηνίαι.
καὶ νὴ Δί’ ἢν ἴδηι γέ που γεγραμμένον
υἱὸν Πυριλάμπους ἐν θύραι Δῆμον καλόν,
ἰὼν παρέγραψε πλησίον κημὸς καλός.
τὸν ἀλεκτρυόνα δ’, ὃς ἦιδ’ ἀφ’ ἑσπέρας, ἔφη
ὀψ’ ἐξεγείρειν αὐτὸν ἀναπεπεισμένον
παρὰ τῶν ὑπευθύνων ἔχοντα χρήματα.
εὐθὺς δ’ ἀπὸ δορπηστοῦ κέκραγεν ἐμβάδας,
κἄπειτ’ ἐκεῖσ’ ἐλθὼν προκαθεύδει πρῲ πάνυ,
ὥσπερ λεπὰς προσεχόμενος τῶι κίονι.
ὑπὸ δυσκολίας δ’ ἅπασι τιμῶν τὴν μακρὰν
ὥσπερ μέλιττ’ ἢ βομβυλιὸς εἰσέρχεται,
ὑπὸ τοῖς ὄνυξι κηρὸν ἀναπεπλασμένος.
ψήφων δὲ δείσας μὴ δεηθείη ποτέ,
ἵν’ ἔχοι δικάζειν, αἰγιαλὸν ἔνδον τρέφει.

He is a heliaphile like no one else,
in love with being a judge,
and he groans if he is not sitting on the first wooden bench.
At night he does not get a speck of sleep;
or if he shuts his eyes a bit, his mind no less
flutters all night long around the waterclock.
From his habit of holding the ballot, he gets up
holding three of his fingers together, just as if
he had offered incense on the new moon's day.
And by Zeus, if he sees written on a gate somewhere
"Demos, son of Pyrilampes, is beautiful," he goes
and writes beside it "Kemos is beautiful."
The cock that crowed from evening, he said,
was tampered with, to call him late,
bribed by officials whose accounts were due.
As soon as supper is done, he shouts for his shoes,
and then goes there early early and sleeps
hanging on to the column like a limpet.
In his bad temper, he assigns
everyone the long [condemning line]
and then comes in like a honeybee or
bumblebee with wax stuck up beneath his nails.

Afraid he might lack ballots with which to judge,
he grows his own pebble beach at home.

On the kemos, see pp. 210–211; on the long condemning line, see pp. 234–235. See scholia on relevant words in lines 90 (**245**), 93 (**313**), 99 (**259**), and 106 (**334**).

107. Schol. Aristophanes, *Wasps*, line 88

φιλοδικαστής· ἦσαν δὲ ἡλιασταὶ τὸν ἀριθμὸν φ′, ἐδίδοντο δὲ αὐτοῖς χρόνον μέν τινα δύο ὀβολοί, ὕστερον δὲ Κλέων στρατηγήσας τριώβολον ἐποίησεν ἀκμάζοντος τοῦ πολέμου τοῦ πρὸς Λακεδαιμονίους. φιληλιαστής· ἀντὶ τοῦ φιλόδικος, ἀπὸ τοῦ μεγίστου δικαστηρίου τῆς ἡλιαίας ὅπερ οὕτω καλεῖται διὰ τὸ ἐν ὑπαιθρίωι εἶναι καὶ ἡλίωι βαλέσθαι.

The correction from δ' to δύο is that of Wilhelm Dindorf.

Dikaphile: there were 500 heliasts, and for a time two obols were given to them. Later, when Kleon became general, as the war with the Lacedaimonians was at its height, he made it three obols. Heliaphile: instead of "trial-lover", [the word is coined] from the largest court in the court system [Heliaia]. It is so named because it is open to the sky and is hit by the sun.

For the second sentence, compare scholia on the *Birds, Clouds, Knights,* and the *Suda.*

108. Aristophanes, *Wasps*, lines 771–772 422 B.C.E.

Βδελυκλέων: καὶ ταῦτα μέν νυν εὐλόγως, ἢν ἐξέχηι
εἵλη κατ' ὄρθρον, ἡλιάσει πρὸς ἥλιον.

Bdelykleon: And so it stands to reason that if the sun comes out at dawn, you will judge these matters in the sun.

On the spelling ἡλιάσει, see MacDowell 1971, p. 158.

109. Schol. Aristophanes, *Wasps*, line 772b, e

(b) εἵλη κατ' ὄρθρον· ... τὸ δ' ἡλιάσει (μήποτε δὲ ψιλῶς προενεκτέον) παρὰ τὴν ἡλιαίαν, πρὸς ἥλιον δικάσειν. ἅμα δὲ παίζει παρὰ τὴν τοῦ ἡλίου ὀνομασίαν. ψυχρῶς δὲ πέπαιχε, φησὶν ὁ Δίδυμος, πρὸς τοὔνομα. ἐπειδὴ γὰρ εἵλη λέγεται ἡ τοῦ ἡλίου αὐγή, ἡλιαία δὲ τὸ δικαστήριον, παίζων ἔφη πρὸς τὸ φιλόδικον ὅτι ἐπειδὰν ἀνάσχηι ὁ ἥλιος, ἡλιάζειν ἐνέσται σοι. οὕτως δὲ οἱ Ἀττικοὶ διὰ τοῦ ι εἵλην λέγουσιν. οὕτως Δίδυμος. (e) δικάσεις, φησίν, πρὸς τὸν ἥλιον καθήμενος. ἔπαιξε δὲ παρὰ τὴν ἡλιαίαν, τὸ μέγιστον δικαστήριον, ὃ ταύτης τῆς ὀνομασίας ἔτυχε διὰ τὸ ἐν ὑπαίθρωι αὐτὸ ἀναπεπταμένον βάλλεσθαι τῶι ἡλίωι.

(b) Ray at dawn: ... The "you will judge" (perhaps to be pronounced with the smooth breathing) derived from the Heliaia, to judge in the sun. At the same time there is a play on the word "sun". He makes a feeble play on the name, Didymos says. Since εἵλη is the ray of the sun, Heliaia the lawcourt, poking fun at the love of trials he said that after the sun has risen it will be possible for you to act as heliast. The Attic writers say εἵλην thus with the iota. Thus Didymos. (e) You will act as a dikast, he says, sitting in the sun. He played on the word "Heliaia", the largest lawcourt, which got this name because it is spread out under the open sky and so is hit by the sun.

110. Aristotle, *Ath. Pol.* 68.1 *ca.* 329–322 B.C.E.

[τὰ μὲν οὖν πολλ]ὰ τῶν δ[ικ]αστηρίων ἐστὶ φ[α........] σο.[.].ασιν, ὅταν δὲ δέ[ηι τὰς δημοσίας γραφ]ὰς ε[ἰ[ς] ᾱ [εἰ]σαγαγεῖν, συν[έρχεται β′ δικαστή]ρια εἰ[ς] τὴν ἡλιαίαν τὰ δ[ὲ μέγιστα... ....] κλε[.]δ' εἰς ϡ καὶ ᾱ τρία [δικαστήρια].

[Most] dikastic panels are of 501. . . . When it is necessary [to introduce] public cases [before 1,000, two dikasteria meet] together in the Heliaia . . . [before] 1,500, three dikasteria.

111. Bekker, *Anecdota Graeca* 1.189.20–21

ἡλιαία καὶ ἡλιάζεσθαι· δικαστήριον ἀνδρῶν χιλίων καὶ ὁ τόπος ἐν ὧι οὗτοι δικάζουσιν.

Heliaia and to serve in the Heliaia: a dikasterion of 1,000 men and the place in which they judge the cases.

Compare *Suda* (**129**).

112. Bekker, *Anecdota Graeca* 1.262.10–13

ἡλιαία· μέγα δικαστήριον Ἀθήνησιν, ἐν ὧι τὰ μέγιστα τῶν δημοσίων πραγμάτων ἐκρίνετο· ἦν δὲ χιλίων πεντακοσίων καὶ ἑνός. συνήιεσαν δὲ οἱ μὲν χίλιοι πεντακόσιοι ἐκ τριῶν φυλῶν.

Heliaia: the great lawcourt in Athens in which the most important public cases were tried. It consisted of 1,501 [dikasts]. The 1,500 came together from three tribes.

Compare Harpokration (**121**).

113. Bekker, *Anecdota Graeca* 1.310.28–311.2

ἐν ποίοις δικαστηρίοις τίνες λαγχάνονται δίκαι; Ἡλιαία. καλεῖται δὲ μέγα δικαστήριον καὶ οἱ χίλιοι δικασταί· ἐν τούτοις ἀρχαιρεσίαι γίνονται καὶ αἱ μέγισται κρίσεις καὶ αἱ διοικήσεις· ἐκαλεῖτο δὲ καὶ μεγάλη ἐκκλησία. ἡλιαία δὲ ἐκλήθη ἤτοι παρὰ τὸ ἐν αὐτῆι ἁλιάζεσθαι, τουτέστιν ἀθροίζεσθαι, ἢ διὰ τὸ ὕπαιθρον εἶναι τὸν τόπον καὶ ἡλιοῦσθαι.

In what courts are what cases tried? [First,] the Heliaia. This is the name of the big court and its thousand dikasts. Here the elections of magistrates are held, and the most important trials and [discussions] of financial administration. It was also called the Great Assembly. It was called Heliaia either because people gathered together in it (ἁλιάζεσθαι = ἀθροίζεσθαι) or because of the fact that the place was open to the sky and the sun shines on it.

There is a confusion here with the κυρία ἐκκλησία (*Ath. Pol.* 43.4). See **133**–**137** for examples of the word *heliaia* used by 4th-century orators in direct quotations from laws; see **132** for an evocation of "heliaia" as venerable and authentic.

114. Demosthenes 23 (*Aristokrates*) 97 — 352 B.C.E.

διόπερ καταρᾶται καθ' ἑκάστην ἐκκλησίαν ὁ κῆρυξ, οὐκ εἴ τινες ἐξηπατήθησαν, ἀλλ' εἴ τις ἐξαπατᾶι λέγων ἢ βουλὴν ἢ δῆμον ἢ τὴν ἡλιαίαν.

Wherefore at each meeting of the assembly, the herald calls down curses not on any who have been deceived but on any speaker who deceives the boule or assembly or heliaia.

115. Demosthenes 24 (*Timokrates*) 21 — 353/2 B.C.E.

τοὺς δὲ νομοθέτας εἶναι ἐκ τῶν ὀμωμοκότων τὸν ἡλιαστικὸν ὅρκον.

The nomothetai are chosen from those who have sworn the heliastic oath.

116. Schol. Demosthenes 24 (*Timokrates*) 21

ἡ Ἡλιαία λέγεται αὐτὸς ὁ τόπος τοῦ μεγάλου δικαστηρίου καὶ τὸ ἄθροισμα αὐτῶν τῶν ἐκεῖσε δικαζόντων. Ἡλιαία δὲ ἐκλήθη ὁ τόπος παρὰ τὸ ἐκεῖσε ἁλίζεσθαι καὶ συναθροίζεσθαι τὸ πλῆθος τῶν δικαστῶν. τὸ γὰρ α εἰς η μεταβέβληται ὡς καὶ πολλαχοῦ. τινὲς δὲ λέγουσιν ἐκ τοῦ ὕπαιθρον εἶναι τὸν τόπον καὶ τὸν ἥλιον ἐκεῖ ἔνδον προσβάλλειν.

"Heliaia" is used of the site of the great lawcourt and of the assembly of dikasts there. The place was called Heliaia from the fact that the mass of dikasts gathered and met there. For the alpha has been changed to eta as in many places. But some say that it is from the fact that the place is open to the skies and the sun shines into it.

117. Schol. Demosthenes 24 (*Timokrates*) 123

τὸ δὲ διχόθεν μισθοφορῆσαι σημαίνει ἐάν τις λαχὼν δικάζειν ὑπὲρ δύο δικαστηρίων μισθοφορήσηι. ἔστι γὰρ ὅτε λαχών τις δικάζειν ἀφικνεῖται πρὸς τὸν ⟨τὸν⟩ μισθὸν διανέμοντα καὶ παρὰ μὲν τοῦ δεῖνος λαμβάνει ὡς εἰς τὴν ἡλιαίαν κεκληρωμένος, παρὰ δὲ τοῦ δεῖνος ὡς εἰς τὸν τρίγωνον.

The phrase "to draw pay from two sources" means that a person allotted to judge draws pay for two courts. [This happens] because sometimes a man allotted to judge comes to the disburser and draws pay from one person as though he had been allotted to the Heliaia, and then from another as though he had been allotted to the Trigonon.

The scholion reflects the system of allotment assumed in Aristophanes, *Ploutos*, lines 1166–1167 (**74**). See Boegehold 1984, *aliter* Hansen 1979, pp. 8–9.

118. [Demosthenes] 47 (*Euergos and Mnesiboulos*) 12 *ca.* 353 B.C.E.

ἡ μὲν γὰρ δίαιτα ἐν τῆι ἡλιαίαι ἦν (οἱ γὰρ τὴν Οἰνῆιδα καὶ τὴν Ἐρεχθῆιδα διαιτῶντες ἐνταῦθα κάθηνται).

The arbitration was in the Heliaia (because the panels of arbitrators for the tribes of Oineis and Erechtheis meet there).

119. *Etymologicum Magnum, s.v.* ἡλιαία 12th century C.E.

ἡλιαία εἰς τὸ ὕπαιθρον προκαθημένων τῶν δικαστῶν· ... ἢ παρὰ τὸ ἁλίζεσθαι τὸ συναθροίζεσθαι, ἁλιαία, καὶ ἡλιαία· ἔστι δὲ τὸ μέγα δικαστήριον Ἀθηναίων ἐν ὧι τὰ δημόσια τῶν πραγμάτων ἐκρίνετο· ἡ βουλὴ συνεστῶσα ἐξ ἀνδρῶν χιλίων· ἡλιάζεσθαι καὶ ἡλίασις ἐστὶ τὸ ἐν ἡλιαίαι δικάζειν.

[It is called] Heliaia since the dikasts took their seats out in the open air ... or from the verb ἁλίζεσθαι, to meet together, ἁλιαία [assembly], and ἡλιαία. It is the great dikasterion of the Athenians in which public matters were judged; the council is made up of 1,000 men. "To serve in the Heliaia" and "service in the Heliaia" is [the same thing as] "to judge in the Heliaia".

Compare Harpokration (**121**) for the last two sentences.

120. Eustathios, *Commentary on Homer, Odyssey* 2.7 12th century C.E.

ἦν δέ φασι καὶ ἀγορὰ Κερκώπων Ἀθήνησι πλησίον Ἡλιαίας, ἔνθα τὰ κλοπιμαῖα ἐπωλοῦντο.

Wachsmuth (1874, II, p. 498, note 2) suggests ἐφ' Ἡλιαίαι.

There was, they say, an Agora of the Kerkopes at Athens near the Heliaia, where stolen goods were sold.

Also see commentary on *Odyssey* 10.552: οἱ Κέρκοπες ἀφ' ὧν καὶ ἀγορὰ καλουμένη Κερκώπων Ἀθήνησιν ἐν Ἡλιαίαι.

121. Harpokration, *s.v.* ἡλιαία καὶ ἡλίασις — 2nd century C.E.

ἡλιαία καὶ ἡλίασις· ἡλιαία μέν ἐστι τὸ μέγιστον δικαστήριον τῶν Ἀθήνησιν, ἐν ὧι τὰ δημόσια τῶν πραγμάτων ἐκρίνετο χιλίων δικαστῶν ἢ χιλίων καὶ φ συνιόντων. συνήιεσαν δὲ οἱ μὲν χίλιοι ἐκ δυοῖν δικαστηρίων, οἱ δὲ χίλιοι πεντακόσιοι ἐκ τριῶν. ἡλιάζεσθαι δὲ καὶ ἡλίασίς ἐστι τὸ ἐν ἡλιαίαι δικάζειν. Λυσίας μὲν ἐν τῶι πρὸς Γλαύκωνα τὴν ἡλιαίαν πολλάκις ὀνομάζει, ἐν δὲ τῶι κατὰ Φιλωνίδου, εἰ γνήσιος, τῶι ἡλιάζεσθαι ἐχρήσατο.

Heliaia and serving in the Heliaia: Heliaia is the greatest court of [all] those at Athens, in which cases affecting the state were tried, 1,000 or 1,500 dikasts assembling for the purpose. The 1,000 came together from two dikasteria, the 1,500 from three. "To serve in the Heliaia" and "service in the Heliaia" is [the same thing as] "to act as dikast in the Heliaia". Lysias in the speech in reply to Glaukon names the Heliaia many times; in that against Philonides, if [it is] genuine, he used the verb "to serve in the Heliaia".

(86) Harpokration, *s.v.* ὁ κάτωθεν νόμος

122. Hesychios, *s.v.* ἀγορὰ Κερκώπων — 5th or 6th century C.E.

ἀγορὰ Κερκώπων· τόπος πλησίον Ἡλιαίας.

Agora of the Kerkopes: a place near the Heliaia.

For the Agora of the Kerkopes, see *Agora* III, nos. 669–673. Its nearness to the Heliaia is the only clue to its location.

123. Hesychios, *s.v.* ἡλιαία τὸ δικαστήριον — 5th century C.E.

ἡλιαία τὸ δικαστήριον. διαφέρει δὲ ἐκκλησία καὶ βουλὴ καὶ ἡλιαία.

Heliaia, the dikasterion. The assembly and the council and the heliaia are distinct from each other.

124. *Lexicon Patmense, s.v.* ἡλιαία
Commentary on Demosthenes 23.28.

ἡλιαία· τὸ μέγα δικαστήριον ἐν ὧι τὰ μέγιστα τῶν δημοσίων πραγμάτων ἐκρίνετο. ἦν δέ ποτε μὲν χιλίων ἀνδρῶν ποτὲ δὲ χιλίων καὶ πεντακοσίων καὶ ἑνός· ἦσαν δὲ οἱ χίλιοι καὶ πεντακόσιοι ἐκ τριῶν δικαστηρίων, οἱ δὲ χίλιοι ἀπὸ δύο δικαστηρίων. Ἐκλήθη δὲ οὕτως ἀπὸ τοῦ ἁλίζεσθαι.

χιλίων is an emendation by K. S. Kontos ("Διορθωτικὰ εἰς τὰς Λέξεις μεθ' Ἱστοριῶν," *BCH* 1, 1877 [pp. 177–181], p. 178).

Heliaia: the great lawcourt in which the most important of public cases were tried. Sometimes it was made up of 1,000 men, at others 1,501; the 1,500 were made up of three dikasteria, the 1,000 from two dikasteria. It has its name from the verb ἁλίζεσθαι, "to assemble".

Compare Harpokration (**121**), the scholion to Demosthenes 24.21 (**116**), and the entry in Bekker, *Anecdota Graeca* (**111**).

(138) Lysias 10.16

(1) Pausanias 1.28.8

(Among the less famous lawcourts) the largest court and the one to which the greatest number assemble is called the Heliaia.

125. Photios, *Lexicon, s.v.* ἡλιαία 9th century C.E.

ἡλιαία· τόπος Ἀθήνησιν, εἰς ὃν συνάγεται δύο δικαστήρια, ὅταν χίλιοι δικάζωσιν.

Heliaia: a place in Athens in which two dikasteria meet together, when 1,000 serve as dikasts.

(2) Pollux 8.121

Well-known lawcourts are the Heliaia; the Trigonon. . . .

126. Pollux 8.123 2nd century C.E.

ἡ ἡλιαία πενταχοσίων· εἰ δὲ χιλίων δέοι δικαστῶν, συνίστατο δύο δικαστήρια, εἰ δὲ πενταχοσίων καὶ χιλίων, τρία.

The Heliaia is composed of 500; if 1,000 dikasts are needed, two dikasteria would meet together, if 1,500, three dikasteria.

127. Stephanos of Byzantion, *s.v.* ἡλιαία 6th century C.E.

ἡλιαία· δικαστήριον Ἀθηναίων· παρὰ τὸ ἀλέες δεῦτε παράγωγον ἁλία καὶ ἡλιαία. ἔστι δὲ τὸ μέγα δικαστήριον τὸ ἐκ τῶν τεττάρων ἡλισμένον δικαστηρίων, ἐκ τοῦ πενταχοσίων καὶ τετραχοσίων καὶ διακοσίων καὶ ἑκατόν. οἱ δὲ ἐκφερόμενοι ἐλέγοντο ἡλιασταί. ἐκ γὰρ τοῦ ἅλις ἁλία γίνεται. καὶ ὡς βία βιάζω καὶ αἰτία αἰτιάζω, οὕτως ἁλία ἁλιάζω, καὶ ἁλιαστὴς ὡς δικαστής, καὶ ἡλιαστής, καὶ κτητικὸν ἡλιαστικὸς παρὰ τὸ ἡλιαστής.

Heliaia: a dikasterion of the Athenians, from the phrase "assemble here", producing *halia* and *heliaia.* It is the great dikasterion made up of the four dikasteria, those [with members] numbering 500, 400, 200, and 100. The members were called heliasts, because from the word ἅλις ["in crowds"] comes ἁλία ["an assembly"]; just as from the noun "force" there is the verb "to force", and from "blame", "to blame", so from "assembly", the verb "to assemble", and [likewise from ἁλία] *haliastes* for *dikastes*, and *heliastes*, and the adjective *heliastikos* from *heliastes.*

For the suggested derivation from ἁλία, see **113**, **116**. The system of four dikasteria, each of different numbers, seems to be a misunderstanding.

128. *Suda* 10th century C.E.

The *Suda* gives five entries under heliastai, heliastes, and heliaia. The first three are practically the same as the scholia to Aristophanes already cited (**99**, **101**, **103**, **105**, and **109**). The fourth entry is a close copy of Harpokration (**121**), and the fifth repeats verbatim the first two sentences of Harpokration.

ἡλιασταί· οἱ ἐν Ἡλιαίαι δικασταί· Ἡλιαία δὲ τὸ μέγιστον δικαστήριον Ἀθήνησιν.

Heliasts: the dikasts in the Heliaia. The Heliaia is the greatest lawcourt in Athens.

The text continues on demagogues and on dikasts' pay as in the scholion on *Knights,* line 255 (**103**).

ἡλιαστής· δικαστής· ἀπὸ μεγάλου δικαστηρίου τῆς Ἡλιαίας. οὕτω δὲ ἐκλήθη διὰ τὸ ἐν ὑπαίθρωι εἶναι τόπωι καὶ ὑπὸ τοῦ ἡλίου βάλλεσθαι.

Heliast; dikast: from the great lawcourt of the lawcourt system. It was so called because of being in a place open to the sky and being hit by the sun. (*Wasps*, line 88, is then cited.)

ἡλιαία· τὸ μέγα δικαστήριον ἐν τῆι Ἀττικῆι καὶ οἱ δικασταὶ ἡλιασταὶ ἐκαλοῦντο.

Heliaia: the great lawcourt in Attica; the dikasts were called heliasts.

ἡλιαία καὶ ἡλιάζεσθαι· βουλὴ συνεστῶσα ἐξ ἀνδρῶν χιλίων. ἐλέγετο δὲ καὶ ὁ τόπος οὕτως ἐν ὧι συνηθροίζοντο. ἡλιάζεσθαι δὲ καὶ ἡλίασίς ἐστι τὸ ἐν ἡλιαίαι δικάζειν.

Heliaia and serving in the Heliaia: a council made up of 1,000 men. The place in which they met was also called Heliaia. *Heliazesthai* and *heliasis* mean "the act of judging in court".

The last sentence repeats verbatim a sentence in Harpokration (**121**).

ἡλιαία καὶ ἡλίασις.

This entry, not given here, repeats verbatim the first two sentences of Harpokration.

129. *Suda, s.v.* ἥλιος — 10th century C.E.

ἥλιος· ἀπὸ τοῦ ἀολλίζεσθαι ἐν ταῖς ἡμέραις.... καὶ ἐν Ἀθήναις δὲ δικαστήριον ἦν ἡλιαία, ἀπὸ τῆς συναγωγῆς τῶν ἀνθρώπων....

The sun: [is derived from a verb that means] assembled in the daytimes.... and in Athens there was a lawcourt, heliaia, from the assembling of people....

130. *IG* I³ 40, lines 71–76 — 446/5 B.C.E.

τὰς δὲ εὐθύνας Χαλκιδεῦσι κατ-
ὰ σφõν αὐτõν ἒναι ἐν Χαλκίδι καθάπερ Ἀθ-
ένεσιν Ἀθεναίοις πλὲν φυγε̃ς καὶ θανάτ-
ο καὶ ἀτιμίας· περὶ δὲ τούτον ἔφεσιν ἒνα-
ι Ἀθέναζε ἐς τὲν ἐλιαίαν τὲν τõν θεσμοθ-
ετῶν.

... for the people of Chalkis, trials resulting from final accountings against their own people are to be at Chalkis, just as those for Athenians are to be at Athens, except for charges where a penalty of exile, death, or loss of citizenship is possible. These are to be referred to Athens, to the heliaia of the thesmothetai.

131. *IG* I³ 71, lines 13–14 — 425/4 B.C.E.

[... ἐσαγογέον δὲ *ho* λα]χὸν κα[ὶ *h*]ο πολέμαρ[χος ...
.... ἐν τ]ε̃ι ἐλιαίαι ...

[An allotted member of the eisagogeis] and the polemarch [are to ...] in the Heliaia

"Heliaia" is restored at line 49. Here it may be interchangeable with "dikasterion". Compare Antiphon 6.21 (**97**).

132. Agora I 7295 (*SEG* XXX 74), lines 99–104 — 270/69 B.C.E.
Honors for Kallias

χειροτονῆσαι δὲ τὸν δ[ῆ]||μον ἤδη τρεῖς ἄνδρας ἐξ Ἀθηναίων ἁπάντων οἵτινες ἐπιμ[ελ]||ήσονται τῆς τε ποιήσεως τῆς εἰκόνος καὶ τῆς ἀναθέσεως· [ε]||ἰσαγαγεῖν δὲ καὶ τοὺς θεσμοθέτας τὴν δοκιμασίαν τῆς δ[ωρ]||εᾶς αὐτῶι εἰς τ⟨ὴ⟩ν ἡλιαίαν ἐπειδὰν αἱ ἡμέραι αἱ ἐκ τοῦ νόμ[ου]|| διεξέλθωσιν·

. . . that the demos now elect three men from all the Athenians to supervise making and setting up the statue; the thesmothetai introduce the dokimasia of the award to him in the heliaia after the days prescribed by law have passed.

Compare *IG* II^2 682, lines 96–98: τοὺς δὲ θεσμοθέτας εἰσαγαγεῖν αὐτῶι τὴν δοκιμασίαν τῆς δωρεᾶς εἰς τὸ δικαστήριον κατὰ τὸν νόμον.

Examples of the use of the word "heliaia" by 4th-century orators in direct quotations from laws are given below. Whether the law in question dated from the time of Solon or from a later revision or from a contemporary decree, such as the law proposed by Timokrates (Demosthenes 24.63 [**135**]), the correct term for Athenian judicial authority is "heliaia". Before the institution of dikastic panels, "the punishment or fine to be assessed by the heliaia" would have been assessed by a court (whatever we may conceive this court to have been). These same punishments and fines, whenever dikastic panels began to function, were judged by a dikastic panel, that is, a subdivision of the heliaia, but in neither case did "heliaia" or "dikasterion" stipulate a locality or building.

133. Demosthenes 21 (*Meidias*) 47 347 B.C.E.

γραφέσθω πρὸς τοὺς θεσμοθέτας ὁ βουλόμενος Ἀθηναίων οἷς ἔξεστιν, οἱ δὲ θεσμοθέται εἰσαγόντων εἰς τὴν ἡλιαίαν τριάκοντα ἡμερῶν ἀφ' ἧς ἂν γραφῆι, ἐὰν μή τι δημόσιον κωλύηι, εἰ δὲ μή, ὅταν ἧι πρῶτον οἷόν τε, ὅτου δ' ἂν καταγνῶι ἡ ἡλιαία, τιμάτω περὶ αὐτοῦ παραχρῆμα, ὅτου ἂν δοκῆι ἄξιος εἶναι παθεῖν ἢ ἀποτεῖσαι.

(The law on physical outrage is being quoted.) [If anyone has committed such an act,] let any Athenian who wishes, and to whom it is permitted, bring a charge before the thesmothetai, and the thesmothetai shall bring it before the Heliaia within thirty days of the indictment, unless some public matter prevents it; in that case whenever it is first possible. Whomever the heliaia condemns shall at once be assessed whatever punishment or fine which he is considered to deserve.

134. Demosthenes 23 (*Aristokrates*) 28 (includes Solon F16) 352 B.C.E.

τοὺς δ' ἀνδροφόνους ἐξεῖναι ἀποκτείνειν ἐν τῆι ἡμεδαπῆι καὶ ἀπάγειν, ὡς ἐν τῶι ἄξονι ἀγορεύει, λυμαίνεσθαι δὲ μή, μηδὲ ἀποινᾶν, ἢ διπλοῦν ὀφείλειν ὅσον ἂν καταβλάψηι. εἰσφέρειν δ' ἐ⟨ς⟩ τοὺς ἄρχοντας, ὧν ἕκαστοι δικασταί εἰσι, τῶι βουλομένωι. τὴν δ' ἡλιαίαν διαγιγνώσκειν.

On the generally accepted emendation, δ' ἐ[ς] for δὲ, see Lipsius 1905–1915, p. 55, note 6.

It shall be lawful to kill homicides in our own territory and to bring them to the authorities, as it says in the axon, but not to maltreat them or demand a fine. Otherwise one owes a payment of twice the damage inflicted. Whoever wants is permitted to bring in to the magistrates those charges that lie within the judicial competence of each [magistracy]. The heliaia shall determine the verdict.

See **83** for the first half of this paragraph.

135. Demosthenes 24 (*Timokrates*) 63 353/2 B.C.E.

ἐὰν δ' ἁλῶι, τιμάτω ἡ ἡλιαία περὶ αὐτοῦ ὅ τι ἂν δοκῆι ἄξιος εἶναι παθεῖν ἢ ἀποτεῖσαι.

If he be convicted, the heliaia is to assess whatever punishment or fine they determine is proper.

This is a quotation from the law proposed by Timokrates.

136. Demosthenes 24 (*Timokrates*) 105 (includes Solon F23d [partial]) 353/2 B.C.E.

δεδέσθαι δ' ἐν τῆι ποδοκάκκηι τὸν πόδα πένθ' ἡμέρας καὶ νύκτας ἴσας, ἐὰν προστιμήσηι ἡ ἡλιαία. . . . δησάντων αὐτὸν οἱ ἕνδεκα καὶ εἰσαγόντων εἰς τὴν ἡλιαίαν, κατηγορείτω δὲ ὁ βουλόμενος οἷς ἔξεστιν. ἐὰν δ' ἁλῶι, τιμάτω ἡ ἡλιαία ὅ τι χρὴ παθεῖν αὐτὸν ἢ ἀποτεῖσαι.

His foot shall be fastened in the stocks for five days and nights if the heliaia adds [such] a further penalty. . . . The Eleven shall put him in bonds and bring him before the heliaia. Anyone who so wishes, to whom it is permitted, may bring a charge against him. If he is convicted, the heliaia shall assess what he must suffer or pay.

This is from the laws on theft, ill treatment of parents, and avoidance of military service.

137. [Demosthenes] 43 (*Makartatos*) 75 *ca.* 341 B.C.E.

ἐὰν δὲ μείζονος ζημίας δοκῆι ἄξιος εἶναι . . . εἰσαγέτω εἰς τὴν ἡλιαίαν. ἐὰν δ' ἁλῶι, τιμάτω ἡ ἡλιαία περὶ τοῦ ἁλόντος, ὅ τι χρὴ αὐτὸν παθεῖν ἢ ἀποτεῖσαι.

If it is determined that a greater penalty is proper . . . the archon is to bring him before the heliaia. If he is then convicted, the heliaia shall determine what he must suffer or pay.

138. Lysias 10 (*Theomnestos*) 16 (contains Solon F15b) 384/3 B.C.E.

δεδέσθαι ἐν τῆι ποδοκάκκηι ἡμέρας πέντε τὸν πόδα, ἐὰν προστιμήσηι ἡ ἡλιαία.

He shall be fastened by his foot in the stocks for five days, if the heliaia adds [such] a further penalty.

Compare **136**, where the same provision is cited by Demosthenes in almost the same words.

Other Buildings Used by Dikastic Panels

Court of the Archon

A court where the archon presides is mentioned in *Wasps* (**139**) as one of the places where heliasts served. A court of the archon is named in an inscription of 421/0 B.C.E. (*IG* I^3 82 [**142**]), and according to Photios (**140**) and the *Suda* (**141**), the court of the archon met in the Odeion. The references all seem to be to a dikastic panel at which the archon presided and not to a building called "the Court of the Archon". The same passage from *Wasps*, if construed as naming the Odeion as third in a series of four places where heliasts judged, is not in accord with Photios, who has the court of the archon meet at the Odeion. Jacoby (*FGrHist* 324 Androtion F59, notes to commentary, p. 151), however, suggests that Aristophanes refers not to four different meeting places but rather to two places, after having named the presiding officials for each. Some heliasts, in his interpretation, would go to the archon at the Odeion, others to the Eleven at the walls. This may be the right interpretation; compare, however, MacDowell 1971, commentary on *Wasps*, line 1109. Photios' statement that the court of the archon met in the Odeion is supported by [Demosthenes] 59.52 (**169**), which shows that cases of alimony were tried there in the 4th century, and by Aristotle (*Ath. Pol.* 56.7), who says that alimony cases were in the competence of the archon. On existing evidence it is not established that the archon presided at trials in the same building in the 5th and the 4th centuries. In 422 B.C.E., trials for which he was responsible could have been held in a stoa or in some other appropriate building that happens not to be named here. By the middle of the 4th century, the court of the archon did meet at the Odeion, at least for some types of cases, and so Photios is correct for that period, at least, and conceivably for the 5th century as well.

139. Aristophanes, *Wasps*, lines 1108–1109 422 B.C.E.

Χορός: οἱ μὲν ἡμῶν οὗπερ ἄρχων, οἱ δὲ παρὰ τοὺς ἕνδεκα,
οἱ δ' ἐν ᾠιδείωι δικάζουσ', οἱ δὲ πρὸς τοῖς τειχίοις

Chorus: Some of us go where the archon [presides], others to the Eleven; some judge in the Odeion, others beside the walls.

140. Photios, *Lexicon*, *s.v.* Ὠιδεῖον 9th century C.E.

Ὠιδεῖον . . . ἐστι δ' ἐν αὐτῶι τὸ δικαστήριον τοῦ ἄρχοντος. διεμετρεῖτο δὲ καὶ ἄλφιτα ἐκεῖ.

Odeion . . . In it is held the court of the archon, and barley was distributed there.

141. *Suda*, *s.v.* Ὠιδεῖον 10th century C.E.

Ὠιδεῖον . . . ἔστι δὲ ἐν αὐτῶι δικαστήριον τοῦ ἄρχοντος. διεμετρεῖτο δὲ καὶ ἄλφιτα ἐκεῖ.

Odeion . . . In it is held the court of the archon. And barley was distributed there.

142. *IG* I^3 82, lines 26–28 421/20 B.C.E.

ἐὰ]|ν δέ τις ἄχσ[ιος εἶ μέζον]ος ζε[μ]ίας τὰς ἐπιβολὰς ποιό[ντ]ον [ὁπόσας ἂν δοκεῖ κ|α]ὶ ἐσαγόν[τον ἐς τὸ δικασ]τέρι[ο]ν τὸ τõ ἄρχοντος.

If a greater penalty is determined to be appropriate, they are to make the fine as great as they think fit and bring the case before the court of the archon.

In these regulations for the Hephaistia, the *hieropoioi* are charged with setting the fine and bringing the charge.

Ardettos

See **171–175**.

Batrachioun and Phoinikioun

Court buildings named after colors can be explained in terms of the complex system described by Aristotle in which allotted dikasts were given staves that matched the colors on some portion of the entrance (*sphekiskos*) which they were to use (**249**). The buildings or parts of buildings so designated may have had official names. A green and a red court are named only by Pausanias.

(1) Pausanias 1.28.8

(Among other, less famous courts) the Batrachioun [Green] and the Phoinikioun [Red] are named after their colors and retain their names to the present day.

Court of the Eleven

(139) Aristophanes, *Wasps*, lines 1108–1109

(156) Harpokration

Kainon

143. Aristophanes, *Wasps*, lines 119–120 422 B.C.E.

Ξανθίας: ὁ δ' αὐτῶι τυμπάνωι
ἄιξας ἐδίκαζεν εἰς τὸ Καινὸν ἐμπεσών.

Xanthias: But drum and all he [Philokleon] would shoot into the New [Court] and act as judge.

144. Schol. Aristophanes, *Wasps*, line 120c

εἰς τὸ Καινὸν ἐμπεσών· τόπος ἐν τῶι δικαστηρίωι οὕτω λεγόμενος. εἰσὶ δὲ δ'· Παράβυστον, Καινόν, Τρίγωνον, Μέσον. τελούμενος οὖν, φησίν, τὰ μυστήρια τῶν Κορυβάντων, παρ' οὐδὲν αὐτὰ θέμενος, κατέχων τὸ τύμπανον ὥρμησεν εἰς τὸ δικαστήριον. ἐν τῶι δικαστηρίωι τόποι ἦσαν τέσσαρες, ὧν ὁ μὲν ἐκαλεῖτο Παράβυστον, ὁ δὲ Καινόν, ὁ δὲ Τρίγωνον, ὁ δὲ Μέσον.

Shoot into the New: a place in the court so called. There are four: Parabyston, Kainon, Trigonon, Meson. And so while performing, he says, the Mysteries of the Corybants, he totally disregarded them and holding the drum rushed into the court. In the court there were four places, one of which was called the Parabyston, one the Kainon, one the Trigonon, one the Meson.

The Kallion

Pollux includes the Kallion "which Androtion mentions" in his list of well-known dikasteria. Photios states that it was named from Kallias who made it, and Bekker has a fragmentary entry on it.

The Kallion and the court of Metichos, according to the lexicographers, were named after private individuals. These may have been donors or architects, as is specifically stated for Metichos. Jacoby (*FGrHist* 324 Androtion F59, notes to commentary, p. 152) assumes that both buildings date from the "reign of Pericles." Neither name is found in a 4th-century or Hellenistic context. The mention of the Kallion by Androtion was probably contained in his *Atthis* and so need not count as a name in use in the 4th century. Jacoby believes that the Kallias for whom the court was named is Kallias, son of Hipponikos, but he admits that this cannot be proved.

The two buildings may well have been known under other names in the 4th century. The Painted Stoa offers a good parallel for a building first named after an individual, Peisianaktos, then called by a descriptive adjective. The court buildings may have had an analogous nomenclature, with the individual's name used for a time and then dropped.

145. Bekker, *Anecdota Graeca* 1.269.33–270.1

Κάλλιον· δικαστήριον Ἀθήνησιν οὕτω καλούμενον ἀπὸ . . .

Kallion: a court in Athens so named from . . .

FGrHist 324 Androtion F59, notes to commentary, p. 152: " . . . there is a gap in the text of the *Anecdota* after ἀπό. The end of the article on Kallion and the opening of the one καλλυντήρια have dropped out."

146. Photios, *Lexicon*, *s.v.* Κάλλιον 9th century C.E.

Κάλλιον· δικαστήριον Ἀθήνησιν ἀπὸ Καλλείου τοῦ πεποιηκότος ἐπώνυμον.

Kallion: a lawcourt at Athens named after Kalleios, who made it.

(2) Pollux 8.121

[Among the well-known lawcourts is] the Kallion, which Androtion mentions.

Pollux as punctuated by Bethe reads "the Kallion of Metichos"; as punctuated by Lipsius (1905–1915, p. 170, note 19) and Jacoby (*FGrHist* 324 Androtion F59, notes to commentary, p. 152), "the (court) of Metichos, Kallion, etc." Both are mentioned as separate courts by the lexicographers. Pollux mentions the court of Metichos again a few lines lower, and the direct article is omitted also before the names Meson and Parabyston. The Kallion and the court of Metichos can be considered separate courts.

The Court near Lykos
See **176–185**.

The Meizon

Pollux lists a court called the Meizon ("the Greater") and states that it was mentioned by Lysias. The fact that this is the only reference to it suggests that Lysias may have used the word as a descriptive adjective of a court rather than as the official title.

(2) Pollux 8.121

Well-known lawcourts are the Heliaia; the Trigonon, which Deinarchos mentions; the Middle; the Parabyston; the Greater. Lysias mentions the Parabyston and the Greater.

The Meson

A court called the Meson ("the Middle") is named by Pollux, by Photios, and in a scholion to Aristophanes. The Middle of the New Courts is named in inscriptions of *ca.* 342/1 B.C.E. and 330–322 B.C.E. See the note following **147** for a suggestion that the Middle Court and the Middle of the New Courts refer to the same building.

(144) Schol. Aristophanes, *Wasps*, line 120c

There are four: Parabyston, Kainon, Trigonon, Meson.

(167) Photios, *Lexicon*, *s.v.* Τρίγωνον

The Trigonon is a dikasterion at Athens, as are the Parabyston and Meson.

(2) Pollux 8.121

Well-known lawcourts are the Heliaia, the Trigonon . . . the Middle.

147. Agora I 1749 (= *Agora* XIX. no. 26) 342/1 B.C.E.

Lines 12–13 (= 365–366): [δικαστήριον] πρῶτον τῶν καιν[ῶν]

The first of the new courts (or, the first court sitting for the new offenses).

Lines 116–117 (= 461–462): δικαστήριον τὸ μέσ[ον τῶ]ν καινῶν

The middle of the new courts (or, the middle court sitting for the new offenses).

These lines come from a fragmentary stele inscribed with annual accounts of the poletai recording sales of confiscated property and leases of silver mines. Certain cases of confiscated property were heard in the courts named. Benjamin D. Meritt ("Greek Inscriptions," *Hesperia* 5,

1936 [pp. 355–441], pp. 393–413) suggests that "new" qualifies offenses (*ibid.*, pp. 405, 408). Dow (1939, p. 23) suggests that "new" applies to buildings. In either case, the proper names of the buildings seem to be First and Middle. If the text does refer to the First and Middle of the New Courts, they are surely not the same as the New Court referred to by Aristophanes some eighty years earlier. But it seems possible that the middle of the New Courts of the inscription is the same as the Middle Court mentioned by the Scholiast, Pollux, and Photios.

148. Agora I 5656 (= *SEG* XXV 180), lines 12–21 *ca.* 330–322 B.C.E.

[Μαιμ]ακτηριῶνος
[– – –]τηι ἐπὶ δέκα· δικαστή-
[ρι]ον μέσον τῶν καινῶν.
[ἐ]πὶ τὸ ὕδωρ Μενεκλῆς Εὐω-
νυμεύς· ἐπὶ τὰς ψήφους
῾Ιεροφῶν ῎Ωαθεν [:] Π[– – –]
φης ῾Αλαιεύς· ᾿Αριστολέων
῾Αλιμούσι : ῾Ιερώνυμος [ἐκ] Κοί
Μ[α]καρεὺς Ξενοφῶντος ᾿Α[να]-
φ[λ]ύστιος

(?)-teenth of Maimakterion; dikasterion: Middle of the New. At the water: Menekles Euonymeus; at the ballots: Hierophon of Oa, – – – of Halai, Aristoleon of Halimousai, Hieronymos of Kos, Makareus Anaphlystios, Xenophon's son.

This notation of a trial, which the polemarch put on the court calendar, stands without a heading or indentation in a list of phiale dedications, all resulting from adjudication of δίκαι ἀποστασίου. See D. M. Lewis, "Attic Manumissions," *Hesperia* 28, 1959, pp. 208–238 and "Dedications of Phialai at Athens," *Hesperia* 37, 1968 [368–380], pp. 369–374. Other published accounts of adjudications likewise find a place on stelai that are principally occupied by other sorts of business. See *IG* II^2 1613, lines 166–310; 1620, lines 32–74; 1623, lines 1–334; 1641 (**163**); 1646 (**159**); 1647; 1670 (**164**); *IG* XI ii 146, B, lines 27–31; Agora I 1749 (**147**), I 3738 (**160**). Cf. Gerhard Thür, "Neuere Untersuchungen zum Prozessrecht der griechischen Poleis. Formen des Urteils," in *Akten des 26. Deutschen Rechtshistorikertages, 22 bis 26 September 1986*, Frankfurt 1987, pp. 467–484. Note also the count of votes at the trial of Sokrates (Diogenes Laertius 2.41–42). See also **342a**.

The Court of Metichos or Metiochos

The court of Metichos apparently was a large structure named after a private individual. It is known only from later writers (Pollux, Hesychios, Photios, and the *Lexeis* published by Bekker in *Anecdota Graeca*), and no 4th-century authorities are cited for it. This suggests, as has been pointed out, that the name was in use only in the 5th century, possibly for a building known later under a different name (see commentary on Kallion, pp. 175–176 above). A building described as large, and as accommodating an allotted 1,000 dikasts, should be where the heliaia, *qua* judging panel composed of two or more panels of 500, sat and as such could also itself have been called the heliaia.

The sources disagree on the spelling of the name, as do modern writers. Pollux and Hesychios give Metichos; the *Lexeis* in Bekker, Metiochos. Photios calls the court Metiocheion but in the following entry describes Metichos in the same phrase as that used in the *Lexeis* for Metiochos. The name Metichos is not attested elsewhere as that of a person in Athens, but Metiochos is. Two are listed by Kirchner: one, *PA* 10132, a son of Miltiades II, and a second, *PA* 10131, a friend of Perikles who was ridiculed, probably in some early comedy, as a politician who had his hand in everything, served as general, inspected roads, bread, flour, and so on (Plutarch, *Precepts of Statecraft* 15.811). Kock (*CAF* III, no. 1325, p. 630), in commenting on the quotation from Plutarch, notes that in trochaic comic verse (if the lines are from comedy) the form should be Metichos (for text, see p. 5, note 9 above). Ernst Fabricius (*RE* XV, 1932, cols. 1407–1408, *s.v.* Metiochos) approves, while Jacoby (*FGrHist* 324 Androtion F59, notes to commentary, p. 152) disagrees. If Metichos is an Athenian name, it can be regarded as possible that Metichos was the overzealous politician of Perikles' time and that he was the man from whom the court was named. Jacoby (*FGrHist* 324 Androtion F59, commentary, p. 166) accepts the identification but chooses the name Metiochos. Lipsius (1905–1915, p. 171, note 20) suggests the identification, as does Fabricius (*loc. cit.*). Assuming as most do that a negative must be restored at **149** below, the description of Metichos or Metiochos as an architect and orator who gave counsel "not of the best" fits the person described in the quotation in Plutarch.

149. Bekker, *Anecdota Graeca* 1.309.17–19

τέμενος Μητιόχου· δικαστήριον, ὀνομασθὲν ἀπὸ Μητιόχου ἀρχιτέκτονος ἢ ῥήτορος τῶν τὰ βέλτιστα συμβουλευσάντων.

Precinct of Metiochos: a lawcourt named after Metiochos, an architect or orator among those who gave excellent counsel.

The negative οὐ is usually restored after τῶν in the second line to correspond with the entry in Photios below, and thus the reading would be "gave counsel not of the best."

150. Hesychios, *s.v.* Μητίχου τέμενος 5th century C.E.

Μητίχου τέμενος· εἴη ἂν τὸ Μητιχεῖον δικαστήριον μέγα, ἐν ὧι προσεκληρώθησαν ⟨χίλιοι⟩ δικασταί.

Precinct of Metichos: This would be the Meticheion, the large lawcourt in which a thousand dikasts were allotted (corrected from "summoned").

151. Photios, *Lexicon*, *s.vv.* Μητιοχεῖον, Μήτιχος 9th century C.E.

Μητιοχεῖον· δικαστήριον.
Μήτιχος· ἀρχιτέκτων καὶ ῥήτωρ τῶν οὐ τὰ βέλτιστα συμβουλευόντων.

Metiocheion: a lawcourt.
Metichos: an architect and orator among those who gave counsel not of the best.

Naber, in his 1864 edition of Photios, prints in the first entry Μητιχεῖον but notes that the codex reads Μητιοχεῖον.

(2) Pollux 8.121

[Among the well-known lawcourts is] that of Metichos. . . . The court of Metichos is large and is named from the architect Metichos.

Parabyston

The Parabyston is included in the two basic lists of Athenian dikasteria and is named by many of the lexicographers. It was the court at which the Eleven presided, a roofed building in the Agora. It was in use at least from the late 5th century into the third quarter of the 4th. The latest specific reference is in *IG* II^2 1646 (**159**), from shortly after the middle of the 4th century B.C.E. A survival in some form into the 2nd century C.E., with the name transferred to another building, may account for Pausanias' assertion that it is in an obscure part of the city; but see "Nomenclature," pp. 6–8 above.

The word appears to contain some clue as to its specific location. LSJ give two meanings for the word, the first "stuffed or forced in", the second "pushed aside or into a corner". In the first meaning, the word is used of a small couch or bed placed beside a larger one (e.g., Harpokration quoting Hypereides [**156**], Pollux 3.43) and also of an uninvited guest crowding in (Timotheos F1 [*PCG* VII], also Athenaeus 6.257a). Both Harpokration and a scholiast commenting on Demosthenes use the word παραπληρώματα ("filling up") in their explanations, the first as the παραβύσματα or παραπληρώματα of freight loads, the second of the filling up of walls during construction, that is, the filling between the two faces. The verbs βύω and παραβύω are used of stuffing (or stopping up), inserting, and plugging, as of stopping up the mouths of orators or plugging one's ears.

For its second meaning, pushed aside or into a corner, LSJ cite Pausanias 1.18.8 on the Parabyston as in an obscure part of town and refer to Timokles *apud* Harpokration (**156**) and Lysias *apud* Pollux (**2**), who only name the court. But whatever may have been the case in Pausanias' time, a court in the Agora could scarcely have been described as in an obscure part of town in the 5th century B.C.E., when it was built and named. LSJ, in a subdivision of this second meaning, cite a metaphorical usage, *viz.* "in a hole and corner". The examples cited for this are the Demosthenes passage; Aristotle, *Topica* 157a4; Lucian, *Necyomantia* (*Menippus*) 17; and Zosimos, *Alchem.* 242B (*Collection des anciens alchémistes grecs*, ed. M. Berthelot, Paris 1888). But "stuffed" or "crowded in" seems to fit better than "pushed aside" or "hole and corner" in the context of the Aristotle passage and equally well in the Lucian. Aristotle is suggesting that at times speeches can be lengthened and items that are of no use be added, as is done by people who write false accounts: "For when there are many things it is not clear in which consists the falsity. Consequently, sometimes the questioners escape notice when they propose things (ἐν παραβύστωι) by stuffing them in, things that proposed by themselves would not be admitted." Lucian, in describing the dead in Hades, says: "You would have laughed if you had seen Mausolus himself, him of the famous monument, so humbly did he lie where he was flung, ἐν παραβύστωι, stuffed in a corner, unnoticed among the rest of the crowd of dead. For whenever Aiakos measures off one's space (he gives at most not over one foot), one must be content to lie in it." Again the sense "crowded in" rather than "secret" seems more appropriate.

"Pushed aside" or "hole and corner" as glosses for the phrase ἐν παραβύστωι may have started with the scholiast's definition as "in secret". If this can be rejected as an error (see note on **154**) found elsewhere only in later lexicographers and probably derived from the scholiast, a basic meaning of "stuffed" or "crowded in beside" is established.

Apparently, then, one should look for a building in the Agora that could be described as stuffed or crowded in beside something else as early as the 420's. Note that Lipsius (1905–1915 p. 172, note 23) suggests that the simplest explanation is "Einbau oder Anbau", a building inserted in another or as an addition. This takes no account (justifiably) of Pausanias' statement that it was in an inconspicuous part of the city. If in fact a Parabyston did survive in some form somewhere in Athens until Pausanias' day, the name may have been a revival.

(62) Antiphon 5 (*Herodes*) 10–11

These passages show that the case was being tried in a covered building in the Agora. This would almost certainly have been the Parabyston, for the defendant was being tried in the heliaistic system as a malefactor (although the charge was actually homicide, which should have been tried in a homicide court); such cases were brought forward by the Eleven (*Ath. Pol.* 52.1), and the Parabyston was the court in which the Eleven presided, according to Harpokration (**156**).

(144) Schol. Aristophanes, *Wasps*, line 120c

There are four [dikasteria]: Parabyston, Kainon, Trigonon, Meson.

(139) Aristophanes, *Wasps*, lines 1108–1109

Some of us go where the archon [presides], others to the Eleven; some judge in the Odeion, others beside the walls.

Those who served with the Eleven presumably went to the Parabyston. See **156**.

152. Bekker, *Anecdota Graeca* 1.292.24–25

παράβυστον· τὸ λάθρα γινόμενον. ἦν δὲ καὶ Παράβυστον δικαστήριον Ἀθήνησιν, ὃ λάθραι ἔκρινεν.

Parabyston: what happens in secret. There was also in Athens a lawcourt, the Parabyston, which judged in secret.

153. Demosthenes 24 (*Timokrates*) 47 353/2 B.C.E.

τῶι δ' οὐκ ἀπέχρησε τοῦτ' ἀδικεῖν μόνον, εἰ μὴ δοθείσης τῆς ἀδείας λέγει καὶ νόμον εἰσφέρει περὶ τούτων, ἀλλὰ καὶ προσέτ' οὐκ εἰς τὴν βουλήν, οὐκ εἰς τὸν δῆμον εἰπὼν περὶ τούτων οὐδέν, ἐν παραβύστωι τῆς βουλῆς μὲν ἀφειμένης, τῶν δ' ἄλλων διὰ τὴν ἑορτὴν ἱερομηνίαν ἀγόντων, λάθρα τὸν νόμον εἰσήνεγκεν.

It was not enough for him [Timokrates] to commit this single crime, namely, that of proposing and bringing forward the law about these matters without having been given permission; he went still further and, saying nothing to the boule or the demos about these matters by stuffing it in with other laws (ἐν παραβύστωι), when the boule stood adjourned and everybody was on holiday in honor of the festival, he introduced his law in secret.

154. Schol. Demosthenes 24 (*Timokrates*) 47

ἐν παραβύστωι· ἀντὶ τοῦ λάθρα. ἀπὸ τῆς μεταφορᾶς τῶν παραπληρωμάτων τῶν ἐμβαλλομένων ἐν ταῖς οἰκοδομίαις ἔνδον καὶ κρύφα τοῦ φαινομένου. βῦσαι τὸ στόμα τῶν ῥητόρων.

By stuffing in: [This phrase is used] instead of "in secret", by metaphor also from the fillings thrown into buildings, within and hidden from sight. [Also] to stop up [plug] the mouth of the orators.

The scholiast's definition of ἐν παραβύστωι as "in secret" was followed by Hesychios, the *Lexeis* (Bekker), and the *Etymologicum Magnum*. With this interpretation of the phrase ἐν παραβύστωι, Demosthenes' sentence seems unnecessarily repetitious, for λάθρα ("in secret") is also included. λάθρα in that case could be omitted, as a gloss inserted from the scholion. If, however, ἐν παραβύστωι means "by stuffing in", λάθρα adds sense.

Is it possible that the phrase ἐν παραβύστωι does refer to the building in which the law was passed in secret? The meeting at which Timokrates proposed his law was one of nomothetai and should have had 1,001 members (paragraphs 26 and 27 of the same oration). Whether this number was in fact present we are not told. The nomothetai were chosen from the dikasts, that is, from those who had taken the heliastic oath. According to Aischines (3.39), in 330 B.C.E. their meetings were called "ekklesia", and so one might expect them to be held on the Pnyx or in the theater. In the one inscription that has survived naming their place of meeting, ἐν [Διονύσου] has been restored (*IG* II^2 140 of 353/2 B.C.E.). These two items of evidence apparently contradict a simple explanation of the phrase in Demosthenes, to the effect that this sudden meeting called by Timokrates and his friends to pass an illegal law in secret was in fact held in the Parabyston.

For the nomothetai, see Busolt and Swoboda 1920, p. 1011 and Kahrstedt 1936, pp. 283–284; D. M. MacDowell, "Law-making at Athens in the Fourth Century B.C.," *JHS* 95, 1975, pp. 62–74; M. H. Hansen, "Athenian *Nomothesia* in the Fourth Century B.C. and Demosthenes' Speech against Leptines," *ClMed.* 32, 1980, pp. 87–104; P. J. Rhodes, "*Nomothesia* in Fourth-Century Athens," *CQ* n.s. 35, 1985, pp. 55–60; and M. H. Hansen, "Athenian *Nomothesia*," *GRBS* 26, 1985, pp. 345–371.

155. *Etymologicum Magnum*, *s.v.* παράβυστον 12th century C.E.

παράβυστον, παρακεκρυμμένον, λάθρα γινόμενον· παρὰ τὸ βύω ὃ σημαίνει τὸ κλείω· σημαίνει γὰρ καὶ τὸ πληρῶ· Ὀδυσσείας δ', νήματος ἀσκητοῖο βεβυσμένον· ἀντὶ τοῦ πεπληρωμένον. ἦν δὲ καὶ παράβυστον δικαστήριον, ὃ λάθρα ἔκρινε.

Parabyston: "concealed, happening in secret". From the verb "stuff", which means "close"; it also means "fill up". *Odyssey* 4 (line 134), "stuffed full of curiously wrought spinning", instead of "filled up". There was also a Parabyston lawcourt, which judged in secret.

The first clause repeats verbatim the entry *s.v.* in the *Suda*. Compare also Bekker (**152**) and Hesychios (**157**). The last sentence repeats almost verbatim the entry in Bekker.

156. Harpokration, *s.v.* παράβυστον 2nd century C.E.

παράβυστον· οὕτως ἐκαλεῖτό τι τῶν παρ' Ἀθηναίοις δικαστηρίων ἐν ὧι ἐδίκαζον οἱ ἕνδεκα. Ἀντιφῶν ἐν τῶι πρὸς Νικοκλέα περὶ ὅρων. μνημονεύουσι δ' αὐτοῦ ἄλλοι τε τῶν κωμικῶν καὶ Τιμοκλῆς ἐν Ὀρεσταυτοκλείδηι. ἐκαλεῖτο δέ τις ἐν τοῖς νυμφικοῖς δωματίοις καὶ κλίνη παράβυστος, ἧς μέμνηται Ὑπερείδης ἐν τῶι κατὰ Πατροκλέους. λέγεσθαι δ' ἔοικε ταῦτα κατὰ μεταφορὰν ἀπὸ τῶν ἐν τοῖς φορτίοις παραβυσμάτων, τουτέστι παραπληρωμάτων.

Parabyston: This was the name of one of the dikasteria in Athens, in which the Eleven pronounced justice. Antiphon [mentions it] in his speech in reply to Nikokles about the boundaries. Timokles, among other writers of comedies, mentions it in his *Orestautokleides*. There was a couch in the bridal chambers called *parabystos*, which Hypereides mentions in his speech against Patrokles. It is probably so called by transference from the use of the word as [additional] stuffings of loads [freight], that is, fillings.

Antiphon's *Nikokles*, if within the range of his datable speeches, cannot be earlier than *ca.* 419 B.C.E. nor later than 411; see Dover 1950, pp. 44–60. Timokles was active in the mid-4th century B.C.E. Compare Pollux (3.43), who says, "There is a couch, or bed (κλίνη), called the wedding bed and another, the παράβυστος, that was spread in the room, so that the bride wouldn't be afraid, as Hypereides said." See also Hesychios (**157**).

157. Hesychios, *s.v.* παράβυστον 5th century C.E.

παράβυστον λάθρα γινόμενον, ἀπόκρυφον. ἀποκεκρυμμένον ἢ μικρὸν κλινίδιον, παρατιθέμενον τῆι μεγάληι. ἔνιοι δὲ δικαστήριον οὕτω καλούμενον.

Parabyston means "happening in secret, concealed"; [for example,] a concealed or small couch placed beside the larger one. Some [say] there is a dikasterion called this.

(1) Pausanias 1.28.8

The Athenians have other, though less famous, courts of justice. The one called Parabyston and Trigonon has its names from the fact that it is in an obscure part of the city—on the most trivial occasions do dikasts convene there—and from its shape.

(167) Photios, *Lexicon*, *s.v.* Τρίγωνον

The Trigonon is a dikasterion at Athens, as are the Parabyston and Meson.

(2) Pollux 8.121

Well-known lawcourts are the Heliaia; the Trigonon, which Deinarchos mentions; the Middle; the Parabyston; the Greater. Lysias mentions the Parabyston and the Greater. The Eleven pronounced judgment in the Parabyston.

158. *Suda*, *s.v.* παράβυστον — 10th century C.E.

Παράβυστον· παρακεκρυμμένον, λάθρα γινόμενον.

Parabyston: concealed, happening in secret.

A second entry in the *Suda* repeats Harpokration (**156**), with the second and third sentences omitted; that is, the *Suda* text jumps from οἱ ἕνδεκα to ἐκαλεῖτο.

159. *IG* II^2 1646, line 12 — after 346/5 B.C.E.

[. . δικα]στήριον τὸ παράβυ[στον. .]

. . . the lawcourt the Parabyston.

This inscription is from a stele containing a fragmentary Delian Amphictyony record. In line 3 τὸ δικασ[τήριον. .] is restored, and in line 8 [πλήρει]ς HHHHΔΔΔΔIII (verb?), that is, there were 443 votes for acquittal. But the text is too fragmentary to tell whether these votes were cast in the Parabyston or in another court. Compare Stumpf (1987, pp. 213–215), who reads the number as 444 and interprets it as the amount of a fine.

160. Agora I 3738 (= *Agora* XIX, no. 24), lines 44–46 — *ca.* 350–340 B.C.E.

[. . . . . . . τάδε ἐπρ]άθη ἀθρο⟨ί⟩ας τῆς τιμῆς ἐπ[ὶ] τῆς Ἀ[ν]
[τιοχίδος ἐνάτης (?)] πρυτανείας Μουνιχιῶνος δικα[σ]
[τήριον τὸ Παράβυστ]ον κυρωτής

These were sold for the full price (lit., paid all at once) in the ninth prytany, that of Antiochis, the month Mounichion, the lawcourt the Parabyston, the ratifier (not named).

A stele containing a fragmentary poletai record recording the sale of confiscated property: M. Crosby, "The Leases of the Laureion Mines," *Hesperia* 19, 1950 [pp. 189–312], p. 237. The restoration "Parabyston" has been suggested because it is the only known name of a court that fits the gap in the stoichedon text. Further, the Eleven, who brought cases before the Parabyston, were responsible for handing over confiscated property to be sold by the poletai (Aristotle, *Ath. Pol.* 52.1 and M. Crosby, "Greek Inscriptions," *Hesperia* 10, 1941 [pp. 14–27], p. 14).

161. Agora A 1668 and A 2011
Dipinti on two separate fragmentary roof tiles.

Πα]ρα[βύστο]
τ̣ο͂ Π̣[αραβύστο]

These are inscriptions painted on fragmentary roof tiles found in the debris of the Square Peristyle at the northeast corner of the Agora Square; see Thompson 1954, p. 60. So few letters of the original remain that any restoration is extremely tentative.

The First of the New Courts
See above under "Meson" (**147**).

Stoa Poikile
Full references to the Stoa Poikile are given in *Agora* III, nos. 47–98. Only the three items showing that it was used at times as a meeting place for a lawcourt, or related business, are repeated here. All three date from the middle or third quarter of the 4th century.

162. Demosthenes 45 (*Stephanos* I) 17 — *ca.* 351 B.C.E.

ἐγίγνετο δ' ἡ δίαιτ' ἐν τῆι ποικίληι στοᾶι, μεμαρτυρήκασι δ' οὗτοι παρέχειν τὸ γραμματεῖον Ἀμφίαν πρὸς τὸν διαιτητήν.

The arbitration took place in the Stoa Poikile, and these men testify that Amphias produced the document for the arbitrator.

The panels of diaitetai, acting for the tribes Oineis and Erechtheis, are said to have met in the Heliaia ([Demosthenes] 47.12 [**118**]). Diaitetai administered oaths at the Delphinion ([Demosthenes] 40.11 [**30**], and Isaios 12.9 [**33**]) and possibly met there. Their meetings may regularly have been held in court buildings or, as in this case, in a building also used as a court.

According to Diogenes Laertius 7.5 (= *Agora* III, no. 63), the Thirty when in power made away with 1,400 citizens in the Stoa Poikile. The meetings at which these citizens were condemned or possibly executed can scarcely be called formal court meetings.

163. *IG* II² 1641, lines 25–33 — mid-4th century B.C.E.

. . . οὗ
τος ἀπέφυγεν παρ
[ὼ]ν καὶ ἀπολογούμ
ενος· τὸ δικαστήρι
ιον ἡ στοὰ ἡ ποικί
λη. τῶν ψήφων αἵ τε
τρυπημέναι: Η: α
ἱ δὲ πλήρεις [:] ΗΗΗ
𐅄ΔΔΔΔΠΙΙΙΙ

This man presented himself for trial and made his defense and was acquitted. The dikasterion [was] the Stoa Poikile. Of the votes, 100 were pierced, 399 were solid.

This inscription comes from a stele with records of the Delian Amphiktyones at Athens; the precise nature of the case is not clear. Another case, whose outcome may have been published with an inscription on stone, was one in which the Delian Amphiktyones were involved. It was tried in the

Parabyston (**159**). The total number of votes is less than the desiderated 501, possibly a result of a reduced total number of potential dikasts (Boegehold 1984, pp. 28–29). Stumpf (1987, pp. 211–213) offers a reason for the publication of the outcome of the trial, namely that the prosecutor wanted to be sure not to be fined for failing to secure 20 percent of the votes. This explanation, however, does not take into account all the other business inscribed on the same stone, which is public and not private.

164. *IG* II^2 1670, lines 34–35 *ca.* 330 B.C.E.

> [. . . . . στοὰ]
> ποικίλη εἰς ἕνα καὶ πε[ντακοσίους δικαστάς].
> . . . Stoa Poikile a [dikastic panel] of five hundred and one.

This inscription is from a stele at Eleusis dealing with building operations. If the restoration is correct, litigation arising from building operations was to be tried in the Stoa Poikile.

The Court beside the Walls

(139) Aristophanes, *Wasps*, lines 1108–1109

> Some of us go where the archon [presides], others to the Eleven; some judge in the Odeion, others beside the walls.

This is the only reference to a court meeting "beside the walls". Note that the word used is τειχίον, not τεῖχος. The former is defined by LSJ, *s.v.*, as " wall", "used of walls of buildings not like τεῖχος of city walls" or of a wall as the fence of a field. The phrase πρὸς τοῖς τειχίοις refers to a meeting place of a court. Aristophanes may have coined the phrase, or he may be repeating a contemporary reference. If the court at the walls was one of the regular meeting places of a heliastic court, its other name(s) may be attested elsewhere; see "Nomenclature," pp. 6–9 above, and p. 173 above. There is no evidence on which to base a specific identification. Compare Lipsius 1905–1915, p. 170: "Dessen Lage mit dem für uns unverständlich Ausdruck πρὸς τοῖς τειχίοις bezeichnet wird."

The Theseion

See **186–187** below.

The Trigonon

A court called the Trigonon is included in the two basic lists, those of Pausanias (**1**) and Pollux (**2**). It is also named by Harpokration (**166**), Photios (**167**), in a scholion to Aristophanes (**144**), and in Bekker's *Anecdota* (**165**). It was so named because of its shape (Harpokration, Pausanias, Bekker). Note that the three authors cited as authorities for the Trigonon, Lykourgos, Menander (*apud* Harpokration [**166**]), and Deinarchos (*apud* Pollux [**2**]), were all active in the second half of the 4th century, a time presumably when the court was in active use.

(144) Schol. Aristophanes, *Wasps* 120

> There are four [dikasteria]: Parabyston, Kainon, Trigonon, Meson.

165. Bekker, *Anecdota Graeca* 1.307.12

> Τρίγωνον· ὄνομα δικαστηρίου, ἀπὸ τοῦ σχήματος.

Trigonon: name of a dikasterion, from its shape.

Ibid., 309.25: "Trigonon, a musical instrument. It also means dikasterion."

(117) Schol. Demosthenes 24 (*Timokrates*) 123

[He] draws pay from one person as though he had been allotted to the Heliaia, and then from another as though he had been allotted to the Trigonon.

166. Harpokration, *s.v.* Τρίγωνον δικαστήριον (includes Lykourgos F5) 2nd century C.E.

Τρίγωνον δικαστήριον· Λυκοῦργος κατ' Ἀριστογείτονος. ὄνομά ἐστι δικαστηρίου, ἴσως καὶ τῶι σχήματι τριγώνου ὄντος. μνημονεύουσιν αὐτοῦ ἄλλοι τε καὶ Μένανδρος ἐν τῆι . . .

Trigonon dikasterion: Lykourgos against Aristogeiton. It is the name of a dikasterion, probably from the fact that it is triangular in shape. Menander among others mentions it in the [name of play lost].

(1) Pausanias 1.28.8

The one called Parabyston and Trigonon has its names from the fact that it is in an obscure part of the city—on the most trivial occasions do dikasts convene there—and from its shape.

167. Photios, *Lexicon*, *s.v.* Τρίγωνον 9th century C.E.

Τρίγωνον· δικαστήριον Ἀθήνησιν, ὡς Παράβυστον καὶ Μέσον.

The Trigonon [is] a dikasterion at Athens, as [are] the Parabyston and Meson.

(2) Pollux 8.121

Well-known lawcourts are the Heliaia; the Trigonon, which Deinarchos mentions.

The Odeion

The Odeion, the one built by Perikles southeast of the Akropolis (Travlos 1971, pp. 387–391), not the later Odeion in the Agora or that of Herodes Atticus, was one of the places in which dikasts sat *ca.* 422 B.C.E. (Aristophanes, *Wasps* [**139**]). Cases of alimony were tried there in the 4th century ([Demosthenes], 59.52 [**169**]; Pollux 8.33 [**170**]; Bekker, *Anecdota Graeca* 1.317.31 [**168**]). The court of the archon met in the Odeion (Photios, *s.v.* Odeion [**140**], repeated by the *Suda* [**141**]). Since the archon was the official responsible for bringing in cases of alimony, this entry agrees with those just cited; see introductory note on the court of the archon, p. 173 above.

(139) Aristophanes, *Wasps*, line 1109

Some judge in the Odeion.

Although a scholiast at *Wasps*, line 1109 states that Aristophanes named the (Periclean) Odeion to show that dikasts were to be found everywhere in Attica, the Odeion was in fact used for court meetings in the 4th century and may well have had the same use in the late 5th century; see introductory note above.

168. Bekker, *Anecdota Graeca* 1.317.31–318.2

Ὠιδεῖον· θέατρον Ἀθήνησιν, ὃ πεποίηκε Περικλῆς εἰς τὸ ἐπιδείκνυσθαι τοὺς μουσικούς· ἐν ὧι καὶ δικαστήριον ἦν σίτου. καὶ ἄλφιτα διεμετρεῖτο ἐκεῖ.

Odeion: a theater at Athens, which Perikles built for musical performances. In it the court for alimony was also [held], and barley meal was distributed there.

A distribution of barley at the Odeion is mentioned in [Demosthenes] 34 (*Phormio*) 37. This same item is repeated in the full texts on the Odeion in Photios (**140**) and the *Suda* (**141**).

169. [Demosthenes] 59 (*Neaira*) 52 *ca.* 340 B.C.E.

λαχόντος δὲ τοῦ Στεφάνου αὐτῶι δίκην σίτου εἰς ᾿Ωιδεῖον, κατὰ τὸν νόμον ὃς κελεύει, ἐὰν ἀποπέμπηι τὴν γυναῖκα, ἀποδιδόναι τὴν προῖκα, ἐὰν δὲ μή, ἐπ᾿ ἐννέ᾿ ὀβολοῖς τοκοφορεῖν, καὶ σίτου εἰς ᾿Ωιδεῖον εἶναι δικάσασθαι ὑπὲρ τῆς γυναικὸς τῶι κυρίωι.

Stephanos brought suit for alimony against him in the Odeion by the law which requires a man, if he repudiates his wife, to return the dowry; otherwise interest accrues at the rate of nine obols, and a legal representative on behalf of the woman can bring a suit for alimony in the Odeion.

The suit for alimony in the Odeion is mentioned again in the deposition two paragraphs further (*ibid.* 54).

(140) Photios

Odeion . . . In it is held the court of the archon.

170. Pollux 8.33 2nd century C.E.

τὰς δ᾿ ἐπὶ τῶι σίτωι δίκας ἐν ᾿Ωιδείωι ἐδίκαζον. σῖτος δέ ἐστιν αἱ ὀφειλόμεναι τροφαί.

They tried cases of sitos in the Odeion; sitos is the living allowance due [someone].

(141) Suda, s.v. Ωιδεῖον

The entry *s.v.* Ωιδεῖον repeats verbatim the sentence given above from Photios (**140**).

DIKASTERIA (?)

The three next entries, Ardettos, the court at Lykos, and the Theseion, if not usual sites for trials, have a place here, since Pollux calls the first two *dikasteria* and Photios says that cases were tried in the Theseion.

Ardettos

The site on the Ardettos Hill where the dikastic oath was administered is called a *dikasterion* by Pollux (**171**), who does not, however, include Ardettos in his basic list of dikasteria. All other ancient and modern authorities seem to agree that Ardettos Hill was the place where the oath was taken.

171. Pollux 8.122 2nd century C.E.

ἐδίκαζον δ᾿ οἱ ὑπὲρ τριάκοντα ἔτη ἐκ τῶν ἐπιτίμων καὶ μὴ ὀφειλόντων τῶι δημοσίωι. ὤμνυσαν δὲ ἐν ᾿Αρδήττωι δικαστηρίωι ᾿Απόλλω πατρῶιον καὶ Δήμητρα καὶ Δία βασιλέα· ὁ δὲ ᾿Αρδηττὸς ᾿Ιλισσοῦ μέν ἐστι πλησίον, ὠνόμασται δὲ ἀπό τινος ἥρωος, ὃς στασιάζοντα τὸν δῆμον ὑπὲρ ὁμονοίας ὥρκισεν.

Those over thirty years of age, in possession of citizens' rights and owing no debts to the state, served as dikasts. They took the oath at the Ardettos lawcourt and swore by Apollo Patroos and Demeter and Zeus Basileus. Ardettos is near the Ilissos and is named for a certain hero, who administered an oath of concord to the people when they were engaged in civil strife.

Since this is the only text in which Ardettos is called a lawcourt, presumably Pollux is in error here. Note also that according to [Demosthenes] 25.151 dikasts swore by Zeus, Poseidon, and Demeter.

172. Bekker, *Anecdota Graeca* 1.443.24–31

Ἀρδηττός· τόπος ἐστὶν Ἀθήνησιν, ἐν ὧι πάντες Ἀθηναῖοι δημοσίαι ὤμνυον τὸν ὅρκον τὸν ἡλιαστικόν. Θεόφραστος δὲ ἐν τοῖς περὶ νόμων καταλελύσθαι τὸ ἔθος τοῦτο λέγει. εἴρηται δὲ Ἀρδηττὸς ἀπὸ Ἀρδήττου ἥρωος ὃς Ἀθηναίους στασιάζοντας εἰς ὁμόνοιαν συνῆψεν. ἐν τούτωι δὴ τῶι χωρίωι ὤμνυον οἱ δικασταὶ τὸν δικαστικὸν ὅρκον. τρεῖς δὲ θεοὺς ὤμνυον, Δία, Δήμητραν καὶ Ἥλιον.

Ardettos: a place in Athens in which all Athenians officially swore the heliastic oath. Theophrastos in his work on the laws says that this custom has been abolished. Ardettos is named for the hero Ardettos, who, when the Athenians were engaged in civil strife, united them in concord. In this place the dikasts swore the dikastic oath. They swore by three gods, Zeus, Demeter, and Helios.

There are two other entries in Bekker: 1.207.2 is an abbreviated form of the above, and 1.183.4 simply describes Ardettos as a hill on which they (that is, Athenians) swore their oaths.

173. Harpokration, *s.v.* Ἀρδηττός — 2nd century C.E.

Ἀρδηττός· Λυσίας ἐν τῶι πρὸς Ἐλπίνην. τόπος Ἀθήνησιν ὑπὲρ τὸ στάδιον τὸ Παναθηναικόν, πρὸς τῶι δήμωι τῶι ὑπένερθεν Ἀγρυλέων. ἐν τούτωι φασὶ δημοσίαι πάντες ὤμνυον Ἀθηναῖοι τὸν ὅρκον τὸν ἡλιαστικόν. ὠνομάσθη δὲ ἀπὸ Ἀρδήττου ἥρωος ἀρχαίου, ὃς Ἀθηναίους πρῶτος ἐξώρκισεν. Θεόφραστος δ᾽ ἐν τοῖς περὶ νόμων δηλοῖ ὡς κατελέλυτο τὸ ἔθος τοῦτο.

Ardettos: [mentioned by] Lysias in his speech in reply to Elpines. A place in Athens above the Panathenaic Stadion near the deme of Lower Agryle. Here they say all Athenians officially swore the heliastic oath. It was named after Ardettos, a hero of old, who first administered an oath to the Athenians. Theophrastos in his work on the laws shows that this custom had been abolished.

174. Hesychios, *s.v.* Ἀρδήττους — 5th century C.E.

Ἀρδήττους· τοὺς ῥαδίως ἐπὶ τοὺς ὅρκους ἰόντας Ἀρδήττους ἐκάλουν. τόπος περὶ τὸν Ἰλισσόν, ἐγγὺς τοῦ Παναθηναικοῦ σταδίου, ἐν ὧι τοὺς ὅρκους ἐποιοῦντο.

Ardettans: They would call those who go easily to oaths Ardettans. [Ardettos] is a place near the Ilissos, close to the Panathenaic stadion, in which they swore their oaths.

175. *Suda, s.v.* Ἀρδήττης, Ἀρδήττου — 10th century C.E.

Ἀρδήττης, Ἀρδήττου· ὄνομα κύριον· καὶ Ἀρδηττὸς τόπος ἐστὶν Ἀθήνησιν, ἐν ὧι πάντες Ἀθηναῖοι δημοσίαι ὤμνυον τὸν ὅρκον τὸν ἡλιαστικόν. Θεόφραστος δὲ ἐν τοῖς περὶ νόμων καταλελύσθαι τὸ ἔθος τοῦτο λέγει.

Ardettes (nominative) and *Ardettou* (genitive), a proper name, and Ardettos is a place in Athens, where all Athenians officially swore the heliastic oath. Theophrastos in his work on the laws says that this custom had been abolished.

The Court near Lykos

A court near (or at) Lykos is included in Pollux's list of well-known dikasteria but not named as a court in any other testimonia. A representation of the hero Lykos, either a statue or painting, stood in a shrine of some sort at or near a court (*Wasps*, lines 389–394 [**176**] and 818–823 [**179**]). Reeds or reed matting surrounded the shrine (*Wasps*, line 394). Lykos received the three-obol pay along with the dikasts (*Lexicon Cantabrigiense*, quoting Isaios, scholia, and lexicographers). The phrase "*Lykou dekas*", "the band of Lykos", probably from a comedy, is a play on the verb *dekazein*, to bribe (Eratosthenes, quoted by Harpokration [**181**]). Dikasts gathered near his shrine before the court opened, and some could be bribed (Eratosthenes, *Lexicon Cantabrigiense* [**183**], Pollux [**2**]). Dikasts were paid at the shrine (scholiast on *Wasps*, line 389 [**177**]).

The phrase Λύκου δεκάς appears to have been the initial point of departure for speculation in antiquity. Eratosthenes, in his work *On Old Comedy* (**181**), may have derived δεκάς from δεκάζειν, "to bribe", and the etymology led him to create the bunches of dikasts who would gather near the shrine of Lykos to sell their votes. Succeeding lexicographers and commentators accepted Eratosthenes' explanation (**2**, **177**, **183**–**185**).

Eratosthenes, quoted by Harpokration, stated that the hero had the form of the animal from which he took his name, the wolf. Pollux and all the later lexicographers follow, but the two scholia to Aristophanes do not. Although modern commentators have accepted the hero's wolf form (Wachsmuth 1890, pp. 374–376; Lipsius 1905–1915, pp. 174–175), ancient commentators may have drawn an inference from the name without knowing of an actual wolf-shaped hero. A hero in the shape of a wolf is anomalous in 5th-century Athens, where other strictly human heros named Lykos were well established. One of these is a son of Pandion and patron of the Lykomedes clan; he is shown, and named, on a red-figured calyx krater from the Akropolis (ARV^2, p. 259, Syriskos Painter, 1). This Lykos can be the one who helped to banish Theseus. The Lykos with his sanctuary near the court might be either of these two, or some other unidentified Lykos. Jessen Gunning (*RE* XIII, 1927, cols. 2398–2401, *s.v.* Lykos, nos. 20 and 21) accepts the court hero as a wolf. Roscher (1894–1897, II.2, cols. 2183–2190, *s.v.* Lykos, nos. 6 and 7) gives separate identities to the hero of the Lykomedes clan and to the court hero, and concludes that "if the hero (of the courts) really was in the form of a wolf, only with difficulty can he be identified with the Lykomedes hero." For further references to various known men and heroes called Lykos, see Boegehold 1967, p. 111.

The notion of Lykos as patron saint or hero of the courts who received the dikast's pay and who must be present at all courts may be a concoction of later commentators, a result of their efforts to explain allusions in comedy. The opening words of Philokleon's prayer (*Wasps*, line 389 [**176**]), ὦ Λύκε δέσποτα, follow the words πατρῴοισι θεοῖσιν, to whom the chorus urges Philokleon to pray. Thus the audience for a split second, upon hearing the first syllable of Λύκε, expects Λύκει', and so the following γείτων ἥρως comes as a surprise. The jest would have added effect if a court were in fact near a sanctuary of Apollo as well as beside a shrine of Lykos. There are benches along the west side of the Agora near the temenos of Apollo Patroos that are consistent with the needs of a 5th-century lawcourt (Fig. 2, Pl. 1). If dikasts ever sat on those benches, and if a heroon or shrine of a hero Lykos or a prominent statue of a wolf stood in the vicinity, an audience might have identified those benches as the dikasterion to which Philokleon has been assigned for the year. Cf. "Court Sites," p. 95.

176. Aristophanes, *Wasps*, lines 387–394 422 B.C.E.

(The chorus urges Philokleon to pray to the ancestral gods of Athens [Apollo, Demeter, and Zeus] and to let himself down from the roof.)

Χορός: οὐδὲν πείσει. μηδὲν δείσῃς. ἀλλ' ὦ βέλτιστε, καθίει
σαυτὸν θαρρῶν κἀπευξάμενος τοῖσι πατρῴοισι θεοῖσιν.

Φιλοκλέων: ὦ Λύκε δέσποτα, γείτων ἥρως· σὺ γὰρ οἷσπερ ἐγὼ κεχάρησαι,
τοῖς δακρύοισιν τῶν φευγόντων ἀεὶ καὶ τοῖς ὀλοφυρμοῖς·
ᾤκησας γοῦν ἐπίτηδες ἰὼν ἐνταῦθ', ἵνα ταῦτ' ἀκροῷο,
κἀβουλήθης μόνος ἡρώων παρὰ τὸν κλάοντα καθῆσθαι.
ἐλέησον καὶ σῶσον νυνὶ τὸν σαυτοῦ πλησιόχωρον·
κοὐ μή ποτέ σου παρὰ τὰς κάννας οὐρήσω μηδ' ἀποπάρδω.

Chorus: Nothing will happen to you. Don't be afraid. Just let yourself down, my friend, confidently, and pray to our ancestral gods.

Philokleon: O Lord Lykos, neighbor and hero! You always rejoice exactly as I do in the tears of the defendants and their wailing cries. You in fact came and settled here on purpose to hear them. And you alone of the heroes wished to sit by the weeping defendant. Pity and save now your companion there, and never again will I piss or fart on your reed matting.

On the interpretation of these lines, compare also "Court Sites," p. 95 above.

177. Schol. Aristophanes, *Wasps*, line 389a–c

(a) πρὸς τοῖς δικαστηρίοις Λύκος ἥρως ἵδρυτο. ἔθυον δὲ αὐτῶι καὶ ἀπένεμον δικαστικὸν μισθόν. (b) ὦ Λύκε δέσποτα· παρὰ τοῖς δικαστηρίοις τὸ τοῦ Λύκου ἱερὸν ἦν καὶ ἡρῷον. ὅθεν φασὶν εἰρῆσθαι Λύκου δεκάς. (c) Λύκου ἡρῷον παρὰ τῶι δικαστηρίωι ἦν, ὧι ἐμέριζον, ὅτε δικαστήρια ἦν, τὸν παρὰ τοῖς λαχοῦσι τῶν Ἀθηναίων δικάζειν δικαστικὸν μισθὸν τριώβολον.

(a) At the dikasteria the hero Lykos was situated. They sacrificed to him and assigned him the dikastic pay. (b) O Lord Lykos: at the dikasteria there was a sanctuary and heroon of Lykos. From whence, they say, is spoken the phrase "the company of Lykos". (c) At the dikasterion there was a heroon of Lykos where, when the dikasteria met, they apportioned the dikastic pay of three obols among the Athenians who had been chosen by lot to serve as dikasts.

178. Schol. Aristophanes, *Wasps*, line 394a, c, d

(a) κάννας· τὰς ψιάθους . . . (c) ψιάθοις δὲ περιπεφραγμένου τοῦ ἡρῴου καὶ ἐστεγασμένου . . .
(d) ὅταν θυσιάσωσιν, περιφράσσουσι ψιάθοις κανναβίναις. κάννας δὲ ἔφη τὰς ψιάθους.

(a) Reeds [reed fencing or matting]: rush mats . . . (c) The heroon was fenced around and roofed with rush mats . . . (d) when they sacrifice, they fence [the heroon] around with hempen mats. By *kannas* he meant the *psiathous*.

See W. K. Pritchett, "The Attic Stelai II," *Hesperia* 25, 1956 [pp. 178–317], pp. 247, 254 for discussion of the words *kanna* and *psiathos*. See **246** and **248** below for *psiathia* as coverings on the benches in a dikasterion.

179. Aristophanes, *Wasps*, lines 818–823 422 B.C.E.
(Bdelykleon is setting up the mock court for his father Philokleon.)

Φιλοκλέων: ἓν ἔτι ποθῶ, τὰ δ' ἄλλ' ἀρέσκει μοι.
Βδελυκλέων: τὸ τί;
Φιλοκλέων: θἠρῷον εἴ πως ἐκκομίσαις τὸ τοῦ Λύκου.
Βδελυκλέων: πάρεστι τουτί, καὐτὸς ἄναξ οὑτοσί.
Φιλοκλέων: ὦ δέσποθ' ἥρως, ὡς χαλεπὸς ἄρ' ἦσθ' ἰδεῖν.

Βδελυκλέων: οἷόσπερ ἡμῖν φαίνεται Κλεώνυμος.
Φιλοκλέων: οὔκουν ἔχει γ' οὐδ' αὐτὸς ἥρως ὢν ὅπλα.

Philokleon: One thing I miss, I am content with the rest.
Bdelykleon: What is it?
Philokleon: The Heroon . . . if you could somehow bring out Lykos's heroon.
Bdelykleon: It is right here. And here is the ruler himself.
Philokleon: O hero lord, how hard you were to see!
Bdelykleon: Exactly like our Kleonymos.
Philokleon: He even doesn't have—although a hero—equipment.

180. Schol. Aristophanes, *Wasps*, lines 819–820

θήρῷον· Τὸ ἱερὸν τοῦ ἥρωος Λύκου ... πάρεστι τουτί· εἰκόνα πινάκιον κομίζει, ἐν ὧι γεγραμμένος ἦν ὁ Λύκος.

The shrine: The hieron of the hero Lykos . . . Here it is: he supplies a picture or tablet on which Lykos is drawn.

181. Harpokration, *s.v.* δεκάζων (includes Eratosthenes, *On Old Comedy*) 2nd century C.E.

δεκάζων· Ἰσοκράτης περὶ τῆς εἰρήνης, ὅ τι ποτὲ τοῦτ' ἐστὶ δῆλον ἅπασιν· Ἐρατοσθένης δὲ ἐν τοῖς περὶ τῆς ἀρχαίας κωμωιδίας, πόθεν τὸ πρᾶγμα εἴρηται δηλοῖ οὕτω λέγων· Λύκος ἐστὶν ἥρως πρὸς τοῖς ἐν Ἀθήναις δικαστηρίοις τοῦ θηρίου μορφὴν ἔχων, πρὸς ὃν οἱ δωροδοκοῦντες κατὰ ι' γιγνόμενοι ἀνεστρέφοντο, ὅθεν εἴρηται Λύκου δεκάς. Ἀριστοτέλης δ' ἐν Ἀθηναίων πολιτείαι Ἄνυτόν φησι καταδεῖξαι τὸ δεκάζειν τὰ δικαστήρια.

Bribing: Isokrates *On the Peace*: What this is, is clear to all. Eratosthenes (writing in the first half of the 3rd century B.C.E.) in his work on the Old Comedy makes clear how the phrase arose, saying this: "Lykos is a hero in the shape of the animal at the dikasteria in Athens, beside whom those who take bribes gathered in groups of ten, whence the phrase 'the company of Lykos'." Aristotle in *Athenaion Politeia* (27.5) says that Anytos introduced the bribing of dikastic panels.

182. Hesychios, *s.v.* Λύκου δεκάς 5th or 6th century C.E.?

Λύκου δεκάς· παροιμιῶδες ἐπεὶ Λύκος ἥρως πρὸς τοῖς ἐν Ἀθήναις δικαστηρίοις ἵδρυτο, τοῦ θηρίου τὴν μορφὴν ἔχων.

The company of Lykos: [said] as a proverb, because the hero Lykos had a sanctuary at the lawcourts in Athens, having the form of the animal.

183. *Lexicon Cantabrigiense* 349.10

Λύκος· ἥρως ἱδρυμένος οὗτος ἦν ἐν τοῖς δικαστηρίοις, ὧι καὶ αὐτῶι τὸ δικαστικὸν ἔνεμον, ὡς Ἰσαῖος ἐν Τεμενικῶι· καὶ Λύκου δεκὰς καλεῖται, ὅτι περὶ τὸ ἀφίδρυμα αὐτοῦ κατὰ δέκα γενόμενοι οἱ δικασταὶ ἐδεκάζοντο.

ἥρως ἱδρυμένος: Dobree; ἤρετο ἱδρύματος: cod.; αὐτῶι: Dobree; αὐτὸ: cod.

Lykos: this was a hero set up in the dikasteria to whom they would give the dikast's pay [dikastikon], as Isaios says in *Temenikon*; and "the company of Lykos" is so called because around his image the dikasts in groups of ten were bribed.

184. Photios, *Lexicon*, *s.v.* Λύκου δεκάς — 9th century C.E.

ἡ Λύκου δεκάς· Λύκος Ἀθήνησι πρὸς τῶι δικαστηρίωι ἥρως μορφὴν ἔχων θηρίου· δεκὰς δὲ τὸ δεκάζεσθαι, πρὸς ὃ ἡ παροιμία, καὶ οἱ πρῶτοι δικασταὶ πρὸς τῶι λυκοειδεῖ ἥρωι ἐκλήθησαν.

ἐκλήθησαν is variously emended to ἐκάθισαν, κατεστάθησαν, or ἐκληρώθησαν.

The company of Lykos: [This refers to] Lykos in Athens at the dikasterion, a hero in the form of the animal; "company" from being bribed, to which the proverb refers, and the first dikasts [to arrive] by the wolflike hero were called [the company of Lykos].

Λύκου δεκάς· ἥρως πρὸς τοῖς Ἀθήνησι δικαστηρίοις τῶν θηρίων μορφὰς ἔχων, πρὸς ὃν οἱ δωροδοκοῦντες κατὰ δέκα συνεστρέφοντο.

The company of Lykos: a hero at the dikasteria in Athens [whose statues have] the form of animals. Beside him those who take bribes rallied in groups of ten.

Λύκου δεκάς· παροιμιῶδες, ἐπεὶ Λύκος ὁ ἥρως ἵδρυτο παρὰ τοῖς δικαστηρίοις, ἔνθα προσήδρευον οἱ συκοφάνται· ἀφώριστο δὲ αὐτῶι τριώβολον τῆς ἡμέρας.

The company of Lykos: proverbial, since Lykos the hero was established at the dikasteria where the sycophants gathered; a triobol a day was set apart for him.

The first entry is repeated almost verbatim in the *Suda* (**185**). Compare Harpokration (**181**) for the second and Hesychios (**182**) for the second and third. The plurals in the second entry reflect a notion that there was a heroon at every court.

(2) Pollux 8.121

(Pollux includes among) well-known lawcourts . . . that at Lykos from which comes the phrase "the company of Lykos". A statue of the hero in the form of the animal was set up there, and formerly those who bribed dikastic panels assembled there.

185. *Suda*, *s.v.* Λύκου δεκάς — 10th century C.E.

ἡ Λύκου δεκάς· παροιμία. Λύκος Ἀθήνησιν πρὸς τῶι δικαστηρίωι ἥρως μορφὴν ἔχων θηρίου, δεκὰς δὲ τὸ δεκάζεσθαι, πρὸς ὃ ἡ παροιμία, καὶ οἱ πρῶτοι δικασταὶ πρὸς τῶι λυκοειδεῖ ἥρωι ἐκλήθησαν.

The company of Lykos: a proverb. Lykos in Athens at the dikasterion was a hero in the form of the animal [the wolf]; "company" [is derived from the verb] from "being bribed", to which the proverb refers, and the first dikasts to arrive beside the wolflike hero were called [the company of Lykos].

See Photios, who gives almost the same entry. The *Suda* in another entry, *s.v.* Λύκου δεκάς, not quoted here, reproduces verbatim the third entry in Photios (**184**). An explanatory note on Lykos follows the entry Λύκου δεκάς, but it offers no new data.

The Theseion

Photios states that the Theseion was a place of asylum for slaves and that lawsuits were also tried there. This same entry is repeated in the *Etymologicum Magnum*. The *Lexeis* in Bekker states simply that it was a place of asylum for slaves. There is no real evidence to suggest that it was ever used as a lawcourt. Lipsius (1905–1915, p. 171, note 21) sees confusion in Photios' statement. Jacoby (*FGrHist* 328 Philochoros F177, notes to commentary, p. 9) thinks ἐλέγοντο δίκαι reflects conversations that slaves, slaves' representatives, and masters had concerning slaves' status; compare K. A. Christensen, "The Theseion: A Slave Refuge," *AJAH* 9, 1984, pp. 23–32.

For full testimonia on the Theseion, see *Agora* III, nos. 339–362.

186. Bekker, *Anecdota Graeca* 1.264.21–22

Θησεῖον· τὸ τοῦ Θησέως ἡρῷιον. ἔστι δὲ ἄσυλον τοῖς οἰκέταις.

Theseion: the hero shrine of Theseus. It is a place of asylum for slaves.

187. Photios, *Lexicon, s.v.* Θησεῖον — 9th century c.e.

Θησεῖον· τὸ Θησέως ἡρῷιον, ὃ τοῖς οἰκέταις ἄσυλον ἦν. ἐλέγοντο δὲ δίκαι καὶ ἐνταῦθα.

Theseion: the hero shrine of Theseus, which was a place of asylum for slaves; lawsuits were also pleaded there.

This same entry is repeated in the *Etymologicum Magnum* (= *Agora* III, no. 349).

ARCHITECTURAL REQUIREMENTS

This section contains testimonia relating to the physical requirements of a dikasterion and selections from Aristotle relating to τὰ δικαστήρια, where the sense of that phrase points to a single court complex. Here there took place the elaborate process of daily allotments that he describes. The texts are grouped under the following headings: structures for the audience or spectators, who although outside could hear the proceedings (**188–200**); entrance and barriers (*kinklis* and *dryphaktoi*, **201–226**); the *bema* (**227–244**); seating arrangements (**245–248**); a pillar (**106**); and a court complex, τὰ δικαστήρια (**249**).

Structures for the Audience or Spectators

Spectators in large numbers would listen to the speeches at the trials (except for cases whose nature required the general public to be kept at a distance). This audience, which was burlesqued as early as 425 b.c.e. in Aristophanes, *Acharnians*, line 915, is often referred to as "those standing around" or "those present outside". Plato, at *Apology* 24e, says "audience"; Antiphon, "private persons". The story told by Plutarch of a seat being found inside for Demosthenes when he was a boy need not imply that those outside could not hear. In cases involving the Mysteries, however, a rope barrier (περισχοίνισμα) was set at a distance of fifty feet from the court building, to keep the uninitiated public from hearing the proceedings (Pollux 8.123, 141 [**199, 200**]).

188. Aristophanes, *Acharnians*, line 915 — 425 b.c.e.

Νίκαρχος: Ἐγὼ φράσω σοι τῶν περιεστώτων χάριν.

Nikarchos: I'll tell you for the sake of the audience.

189. Aischines 2 (*The False Embassy*) 5 — 343 b.c.e.

εἰ γάρ τις ἢ τῶν ἔξωθεν περιεστηκότων πέπεισται, σχεδὸν δ' οἱ πλεῖστοι τῶν πολιτῶν πάρεισιν, ἢ τῶν δικαζόντων ὑμῶν, ὡς ἐγὼ τοιοῦτόν τι διαπέπραγμαι. . . .

For if any man among those standing around outside, and almost the whole of the citizen body is present, or if anyone of you who are dikasts is convinced that I have done such a deed. . . .

(229) Aischines 3 (*Ktesiphon*) 56

And so . . . for me to answer you, Demosthenes, in the presence of all the dikasts and of all the other citizens who are standing around outside, and of all those Greeks whose concern it is to listen to this case—and I see not a few here, but more in fact than anyone remembers ever being present at a public trial—I answer . . .

(231) Aischines 3 (*Ktesiphon*) 207

And I should not be surprised if he should turn around and abuse those standing around outside, claiming that those who have been counted up and certified as oligarchs . . . have come to the prosecutor's bema, . . .

190. Antiphon 6 (*Choreutes*) 14 419/18 B.C.E.

πολλοὶ τῶν περιεστώτων τούτων τὰ μὲν πράγματα ταῦτα πάντα ἀκριβῶς ἐπίστανται.

Many of these men who are standing outside around [this court] know all of this well.

191. Antiphon 6 (*Choreutes*) 24 419/18 B.C.E.

καὶ ταῦτα ἐμοῦ προκαλουμένου καὶ λέγοντος ἐν τῶι δικαστηρίωι, οὗ καὶ αὐτοὶ οἱ δικασταὶ καὶ ἕτεροι ἰδιῶται πολλοὶ μάρτυρες παρῆσαν.

And I made this challenge in the dikasterion, where the dikasts themselves and many other private persons were present as witnesses.

See **97** above for a fuller text.

192. Deinarchos 1 (*Demosthenes*) 66 323 B.C.E.

τί γὰρ ἐροῦμεν, ὦ Ἀθηναῖοι, πρὸς τοὺς περιεστηκότας ἐξελθόντες ἐκ τοῦ δικαστηρίου ἐάν, ὃ μὴ γένοιτο, παρακρουσθῆτε ὑπὸ τῆς τούτου γοητείας;

What shall we say, Athenians, as we come out of the dikasterion to those standing around if, which I hope does not happen, you are led astray by his witchcraft?

193. Deinarchos 2 (*Aristogeiton*) 19 323 B.C.E.

ὥστε τὸ πολλάκις λεγόμενον ἀληθὲς εἰπεῖν ἔστιν, ὅτι περὶ μὲν τούτου τὴν ψῆφον ὑμεῖς μέλλετε φέρειν, περὶ δ' ὑμῶν οἱ περιεστηκότες καὶ οἱ ἄλλοι πάντες.

And so you can say what is often said is true, that while you are about to judge the defendant, those standing around [outside] and all others besides are about to judge you.

194. Demosthenes 18 (*On the Crown*) 196 330 B.C.E.

ἔστι δὲ ταυτὶ πάντα μοι τὰ πολλὰ πρὸς ὑμᾶς ἄνδρες δικασταὶ καὶ τοὺς περιεστηκότας ἔξωθεν καὶ ἀκροωμένους . . .

All this [long argument] I intend chiefly for you dikasts and for those standing around outside and listening [because a short clear answer would be enough for him].

195. Demosthenes 30 (*Onetor* I) 32 362/1 B.C.E.

οἵ τε γὰρ ἐν τῶι δικαστηρίωι τότε δικάζοντες καὶ τῶν ἔξωθεν παρόντων πολλοὶ συνίσασιν.

Those who were then serving as dikasts in the dikasterion and many of those present outside know these facts well.

Compare Demosthenes 54.41.

196. Hypereides 5 (*Demosthenes*) 22 323 B.C.E.

ἀλλ' ὑμεῖς μὲν ἠσχύνεσθε ἐπὶ [– – –]
τ]οὺς περιεστηκότας [τῶ]ν Ἑλλήνων, ὅτε
[τινῶ]ν κατεχειρο[τον]εῖτε.

You, O dikasts, used to be ashamed . . . those of the Greeks who were standing around when you passed sentence on certain persons.

The text is fragmentary.

197. Isaios 5 (*Dikaiogenes*) 20 *ca.* 389 B.C.E.

καίτοι εἰ μὴ ἐναντίον μὲν τῶν δικαστῶν, πεντακοσίων ὄντων, ἐναντίον δὲ τῶν περιεστηκότων ἠγγυᾶτο, οὐκ οἶδ' ὅ τι [ἂν] ἐποίησεν.

See Wyse, p. 429, on [ἂν].

If he was not giving surety before the dikasts, of whom there were 500, and before those standing around, I do not know what he did.

198. Plutarch, *Demosthenes* 5.3 1st–2nd century C.E.

(The young Demosthenes had persuaded his tutor to take him to the trial where Kallistratos was speaking on Oropos.)

ὁ δὲ ἔχων πρὸς τοὺς ἀνοίγοντας τὰ δικαστήρια δημοσίους συνήθειαν, εὐπόρησε χώρας ἐν ἧι καθήμενος ὁ παῖς ἀδήλως ἀκροάσεται τῶν λεγομένων.

The [tutor,] who was acquainted with the public servants who opened the dikasteria, found a place where the boy could sit unseen and listen to what was said.

199. Pollux 8.123–124 2nd century C.E.

. . . οὗ ὕστερον μυστικῶς δικάζοντες ἦσαν ἐκ τῶν ἐπωπτευκότων. τὸ δὲ δικαστήριον περιεσχοινίζετο, τοῦ μὲν βασιλέως παραγγείλαντος, τῶν δὲ θεσμοθετῶν πληρούντων τὸ δικαστήριον. τὸ δὲ περισχοίνισμα ἀπὸ πεντήκοντα ποδῶν ἐγίγνετο. καὶ οἱ ὑπηρέται ὑφειστήκεισαν, ὅπως μηδεὶς ἀνεπόπτευτος προσίηι.

. . . where later when they were trying cases about the Mysteries a panel was composed of initiates in the highest Mysteries. The court was roped off; the basileus gave the order and the thesmothetai manned the court. The rope barrier was at a distance of fifty feet, and the attendants were stationed to see that no person approached who had not been initiated.

Some text is missing before the first phrase. See *Agora* III, nos. 529–536, for full testimonia on *perischoinisma.*

200. Pollux 8.141 2nd century C.E.

περισχοινίσαι δὲ τὸ δικαστήριον, ὁπότε περὶ μυστικῶν δικάζοιεν, ἵνα μὴ προσίηι μηδεὶς ἀνεπόπτευτος ὤν.

To rope off the court, [this was done] when they would try cases which involved the Mysteries, so that no one could enter who was not initiated in the highest Mysteries.

Kinklis and Dryphaktoi (Gate and Fence)

Scholiasts and lexicographers all agree that kinklis and dryphaktoi were parts of a dikasterion. Kinklis was the door of the dikasterion (Harpokration [**220**]). It was the dikasterion door that the Romans call *kankellotai* (Pollux [**226**] and Schol. Aristophanes, *Wasps*, line 124 [**205**], *Knights*, line 641 [**202**]). Kinklis is the same as the dryphaktoi, a fence or enclosing barrier of some sort (Schol. Aristophanes, *Wasps*, lines 386 [**207**], 844 [**213**]).

Dryphaktoi are fences or railings of the dikasterion (Schol. Aristophanes, *Wasps*, line 552 [**208**]). A dryphaktos is the plank or bar stretched alongside the dikasts (Schol. Aristophanes, *Wasps*, line 830 [**212**]). Dryphaktoi are the doors or *kankeloi* of a dikasterion or the barriers or encircling walls (Hesychios [**221**]).

The confusion between doors and barriers of some sort is understandable when one looks at the classical sources. A kinklis of a dikasterion is referred to three times by Aristophanes: Philokleon before daybreak appeared at the kinklis (*Wasps*, line 124 [**204**]); no thesmothetes will close the kinklis if the dikast arrives late (*Wasps*, line 774 [**210**]); and the heliast crept towards the kinklis (F216 [*PCG* III.2]). In Aristotle's *Athenaion Politeia*, the dikast enters inside the kinklis after he has received his balanos but before he moves on to the courtroom where he is to sit. [Demosthenes] 25 (**218**), in referring to the weak kinklis of the Bouleuterion, seems to imply the presence of a similar kinklis in the dikasterion where he is speaking.

Dryphaktoi of a dikasterion are referred to three times by Aristophanes: Philokleon asks to be buried under the dryphaktoi (*Wasps*, line 385 [**206**]); suppliants wait for him at the dryphaktoi before he enters the dikasterion (*Wasps*, line 552 [**208**]); and Philokleon demands a dryphaktos, the first of all "our sacred things", before the mock trial can begin (*Wasps*, line 830 [**211**]), and some kind of enclosure for pigs is brought as a substitute (*Wasps*, line 844 [**211**]).

The kinklis and dryphaktoi of the Bouleuterion appear in Aristophanes' *Knights*, and the closely contemporary references to those of a dikasterion in *Wasps* ought to be similar constructions. In *Knights*, lines 640–641 (**201**), the Sausage-seller, having followed Paphlagon to the Bouleuterion and listened to his speech, says that he shattered the kinklis with a blow from his fundament and then addressed the boule, and when the councillors demanded that the meeting be dismissed, they jumped over the dryphaktoi on every side (ὑπερεπήδων τοὺς δρυφάκτους πανταχῆι, lines 674–675 [**201**]). Dryphaktoi in the Bouleuterion are also mentioned by Xenophon when he describes the liquidation of Theramenes in 404 B.C.E. Kritias ordered the swordsmen "to take their stand at the dryphaktoi where the boule could clearly see them. . . . The boule remained silent, seeing that the men at the dryphaktoi were of the same kind as Satyros and that the space in front of the Bouleuterion was full of guards" (*Hellenika* 2.3.50 and 55; see *Agora* III, no. 407 for the text).

The dryphaktoi of the Bouleuterion were some kind of railing or barrier low enough to be jumped over and to be seen over and through, behind which the members of the council sat. The word is used elsewhere with a similar meaning. According to Plutarch, at the time of an ostracism part of the Agora was fenced around in a circle with dryphaktoi (*Aristeides* 7.7–8; see *Agora* III, no. 532 for text). Polybios uses the word in the singular for a railing of some sort that was knee high along the side of a "raven" (engine for grappling ships) on which the soldiers rested their shields (1.22.6 and 10). In Aristotle's *Ath. Pol.* 50.2, among the duties of the *astynomoi* is seeing that dryphaktoi did not stretch out over the road (καὶ δρυφάκτους ὑπὲρ τὴν ὁδὸν ὑπερτείνειν). Here the word is often translated as "balconies" but might equally well be interpreted as any kind of wooden structure projecting out from the houses. This passage is perhaps the source of the "wood projecting from buildings" in the scholia to *Knights*, line 675 (**203**) and *Wasps*, line 386 (**207**). The word itself makes it clear that dryphaktoi, at least originally, were made of wood, although not necessarily of oak (see LSJ, *s.v.* δρῦς).

The dryphaktoi of the dikasterion of *Wasps*, lines 552–553 (**208**) could have been a wooden barrier or railing that kept the public from entering the court proper. It may have been inside the building, as in the Bouleuterion, or at the entrance. Note that there is no contemporary evidence of dryphaktoi forming any part of the elaborate court complex required for the allotment system of the second half of the 4th century.

The exact position and function of the kinklis of the Bouleuterion is not certain from the passage in the *Knights*. After reaching the Bouleuterion and hearing some of Paphlagon's speech, the Sausage-seller breaks the kinklis with a physical blow or by crepitation and then starts addressing the boule. It is clearly a barrier or gate of some kind that one has to go through to reach a speaking position, whether that be beside the bema or simply inside the dryphaktoi.

In a building inscription for the Arsenal of Peiraieus of 347/6 B.C.E. (*IG* II^2 1668, line 65), the contractor is instructed to fill (block) each intercolumniation with two stone orthostates three feet high and to place in between them a kinklis that could be closed (καὶ ἐν τῶι μεταξὺ κιγκλίδα ἐπιθήσε[ι] κλειομένην).

The word *kinklis* is related to *kinklos*, a dabchick or grebe that wags its tail, and to the verb κιγκλίζω, defined as "to wag the tail or change constantly" (LSJ). A swinging door or gate is consonant with a basic meaning for kinklis. The meaning "lattice work" given by dictionaries and commentators may derive from observation that lattice work would often be the material of a swinging gate. One ancient commentator (Schol. Aristophanes, *Knights*, lines 641f [**202**]) describes the kinklis as though he sees it.

The kinklis of the Bouleuterion was therefore a swinging, latticed gate, probably in the dryphaktoi, that was closed after the meeting began and so, for instance, had to be broken open for the illegal entry of the Sausage-seller. The kinklis of a dikasterion was likewise a swinging gate, and in the second half of the 4th century it was an entrance or gate to the outer enclosure rather than to the meeting place of a specific dikastic panel. For discussion of the two terms, see Dow 1939, pp. 18–22; compare F. Salviat, "Dédicace d'un τρύφακτος par les Hermaïstes Déliens," *BCH* 87, 1963 [pp. 252–264], pp. 259–264; G. Roux, "Aristophane, Xénophon, le Pseudo Démosthène et l'architecture du bouleutérion d'Athènes," *BCH* 100, 1976, pp. 475–483; and Rhodes 1972, pp. 33–44.

201. Aristophanes, *Knights*, lines 640–642, 674–675 — 424 B.C.E.

(The Sausage-seller speaks, describing the scene at the Bouleuterion.)

κᾆτα τῶι πρωκτῶι θενὼν
τὴν κιγκλίδ' ἐξήραξα, κἀναχανὼν μέγα
ἀνέκραγον·...

Then with my vent I hit the kinklis and shattered it; and opening my mouth wide I shouted....

ἐκεκράγεσάν τε τοὺς πρυτάνεις ἀφιέναι·
εἶθ' ὑπερεπήδων τοὺς δρυφάκτους πανταχῆι·

The councillors shouted out that the prytaneis should dismiss the meeting; then they jumped over the dryphaktoi on every side.

Note that the kinklis and dryphaktoi referred to above are at the Bouleuterion, not a dikasterion.

202. Schol. Aristophanes, *Knights*, line 641a, f

(a) τὴν κιγκλίδ'· τὴν θύραν, τὸ κάγκελον τοῦ δικαστηρίου. ἰδίως δὲ τὰς διπλᾶς θύρας οὕτω κλητέον, ἅς τινες δικλίδας φασίν. ἢ κιγκλὶς ἰδίως ἡ τρύπη, δι' ἧς ἡ κλεὶς πέμπεται. (f) αἱ τοῦ δικαστηρίου θύραι ἐπικειμένας εἶχον ἔξωθεν ἑτέρας, οὐ διὰ συμφυνῶν σανίδων ἀλλ' ἐκ κιγκλίδων συγκειμένας ἵνα διαφανεῖς οὖσαι καὶ διῃρημέναι εἰς πλείους ὀπὰς ἀκωλύτως ὁρᾶν παρέχοιεν τοῖς ἐκτὸς ἐπὶ τὰ ἔνδον.

(a) I shattered the kinklis: the door, the bar of the dikasterion. Specifically double doors are to be called thus, which some name folding doors. Or kinklis is specifically the hole through which the key is sent. (f) The doors of the court had other doors added from outside. These were put together not out of attached boards but from latticed gates. These, since they could be seen through and were divided into a number of openings, provided people from outside an unobstructed view inside.

203. Schol. Aristophanes, *Knights*, line 675b

τοὺς δρυφάκτους· τὰ νῦν ταβλώματα καλούμενα. τὰ τῶν οἰκοδομημάτων ἐξέχοντα ξύλα· ἢ τὰ κάγκελα δρυόφρακτός τις ὤν. τουτέστι ὁ ἐκ δρυῶν φραγμός. οἱ γὰρ ἀρχαῖοι πᾶν δένδρον δρῦν ἐκάλουν, ὥσπερ καὶ ἀκρόδρυα τὰ ἄκρα τῶν δένδρων.

The dryphaktoi: now called *tablomata*. The wooden parts projecting from buildings or the bars, a wooden fence, that is, a fence of wood [oak]. For the ancients called every tree a *drys*, for example, *akrodrya* of the tops of trees.

Compare the Scholion on *Wasps*, line 386 (**207**). *Akrodrya*, in fact, means the fruit growing on the outermost branches of trees, of fruit trees in general (see LSJ, *s.v.* ἀκρόδρυα).

204. Aristophanes, *Wasps*, line 124 — 422 B.C.E.
(Xanthias describes Philokleon.)

ὁ δ' ἀνεφάνη κνεφαῖος ἐπὶ τῆι κιγκλίδι.

Before daybreak he appeared at the kinklis.

205. Schol. Aristophanes, *Wasps*, line 124c

ἐπὶ τῆι κιγκλίδι· ἀντὶ τοῦ, ἐν τῶι δικαστηρίωι ὁ πατήρ. κιγκλὶς γὰρ ἡ θύρα τοῦ δικαστηρίου, ἣν καὶ καγκελωτὴν καλοῦσι. . . .

At the kinklis: instead of [saying] "his father in the lawcourt." For kinklis is the door of the dikasterion, which they also call *kankelotes*. . . .

206. Aristophanes, *Wasps*, lines 385–386 — 422 B.C.E.
(Philokleon appeals to the chorus, fearing disaster in his efforts to escape.)

. . . ἤν τι πάθω 'γώ,
ἀνελόντες καὶ κατακλαύσαντες θεῖναί
μ' ὑπὸ τοῖσι δρυφάκτοις.

. . . If anything happens to me, take me up and mourn for me, and bury me under the dryphaktoi.

207. Schol. Aristophanes, *Wasps*, line 386b–c

(b) ἀνελόντες καὶ κλαύσαντες· ἐὰν συμβῆι με πεσόντα ἀποθανεῖν ἐν τῶι δικαστηρίωι με θάψατε. (c) δρύφακτα ἐλέγετο, ἐνταῦθα δὲ τὰ ταυλώματα τοῦ δικαστηρίου, καὶ τὰ περιφράγματα διὰ τὸ ἐκ ξύλων καὶ σανίδων τῶν ἐκ δρυὸς εἶναι κατεσκευασμένα. λέγει δὲ κἀνταῦθα ἀπὸ μέρους τὸ δικαστήριον.

(b) Take me up and mourn: if it happens I fall and die, bury me in the dikasterion. (c) dryphakta was mentioned. Here the tablomata of the dikasterion and the encircling fences, because they are constructed of timbers and planks of oak. The dikasterion here is called by the name of its part.

Compare Schol. Aristophanes, *Wasps*, line 349, (**339**), where dryphaktoi are also called *tablota*.

208. Aristophanes, *Wasps*, lines 552–553, 560–561 422 B.C.E.
(Philokleon expatiates on the joys of being a dikast.)

ὃν πρῶτα μὲν ἕρποντ' ἐξ εὐνῆς τηροῦσ' ἐπὶ τοῖσι δρυφάκτοις
ἄνδρες μεγάλοι καὶ τετραπήχεις·

εἶτ' εἰσελθὼν ἀντιβοληθεὶς καὶ τὴν ὀργὴν ἀπομορχθείς,
ἔνδον τούτων ὧν ἂν φάσκω πάντων οὐδὲν πεποίηκα. . . .

When I first crawl out of bed, great tall fellows attend me at the dryphaktoi . . . [bowing before me and begging for acquittal]. . . .

Then, after I have been implored and my anger is wiped away, I go inside and do not do any of all the things I say. . . .

209. Schol. Aristophanes, *Wasps*, line 552b

τοῖς δρυφάκτοις· τοῖς περιφράγμασι τοῦ δικαστηρίου.

Dryphaktoi: Fences (or railings) of the dikasterion.

210. Aristophanes, *Wasps*, lines 774–775 422 B.C.E.
(Bdelykleon is describing the joys of a court at home.)

κἂν ἔγρηι μεσημβρινός,
οὐδείς σ' ἀποκλείσει θεσμοθέτης τῆι κιγκλίδι.

And if you wake at noon, no thesmothetes will close you out with the kinklis.

211. Aristophanes, *Wasps*, lines 830–831, 844 422 B.C.E.
(Philokleon, during preparations for the mock trial, asks the following.)

ἄνευ δρυφάκτου τὴν δίκην μέλλεις καλεῖν,
ὃ πρῶτον ἡμῖν τῶν ἱερῶν ἐφαίνετο;

Are you about to start a trial without a dryphaktos, which was the first of all our sacred things to be revealed?

(Philokleon goes to look for a substitute, returns, and says the following.)

Βδελυκλέων: τουτὶ τί ἐστι;
Φιλοκλέων: χοιροκομεῖον Ἑστίας

Bdelykleon: What have you there?
Philokleon: Hestia's pigpen.

On Hestia's pigpen, see **213** below.

212. Schol. Aristophanes, *Wasps*, line 830

ἄνευ δρυφάκτου· Δρύφακτος τὸ παραγενόμενον ξύλον τοῖς δικασταῖς.

Without a dryphaktos: dryphaktos is the wood [plank or bar] alongside the dikasts.

213. Schol. Aristophanes, *Wasps*, line 844a–b

χοιροκομεῖόν ἐστιν ἀγγεῖόν τι κανονωτὸν ὅπου οἱ χοῖροι τρέφονται. ἑστίας δὲ, ἐπεὶ ἐπὶ τῆς ἑστίας τρέφουσι χοίρους. εἰσφέρει δὲ τοῦτο ἀντὶ δρυφάκτου, ἢ κιγκλίδος. ἐν τῆι Λυσιστράτηι κλοιὸν μᾶλλον ἢ πάσσαλον ἐμφαίνει, ὡς καὶ τούτου ὁμοίως λεγομένου, ὅπου ὁ χοῖρος δέδεται. (b) ἔξεισιν ὁ ἕτερος τῶν οἰκετῶν ἀντὶ δρυφάκτων χοιροκομεῖον ἔχων. ἔστι δὲ τὸ καλούμενον ζωγρεῖον κανονωτόν, ὅπου οἱ χοῖροι τρέφονται.

A *choirokomeion* is a pot [cage] furnished with crossbars where pigs are reared. "Hestia", because they raise pigs on the hearth. He brings in this instead of a dryphaktos or kinklis. In *Lysistrata* (line 1073) he indicates (or exhibits?) a collar or peg, since the place where the pig is tethered is called by this name likewise. (b) The other servant appears on stage with a *choirokomeion* instead of dryphaktoi. It is the cage called *zogreion* with cross bars where pigs are reared.

Gerald Lalonde ("Topographical Notes on Aristophanes," in *Thompson Studies* [pp. 77–81], pp. 77–79) reviews interpretations of "Hestia's pigsty".

214. Aristophanes, *Wasps*, line 891 422 B.C.E.

(Bdelykleon pretends to be a presiding magistrate or a herald at the beginning of the mock trial.)

εἴ τις θύρασιν ἡλιαστής, εἰσίτω.

If any heliast is at the doors, let him enter.

215. Schol. Aristophanes, *Wasps*, line 891

Βδελυκλέων μιμεῖται τὸν κήρυκα.

Bdelykleon is imitating the herald.

216. Aristotle, *Ath. Pol.* 65.1 *ca.* 329–322 B.C.E.

αὐ[τ]ὸ[ς δὲ δείξα]ς πᾴλιν τ[ῶι ὑ]πηρέτηι εἶ[τ'] ἐ[ντὸς εἰσέρχετ]αι τῆς κ[ι]γκλ[ί]δος.

See **249** below for full text of this paragraph.

[The dikast] again shows [the balanos] to the attendant and goes inside the kinklis.

Note that the dikast has just received the balanos with the letter of the court to which he is assigned. Immediately after entering inside the kinklis, an attendant, presumably the same to whom he shows the balanos, gives him a colored staff. Then the dikast proceeds to the particular court whose lintel is painted with the same color as his staff. *Kinklis* in this passage appears to be an entrance in the enclosure around the court area and not an entrance to a specific court meeting place.

The word *kinklis* as used in this text (note that the text is fragmentary, but the reading *kinklidos* seems highly probable) could be interpreted as a barrier around the enclosure rather than a specific entrance or gate. Generally, however, *kinklis* seems to mean a gate of some kind or a light, removable barrier.

217. Bekker, *Anecdota Graeca* 1.271.33

κιγκλίδες· δρύφακτοι, οἱ νῦν καλούμενοι κάγκελοι.

Kinklides: dryphaktoi, which are now called bars [barriers].

218. [Demosthenes] 25 (*Aristogeiton* I) 23 *ca.* 325 B.C.E.?

(The author is citing examples of orderliness and dignity ensured in public life by the laws.)

τὸ τὴν βουλὴν τοὺς πεντακοσίους ἀπὸ τῆς [ἀσθενοῦς] τοιαυτησὶ κιγκλίδος τῶν ἀπορρήτων κυρίαν εἶναι, καὶ μὴ τοὺς ἰδιώτας ἐπεισιέναι·

The fact that the Council of the 500 is in control of secret matters as a result of a [weak] kinklis such as this, and that private persons do not push in.

The speaker is describing the Bouleuterion, but the deictic τοιαυτησί points to a kinklis associated with the court in which he was speaking.

219. *Etymologicum Magnum, s.v.* κιγκλίς 12th century C.E.

κιγκλίς· ἡ καγκελοθυρίς, θύρα δικτυωτή. Μάλιστα δὲ ἐπὶ τῶν δικαστηρίων τοιαῦται ἦσαν, ἵνα ταχέως ἀνοίγωνται καὶ κλείωνται· συνεχῶς γὰρ εἰσήιεσαν καὶ ἐξήιεσαν.

Kinklis: the door of the bar, a latticed door. Especially at the lawcourts, they were of this kind so that they might be opened and shut quickly; for [the dikasts] were continually coming in and going out.

220. Harpokration, *s.v.* κιγκλίς 2nd century C.E.

κιγκλίς· Δημοσθένης ἐν τῶι κατὰ Ἀριστογείτονος. αἱ τῶν δικαστηρίων θύραι κιγκλίδες ἐκαλοῦντο. Ἀριστοφάνης Δαιταλεῦσιν· ὁ δ' ἡλιαστὴς εἷρπε πρὸς τὴν κιγκλίδα.

Kinklis: [The word appears in] Demosthenes in his speech against Aristogeiton (25.23). The doors of the dikasteria are called *kinklides*. Aristophanes in the *Banqueters* (F216 [*PCG* III.2]) [says] "the heliast crept towards the kinklis."

Banqueters was produced in 427 B.C.E., and this is our earliest reference to the κιγκλίς. Note that [Demosthenes] (see **218** above) refers to the kinklis of the Bouleuterion, not of the dikasteria.

221. Hesychios, *s.v.* ἀδρύφακτον 5th or 6th century C.E.?

ἀδρύφακτον· ἄνευ δικαστηρίου. ἢ ἀφύλακτον, ἀτείχιστον.

Without a dryphaktos: without a dikasterion, or unguarded, unwalled.

δρύφακτοι· αἱ τοῦ δικαστηρίου θύραι ἢ κάγκελοι, ἢ τὰ διαφράγματα, ἢ τὰ περιτειχίσματα.

Dryphaktoi: the doors or bars of a dikasterion, or the barriers [fences] or encircling walls.

Compare Schol. Aristophanes *Wasps*, lines 386 (**207**) and 552 (**209**).

222. *Lexicon Patmense, s.v.* κιγκλίς

Commentary on [Demosthenes] 25.23.

κιγκλίς· τὸ κάγκελλον τοῦ δικαστηρίου.

Kinklis: the bar of the dikasterion.

223. Pollux 4.37 2nd century C.E.

Pollux, in a list of abusive words and phrases, includes the following:

πρὸς ἡδονὴν δημηγορῶν, παρὰ τῆι κιγκλίδι ζῶν ἀεί, παρὰ τὸν δρύφακτον ποιούμενος τὸν βίον, παρὰ τὴν κλεψύδραν.

Addressing the demos to please them, living always at the kinklis, making one's living beside the dryphaktos, beside the klepsydra.

224. Pollux 7.122 2nd century C.E.

(Pollux lists the various parts of a house.)

καὶ κιγκλίδες δὲ εἴδη θυρῶν.

And kinklides are a kind of doors.

225. Pollux 8.17 2nd century C.E.

τάχα δὲ τῶν τοῦ δικαστηρίου μερῶν ἐστὶ καὶ κιγκλὶς καὶ δρύφακτος.

Probably both kinklis and dryphaktos are parts of a dikasterion.

This sentence is from a paragraph that lists dikastic equipment, such as symbola, klepsydra, and so on; see **250** for full text.

226. Pollux 8.124 2nd century C.E.

αἱ μὲν οὖν τῶν δικαστηρίων θύραι κιγκλίδες ἐκαλοῦντο, ἃς οἱ Ῥωμαῖοι καγκελλωτὰς λέγουσιν.

The doors of dikasteria were called *kinklides*, which the Romans call *kankellotai*.

THE BEMA

According to Aristophanes, suppliants sat on the bema (*Ploutos*, lines 382–384 [**236**]), mixing bowls and pitchers could have been placed on it (*Ecclesiazusae*, line 677 [**64**]), and old men in imagining themselves as defendants include it as characteristic furniture (*Acharnians*, line 683 [**233**]), if the scholiast is correct in identifying the stone with the bema.

Speakers and witnesses came up and went down from the bema (e.g., [Lysias] 20.29 [**243**], Aischines 2.59 [**227**] and 143 [**228**]). There was room on it for a fair number of people (*Ploutos*, lines 382–384, Aischines 2.143, 3.257 [**232**]). The voting urns stood on or beside it (Demosthenes 19.311 [**240**]).

In the second half of the 4th century there are attested a bema of the defendant and one of the prosecutor, as well as the speaker's bema. For the bemas of the contending parties, see Aischines 3.207 (**231**), [Demosthenes] 48.31 (**241**), and Schol. Demosthenes 19.120 (**239**).

Bema, as speaker's platform, also designates the places occupied by prosecutor and defendant, and at times by their witnesses and supporters. In a building used regularly as a court, one might find raised areas or platforms for speakers. *Bema* seems to have been used occasionally for this whole area or platform in front of the court (*Ecclesiazusae*, *Ploutos*). In other buildings such as the Stoa Poikile, where cases were sometimes tried, the speakers' tribunals could have been temporary wooden structures.

The bema was sometimes called the *lithos* (*Acharnians*, line 683 with scholion [**233–234**], and Schol. *Ecclesiazusae*, line 677 [**235**]), possibly a borrowing from the usage at the Pnyx, where the speaker's platform was normally called "the stone". The speaker's platform in permanent court buildings may have been of stone.

227. Aischines 2 (*The False Embassy*) 59 343 B.C.E.

παρελθών, τοίνυν, Δημόσθενες, ἐπὶ τὸ βῆμα τοῦτο ἐν τῶι ἐμῶι λόγωι, ... καταβαίνω καὶ θανάτου τιμῶμαι.

Come forward, then, Demosthenes, to this bema using the time given to my speech... [If any evidence is offered which contradicts my charges] let me step down and be sentenced to death.

228. Aischines 2 (*The False Embassy*) 143 343 B.C.E.

ὅτι δ' ἀληθῆ λέγω, κάλει μοι Μνάσωνα τὸν Φωκέα καὶ τοὺς συμπρέσβεις, καὶ τοὺς ἀπὸ τῆς τῶν Βοιωτῶν φυγῆς ἡιρημένους. ἀνάβηθι δεῦρο, Λίπαρε καὶ Πυθίων, καὶ τὴν αὐτὴν ἀπόδοτέ μοι χάριν εἰς τὴν τοῦ σώματος σωτηρίαν, ἥνπερ ἐγὼ ὑμῖν.

To prove that I am telling the truth, call Mnason the Phokian and his fellow ambassadors, and call the delegates chosen by the Boiotian exiles. Come up here, Liparos and Pythion, and do me the same favor that I did you, with the aim of saving a life.

229. Aischines 3 (*Ktesiphon*) 55–56 330 B.C.E.

κἂν μὴ θέλω ἀποκρίνασθαι, ἀλλ' ἐγκαλύπτωμαι καὶ ἀποδιδράσκω, ἐκκαλύψειν μέ φησι προσελθὼν καὶ ἄξειν ἐπὶ τὸ βῆμα καὶ ἀναγκάσειν ἀποκρίνασθαι.

ἵν' οὖν μηθ' οὗτος ἰσχυρίζηται ὑμεῖς τε προειδῆτε ἐγώ τε ἀποκρίνωμαι, ἐναντίον σοι τῶν δικαστῶν, Δημόσθενες, καὶ τῶν ἄλλων πολιτῶν, ὅσοι δὴ ἔξωθεν περιεστᾶσι, καὶ τῶν Ἑλλήνων, ὅσοις ἐπιμελὲς γέγονεν ἐπακούειν τῆσδε τῆς κρίσεως, ὁρῶ δὲ οὐκ ὀλίγους παρόντας, ἀλλ' ὅσους οὐδεὶς πώποτε μέμνηται πρὸς ἀγῶνα δημόσιον παραγενομένους, ἀποκρίνομαι, ὅτι ...

And if I am not willing to answer, but cover up my face and run away, [Demosthenes] says he will come and uncover me and bring me to the bema and force me to answer.

And so for him not to persist, and for you to know in advance, and for me to answer you, Demosthenes, in the presence of all the dikasts and of all the other citizens who are standing around outside, and of all those Greeks whose concern it is to listen to this case—and I see not a few here, but more in fact than anyone remembers ever being present at a public trial—I answer you that ...

230. Aischines 3 (*Ktesiphon*) 165 330 B.C.E.

ἐνταῦθ' ἡμῖν ἀπόδειξιν ποιῆσαι, Δημόσθενες, τί ποτ' ἦν ἃ ἔπραξας, ἢ τί ποτ' ἦν ἃ ἔλεγες· καὶ εἰ βούλει, παραχωρῶ σοι τοῦ βήματος ἕως ἂν εἴπῃς.

At this point, Demosthenes, give us an account of whatever it was you did then, or whatever you were saying. If you want, I will yield the bema to you while you tell.

A few sentences below, *ibid.* 167, Aischines uses *bema* for the speaker's platform at the Pnyx, as he also does earlier in this same oration, 145–146.

231. Aischines 3 (*Ktesiphon*) 207 330 B.C.E.

οὐκ ἂν θαυμάσαιμι δέ, εἰ μεταβαλόμενος τοῖς ἔξωθεν περιεστηκόσι λοιδορήσεται, φάσκων τοὺς μὲν ὀλιγαρχικοὺς ὑπ' αὐτῆς τῆς ἀληθείας διηριθμημένους ἥκειν πρὸς τὸ τοῦ κατηγόρου βῆμα, τοὺς δὲ δημοτικοὺς πρὸς τὸ τοῦ φεύγοντος.

And I should not be surprised if he turns around and abuses those standing around outside, and claims that those who have been counted up and certified as oligarchs by truth itself have come to the prosecutor's bema, and that the friends of the people have come to that of the defendant.

232. Aischines 3 (*Ktesiphon*) 257 330 B.C.E.

ὅταν δ' ἐπὶ τελευτῆς ἤδη τοῦ λόγου συνηγόρους τοὺς κοινωνοὺς αὐτῶι τῶν δωροδοχημάτων παραχαλῆι, ὑπολαμβάνετε ὁρᾶν ἐπὶ τοῦ βήματος, οὗ νῦν ἑστηκὼς ἐγὼ λέγω, ἀντιπαρατεταγμένους πρὸς τὴν τούτων ἀσέλγειαν τοὺς τῆς πόλεως εὐεργέτας....

But when now at the end of his speech he calls forward as supporters the men who share his bribes, suppose you see on the bema, where now I am standing as I speak, the benefactors of the city drawn up against the insolence of these men....

233. Aristophanes, *Acharnians*, lines 683–684 425 B.C.E.

(The old men of the chorus picture themselves as defendants being pushed around by bright young men.)

τονθορύζοντες δὲ γήραι τῶι λίθωι προσέσταμεν,
οὐχ ὁρῶντες οὐδὲν εἰ μὴ τῆς δίκης τὴν ἠλύγην.

Mumbling in old age we stand beside the stone, seeing nothing but the fog of justice.

234. Schol. Aristophanes, *Acharnians*, line 683b–c

(b) τῶι λίθωι· τῶι βήματι. (c) τῶι λίθωι· τῶι ἐν τῆι πνυκὶ δικαστηρίωι.

(b) Stone: the bema. (c) Stone: the dikasterion in the Pnyx.

Wachsmuth (1874, p. 372) and Sommerstein (*The Comedies of Aristophanes*, I, *Archarnians*, Westminster 1984, p. 190) see the stone beside which the old men stood as the stone on which the votes were counted (*Wasps*, line 333 [**262**]). Lipsius (1905–1915, p. 173, note 31) believes that the stone in this passage is in fact the bema, that the word was borrowed from the usage at the Pnyx, and that this view is supported by the Scholion to *Ecclesiazusae*, line 677.

(64) Aristophanes, *Ecclesiazusae*, lines 677–679

(Blepyros asks Praxagora to what use she will put the bema [when the dikasteria and stoas are turned into dining halls]. She replies that she will set the mixing bowls and pitchers on it.)

235. Schol. R, Aristophanes, *Ecclesiazusae*, line 677 (ed. Dübner)

βῆμα· ὁ λίθος ἐν τῶι δικαστηρίωι.

Bema: the stone in the dikasterion.

236. Aristophanes, *Ploutos*, lines 382–384 388 B.C.E.

(Blepsidemos pretends to see in the near future a man being tried in court.)

ὁρῶ τιν' ἐπὶ τοῦ βήματος καθεδούμενον,
ἱκετηρίαν ἔχοντα μετὰ τῶν παιδίων
καὶ τῆς γυναικός....

I see someone seated on the bema holding a suppliant branch with his children and wife [beside him]....

237. Bekker, *Anecdota Graeca* 1.219.28–31

βῆμα· πλείονα σημαίνει κοινότερον. ἔστι δὲ οὕτω πως καὶ τὸ λογεῖον, ὥσπερ καὶ τὸ ἐν ἐκκλησίαι καὶ τὸ ἐν δικαστηρίοις. ἴσως δὲ καὶ τὸ ἐκκύκλημα. ἦν δὲ καὶ ἐν Ἀρείωι πάγωι βῆμα.

Bema: it commonly has many meanings. It is as here in some sense the speakers' place on stage, like the one in the ekklesia and the dikasteria. It may also be the [theatrical machine called] *ekkyklema.* There was also a bema on the Areopagos.

Compare Hesychios (**242**).

238. Demosthenes 19 (*The False Embassy*) 120 343 B.C.E.

ἀπόκριναι γὰρ δεῦρ' ἀναστάς μοι.

Now stand up here and answer me.

239. Schol. Demosthenes 19 (*The False Embassy*) 120

ἀπόκριναι· δύο βήματα ἦν, τοῦ κατηγόρου καὶ τοῦ ἀπολογουμένου, καὶ τοῦ ἑνὸς λέγοντος ἐκαθέζετο ὁ ἕτερος, ἕως οὗ εἴπηι.

Answer: there were two bemas, that of the prosecutor and that of the defendant, and while one [of the men] was speaking, the other sat until it was his turn to speak.

240. Demosthenes 19 (*The False Embassy*) 311 343 B.C.E.

νῦν τοίνυν ὑμᾶς οὐκ εἰς Πελοπόννησον δεῖ πρεσβείαν πέμπειν, οὐδ' ὁδὸν μακρὰν βαδίσαι, οὐδ' ἐφόδι' ἀναλίσκειν, ἀλλ' ἄχρι τοῦ βήματος ἐνταυθὶ προσελθόνθ' ἕκαστον ὑμῶν τὴν ὁσίαν καὶ δικαίαν ψῆφον ὑπὲρ τῆς πατρίδος θέσθαι. . . .

And so there is no need for you to send an embassy to the Peloponnesos, or make a long journey, or spend travel money, just come up to this bema each one of you and cast a righteous vote for your fatherland. . . .

241. [Demosthenes] 48 (*Olympiodoros*) 31 *ca.* 342–340 B.C.E.

καὶ οὑτοσὶ Ὀλυμπιόδωρος ἠγωνίζετο πρῶτος, καὶ ἔλεγεν ὅ τι ἐβούλετο, καὶ μαρτυρίας παρείχετο ἃς ἐδόκει τούτωι· κἀγώ, ὦ ἄνδρες δικασταί, σιωπῆι ἐκαθήμην ἐπὶ τοῦ ἑτέρου βήματος.

And Olympiodoros here spoke first and said what he wished and presented the evidence he liked, and I, O dikasts, sat on the other bema in silence.

242. Hesychios, *s.v.* βῆμα 5th or 6th century C.E.?

βῆμα· πλείονα μὲν σημαίνει κοινότερον. ⟨ἔστι⟩ δὲ οὕτως καὶ τὸ λογεῖον ὥσπερ ⟨καὶ τὸ⟩ ἐν ἐκκλησίαι καὶ δικαστηρίωι. σημαίνει δὲ καὶ τὸ ἐκκύκλημα. ἦν δὲ καὶ ἐν Ἀρείωι πάγωι ⟨βῆμα⟩.

Bema: Commonly it has several meanings. It is thus the speakers' platform (or stage), as in the ekklesia or dikasterion. It also means the ekkyklema. There was also a bema on the Areopagos.

Compare Bekker (*Anecdota Graeca* 1.219.28–31 [**237**]), who has almost the same entry.

243. [Lysias] 20 (*Polystratos*) 29 410 B.C.E.?

καί μοι ἀνάβητε δεῦρο.

And come up here to me.

The orator is speaking, no doubt, from the bema.

244. *Suda, s.v.* βῆμα 10th century C.E.

There are two entries under *bema:* the first essentially repeats the Scholion to *Ecclesiazusae*, lines 677–678 and the quotation of the lines; the second follows.

βῆμα· δικαστικὴ τράπεζα. οὐ μακρὰν δὲ τῶν πυλῶν τὸ δικαστικὸν βῆμα προσέταξε δοθῆναι.

Bema: the table of the dikasterion. Not far from the gates he ordered the dikastic bema to be provided.

We are not told who gave the order or why.

SEATING ARRANGEMENTS

Literary testimonia give little definite information about the seating arrangements in the lawcourts. The dikasts probably sat on wooden planks or benches; at least those in the first row did (Aristophanes, *Wasps*; Hesychios).

There is reason to suppose that after *ca.* 409 B.C.E. dikasts sat in lettered sections as did the council; see "Tokens," pp. 71–72 above. Some of the entrance steps of South Stoa II have large single letters inscribed on them. The blocks of these steps, along with the inscribed letters (which in South Stoa II have no discernible order or function), originally belonged in the Square Peristyle, where they may have designated seating bays; see pp. 109–113 above.

(106) Aristophanes, *Wasps*, lines 89–90

And [Philokleon] groans if he is not sitting on the first wooden bench.

245. Schol. Aristophanes, *Wasps*, line 90a

ἢν μὴ 'πὶ τοῦ πρώτου· Ξύλον ὃ ἡμεῖς βάθρον. καὶ ἐν Ἀχαρνεῦσιν ἐλθόντες ἀλλήλοισι περὶ πρώτου ξύλου.

If not on the first: "Plank" is what we call "bench". Also in the *Acharnians* (line 25) "coming in [they jostle] one another for the first plank."

In the *Acharnians* the reference is to the Pnyx. A scholion thereto adds that the seats in the Pnyx were in fact of stone, citing *Knights*, lines 754 and 783.

246. Hesychios, *s.v.* ψιάθια 5th or 6th century C.E.?

ψιάθια· τὰ ἐν τοῖς δικαστηρίοις ἐπὶ τῶν καθεδρῶν ἐπιστορνύμενα.

Rush mats: the coverings on the seats in the dikasteria.

247. Pollux 4.121 2nd century C.E.

(Pollux is listing theatrical terms in this section).

πρῶτον δὲ ξύλον ἡ προεδρία, μάλιστα μὲν δικαστηρίων, ἐφ' ὧν καὶ τὸν πρῶτον καθίζοντα πρωτόβαθρον Φερεκράτης εἴρηκεν ὁ κωμῳδοδιδάσκαλος· ἴσως δ' ἂν καὶ ἐπὶ θεάτρου κατὰ κατάχρησιν λέγοις.

The name Epikrates also has manuscript authority. Compare Epikrates F11 (*PCG* V).

The first plank is the front seat, especially of the dikasteria, with a view to which the comic poet Pherekrates calls the man who sits first "the first bench man". By analogy you might say it also in connection with the theater.

248. Pollux 8.133 2nd century C.E.

ἐκάλουν δὲ τὴν προεδρίαν καὶ πρῶτον ξύλον, καὶ μάλιστα ἐν τῶι δικαστηρίωι τὴν πρώτην καθέδραν. τὰ δ' ὑποστορνύμενα τοῖς δικασταῖς ἐπὶ τῶν ἑδρῶν ψιάθια ἰδίως ὠνομάζετο.

They called the front seat also the "first plank", and especially in the dikasterion the "first seat". The coverings on the seats for the dikasts were properly called *psiathia.*

Compare Hesychios, cited above (**246**). For the word *psiathos*, see also **178**.

(106) Aristophanes, *Wasps*, lines 104–105
(Xanthias describes Philokleon's habits.)

And then goes [to the dikasterion] early early and sleeps hanging on to the column like a limpet.

The column, *kion*, is presumably at or near the entrance to a known court building.

Ta Dikasteria (A Court Complex)

The plan of the single court complex, τὰ δικαστήρια, needed for the complicated process of sortition described by Aristotle may have been a relatively simple one: an enclosing fence in which there were ten entrances, one for each tribe, and three or four buildings, possibly stoas, in which trials could be held. Kinklides (swinging gates) controlled the ten entrances to the enclosure. Courts were distinguished by lintels (or some other architectural element) that were painted different colors. These are specific requirements named by Aristotle. Structural needs for individual courts would be the same as those for any other courtroom, *viz.*, benches for dikasts, space for spectators around, a bema; in short, the items already discussed in this section. Much early speculation on the overall plan of this complex is irrelevant now that Sterling Dow has shown that the word "kleroterion" always means "allotment machine" and not "allotment room"; see "Kleroterion," pp. 58, 230–234.

This system of daily sortition and a complex of courts was established sometime around 340 B.C.E.; see "Structures" (pp. 14–15 above) and "Three Court Days" (pp. 36–38 above). Aristotle's account, dating from shortly after that time, reads as if he were describing a recent innovation.

The routine as described seems to imply that dikasts went only to those courtrooms that were part of the complex. They could not go out into the open Agora or the streets after having been chosen and assigned to a specific courtroom. But these constraints obviously could not apply if trials were held on the same day at the Stoa Poikile (**163**, **164**) and at the Odeion (**168**–**170**); the two buildings cannot have been included at the same time in a single complex (Fig. 1). Another building, however, the Heliaia, was still being used, for Aristotle states that when two or three dikasteria of 500 each were needed for a single trial, the trial was held at the Heliaia. And so the complex may have been built around or connected with an existing Heliaia, or it may have been possible to combine the courts in the complex to constitute a Heliaia. Again, it may be that Heliaia and complex were used on alternate days. References to contemporaneous use of the Heliaia therefore do not point to a venue outside the complex. Three (or four) courts are named as in use in the second half of the century, *viz.*, the First and Middle of the New Courts and one called both Trigonon and Parabyston. The first two can have been two courtrooms of the complex. The third, the Trigonon/Parabyston, seems also a likely candidate. A fourth court can be postulated, since the Middle of the New Courts might have besides a First, a Third. But the Trigonon/Parabyston may have been the putative Third. The Green and Red Courts, named by Pausanias, belonged in their original form to the complex.

249. Aristotle, *Ath. Pol.* 63.1–2, 4–5; 64.1; 65–66.1 *ca.* 329–322 B.C.E.

63 Τὰ δὲ {τὰ} δικαστήρια [π]ληρ[οῦ]σιν οἱ θʹ ἄρχοντες κατὰ φυλάς, ὁ δὲ γραμματεὺς τῶν θεσμοθ[ετῶν τῆς] δεκάτης φυλῆς. εἴσοδοι δέ εἰσιν ε[ἰς] τὰ δικαστ[ή]ρια δέκα, μία τῆι φυλῆι ἑκάστηι, καὶ κλη[ρωτήρι]α εἴκοσι, δύο̣ τ̣ῆι φυλῆι ἑκάστηι, καὶ κιβώτια ἑκατὸν, δέκα τῆι φυλῆι ἑκάστηι, καὶ ἕτερα κιβώτια, [εἰς ἃ ἐμ]βάλλεται τῶν λαχόντων δικαστῶν τὰ π[ι]ν[ά]κια, καὶ ὑδρίαι δύο. καὶ βακτηρίαι παρατίθενται κατὰ τὴν ε[ἴ]σ[οδον] ἑκάστην, ὅσοιπερ οἱ δικασταί, καὶ βάλανοι εἰς τὴν ὑδρίαν ἐμβάλλονται ἴσαι ταῖς βακτηρίαις, ἐγ[γ]έγραπται δʼ ἐν ταῖς βαλάνοις τῶν στοιχείων ἀπὸ τοῦ ἑνδεκάτου τοῦ λʹ {τριακοστοῦ}, ὅσαπερ ἂν μέλληι τὰ δικαστήρια πληρωθήσεσθαι . . . ἔχει δʼ ἕκαστος δικαστὴς τὸ πινάκιον πύξινον, ἐπιγεγραμμένον τὸ ὄνομα τὸ ἑαυτοῦ πατρόθεν καὶ τοῦ δήμου, καὶ γράμμα ἓν τῶν στοιχείων μέχρι τοῦ κ· νενέμηνται γὰρ κατὰ φυλὰς δέκα μέρη οἱ δικασταί, παραπλησίως ἴσοι ἐν ἑκάστωι τῶι γράμ[μ]ατι.

ἐπειδὰν δὲ ὁ θεσμοθέτης ἐπικληρώσηι τὰ γράμματα, ἃ δεῖ προσπαρατίθεσθαι τοῖς δικαστηρίοις, ἐπέθηκε φέρων ὁ ὑπηρέτης ἐφʼ ἕκαστ[ο]ν τὸ δικαστήριον τὸ γράμμα τὸ λαχόν.

64 τὰ δὲ [κιβώ]τια τὰ δέκα κ[εῖται] ἐν τ[ῶι ἔμ]προσθεν [τ]ῆς εἰσόδου καθʼ ἑκάστην τὴν [φυ]λήν . . .

See **325** below for the continuation of this chapter.

65 αὐ[τ]ὸ[ς δὲ δείξ]ας πά̣λιν τ[ῶι ὑ]πηρέτηι εἶ[τʼ] ἐ[ντὸς εἰσέρχετ]αι τῆς κ[ι]γκλ[ί]δος. ὁ δʼ ὑπηρέτης [δίδωσιν αὐτῶ]ι [β]ακτηρίαν ὁμόχρων τῶι δικαστ[ηρίωι, οὗ τὸ] αὐτὸ [γ]ράμμα ἐσ[τὶν] ὅπερ ἐν τῆι βαλάνωι, ἵνα [ἀναγ]καῖον ἦι αὐτῶι εἰσελθεῖν εἰς ὃ εἴληχε [δικασ]τήριον· ἐὰν γὰρ εἰς ἕτερον εἰ[σ]έλ[θηι], ἐξε[. . . .] . . δ̣ι̣ὰ̣ τὸ χρῶμα τὸ [τ]ῆς βακτηρίας. τοῖς [γὰρ δι]καστηρίοις χρώμα[τ]α ἐπιγέγραπται [ἑκάσ]τωι ἐπὶ τῶι σφηκίσκωι τῆς εἰσ[όδ]ου. ὁ δ[ὲ λαβὼ]ν τὴν βακτηρίαν βαδίζει εἰς [τὸ] δικασ[τήριο]ν τὸ ὁμόχρων μὲν τῆι βακτηρίαι, ἔχ[ον δὲ τ]ὸ αὐτ[ὸ] γράμμα ὅπερ ἐν τῆι βαλάνωι. ἐ̣πειδ̣[ὰν δʼ εἰσ]έλθηι, παραλαμβάνει σύμβολον δη[μοσίαι] παρὰ τοῦ εἰλη[χό]τος ταύτη[ν τ]ὴν ἀ[ρχὴν. ε]ἶ̣τ̣α τήν τε [β]άλα[νον καὶ] τὴν βακτηρίαν ⟨ἀποτιθέασιν⟩ [ἐν τῶι δ]ικαστηρίωι [το]ῦτο[ν] ⟨τὸν⟩ τρόπον ε[ἰ]σελ[ηλυθό]τες. τοῖς δʼ ἀπο[λα]γχάνουσι[ν] ἀποδιδ[όασιν] οἱ ἐμπῆκτ[αι τ]ὰ πινάκια. οἱ δὲ ὑπη[ρέται] οἱ δημόσι[ο]ι ἀπ[ὸ] τ̣ῆ̣ς φυλῆς ἑκάστης π[αραδι]δόασιν τὰ κ[ι]βώτια, ἓν ἐπὶ τὸ δικα[στήρ]ιον ἕκαστον, ἐν ὧι ἔνεστιν τὰ ὀνόματ[α τῆ]ς φυλῆς τὰ ὄντα ἐν ἑκάστωι τῶ[ν] δ[ι]κασ[τηρί]ων. παραδιδόασι δὲ τοῖς εἰληχό[σι] τὸ πά̣λ̣[ιν] διδόναι τοῖς δικασταῖς ἐν ἑκάστωι τῶι δικαστηρίωι ἀριθμῶι ⟨πέντε⟩ τὰ πινάκια, [ὅ]πως ἐκ τούτων [κ]αλοῦντες ἀπο[δ]ιδῶσι τὸν μι[σ]θόν.

66 ἐ[π]ειδὰν δὲ πάντα πλή[ρ]η ἦι τὰ δικαστήρια, τίθεται ἐν τῶι πρώτω[ι τ]ῶν δικαστηρ[ί]ων βʹ κληρωτήρια καὶ κύβοι χαλκοῖ, ἐν οἷς ἐπιγέγραπται τὰ χρώματα τῶν δ[ι]κα[σ]τηρίων, καὶ ἕτεροι κύ[β]οι, ἐν οἷς ἐ[στι]ν τῶν ἀρχῶν τὰ [ὀ]νό[μ]ατα ἐπιγεγραμμέν[α]. λα[χ]όντες δὲ τῶν θεσ[μ]οθετῶν δύο χωρὶς ἑκατέρων τοὺς κύβους ἐμβάλλουσιν, ὁ μὲν τὰ χρώματα ε[ἰς τ[ὸ ἓν] κλη[ρ]ωτήριον, ὁ δὲ τῶν ἀρχῶν τὰ ὀνόματα ε[ἰς τ]ὸ ἕτερον. ἣ δʼ ἂν πρώτη λάχηι τῶν ἀρχῶν, αὕτ[η] ἀναγορεύεται ὑπὸ [τοῦ] κήρυκος ὅτι χρήσε[τ]α[ι] τῶι πρώτωι [λ]αχόντι δικ[αστηρίωι, ἡ δὲ δευτέ]ρ[α τῶι δ]ευτέρω[ι], καὶ οὕ[τω ταῖς λοιπαῖς ἵ]να [μηδ]εμία προειδ[ῆι τίνι αὐτῶν χρήσεται], ἀλλʼ [οἷο]ν ἂν λά[χ]ηι ἑκάσ[τη, τούτωι χρήσεται].

The nine archons by tribes fill the dikasteria, and the secretary of the thesmothetai represents the tenth tribe. There are ten entrances to the dikasteria, one for each tribe, and twenty kleroteria, two for each tribe, and one hundred boxes, ten for each tribe, and other boxes where they put the pinakia of the dikasts who have been chosen by lot, and two hydriai. At each entrance, staves are placed equal in number to the dikasts [required], and acorns [balanoi] are put in the hydria, equal in number to the staves, and there is written on the acorn one letter of the alphabet starting with the eleventh, lambda, as many as the dikastic panels that are to be filled. . . . Each dikast has his boxwood pinakion inscribed with his name, patronymic, and deme, and one letter of [the alphabet] up to kappa, for the dikasts are divided into ten sections distributed over the tribes, with about the same number in each letter [section].

After the thesmothetes has chosen by lot the letters which are to be attached to the dikasteria, the attendant takes the allotted letter and places it on the proper dikasterion.

The ten boxes lie in front of the entrance for each tribe . . . (See pp. 231–232 below for continuation of this chapter giving further details of the allotment process.)

[The dikast] again shows his acorn to the attendant and goes inside the gate [kinklis]. The attendant gives him a staff of the same color as the court which has the same letter as that on his acorn, so that he must go into the court to which he has been assigned by lot. If he goes into another, he is detected by the color of his staff. For at each of the dikasteria, a color is painted on the lintel of the entrance. When the dikast takes the staff, he walks into the court that has the same color as his staff and the same letter as the acorn. After he goes in, he receives an official token from the person allotted this task. Then after they have entered the courtroom in this way, they put aside the acorn and the staff. The ticket-inserters [*empektai*] give back the pinakia to those who have not been allotted as dikasts. The public attendants from each tribe hand on the boxes, one for each dikasterion, in which are the tribe's names of the men in each dikasterion. And they hand them over to the dikasts who have been chosen by lot to return the pinakia to the dikasts; [five] in number in each dikasterion, so that they can call out the names from these and give out the pay.

When all the dikasteria are full (when the panels are complete), two kleroteria and bronze dice [kuboi] on which the colors of the dikasteria are painted are placed in the first of the dikasteria, also other dice on which are inscribed the names of the magistrates. Two of the thesmothetai chosen by lot throw in the dice separately: one throws the colored dice into one kleroterion, the other the names of the magistrates into the other. The magistrate whose name is first drawn is thereupon proclaimed by the herald as assigned to the dikasterion that is first drawn, and the second to the second, and similarly with the rest, so that no magistrate knows in advance at which dikasterion he will officiate. He officiates wherever he has been allotted.

COURT EQUIPMENT: MINOR MOVABLE OBJECTS

This section starts with two general lists of dikastic equipment given by Pollux (**250**, **251**) in addition to that of Aristotle (**249**). The testimonia on specific items are arranged as follows:

Objects needed in the process of voting: kados, kadiskos, kemos, ballots, trays, abacus, stone, **163**, **249–287**, **317**.
Echinos, **250**, **251**, **288–305**.
Klepsydra, **79**, **250**, **251**, **306–323**.
Kleroterion, **64**, **79**, **249**, **251**, **266**, **268**, **324–333**.
Pinakion, **249**.
Pinakion timetikon, **106**, **250**, **334–336**.
Sanides, **337–342**.
Dikastic staff and symbolon, **70**, **249**, **250**, **276**, **343–351**.
Tablet and stylus, **304**, **352–355**.

250. Pollux 8.16–18, 20 2nd century C.E.

σκεύη δὲ δικαστικὰ σύμβολον, βακτηρία, πινάκιον τιμητικόν, μάλθη, ἧι καταλήλιπτο τὸ πινάκιον, ἐγκεντρίς, ἧι εἷλκον τὴν γραμμήν· μακρὰ δὲ ἐκαλεῖτο ἣν καταδικάζοντες εἷλκον. κημός, καδίσκος, ἐχῖνος, ψῆφος, κλεψύδρα, χοιρῖναι. πάλαι γὰρ χοιρίναις ἀντὶ ψήφων ἐχρῶντο, αἵπερ ἦσαν κόγχαι θαλάττιοι. αὖθις δὲ καὶ χαλκᾶς ἐποιήσαντο κατὰ μίμησιν. καὶ σφόνδυλοι δὲ ἐκαλοῦντο αἱ ψῆφοι αἱ δικαστικαὶ χαλκοῦ πεποιημέναι. καδίσκος μὲν οὖν ἐστι τὸ ἀγγεῖον ὧι τὰς ψήφους ἐγκαθίεσαν, κημὸς δὲ δι' οὗ κατήιεσαν αἱ ψῆφοι ἐπικειμένου τῶι καδίσκωι, ἐχῖνος δὲ οὗ μαρτυρίαι ἐμβληθεῖσαι κατεσημαίνοντο. τάχα δὲ τῶν τοῦ δικαστηρίου μερῶν ἐστὶ καὶ κιγκλὶς καὶ δρύφακτος. ἔνιοι δ' οἴονται καὶ ἀνάγκην σκεῦος εἶναι δικαστικόν, εἰπόντος Ἀριστοφάνους

οὐκ εἶ λαβὼν θύραζε τὰ ψηφίσματα
καὶ τὴν ἀνάγκην ἐς κόρακας ἐντευθενί;

καὶ φρυκτοὶ δὲ ἐκαλοῦντο αἱ ψῆφοι αἱ δικαστικαί, ὅθεν καὶ φρυκτή τις ψῆφος, ἧι εἰς τὰ ἐναντία ἐχρῶντο. . . .
τῶν μὲν δικαστικῶν ὀνομάτων ἐστὶν αὐτὸ τοῦτο, δικαστικόν. ἦν δὲ τοῦτο τὸ τριώβολον ὁ τῶι δικαστῆι διδόμενος μισθός.

Dikastic equipment: token, staff, assessing tablet, wax with which the tablet was smeared, stylus with which they drew the line. The line which they drew to condemn was called "long". Hopper, urn, jar, ballot, klepsydra, shells; for long ago instead of ballots they used seashells. Then again later they made them of bronze in imitation. The dikastic ballots [*psephoi*] made of bronze were also called vertebrae [*sphondyloi*]. The urn is the pot in which they placed the ballots; the hopper, the apparatus through which the ballots dropped when it had been placed on the urn; echinos, [the jar] in which testimony was placed and sealed. Probably both kinklis and dryphaktos are parts of a dikasterion. Some think that an ananke is part of the dikastic equipment, since Aristophanes (F601 [*PCG* III.2]) says:

Get out and take the decrees and the ananke the hell out of here.

And dikastic ballots were called *phryktoi* [roasted beans], whence the phrase a "phrykte ballot", which they used for the opposite. . . . Among the dikastic words there is this one, dikastikon; this was the triobol, the pay given to the dikast.

Compare Hesychios, *s.v.* ἀνάγκη: ἀνάγκη· δικαστικὴ κλεψύδρα (Necessity: dikastic klepsydra).

251. Pollux 10.61 — 2nd century C.E.

Δικάζειν μὲν οὖν ὁπότε δέοι, σκεύη ἂν εἴη δικαστικὰ κλεψύδρα καὶ προχοίδιον καὶ δίσκοι καὶ ψῆφοι, καὶ ἡλίσκος ἐπικρούειν τὴν κλεψύδραν. τὸν γὰρ ἧλον καὶ ἡλίσκον ἐν Ἥρωσιν Ἀριστοφάνης κέκληκεν. οὕτω γὰρ τὰ Ἀττικά· κημοὶ καὶ καδίσκοι καὶ ἐχῖνοι. κιβώτια δ' ἴσως γραμματοφόρα καὶ γραμματεῖα καὶ κάλαμοι γραφεῖς καὶ κληρωτήριον. εἰ γὰρ καὶ ἐπὶ τοῦ τόπου ἔοικεν εἰρῆσθαι τοὔνομα ἐν τῶι Γήραι Ἀριστοφάνους, ἀλλὰ καὶ ἐπὶ τοῦ ἀγγείου ἂν ἐναρμόσειεν.

Now when a case had to be tried, court equipment would be a klepsydra, a jug, trays, and ballots, and a little nail to hammer into the klepsydra; for Aristophanes in the *Heroes* (F328 [*PCG* III.2]) called the nail "the little nail". Attic terms include hoppers, urns, and echinoi. There are also boxes, possibly with letters, and tablets and reed-pens and kleroterion; although the word "kleroterion" in Aristophanes' *Geras* (F152 [*PCG* III.2]) seems to refer to the place, it would also be fitting in reference to the vessel.

Equipment Used in Voting: Urns, Ballots, and Trays

Dikasts, as far as is known, voted by ballot, not by show of hands, at both public and private trials. Three different procedures are attested in literature for casting ballots in court. A fourth method (presumably the earliest) can be seen in red-figured vase paintings in which Homeric heroes deposit pebbles openly on an altar (see Plate 23 and commentary to **21**). In the earliest method of those attested in literature, two urns were used: one urn, the one situated farthest from the dikasts, was for acquittal; the other, nearer to the dikasts, was for conviction (see *Wasps*, lines 981–991 [**271**];

Phrynichos, quoted by Harpokration [**279**]; and Lysias [**284**, a travesty of a court trial actually in the Bouleuterion]). Aristophanes, *Wasps*, lines 166–167 (**335**), alludes to a contemporary method, one in which wax tablets were inscribed with long or short lines. In the later method, that to which Aischines alludes and which Aristotle describes in the *Athenaion Politeia*, one urn was for valid votes, one for discards. This last method required the differentiated ballots which we find as bronze disks with pierced or solid axles (pp. 82–90 above). Dates for changes from pebbles to seashells and tablets to bronze ballots are not known. Aischines' reference to hollow and solid ballots (345 B.C.E.), and therefore inferentially to valid and invalid urns, is the earliest reference to that method. Under the previous method, that where the container rather than the shape of the ballot distinguished "innocent" from "guilty", secrecy of voting may have been maintained by kemos; see "Three Court Days," pp. 28–29 and Illustration 1 above for a conjecture as to its use.

If the question to be voted on was one of guilt or of innocence, two urns sufficed. In some private cases, such as inheritance suits, where claims and counter claims were involved, varying numbers of urns were used, such as the one and two mentioned by Isaios and the four in [Demosthenes] (**278**).

The urns that served as receptacles for the ballots are variously called *kadoi*, *kadiskoi*, *hydriai*, or *amphoreis*. Pollux says that the Athenian word for them was kadiskoi. Only Aristophanes (*Birds*, lines 1032, 1053 [**253**]) uses kadoi in this sense. Xenophon calls voting urns used at a meeting of the assembly hydriai, as do lexicographers. A red-figured cup in Dijon (*ARV*[2] 829, no. 37, identified by Dietrich von Bothmer ["Two Bronze Hydrias in Malibu," *J. Paul Getty Museum Journal* 1, 1975, pp. 15–22] as by the Steiglitz Painter) shows hydriai in use at a balloting (Pl. 5). It is noteworthy that a scholion to Aristophanes, *Wasps*, line 95 describes the grip on a ballot as being effected by thumb, forefinger, and middle finger, just as it is by two seated voters in the painting. (Margot Schmidt ["Dionysien," *AntK* 10, 1967, p. 80] speculatively relates the voting scene on the Dijon cup to the Dionysia but cites no clues or emblems in the scene to support the association.) The bronze and wooden receptacles described by Aristotle are called amphoreis, and this terminology is repeated by Pollux. But contemporary use (Lykourgos [**283**], Isaios [**282**], *et al.*) suggests that kadiskos was also a proper word in the 4th century as it was in the late 5th (*Wasps*, lines 320 [**260**], 852 [**269**]). Once the urns are described as *stamnoi* (Schol. *Wasps*, line 752 [**268**]), twice as *kalpis* (Schol. *Wasps*, line 106 [**334**], line 321b–c [**261**]). Both vessels are thought to be similar to a kados in shape. In two other scholia (to *Wasps*, lines 674 [**266**] and 752 [**268**]), they are called *klerotris*, surely in error, for klerotris is a variant of kleroterion (see Dow 1939, pp. 14–15).

For a discussion of the shape of kadoi and kadiskoi, see D. Amyx, "The Attic Stelai III," *Hesperia* 27, 1958 [pp. 163–310], pp. 186–190. Used largely for drawing water from wells, they are relatively squat, with a flat base, two handles, spreading lip, and medium-sized mouth. The shape lends itself to use as a receptacle for ballots. A hopper or pierced lid (see below), through which only one vote could pass, might fit into or over the spreading lip. The mouth is large enough so that when the lid was removed the ballots could be poured out easily with no danger of any being left behind uncounted. As Amyx points out (*op. cit.*, p. 188, note 16), this shape in Athens in Hellenistic and Early Roman times is represented by basket-handled water jars, which except for the basket handle are very like a balloting urn shown on a relief from Smyrna (J. E. Harrison, *Mythology and Monuments of Ancient Athens*, London/New York 1890, p. 423, fig. 35). On the word *kados*, see A. Aloni, "Osservazione su gr. κάδος," *Acme* 6, 1983, pp. 43–49.

The five bronze ballots found between two upright tile water channels in Building A have no obvious relation to urns or kadiskoi described as in use at trials. All the ballots had solid axles, and the homogeneity, if not accidental, could point to the sometime presence of an urn for acquittal. If the two tiles served, for instance, as base for a table that held a voting urn, the ballots in that case may have dropped between them out of sight. Rhys Townsend, however, conjectures plausibly that the tiles are remains of a lined pit in which equipment was stored; see p. 105 above.

Κημός is a word used in widely varying senses (see *RE* XI, 1921 [cols. 157–162], col. 157, *s.v.* κημός [A. Schenkl]). In judicial contexts, a kemos, according to Pollux, scholiasts, and lexicographers, was a fixture placed on the kadiskos through which the ballots were dropped. Aristophanes uses the word three times in the *Wasps*: Philokleon longs to stand by the kemoi as the last of those to vote (lines 754–755 [**267**]). The other two occurrences, at lines 99 (**106**) and 1339 (**274**), give no particular clue to the meaning of the word. In Aristophanes' *Knights*, line 1150 (**255**), Demos threatens to use the kemos as a probe to make miscreants disgorge their spoils. The word in other contexts can mean "muzzle". According to a scholion to Aristophanes, *Knights*, line 1150 (**256**), Kratinos in the *Laws* (F140 [*PCG* IV]) described a kemos, presumably that of the lawcourts, as a strainer made of rushes. The same scholion describes it as of wickerwork or basketry (πλέγμα), as does the scholion on *Wasps*, line 99 (**259**), which adds that it is wider at the top, narrower at the bottom. In Bekker (**277**) it is also described as wickerwork and like a funnel or strainer. Nowhere is it said specifically that the kemos lets only one ballot pass through; its function may in fact have been to preserve secrecy (see, e.g., Ill. 1 on p. 29 above). It was therefore a wholly different piece of equipment from the pierced lid noted by Aristotle (**276**).

According to Pollux 8.16 (**250**), musselshells (*choirinai*) were first used as ballots, then pebbles (*psephoi*), and then bronze whorls, also called psephoi. Ballots are called choirinai in *Wasps*, lines 333 (**262**) and 349 (**338**), in *Knights*, line 1332 (**257**), and in a scholion to *Knights*, line 1150 (**256**). They are also referred to as psephoi in *Wasps*, line 109 (**106**). By the late 5th century, the word *psephos* was generally used for ballot, but one cannot be certain what the actual object was. Philokleon's need for a private beach in order never to be short of psephoi (*Wasps*, lines 109–110 [**106**]) points to another, earlier use of the word *psephos*, namely, "pebble". There is no convincing evidence to suggest that black and white pebbles or black and white beans were ever used as distinguishing ballots in Athenian lawcourts. See, however, a scholion to Aristophanes, *Wasps*, line 106 (**334**) and Schol. Demosthenes 24.150. Compare Lipsius 1905–1915, pp. 920–921.

Aristotle (*Ath. Pol.* 68.4 [**276**]) states that the ballots (psephoi) were distributed to the dikasts from a lampstand (*lychneion*). The diskoi (trays) named by Pollux 10.61 (**251**) among dikastic furnishings may also have carried ballots.

In the late 4th century the ballots were counted on a counting board (abacus), which had the same number of holes as there should have been ballots (*Ath. Pol.* 69.1). In the late 5th century the ballots were counted on a stone, perhaps a stone table of some sort (*Wasps*, lines 333–334 [**262**]). The dikasts apparently came forward to vote at voting urns at the front of the court. The abacus may likewise have been at the front of the court.

Testimonia on words concerning voting procedure are presented here as a single unit and alphabetized by author, rather than arranged by the individual words such as *kados*, *psephos*, and so on.

252. Aischines 1 (*Timarchos*) 79 — 345 B.C.E.

εἰ . . . ὁ δὲ κῆρυξ οὑτοσὶ ὁ νυνὶ παρεστηκὼς ἐμοὶ ἐπήρωτα ὑμᾶς τὸ ἐκ τοῦ νόμου κήρυγμα, τῶν ψήφων ἡ τετρυπημένη, ὅτωι δοκεῖ πεπορνεῦσθαι Τίμαρχος, ἡ δὲ πλήρης ὅτωι μή, τί ἂν ἐψηφίσασθε;

If the herald here who is now standing next to me had announced as prescribed by law: "Of the ballots, the pierced one is to be cast by the dikast who believes that Timarchos has been a prostitute, the solid by him who does not," how would you have voted?

253. Aristophanes, *Birds*, lines 1032, 1053 414 B.C.E.

(An Inspector has come in, interrupting the process of organizing Cloudcuckooland. Peisthetairos is addressing the Inspector in both lines cited.)

οὐκ ἀποσοβήσεις; οὐκ ἀποίσεις τὼ κάδω;

Buzz off. Take away the two urns. . . .

ἐγὼ δὲ σοῦ γε τὼ κάδω διασκεδῶ.

I will scatter your two urns.

254. Schol. Aristophanes, *Birds*, line 1032

τὼ κάδω· τοὺς κάδους τοὺς ἀμφορίσκους, εἰς οὓς τὰς ψήφους καθιᾶσιν.

The kadoi: kadoi, amphoralike vessels in which they place the votes.

255. Aristophanes, *Knights*, lines 1145–1150 424 B.C.E.

(Demos is boasting.)

τηρῶ γὰρ ἑκάστοτ' αὐ-
τοὺς οὐδὲ δοκῶν ὁρᾶν
κλέπτοντας· ἔπειτ' ἀναγ-
κάζω πάλιν ἐξεμεῖν
ἅττ' ἂν κεκλόφωσί μου
κημὸν καταμηλῶν.

Because I watch them every time
they steal, although not
seeming to see them; then
I make them vomit up again
whatever they have stolen from me,
probing with the hopper.

256. Schol. Aristophanes, *Knights*, line 1150

(a) κημόν. κημὸς ὁ κάδος τῶν δικαστῶν, ἔνθα ἔβαλλον τὰς ψήφους. Ἄλλως. κημὸς ὁ ἐπὶ τοῦ καδίσκου, εἰς ὃν τὰς ψήφους καθίεσαν ἐν τοῖς δικαστηρίοις. Κρατῖνος δὲ αὐτὸν ἐν Νόμοις σχοίνινον ἠθμὸν καλεῖ. τοιοῦτος γὰρ ἐγίγνετο καὶ ἦν παρόμοιος χώνῃ, ὡς καὶ Σοφοκλῆς ἐν Ἰνάχωι. ὕστερον δὲ ἀμφορεῖς δύο ἵσταντο ἐν τοῖς δικαστηρίοις, ὁ μὲν χαλκοῦς, ὁ δὲ ξύλινος. καὶ ὁ μὲν κύριος ἦν, ὁ δὲ ἄκυρος. ἔχει δὲ καὶ ὁ χαλκοῦς, ὥς φησιν Ἀριστοτέλης, διερρινημένον ἐπίθεμα, εἰς τὸ αὐτὴν μόνην τὴν ψῆφον καθίεσθαι. πρὸς τοῦτο οὖν ὁ κημός. ἀντὶ δὲ ψήφων ταῖς χοιρίναις οἱ δικασταὶ ἐχρῶντο. αὗται δὲ κόγχαι τινές εἰσιν, ὥς φησιν Ἐπαφρόδιτος ἐν ταῖς λέξεσιν. . . . (b) καταμηλῶν· καταμηλοῦν μὲν ἔλεγον τὸ τὴν μήλην καθίεσθαι ὑπὸ τοῦ ἰατροῦ εἰς τὸν λαιμόν, ὡς ποιοῦσι καὶ οἱ ἐμοῦντες. κημὸς δὲ ἐκαλεῖτο τὸ ἐπιτιθέμενον πλέγμα τῶι καδίωι δι' οὗ οἱ δικασταὶ καθίεσαν τὰς ψήφους.

Kemos: kemos is the urn [kados] of the dikasts where they cast their ballots. Another explanation is that kemos is the object on the kadiskos into which they cast their ballots in the lawcourts. Kratinos in the *Laws* (F140 [*PCG* IV]) calls it a strainer made of rushes. It was like this and very like a funnel, as Sophokles has it in *Inachos* (F295 *TrGF*). Later, two amphoras were set in the dikasteria, one of bronze, one of wood; one was valid, one invalid. The bronze one, as Aristotle says, has a pierced cover so that only the vote itself could be dropped in. The kemos consequently was designed to do this. Instead of psephoi [pebbles, ballots] the dikasts used choirinai. These are a kind of musselshell, as Epaphroditos says in his *Lexeis*.... (b) "Using as probe": by "using as probe" they meant the insertion by a doctor of a probe into the throat, as people do when vomiting. The plaited attachment on the urn was called kemos. Through it dikasts inserted their ballots.

Kratinos was an older contemporary of Aristophanes. Epaphroditos wrote in the time of Nero. The scholiast's equation of *kemos* with *kados* notes a synecdoche. Aristotle's pierced cover has a different function from that of the original funnel-shaped kemos, for the kemos maintained secrecy of balloting, while the pierced cover was a control over the number of ballots that could be cast at one time. The phrase σχοίνινον ἠθμόν, quoted here from Kratinos, is also given by Hesychios; see **281**.

257. Aristophanes, *Knights*, lines 1331–1332 424 B.C.E.
(The Sausage-seller rejoices at the rejuvenation of Demos.)

ὅδ' ἐκεῖνος ὁρᾶν τεττιγοφόρος, τἀρχαίωι σχήματι λαμπρός
οὐ χοιρινῶν ὄζων, ἀλλὰ σπονδῶν, σμύρνηι κατάλειπτος.

See where he stands, wearing the cicada, splendid in the old-fashioned style, redolent not of ballots [choirinai] but of peace, and anointed with myrrh.

258. Schol. Aristophanes, *Knights*, line 1332a

οὐ χοιρινῶν ὄζων· ὅτι χοιρίναις ἐχρῶντο πρότερον πρὸ τῶν ψήφων. εἰσὶ δέ τινες κόγχαι θαλάσσιαι.

Not smelling of choirinai: for they used choirinai before psephoi [pebbles]. They are a kind of seashell.

259. Schol. Aristophanes, *Wasps*, line 99a–b

(a) κημός ἐστι πλέγμα τι, δι' οὗ τὴν δικαστικὴν ψῆφον καθίεσαν. (b) κημὸς καλός· κημὸς καλεῖται τὸ τοῖς καδίσκοις ἐπιτιθέμενον, δι' οὗ τὰς ψήφους καθίεσαν, ἵνα μὴ ὀλισθάνωσιν. ἔστι δὲ πλέγμα τι δικτυῶδες καὶ ἠθμῶδες, ἄνωθεν πλατύ, κάτωθεν στενόν.

(a) Kemos is a wicker object through which they drop the dikastic ballot. (b) Lovely hopper: the thing set on the voting urns, through which they would drop their ballots so that they would not slip. It is a wicker-plaited [attachment] like a net and a sieve, wide at the top, narrow at the bottom.

See **106** above for Aristophanes' text.

260. Aristophanes, *Wasps*, lines 320–322 422 B.C.E.
(Philokleon addresses the chorus of heliasts from the roof.)

βούλομαί γε πάλαι μεθ' ὑ-
μῶν ἐλθὼν ἐπὶ τοὺς καδί-
σκους κακόν τι ποιῆσαι.

I have wanted for so long to go with you to the urns [kadiskoi] and do some harm.

261. Schol. Aristophanes, *Wasps*, line 321b–c

(b) καδίσκους εἶπεν ὑποκοριστικῶς τὰς κάλπεις, ἔνθα τὰς ψήφους καθίεσαν δικάζοντες. ἐκ τούτου δὲ δηλοῖ τὴν ἐπὶ τὸ δικαστήριον ἄφιξιν. (c) ἐπὶ τοὺς καδίσκους· τοὺς ἐν τῶι δικαστηρίωι κάδους, ἐν οἷς τὰς ψήφους καθίεσαν, νῦν καδίσκους ὑποκοριστικῶς λέγει. ὀνομάζει δὲ ἀπὸ μέρους τὸ δικαστήριον, ὡς καὶ πρότερον κλεψύδραν αὐτὸ εἴρηκεν ἀπὸ τοῦ κειμένου ἐν αὐτῶι ἀγγείου, πρὸς ὃ οἱ ῥήτορες ἔλεγον.

(b) He used *kadiskoi* as a diminutive for the *kalpeis* [urns], where they dropped their votes in judgment. By this [expression] he means "arrival at the dikasterion". (c) To the kadiskoi: the kadoi in the dikasterion in which they drop the votes. He is using the diminutive, and he names the dikasterion from its part, just as earlier he said it is a klepsydra, from the vessel set in the court against whose [regulation of time] the orators spoke.

262. Aristophanes, *Wasps*, lines 333–334 422 B.C.E.
(Philokleon is speaking.)

ἢ δῆτα λίθον με ποίησον ἐφ' οὗ
τὰς χοιρίνας ἀριθμοῦσιν.

Or make me the stone on which they count the votes [choirinai].

This is the only certain reference to a stone on which the votes were counted. The stone beside which the old men stood during a trial in *Acharnians*, line 683 (**233**), was probably the bema.

263. Schol. Aristophanes, *Wasps*, line 333a

τὰς δικαστικὰς ψήφους· εἰσὶ δὲ ὥσπερ κογχύλια λεπτά, οἷς πρότερον ἐχρῶντο ἀντὶ ψήφων οἱ δικασταὶ πρὸ τῆς εὑρέσεως τῶν κυάμων. οἱ δέ φασι καὶ παρὰ τὰς πέτρας αὐτὰς ἔχειν τὴν ὀνομασίαν, ἐξ ὧν ἐκλέγουσι τὰ κογχύλια· χοιρίδες δὲ αἱ πέτραι.

The dikastic ballots [psephoi]. They are like small shells which formerly the dikasts used instead of ballots, before the discovery of beans. Others say that they have their name from the stones from which they gather the shells. Choirides are stones.

An attempt to explain χοιρίνας that confuses the instruments of allotment (beans) with those of voting (shells or pebbles?).

264. Aristophanes, *Wasps*, lines 673–674 422 B.C.E.
(Bdelykleon is describing the miserable life of the dikasts.)

οἱ δὲ ξύμμαχοι ὡς ᾔσθηνται τὸν μὲν σύρφακα τὸν ἄλλον
ἐκ κηθαρίου λαγαριζόμενον καὶ τραγαλίζοντα τὸ μηδέν . . .

When our allies have seen the rest of the rabble getting a poor living out of the ketharion and eating nothing . . .

For *ketharion*, see **266** below.

265. Schol. Aristophanes, *Wasps*, line 673

Σύρφακα· τὸ ἱκανὸν πλῆθος τῶν δικαστῶν τὸ συρφετῶδες

Rabble: the full crowd of dikasts, rabblelike.

266. Schol. Aristophanes, *Wasps*, line 674a–e

(a) ἐκ κηθαρίου· ἤγουν ἐξ εὐτελῶν τρεφόμενον. τὸ κηθάριον γὰρ πλέγμα ἐστὶ κανισκῶδες ἐπιτιθέμενον τῆι κληρωτρίδι τῶν ψήφων. . . . (b) κήθια κηθάρια λέγει τὰ ὀξύβαφα, ἐξ ὧν τοὺς κύβους ἠφίεσαν. πλεκτὰ δὲ ἦν καὶ ταῦτα. (c) ἐκ κηθαρίου· τὰ ἐκπέταλα τρύβλια, ἃ Εὐφρόνιος κήθια. . . . οὐκ ἔστι δέ, ἀλλ' ἀγγεῖον πλεκτόν, εἰς ὃ τὰς ψήφους καθιᾶσιν, τὸ κήθιον, οἷον ὡς ἀπὸ τοῦ ψηφηφορεῖν οὖν μόνον ⟨τρεφόμενον⟩. . . . (d) ἴσως ἂν οὖν λέγοι ἤτοι ἐκ τῶν ἀγγείων τῆς ψήφου ἀποξύοντας τὸν μισθὸν ἢ ἐξ ἄγγους τινὸς πλεκτοῦ, οἷον ὁ κάρταλος, τραγαλιζομένους, ὡς ἂν πένητας. (e) λαγαριζόμενον δὲ ἀντὶ τοῦ ἀποξύοντα, ὡς ἀπὸ τῶν δικαστικῶν ἀγγείων. ταῦτα δὲ ὡς περὶ πενήτων.

(a) Out of the ketharion: nourished badly (cheaply). Ketharion is the basketlike wickerwork object placed on the klerotris for the votes. . . . (b) *kethia* means the small saucers from which they would release the dice. These were wickerwork. (c) Out of the ketharion: the open bowls, which Euphronios (F65: K. Strecker, *De Lycophrone Euphronio Eratosthene comicorum interpretibus*, Greifswald 1884) calls *kethia*. . . . It is not this, but a wickerwork vessel in which they drop the ballots, the *kethion*, as if they [made their living] only from casting votes. . . . (d) Perhaps he means scraping off their pay from the vessels for the ballots, or eating like poor folk from some sort of woven object like a basket. (e) "Getting a poor living" instead of "scraping off" from the dikastic vessels. This is as though [he is talking] about poor people.

Where the commentary associates a ketharion with a kemos, and a klerotris with a receptacle for ballots, the scholiast is in error. Compare Schol. Aristophanes, *Wasps*, line 752a (**268**), where *klerotris*, also misidentified as a receptacle for votes, is probably a variant for *kleroterion*. The ketharion may have held dice in a process of allotment (see Dow 1939, pp. 14–15). This interpretation makes sense of Aristophanes, *Wasps*, lines 673–674 (**264**), if allotments determined the livelihood of heliasts as early as 422 B.C.E.

267. Aristophanes, *Wasps*, lines 751–755 422 B.C.E.
(Philokleon expresses his longing to serve as dikast.)

κείνων ἔραμαι, κεῖθι γενοίμαν
ἵν' ὁ κῆρύξ φησι, τίς ἀψήφι-
στος; ἀνιστάσθω.
κἀπισταίην ἐπὶ τοῖς κημοῖς
ψηφιζομένων ὁ τελευταῖος.

These are the things I love, that's where I want to be, where the herald says, "Who has not voted? Let him arise." I wish I could stand by the hoppers, as the last of the voters.

268. Schol. Aristophanes, *Wasps*, line 752a–b

(a) τίς ἀψήφιστος; ἔνθα ἐν ταῖς δημοσίαις δίκαις εἰς ταὐτὸ συναγόμενοι οἱ δικασταὶ τοῦ κήρυκος τὴν κληρωτρίδα προσφέροντος ἔβαλον τὰς ψήφους. ἔνιοι δὲ ἔσθ' ὅτε ὑπὸ φιληδίας κατεῖχον αὐτάς. (b) ἐνίοτε μέν, φησίν, ἔφερον στάμνον καὶ ἐνέβαλλον καθήμενοι οἱ δικασταὶ τὰς ψήφους, ἐνίοτε δὲ καὶ αὐτοὶ ἐγειρόμενοι ἔβαλλον. τοῦτο οὖν λέγει, ὁ μὴ ἐψηφοφορηκὼς ἐγερθεὶς βαλλέτω.

(a) Who has not voted? In the public trials, the dikasts gathered together in the same place and cast their ballots when the herald offered the klerotris. Some sometimes kept them for pleasure. (b) At times, he says, they carried around the stamnos and the dikasts cast their ballots seated; other times they got up and cast them. This means then, whoever has not voted let him get up and cast his ballot.

Klerotris is probably a variant of *kleroterion*, and the word is misused by the scholiast here. See comment on **266**. Voters on a red-figured cup from Dijon are either standing or sitting; see Plate 5.

269. Aristophanes, *Wasps*, lines 852–859 422 B.C.E.

(At the beginning of the mock trial Philokleon has just asked what case is first and Bdelykleon interrupts.)

Βδελυκλέων: ἐς κόρακας, ὡς ἄχθομαι,
ὁτιὴ 'πελαθόμην τοὺς καδίσκους ἐκφέρειν.
Φιλοκλέων: οὗτος σὺ ποῖ θεῖς;
Βδελυκλέων: ἐπὶ καδίσκους.
Φιλοκλέων: μηδαμῶς.
ἐγὼ γὰρ εἶχον τούσδε τοὺς ἀρυστίχους.
Βδελυκλέων: κάλλιστα τοίνυν· πάντα γὰρ πάρεστι νῷν
ὅσων δεόμεθα, πλήν γε τῆς κλεψύδρας.
Φιλοκλέων: ἡδὶ δὲ δὴ τίς ἐστιν; οὐχὶ κλεψύδρα;
Βδελυκλέων: εὖ γ' ἐκπορίζεις αὐτὰ κἀπιχωρίως.

Bdelykleon: Damn me to hell! I forgot to bring the voting urns (kadiskoi).
Philokleon: Hey! Where are you going?
Bdelykleon: For the urns.
Philokleon: Don't bother. I got these ladles.
Bdelykleon: That's beautiful. Then we have everything we need except for the klepsydra.
Philokleon: What is this? Isn't it a klepsydra?
Bdelykleon: You are providing well and just like home.

270. Schol. Aristophanes, *Wasps*, line 855a–c

(a) ἀρυστίχους· ἀρύστιχος καὶ ἄρυστις καὶ ἀρυστήρ. ἀγγεῖόν ἐστιν ὧι ἔστιν ἀρύσασθαι ἐπιτήδεια οἷον κοτύλη, ἢ κύαθος. (b) ἐγὼ γὰρ εἶχον ἀρυστίχους· πρὸς τὴν διαψήφισιν. ἀρυστίχους δὲ οὓς ἐνίοτε κοτυλίσκους. (c) ἀρυστίχους τὰς οἰνοχόας εἴρηκεν, ἀπὸ τοῦ ἀρύειν· ἔνθεν καὶ ἀρύταινα.

(a) Ladles: *arystichos* and *arystis* and *aryster*, a vessel such as a cup or small ladle with which they draw what they need. (b) I got these ladles: for the voting. *Arystichoi*, which sometimes people called *kotyliskoi* [small cups]. (c) By *arystichoi* he means oinochoai [wine pitchers], from the verb *aryein* [to draw], whence also the word *arytaina*.

271. Aristophanes, *Wasps*, lines 986–991 422 B.C.E.

(Bdelykleon guides Philokleon through the voting procedure at the close of a mock trial.)

Βδελυκλέων: ἴθ', ὦ πατρίδιον, ἐπὶ τὰ βελτίω τρέπου.
τηνδὶ λαβὼν τὴν ψῆφον ἐπὶ τὸν ὕστερον
μύσας παρᾷξον κἀπόλυσον, ὦ πάτερ.
Φιλοκλέων: οὐ δῆτα· κιθαρίζειν γὰρ οὐκ ἐπίσταμαι
Βδελυκλέων: φέρε νύν σε τηιδὶ τὴν ταχίστην περιάγω.
Φιλοκλέων: ὅδ' ἔσθ' ὁ πρότερος;
Βδελυκλέων: οὗτος.
Φιλοκλέων: αὕτη 'ντευθενί.

Bdelykleon: Dear dad, take a turn for the better. Take this ballot and dart past to the farther [urn] with your eyes shut and acquit him, O father.

Philokleon:	No, not that. I don't know how to play the lyre.
Bdelykleon:	Come now, I will lead you to it the quickest way.
Philokleon:	Is this the nearer?
Bdelykleon:	This one.
Philokleon:	In she goes.

"I don't know how to play the lyre" (also at line 959) means "I have no pretensions to being καλὸς κ' ἀγαθός: I'm just plain folks." Themistokles gave the expression a notable turn (*FGrHist* 392 Ion of Chios F13).

272. Schol. Aristophanes, *Wasps*, line 987a–b

(a) τηνδὶ λαβὼν τὴν ψῆφον· τὴν τετρυπημένην αὐτῶι δείκνυσι ψῆφον. δύο γὰρ ἀμφορεῖς εἰσιν, ὧν ὁ μὲν κύριος λεγόμενος χαλκοῦς, εἰς ὃν τὴν κυρίαν ψῆφον καθίεσαν οἱ δικασταί, ἢ καταδικάζοντες, ἢ ἀπολύοντες. ὁ δὲ ἕτερος ξύλινος, εἰς ὃν τὰς ἀκύρους καθίεσαν. ὁπότε δὲ πάντες διεψηφίσαντο εἰς τὸν χαλκοῦν κάδον, διηριθμοῦντο αἱ ψῆφοι, καὶ κατεδίκαζον μὲν αἱ τετρυπημέναι, ἀπέλυον δὲ αἱ πλήρεις. δεῖται οὖν αὐτοῦ ἵνα τὴν τετρυπημένην εἰς τὸν ὕστερον τὸν ἄκυρον καταθῆι καὶ ἀπολύσηι τὸν ἀπολογούμενον. φαίνονται δὲ συνήθως καλοῦντες τὸν μὲν κύριον ἀμφορέα πρότερον, τὸν δ' ἕτερον ὕστερον. (b) εἰς τὸν ὕστερον καδίσκον τὴν ἀποδοκιμάζουσαν ἐνέβαλον ψῆφον.

(a) "Take this ballot": he shows him the pierced ballot. For there are two amphoras; the one called valid is of bronze, in which the dikasts would cast the valid vote whether for condemnation or acquittal. The other is of wood, in which they would drop the invalid votes. When all had voted in the bronze kados, the votes were counted and classified, and the pierced votes would condemn, the solid acquit. He begs him to place the pierced one in the farther invalid [urn] and acquit the defendant. It is obvious that they customarily call the valid amphora the earlier, the other invalid one the later. (b) They placed the rejecting ballot in the farther kadiskos.

Scholiast (a) describes a voting procedure of the second half of the 4th century, derived from Aristotle, *Ath. Pol.* 68.3 (**276**), which does not apply to the present scenario. A scholion to line 988 (not quoted here) makes the same error in saying that Philokleon was persuaded to cast his ballot into the ἄκυρον κάδον, the invalid urn. ἀποδοκιμάζω in (b) might be the appropriate word in a certain kind of trial.

273. Schol. Aristophanes, *Wasps*, line 991a–b, e

(a) ὅδ' ἔσθ' ὁ πρότερος· ὁ καδίσκος, ὅπου αἱ τῶν καταδικαζομένων ψῆφοι ἐβάλλοντο. (b) ἐναλλάσσει τὰς χεῖρας, περιφέρων τὰς ὑδρίας, ἵνα ἀγνοήσας ἀποδοκιμάσηι εἰς τὸν ὕστερον καδίσκον τὴν ἀποδοκιμάζουσαν ἐμβαλὼν ψῆφον. . . . (e) αὕτη 'ντευθενί· Δύο καδίσκοι τῶν ψήφων ἦσαν, εἷς μὲν ἐλέου, ὁ ὀπίσω, ἕτερος δέ, ὁ ἔμπροσθεν, θανάτου. . . .

(a) Is this the nearer: the kadiskos where the ballots for condemnation were cast. (b) He changes hands, moving the hydriai around so that without knowing it he [Philokleon] acquits [the defendant] by throwing into the farther kadiskos the ballot for acquittal. . . . (e) "In she goes": there were two kadiskoi for ballots, one for pity, the one behind, and the other, the one in front, for death. . . .

274. Aristophanes, *Wasps*, line 1339 422 B.C.E.
(Philokleon decides to give up the dikastic life and turn to other pleasures.)

τάδε μ' ἀρέσκει· βάλλε κημούς.

These please me. Throw away the hoppers.

275. Schol. Aristophanes, *Wasps*, line 1339

βάλλε κημούς· βάλλε ἐς κόρακας τὰ δικαστικὰ σκεύη.

Throw away the kemoi: throw out the dikastic equipment to the crows.

276. Aristotle, *Ath. Pol.* 68.2–69.2 *ca.* 329–322 B.C.E.

[ψῆφοι δέ] εἰσι[ν] χαλκαῖ αὐλίσκον [ἔχουσαι ἐν τῶι μέσωι, αἱ μ]ὲ[ν] ἡμίσειαι τετρυπ[ημέναι, αἱ δὲ ἡμίσ]ει[αι πλή]ρει[ς· ο]ἱ δὲ λαχόντες [ἐπὶ τὰς ψήφους, ἐπειδὰν] εἰρη[μένοι ὦσιν οἱ λόγοι, παραδιδόασιν ἑ]κάστωι τῶν δικαστῶ[ν δύο ψήφους, τετρυπ]ημέν[η]ν καὶ πλήρη, [φανερὰς ὁρᾶν τοῖς ἀντιδί]κο[ις, ἵ]να μήτε πλή[ρεις μήτε τετρυπημένα]ς ἀμφοτέρας λαμβάν[ωσιν. ὁ δὲ ταύτην τὴν ἀρχὴ]ν ε[ἰ]ληχὼς ἀπολα[μβάνει τὰ σύμβολα, ἀν]θ' ὧ[ν] εἷς ἕκαστος ψηφιζ[όμενος λαμβάνει σύμβολο]ν [χ]αλκοῦν [μετὰ] τοῦ γ, ἀποδιδοὺς γὰρ γ' λαμβάνει, ἵ[να] ψηφί[ζωντ]αι πάντες· οὐ [γὰ]ρ ἔστι λαβεῖν σ[ύ]μβολον [οὐδεν]ί, ἐὰν μὴ ψηφίζηται. εἰσὶ δὲ ἀμφ[ο]ρεῖς [δύο κεί]μενοι ἐν τῶι δικαστηρίωι, ὁ μὲν χαλκοῦς, [ὁ δὲ ξύ]λινος, διαιρετοὶ [ὅ]πως μὴ λ[άθ]ηι ὑποβάλλων [τις ψή]φους, εἰς οὓς ψηφίζονται οἱ δικαστα[ί], ὁ μὲν [χαλκοῦς] κύριος, ὁ δὲ ξύλινος ἄκυρος, ἔχω[ν] ὁ χαλ[κοῦς] ἐπίθημα διερρινημένο[ν], ὥστ' αὐτὴν [μόνη]ν χωρεῖν τὴν ψῆφον, ἵνα μὴ δύο ὁ αὐτὸς [ἐμβάλ]λῃι. ἐπειδὰν δὲ διαψηφίζεσ[θ]αι μέλ[λ]ωσιν [οἱ δικα]σταί, ὁ κῆρυξ ἀγορεύει πρῶτον, ἂν ἐπισκή[πτων]ται οἱ ἀντίδικο[ι] ταῖς μαρτυρίαις· [ο]ὐ γὰρ [ἔστιν] ἐπισκήψασθαι, ὅταν ἄρξωνται διαψη[φίζε]σθαι. ἔπειτα πάλιν ἀνακηρύττει ἡ τε[τρυπη]μένη τοῦ πρότερον λ[έ]γοντος, ἡ δὲ πλή[ρης το]ῦ ὕστερον λέγοντος. ὁ δὲ δικαστὴς λα[βὼν ἅμα] ἐκ τοῦ λυχνείου τὰς ψήφους, πιέζων τὸν [αὐλίσκο]ν τῆς ψήφου καὶ οὐ δεικνύων τοῖς ἀ[γωνιζο]μένοις [οὔτε τ]ὸ τετρυπημένον [οὔτε τ]ὸ πλῆρες, ἐμβάλλει τὴν μὲν κυρί[α]ν εἰς [τὸν χαλ]κοῦν ἀμφορέα, τὴν δὲ ἄκυρο[ν] εἰς [τὸν ξύ]λινον. πάντες δ' ἐπειδὰν ὦσι διε[ψηφι]σμένοι, λαβόντες οἱ ὑπηρέται [τὸν ἀ]μφορέα τὸν κύριον, ἐξερῶσι ἐπὶ ἄβα[κα τρ]υπήματα ἔχοντα ὅσαιπερ εἰσὶν αἱ ψῆ[φοι, [καὶ τ]αῦτα ὅπ[ως] αἱ κύρ⟨ιαι προ⟩κείμεναι [[κ]] εὐαρίθμη[τοι ὦσι]ν, καὶ τὰ [τρ]υπητὰ καὶ τὰ πλήρη {δηλονότι [τοῖς ἀν]τιδίκοις}. οἱ δὲ ἐπὶ τὰς ψήφους εἰλη[χότε]ς δια[ριθ]μ[οῦ]σιν αὐτὰς ἐπὶ τοῦ ἄβακος, [χωρὶ]ς μὲν [τ]ὰς πλήρεις, χω[ρ]ὶς δὲ τὰς τετ[ρυπ]ημένας. καὶ ἀναγορεύει ὁ κῆρυξ τὸν ἀ[ριθ]μὸν τῶν ψήφων, τοῦ μὲν διώκ[ον]τος τὰς τετρυπημένας, τοῦ δὲ φε[ύ]γον[τος τ]ὰς πλήρεις· ὁποτέρωι δ' ἂν πλείους γένων[ται, ο]ὗτος νικᾶι, ἂν δὲ ἴσαι ὁ φ[εύ]γων. ἔ[πειτ]α πάλιν τιμῶσι, ἂν δέηι τιμῆσαι, τὸν αὐτὸν τρόπον ψηφιζόμενοι, τὸ μὲν σύμβολον ἀποδιδόντες, βακτηρίαν δὲ πάλιν παραλαμβάνοντες. ἥ τε τίμησίς ἐστιν πρὸς ἡμίχουν ὕδατος ἑκατέρωι, ἐπειδὰν δὲ αὐτοῖς ἦι δεδικασμένα τὰ ἐκ τῶν νόμων, ἀπολαμβάνουσιν τὸν μισθὸν ἐν τῶι μέρει οὗ ἔλαχον ἕκαστοι.

The ballots are bronze with a tube in the middle, of which half are pierced, half solid. Those who have been allotted to [administer] the ballots, after the speeches have been delivered, give to each dikast two ballots, one pierced and one solid; they are given openly in such a way that the opposing parties can see that no one receives both solid or both pierced. He who was chosen by lot for this task takes the symbola; in exchange for these every single dikast upon voting receives a bronze symbolon marked with a three, for on surrendering this he receives three [obols], so that all will vote. For it is not possible for anyone to receive a symbolon unless he votes.

There are two amphoras in the dikasterion, one of bronze, one of wood, into which the dikasts cast their ballots; they can be taken apart so that no one will be able to put ballots in surreptitiously. The bronze is the valid one, the wooden the invalid; the bronze one has a lid pierced in such a way that only one ballot can go through; thus no one can drop in two ballots.

When the dikasts are about to vote, the herald first asks if the parties challenge the testimony, for it cannot be challenged after they have started to vote. Then again the herald proclaims: "The pierced one for the first speaker, the solid one for the second." The dikast takes the ballots from the lampstand and, holding the tube of the ballot without showing either the pierced or the solid end to the litigants, casts the valid one into the bronze amphora, the invalid into the wooden one. When all have voted, the attendants take the valid amphora and empty it onto a counting board which has as many holes as there are ballots; this so that the valid ballots set out can be easily counted, both the pierced and the solid {obviously, to the litigants}. Those who have been allotted to [administer] the ballots count them on the board, the solid separately and the pierced separately. And the herald announces the number of votes, the pierced for the prosecutor, the solid for the defendant. Whoever receives the most votes wins; if an equal number, the defendant wins. Afterwards they assign the penalty, if it is necessary to do so, voting again in the same way, giving back the [pay] symbolon and receiving again the staff. The penalty [speech] is timed at half a chous of water for each side. After the adjudications are complete, they receive their pay by turn as each has been allotted.

277. Bekker, *Anecdota Graeca* 1.275.25

κημός· πλέγμα τι ἐκ σχοινίων, ἐπιτιθέμενον τῆι ὑδρίαι παρόμοιον χώνηι ἢ ἠθμῶι, δι' οὗ τὰς δικαστικὰς καθίεσαν ψήφους.

καδίσκοι· ὑδρίαι χαλκαί, εἰς ἃς καθίεντο αἱ ψῆφοι τῶν δικαζομένων.

Kemos: a plaited attachment of ropes, placed on the hydria, like a funnel or strainer, through which they dropped the dikastic ballots.

Kadiskoi: bronze hydriai into which the ballots of the litigants were dropped.

The word *hydria* is also used in describing the voting urns of the dikasteria in the scholion to *Wasps*, line 991 (**273**) and by Hesychios, *s.v.* σχοίνινος ἠθμός (**281**). Xenophon (*Hellenika* 1.7.9 [**287**]) calls the urns used for votes at a special meeting of the assembly *hydriai*.

278. [Demosthenes] 43 (*Makartatos*) 10 *ca.* 341 B.C.E.?

καδίσκων τεττάρων τεθέντων κατὰ τὸν νόμον.

Four kadiskoi were set in place according to the law.

A complicated case of inheritance is involved, the same one argued in Isaios 11 (**282**). Numbers of voting urns used in the varying claims and counter-claims in private suits can apparently vary. The procedure is not clear. The word *kadiskos*, meaning "voting urn", is found in two other Demosthenic orations, but in neither case is the urn being used in a dikasterion. It is used at a meeting of demesmen ([Demosthenes] 57 [*Euboulides*] 13, 345 B.C.E.) and a meeting of the ekklesia ([Demosthenes] 59 [*Neaira*] 90, *ca.* 340 B.C.E.).

(317) Eustathios, *Commentary on Homer, Iliad*

On the noise a ballot makes as it falls into the urn, Eustathios preserves the onomatopoeic word κύξ.

279. Harpokration, *s.v.* καδίσκος 2nd century C.E.

καδίσκος· Ἰσαῖος ἐν τῶι περὶ τοῦ Ἁγνίου κλήρου. ἀγγεῖόν τι εἰς ὃ ἐψηφοφόρουν οἱ δικασταὶ οὕτως ἔλεγον. Φρύνιχος Μούσαις· ἰδού, δέχου τὴν ψῆφον, ὁ καδίσκος δέ σοι, ὁ μὲν ἀπολύων οὗτος, ὁ δὲ ἀπολλὺς ὁδί.

Kadiskos: [this is mentioned by] Isaios in the speech about the inheritance of Hagnias (11). So they called a vessel into which the dikasts cast their ballots. Phrynichos in *The Muses* (F33 [*PCG* VI]): "See, take the ballot, here is the kadiskos, this one for acquittal, that for condemnation."

See **282** below for the passage from Isaios. *The Muses* by Phrynichos was produced in 405 B.C.E. The second and third sentences, including the quotation from Phrynichos, are given essentially in the *Suda*, *s.v.* καδίσκος.

280. Hesychios, *s.v.* καδίσκοι — 5th or 6th century C.E.?

καδίσκοι· σιπύαι, εἰς ἃς τὰ ἱερὰ ἐτίθεσαν, καὶ τὰ ἀγγεῖα εἰς ἃ τὰς ψήφους ἔφερον.

Kadiskoi: meal-tubs in which they placed sacred things and the vessels in which they cast their ballots.

281. Hesychios, *s.v.* σχοίνινος ἠθμός — 5th or 6th century C.E.?

σχοίνινος ἠθμός· δι' οὗ τὰς ψήφους οἱ δικασταὶ εἰς τὰς ὑδρίας καθιᾶσιν.

Rush strainer: through which the dikasts drop the ballots into the hydriai.

Compare Schol. Aristophanes, *Knights*, line 1150 (**256**).

(163) *IG* II^2 1641, lines 25–33

This man presented himself for trial and made his defense and was acquitted. The dikasterion [was] the Stoa Poikile. Of the votes, 100 were pierced, 399 were solid.

IG II^2 1646 (**159**) also records a count of ballots.

282. Isaios 11 (*Hagnias*) 21 — *ca.* 380–378 B.C.E.

τῆι μὲν γὰρ Εὐβουλίδου θυγατρὶ καὶ τῆι Ἁγνίου μητρὶ πρὸς ἡμᾶς ἀγωνιζομέναις, μὴ κατὰ ταὐτὸ ἀμφισβητούσαις, ἐνῆν ποιήσασθαι συνθήκας, ἂν ἡ ἑτέρα νικᾶι, μετεῖναί τι καὶ τῆι ἡττηθείσηι· καδίσκος γὰρ ἔμελλεν ἑκατέραι τεθήσεσθαι. τὸ δ' ἡμέτερον οὐ τοιοῦτον ἦν, ἀλλ' ἓν τὸ γένος, δύο δὲ λήξεις, ἡμικληρίου ἑκατέρωι· τοῖς δὲ κατὰ ταὐτὰ ἀμφισβητοῦσιν εἷς τίθεται καδίσκος, οὗ οὐκ ἂν ἦν τὸν μὲν ἡττᾶσθαι τὸν δὲ νικᾶν.

Because Euboulides' daughter and Hagnias' mother, since they were not litigating on the same basis, when they were in litigation with us, could make an agreement that whoever wins, a share goes to the one who loses, because a ballot container was going to be set up for each of them. But our case was not the same. The family is a unit, and there are two applications to be put in possession of the inheritance, each to half. But for persons who are making application on the same basis, one vote container is set up, and in that case it would be impossible for one person to lose and the other to win.

See the comment on [Demosthenes] 43.10 (**278**). A kadiskos is also mentioned in section 23 of this same oration. This is the oration cited by Harpokration in his definition of kadiskos (**279**).

283. Lykourgos (*Leokrates*) 149 — 330 B.C.E.

ὑμῶν δ' ἕκαστον χρὴ νομίζειν τὸν Λεωκράτους ἀποψηφιζόμενον θάνατον τῆς πατρίδος καὶ ἀνδραποδισμὸν καταψηφίζεσθαι, καὶ δυοῖν καδίσκοιν κειμένοιν τὸν μὲν προδοσίας, τὸν δὲ σωτηρίας εἶναι, καὶ τὰς ψήφους φέρεσθαι τὰς μὲν ὑπὲρ ἀναστάσεως τῆς πατρίδος, τὰς δ' ὑπὲρ ἀσφαλείας καὶ τῆς ἐν τῆι πόλει εὐδαιμονίας.

Each one of you should believe that if you acquit Leokrates you condemn your fatherland to death and slavery, that "of the two urns", one stands for betrayal, the other for survival, and that you are casting your ballots in one urn for the desolation of your fatherland, in the other for happiness and security in the city.

Lykourgos asks the dikasts to envision two containers, one for condemnation, the other for acquittal. This way of voting, however, is that of earlier times (see **271**, **279**) and not that of the 340's and after (see **252**, **276**). For the suggestion that Lykourgos has introduced an anachronism in the course of quoting from earlier poetry, see A. Boegehold, "Lykourgos 1.149," *CP* 80, 1985, pp. 132–135. The phrase "of the two urns" is set in quotation marks as a suggestion that the Greek phrase δυοῖν καδίσκοιν κειμένοιν may be a quotation.

284. Lysias 13 (*Agoratos*) 37 *ca.* 399 B.C.E.

ἡ δὲ κρίσις τοιαύτη ἐγίγνετο, οἵαν καὶ ὑμεῖς αὐτοὶ ἐπίστασθε. οἱ μὲν γὰρ τριάκοντα ἐκάθηντο ἐπὶ τῶν βάθρων, οὗ νῦν οἱ πρυτάνεις καθέζονται· δύο δὲ τράπεζαι ἐν τῶι πρόσθεν τῶν τριάκοντα ἐκείσθην· τὴν δὲ ψῆφον οὐκ εἰς καδίσκους ἀλλὰ φανερὰν ἐπὶ τὰς τραπέζας ταύτας ἔδει τίθεσθαι, τὴν μὲν καθαιροῦσαν ἐπὶ τὴν ὑστέραν, ὥστε ἐκ τίνος τρόπου ἔμελλέ τις αὐτῶν σωθήσεσθαι; ἑνὶ δὲ λόγωι, ὅσοι εἰς τὸ βουλευτήριον [[ἐπὶ τῶν τριάκοντα]] εἰσῆλθον κριθησόμενοι, ἁπάντων θάνατος κατεγιγνώσκετο καὶ οὐδενὸς ἀπεψηφίσαντο, πλὴν Ἀγοράτου τουτουί·

What sort of trial it was you yourselves know. The Thirty were sitting on the benches where the prytaneis sit now. Two tables stood in the area in front of the Thirty, and you had to cast your vote not in voting urns but openly on these tables, a vote to convict on the farther table. Under such circumstances, how was any of them going to survive? In a word, everyone who came into the bouleuterion to be judged was condemned to death, and no one was acquitted, except for Agoratos here. (The bracketed words appear to be a gloss.)

Any vote regarding the rights of a single citizen had to be secret. The open balloting was therefore a blatant wrong. In addition to that wrong, however, a second can be discerned. Throughout various changes in methods of voting, one rule of precedence seems to have remained unchanged. A dikast's first option was to find the defendant guilty, his second was to find the defendant innocent. Lysias alludes to a perversion of this order when he says, "... vote to convict on the farther table." Because the order of precedence is a constant, he does not need to add the balancing clause that would place votes to acquit on the nearer table. Compare Aristophanes, *Wasps*, line 987 (**271**) with MacDowell 1971.

285. Photios, *Lexicon*, *s.v.* καδίσκος 9th century C.E.

καδίσκος· οὗ αἱ ψῆφοι τῶν δικαστῶν βάλλονται.

Kadiskos: where ballots of the dikasts are thrown.

(250) Pollux 8.16–18

286. Pollux 8.123 2nd century C.E.

ψήφους δ' εἶχον χαλκᾶς δύο, τετρυπημένην καὶ ἀτρύπητον, καὶ κάδον, ὧι κημὸς ἐπέκειτο, δι' οὗ καθίετο ἡ ψῆφος. αὖθις δὲ δύο ἀμφορεῖς, ὁ μὲν χαλκοῦς ὁ δὲ ξύλινος, ὁ μὲν κύριος ὁ δ' ἄκυρος· τῶι δὲ χαλκῶι ἐπῆν ἐπίθημα μιᾶι ψήφωι χώραν ἔχον.

They had two bronze ballots, one pierced and one unpierced, and an urn on which a hopper was placed, through which the ballot was dropped. Again there were two amphoras, one of bronze and one of wood, one valid and one invalid; a cover with space for one vote was placed on the bronze one.

(251) Pollux 10.61

287. Xenophon, *Hellenika* 1.7.9 5th–4th century B.C.E.

(At a meeting of the ekklesia after the battle of Arginousae a travesty of dikastic procedures was enacted.)

θεῖναι δὲ εἰς τὴν φυλὴν ἑκάστην δύο ὑδρίας· ἐφ' ἑκάστηι δὲ τῆι φυλῆι κήρυκα κηρύττειν, ὅτωι δοκοῦσιν ἀδικεῖν οἱ στρατηγοί ... εἰς τὴν προτέραν ψηφίσασθαι, ὅτωι δὲ μή, εἰς τὴν ὑστέραν.

They set up two hydriai for each tribe; to each tribe the herald announced that whoever thought the generals were guilty... was to cast his ballot in the nearer one, and whoever thought them not guilty in the farther.

Echinos

An essay on the echinos will be found on pp. 79–81 above.

288. Aristophanes, *Wasps*, lines 1435–1437 422 B.C.E.

Φιλοκλέων: ... ἐν Συβάρει γυνή ποτε
κατέαξ' ἐχῖνον.
Κατήγορος: ταῦτ' ἐγὼ μαρτύρομαι.
Φιλοκλέων: οὑχῖνος οὖν ἔχων τιν' ἐπεμαρτύρατο.

Philokleon: ... In Sybaris once a woman broke an echinos.
Prosecutor: I call you to witness this.
Philokleon: And so the echinos, since he had a friend, called him to witness.

289. Schol. Aristophanes, *Wasps*, line 1436

κατέαξ' ἐχῖνον· χύτρας εἶδος ὁ ἐχῖνος. ἄγγος τι χαλκοῦν, ἢ καὶ ἐκ κεράμου, εἰς ὃ καθιᾶσιν οἱ διαιτηταὶ τὰ γραμματεῖα τῶν μαρτυρίων, ἅ τινες ἐμαρτύρησαν, καὶ κατασημηνάμενοι μετὰ ταῦτα, εἰ ἐγκληθείη ἡ δίαιτα, τοῖς δικασταῖς ἐπεδίδουν. τοῦ δ' ἄγγους τούτου καὶ Δημοσθένης μνημονεύουσι καὶ Ἀριστοτέλης.

Broke an echinos: the echinos is a kind of chytra. It is a kind of bronze vessel, also of terracotta, in which the diaitetai deposit written texts of testimony which people have given. The diaitetai seal it, and afterwards, if an appeal was made against the decision of the diaitetai, they [the diaitetai] handed the echinos over to the dikasts. Demosthenes and Aristotle mention this vessel.

290. Aristotle, *Ath. Pol.* 53.2–3 *ca.* 329–322 B.C.E.

(The author describes private cases handed over to the diaitetai by the Forty.)

ἂν δ' ὁ ἕτερος ἐφῆι τῶν ἀντιδίκων εἰς τὸ δικαστήριον, ἐμβαλόντες τὰς μαρτυρίας καὶ τὰς προκλήσεις καὶ τοὺς νόμους εἰς ἐχίνους, χωρὶς μὲν τὰς τοῦ διώκοντος, χωρὶς δὲ τὰς τοῦ φεύγοντος, καὶ τούτους κατασημηνάμενοι, καὶ τὴν γνῶσιν τοῦ διαιτητοῦ γεγραμμένην ἐν γραμματείωι προσαρτήσαντες, παραδιδόασι τοῖς δ' τοῖς τὴν φυλὴν τοῦ φεύγοντος δικάζουσιν. οἱ δὲ παραλαβόντες εἰσάγουσιν εἰς τὸ δικαστήριον, τὰ μὲν ἐντὸς χιλίων εἰς ἕνα καὶ διακοσίους, τὰ δ' ὑπὲρ χιλίας εἰς ἕνα καὶ τετρακοσίους. οὐκ ἔξεστι δ' οὔτε νόμοις οὔτε προκλήσεσι οὔτε μαρτυρίαις ἀλλ' ἢ ταῖς παρὰ τοῦ διαιτητοῦ χρῆσθαι ταῖς εἰς τοὺς ἐχίνους ἐμβεβλημέναις.

If either litigant appeals to the dikasterion, the diaitetai put the depositions and challenges and the laws in echinoi, a separate one for the prosecutor, another for the defendant, seal them, and attach the decision of the arbitrator written on a tablet. They hand the echinoi over to the four [of the Forty] who serve as judges for the tribe to which the defendant belongs. The four, when they have received them, bring the case before the dikasterion; before a jury of 201 if less than a thousand [drachmai are involved], a jury of 401 if more than a thousand. It is not permitted to use any laws or challenges or depositions other than those placed in the echinoi by the arbitrator.

291. Bekker, *Anecdota Graeca* 1.258.3–6

ἐχῖνος· καδίσκος χαλκοῦς εἰς ὃν αἵ τε μαρτυρίαι καὶ αἱ προκλήσεις ἔγγραφοι ἐνεβάλλοντο ὑπὸ τῶν δικαζομένων. καὶ κατεσημαίνετο ὁ ἐχῖνος, ἵνα μηδεὶς κακουργήσηι μετὰ τὸ ἅπαξ ἐμβάλλεσθαι.

Echinos: a bronze kadiskos in which the written testimony and challenges were placed by the litigants. The echinos was sealed so that no one could tamper [with the contents] after they had once been put in.

Another entry in Bekker's *Anecdota Graeca* (1.189.5) defines echinoi by metonymy as the documents (γραμματεῖα) which they handed over to the dikasts.

292. Demosthenes 39 (*Boiotos* I) 17 349/8 B.C.E.

ταῦτα δ' εἰ μὴ σεσημασμένων ἤδη συνέβη τῶν ἐχίνων, κἂν μάρτυρας ὑμῖν παρεσχόμην.

If this had not happened after the echinoi had already been sealed, I would have brought witnesses [to prove it].

293. Demosthenes 45 (*Stephanos* I) 17 *ca.* 351 B.C.E.

ἐγίγνετο δ' ἡ δίαιτ' ἐν τῆι ποικίληι στοᾶι, μεμαρτυρήκασι δ' οὗτοι παρέχειν τὸ γραμματεῖον Ἀμφίαν πρὸς τὸν διαιτητήν. οὐκοῦν εἴπερ ἀληθὲς ἦν, ἐχρῆν αὐτὸ τὸ γραμματεῖον εἰς τὸν ἐχῖνον ἐμβαλεῖν καὶ τὸν παρέχοντα μαρτυρεῖν, ἵν' ἐκ τῆς ἀληθείας καὶ τοῦ τὰ σημεῖ' ἰδεῖν οἱ μὲν δικασταὶ τὸ πρᾶγμ' ἔγνωσαν.

The arbitration took place in the Stoa Poikile. These men testify that Amphias produced the document for the arbitrator. If in fact it was genuine, the document itself should have been put in the echinos and the man providing it should have testified [that he had done so], so that the dikasts could judge the question on the basis of the truth and having seen the seals.

When Apollodoros says that "the document itself" ought to have been put in the echinos, he presumably means the true, authentic text. The physical object in question may in fact have been a copy; see **290**, **296**.

294. Demosthenes 45 (*Stephanos* I) 57–58 *ca.* 351 B.C.E.

τὴν γὰρ μαρτυρίαν ἣν ᾤιμην εἶναι καὶ δι' ἧς ἦν ὁ πλεῖστος ἔλεγχός μοι, ταύτην οὐχ ηὗρον ἐνοῦσαν ἐν τῶι ἐχίνωι. τότε μὲν δὴ τῶι κακῶι πληγεὶς οὐδὲν ἄλλ' εἶχον ποιῆσαι πλὴν ὑπολαμβάνειν τὴν ἀρχὴν ἠδικηκέναι με καὶ τὸν ἐχῖνον κεκινηκέναι.

I did not find in the echinos the testimony that I thought was there and that was my most important refutation. At that time, hurt by the ill stroke, I could only assume that the magistrate had wronged me and had tampered with the echinos.

295. [Demosthenes] 47 (*Euergos and Mnesiboulos*) 16

ἐπειδὴ τοίνυν σοι τότε οὐ παρῆν ἡ ἄνθρωπος, ἀλλὰ πρότερον ἐσημάνθησαν οἱ ἐχῖνοι, ὕστερον ἔστιν ὅπου ἤγαγες τὴν ἄνθρωπον εἰς τὴν ἀγορὰν ἢ εἰς τὸ δικαστήριον;

Since, therefore, the woman was not with you at the time, and the echinoi had previously been sealed, did you take her later into the Agora or into the dikasterion?

There is another reference to sealing of echinoi at Demosthenes 54 (*Konon*) 27.

296. [Demosthenes] 48 (*Olympiodoros*) 48 343/2 B.C.E.

ἐγὼ γὰρ τοῦτον προὐκαλεσάμην καὶ ἠξίωσα ἀκολουθῆσαι ὡς Ἀνδροκλείδην, παρ' ὧι κεῖνται αἱ συνθῆκαι, καὶ κοινῆι ἐκγραψαμένους ἡμᾶς τὰς συνθήκας πάλιν σημήνασθαι, τὰ δὲ ἀντίγραφα ἐμβαλέσθαι εἰς τὸν ἐχῖνον, ὅπως ἂν μηδεμία ὑποψία ἧι.

I challenged him and demanded that we go to Androkleides, with whom we had deposited the agreement, make copies of the agreement in common, have them sealed again, and put the copies in the echinos so that there would be no reason for suspicion.

297. Demosthenes 49 (*Timotheos*) 65 362 B.C.E.

βούλομαι τοίνυν ὑμῖν καὶ περὶ τῆς προκλήσεως τοῦ ὅρκου εἰπεῖν, ἣν ἐγὼ τοῦτον προὐκαλεσάμην καὶ οὗτος ἐμέ. ἐμβαλομένου γὰρ ἐμοῦ ὅρκον εἰς τὸν ἐχῖνον, ἠξίου οὗτος καὶ αὐτὸς ὀμόσας ἀπηλλάχθαι.

I want to tell you therefore about how I challenged his oath, and he challenged mine, because after I had put [a written copy of] my oath in the echinos, he thought that by taking an oath himself he would be free and clear.

298. Erotian, p. 41, no. 79 1st century C.E.

ἐχῖνον καινόν· χύτραν καινήν. ἔστιν ἐχῖνος χύτρας εἶδος μεγαλοστόμου καὶ μεγάλης. μέμνηται τῆς λέξεως καὶ Εὔπολις καὶ Μένανδρος ἐν 'Επιτρέπουσι καὶ Φιλήμων ἐν Μυρμιδόσι.

New echinus: new chytra. Echinus is a kind of large, big-mouthed chytra. Eupolis (F453, [*PCG* V]) and Menander in his *Arbitrators* (F4) record the word, as does Philemon in *Myrmidons* (F26, [*PCG* VI]).

299. Harpokration, *s.v.* ἐχῖνος 2nd century C.E.

ἐχῖνος· ἔστι μὲν ἄγγος τι εἰς ὃ τὰ γραμματεῖα τὰ πρὸς τὰς δίκας ἐτίθεντο· Δημοσθένης ἐν τῶι πρὸς Τιμόθεον μνημονεύει τοῦ ἄγγους τούτου καὶ Ἀριστοτέλης ἐν τῆι Ἀθηναίων πολιτείαι καὶ Ἀριστοφάνης Δαναίσιν.

Echinos: it is a kind of vessel into which the documents relating to the trials were placed. Demosthenes in the speech in reply to Timotheos mentions this vessel and Aristotle in the *Athenaion Politeia*, as does Aristophanes in the *Danaids* (F274 [*PCG* III.2]).

300. Hesychios, *s.v.* ἐχῖνοι 5th or 6th century C.E.?

ἐχῖνοι· πέμμα νησιωτικόν, ὡς πλακοῦς. καὶ κοιλίας μέρος τῶν μηρυκαζομένων ζώων. καὶ τῶν πτηνῶν ἡ κοιλία. καὶ σκεῦος μαγειρικόν . . . καὶ τῶν κιονοκράνων μέρος . . . καὶ λοπάς.

Echinoi: an island dish like flat-cake, and part of the belly of ruminant animals and the belly of birds. Also a cooking utensil . . . and part of a column capital . . . and lopas [which usually means stewpot].

In a list of many different meanings for echinos, "cooking utensil" and "lopas" (stewpot) are listed separately as though they were not the same thing. "Repository for evidence", however, does not appear in this list, as it does in Bekker, *Anecdota Graeca*; Harpokration; and Photios (**291**, **299**, **302**).

301. *Lexicon Patmense, s.v.* ἐχῖνος
Commentary on [Demosthenes] 48.48

ἐχῖνος· ἀγγεῖόν τι χαλκοῦν ἐν ὧι ἀπετίθεσαν τὰς μαρτυρίας καὶ τὰς προκλήσεις οἱ δικαζόμενοι.

Echinos: a bronze vessel in which litigants would keep testimonies and challenges.

302. Photios, *Lexicon, s.v.* ἐχῖνος — 9th century C.E.

ἐχῖνος· Καδίσκος τίς ἐστι χαλκοῦς, εἰς ὃν αἵ τε μαρτυρίαι καὶ αἱ προκλήσεις ἔγγραφοι ἐνεβάλλοντο ὑπὸ τῶν δικαζομένων, καὶ κατεσημαίνοντο ἵνα μηδεὶς κακουργήσηι περὶ τὰ ἐμβαλλόμενα. . . . ἐχῖνοι· οἱ μὲν χαλκοῖ, οἱ δὲ ἐκ κεράμου· εἰς οὓς καθιᾶσιν οἱ διαιτηταὶ τὰ γραμματεῖα τῶν μαρτυριῶν ἅ τινες ἐμαρτύρησαν καὶ κατασημηνάμενοι μετὰ ταῦτα, εἰ ἐγκληθείη ἡ δίαιτα, τοῖς δικασταῖς ἐπεδίδουν.

Echinos: it is a kind of bronze kadiskos, in which the written testimony and challenges were placed by the litigants, and they were sealed so no one would tamper with the contents. . . . Echinoi: some are of bronze, others of terracotta, in which the diaitetai deposit the texts of the testimony that people have given. The diaitetai sealed it and afterwards, if an appeal was made against the decision of the diaitetai, they [the diaitetai] handed the echinos over to the dikasts.

Compare scholion to *Wasps*, line 1436 (**289**) for the same entry.

303. Pollux 6.91 — 2nd century C.E.

ἐχῖνος δὲ χύτρας εἶδος ἦν.

An echinos was a kind of cooking pot [chytra].

This is included in a passage naming various dishes and pots used for cooking. An echinos is also mentioned in Pollux 10.95, which gives another similar list of cooking pots.

(250) Pollux 8.17

(251) Pollux 10.61

304. Theophrastos, *Characters* 6.8 (ἀπονοίας [Recklessness]) — *ca.* 321–318 B.C.E.

ἱκανὸς δὲ καὶ δίκας τὰς μὲν φεύγειν, τὰς δὲ διώκειν, τὰς δὲ ἐξόμνυσθαι, ταῖς δὲ παρεῖναι ἔχων ἐχῖνον ἐν τῶι προκολπίωι καὶ ὁρμαθοὺς γραμματιδίων ἐν ταῖς χερσίν·

He is apt at being defendant in some trials and prosecutor in others, at excusing himself from some trials on oath, and at being present at others with an echinos at his chest and stacks of writing tablets in his hands.

In what way these are the characteristics of the Reckless Man is noted at "Echinos," pp. 79–80 above. Jeffrey Rusten (Theophrastos, *Characters*, p. 75) translates ἀπονοίας "Shamelessness".

305. Agora P 28470, lines 1–4 — 4th–3rd century B.C.E.

[- - -] δ̣ε̣: τετταρ̣[. . .]ν: ἐκ[- - -]
[- - - δ]ιαμαρτυρία· ἐξ ἀνακρίσεως
[- - -]ν κακώσεω[ς - - -]
[- - -]ιδ̣ι̣[- - -]ρ: ἐπέ̣θ[ηκε]

. . . four . . . from . . .
. . . diamartyria from anakrisis . . .
. . . abuse . . .
. . . put [the lid] on . . .

For a version of the text on this echinos lid with full restorations *exempli gratia*, as well as an explanation of the terms, see pp. 79–81 above.

KLEPSYDRA

An essay on the klepsydra as used in lawcourts will be found on pp. 77–78 above.

306. Aeneas Tacticus 22.24–25 *ca.* 357 B.C.E.

. . . πρὸς κλεψύδραν χρὴ φυλάσσειν, ταύτην δὲ συμμεταβάλλειν διὰ δεχημερίδος. μᾶλλον δὲ αὐτῆς κεκηρῶσθαι τὰ ἔσωθεν, καὶ μακροτέρων μὲν γιγνομένων τῶν νυκτῶν ἀφαιρεῖσθαι τοῦ κηροῦ, ἵνα πλέον ὕδωρ χωρῆι, βραχυτέρων δὲ προσπλάσσεσθαι, ἵνα ἔλασσον δέχηται.

. . . One ought to set the night watches by the klepsydra, and this should be reset every ten days. But a better plan is to smear the interior [of the klepsydra] with wax and then to remove some of the wax when the nights grow longer, so that it will hold more water, and when the nights grow shorter to add more wax so that it will hold less.

The klepsydra recommended for timing the night watches, onto which wax could be added and removed, may be the same type of open pot as that used in the Athenian council or lawcourts (Young 1939, p. 274).

307. Aischines 2 (*The False Embassy*) 126 345 B.C.E.

πρὸς ἕνδεκα γὰρ ἀμφορέας ἐν διαμεμετρημένηι τῆι ἡμέραι κρίνομαι.

[There is still time] for in a measured day my hearing is assigned eleven amphoras.

308. Schol. Aischines 2 (*The False Embassy*) 126

φασὶν ὅτι τὰς ἡμέρας τοῦ Ποσειδεῶνος μηνὸς ἐκλεξάμενοι οἱ Ἀθηναῖοι ὡς συμμέτρους καὶ δυναμένας κατέχειν ἕνδεκα ἀμφορέας πρὸς αὐτὰς καὶ ταῖς ἄλλαις ἡμέραις ἐσκεύαζον τὴν κλεψύδραν, μεγάλου πράγματος δηλονότι ἀγωνιζομένου. ἀπενέμοντο δὲ οἱ ἕνδεκα ἀμφορεῖς κατὰ τὸ τρίτον τοῖς ἀντιδίκοις καὶ τοῖς δικασταῖς.

They say that the Athenians chose the days of the month Posideon as in the right measure to hold eleven amphoras and fixed the klepsydra by these days for the other days as well on an occasion when it was clear that an important matter was being contested. Eleven amphoras were assigned, one-third to [each of] the litigants and to the dikasts.

309. Aristophanes, *Acharnians*, lines 692–693 425 B.C.E.
(The old men of the chorus picture themselves as defendants in a lawsuit.)

ταῦτα πῶς εἰκότα, γέροντ' ἀπολέσαι, πολιὸν ἄνδρα,
περὶ κλεψύδραν.

How can it be seemly to destroy an old gray-headed man beside the klepsydra?

310. Schol. Aristophanes, *Acharnians*, line 693 (693a)

κλεψύδραν· ἀντὶ τοῦ ἐν τῶι δικαστηρίωι. ἡ γὰρ κλεψύδρα ἀγγεῖόν ἐστιν ἔχον μικροτάτην ὀπὴν περὶ τὸν πυθμένα, ὅπερ ἐν τῶι δικαστηρίωι μεστὸν ὕδατος ἐτίθετο, πρὸς ὃ ἔλεγον οἱ ῥήτορες.

Klepsydra: instead of saying "in the dikasterion". For a klepsydra is a vessel with a very small hole near the base which, full of water, would be placed in the lawcourt and by which the orators spoke (i.e., were timed).

Compare Schol. Aristophanes, *Wasps*, line 321 (**261**) and the *Suda* (**323**) for similar notes on the klepsydra.

311. Aristophanes, *Birds*, lines 1694–1696 414 B.C.E.

ἔστι δ' ἐν Φαναῖσι πρὸς τῆι
Κλεψύδραι πανοῦργον ἐγ-
γλωττογαστόρων γένος.

At Phanae ["Land of Indictments"] by Klepsydra there is a criminal race that fills its belly by means of its tongue.

312. Schol. Aristophanes, *Birds*, line 1695a

(A scholiast first explains the play on words of Φαναῖσι, a place name that recalls the verb φαίνειν, to bring an indictment or information against. He then mentions Klepsydra as a spring and concludes with the following.)

ἔπαιξε δὲ πάλιν διασύρων τοὺς Ἀθηναίους ὡς φιλοδίκους, ἐπεὶ καὶ ἐν τῶι δικαστηρίωι ἐστὶ κλεψύδρα, κατασκεύασμά τι ὥσπερ ὡρονομικόν.

Again he jested, ridiculing the Athenians as lovers of lawsuits, for in the dikasterion there is also a klepsydra, a contrivance of some sort like a time measurer.

313. Schol. Aristophanes, *Wasps*, line 93

See **106** for the text of Aristophanes.

περὶ τὴν κλεψύδραν· ἀντὶ τοῦ περὶ τὸ δικαστήριον. κλεψύδρα γὰρ ἀγγεῖον τετρημένον, ἐν ὧι ὕδωρ ἔβαλλον καὶ εἴων ῥεῖν ἄχρι τινὸς ὀπῆς, καὶ οὕτως ἔπαυον τὸν ῥήτορα. τοῦτο δὲ ἐποίουν διὰ τὸ φλυαρεῖν τὸν λέγοντα καὶ ἐμποδίζειν ἄλλοις θέλουσι λέγειν, ἵνα τὰ σπουδαῖα λέξας ἐξέλθηι.

"Around the klepsydra" instead of "around the dikasterion". A klepsydra is a pierced pot into which they would pour water and let it flow to a certain hole. That way they would stop the speaker. They would do this because speakers were speaking nonsense and obstructing others wishing to speak; the object was that a speaker say what was important and leave.

314. Schol. Aristophanes, *Wasps*, lines 857–858

See **269** for the text of Aristophanes.

κλεψύδρας· ἀγγείου· κλεψύδρα ἦν δὲ καὶ κρήνη ἐν τῆι Ἀττικῆι, ἥτις Ἐμπεδὼ προσηγορεύετο. σημαίνει δὲ τὸ σκεῦος νῦν. ἤδι δέ τίς ἐστιν; Μήποτε τὸ αἰδοῖον αὐτῶι δείκνυσιν ὁ πρεσβύτης, ὅτι οὐρεῖ ὡς ἡ κλεψύδρα. ἀμὶς γὰρ αὐτῶι παράκειται.

Klepsydra: pot. Klepsydra is also a spring in Attica which was called Empedo as well. Here klepsydra means the pot. What is this? Perhaps the old man is showing his private part to him because he passes water as the klepsydra does; for a chamber pot is set beside him.

Bdelykleon had previously (line 807) provided his father with an *amis*, a chamber pot.

315. Aristotle, *Ath. Pol.* 67.2–3, 69.2 *ca.* 329–322 B.C.E.

εἰσὶ δὲ κλεψύδ[ραι] αὐλ[ίσκους] ἔχουσαι ἔκρους, εἰς ἃς τὸ ὕ[δω]ρ ἐγχέ[ουσι, πρ]ὸς ὃ δεῖ λέγειν {καὶ} τὰς δ[ί]κας. δί[δοτα]ι δὲ δεκά[χους τ]αῖς ὑπὲρ πενταχισχιλίας [δραχ]μὰς καὶ [τρίχο]υς τῶι δ[ευτέρωι] λό[γω]ι, ἑπτάχους δὲ ταῖ[ς] μέχρι πεν[τ]α[κι]σχ[ιλί]ων καὶ δίχους, [πεν]τάχους δὲ τα[ῖς] ἐν[τὸς] ᾱͅ καὶ δίχους, ἑξάχους [δὲ] τα[ῖς] διαδικα[σία]ις, [καὶ ὕστ]ερον λόγος οὐκ ἔστιν ο[ὐδ]εί[ς]. ὁ δ' ἐφ' [ὕδ]ωρ [εἰληχ]ὼς ἐπιλαμβάνει τὸν α[ὐλίσκον, ὅταν ψήφισμα ἢ] νόμον ἢ μαρ[τυρίαν ἢ σύμβολον ὁ γραμ]ματεὺς ἀναγιγ[νώσκειν μέλληι. ὅταν δ'] ἢ[ι πρὸ]ς διαμεμετρημ[ένην τὴν ἡμέραν] ἡ δ[ίκη τό]τε δὲ οὐκ ἐπιλαμβ[άνει τὸν αὐλίσκον ἀλλὰ δίδοτα]ι τ[ὸ ἴσο]ν ὕδωρ τῶι τε κατ[ηγοροῦντι καὶ τῶι ἀπο]λογ[ουμ]ένωι. διαμε[τρεῖται δὲ πρὸς τὰς ἡμέ]ρα[ς τοῦ] Ποσιδεῶνος [μηνός].... 69.2 ἥ τε τίμησίς ἐστιν πρὸς ἡμίχουν ὕδατος ἑκατέρωι.

MacDowell (1985, pp. 525–526) wishes to emend πρὸς ἡμίχουν at 69.2 to πρὸς ἥμισυ.

(67.2–3) There are klepsydras with small tubes for outflow into which they pour the water against [whose flow] the litigants must speak at their trials. Ten choes are given for cases involving over 5,000 drachmai and three choes for the second speech, seven choes for those up to 5,000 drachmai and two choes for the second speech, five choes for those under 1,000 and two choes for the second speech, and six choes for suits involving rival claims for which there is no second speech. He who has been chosen by lot to measure the water stops up the tube when the secretary is about to read a statute or law or testimony or agreement. But when the trial is by "measured day", then he does not stop up the tube. Instead, an equal amount of water is given to prosecution and defense. The day is measured in accordance with the days of the month Posideon.... (69.2) Each party has one-half a chous for the penalty.

Other references to the man allotted to the water: Pollux 8.113 (**322**), Agora I 5656 (**148**).

316. Aristotle, *Poetica* 1451a8 *ca.* 335–322 B.C.E.?
(In a discussion of the length of a story or plot, Aristotle says the following.)

εἰ γὰρ ἔδει ἑκατὸν τραγωιδίας ἀγωνίζεσθαι, πρὸς κλεψύδρας ἂν ἠγωνίζοντο.

If it were necessary to perform a hundred tragedies, they would be performed by klepsydra.

See also the scholion to Aristophanes, *Ecclesiazusae*, line 1089 (ed. Dübner). In a somewhat garbled explanation of the law of Kannon there is the sentence Κρατῖνος δὲ καὶ πρὸς κλεψύδραν κελεῦσαι: Kratinos [says that the law of Kannon] orders [?? to take place] by klepsydra.

(79) Athenaeus 14.640b–c
Klepsydras are included in a list, quoted from Euboulos, of objects all sold together at the same place in Athens.

317. Eustathios, *Commentary on Homer, Iliad* 768.12 (= Z:774.20–775.1) 12th century C.E.

βλόψ μέντοι τὸ μονοσύλλαβον συνέσταλται. ὅπερ ἐστὶν ὁ τῆς κλεψύδρας ἦχος μιμητικῶς κατὰ τοὺς παλαιούς. ὥσπερ, φασί, καὶ κὺξ ἐπὶ τῆς ψήφου κατὰ μίμησιν καὶ αὐτό.

Hesychios (Latte), *s.v.* κόγξ, may add πάξ.

But the monosyllable βλόψ, which according to the ancients is an imitation of the sound of the klepsydra, is pronounced short. Likewise, they say, κύξ is an imitation in the case of the ballot.

The onomatopoeic words may be inventions of a comic playwright who, like Aristophanes with his *Wasps*, featured a lawcourt in his plot. See A. Boegehold, "Two 'Fragmenta Dubia Incertae Sedae' Possibly from Old Comedy," *CQ* n.s. 41, 1991, pp. 247–248. βλόψ should be the sound water makes upon hitting water in another container. κύξ can be the sound a ballot makes as it hits the side or bottom of the voting urn.

318. Herodas, *Mimes* 2.42–43 — 3rd century B.C.E.

(In the course of a mock trial, the prosecutor addresses the attendant.)

καὶ σὺ τὴν ὀπὴν βῦσον
τῆς κλεψύδρης.

And you plug the hole of the klepsydra [while the attendant reads the law].

319. Hesychios, *s.v.* κλεψύδρα — 5th or 6th century C.E.?

κλεψύδρα· . . . ⟨σημαίνει δὲ καὶ τὸ σκεῦος⟩, ὡρολόγιον, ὄργανον, ἐν ὧι αἱ ὧραι μετροῦνται.

Klepsydra: [is the spring Empedo] . . . it also means the vessel, clock, instrument, in which the hours are measured.

320. Lucian, *Piscator* 28 — 2nd century C.E.

ἔγχει τῶι ἀπολογουμένωι. σὺ δὲ ὁ Παρρησιάδης λέγε ἤδη ἐν τῶι μέρει· σοὶ γὰρ τὸ ὕδωρ ῥεῖ νῦν.

Philosophy speaking [to Parresiades, or Candorson]: Pour in the water for the defendant. Now, Candorson, make your speech in turn, for the water is now running for you.

321. Schol. Lucian, *Piscator* 28

ἐν τῶι μέρει ἀντὶ τοῦ, τὸ σὸν μέρος· ῥεῖ γὰρ ἤδη τὸ κατὰ σὲ ὕδωρ ἀπὸ τοῦ δικαστικοῦ ἀμφορέως· ἰστέον γὰρ ὡς τοὺς πολλοὺς ἐπισχεῖν βουλόμενοι τῆς ἀπεράντου φλυαρίας οἱ δικασταὶ τῶν ῥητόρων, ὑδρίας ὕδατος πληροῦντες διά τινος διατρήματος παρεῖχον τῶι ὕδατι ἔκροιαν, κελεύοντες τὸν ῥήτορα λέγειν ἐν ἀρχῆι τῆς ἀφέσεως τοῦ κρουνίσκου. ἅτε οὖν πρὸς μέτρον τοῦ ὕδατος τὸν λόγον ποιούμενοι συνέτεμνον τὸν λόγον.

"In turn" instead of "your turn", because now the water that times you is running out of the dikastic vessel. Note that the dikasts, because they wanted to restrain most orators from endless nonsense, filled a water jar with water and gave it an outflow by means of a hole. They told the orator to begin speaking with the unstopping of the cock. And the orators, since they were making their speech by the measure of the water, would cut their talk short.

(250) Pollux 8.16

322. Pollux 8.113 — 2nd century C.E.

ἦν μέντοι καὶ κρηνοφυλάκιον ἀρχή, δηλούσης τὸ ἔργον αὐτῆς τῆς ἐπικλήσεως. καὶ λέων δέ τις ἐκαλεῖτο κρηνοφύλαξ, χαλκοῦ πεποιημένος ἐπὶ κρήνης τινός, δι' οὗ τὸ ὕδωρ ἐφέρετο ἐν ταῖς πρὸς ὕδωρ δίκαις· ἐπιμελητὴς δέ τις κληρωτὸς ἐγίνετο, ὃς καὶ ἐκαλεῖτο ὁ ἐφ' ὕδωρ, ὁ παραφυλάττων τὴν ἰσότητα τῆς κλεψύδρας.

There was also a magistracy called fountain guardianship; the name shows the function. There was a lion called the guardian of the spring, [a statue] made of bronze at a certain fountain, and through the lion water was conveyed at trials that were timed by water. The man responsible was chosen by lot, and he was called the man at the water, the one who protected the equitable functioning of the waterclock.

See p. 75, note 21 above for commentary.

(251) Pollux 10.61

323. *Suda, s.v.* κλεψύδρα 10th century C.E.

κλεψύδρα· ὄργανον ἀστρολογικόν, ἐν ὧι αἱ ὧραι μετροῦνται, καὶ ὄνομα ἑταίρας, καὶ δικαστήριον ἡ κλεψύδρα, καὶ ἀγγεῖον ἔχον μικροτάτην ὀπὴν περὶ τὸν πυθμένα, ὅπερ ἐν τῶι δικαστηρίωι μεστὸν ὕδατος ἐτίθετο, πρὸς ὃ ἔλεγον οἱ ῥήτορες.

Klepsydra: an astronomical instrument by which the hours are measured; also the name of a courtesan. The klepsydra [means] lawcourt: a vessel with a very small hole near the base which would be placed full of water in the lawcourt, and the orators would speak in accordance with it.

This is the second entry in the *Suda, s.v.* κλεψύδρα; the first describes the spring. This entry from ἀγγεῖον is a repetition verbatim of the scholion to Aristophanes' *Acharnians*, line 693 (**310**).

KLEROTERION

A κλῆρος is a lot, and a κληρωτήριον is an implement by which allotments were effected. An allotment can be a simple matter: one can, for instance, shake lots in a helmet to see which one jumps out first. For general purposes of Athenian administration, however, and in particular the requirements of dikastic assignments, something more complex and substantial was needed. Although the earliest securely dated mention of a kleroterion is that in Aristophanes' *Ecclesiazusae*, an explicit reference in Aristophanes' *Geras* (**251**) may be slightly earlier; see G. Kaibel in *PCG* III.2, p. 89; compare Boegehold 1984, p. 24, with note 11. A reference to a κηθάριον in Aristophanes' *Wasps* (**264**) may be an index to use of kleroteria in the 420's, since that small receptacle is plausibly identified by later authorities as an appurtenance of the kleroterion. At Athens, fragments of marble kleroteria come from a time as late as the 2nd century B.C.E.: *Agora* XIV, p. 70. Outside Athens, kleroteria are attested in Roman times; see Dow 1939, p. 14.

The size and shape of a kleroterion was a matter of guesswork until 1939, when Sterling Dow (Dow 1939) recognized how chapters 63–66 in Aristotle's *Athenaion Politeia* could be used to reconstruct a whole allotment machine from a few ancient fragments of worked marble that had been found at Athens. These fragments, most of them from the 2nd century B.C.E., were distinguished principally by vertical rows of slots, one fragment with one row (Dow 1937, no. I), one with two (no. II), one with six (no. VI), and one with ten (no. X). Dow, using Aristotle's description of kleroteria functioning, put together from them a convincing restoration of a 4th-century kleroterion; see Illustration 3.

The implement in Aristotle's account is essentially a stele into which five vertical rows of slots were cut. To one side of this stele, a pipe or tube with a funneled opening at top completes the scheme. To function, it needs only a certain number of differentiated balls or dice, which will be put in the pipe, and a number of plaques (that is to say, pinakia) to put in the slots; see "Balls," pp. 65–66 above, and "Pinakia," pp. 59–64 above. The stele can be made of wood or stone, the balls or dice of bronze or terracotta, the pinakia of bronze or boxwood. The pipe or tube can be fastened to the stele or run through a vertical boring, as can be seen in some of the marble examples (Dow 1937, nos. I and II). With a sketch of the apparatus in a properly assembled restoration, it is possible to follow Aristotle's description of the procedure (see, for example, the description in "Three Court Days," pp. 59–64 above). Later scholars preserve the following as names of containers in which balls or dice were shaken: κηθίς, κήθιον, κηθάριον, ὀξύβαφος, τρύβλιον; see **266**.

Sterling Dow had been preparing a final publication of kleroterion fragments found at Athens before his death in January 1995. The following studies can serve as introduction until means can be found to complete Dow's work. A fragment found recently in excavations conducted by the Greek Archaeological Service is presented on p. 58 and Plate 6.

S. Dow 1937; 1939; *RE* Suppl. VII, 1940, cols. 322–328, *s.v.* Kleroterion (S. Dow); 1963.

J. D. Bishop, "The Cleroterium," *JHS* 90, 1970, pp. 1–14.

Agora XIV, pp. 52–54, 70.

A. Boegehold 1984.

E. S. Staveley 1972.

(64) Aristophanes, *Ecclesiazusae*, lines 681–683

Blepyros: Where will you put the kleroteria?
Praxagora: I will put them in the Agora, set them up beside Harmodios, and allot everybody until each man gets his lot and goes off happy knowing in what letter he is dining.

324. Schol. Aristophanes, *Ecclesiazusae*, line 681

κληρωτήρια· τὰς κληρωτὰς ἀρχάς.

Kleroteria: the allotted magistracies.

A misunderstanding on the part of the scholiast.

(266) Schol. Aristophanes, *Wasps*, line 674a

... Ketharion is the basketlike wicker object placed on the klerotris for the votes ...

Klerotris is probably a variant for the word *kleroterion*, and its identification as a receptacle for votes is probably an error; see comment on **266**.

(268) Schol. Aristophanes, *Wasps*, line 752a

... the dikasts ... cast their ballots when the herald offered the klerotris.

See comment on **266**.

(249) Aristotle, *Ath. Pol.* 63.2

There are ten entrances to the dikasteria, one for each tribe, and twenty kleroteria, two for each tribe, and one hundred boxes, ten for each tribe.

325. Aristotle, *Ath. Pol.* 64 *ca.* 329–322 B.C.E.

τὰ δὲ [κιβώ]τια τὰ δέκα κ[εῖται] ἐν τ[ῶι ἔμ]προσθεν [τ]ῆς εἰσόδου καθ' ἑκάστην τὴν [φυ]λήν, ἐπιγέ[γ]ραπται δ' ἐπ' αὐτῶν τὰ στοιχεῖα μέχρι [το]ῦ κ. ἐ[π]ειδὰν δ' ἐμβάλωσιν οἱ δικαστ[αὶ τὰ] πιν[ά]κια εἰς τὸ κιβώτι[ον], ἐφ' οὗ ἂν ᾖ[ι ἐπιγεγρα]μμένον τὸ γράμ[μ]α τὸ αὐτὸ ὅπ[ερ ἐπὶ τῶι π]ιναχίωι ἐστὶν α[ὐτ]ῶι τῶν στοιχ[είων, δια]σείσαντος τοῦ ὑ[πη]ρέτου ἕλκ[ε]ι [ὁ θεσμο]θέτης ἐξ ἑκάσ[τ]ου τοῦ κιβωτ[ίου πιν]άκιον ἕν. οὗτος δὲ καλεῖται ἐμ[πήκτ]ης, καὶ ἐμπήγνυσι τὰ πινάκια [τὰ ἐκ το]ῦ κιβωτίου εἰς τὴν κανονίδ[α, ἐφ' ἧς τὸ α]ὐτὸ γράμμα ἔπεστιν ὅπερ ἐπὶ τοῦ [κιβωτίο]υ, [κληροῦται δ'] οὗτος, ἵνα μὴ ἀεὶ ὁ αὐτὸς ἐμπ[ηγνύων] κακουργῆι. εἰσὶ δὲ κανονίδες [πέντε ἐ]ν ἑκάστωι τῶν κληρωτηρίων. ἐ[πειδὰν δ'] ἐμβάληι τοὺς κύβους, ὁ ἄρχων τὴν φυλὴν κληρ[οῖ κατὰ κ]ληρωτήριον. εἰσὶ δὲ κύβοι χα[λκοῖ, μ]έλανες καὶ λευκοί. ὅσους δ' ἂν δέηι [λαχεῖν] δικαστάς, τοσοῦτοι ἐμβάλλοντ[αι λε]υκοί, κατὰ πέντε πινάκια εἷς, οἱ δὲ [μέλ]ανες τὸν αὐτὸν τρόπον. ἐπειδὰν ἐ[ξαιρῆι] τοὺς κύβους, καλεῖ τοὺς εἰληχότας ὁ κ[ῆρυξ]. ὑπάρχει δὲ καὶ ὁ ἐμπήκτης εἰς τὸν ἀ[ριθμό]ν. ὁ δὲ κληθεὶς καὶ ὑπακούσας ἕλκει β[άλανο]ν ἐκ τῆς ὑδρίας, καὶ ὀρέξας αὐτήν, [ἄνω ἔχ]ων τὸ γράμμα, δ[εί]κνυσιν πρῶτ[ον μὲν] τῶι ἄρχοντι τῶι ἐφεστηκότι. ὁ δὲ ἄρχων [ἐπειδ]ὰν ἴδηι, ἐμβάλλει τὸ πινάκιον α[ὐ]τοῦ [εἰς τὸ] κιβώτιον, ὅπου ἂν ἦι ἐπιγεγραμ[μέν]ον τὸ αὐτὸ στοιχεῖον ὅπερ ἐν τῆι βαλ[άνωι, ἵ]ν' εἰς οἷον ἂν λάχηι εἰσίηι καὶ μὴ εἰς ο[ἷο]ν ἂν βούληται, μηδὲ ἦι συναγαγεῖν [εἰς] δικαστήριον οὓς ἂν βούληταί τις. πα[ράκει]ται δὲ τῶι ἄρχοντι κιβώτια, ὅσαπερ [ἂν μ]έλληι τὰ δικαστήρια πληρωθήσεσθα[ι, ἔχ]οντα στοιχεῖον ἕκαστον, ὅπερ ἂν [ἦι τὸ] τοῦ δικαστηρίου ἑκάσ[του] εἰληχός.

The ten boxes lie in front of the entrance for each tribe. On them are inscribed the letters as far as kappa. After the dikasts have thrown their pinakia into the box on which is written the same letter as is on the pinakion itself, the attendant shakes them, and the thesmothetes draws one pinakion from each box. This dikast is called the inserter and he inserts the pinakia from the box into the column of slots on which is the same letter as that on the box. He [the inserter] is chosen by lot, so that the same person does not always insert the pinakia and cheat. There are five columns of slots in each of the kleroteria. When he has thrown in the dice, the archon draws lots for tribe members on the kleroterion. The dice are bronze, black and white; as many white ones are thrown in as [the number of] dikasts needed to be chosen, a single white one for each five pinakia, and the black dice in the same way. After he draws out the dice, the herald calls those who have been allotted to serve. The inserter is included in the number [of those accepted as dikasts]. The man who has been called answers and draws a balanos from the hydria. He holds it out with the letter upward and shows it first to the archon in charge; when the archon has seen it, he throws the man's pinakion into the box that has the same letter written on it as the one on the balanos, so that the man goes into the court to which he is allotted and not into whatever court he likes, and so that no one can assemble in a court whatever dikasts he likes. Beside the archon are as many boxes as there are courts to be filled, each marked with the letter which is assigned by lot to each court.

(249) Aristotle, *Ath. Pol.* 66.1

When all the dikasteria are full (when the panels are complete), two kleroteria and bronze dice on which the colors of the dikasteria are painted are placed in the first of the dikasteria, also other dice on which are inscribed the names of the magistrates. Two of the thesmothetai chosen by lot throw in the dice separately: one throws the colored dice into one kleroterion, the other the names of the magistrates into the other.

326. Athenaeus 10.450b, c — 2nd–3rd century C.E.
(contains Euboulos F107 [ed. Hunter] lines 23–27 = Euboulos F106 [*PCG* V], lines 21–25)

ἔστιν ἄγαλμα μεμυκὸς ἄνω, τὰ κάτω δὲ κεχηνός,
εἰς πόδας ἐκ κεφαλῆς τετρημένον ὀξὺ διαπρό,
ἀνθρώπους τίκτον κατὰ τὴν πυγὴν ἕν' ἕκαστον,
ὧν οἱ μὲν μοίρας ἔλαχον βίου, οἱ δὲ πλανῶνται,
αὐτὸ δ' ἕκαστος ἔχων αὐτόν, καλέω δὲ φυλάττειν

ταῦτα δ' ὅτι κληρωτικὸν σημαίνει ὑμεῖς διακρίνατε, ἵνα μὴ πάντα παρὰ τοῦ Εὐβούλου λαμβάνωμεν.

See Hunter 1983, p. 207 for comment on the text of line 27.

There is a statue that is closed on top, open at bottom, bored sharply through from head to foot, giving birth to people at its rump, each one in his turn, and some of them are allotted the right to live, while others wander . . . (textual uncertainty here)

You can judge for yourselves that this signifies the *klerotikon*, for I do not want to cite all that Euboulos says.

Euboulos is a Middle Comedy poet of the mid-4th century, and *klerotikon* is a variant of *kleroterion*. See Dow 1939, p. 11; compare Kroll (1972, p. 6), who says the play can be as early as the 380's.

(79) Athenaeus 14.640b–c
Kleroteria are included in a list, quoted from Euboulos, of objects all sold together in the same place in Athens.

327. Bekker, *Anecdota Graeca* 1.47.13

κληρωτήρια· ἔνθα κληροῦνται οἱ δικασταί.

Kleroteria: where the dikasts are chosen by lot.

328. Hesychios, *s.v.* κυαμῶι πατρίωι — 5th or 6th century C.E.?
(contains Sophokles, F404 [ed. Radt] = 266 N^2 = 288 Pearson)
(The lexicographer, in explaining the phrase "by ancestral bean", cites some analogous uses of the word "bean" as instrumental of an allotment.)

Σοφοκλῆς Μελεάγρωι. ὡς καὶ τῶν Αἰτωλῶν τὰς ἀρχὰς κυαμευόντων. διεκλήρουν δὲ αὐτὰς κυαμῶι καὶ ὁ τὸν λευκὸν λαβὼν ἐλάγχανεν. ἀνάγει δὲ τοὺς χρόνους ὡς καὶ ἐν 'Ινάχωι κυαμόβολον δικαστήν.

Sophokles in *Meleager*. As though the Aitolians also allot their magistracies. They would allot them by bean, and the man who got a white [bean] was allotted. Sophokles modernizes as he also does in *Inachos* with the phrase "dikast by cast of the bean".

The phrase from Sophokles, *Inachos* has been variously emended. δικαστήν is accepted here for δικιστήν, and as far as other attempted emendations go, none dislocates the conjunction of allotment procedures with "dikast". In other entries, *viz.*, κυαμοτρώξ and κυαμῶι δικαστικῶι, Hesychios confuses voting procedures with allotment procedures.

329. Plutarch, *Moralia, Old Men in Public Affairs* 18 (793d) — 1st–2nd century C.E.

πρεσβύτηι δὲ κομιδῆι, κἂν τὸ ἄδοξον ἀφέλῃς, ἐπίπονος καὶ ταλαίπωρος ἡ πρὸς πᾶν μὲν ἀεὶ κληρωτήριον ἀπαντῶσα φιλαρχία, παντὶ δ' ἐφεδρεύουσα δικαστηρίου καιρῶι καὶ συνεδρίου πολυπραγμοσύνη. . . .

But for a man who is quite old, even if you subtract the lack of glory, that love of office that always responds at every kleroterion, that busy restlessness that lies in wait for every chance to serve in a lawcourt or synedrion, are toilsome and miserable. . . .

330. Pollux 9.44 2nd century C.E.

λογιστήριον, ἵνα οἱ λογισταὶ συνεκάθιζον· κληρωτήριον, ἵνα οἱ κληρωταί.

Logisterion, where the logistai would sit down together; kleroterion, where those chosen by lot [would sit down together].

In this passage, Pollux is listing public meeting places and erroneously includes a kleroterion as a place.

(251) Pollux 10.61

331. *Suda, s.v.* κληρωτήρια 10th century C.E.

κληρωτήρια· αἱ κληρωτικαὶ ἀρχαί, αἱ κληρωτρίδες.

Kleroteria: the allotted magistracies, the klerotrides.

This entry continues with a quotation of Aristophanes, *Ecclesiazusae*, lines 675–690 (**64**). It has affinities with two erroneous scholia; see **266** and **324** above.

332. *IG* II^2 972, lines 10–12 159/8 or 158/7 B.C.E.

[ἀν]αγράψαι δὲ τόδε [τὸ ψήφισμα τὸν γραμματέα τὸν κατὰ
[πρυτανείαν . . . . εἰς] κληρωτήριον λίθι[νον καὶ
[στῆσαι αὐτὸ ἐν τῶι τεμένει . . .]

The secretary of the prytaneis is to inscribe this decree on a stone kleroterion and set it up in the sanctuary. . . .

From a fragmentary prytany decree in honor of Ptolemais, this is published as number 80 in Dow 1937. No trace of any cutting for a kleroterion is preserved on the back (*ibid.*, p. 207).

333. Agora I 2539, lines 28–33 159/8 or 158/7 B.C.E.

[ἀναγράψαι δὲ τόδε] τὸ ψήφισμ[α τὸν γρ-
[αμματέα τὸν κατὰ πρυτανε]ίαν εἰς κληρ[ωτήρι]-
[ον λίθινον καὶ στῆσαι αὐ]τὸ ἐν τῶι τεμ[ένει ca. 3]
[. . . . . . .15. . . . . . . εἰς δ]ὲ τὴν ἀναγραφ[ὴν καὶ τὴν]
[ἀνάθεσιν τοῦ κληρωτηρί]ου μερίσαι τὸ[ν ταμίαν]
[τῶν στρατιωτικῶν τὸ γ]ενόμενον ἀνάλ[ωμα].

The secretary of the prytaneis is to inscribe this decree on a stone kleroterion and set it up in the sanctuary . . . the military treasurer is to pay the cost for the inscribing and erection of the kleroterion.

From a fragmentary prytany decree in honor of Erechtheis, this is published as number 79 in Dow 1937. Slots of the kleroterion are preserved on the backs of the fragments (*ibid.*, pp. 206–207).

PINAKION

(249) Aristotle, *Ath. Pol.* 63.1–2, 4–5; 65

PINAKION TIMETIKON (ASSESSING TABLET)

Philokleon demands an assessing tablet, *pinakion timetikon* (*Wasps*, line 167 [**335**]), and Xanthias says that Philokleon returns with wax under his nails from punishing all with the long line (*Wasps*, lines 106–108 [**106**]). Pollux and scholia to Aristophanes add that the long line was used for condemnation, the short for acquittal. Hippodamos of Miletos recommended that judicial decisions be written on tablets (πινάκια), and he may have had Athens in mind (Aristotle, *Politics* 1268a1–6). There is no mention of such tablets in the 4th-century orators. They may have been in use for a short period only (Lipsius 1905–1915, p. 927), used on a second vote when the dikasterion was deciding between two recommended punishments: that offered by the prosecutor (severe) and that offered by the defendant (mild).

The lexicographers, Hesychios, Photios, and the *Suda*, under the heading μακρὰ γραμμή (or γραμμὴ μακρά in Photios, *Lexicon* I), give the same information as that found in Pollux and the scholia. These entries are not included here.

These pinakia are not to be confused with the dikasts' pinakia (*Ath. Pol.* 63.4 [**249**]) used in the process of allotment, nor with the tablets on which depositions can be composed at home ([Demosthenes] 46.11 [**354**]), nor with wax-lined pinakia on which responses to challenges were written ([Demosthenes] 46.11).

(106) Aristophanes, *Wasps*, lines 106–108
(Xanthias describes the habits of Philokleon.)

In his bad temper, he assigns everyone the long [condemning line] and then comes in like a honeybee or bumblebee with wax stuck up beneath his nails.

334. Schol. Aristophanes, *Wasps*, line 106a–c

(a) εἰώθασιν οἱ καταδικάζοντες ἐν τῶι γραμμιτιδίωι μακρὰν γραμμὴν ἕλκειν. (b) τιμῶν τὴν μακράν· Προείρηται ὑπὲρ τοῦ τοὺς δικαστὰς ἐν πινακίωι, ἤτοι ἐπὶ σανίδος κηρῶι ἀληλιμμένης, ὁπότε καταλαμβάνοιέν τινα τῶι τολμήματι, ἕλκειν μακρὰν γραμμήν, ὁπότε δὲ ἀπολύοιεν, βραχεῖαν, καὶ ἑξῆς: δότε μοι ξίφος ὅπως τάχιστ', ἢ πινάκιον τιμητικόν. τοῦτο δὲ ἐποίουν μετὰ τὸ ἀποβλέψαι εἰς τὰς ψήφους τὰς ἐν τῆι κάλπιδι. εἰ γὰρ ἑώρων τὰς μελαίνας πλείους, ἐχάραττον τῶι ὄνυχι τὴν μακράν, εἰ δὲ τὰς λευκάς, τὴν βραχεῖαν. (c) . . . ὅτε δὲ πλείους ἦσαν αἱ λευκαί, ὁ διώκων ἐνίκα, ὁ φεύγων δ', ἣν πλείους αἱ μέλαιναι, κατεκρίνετο.

(a) Those voting to convict used to draw a long line on the small tablet. (b) "To assign the long line": It has been said before with reference to the fact that the dikasts drew a long line on a tablet or board covered with wax, when they judged a person guilty of the deed, a short line, when they acquitted. (See also line 167 [**335**]) "give me a sword as quickly as possible, or an assessing tablet." They did this after looking at the votes in the urn [kalpis]. If they saw a majority of black votes, they scratched a long line with their nail; if of white, a short one. (c) . . . When there were more white ballots, the prosecutor won; if more black, the defendant was condemned.

The last sentence as it stands is confused: in either case the prosecutor wins. See the *apparatus criticus* in the edition of W. J. W. Koster on attempts to emend the text. Black and white ballots are not attested in any case as having been used in lawsuits in the 5th and 4th centuries.

335. Aristophanes, *Wasps*, lines 166–167 422 B.C.E.
(Philokleon in his frustration parodies tragedy as he expostulates to Bdelykleon.)

πῶς ἄν σ' ἀποκτείναιμι; πῶς; δότε μοι ξίφος
ὅπως τάχιστ', ἢ πινάκιον τιμητικόν.

How shall I slay thee, how? Give me a sword as quickly as possible, or an assessing tablet.

336. Schol. Aristophanes, *Wasps*, line 167b

τιμητικόν· καταδικαστικόν, ὅπου τὴν μακρὰν χαράσσοντες κατεδίκαζον, ἢ τὴν μικράν, καὶ ἀπέλυον.

Assessing: condemnatory, where by drawing the long line they would condemn, or by drawing the short, acquit.

(250) Pollux 8.16

Sanides (Notice Boards)

Sanides, boards or tablets, are mentioned twice in the *Wasps* (lines 349 and 848) in connection with a lawcourt. The scholia offer various meanings, understandably, since the word is generic and changes with context. Sometimes it meant "notice boards" on which upcoming trials were posted (**338–340**), but at other times the sense is not so clear (**338**, **339**). See James Sickinger ("A Note on *Wasps* 349," *CQ* n.s. 41, 1991, pp. 529–532), who argues that the sanides in question at that point refer to the dryphaktoi, the grill that separates court area from spectators generally.

337. Aischines 3 (*Ktesiphon*) 199–200 — 330 B.C.E.

ὥσπερ γὰρ ἐν τῆι τεκτονικῆι, ὅταν εἰδέναι βουλώμεθα τὸ ὀρθὸν καὶ τὸ μή, τὸν κανόνα προσφέρομεν, ὧι διαγιγνώσκεται, οὕτω καὶ ἐν ταῖς γραφαῖς ταῖς τῶν παρανόμων παράκειται κανὼν τοῦ δικαίου τουτὶ τὸ σανίδιον, τὸ ψήφισμα καὶ οἱ νόμοι.

For just as in carpentry, when we want to know what is straight and what is not, we apply a straight edge, by which a determination is made, so in the case of indictments for illegal motions we have available as measure of what is right this notice board, which is to say, the [illegal] statute and the laws [that were broken].

338. Aristophanes, *Wasps*, line 349 — 422 B.C.E.

Βδελυκλέων: οὕτω κιττῶ διὰ τῶν σανίδων μετὰ χοιρίνης περιελθεῖν.

Bdelykleon: That's how much I crave to walk through the boards [and into the dikasterion] with my ballot.

339. Schol. Aristophanes, *Wasps*, line 349

διὰ τῶν σανίδων· τῶν δρυφάκτων τῶν ταβλωτῶν τοῦ δικαστηρίου, ἵνα λέγηι ἐπιθυμῶ ἐν τῶι δικαστηρίωι ἐλθεῖν. ἢ [τῶν] σανίδων φησὶ τῶν περιεχουσῶν τὰ ὀνόματα τῶν εἰσαχθησομένων εἰς τὸ δικαστήριον, ποῖον δεήσει πρῶτον εἰσαχθῆναι καὶ κατὰ τάξιν.

"Through the boards [sanides]": the dryphaktoi, tablota, of the dikasterion; he means "I long to walk in the dikasterion." Or by sanides he means the notice boards that have the names of those who are going to be prosecuted, who is to be prosecuted first and [so on], in order.

The second suggestion in the scholion, that the sanides are notice boards, has been generally accepted. But see the introductory note above. The scholia to *Wasps*, line 386 (**207**) and *Knights*, line 675 (**203**) explain dryphaktoi as tablota.

340. Aristophanes, *Wasps*, line 848 — 422 B.C.E.

(Bdelykleon is speaking as he is getting ready for the mock trial.)

φέρε νῦν, ἐνέγκω τὰς σανίδας καὶ τὰς γραφάς.

Come on now, let me bring the notice boards [sanides] and the indictments.

341. Schol. Aristophanes, *Wasps*, line 848

τὰς σανίδας· σανίδας φησὶν ἐν αἷς ἔγραφον τὴν μακρὰν ἢ τὴν βραχεῖαν τῆς δίκης.

Sanides: By sanides he means the objects on which they used to write the long or short [line] for the punishment.

The scholiast here identifies the sanides with the pinakia or sanides used by dikasts in fixing a penalty; see Schol. *Wasps*, line 106 (**334**), and Pollux 8.16 (**250**). The meaning "notice boards" or "cause lists" seems more appropriate in the text; see Schol. *Wasps*, line 349 (**338**).

342. Isokrates 15 (*Antidosis*) 237–238 — mid-4th century B.C.E.

ἐν γὰρ ταῖς σανίσι ταῖς ὑπὸ τῶν ἀρχόντων ἐκτιθεμέναις ἀναγκαῖόν ἐστιν ἐν μὲν ταῖς τῶν θεσμοθετῶν ἀμφοτέρους ἐνεῖναι, τούς τε τὴν πόλιν ἀδικοῦντας καὶ τοὺς συκοφαντοῦντας, ἐν δὲ ταῖς τῶν ἕνδεκα τούς τε κακουργοῦντας καὶ τοὺς τούτοις ἐφεστῶτας, ἐν δὲ ταῖς τῶν τετταράκοντα τούς τ' ἐν τοῖς ἰδίοις πράγμασιν ἀδικοῦντας καὶ τοὺς μὴ δικαίως ἐγκαλοῦντας.

In the notice boards that the archons set out, those of the thesmothetai must have in them [the names of] both men who wrong the city and extortionists, and the notice boards of the Eleven, names of both criminals and their bosses, and the notice boards of the Forty, names of men who do wrong in private transactions and men who make unjust accusations.

342a. *POxy* 2087, lines 16–18 — 2nd century C.E.

Αἰά[κ]ιον κ(αὶ) ἡ Θόλος ο[ὗ] φασι [τ]ὸν Αἰακὸν
οἰκῆσ[α]ι, Θό[λο]ς δ(ὲ) ὅπου δει[πν]ει ἡ πρυτα-
νέου[σ]α φυλή, [ἐν δ(ὲ)] τῶι Αἰακίωι δίκ(αι) ἀ(να)γράφον|ται

Aiakeion and Tholos, where they say Aiakos dwelt. Tholos is where the prytanizing tribe dines. Notices of trials are published in the Aiakeion.

The Greek text, from a fragmentary lexicon, is that proposed by R. S. Stroud, "The Aiakeion and Tholos of Athens in *POxy* 2087," *ZPE* 103, 1994, pp. 1–9. Stroud sees the two structures as separate. The notice does not tell whether preliminary notices are meant (like those posted by the Eponymous Heroes) or judgments (like those in, e.g., **148** and **163**).

The Dikastic *Bakteria* (Staff) and Symbolon

Dikastic symbola or tokens are discussed at "Bronze Tokens," pp. 67–76 above.

(70) Aristophanes, *Ploutos*, lines 277–278

Now that you have been allotted your letter to act as judge in the grave, go. Charon is handing out the token.

343. Schol. Aristophanes, *Ploutos,* line 277

τὸ δὲ ὁ Χάρων τὸ ξύμβολον δίδωσι, τοιοῦτόν ἐστι. τοῖς λαχοῦσι δικάσαι εἰσελθοῦσιν ἑκάστωι σύμβολον δίδοται δημόσιον παρὰ τῆς ἐπὶ τούτωι εἰληχυίας ἀρχῆς, ἵν' οἱ ἐξιόντες καὶ τοῦτο προσφέροντες λαμβάνοιεν τὸν δικαστικὸν μισθόν.

The phrase "Charon gives the symbolon" is some such thing as this: an official symbolon is given by the official allotted this task to each man chosen by lot to serve as judge as he comes in, so that on going out by offering this token he would receive the dikastic pay.

(249) Aristotle, *Ath. Pol.* 65.3

After he [the dikast] goes in, he receives an official token from the person allotted this task.

This is quoted in a scholion to *Ploutos,* line 278, not given here.

(276) Aristotle, *Ath. Pol.* 68.2 and 69.2

He who was chosen by lot for this task takes the symbola; in exchange for these every single dikast upon voting receives a bronze symbolon marked with a three, for on surrendering this he receives three [obols], so that all will vote. For it is not possible for anyone to receive a symbolon unless he votes.... Afterwards they assign the penalty, if it is necessary to do so, voting again in the same way, giving back the symbolon and receiving again the staff.

344. Bekker, *Anecdota Graeca* 1.185.4–6

βακτηρία καὶ σύμβολον· ῥάβδον κατεῖχον οἱ δικάζοντες, καὶ σύμβολον ἐλάμβανον ἀντιδιδόντες διὰ τὸ κομίσασθαι τὸ τριώβολον.

Staff and symbolon: those serving as judges would keep a baton, and they would get a token which they would give back on receipt of the triobol.

345. Bekker, *Anecdota Graeca* 1.300.32–301.3

σύμβολον· σημαίνει μὲν τὰ σημεῖα.... εἰδικῶς δὲ τὸ σύμβολον δηλοῖ γραμματεῖόν τι ὃ ἐλάμβανε τῶν δικαστῶν ἕκαστος εἰσιὼν εἰς τὸ δικαστήριον, ὅ ἐστι πινάκιον.

Symbolon: it means the signs.... Specifically, *symbolon* signifies a tablet that each of the dikasts received as he went into his lawcourt, that is, a ticket [pinakion].

There is confusion here: a symbolon is not a pinakion.

346. Demosthenes 18 (*On the Crown*) 210 — 330 B.C.E.

καὶ παραλαμβάνειν γ' ἅμα τῆι βακτηρίαι καὶ τῶι συμβόλωι τὸ φρόνημα τὸ τῆς πόλεως νομίζειν ἕκαστον ὑμῶν δεῖ....

And each of you ought to believe that along with the staff and symbolon you receive the resolution of the city....

347. Hesychios, *s.v.* σύμβολον — 5th or 6th century C.E.?

σύμβολον· σημεῖον ... καὶ τὸ διδόμενον τοῖς εἰσιοῦσιν εἰς τὸ δικαστήριον.

Symbolon: a sign ... and the object given to those entering the lawcourt.

348. *Lexicon Patmense, s.v.* βακτηρία
Commentary on Demosthenes 18.210.

βακτηρία· ῥάβδος ὁμόχρους τῶι δικαστηρίωι ἣν ἐλάμβανε σύμβολον τῆς χειροτονίας ὁ δικάζειν λαχών.

Staff: a baton of the same color as the lawcourt: a man chosen by lot to serve as judge received it as a sign [symbolon] of his vote by hand.

The identification of the staff as symbolon is confused. χειροτονία, the vote by hand, was customary in the ekklesia but not in the dikasteria, where the vote was secret.

349. Athenaeus 6.244d5–7 (contains Machon Comicus F5 [ed. Gow], lines 43–45) 260–250 B.C.E.

τοὔψον δὲ σέβεται τοῦτο καὶ δέδοικέ πως·
οὐδ' ἔστιν αὐτῶι πάτριον ὄντ' ἀσύμβολον
ἰχθὺν ἔχοντα ψῆφον ἀδικεῖν οὐδένα.

He respects this fish and is, in a way, afraid of it. It is not ancestral custom in his country for a person who has not made a contribution (or who does not have a token that authorizes him to sit in judgment) to do wrong to any fish with a stone (or ballot).

Machon describes an elegant dinner at which a parasite named Archephron surprises his host by not eating one sort of fish. The fish in question is a goby, which has a sucker by which it attaches itself to stones. Machon's play on words starts with λοπάς in line 30, the vessel in which the gobies are served. *Lopas* suggests "echinos" (**300**). Next, *asymbolon* describes Arkhephon accurately as a parasite, one who has not contributed money or food or drink to the dinner, but plays at the same time on *symbolon*, the dikastic token (**343–351**). *Psephon* consequently is both the stone to which a goby attaches itself and a ballot, widely recognized as an instrument of power at Athens. See A. Boegehold, "Machon, Frag. 5 (Gow)," *AJA* 90, 1986, pp. 43–44.

350. Photios, *Lexicon, s.v.* σύμβολον 9th century C.E.

σύμβολον· ὃ ἐλάμβανον οἱ δικασταὶ εἰς τὸ δικαστήριον εἰσιόντες, εἶτα τοῦτο δόντες τὸ δικαστικὸν ἐκομίζοντο.

Symbolon: that which the dikasts would receive upon entering their lawcourt. Then they would give this up and receive the dikastikon.

This entry is repeated verbatim in the *Suda, s.v.* σύμβολον, with the apparently erroneous addition ἦσαν δὲ τὸν ἀριθμὸν ἀπὸ τοῦ α' ἕως τοῦ κ', "they were numbered from alpha to kappa" (see pp. 67–76 above).

(250) Pollux 8.16

351. *Suda, s.v.* βακτηρία καὶ σύμβολον 10th century C.E.

βακτηρία καὶ σύμβολον· οἱ λαχόντες δικάζειν ἐλάμβανον παρὰ τῶν δημοσίων ὑπηρετῶν σύμβολον καὶ βακτηρίαν, καὶ οὕτως ἐδίκαζον, ... τὸ μέντοι σύμβολον μετὰ τὴν κρίσιν ἀποδιδοῦντες ἐκομίζοντο τριώβολον· ὅπερ καὶ δικαστικὸν γέγονεν.

Staff and symbolon: those chosen by lot to serve as judges received from the public attendants a token [symbolon] and a staff, and thus they served as judges ... After the trial, they returned the symbolon and received the triobol; this was the dikastic pay [dikastikon].

Tablet and Stylus

Writing tablets were used by Athenians for most kinds of writing. In the 4th century, a number of uses had to do with court procedure. The tablets, variously called πίναξ, πινάκιον, γραμματεῖον, and γραμματείδιον, might be coated with wax (μάλθη) or whitened with gypsum (λελευκωμένον). A stylus (γραφίς) was the writing implement. (MacDowell [1971, commentary to *Wasps*, line 467] sees ἐγκεντρίς as a punning way of saying "stylus".) Made of bone, bronze, or ivory, the stylus had a point at one end to scratch letters in the wax and a flange at the other to erase letters by smoothing the wax. Rhys Townsend (*Agora* XXVII, p. 41, note 37) lists eight styli that were found in the general area of the Square Peristyle and its predecessors. Two of these, BI 658 and BI 711, are shown on Plate 22.

In procedures having to do with courts, some attested uses of tablets are as follows: A magistrate's original disposition of a case might be recorded on a wax tablet (Aristophanes, *Clouds*). Compare a tablet containing an informer's communication: [πίνα]κα τε̃ς μενύσεος (*IG* I^3 34, line 72 and Lipsius 1905–1915, p. 201 with note 80, p. 813, note 34; likewise notes taken in the course of a trial, [Demosthenes] 46.11, and testimonies, [Demosthenes] 34.36–37). A deposition might be prepared at home by being written on a whitened tablet ([Demosthenes] 46.11).

Letters written into a wax tablet would not be expected to last. Strepsiades stresses the fugitive nature of such texts when he wants to melt away a notice of a suit against himself (Aristophanes, *Clouds*, lines 768–772). His reasoning is not unlike that imputed to Alkibiades by Chamaileon, Athenaeus 9.407b–c, where Alkibiades seems to be able to disintegrate a lawsuit by moistening his finger and erasing the notice from a whitened board.

352. Aristophanes, *Clouds*, lines 768–772 — 423 B.C.E.

Σωκράτης: τὴν ὕαλον λέγεις;
Στρεψιάδης: ἔγωγε.
Σωκράτης: φέρε τί δῆτ' ἄν,
Στρεψιάδης: εἰ ταύτην λαβών,
ὁπότε γράφοιτο τὴν δίκην ὁ γραμματεύς
ἀπωτέρω στὰς ὧδε πρὸς τὸν ἥλιον
τὰ γράμματ' ἐκτήξαιμι τῆς ἐμῆς δίκης.

Sokrates: You mean the glass?
Strepsiades: Yes.
Sokrates: What would . . .
Strepsiades: I'd take it and when the secretary was writing up the suit, I'd stand off toward the sun like this and melt the letters of my suit.

353. Demosthenes 45 (*Stephanos* I) 44 — mid-4th century B.C.E.

διὰ ταῦθ' ὁ νόμος μαρτυρεῖν ἐν γραμματείωι κελεύει ἵνα μήτ' ἀφελεῖν ἐξῆι μήτε προσθεῖναι τοῖς γεγραμμένοις μηδέν.

For this reason the law requires testimony to be written on a tablet, so that nothing can be added or subtracted from what has been written.

Compare [Demosthenes] 46.6.

354. [Demosthenes] 46 (*Stephanos* II) 11 mid-4th century B.C.E.

ἔτι τοίνυν κἂν ἀπὸ τοῦ γραμματείου γνοίη τις, ἐν ὧι ἡ μαρτυρία γέγραπται, ὅτι τὰ ψευδῆ μεμαρτύρηκεν. λελευκωμένον τε γάρ ἐστιν καὶ οἴκοθεν κατεσκευασμένον. καίτοι τοὺς μὲν τὰ πεπραγμένα μαρτυροῦντας προσήκει οἴκοθεν τὰς μαρτυρίας κατεσκευασμένας μαρτυρεῖν, τοὺς δὲ τὰς προκλήσεις μαρτυροῦντας, τοὺς ἀπὸ ταὐτομάτου προσστάντας, ἐν μάλθηι γεγραμμένην τὴν μαρτυρίαν, ἵνα, ἐάν τι προσγράψαι ἢ ἀπαλεῖψαι βουληθῆι, ῥάδιον ἦι.

You can tell moreover from the tablet on which his testimony is written that he has given false evidence. It has been whitened, that is, prepared [ahead of time] at home. And yet it is witnesses to transactions who should use prepared testimony, while those who testify in response to a challenge, namely those who step forward extemporaneously, should use testimony written in wax to make it easier to add or erase something.

355. Demosthenes 54 (*Konon*) 37 mid-4th century B.C.E.

τοίχους τοίνυν διορύττοντες καὶ παίοντες τοὺς ἀπαντῶντας, ἆρ' ἂν ὑμῖν ὀκνῆσαι δοκοῦσιν ἐν γραμματειδίωι τὰ ψευδῆ μαρτυρεῖν ἀλλήλοις οἱ κεκοινωνηκότες τοσαύτης καὶ τοιαύτης φιλαπεχθημοσύνης;

Do you think that in the course of breaking into houses and beating whoever gets in their way they would hesitate to attest to their lies for each other in a tablet, men who have in common so much of that kind of quarrelsomeness?

(304) Theophrastos, *Characters* 6.8 (ἀπονοίας [Recklessness])

DEPOSIT LIST

Additional information on these deposits will be found in other volumes of the *Agora* series. Where a deposit has several fillings, not all are listed; only the relevant one is listed here. The general location of the deposits can be seen on the plan (Fig. 4).

B 19:4 Pit	4th century B.C.	**P 13**
E 14:1 Cistern	3rd century B.C.	**B 35, B 36**
G 11:2 Well	Accumulated use from late 2nd century B.C.E. to early 6th century C.E.	**B 5**
G 14:2 Well	Gradual accumulation of 4th, 3rd, and 2nd centuries B.C.E.	**B 7**
H 12:11 Well	Beginning of 4th century B.C.E.	**M 1; BB 2–BB 7; CB 1**
J 5:1 Well	2nd half 4th century B.C.E.	**B 18–B 20**
J 18:2 Well	1st–3rd century C.E.	**B 39**
K 9–10:1	1st century C.E.	**B 54**
Q 8:3 Ballot Deposit	*Ca.* 300 B.C.E.	**B 12–B 17; BB 8; T 1**
Q 17:7 Well	3rd–6th century C.E.	**B 21**

Comparatively few dikastic small finds come in dated deposits, and of these few several are dated and irrelevant. Where the fill from which other small finds come is generally pure (e.g., 4th century) a date may accompany the grid designation. The distribution of the small finds, identified by Agora inventory numbers, is clear from the plan in Figure 4.

CONCORDANCE OF CATALOGUED OBJECTS

(Asterisk [*] designates an inventory number of the Greek Archaeological Service, not an Agora inventory number)

Agora Inv. No.	*Agora XXVIII No.*
Bronze	
B 12	**P 11**
B 43	**B 7**
B 54	**B 46**
B 56	**P 1**
B 60	**P 8**
B 62	**P 4**
B 72	**B 47**
B 76	**P 20**
B 99	**B 48**
B 100	**B 23**
B 105	**BB 1**
B 110	**P 12**
B 111	**P 10**
B 146	**B 1**
B 157	**B 24**
B 165	**B 25**
B 166	**B 26**
B 182	**B 2**
B 233	**B 35**
B 234	**P 36**
B 242	**P 3**
B 255	**B 27**
B 295	**B 37**
B 355	**B 38**
B 429	**B 3**
B 430	**B 49**
B 431	**B 4**
B 449	**B 39**
B 493	**B 5**
B 500	**BB 2**
B 539	**BB 3**
B 540	**BB 4**
B 541	**BB 5**
B 582	**B 28**
B 593	**BB 6**
B 594	**BB 7**
B 697	**B 29**
B 698	**B 30**
B 699	**B 31**
B 700	**P 12**
B 728	**B 8**
B 783	**B 9**
B 790	**B 40**
B 791	**B 41**
B 822	**P 2**
B 847	**P 13**
B 863	**P 21**
B 871	**B 42**
B 898	**P 16**
B 947	**B 6**
B 969	**B 43**
B 974	**P 5**
B 987	**P 17**
B 988	**B 32**
B 992	**B 10**
B 1000	**B 11**
B 1003	**P 15**
B 1013	**B 44**
B 1028	**P 22**
B 1047	**P 7**
B 1055	**B 12**
B 1056	**B 13**
B 1057	**B 14**
B 1058	**B 15**
B 1059	**B 16**
B 1060	**BB 8**
B 1061	**B 17**
B 1078	**B 33**
B 1083	**P 18**
B 1086	**B 34**
B 1104	**P 14**
B 1124	**T 22**
B 1125	**T 16**
B 1126	**T 41**
B 1127	**T 42**
B 1129	**T 33**
B 1130	**T 34**
B 1132	**T 2**
B 1133	**T 6**
B 1135	**T 10**
B 1136	**T 44**
B 1137	**T 18**
B 1138	**T 39**
B 1140	**T 24**
B 1146	**T 38**
B 1154	**T 21**
B 1156	**T 31**
B 1158	**T 15**
B 1159	**T 25**
B 1160	**T 36**
B 1161	**T 37**
B 1163	**T 13**
B 1164	**T 20**
B 1165	**T 9**
B 1166	**T 28**
B 1167	**T 27**
B 1168	**T 35**
B 1169	**T 11**
B 1170	**T 12**
B 1171	**T 26**
B 1172	**T 3**
B 1173	**T 29**
B 1174	**T 17**
B 1175	**T 19**
B 1176	**T 1**
B 1177	**T 14**
B 1179	**T 7**
B 1212	**P 6**
B 1230	**B 45**
B 1235	**B 21**
B 1260	**T 23**
B 1261	**T 40**
B 1262	**T 4**
B 1263	**T 8**
B 1276	**P 24**
B 1352	**P 9**
B 1357	**B 22**
B 1374	**B 18**
B 1375	**B 19**
B 1379	**BB 9**
B 1380	**B 20**
B 1397	**P 19**
B 1485	**P 23**
B 1564	**T 5**
B 1626	**T 30**
B 1644	**T 43**
Iron and Lead	
IL 578	**B 50**
IL 579	**B 51**
IL 971	**B 52**
IL 1075	**B 53**
IL 1161	**T 32**
IL 1266	**B 54**
Marble	
*ΠΛ 367	**K 1**
Terracotta	
MC 856	**CB 1**
P 2084	**M 1**
P 28470	**E 1**

CONCORDANCE OF TESTIMONIA

INDEX

Numbers in plain type refer to pages; those in boldface indicate testimonia. Only the commentaries to the latter are cited in the index. The testimonia themselves are not indexed.

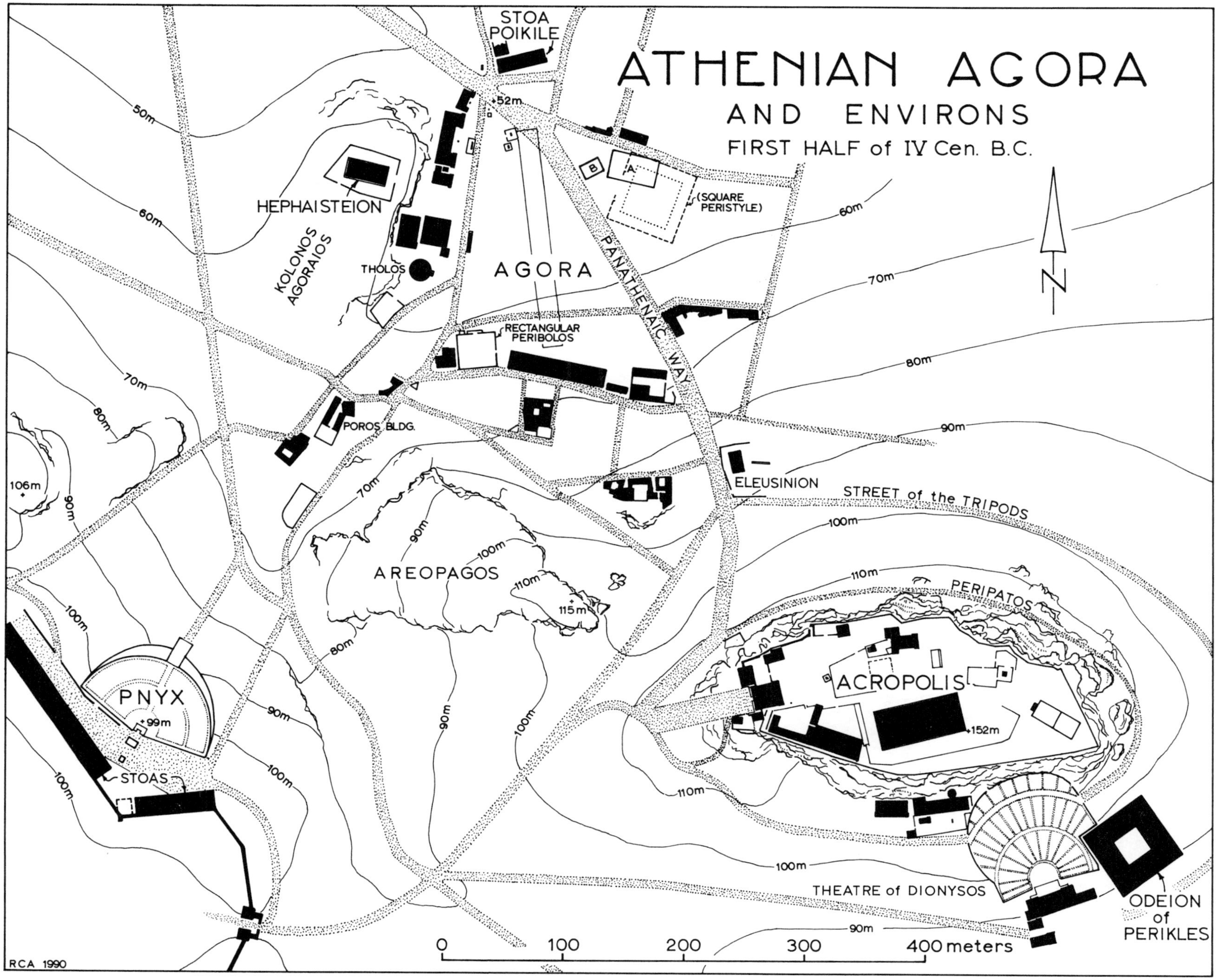

The Athenian Agora and environs, first half of the 4th century B.C.E.

FIGURE 2

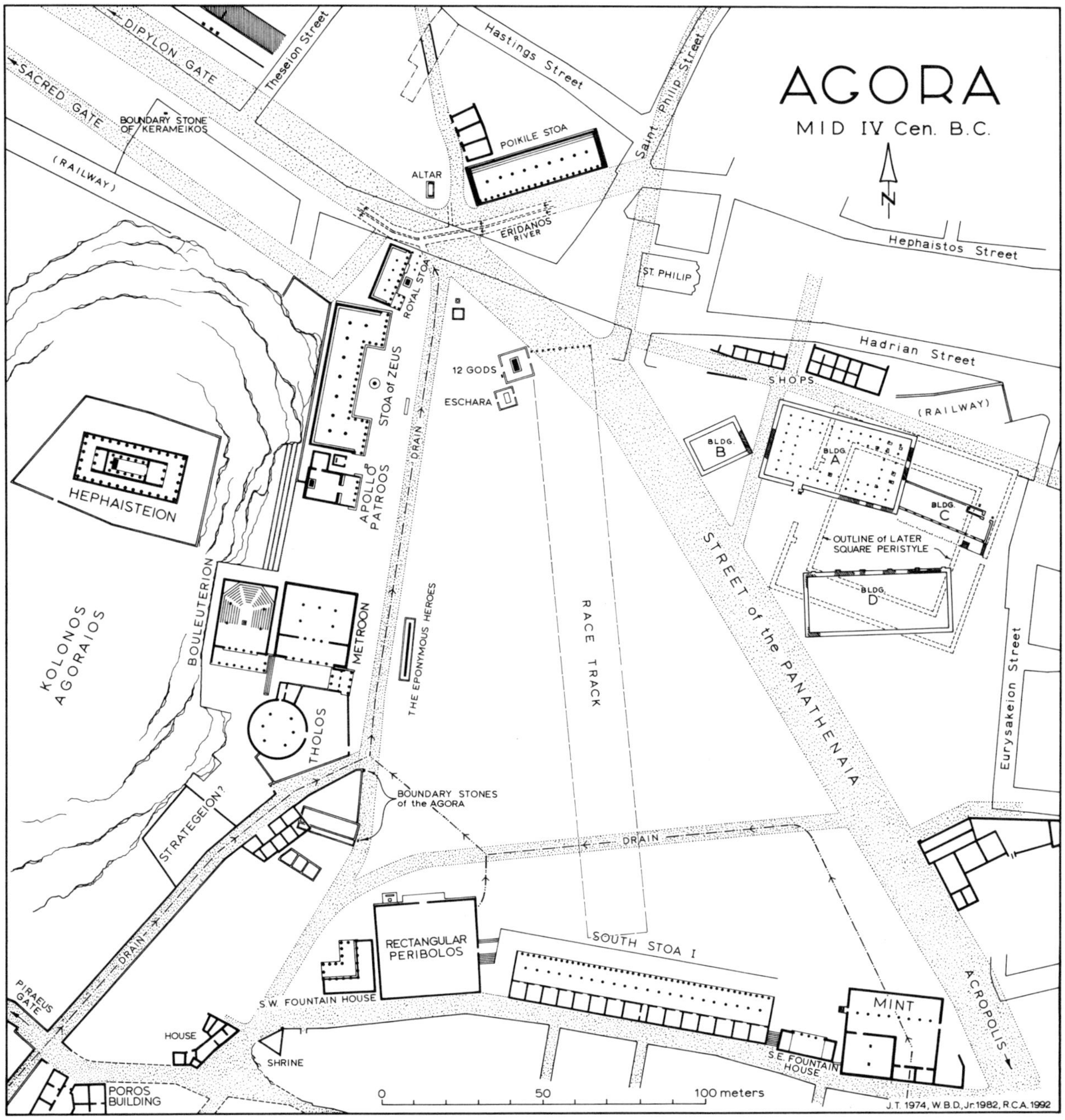

The Athenian Agora, mid-4th century B.C.E.

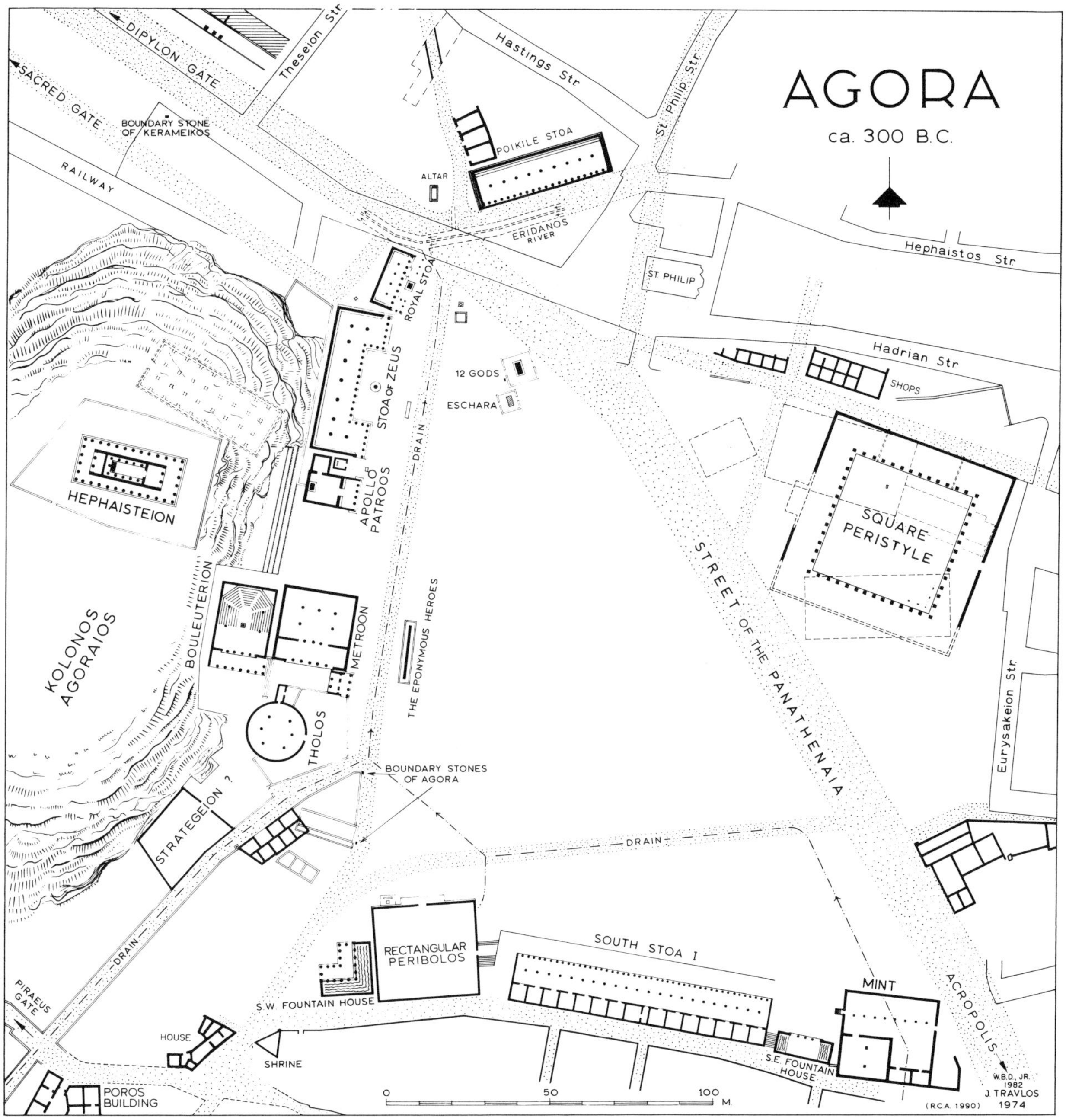

The Athenian Agora *ca.* 300 B.C.E.

FIGURE 4

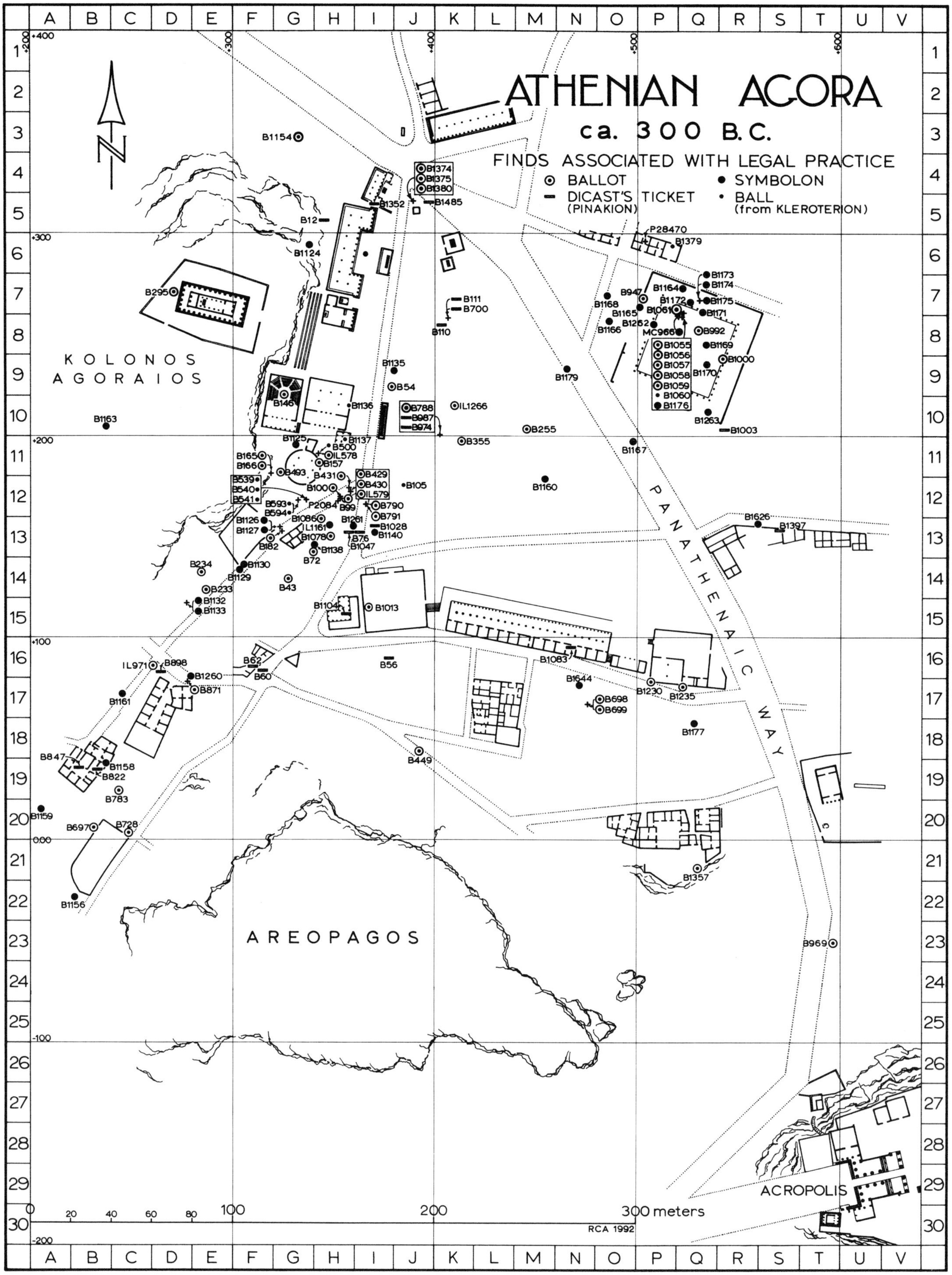

Findspots of dikastic equipment in the Athenian Agora

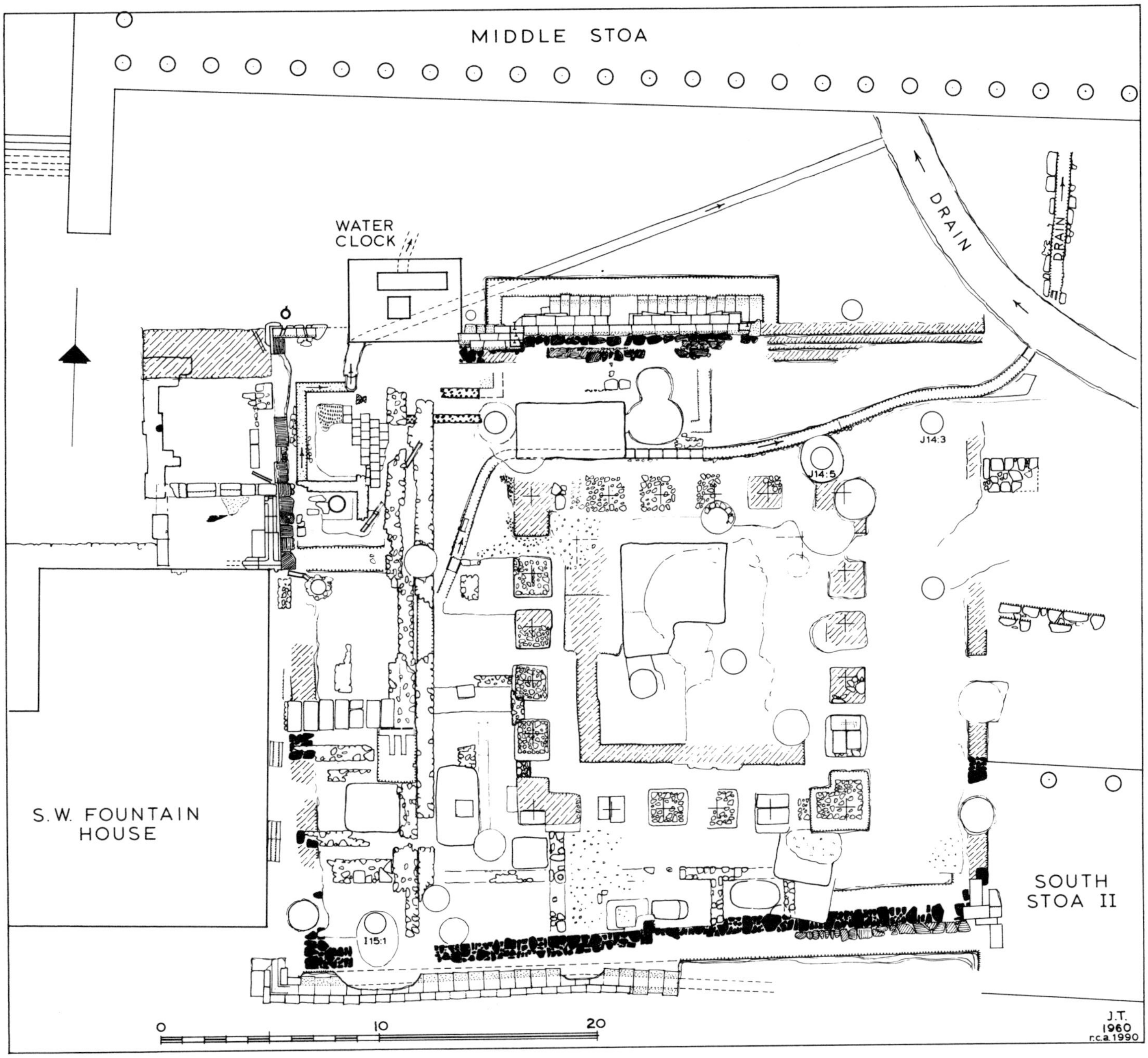

Rectangular Peribolos (? Heliaia), actual-state plan (incomplete)

FIGURE 6

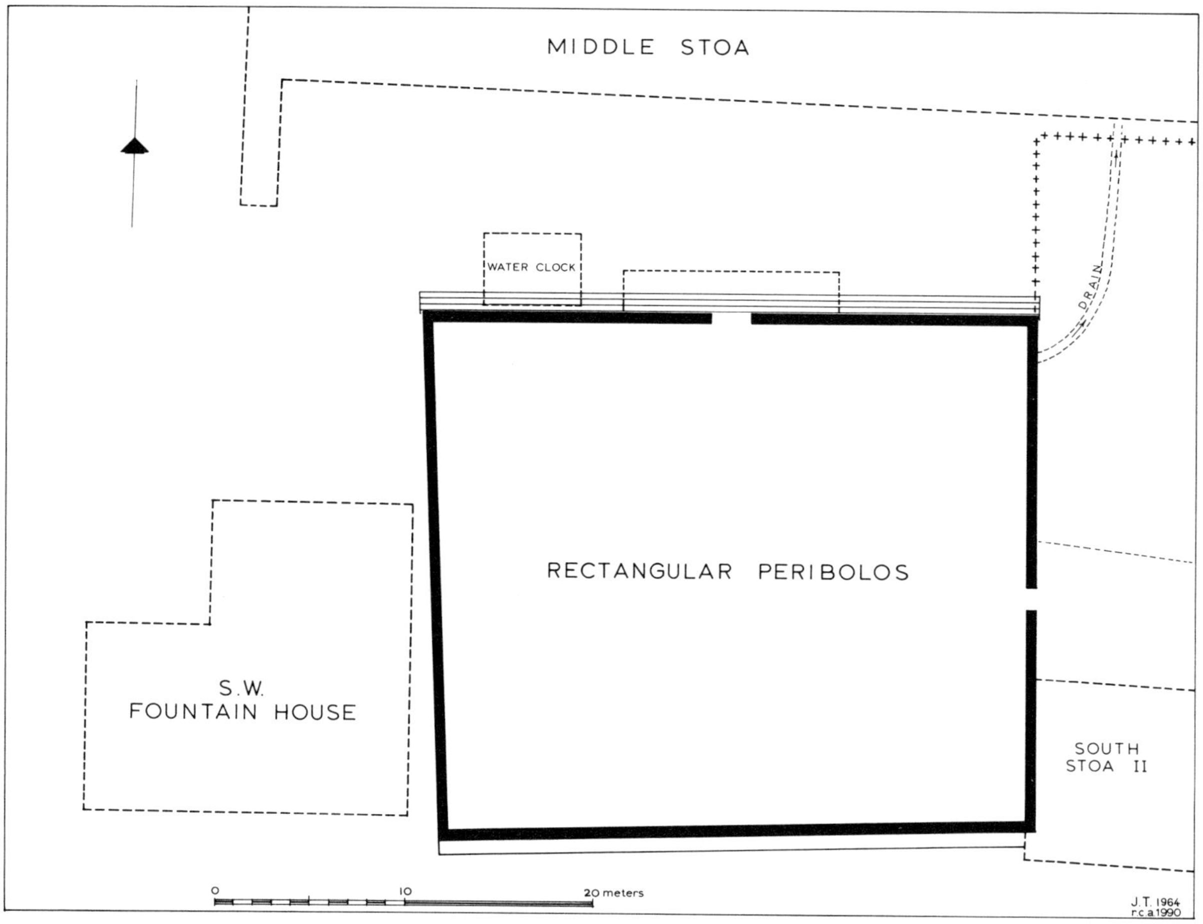

a. Original form

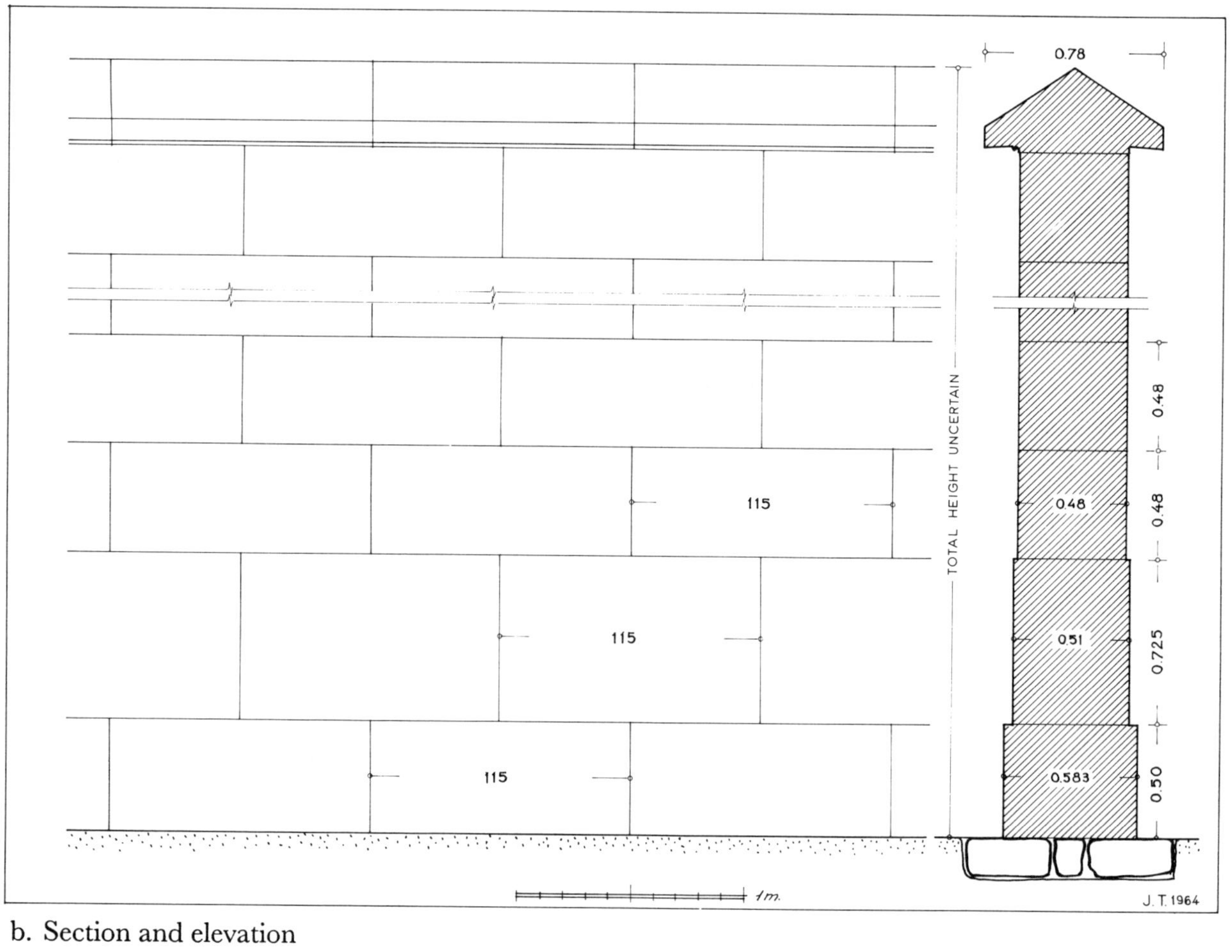

b. Section and elevation

Rectangular Peribolos (? Heliaia)

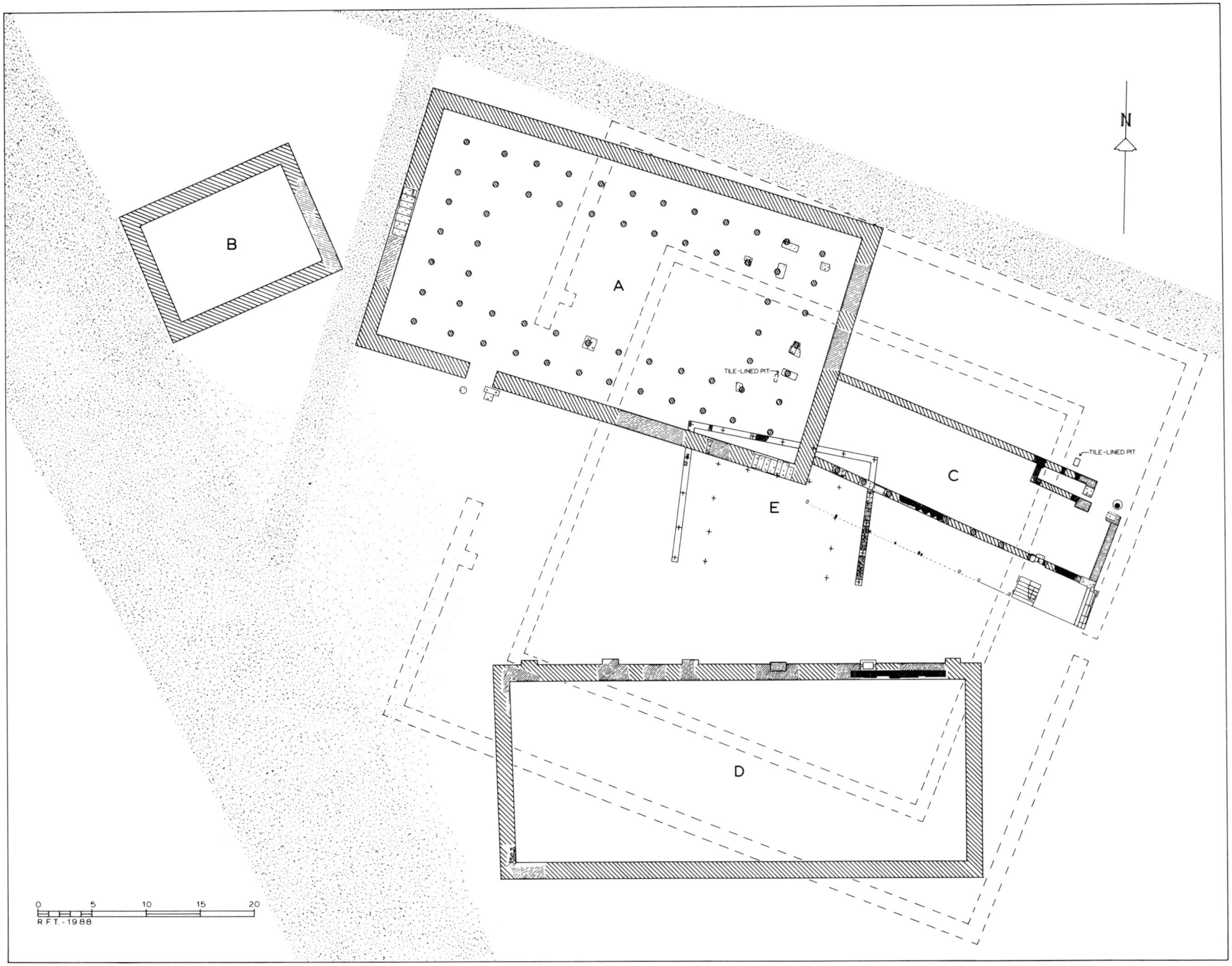

The Predecessors to the Square Peristyle, Buidings A–E, actual-state plan with restorations

FIGURE 8

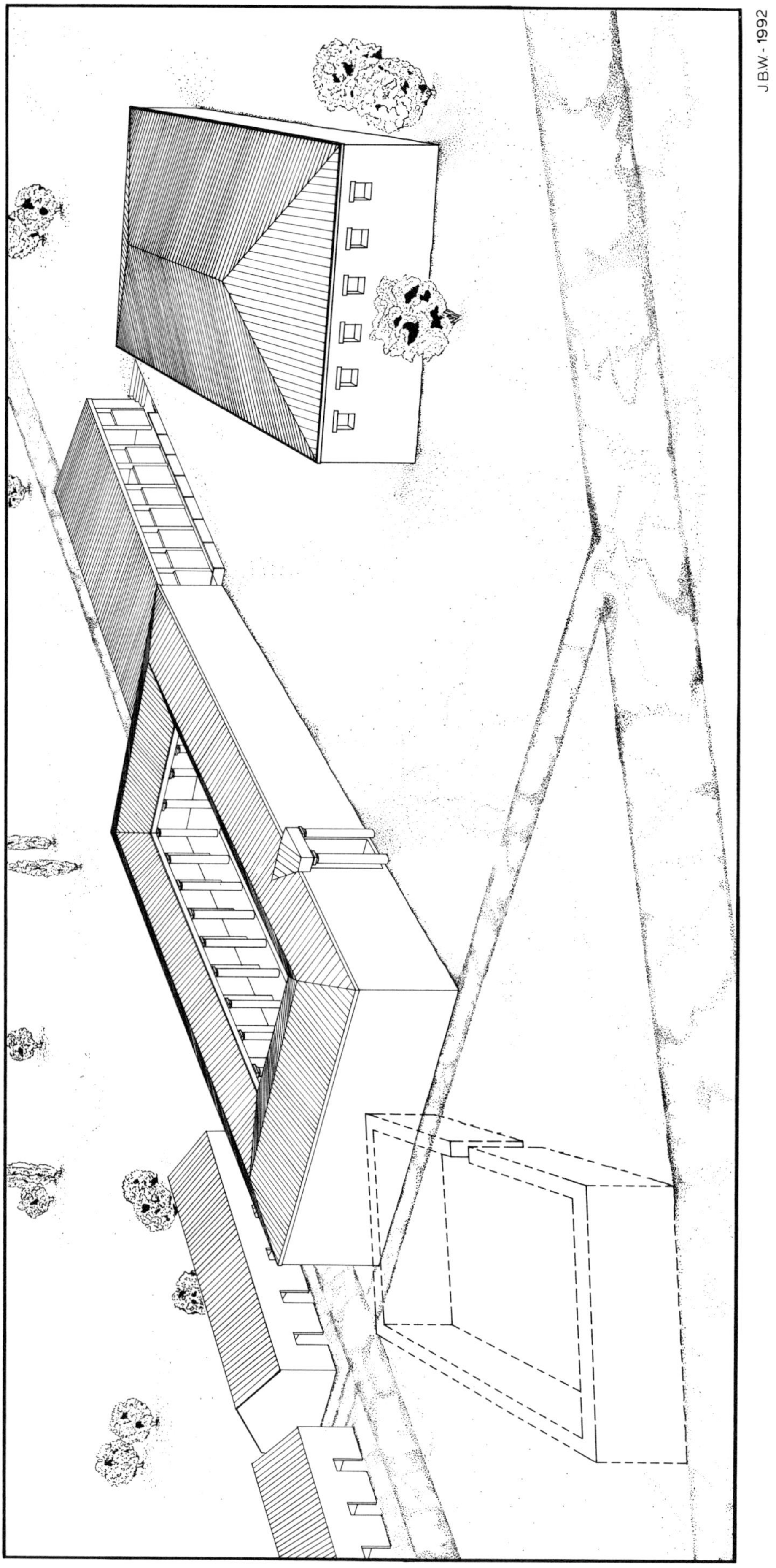

The Predecessors to the Square Peristyle, Buidings A–D, reconstructed

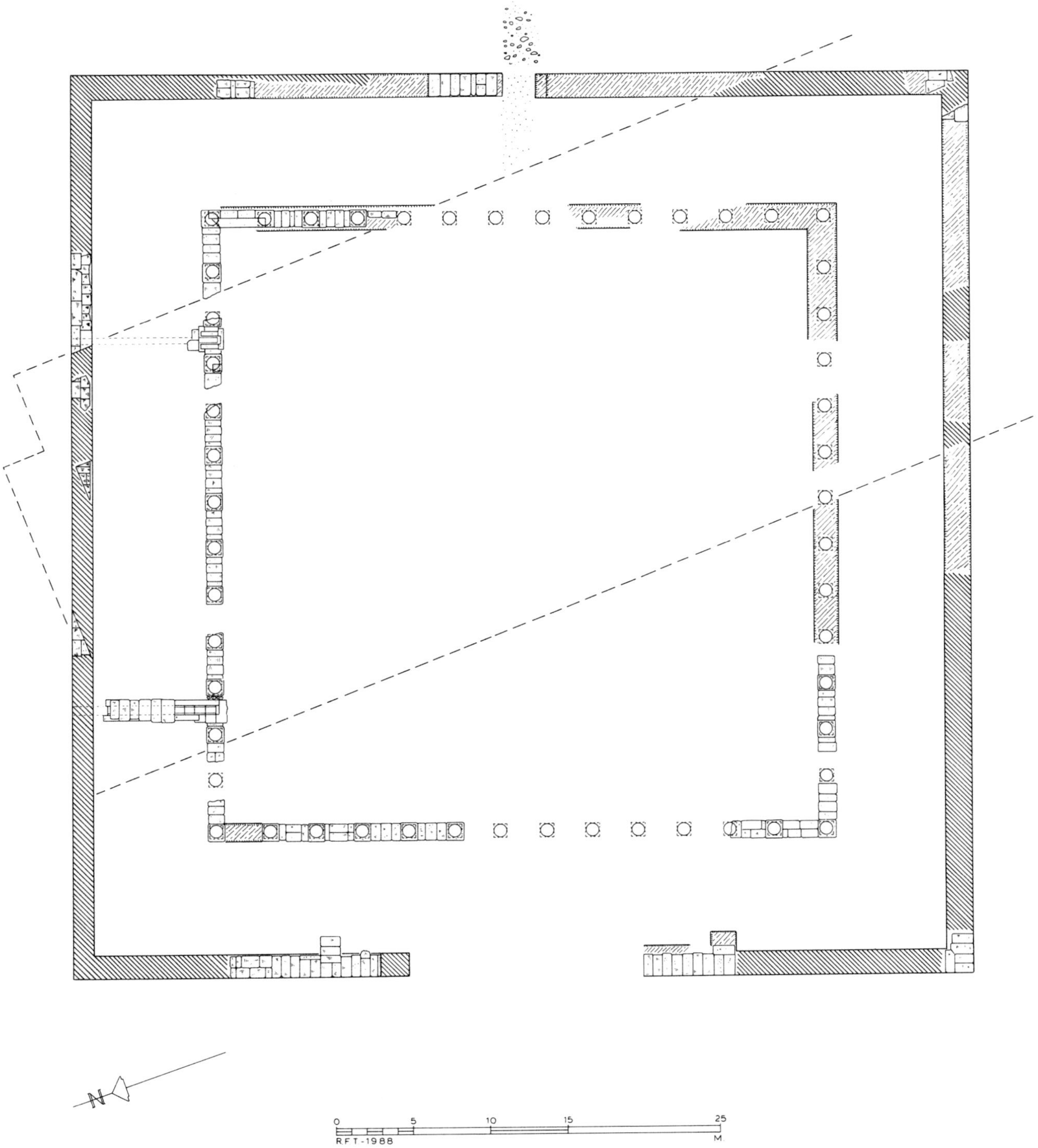

Square Peristyle, actual-state plan with restorations

FIGURE 10

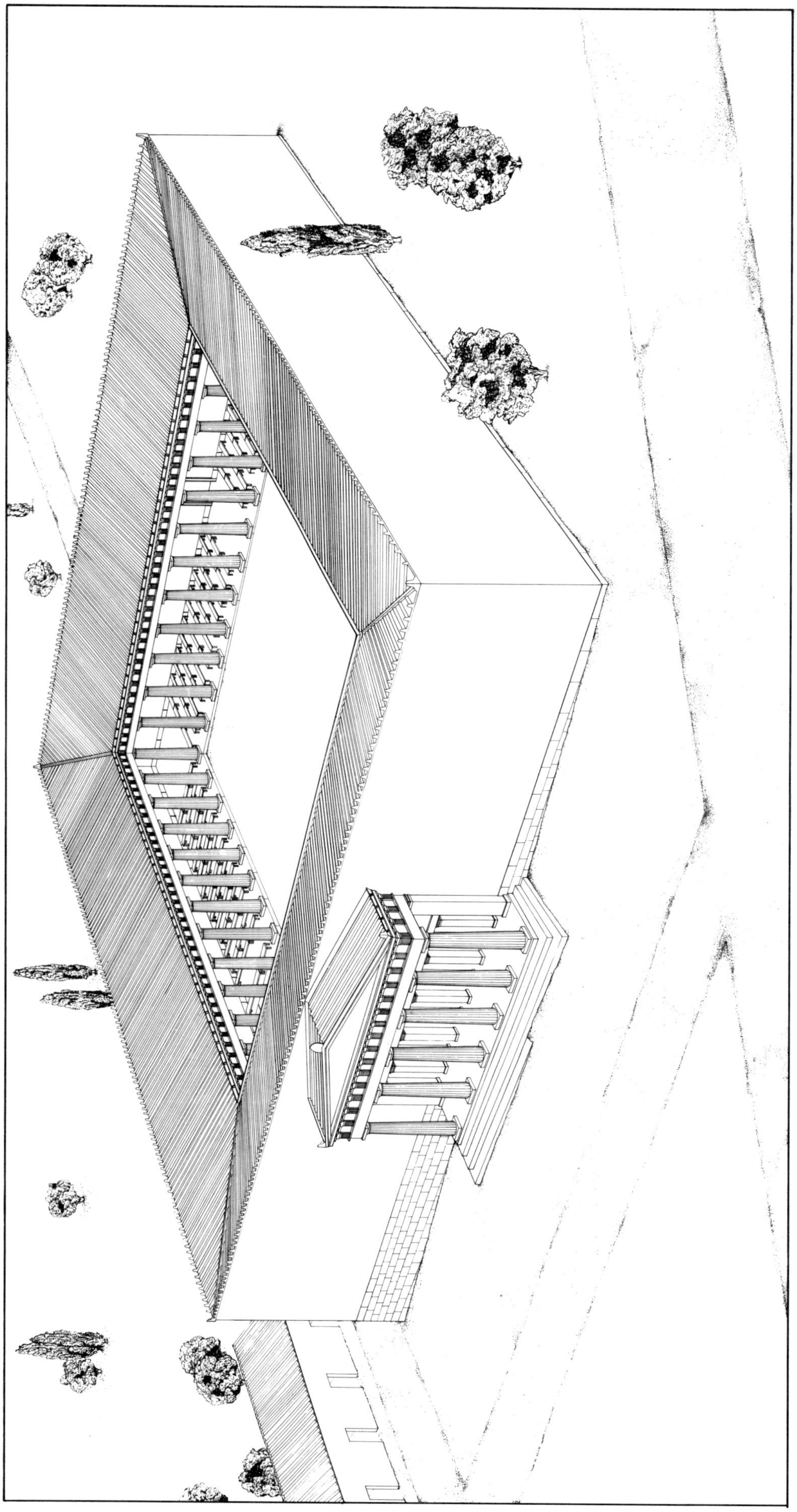

Square Peristyle, reconstructed

PLATES

a. Eastern slope of the Kolonos Agoraios, from the east

b. Eastern slope of the Kolonos Agoraios, from the south

Poros benches

a. View from the east

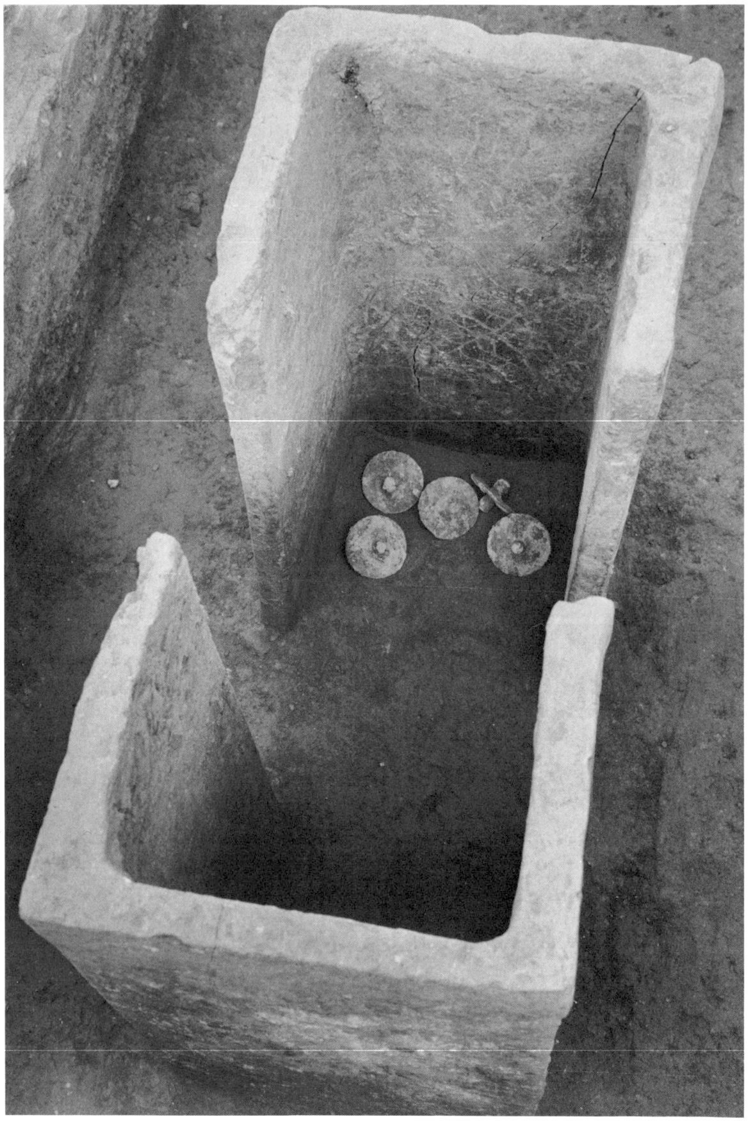

b. View from the south

Terracotta water channels enclosing the "Ballot Deposit"

a. Northeast corner showing reused intercolumnar step blocks and stylobate blocks from the Square Peristyle

b. Stylobate block with omicron on face

a. zeta

b. eta

c. iota

d. kappa

e. mu

f. omicron

g. rho

Letters in step blocks of Square Peristyle reused in South Stoa II

a. Side A

b. Side B

Dijon Cup, with men voting

a. **K 1**

b. Dow 1937, no. X

Kleroteria

P 1

P 2

P 3

P 4

P 5

P 7

P 8

P 10

P 9

P 11

P 12

P 12

Pinakia

Scale 1:1

P 13

P 14

P 15

P 16

P 17

P 18

P 19

P 20

P 21

P 22

P 23

P 24

Pinakia

Scale 1:1

BB 1

BB 2

BB 3

BB 4

BB 5

BB 6

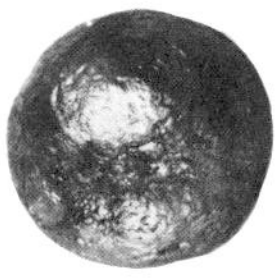
BB 7

BB 8

BB 9

CB 1

Balls **BB 1–BB 9, CB 1**

T 1

T 2

T 3

T 4

T 5

T 6

T 7

Tokens **T 1–T 7**

Scale 1:1

PLATE 10

T 8

T 9

T 10

T 11

T 12

T 13

T 14

T 15

T 16

T 17

T 18

T 19

Tokens

Scale 1:1

T 20

T 21

T 22

T 23

T 24

T 25

T 26

T 27

T 28

T 29

T 30

T 31

B 1141

Tokens

Scale 1:1

PLATE 12

T 32

T 33

T 34

B 1131

T 35

T 36

T 37

T 38

T 39

T 40

T 41

T 42

T 43

T 44

Tokens

Scale 1:1

a. Models

b. Drawing, **M 1** restored

c. **M 1** (1:2)

Klepsydra **M 1**

a. Fragment of inscribed lid

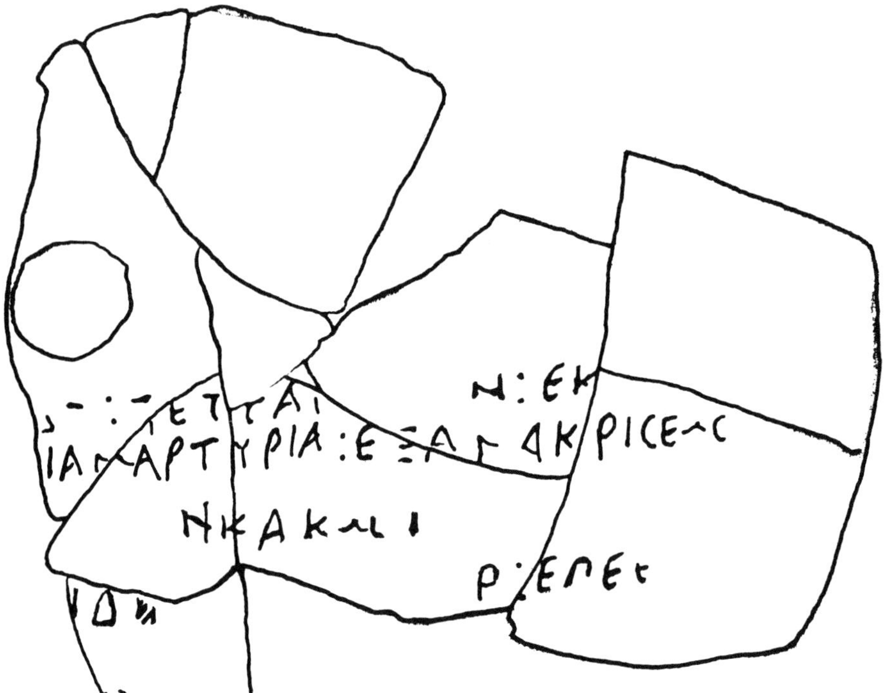

b. Drawing (Alan Boegehold)

B 1

B 2

B 3

B 4

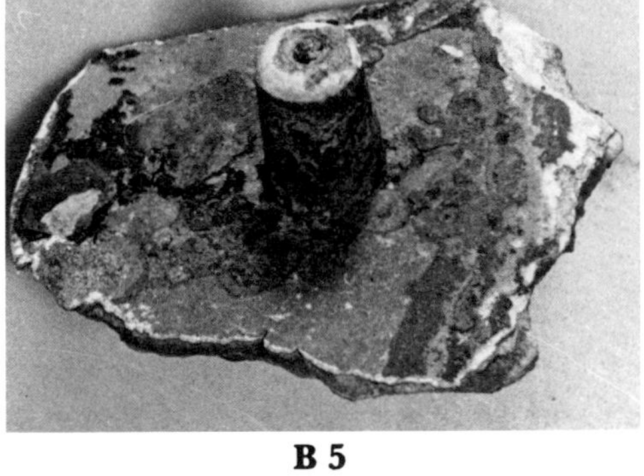

B 5

B 6

B 7

Ballots

Scale 1:1

B 8

B 9

B 10, obverse

B 10, reverse

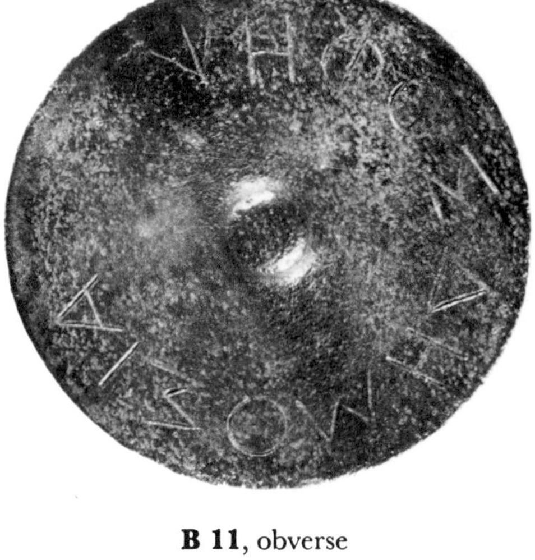

B 11, obverse

B 11, reverse

Ballots

Scale 1:1

B 12, obverse

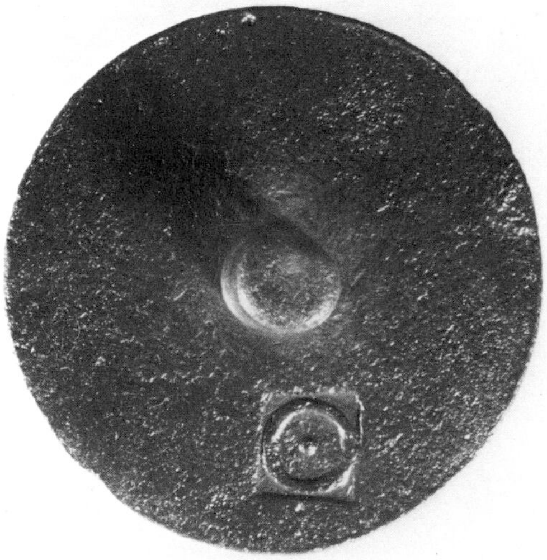

B 12, reverse

B 14, obverse

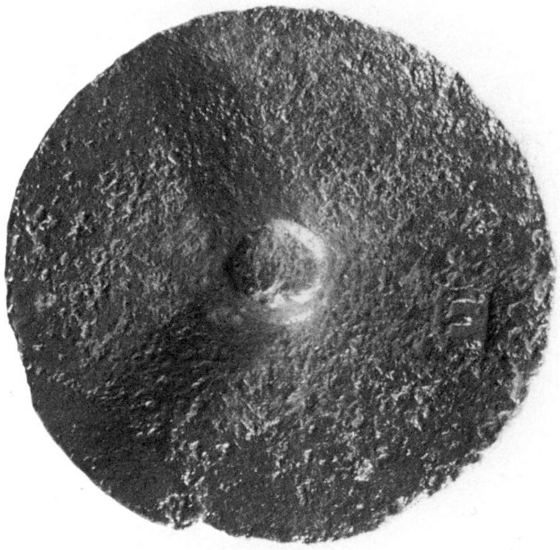

B 14, reverse

B 13

B 17

Ballots

Scale 1:1

B 15, obverse

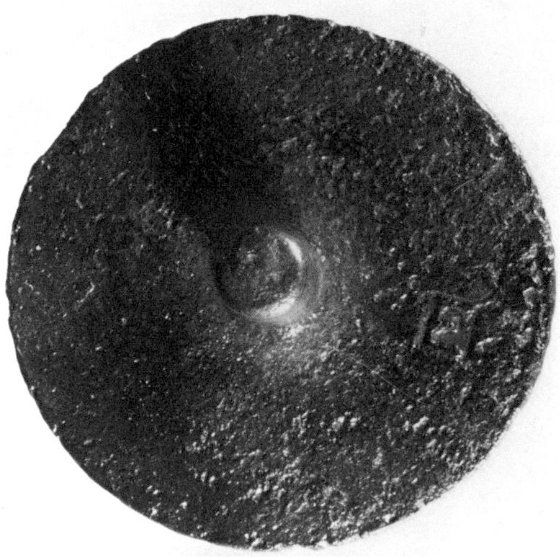

B 15, reverse

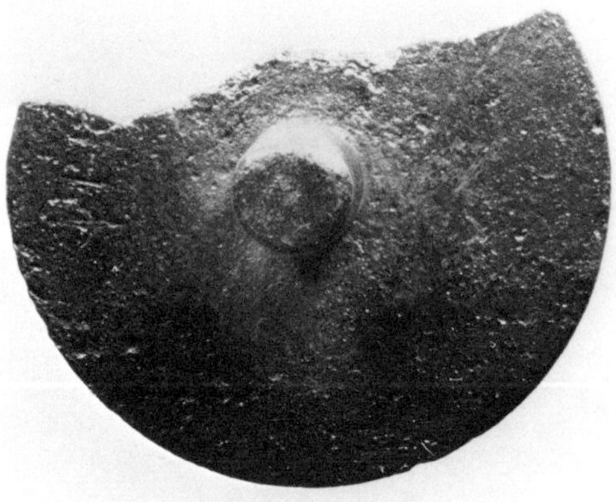

B 16, obverse

B 16, reverse

B 18

B 19

Ballots

Scale 1:1

B 20

B 21

B 22

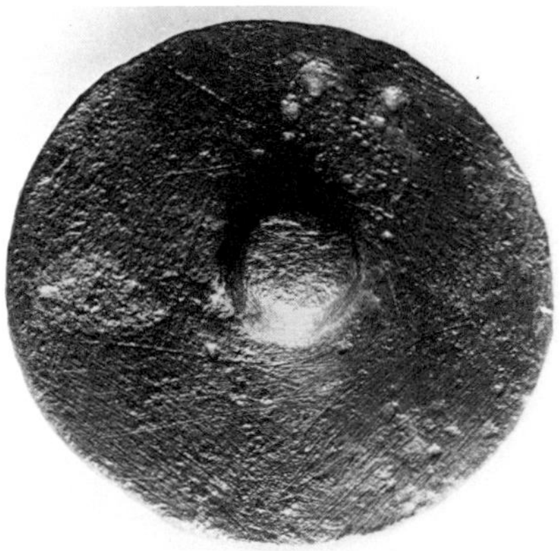

B 23

B 24

B 25

B 26

B 27

Ballots

Scale 1:1

PLATE 20

B 28

B 29

B 30

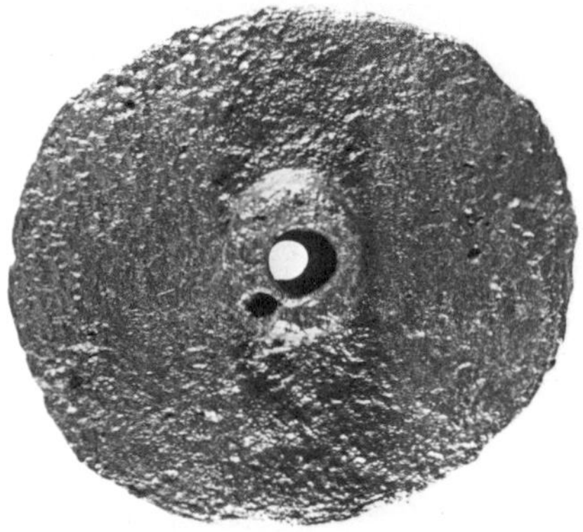
B 31

B 32

B 33

B 34

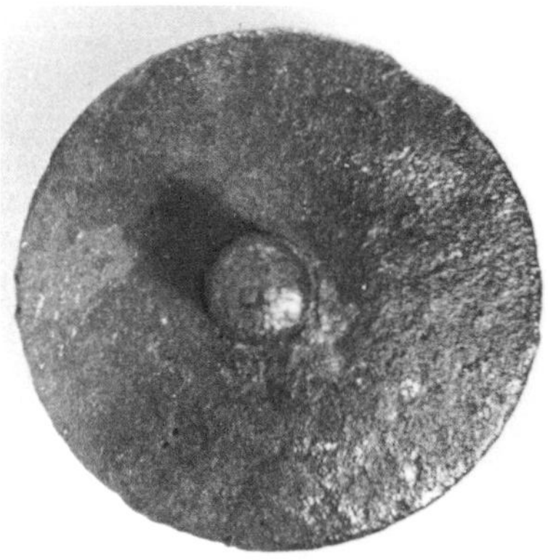
B 35

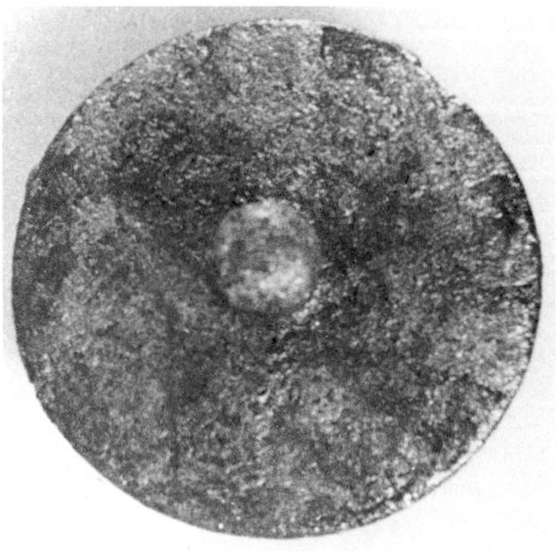
B 36

Ballots

Scale 1:1

B 37

B 38

B 39

B 40

B 41

B 42

B 43

B 44

B 45

Ballots

Scale 1:1

Ballots **B 46–B 54**

B 46

B 47

B 48

B 49

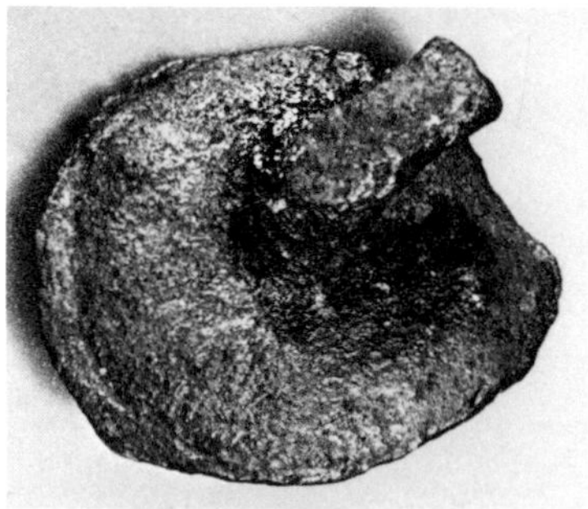

B 50

B 51

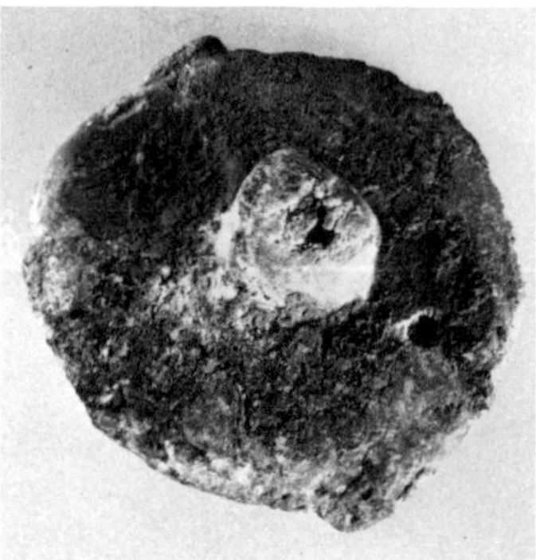

B 52

B 53

B 53

B 54

BI 658

BI 711

Styli **BI 658**, **BI 711**

Scale 1:1

Cup by Douris, with κρίσις ὅπλων